The U.S. Navy's
"Interim" LSM(R)s
in World War II

The U.S. Navy's "Interim" LSM(R)s in World War II

Rocket Ships of the Pacific Amphibious Forces

Ron MacKay, Jr.

Foreword by
Captain Wayne P. Hughes, Jr., USN (Ret.)

McFarland & Company, Inc., Publishers
Jefferson, North Carolina

Library of Congress Cataloguing-in-Publication Data

Names: MacKay, Ron, author.
Title: The U.S. Navy's "Interim" LSM(R)s in World War II : rocket ships of
the Pacific Amphibious Forces / Ron MacKay, Jr. ; foreword by Captain
Wayne P. Hughes, Jr., USN (Ret.).
Other titles: Rocket ships of the Pacific Amphibious Forces.
Description: Jefferson, North Carolina : McFarland & Company, Inc.,
Publishers, 2016 | Includes bibliographical references and index.
Identifiers: LCCN 2016012102 | ISBN 9780786498598 (softcover : acid free paper) ∞
Subjects: LCSH: World War, 1939–1945—Amphibious operations. | Landing craft—
United States—History—20th century. | Amphibious assault ships—
United States—History—20th century. | World War, 1939–1945—Campaigns—
Pacific Area. | World War, 1939–1945—Naval operations, American.
Classification: LCC D784.52.U6 M333 2016 | DDC 940.54/5973—dc23
LC record available at http://lccn.loc.gov/2016012102

British Library cataloguing data are available

Front cover: USS *LSM(R) 196*, USS *LSM(R) 197*, USS *LSM(R) 198* and USS
LSM(R) 199 firing rockets in Kerama Retto, Okinawa, 26 March 1945 (U.S. Navy)

Printed in the United States of America

*McFarland & Company, Inc., Publishers
Box 611, Jefferson, North Carolina 28640
www.mcfarlandpub.com*

In memory of
RdM2c Ronald Reyner MacKay,
USNR, and those who served

Table of Contents

Foreword

by Captain Wayne P. Hughes, Jr., USN (Ret.)

This book about a single class of warships in World War II is history at its best: impeccable primary research into the source documents; interviews with all the officers and enlisted men who served in the LSM(R) fleet whom Ron MacKay could find; a superb collection of photos; and a set of maps to help the reader visualize the many actions off Okinawa. MacKay has written a constrained and factual interpretation of the events from program inception; to the rapid class design and construction; to the adventurous trips from Charleston, South Carolina to the Western Pacific; and finally the varied operations in the lengthy and harrowing two-and-a-half month Okinawa Campaign in the spring of 1945. As with the best of historians, MacKay makes no attempt to either exaggerate or denigrate the contributions of the U.S. Navy's first twelve rocket ships in fulfilling their destiny and confronting the dangers they were subjected to.

An expected limitation of the rockets they carried was their range—5,000 yards, more or less. An expected advantage was the ability of each vessel to fire a salvo of three hundred rockets almost instantaneously, or to fire small salvoes of five to twenty rockets for an extended time, as they frequently did for harassing fire, often at night, and then in both cases rearming the launchers from substantial magazines and firing again.

MacKay excels at putting rocket fire accuracy in proper perspective: no theoretical performance here, and no single point conclusion. The best takeaway was that everyone was learning "on the job." MacKay describes how the ships were swiftly built with deficiencies uncovered later and the crews were hastily assembled and bonded. They used every opportunity to practice fire, but no conclusive measure of performance was possible until the LSM(R)s arrived at Okinawa and started firing purposefully at enemy targets of many descriptions.

The two most valuable conclusions about performance are still apt for modern missile warfare today. First, as the crews became experienced in action their accuracy improved and their types of employment broadened, especially when the LSM(R)s were teamed with big cruisers and battleships. (Of course close air support was vital, too, but the value of CAS in different campaigns would take a separate book, and one as detailed as the present work.)

The second conclusion is that the theater commanders and staffs were also learning as they went, especially about the breadth of potential of the deadly, barrage-capable little rocket ships. MacKay describes a regrettable distraction before the commanders fully understood

1

the LSM(R)s' value in salvo firing and inshore patrol. After the initial landings some of the little ships were sent out on radar picket duty, and teamed with destroyers and other small vessels early in the Okinawa Campaign when the Japanese kamikazes began attacking in large numbers and the threat was at its peak. It was good to spread the suicide bombers' targets with ships to supplement the destroyer pickets that carried the critical air search radars, but the LSM(R)s had too much future importance as rocket ships in planned operations later in April, May, and early June to serve as mere targets and personnel rescue vessels on picket station. Fortunately this misapplication of value did not last long.

Every reader will find out things he ought to know. I learned the Okinawa campaign was really a series of landings on *many* islands in the archipelago around the big island. It was also fascinating to read the sailors' experiences watching rocket propelled, aircraft launched "Baka" bomb suicide attacks at speeds none had ever seen before, by the fastest manned platforms anyone had ever faced. I was delighted to find mention by MacKay of a little-known fact, which was that a very large number of suicide boats were also built by the Japanese army and navy. Unlike the aircraft, the boats were almost totally ineffective, partly because of inshore patrols such as those conducted by the LSM(R)s. As a result of the boats' ineffectiveness their existence has gone almost unnoticed by historians. Technological failures as a part of war don't get the attention they deserve.

Written in loving detail, while retaining the swift pace of the narrative, this book is unique in carrying a single class of combat vessel from its inception, to its rapid redesign from existing LSM blueprints, to priority construction of the entire class in just two-and-a-half months, to their hasty but time-consuming deployment from the U.S. East Coast to the Western Pacific. Then we are shown that there is nothing like real combat to advance them from theoretical employment to real operations, in all their practical variety. Lastly we see the LSM(R)s return to the states at war's end, their crews of mostly reservists discharged, and in short order the ships sold off or broken up.

This book is unique and all the more valuable because the author has, in one narrative, described the full lifetime of a warship class, and one that saw lots of intensive combat. Would that we had seen the need and built the rocket ships in 1942 as the Royal Navy had done for the European theater. At the Naval Postgraduate School we have established a Littoral Operations Center, linked to industry and international governments. Our intent is to help anticipate the kinds of dangerous operations, amphibious or otherwise, the U.S. and allied navies will be subjected to. The Japanese Baka bomb was merely a foretaste of missile warfare in the future and the increasing roles of autonomous vehicles of all descriptions that do not need a suicide pilot.

Dean emeritus and Captain Wayne Hughes USN (Ret.) has been on the Naval Postgraduate School faculty since 1979. He has taught many subjects, including naval tactics, military command and control, and joint campaign analysis. He is author or editor of several books, and has articles in the Encyclopædia Britannica *and the* Encyclopedia of Military History. *His awards include Fellow of the Military Operations Research Society and Distinguished Technology Fellow of Singapore.*

Preface and Acknowledgments

The twelve "Interim" LSM(R)s were uniquely evolutionary and revolutionary in American naval history. These improvised warships were the United States Navy's first true rocketships—their *raison d'être*—and the ultimate progression of U.S. naval rocket warfare in World War II. This book is a comprehensive operational history of the original twelve "Interim" LSM(R)s of World War II. (While the title of this work uses the more commonly seen "rocket ship," within the text I refer to the LSM(R)s as "rocketships," in the same manner as one refers to "battleships," "minesweepers" and "warships.")

My lifelong interest in the U.S. Navy's LSM(R)s was kindled as a youngster. I was fascinated by my father's vivid reminiscences from World War II, and he inspired my love of history. I sought to learn more about these unusual rocketships over the intervening years, but no book or definitive work existed on the LSM(R)s. That which had been published, unfortunately, was diffuse, piecemeal, and too-often erroneous.

The LSM(R), or Landing Ship, Medium (Rocket), was conceived to deliver maximum firepower from the seas to enemy targets ashore. The original LSM(R)s, so-called "Interim," were the first of an entirely new class of U.S. Navy commissioned warship and the forerunners of generations of rocket-firing ships. These dozen rocketships were hybrid amphibious landing ships rushed to the Pacific in World War II, where their heavy rocket bombardments devastated Japanese forces on Okinawa in 1945. While fighting the murderous Kamikazes on distant radar picket lines, the LSM(R) sailors rose to legendary status in the annals of American naval history.

The genesis of this book was sparked by the worldwide 50th anniversary observances of the Second World War. Memorials and tributes honored America's "Greatest Generation," those who first struggled through the Great Depression and then answered the call to defend their nation amidst the world-changing cataclysm of World War II. Veterans published memoirs and recounted wartime experiences in newspapers and on television, some baring their souls for the first time since the war ended. Simultaneously, countless government wartime documents that were never before available were being declassified. Heightened public awareness and renewed interest in the milestones of World War II also revitalized historical scholarship, which spanned the renowned and arcane alike.

Within this milieu, LSM(R) veterans, like many World War II–era servicemen nationwide, began holding reunions which my father and I also attended. By then a Navy veteran myself, I was privileged to befriend many of my father's former shipmates and scores of other LSM(R) veterans and families. Here the distant past truly became living history. The wartime service of these proud rocketship sailors clearly equaled others chronicled throughout U.S. Navy history. Yet I came to fear their deeds and legacies would be forever lost if not actively preserved for future generations.

This imperative compelled my vision for this book, which culminates more than twenty years of research, study, and writing based upon innumerable declassified wartime documents. Its capstone is the interviews, correspondence, personal journals and rare photographs so generously contributed by former LSM(R) officers and enlisted men and their families.

Lost, missing, or destroyed documentation was the most serious problem during research. Irreplaceable operational records were lost when *LSM(R)s 190, 194,* and *195* were sunk by Kamikaze aircraft in May 1945 during the Okinawa operation. From that same time period, several months of LSM Flotilla Nine war diaries remain unaccounted for in the National Archives at College Park, Maryland. Further alarming in hindsight, countless documents were destroyed or discarded when the peacetime U.S. armed forces downsized after the war.

By far, the most persistent problems posed by wartime documentation were quality and reliability. Under-reporting was common not only among the LSM(R)s but throughout the amphibious forces generally. Ship's daily logs and war diaries were frequently terse, sometimes omitted important details, and occasionally misreported facts. Action reports, which describe specific enemy encounters and ship operations, ran the qualitative gamut as well. Not of small concern, this writer was cautioned more than once of records edited during the war due to fears of potential legal or disciplinary repercussions.

Recourse was to consult and crosscheck a wide range of contemporary sources, most of which are official reports and records from an array of U.S. Navy warships, senior naval and military commanders, civilian governmental agencies and private contractors. In exceptional instances, veterans and family members provided copies of rare official documents otherwise unknown to exist. Many additional questions were resolved by the LSM(R) sailors themselves, to be sure, from whom I sought the broadest firsthand accounts. Here special recognition is owed to the gutsiness of those who kept personal journals (and cameras), despite risks under strict Navy wartime censorship regulations, which capture priceless glimpses of "real time history." Equally vital to this book, LSM(R) veterans offered remarkable personal experiences during interviews, through correspondence, and in memoirs, so to the greatest extent possible, full quotations are honored as originally expressed with minimal editing.

Because the focus of this book is the operational history of the "Interim" LSM(R)s, its scope imposed limitations on much of great historical significance. Grand strategy, tactical analyses, rocket science, and the Kamikaze operations are but examples of complex human technical and technological endeavors about which volumes have been expertly written at length and in depth. Of necessity, therefore, such weighty matters were distilled to within the contexts of the "Interim" LSM(R)s. Should the reader wish to delve deeper, numerous sources are cited in chapter notes and in the bibliography.

Chapters in this book are organized chronologically, although a strictly progressive narrative was not always possible. Overlapping storylines were unavoidable because LSM(R)s were often deployed in small groups, for examples, among convoys, during rocket runs, and on patrols. (One should also bear in mind that LSM(R) sailors often did not know what other LSM(R)s were doing in different places at the same time). So to aid continuity and minimize repetition, such independent deployments and operations are sub-sectioned within chapters.

A glossary defines abbreviations, acronyms, and terminology. Appendices provide supplemental information about ship characteristics, crew complements, painting and camouflage, and ships' data.

I wish thank those LSM(R) officers and enlisted men whose personal support and selfless contributions brought this book to life:

USS *LSM(R) 188*
Charles H. Billings, Allison D. Gray, Robert R. Wise.

USS *LSM(R) 189*
Commanding Officer James M. Stewart, Earl E. Bishop, J. Edward Briand, Harry J. Coffman, Joseph M. Farrar, F. Donald Moore.

USS *LSM(R) 190*
Gordon E. Etter, John E. Hall, William J. Nuber, George O. Spencer, Lyle S. Tennis, Leroy E. Vanderhoof.

USS *LSM(R) 191*
Edward E. Bowden, Donald G. Burns, Roy J. Moceri, Laurie R. Russell, Joe B. Smith, Andrew J. Vescova.

USS *LSM(R) 192*
Commanding Officer Neal B. Hadsell, Victor C. Anderson, Heik K. Davitian, LeRoy Donaldson, Harold J. Franssen, Robert J. Frist, Robert W. Landis, James C. MacBeth, Ronald R. MacKay, Raymond J. North, Joseph A. Raulinaitis, Russell D. Wydeen.

USS *LSM(R) 193*
Earl F. Hjelmberg, E. Wesley Murbach, Mike E. Shardelman, Louis B. Strong, Robert F. Tuve, Paul S. Vaitses, Jr., Hugh B. Wallace.

USS *LSM(R) 194*
Commanding Officer Allan M. Hirshberg, Steve A. Gatto, Harvey M. McGehee, Jr., John M. Stinson.

USS *LSM(R) 195*
Loren F. Bell, Harold C. Catchpole, William J. Ernst, John B. Francis, Terence W. Listen, David P. Murillo, Frank E. Pizur.

USS *LSM(R) 196*
Richard J. Antioch, Clyde L. Butler, Preston E. Greene, Kelly K. Kirchner, David Mallery, Karl G. Matchett, Bruce A. McDaniel, E. Doug Moyer, Jr., Jack P. Shedd, Leonard A. VanOteghem.

USS *LSM(R) 197*
Clyde J. Blue, Louis DeJessie, Lawrence J. Low, Leslie W. Taylor, Lawrence Willison.

USS *LSM(R) 198*
Louis E. Gobeille, Eugene H. Milotz, Peter C. Rendina.

USS *LSM(R) 199*
   Jay S. Farley, George E. Passey.

USS *LC(FF) 535*
   Commanding Officer Himus S. Sims, Harold J. Ball, Robert W. Cox, John K. Harlow.

Captain Wayne P. Hughes, Jr., USN (Ret.), most graciously penned the excellent foreword. Captain Hughes is Professor Emeritus of Operations Research and teaches tactical analysis at the Naval Postgraduate School, Monterey, California. Following 30 years' active duty in the U.S. Navy, Captain Hughes is the acknowledged preeminent authority on naval power and author of the acclaimed landmark works, *Fleet Tactics: Theory and Practice* and *Fleet Tactics and Coastal Combat*.

No author works in a vacuum. Many aided this work immeasurably by sharing recollections and insights and by contributing memoirs, historical documents and photographs: Douglas G. Aitken, Roy S. Andersen, Bill Barthel, David and Kathleen Bassett, Linda E. Behrendt, Robert S. Benner, Earl Blanton, the Boak family, Edward J. Buliavac, Edward H. Burtt, Tim Colton, Robert W. Erlbacher II, Robert Glass, Jacquelyn Marie (Thomas) Guss, Shirley Hadsell, Jack E. Johnson, Allen B. Koltun, Donald Lowy, Ruth Lowy, Barbara Stewart Lyle, Alvin C. "Rusty" McNabb, John A. McNeill, Chuck Major, Russell H. McDonald, Sr., Betty Meeusen, Laura Nelle O'Callaghan, Palmer W. Olliff, Louis H. Parker, William W. Richardson, Kenneth E. Roberts, Stephen S. Roberts, Ron Swanson, Tony Teal, Jana A. Teehan, John B. Tombaugh, Edward Trautwein, Reverend Lawrence Weed, Laurie Woodson White, Andrew B. Wilson, Julia Woodson, and Barry Zerby.

Special acknowledgements are due both past and present Archivists of the National Association of USS LCS(L) 1–130. Raymond A. Baumler, a Quartermaster on *LCS(L)(3) 14* during World War II, encouraged and supported my pursuit from its earliest beginnings. Ray embodied a keen sense of history with rare energy and enthusiasm, which in turn buoyed my own work throughout many trials. His correspondence caused my files to literally overflow with a wealth of historical documents and useful resources. Ray's successor Robin L. Rielly— former Marine, martial arts expert, prodigious author, professional photographer, longtime colleague and steadfast friend—has been the single most important influence behind this long-overdue book, after that of my late father. A noted authority on U.S. amphibious warfare of World War II, Rob's scholarship is of the highest measure, and one I strove to meet. I remain grateful to Rob as well for allowing me to reprint his fine radar picket stations diagram, and for unearthing many amazing never-before-published LSM(R) photographs from the National Archives.

Renowned naval illustrator and author A.D. Baker III graciously granted me permission to reprint his excellent LSM(R) illustration, and he very kindly loaned me his collection of LSM(R) photographs. I ever appreciate Mr. Baker, moreover, for sharing his exceedingly rare "Interim" LSM(R) booklet of ship plans.

Arthur L. Storbo tirelessly proofread every iota of every revision of my manuscript with admirable tenacity. Art, a retired civil engineer with CH2M Hill consultants, brought his scientific acumen and contagious good cheer to this massive undertaking, for which I am indebted a thousandfold.

I take the profoundest personal pride in the fact that my brother, John C. MacKay, contributed several fine illustrations to this work.

Through thick and thin, finally, my ever-patient wife Debbie persevered in spite of my single-minded obsession with this book—even when I used "big words."

In sum, this work is presented from the LSM(R)s' perspective, as it were, although no single rocketship, crew, or sailor typified all. My lasting regret is that so many of our "Greatest Generation" passed on before this book saw print.

Responsibility for the accuracy and contents of this work rests solely with the author.

Introduction

LIFE magazine famously heralded the LSM(R)s as having "the combined firepower of two mammoth Iowa-class battleships."[1] Infamously, Tokyo Rose predicted oblivion for these "super dreadnaughts"[2] at the hands of the Imperial Japanese Navy. Called the "meanest little ships in the fleet,"[3] and even "rocket-firing guinea pigs,"[4] LSM(R)s were hailed as the destroyers' "best friend."[5]

In the autumn of 1944, the LSM(R)s, or Landing Ship, Medium (Rocket)s, were pressed into service as stopgap (hence "Interim") weapons platforms against Imperial Japan. These rocket-firing warships were engineered upon the conventional LSM design and structurally reconfigured in Charleston Navy Yard, Charleston, South Carolina. Function followed form. Prospective crews knew nothing about their new warships bristling with rocket launchers, advanced radar and unusual ordnance. Fleet Admiral Chester Nimitz requested the LSM(R)s to be expedited operationally as warfare intensified in the Pacific theatre.[6] Their primary mission was close-in rocket bombardment during amphibious invasions. Yet the LSM(R)s would see more desperate fighting in four fateful months at Okinawa in 1945 than most "Blue Water" ships-of-the-line encounter over a lifetime.[7]

Rockets were not new to naval warfare. Great Britain was first to tactically exploit shipborne rockets in the early 19th Century during the Napoleonic Wars in Europe and the American War of 1812. Indeed, Francis Scott Key forever immortalized the Royal Navy's HMS *Erebus*, herself a converted rocketship, in "The Star-Spangled Banner" when he recalled "the rocket's red glare" during the failed British seaborne assaults of Fort McHenry in Baltimore, Maryland, during 13–14 September 1814. Erratic flight and inaccuracy, however, limited the destructive effectiveness of these early rockets, although their dramatic brilliance proved useful as a terrorizing weapon.[8]

Remarkable in hindsight, the U.S. Navy had no rockets in its inventory before the Japanese attack on Pearl Harbor on 7 December 1941. But with breathtaking speed, the United States launched a crash program of scientific research and development that quickly proved rockets as viable weapons against enemy forces on foreign shores. Navy experimentation soon led to retro-fitting a plethora of boats, crafts and ships with rockets and launchers in almost all theatres of naval operations. Still, rocket barrages were of limited duration and concentration due to equally limited stowage capacities and deck spaces for launchers, so rockets remained secondary weapons to conventional naval guns. Put simply, these were gunships with rockets. The LSM(R)s, in contrast, were rocketships with guns.

The "Interim" LSM(R)s were the pinnacle of U.S. naval rocket warfare during World

War II,[9] and validated the vital importance of maximum fire support in the Fleet. Their wartime legacy presaged the postwar rocket- and guided-missile destroyers and cruisers. Genealogical descendants, called "Ultimate" LSM(R)s, served in the Korean War and Vietnam War as well as in foreign navies. Of direct lineage was the Inshore Fire Support rocketship USS *Carronade IFS 1* of the mid–1950s. Today, the proposed new "arsenal ship," a technologically modern LSM(R) in essence, is seen as a critically missing fire support adjunct to the 21st century U.S. Navy.[10]

The conceptual origins of the LSM(R) evolved under Fleet Admiral Ernest J. King, who encouraged accelerated developments in amphibious fire support.[11] As both Chief of Naval Operations (CNO) and Commander in Chief, United States Fleet (COMINCH), King wielded near-absolute authority over U.S. naval shipbuilding programs during World War II. Seeking American mastery of the seas and victory over her enemies, Admiral King's outlook was if a ship should be built, then it would be built.[12] Hence a proposed "LSM Rocket Ship" program fit well within his strategic calculus of capturing China's island of Formosa, modern day Taiwan.

Admiral King argued strongly that seizing Japanese-held Formosa was critical for isolating and ultimately defeating Imperial Japan.[13] Indeed, Admirals King and Nimitz projected the amphibious assault of Formosa, codenamed Operation Causeway, for February-March 1945.[14] But Formosa is a distant and formidable island, slightly more in square miles than Maryland and Delaware combined, and the U.S. Army objected that it did not have enough soldiers to support such a massive, far-reaching operation.[15] Facing increasingly stubborn resistance from the Army by late September 1944, Adm. King reluctantly dropped his insistence upon taking Formosa and acquiesced to Generals George C. Marshall and Douglas MacArthur, who argued instead for the capture of Luzon Island in the Philippines followed by Iwo Jima and Okinawa. Immediately, the U.S. Joint Chiefs of Staff (JCS) issued a directive on 3 October 1944 instructing military staffers to draft operational plans.[16] With Formosa tabled, the "LSM Rocket Ships" were redirected for the Iwo Jima operation set for February 1945.[17] But fateful delays precluded their participation, so Okinawa, Operation Iceberg, was destined as the LSM(R)s' baptism of fire.[18]

The dozen rocketships would support numerous Army and Marine amphibious landings, shoreline skirmishes, and inland battles with devastating rocket runs among the Okinawa archipelago. And yet the rocketships repulsed speedy Japanese attack boats laden with explosives; disrupted enemy troops and installations; rescued burning or crippled warships; recovered hundreds of survivors stranded at sea; and deployed as anti-submarine hunter-killers. But casualties were staggering. Three LSM(R)s were sunk, a fourth crippled, and two more grazed by Kamikaze airplane crashes, and one other was blasted by devastating shore fire. Four rocketships earned Navy Unit Commendations and another was awarded the esteemed Presidential Unit Citation. Only President Harry S. Truman's decision to drop the atomic bombs on Hiroshima and Nagasaki saved the surviving LSM(R) sailors from the hellish inferno of invading homeland Japan.

CHAPTER 1

"LSM Rocket Ships"

On 6 September 1944, the Deputy Chief of Staff[1] for Fleet Admiral Ernest J. King (Commander-in-Chief, United States Fleet, and Chief of Naval Operations) wrote a confidential memorandum to the Vice Chief of Naval Operations[2] calling for a unique "LSM Rocket Ship":

> It is desired that plans be prepared for the conversion of an LSM for use as a rocket ship. These plans will be submitted to Commander in Chief, United States Fleet, for consideration at the earliest practicable date. The ultimate number of LSM hulls to be so converted will be determined later. C. M. Cooke, Jr.[3]

On Admiral King's approval, a readiness deadline[4] was set for 1 January 1945. This new class of warship would become the "Interim" LSM(R), or Landing Ship, Medium (Rocket), the United States Navy's first rocketship and penultimate wartime amphibious fire support ship.[5]

On 29 September, three weeks after Adm. Charles M. Cooke's initial memo, the U.S. Navy's Bureau of Ships (BuShips) directed Gibbs & Cox, Inc., the naval architecture and engineering design agent, to prepare working plans for unprecedented conversions of LSMs to "LSM Rocket Ships."[6]

Only days after beginning preliminary designs, on 6 October the Bureau of Ships provided Gibbs & Cox Company essential data permitting detailed engineering.[7] The following day, BuShips sent a confidential memorandum to the Chief of Naval Operations (via Bureau of Ordnance) affirming general agreements on the configuration of the new rocket-firing landing ship, after conferences between representatives from the Commander-in-Chief U.S. Fleet, Vice Chief of Naval Operations, Bureau of Ordnance, and Bureau of Ships. Sets of preliminary plans, "to permit quick conversion," were forwarded that also suggested general arrangements for rocket launchers and rocket stowage. Specific requirements were outlined under armament, ammunition, and accommodations:

Armament:
76–4-rail launchers for 5" aircraft rockets (total 304 rails);
30–6-rail launchers for 5" aircraft rockets (total 180 rails);
1–5"/38 cal. destroyer type mount;
4–20mm single mounts.

Ammunition:
350 rounds 5" ammunition;
6,000 rds./bbl. [rounds per barrel]–20mm ammunition;

11

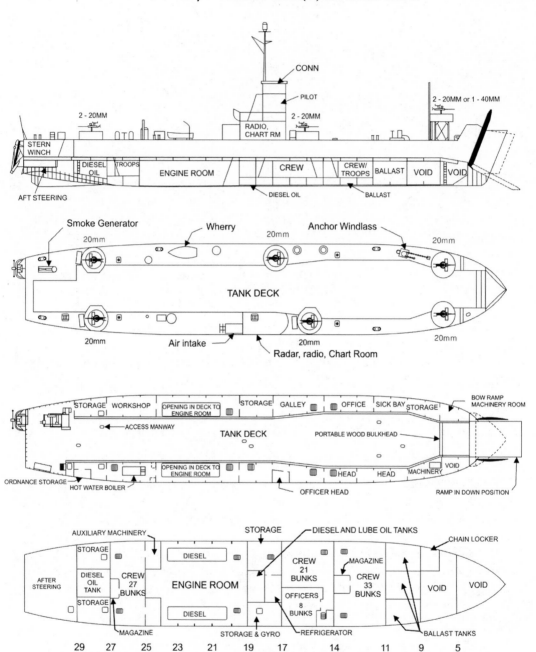

General arrangements of a conventional LSM, or Landing Ship, Medium (used with permission from John C. MacKay).

  3,000 rounds–5" aircraft rockets made up as follows:
  300 rds. assembled ready service;
  2700 rds. unassembled in separate magazines.

Accommodations:
7 officers (including division commander);
81 crew.

The BuShips memo of 7 October concluded, "Working plans are being developed as quickly as possible ... in order that the ships may be converted immediately on receipt of a directive to do so. It is requested that the Bureau [of Ships] be advised as promptly as possible if these ships are to be converted in order that material procurement may be undertaken in time to meet desired dates of completion."[8]

A final imprimatur was the Pacific Fleet's urgent request in October 1944, asking for the 12 rocket-firing support ships based on BuShips' proposal.[9] This preliminary design outline would conform closely with the final configuration of the of LSM(R)188-Class.

Within three weeks, in a remarkable feat of engineering, Gibbs & Cox submitted 76 working drawings to Bureau of Ships on 25 October. These, in turn, were expedited via special messenger to Charleston Navy Yard, South Carolina, a mere 24 hours after approval from the Supervisor of Shipbuilding.[10] Among the half-dozen shipyards contracted to build LSMs, or Landing Ship, Mediums, Charleston Navy Yard, alone, was a U.S. naval base, which assured enhanced security for this new, secretive program. The next steps were to select the ships for conversion and determine the crews to man them.

The LSMs

Beginning late 1943 until mid 1945, literally dozens of Landing Ships, Medium were in various stages of construction among six shipyards across the nation. At any given moment, LSMs were on building ways, in dry docks, and at docksides in shipyards, while more LSMs were being fitting out, commissioned, undergoing builders' sea trials and shakedown cruises. All were destined for war in the Pacific.

Amphibious ships, crafts, and vehicles became highest priorities for the United States Navy in America's total war against Imperial Japan.[11] The vast Pacific Ocean, and the great distances between Japanese-held islands, required shallow-draft vessels capable of approaching and landing on enemy-held beachheads to deploy American fighting men, war machines, and equipment. This imperative led to wide-ranging, innovative designs, resulting in a veritable alphabet soup of amphibious classifications.[12] To meet the Navy's wartime requirements and deadlines, much work was sub-contracted to numerous commercial companies, which pre-fabricated smaller sub-sections that were transported to the primary shipyards for final assembly.[13]

The LSM evolved in the fall of 1943 from the U.S. Navy's proposed criteria for an intermediate tank-carrying amphibious craft, smaller than the 345-foot LST (Landing Ship, Tank), yet larger than the 120-foot LCT(6) or Landing Craft, Tank (Mark 6). Ideally, the design would be a strong, ballasted cargo vessel, able to navigate and beach among smaller islands, yet also span open seas fast enough to maintain convoy speeds. It also had to transport the largest American tanks, provide living spaces for vehicle crews, and accommodate two infantry platoons.

The Bureau of Ships developed conceptual designs in August 1943 for a 196-foot vessel with a flat bottom for beaching, an open main (also called a well or tank well) deck, running

Landing Ships, Medium served only in the Pacific Theatre during World War II. LSMs first saw combat operations in the Southwest Pacific in late 1944. Here *LSMs 18* and *51* offload Army trucks, tanks and artillery in Ormoc Bay, Leyte, Philippines, on 7 December 1944 (official U.S. Navy photograph).

from the bow through most of the length of the ship for vehicles and cargo, a conning tower offset starboard amidships to maximize transport capacity, and a flat nose with an LCT-type dropping bow ramp. Its broad bow was a drawback, however, because it pushed against rather that cut through water, so it was replaced with the LST-type "clamshell" bow doors with a drawbridge-style ramp, which added about six feet to overall length. Final dimensions were 203-feet length and 34-feet beam. LSM crews were nominally four officers and 54 enlisted men.

    This new configuration was initially designated the LCT(7), or Landing Craft, Tank (Mark 7), 1501 Class,[14] for which the Bureau of Ships awarded contracts to U.S. shipyards by mid–September 1943.[15] The design agent was Gibbs & Cox Company, whose naval engineers would be central to designing the future LSM(R)s, as well.[16] The new design proved not so much a craft as a ship, however, so by 19 November 1943, the classification was changed to LSM, or Landing Ship, Medium.[17]

    The LSM was assigned four interrelated missions: first, to land manned tanks, vehicles, and infantry forces on enemy shores; second, to retract from shore; third, to re-embark troops and equipment from beaches; fourth, serve as a small freighter across oceans and among islands.[18]

LSMs had several general levels, from lowest to highest, the Inner Bottom, Skegs, Hold, Main Deck (also called the Well or Tank Deck), Superstructure Deck (including the Radar-Radio-Chart Room, often called the Radio or Radar Shack), Bridge Deck, Wheelhouse Deck, and Conn.

Below the waterline, the Inner Bottom contained numerous seawater ballast tanks with electric pumps for shifting the ship's level and buoyancy during beaching and un-beaching operations. Ballast tanks could be used also for extra diesel fuel storage as needed. Forward draft fully loaded was about four feet and aft draft about seven feet. Freeboard forward was thirteen feet and aft was ten feet.

Above the Inner Bottom was the Hold, still below the waterline, with compartments for the engines, fuel tanks, berthing and messing spaces, after steering, and stowage.

The Main Deck, in which vehicles and cargo were carried, was about four feet above the waterline. Enclosed lengthwise on both port and starboard sides, numerous compartments housed equipment, stowage, washrooms (or heads, in Navy parlance), and work spaces.

The Superstructure Deck was about 12 feet above waterline, and the height from the Superstructure Deck to the top of the Conn was 22.5 feet. The Conning Tower was offset starboard amidships, including the Chart Room and Radio/Radar Shack. Upper levels were the Bridge Deck, the Wheelhouse (or Pilot House), and finally the Conn, sometimes called the Open or Flying Bridge, where the signalman's light was some 36 feet above sea level. Offset abaft the Conn was the main mast and yard arm, arrayed with lights, horn, radio and radar equipment, and signal flag lanyards attached to the flag bag on the Bridge Deck below.

LSMs were powered by two, opposing 16-cylinder diesel engines. The initial design called for Fairbanks-Morse 38D81/8 × 10, but an option soon allowed the General Motors 16–278A, installed at Charleston Navy Yard, both of which were utilized in submarines and destroyer escorts. Sealift capacity was 165 tons, for 5 medium or 3 heavy tanks, or 6 LVTs (Landing Vehicle, Tracked), or 9 army DUKW amphibian trucks.[19]

Defensive ordnance for conventional LSMs were six, single-barrel 20mm guns in gun tubs (or gun shields) on the superstructure deck: two, opposed port and starboard near the fantail; two, opposed port and starboard amidships; two, opposed port and starboard immediately abaft the raised forecastle. A subsequent version replaced the two forward 20mm guns with a single 40mm in a large gun tub atop the forecastle. Some LSMs also saw *ad hoc* field modifications during the course of the war.

Amphibious Training Base, Little Creek, Virginia

The Amphibious Training Base at Little Creek, Virginia, was operational in summer 1942 under the U.S. Atlantic Fleet, and became a specialized LSM training facility in January 1944.[20] (Coincidentally, the following year, in May 1945, the base commander, Captain Charles F. Macklin, Jr., would assume command of the new "Ultimate" LSM(R)s of LSM(R) Flotilla Eighteen.)

From across the nation, prospective LSM sailors arrived at Little Creek and were formed in training companies with a nucleus of 48 enlisted men (fourteen in Deck Group, seventeen in Engine Group, seventeen in Ships Control Group) and 4 officers (Commanding, Executive, Engineering, Gunnery). Four (originally ten) weeks of training ashore and afloat emphasized LSMs in particular, and landing craft operations generally. Classes included engines and ship's equipment, ordnance and gunnery, damage control and firefighting, battle station drills and watch standing as well as First Aid and lifesaving, hygiene and physical training, and, of course, marching. Upon graduation, officers and enlisted crews usually remained as a unit en route receiving stations, where training and drilling continued while LSMs were readied with commissionings, outfitting, sea trials, shakedowns, and final deployment.

The Secretary of the Navy acknowledged the special status of the Amphibious Forces, authorizing enlisted personnel to wear the scarlet and gold shoulder patch insignia, embroidered with an eagle perched above a submachine gun that crossed the shank of an anchor.[21] Yet assignment to landing ships and craft was anything but respected by the "Blue Water" Navy, because amphibious duty was considered a career-ender for officers and a dead end for misfits. "As you know," confided former Lieutenant Neal Hadsell, "there was little love lost between 'the real Navy' and the Amphibs. We were second class all the way as far as ships of the line were concerned. It was common for any enlisted man or officer that screwed up to be assigned to the Amphibs as a form of punishment. I had several crew members in that category on my LCT. I think there were several rejects on the [LSM(R)] 192 also. Our flotilla commander was in this class also I understand."[22] Unlike the traditional fleet, moreover, the Amphibious Force was also seen as expendable.[23] "But in the course of the war, ironically, the amphibious fleet proved to be 'the closest to the enemy with the mostest' of any ships in the Navy," affirmed Admiral George C. Dyer, biographer of Admiral Richmond Kelly Turner.[24]

In hindsight, reflected Paul S. Vaitses, Jr., then a Lieutenant (Junior Grade) who got his "sea legs" aboard battleship *Massachusetts BB 59*, "Scarcely had we dreamed back in July 1944 at Little Creek, Virginia, where the Navy assembled its crews for amphibious training, that we were to be chosen for the important job of testing these revolutionary craft [i.e., LSM(R)s] for use in the final all-out drive against the Japanese. At the amphibs base, we were merely readied for duty on regular LSMs (Landing Ship Medium) as were hundreds of other crews." But, he hastened, "Of course, much of the time spent at Little Creek had been wasted as far as preparation for this type of duty went."[25]

Charleston Navy Yard, Charleston, South Carolina

Charleston Navy Yard (CNY) reached its height of activity in 1944 with the largest workforce in South Carolina. Over 25,000 people were employed by the Navy Yard, many working nine-hour, six-day schedules among three shifts. Sunday was a day off, although many worked that day as well.[26] Average LSM production rates, from keel layings to launchings, were about 30 days; rates between launchings and commissionings averaged another 48 days.

In January 1944 CNY started laying keels for the new LSMs, built side-by-side in pairs or "sister ships," followed some four weeks by dual ceremonial public launchings, after which work continued up to and after commissionings. LSMs were built so rapidly and in such large numbers, in fact, that keel layings, launchings and commissionings occurred on an almost weekly rotation and oftentimes out of numerical order. By fall 1944, remarked Rear Admiral

Landing Ships, Medium were built in pairs at Charleston Navy Yard in South Carolina. *LSM 188* **is being launched, and minutes later sister ship** *LSM 189* **was launched after dual christening ceremonies on 12 September 1944 (official U.S. Navy photograph).**

Jules James, USN, both Commandant of the Charleston Navy Yard and Commandant of the Sixth Naval District, "Our activities here have been on the increase and we are building ships faster than ever, paying no attention to the many rumors that the war is almost over…"[27]

Yet few among the prospective LSM companies at Charleston were aware of the intense, secretive shipyard conversion work on their future rocketships. Motor Machinist Mate Allison Gray, an original crew member known as a "plank owner" on *LSM 188*, recalled nothing being said about their new LSM Rocket Ship. "None of us to our knowledge had any hint of what was going on. [But] This probably was planned this way."[28] Bruce McDaniel, Quartermaster-Striker assigned to *LSM 196* added, "…most of us never saw much of the [*LSM*] *196* before we were ready to leave [Charleston]…"[29] Lt. (jg) Paul S. Vaitses of *LSM 193* affirmed that this was as true for officers as for enlisted men: "To make matters worse, the ship was practically inaccessible until almost commissioning time because of the work going on aboard. All we could do was to send the gun crews to loading drills, the cooks to cooking school, the

CONFIDENTIAL

2556-44   U. S. Navy Yard, S. C., September 12, 1944.
LSM 188 after Launching.

The 12 "Interim" LSM(R)s were originally configured as conventional Landing Ships, Medium, including the forward ramp and "clam shell" bow doors, as seen by *LSM 188* on launching day 12 September 1944 (official U.S. Navy photograph).

signalmen and quartermasters to their daily drills, and just hope to God the engineering gang and the seamen wouldn't go AWOL before the ship was completed."[30] This also became a concern to Commander Dennis L. Francis, who, after assuming command of the twelve LSM(R)s, complained that crews lacked sufficient training and familiarization with their new rocketships, which directly affected the flotilla's combat readiness.[31]

Although remarkable in hindsight, some officers assigned commanders of amphibious landing ships, including *LSMs 191, 192, 194,* and *195,* were only Lieutenants (Junior Grades), and most were naval reservists. Allan M. Hirshberg of *LSM 194* related a not-so-uncommon experience: "I was first to be assigned as an Exec Officer, but after a great deal of discussion at staff level, I was given command, and spot-promoted to full Lieutenant, there not being enough senior officers with previous sea and/or amphibious experience."[32] Most commanding officers, however, were lieutenants with wartime experience under their belts, such as naval reservist Lt. Dennis D. O'Callaghan of *LSM 196,* who had served in the Atlantic Theatre, including Armed Guard service aboard a Liberty ship off North Africa. Uniquely, Lt. John M. Cooper, commanding sister ship *LSM 197,* was "Regular Navy," but one who had advanced from an enlisted chief petty officer until selected for naval commission, known in Navy parlance as a "mustang."

Lt. James M. Stewart of *LSM 189* reflected upon the spectrum of naval officers at the time: "I believe the officers were selected by chance [to man the LSM(R)s]. They were all college graduates. [The Navy] selected lawyers, teachers, administrators and engineers. They were teachable and, like myself in the beginning, didn't know the port from the starboard side of the ship, the upstairs from topside, the head from the Captain, but they learned."[33] Stewart, an attorney, had volunteered for active duty in the naval reserves when war began and, after graduating midshipman's school with a commission—a so-called "ninety-day wonder"—he served in the Aleutian Islands of Alaska in patrol craft and minesweepers.[34]

Prospective skipper Lt (jg) Neal B. Hadsell, captained an LCT in the South Pacific until ordered stateside to command "LSM Crew 7269" at Little Creek. Thereafter, he received "Restricted" change of duty orders on 11 October 1944, directing him and three subordinate officers to escort their enlisted 48-man "LSM" crew to the Charleston Navy Yard Receiving Station. The next day, Hadsell was provided government quarters in the Citadel Barracks at the Military College of South Carolina, and over the next five weeks assigned "temporary duty in connection with fitting out the U.S.S. *LSM 192* and for duty on board when commissioned."[35]

"Staying at The Citadel was a very enjoyable experience because our living conditions were excellent and we had a lot more freedom than we have had at the base," recalled Paul S. Vaitses, Jr., prospective Executive Officer for sister ship *LSM 193*, "but were cautioned to be prompt in reporting for duty at 0800 at the shipyard each weekday morning."[36]

Prospective enlisted LSM crewmen, on the other hand, found barracks capacities in Charleston often filled and unable to accommodate all the newly-reporting naval personnel. In one instance, while awaiting completion of *LSM(R) 196*, Quartermaster-striker Bruce A. McDaniel recalled he and other sailors were temporarily quartered at the U.S. Coast Guard Station on the Ashleigh River, amidst a collection of old brick buildings which were once used in previous years for processing and shipping rice.[37]

Meantime, "Our days at Charleston Navy Yard were utilized in learning about the LSM in general and then the conversion to an LSM(R)," said Lyle Tennis, a naval reserve ensign assigned to then-*LSM 190*. "Some of our early learning was classroom instruction supplemented by bringing all manuals up-to-date. As Communications and Stores Officer, I had to supervise those rates as they made official corrections and additions to the manuals. As time progressed, we all got hands-on training on equipment relating to our area—the radarmen, radiomen, signalmen, quartermasters, yeomen, and storekeepers all had time allotted for work and learning."[38] Some spent time in the *Wyoming AG 17*, a pre–World War I former battleship serving as an auxiliary gunnery training ship.

About two-thirds of the future LSM(R) crews averaged less than a year's active duty with the Navy.[39] "Moreover," said Paul S. Vaitses, Jr., citing *LSM(R) 193* as an example, "with only three officers and eleven men out of the entire ship's company claiming any previous sea duty, to say nothing of having seen real action, we faced a frightful task to whip such a green crew into shape. As the skipper put it, only a handful of us had 'ever heard a shot fired in anger.'"[40] Allan M. Hirshberg, still only prospective Commanding Officer of *LSM 194*, recalled thinking at the time, "'This crew from Officer core to enlisted men is as inexperienced as is possible.' I believe less than ten percent of the crew had ever been to sea before. For example, as we were leaving Charleston the helmsman was chasing the compass in steering his course."[41]

Caltech and the U.S. Navy

The "LSM Rocket Ship" and the U.S. Navy's entire rocket program were made possible by the scientists and engineers at California Institute of Technology in Pasadena, California.

When the United States was preemptively attacked by the Imperial Japanese Navy on 7 December 1941, American naval forces had no rocket weapons nor, for that matter, had the U.S. Navy shown much interest in rocket technology between the wars.[42] In contrast, as early as 1940, rockets were in production for military purposes in Great Britain, the Soviet Union, and Nazi Germany.[43]

During the quarter century between world wars, Dr. Robert H. Goddard, later considered the founding father of modern rocketry, persistently proposed scientific rocket programs to the Navy and War Departments. Of those contracted, funding was limited and lacked enthusiasm. In the end, the U.S. Navy terminated each of Goddard's rocket projects, and all but dismissed rockets as significant to the Fleet.[44]

But in the years immediately preceding World War II, a small number of prescient American scientists pressed for U.S. military technical and scientific research.[45] Alarmed by world events and growing international crises, leading scientists, including Drs. Richard C. Tolman, Charles C. Lauritsen, Clarence N. Hickman, John T. Tate, Frederick L. Hovde, James B. Conant and Vannevar Bush, foresaw American civilian scientific expertise spurring the U.S. military's technological inertia. After great persistence, their proposal was finally presented to President Franklin D. Roosevelt to establish an agency that would mobilize science to aid national defense. With his presidential scrawl, "OK-FDR," the National Defense Research Committee (NDRC) was formed in June 1940 headed by Dr. Bush. A year later, a unit of NDRC was formed which would have far-reaching influence, the Office of Scientific Research and Development (OSRD), uniting American scientific, engineering and industrial resourcefulness. Under the aegis of OSRD, a department known simply as Division 3 oversaw the research and development of rocketry, including the Fin-stabilized ("Finner") and Spin-stabilized ("Spinner") rockets and launchers subsequently mounted on the twelve "Interim" LSM(R)s.[46]

NDRC and OSRD worked closely with the Bureau of Ordnance, the Bureau of Ships, and the Signal Corps.[47] Universities and private companies were contracted for various aspects of rocket research and development.[48] The British, too, helped the American rocket program, most creditably during its early stages. In fall of 1940, a scientific mission from Great Britain, sanctioned by their government, shared heretofore secret rocket research with their American counterparts. Upon forming an intergovernmental academic alliance, the British provided valuable data that allowed the Americans to quickly leap ahead in areas of rocketry and other scientific endeavors. While Great Britain lacked sufficient technical manpower with limited research facilities and resources, they could thereafter count on America's reciprocation.[49]

Yet perhaps no single institution had a greater impact upon or contribution to the U.S. Navy rocket program than the California Institute of Technology (known as Caltech or CIT) in Pasadena, California.[50] Under government Contract OEMsr-418, Caltech served as the

U.S. Navy's *de facto* naval rocket program during World War II.[51] So close were the ties, in fact, Caltech scientist Dr. William Fowler once remarked, "...the upshot was that a large part of Caltech literally became a branch of the Bureau of Ordnance."[52]

Forward-firing finned aircraft rockets were first developed and tested for the U.S. Navy by Caltech in 1943, initially designed to puncture German submarine hulls. Caltech undertook manufacturing rockets as a wartime stop-gap measure, meanwhile, until contractors could assume production. As the German submarine threat diminished in the Atlantic, 5.0-inch Aircraft Rockets assumed greater importance for U.S. naval aviation and amphibious forces. Large quantities of Finners were manufactured and widely distributed throughout the Pacific theatre until the end of the war.[53]

From mid–1942, Caltech and the U.S. Navy and Marine Corps became increasingly interested in forward-launched naval rockets for beach barrages immediately prior to amphibious landings.[54] A problem during Pacific island assaults was the brief lull after American naval gunfire and air support were lifted prior to troops hitting the beach from landing craft. This critical hiatus thus allowed the Japanese to mobilize defense forces for disastrous counter fires against the assaulting Army infantry and Marines.

A solution was to mount launchers with barrage rockets aboard shallow-draft amphibious vessels, which closed beachheads with sustaining fires on the enemy ashore, as troop-carrying landing craft landed on the beaches. Here, the capacity to concentrate firepower over a broad area was deemed of greater importance than pin-point accuracy, so dispersion[55]—or rocket scatter—was not viewed as especially significant.[56] The idea of mounting barrage rockets in landing craft was thought born early 1942 in Great Britain, some crediting Royal Navy commando Colonel H. F. G. Langley, Royal Artillery, of the British Combined Operations Headquarters (COHQ).[57]

Indeed, a predecessor was the Royal Navy's LCTR (Landing Craft, Tank, Rocket),[58] converted from the larger British-designed LCT. LCTRs accommodated 5-inch British Army rockets in launchers, fixed in forward train and elevation, and supported by a temporary raised structure above the well deck. The numbers of rocket launchers among the several LCTR iterations ranged between 800 and 1,044, with stowage capacities of 4,000 to 5,000 rockets. However, a design deficiency was the inability to correct the line of fire, since LCTRs launched their entire deck loads of rockets at once. Under an unusual reverse Lend-Lease program, 14 British LCTRs were loaned to the U.S. Navy and manned by American sailors for operations in the Atlantic and Mediterranean Theatres from September 1943 to October 1944. Sailing under U.S. flag, each American LCTR billeted two naval officers and 17 enlisted men under the U.S. LCTR Group, Gunfire Support Craft, 11th Amphibious Force.[59]

By May 1943, the U.S. Navy Bureau of Ordnance called for a ship-to-shore bombardment rocket with a minimum range of 10,000 yards and propelled by a 3.25-inch diameter rocket motor. Caltech responded by producing a series of increasingly powerful and durable 5.0-inch Fin-stabilized Aircraft Rockets, which scientists and engineers referred to as "Finners." The Naval Gun Factory at Washington Navy Yard also participated in limited production and testing under the Bureau of Ordnance.[60] Several barrage rocket and launcher designs, developed by Caltech, became widely produced and deployed in the Pacific for amphibious island assaults. Ballistite was the propellant used in virtually all U.S. Navy rockets.[61]

Caltech also began studies of fin-less "rotating" or "spinning" rockets,[62] in spring of 1943 because, as one scientist remarked, "The most exasperating thing about fin-stabilized rockets is the infrequency with which they go in the direction that they are aimed."[63] This dispersion (or rocket scatter) diminished accuracy, since rocket flight paths were affected not only by surface and atmospheric conditions, but also from occasional collisions in flight. The weight and relative bulkiness of fin-stabilized rockets during handling and storage were negative factors, as well.[64]

Intense research sought a more accurate and powerful rocket—sans tailfins—that self-stabilized in flight, not unlike a bullet fired from a rifled barrel. Experimentation found the preferred means for inducing rotation, by forcing propellant exhaust gases through inclined nozzles, pre-set at a given angle, in the tail of the rocket.[65] These were called Spin-stabilized Rockets or SSRs, sometimes referred to as "Spinners."

The numbers and types of Spinners tested and developed took many forms and combinations. By war's end, over thirty kinds of 5.0-inch SSRs were developed alone using the same artillery head in the 5.0-inch ARs.[66] Caltech also developed a Spinner gravity-fed launcher from a design borrowed from the earlier Mark 7 Launcher, used widely in the Pacific among LCI and LCS gunboats with 4.5" barrage rockets. Meantime, California Institute of Technology continued serving in the rocket manufacturing business, as stopgap supplier of the Navy's rapidly increasing demands for Spinners, until American commercial industries took over.[67]

Thus building upon experiences gained from the Royal Navy's LCTRs and the U.S. Navy's early rocket-firing amphibious crafts, the new "LSM Rocket Ship" integrated air-to-surface and surface-to-surface rocket and launcher technologies for concentrated ship-to-shore fire support. Fin-stabilized Aircraft Rockets with rail launchers ushered the *LSM(R) 188* Class, and Spin-stabilized Rockets with gravity-fed launchers augured the *LSM(R) 196* Class.

LSMs to "LSM Rocket Ships"

Six days after the Bureau of Ships proposed the "LSM Rocket Ship," the Chief of Naval Operations sent a confidential letter dated 13 October 1944—coinciding with the U.S. Navy's 169th birthday—directing Bureau of Ships and Bureau of Ordnance to expedite the conversion of twelve LSMs[68] to the new—but as yet unofficial—classification of LSM(R): "It is desired that *LSMs 188–199* now building at Navy Yard, Charleston, be converted ... with priority equal to repairs, and that all material and work be prosecuted as urgently as possible." This directive is notable because it reveals the Navy still intended all twelve ships mounted with launchers for Fin-stabilized Aircraft Rockets (AR), which actually defined the *LSM(R) 188* Class.

The CNO directive concurred with most of BuShips earlier recommendations for the LSM conversions, but "amended to include an interim armament for twelve (12) LSM Rocket Ships as follows":

76—4 rail launchers fixed in train and elevation, mounted on the covered well deck.

30—6 rail launchers (pre-set in elevation) mounted along starboard and port rails and capable of rotating inboard to a securing position from an outboard firing position.

1—5"/38 cal. D.P. gun (750 f.s., 1200 f.s., 2600 f.s. muzzle velocities) mounted aft on centerline.

1—Mark 51 director.

2—40 mm. singles. One forward of bridge structure, starboard side, raised sufficiently to clear loaded rocket launchers when in firing positions, the other on the forecastle-head.

3—20 mm. guns.

3000 rocket capacity magazines for 3.5" aircraft rockets with 5" H.E. Head.

Concluding, "Until otherwise advised, it is desired that these craft be identified by the designation LSM(R).... The additional personnel required as result of this change in ordnance has not been included in any previous directive. By copy of this letter the Chief of Naval Personnel is requested to determine the complement and furnish trained personnel for manning these special vessels.[69]

The CNO directive is also notable for its qualifying reference to "interim armament," clearly alluding to future LSM(R)s possessing "ultimate armament." Remarkably, a mission statement for these new rocketships was never formalized.

Acting on the CNO's recommendation, the following week Secretary of the Navy James Forrestal directed these twelve rocket-firing LSMs be reclassified and commissioned as "LSM(R)," effective 18 October 1944.[70]

By 21 October, the Bureau of Naval Personnel issued the directive, "LSM—Officer and Enlisted Complement," enumerating crew billeting in the *LSM(R)s 188–199* for five commissioned officers and 76 enlisted men.[71] After ships' commissionings, however, six officers were typically assigned to each rocketship, while the numbers of enlisted remained close to the NavPers directive. To the consternation of prospective commanding officers, however, many of the supplemental enlisted men and officers were only actually reporting to their LSM(R)s by the days of commissionings.

One officer was Ensign Lawrence J. Low, USNR: "I reported to the [*LSM(R)*] *197* for duty on 8 December 1944, the day she was commissioned. In fact, I never made it into the official crew photo that was taken dockside on that date. The same may be true of some of the other Gunnery Officers. I recall the confusion, as you have reported it, that existed with the LSM(R) crews (from the skippers on down) as to what their future roles were to be. As a matter of fact, the group of us reporting in from the crash rocket course at American University in early December had the latest clues as to how the ships would conduct their future rocket firing missions simply based on the performance characteristics of the rockets themselves. Needless to say, there were varied reactions among the ship's officers and enlisted men (not altogether positive) ... and this was before any of us knew about Roger Peter stations or kamikazes."[72]

Conversions

The twelve "LSM Rocket Ships" began as conventional LSMs, including "clam shell" bow doors, landing ramps, and open well decks. At launchings, however, the absence of the distinctive round conning tower gave a strangely unnerving appearance; instead, arising from the well deck was a temporary mast with yardarm. Ships were painted gray overall, and the official ceremonies were semi-public albeit by invitation only, but none of the ships' prospective officers or enlisted men was present. (The launchings of *LSM 188* and *LSM 197* were noteworthy if for no other reason than their sponsors were wives of the sitting governors of South Carolina and North Carolina, respectively. After the war, interestingly, the former commanding officer of *LSM(R) 198* would be elected governor of South Carolina).[73]

Once launched and floated, tugs maneuvered the medium landing ships to docksides, within reach of large overhead shipyard cranes where much fitting, cutting, grinding, and welding continued, although progress varied.[74] From late October into November 1944, the forward ramps were removed, the large bow doors with lower bow door flaps were welded watertight from inside, and their outer exposed seams covered with long strips of thin, narrow steel plates, also welded watertight.

The "Interim" LSM(R)s shared many fundamental LSM design characteristics: an Inner Bottom (900 Level), Skegs (300 Level), Hold (200 Level), Main Deck (100 Level), Superstructure Deck including the Radar-Radio-Chart Room (01 Level), Bridge Deck (02 Level), Wheelhouse (03 Level), and Conn (04 Level). Similarly, frames (or "ribs") were numbered forward to aft from 0 to 41 with varying spacings; portside compartments were even-numbered, and starboard side compartments odd-numbered.

The LSM(R)'s Inner Bottom remained unaltered, enclosing water ballast tanks and internal pumping systems which could be used for extra diesel fuel capacity. The Hold was also identical to LSMs, with forward void and ballast tanks, and separate berthing and messing spaces for officers and enlisted. The Hold also comprised 20mm magazines, refrigeration and general stores compartments, engine room with two General Motors 16–278A, diesel storage and lube oil settling tanks, auxiliary machinery spaces, and aft Landing Force berthing space. Not least, deep in the Hold under the fantail was the Steering Gear Flat (C-206E), also known as After Steering with a "Trick Wheel," for emergency manual steering.

In the LSM(R)s, the Main Deck's tank wells were extensively revised, requiring structural support for the numerous additional bulkheads and compartments. The Forward Rocket Assembly Room (A-103¼ M) with ready service stowage was at Frames 8–12, Amidships Rocket Assembly Room (A-104¼ M) at Frames 14–16, and Aft Rocket Assembly Room (B-102 M) with ready service stowage at Frames 21–24¾, each with a rocket assembly table. Rocket fins were stowed in the three rocket assembly rooms, adjacent to separate magazines for rocket fuses, rocket bodies, and rocket motors. A Forward 40mm Magazine and Ammunition Stowage (A-101¼ M) compartment assumed the general area of the removed bow door, and the aft tank well became a 5"/38 Caliber Powder Magazine (C-102⅛ M) and 5"/38 Caliber Projectile Stowage and Handling Room (C-102¼ M). A division commander's cabin (A-105L) was also added center amidships. For temperature control of the rocket magazines, internal lighting, wiring, piping, insulation, ventilation ducting and venting hoods were added or modified with the new compartmentation.

General internal arrangement of an "Interim" LSM(R) (used with permission from John C. MacKay).

Lengthwise, port and starboard compartments opposed the Main or Well Deck, similar to a conventional LSM. From the forward starboard side, bow door machinery were removed to become extra stowage space, followed by the crew's washroom (or head), the officers' washroom, the upper level engine room and passage, boiler room, ordnance stores, damage control locker, and aft vegetable locker. From the forward port side, ramp gate machinery were removed to become extra stowage space, followed by the Bosun's Locker, 750-pound port bow anchor and windlass machinery room, sick bay, galley and galley stores, the upper level engine room and passage, machine workshop, and aft Engineer's stores. The 2,000-pound stern anchor and fantail winch with windlass remained in place, as well.[75]

The LSM(R) Well Deck was entirely covered by mild steel plate, faired with the Superstructure Deck from Frame 27 forward to the Forecastle's sloping bulkhead at Frame 5, becoming a full Weather Deck but often called the Rocket Deck. The after Superstructure Deck from Frames 27 to 39 was raised 12 inches, with structural reinforcement and covered with mild steel plate, for a topside deck foundation where the 5"/38 gun was installed on the longitudinal centerline at Frame 28. For access to and from the lower 5"/38 Handling Room, a 2-foot by 6-foot watertight hatch was added athwartship at Frame 34. A portside opening in the aft deck plating allowed the anchor cable to draw freely between the stern anchor and the winch/windlass, mounted below on the aft portside Well Deck.

On the Superstructure Deck, forward of the 5"/38 gun, was a Mark 51 Gun Director Tower with ladder, centered over Frame 25¼ with overall height of 15 feet. Three 2-foot by 6-foot longitudinal watertight hatches were centered at Frames 10, 15 and 23 above the Forward, Amidships and Aft Rocket Assembly Rooms. Along the gunwales, the forward portside #1 20mm AA gun shield (or gun tub) remained at Frame 17; the aft portside #2 20mm AA gun tub was shifted 30 feet forward to Frame 25½; and the starboard #3 20mm AA gun tub was shifted 17 feet forward to Frame 25½. At Frame 15, directly forward of the Conning Tower, the #2 40mm gun tub was raised with support framework to the Bridge Deck level. The Forecastle Deck was lowered to five feet above the Superstructure Deck, above which the #1 40mm gun tub was shifted forward to the very stem of the bow. The Conning Tower remained identical to a conventional LSM, but the portside horizontal yardarm on the mainmast was shortened to clear rocket flight paths.

Reactions to the shipyard conversions ranged from surprise to frustration. Lt.(jg) Paul S. Vaitses, Jr., recalled, "It was after we had been shipped to Charleston, SC, in October [1944] that we discovered what Fate had in store for us. There we had expected to board and commission our newly completed landing ships and enjoy a leisurely cruise back up to Little Creek before sailing for the Pacific. What a rude awakening we had!"

Wandering down to the docks at the Charleston, SC, Navy Yard the day after our arrival, Lt. Don Boynton, USNR, the skipper, and I proceeded to look for the number *193* which had just been designated as our ship in our BuPers [Navy Bureau of Personnel] orders. We were much aghast when we found her, for the workmen were hard at it with acetylene torches cutting down her forecastle and slicing up her tank deck. Welders were sealing up her bow doors, while countless yard superintendents huddled nearby over blueprints.

"Looks like they got pretty far along before they discovered what the hell was wrong!" dryly commented the skipper, with his scornful Purdue [University] air.

"Anyhow, it's unanimous," I pointed out, waving my arm in the direction of several more LSMs astern and outboard of our ship undergoing the same treatment.

In no time, a conference in the Captain-of-the-Yard's office and a good look at the blueprints brought us up to date on the situation.[76]

On the other hand, Lt. Neal B. Hadsell, prospective commanding officer of *LSM 192*, found that he had to investigate on his own to learn more about his future LSM rocket ship. "The first I heard about such a ship was from Navy Yard workers. I went down to the dock each morning to see what was happening toward completion. I got down there one morning and there were no workers in sight anywhere. I thought I had somehow gotten mixed up on the days. The next day was the same. I inquired at the Port Director's Office and got no straight answer."

"I had real trouble finding out anything that was going on," continued Hadsell. "No one really wanted to talk officially. My best source of information was the work crew. They were always glad to talk and usually you could count on what they had to say."

> The third day I found two workmen aboard the *192* measuring and marking bulkheads and decks. I asked them what was happening. One, with a little notebook, said he had been in Washington for a meeting where the group was told that 12 LSMs would be modified to carry rockets. There were no usable plans yet but he had copied some measurements of changes so that work could begin on the changes. The modification began immediately but as I remember specific plans and full-scale work did not begin for a couple of weeks. Information was so sketchy early on that it was difficult to form any conclusion. Being something brand new there was some concern about how things would work out and what kind of assignments we might draw.[77]

Rear Admiral Jules James, Charleston Navy Yard Commandant, allowed an additional 15 days of shipyard work for the conversions of the first pairs of rocketships (in his initial weekly progress reports, James referred to the ships as "USS *LSM 188* (Modified)," "USS *LSM 189* (Modified)," and so on).[78] But speed demanded for the LSM conversions caused mixed reactions from the ships' commanding officers, suggesting the directives and scope of the work were not fully known or disclosed.[79] One prospective LSM captain stated: "Delay in the date of completion is anticipated due to conversion…. Enlisted personnel have been assembled and seemingly are satisfactory unless the Bureau [of Personnel] increases the complement due to conversion…." One other prospective LSM skipper commented, "The construction was progressing satisfactorily for this ship in accordance with original plans. Due, however, to the conversion of this ship, it is believed there will be some delay…. Our officer and enlisted complement [of four officers and 48 enlisted men], it is felt, will be inadequate to man all stations…. When information is available on type of ordnance equipment to be installed on conversion, additional training will be necessary for officers and men manning same." Yet another future LSM commander lamented, "Due to conversion no accurate estimate of date of delivery can be made at this time."[80]

All landing ships underwent a deperming (or degaussing) process to eliminate the magnetic fields of the steel hulls which would otherwise attract and detonate enemy magnetic floating mines. Per a CNO directive for the twelve rocketships, BuShips ordered work, beginning with *LSM 188*, to replace the standard LSM SO-8 radar with the improved SU-1 surface search radar. As a result, Navy Yard Commandant Admiral James informed the CNO that radar replacements would require an extension of the fitting out periods by almost another week.[81] Meanwhile, inclining tests were performed on the *LSM 189* in dry dock to measure and evaluate a fully-loaded LSM(R)'s stability and centers of gravity.[82]

Prior to commissionings, the neophyte LSM(R)s underwent simultaneous Builder's Trials by shipyard representatives, and Acceptance Trials overseen by a Sub-Board of Inspection and Survey with naval personnel. The Builder's Trials consisted of extensive testing and data collection of machinery and engines, steering, and the distilling plant. While underway, each ship was tested for full power runs, backing trials, steering trials at full power, anchoring trials, and material inspection. The Acceptance Trials, reviewed by Navy inspectors with expertise in engineering, radar, radio, ordnance and hull construction, checked the quantity and quality of the ship's completion, and filed reports outlining discrepancies and recommendations. Commanding officers would also submit additional inspection reports on discrepancies to the CNO via the Navy Yard Commandant for corrective measures.

Yet, even after commissionings, shipyard inspectors, welders and fitters, and work parties were busy aboard each ship around the clock, and sometimes up to the last minute before sailing. Liberty ashore became less frequent, and soon cancelled altogether, with crews restricted to ships. However, the unintended consequences of the urgency with which these "LSM Rocket Ships" were pushed, resulted in uneven qualities of workmanship and disparate levels of completion.[83]

The LSM(R) 188 *Class*

The *LSM(R) 188* Class was distinguished by the Mark 36 rocket launchers and the Mark 30 rocket launchers.

*LSM(R)*s *188* through *195* were outfitted with 75 Mark 36 Mod 0 Rocket Launchers holding 300 5.0-inch Fin-stabilized Aircraft Rockets (AR), and 30 Mark 30 Mod 0 Shipboard Aircraft Rocket Launchers holding 180 5.0-inch Fin-stabilized Aircraft Rockets.

Rockets were launched by the gunnery officer, using the Firing Panel Mark 17 Mod 0 mounted in the open Conn:

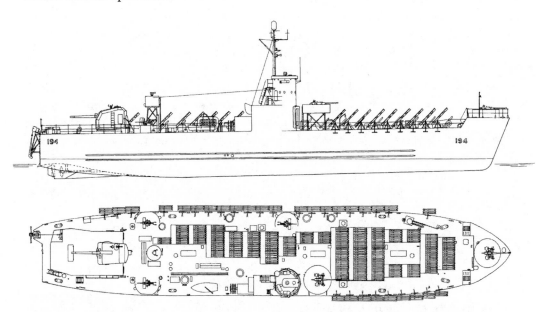

LSM(R) 194 plan and side views show Mark 30 and Mark 36 Rocket Launcher arrangements on "Finner" LSM(R)s 188 through 195 (Norman Friedman, *U.S. Amphibious Ships and Craft: An Illustrated Design History*, Annapolis: Naval Institute Press, 2002, page 250; reprinted with permission from A. D. Baker III).

The control panel usually incorporates a safety plug, master power switch, indicator lamp, push-button firing switch, and individual push buttons or a selector switch for the circuits to the launchers…. The safety plug, which is removable, should be carried by the loader while at the launcher. As an additional precaution, the firing switch should be of a spring type which is normally open. Thus, inadvertent fire will result only if there is both an act of omission (failure to remove safety plug) and of commission (manipulation of firing button).[84]

Mark 36 Launcher

The Mark 36 Mod 0 Launcher was a welded steel framework, grouping four single rails to form a launcher bank, fixed for train and 45° quadrant elevation (QE). Train of fire was accomplished by steering (or aiming) the entire ship toward its target. A deflector, mounted on the deck behind each Mark 36 launcher bank,

Firing Panel Mk 17 Mod 0 with Safety Plug Type B

The Mark 17 Firing Panel was mounted in the "Flying Bridge" atop conning towers of LSM(R)s 188 through 195. Gunnery officers had custody of a Safety Plug Type B (Department of the Navy, Bureau of Ordnance, *Missile Launchers and Related Equipment Catalog OP 1855*, 1 June 1953, page 319).

channeled rocket exhausts upward and aft. Launcher weight unloaded was 600 lb. Launchers were provided by the Bureau of Ordnance.

Mark 36 launchers were arranged in varying banks and rows in relation to ship's centerline, and conformed to the deck and superstructure for safe firing clearances and access for loading and maintenance. Insulated electrical leads connected the launchers to the Firing Panel Mark 17 Mod 0 mounted in the LSM(R) conning tower.

The Mark 36 launcher evolved from Caltech's first successful forward-firing aircraft rocket launcher, the single Mark 4 Rail Launcher, commonly called a "T-slot" launcher developed and tested in 1943. Each rail was 70.0 inches long of box-like design, measuring 3.5 inches wide by 3.6 inches deep with a ⅜-inch lengthwise slot. Rails were light Dural aluminum metal, weighing approximately 14 pounds, and gradually tapered toward the forward or upper end to about 1.75 inches.[85] Two button-type lug bands, attached to each rocket, aligned with the rail's slot and guided the projectile into firing position. Each launcher bank had an electrical circuit box from which an electrical cable adaptor, called a "pigtail," plugged into the rocket motor's tail.

Each "Finner" LSM(R) could launch a maximum deck load of 480 ARs in 30 seconds. Manual load and reload times varied between 1-½ and 2-¾ hours and required all hands.[86]

Mark 30 Launcher

The Mark 30 Mod 0 Shipboard Aircraft Rocket Launcher was mounted on a tripod stand, and manually adjusted and locked for loading, train, and elevation.[87] 30 launchers were welded on the gunwales: 9 mounted along the starboard bow, 21 mounted along the entire port side.

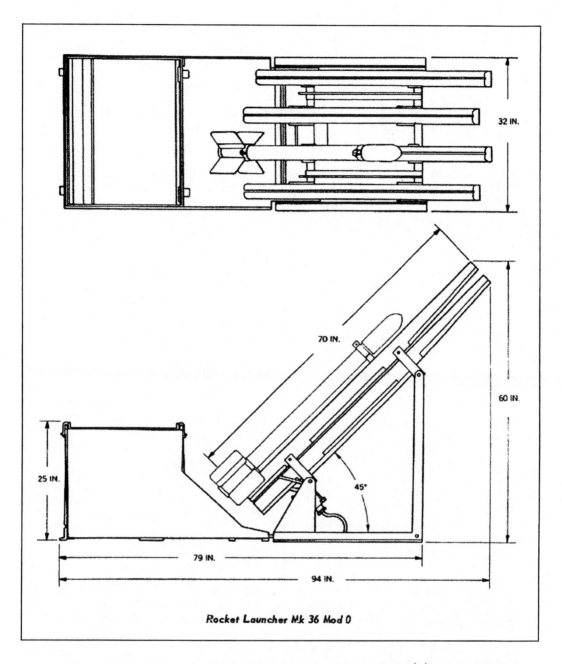

75 Mark 36 Mod 0 Rocket Launcher banks were mounted on "Interim" *LSM(R)*s 188 through 195. Launcher train and elevation were fixed at nominal 45° quadrant elevation (QE). Behind each launcher, a concave deflector channeled rocket blasts upward and aft (Department of the Navy, Bureau of Ordnance, *Missile Launchers and Related Equipment Catalog OP 1855*, 1 June 1953, page 126).

The Mark 30 launcher was a Caltech adaptation, developed in 1944, utilizing three 90.0-inch I-beam-like guides in parallel array. Two button-type lug bands, attached to each rocket, aligned with upper and lower T-slots, which held six Fin-stabilized Aircraft Rockets. Launcher weight unloaded was approximately 450 pounds of steel construction.

Each launcher bank had an electrical circuit box from which an electrical cable adaptor,

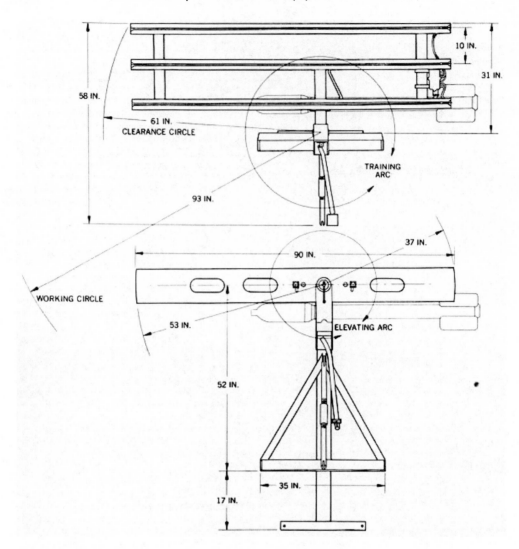

30 Mark 30 Mod 0 Rocket Launchers were mounted on "Interim" *LSM(R)s 188* through *195*. Launcher train and elevation were adjusted manually (Department of the Navy, Bureau of Ordnance, *Missile Launchers and Related Equipment Catalog OP 1855*, 1 June 1953, page 112).

a "pigtail," plugged into the rocket motor's tail. Insulated electrical leads connected the launchers to the Firing Panel Mark 17 Mod 0 in the LSM(R) conning towers. Launchers were provided by the Bureau of Ordnance.

However, the Mark 30 launchers interfered with sector fires from the port amidships and port quarter 20mm guns, blocking gun tracking and depression against air or surface targets. Launchers also became easily entangled or damaged when tying close alongside ships or docks, so all were removed by mid–April 1945 at Okinawa.

5.0-inch Fin-stabilized Aircraft Rocket (AR)

The 5.0-inch Fin-stabilized Aircraft Rocket (AR) Mark 1 averaged 65.0 inches long and weighed about 85 pounds. The AR reached a velocity of approximately 710 feet per second

S1c William R. Toy and F1c Leo H. Gannon load a 5-inch Fin-stabilized Aircraft Rocket (AR) into a Mark 30 Rocket Launcher on *LSM(R) 190* in Charleston Navy Yard, Charleston, South Carolina, circa late 1944 (official U.S. Navy photograph).

with a range of about 4000 yards.[88] Nominal dispersion, or rocket scatter at the impact point, was above 15 mils and ranged upwards of 30 mils due to sea, atmospheric and other conditions. (One mil approximates a 1-yard deflection in 1,000 yards).[89]

Primary components[90] consisted of a Rocket Head, Rocket Motor, and Nose Fuse:

- The Mark 1 Mod 0 Rocket Head[91] was a modified 5.0-inch Mark 35 antiaircraft shell 17 inches long and weighed about 50 pounds, including eight pounds of TNT and a base fuse within;
- The Mark 7 Mod 0 Rocket Motor was 3.25-inch diameter and approximately 46 inches long and weighed about 35 pounds;
- The Mark 149 Mod 0 Nose Fuse was specifically designed for AR rockets[92] with a small propeller at the tip that rotated rapidly in the air stream to arm the fuse after its protective cap was removed.

Rounds were stored in ships' magazines fully assembled (motors plus bodies), less fuses stowed separately; fuses were not installed until after the rounds were carried or passed "bucket brigade" fashion to the rocket deck before manual loading into the launchers.[93] Two

LSM(R) 190 rocket launchers with 5-inch Fin-stabilized Aircraft Rockets (ARs) near Charleston Navy Yard, Charleston, South Carolina, circa late 1944 (official U.S. Navy photograph).

button-type suspension lug bands attached lengthwise to the rocket motor, which aligned the 5.0-inch Fin-stabilized Aircraft Rocket with the T-slot Mark 4 Rail Launchers. ARs came with a short electrical cord with a push-on "pigtail" adapter, which connected the rear exhaust nozzle to the electrical circuit box on its launcher.[94]

For transport, Aircraft Rockets were packaged as sub-assemblies: the 3.25-inch Rocket

Motor was shipped four per box including four unattached Rocket fin-tails, the 5.0-inch Rocket Head was shipped two per box, and Fuses shipped separately.[95]

LSM(R)s 188 through *195* stowage capacity was 4,400 Fin-stabilized Aircraft Rockets (ARs) per ship.[96] Henceforth, Caltech scientists and engineers often referred to these rockets as "Finners."

Radar and Ordnance

The SU-1 Radar was a medium-power surface search radar easily recognizable by its distinctive large-domed hood atop the mainmast. Radar sets had two scopes visually monitored by a single radar operator: an "A" scope on the left side for determining the range of a target relative to the ship, and a "PPI" or Planned Position Indicator on the right side for determining both range and heading relative to the ship. Accuracy was +/- one-half mile at 80 miles.[97] The SU-1 detected both surface and air targets and aided ship's control during rocket runs. This radar system was uniquely outfitted to LSM(R)s among the amphibious forces.

Conventional ordnance of the *LSM(R) 188* Class comprised a single 5"/38 gun, two 40mms, and three 20mms with firing sectors of ten-degree overlaps:

The 5-inch 38 caliber gun mounted on the fantail was a dual purpose (DP) Mark 12 gun in a Mark 30 Mount, with an automated ammunition hoist, that required 16 men.[98] When selected, the Mark 51 Mod 3 Director mounted in the adjacent gun director tower, operated by one man, visually tracked targets through its Mark 14 gyro lead-computing gun sight to electrically direct 5"/38 fires.

Two single-barrel 40mm Bofors were each mounted in gun tubs on the forecastle and directly forward of the Conn, and each gun required seven men. Pipe rail limit stops blocked the gun barrels from aiming into the ship.

Three single-barrel 20mm Oerlikons on Mark 10 Mounts, one each mounted fore and aft along the port side gunwales and one mounted along the starboard gunwale, required three men per gun. Each gun mounted a Mark 14 gyro lead-computing gun sight.

(Conventionally, port side guns are assigned even numbers and starboard side guns are assigned odd numbers. LSM(R) gunnery officers sometimes ignored this practice, however.)

The Navy extensively trained the LSM(R)s' future gunnery officers after midshipman schools at civilian universities. Specialized training included General Ordnance School at the Naval Gun Factory in Washington, D.C.; Ammunition Handling School in Hingham, Massachusetts; Demolition Research Unit at Fort Pierce, Florida; Gunners Mates School in Pontiac, Michigan; Anti-Aircraft Training Centers in Great Lakes, Illinois, and Dam Neck, Virginia; and Bomb Disposal and Rocket Schools at American University, Washington, D.C.

LSM(R)s 188 *and* 189 *Structural Firing Tests: 20 November 1944*

As the first pair of new "LSM Rocket Ships" neared completion, the Navy Department in Washington wanted to see results. Bureau of Ships representatives therefore arranged with Charleston Navy Yard's commandant to be present for the Builder's Trials of *LSM(R) 188*, which were delayed until the entourage arrived.[99]

LSM(R) gun crew with single 40mm Bofors anti-aircraft gun mounted in a raised gun tub forward of conning tower. Note the fore and aft pipe rail limit stops, which block the gun barrel from aiming into the ship (official U.S. Navy photograph).

Early Monday morning of 20 November, naval inspectors, staff officers, and select shipyard employees embarked two rocketships to observe the first structural firing tests. Among those boarding *LSM(R) 188* was OTC (Officer in Tactical Command) Commander Dennis L. Francis, USN, Commanding Officer of LSM Flotilla Nine, with second in command Lieutenant (soon to be Lieutenant Commander) John H. Fulweiler, USNR, Commander of LSM(R) Group 27. Others embarked *LSM(R) 189*, including the prospective commanding officers of *LSM(R)s 190, 191, 194* and *195*.[100]

Crews busily assembled and loaded rockets into launchers, but the weather and visibility was poor this morning. U.S. Navy blimps, which monitored activities along the coasts, was unable to go aloft and queried, "Blimp cannot accompany you, will you carry out schedule anyway?"

After noontime, the two LSM(R)s weighed anchors and steamed down Charleston's Cooper River toward Sullivan Island, the designated firing practice area. Visibility increased shortly after arriving in the fire zone, and permission was granted to commence firing. 20mm and 40mm gunners fired several hundred rounds, followed by a handful of rounds fired from each 5"/38 gun.

Top: LSM(R) 188 was the first "Finner" rocketship fitted with Mark 30 and Mark 36 Rocket Launchers and designated the LSM(R) 188 Class. Note the missing domed SU-1 Radar during builder's sea trials off Charleston, South Carolina, circa late 1944. *Bottom:* LSM(R) firing rockets off Charleston, South Carolina, circa late 1944 (official U.S. Navy photograph).

Topside LSM(R) personnel were evacuated from the rocket deck before rocket runs due to the dangerous rocket exhaust blasts and swirling debris (official U.S. Navy photograph).

In mid-afternoon, all unnecessary personnel were ordered to clear topsides before rocket fire. *LSM(R) 189* initiated the trials, firing salvos from among a hundred Aircraft Rockets (AR) over the next 45 minutes. During the following hour, *LSM(R) 188* launched salvos from her fully loaded rocket deck—480 in all—from both Mark 36 and Mark 30 launchers. Only ten rockets failed to fire, deemed due to improper electrical connections, and lowered over the side.[101] "When firing rockets," recalled Motor Machinists Mate Burton E. Weed, "all the men on the decks [*sic*] would have to go below decks because the heat of all the rockets going off was too much. When we came back up we had to step or dance around as the heat would come right through our shoes—like walking across a hot blacktop street in bare feet."[102]

Upon completion of the test firings, the Navy Yard Commandant commended the rocketships' commanding officers: "Very good show. Well done," then added, "Congratulations to Mr. Fulweiler."[103]

"Moving in High Gear"

During marathon-like work parties, loading munitions aboard the rocketships could take as little as 13 hours, but as much as 30 hours straight.[104] Deperming, navigation equipment

Top: Starboard bow view of *LSM(R) 194* during sea trials near Charleston Navy Yard, Charleston, South Carolina, circa late 1944. In the shipyard, LSM(R)s were painted modified tropical camouflage Measure 31, Design 10L ("L" for Landing Craft), in matte black and several shades of matte green with "blended dots" between colors. *Bottom:* Port side view of *LSM(R) 194* on the Cooper River approaching the John P. Grace Memorial Bridge (built 1929, demolished 2005–2007) off Charleston Navy Yard, Charleston, South Carolina, circa late 1944 (official U.S. Navy photograph).

checks, drills, gunnery practice and rocket firings, ship handling and tactical formations, and loading fresh and dry provisions, consumed much of the remainder of time before reporting to the fleet. But replacements of the LSM-type SO-8 radars with the new SU-1 radars were taking longer than anticipated, and a second extension by several days' time was authorized by the CNO.

Initial stowed ammunition allotments were 3,000 rocket motors, rocket bodies, and rocket fuses; 300 rounds of 5"/38 projectiles and powder cases; 200 boxes of 40mm rounds; 96 boxes of 20mm rounds; and numerous small arms ammo and pyrotechnics. Testing of ordnance was curtailed, nevertheless, due to restrictions in lower Charleston harbor, so guns, rockets and launchers were either test-fired during sea trials after commissionings, or while underway leaving Charleston Navy Yard.

"By the middle of November," recalled Paul S. Vaitses, Jr., of *LSM(R) 193*, "things were moving in high gear. No one knew it at the time, but we were tentatively earmarked for the Iwo Jima campaign, scheduled for early in 1945, and Washington wanted us finished and en route to the Pacific by the first of December [1944]. How we ever did accomplish that without leaving some one or something important behind, I shall never know." He continued,

> One Monday, we gave our ship her yard trials. Three days later, on November 22, with her green and black camouflage paint job still wet, we proudly commissioned her the USS *LSM(R) 193*—in a brief double ceremony with her sister ship, the *192*. From then on, for a solid week, chaos and confusion reigned aboard our fair vessel. To this day, the memory of that hectic period makes me marvel at our ultimate return to sanity. I know we could not have been sane while it was going on. During that sleepless, frantic week we loaded the ship with complete equipment and supplies, took on a full load of 5" machine gun, and rocket ammunition, plus a capacity fuel supply. Each time we came back to the yard docks, the workmen swarmed back aboard to make last minute alterations. In between loading operations and yard periods, we sandwiched a three day, so-called "shake down" cruise. This shakedown only meant taking the ship out a few miles to sea to test fire our guns and rockets. My most vivid recollection of this period was the first time we fired a salvo of rockets. The twelve screaming projectiles roared so close by the conning tower that they blew the skipper's cap overboard. From then on helmets were the order of the day.[105]

"Scheme E"

The Navy Department in Washington, meanwhile, took stock of the culminating research and development of Spin-stabilized Rockets (SSRs), and drafted a memo to include the SSR launchers on some of the twelve "LSM Rocket Ships" still under conversion at the Charleston Navy Yard in South Carolina. On 26 October, the Bureau of Ships proposed a general arrangement plan, adapting the advanced Mark 51 Spin-stabilized rocket launchers as LSM(R) alternate designation "Scheme E." BuShips advised design agent Gibbs & Cox that working plans for this new rocketship were urgent, and a day later the Navy outlined its requirements. In the space of only eight days, G&C produced 75 detailed plans by 3 November, including

Opposite, top: Stern view of *LSM(R) 194* on Cooper River near Charleston Navy Yard, Charleston, South Carolina, circa late 1944. "Interim" LSM(R)s retained the LSM stern anchor, cradle, and windlass. Note the shortened portside yard arm from the main mast to clear rocket fire. *Opposite, bottom:* Bow view of *LSM(R) 194* near Charleston Navy Yard, Charleston, South Carolina, circa late 1944. The bow door openings were covered by long, narrow steel plates and welded shut (official U.S. Navy photograph).

revisions of the weather/rocket deck, supporting structures, ammunition handling, and stowage arrangements.[106]

On 3 November in Washington, a conference convened representatives from CNO, COMINCH, BuShips and BuOrd in Rear Admiral Walter S. DeLany's office, Admiral King's Assistant Chief of Staff for Readiness. Recalling the CNO's directive of 13 October 1944[107] for conversions of *LSMs 188–199* with Mark 30 and Mark 36 Fin-stabilized launchers, this meeting authorized the new Mark 51 Spin-stabilized launchers, but only for the last four rocketships, *LSMs 196–199*. The following day, Bureau of Ships submitted a confidential letter to the CNO with ordnance changes and anticipated shipyard delays:

85 Mark 51 modification zero launchers (automatic type);
1—5"/38 cal. D.P. gun (750 f.s., 1200 f.s., 2600 f.s. muzzle velocities) mounted aft on centerline;
1—Mark 51 director
2—40mm singles. One forward of bridge structure, starboard side, raised sufficiently to clear loaded rocket launchers when in firing positions, the other on the forecastle-head;
3—20mm guns;
7140 rocket capacity magazines for 5" spin-stabilized rockets.

The BuShips directive concluded, "This change in armament will result in a delay of approximately three weeks for *LSM(R) 196–199*, inclusive. The Bureau understands that this delay is acceptable. The conversion of LSMs to Rocket Ships, in accordance with the directive [of 13 October 1944] will result in a setting back of the remainder of the LSM program at the Charleston Navy Yard by five ships. The change in the conversion of the last four rocket ships in accordance with the conference [on 3 November] will result in a further setback of one or two vessels. The Bureau will endeavor to make up this loss of LSMs in later months."[108]

This 4 November 1944 directive effectively created a new *LSM(R) 196* Class, whose design and construction would resemble the *LSM(R) 188* Class with almost-imperceptible exceptions. These "Scheme E" rocketships would share identical conventional ordnance with the *LSM(R) 188* Class: a single 5"/38 gun, two single 40mms, and three single 20mms. But stowage bins and ready service racks were redesigned to stow the shorter SSRs, and the entire length of the Rocket Deck, mounted with Mark 51 launchers, was raised 12 inches above the Superstructure level for additional clearance below deck.

By mid–November, *LSMs 196, 197, 198* and *199* were already seeing extensive conversion, with commissionings still scheduled for the last days of the month. But the new BuShips directive, modifying these final four LSMs into "Scheme E" conversions, protracted shipyard work by about three weeks, so paired commissioning dates were revised for 15 and 22 December 1944, respectively.

Fabrication of the Mark 51 SSR launchers was accelerated under contract with Consolidated Steel Corporation in Orange, Texas, and rapidly shipped to Charleston Navy Yard for final inspection, installation and testing. Each of the four latter LSMs was allotted 85 Mark 51 launchers, plus ten spares. The launchers' rushed shipments also allowed rollbacks of shipyard commissioning dates by a week for *LSM(R)s 196* and *197* to 8 December; and by ten full days for *LSM(R)s 198* and *199* to 12 December.

The four Spinner LSM(R)s were the first U.S. Navy warships designed for Mark 51

Automatic Launchers. Yet the intense pressure to expedite the SSR launchers resulted in poor production workmanship, and would cost valuable time in the long run due to unavoidable, remedial rework.

The LSM(R) 196 *Class*

The *LSM(R) 196* Class was distinguished by the Mark 51 rocket launchers.

LSM(R)s 196 through *199* were outfitted with 85 Mark 51 Mod 0 Automatic Launchers holding 1,020 5.0-inch Spin-stabilized Rockets (SSR).

Rockets were launched by the gunnery officer using the Firing Panel Mark 19 Mod 0, mounted in the open Conn, with three primary features: a port to accept a safety plug, inserted to activate the electrical circuits; a rotating panel dial to select rocket launcher banks; and a firing button. Numbers corresponded with the electrical leads to banks of rocket launchers. The panel dial was turned to a numbered position, visible through the fire selector switch window, then an adjacent button was pressed to fire the selected banks of rockets.[109]

Mark 51 Automatic Launcher

The Mark 51 Mod 0 Automatic Launcher was a formed and welded tubular steel framework with angle iron and metal subassemblies. The launcher was fixed for train and manually adjusted and locked at 30°, 35°, 40,° or 45° elevations, but 45° quadrant elevation (QE) was the optimum setting. Train of fire was accomplished by steering (or aiming) the entire ship toward its target. Launcher weight

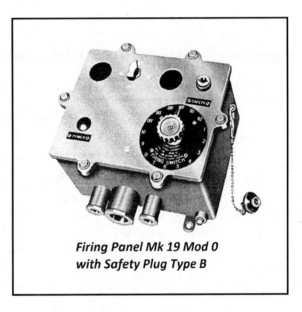

Firing Panel Mk 19 Mod 0 with Safety Plug Type B

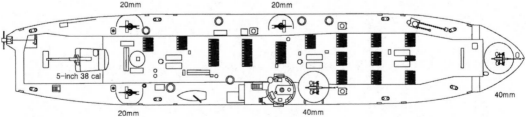

Top: **The Mark 19 Firing Panel was mounted in the "Flying Bridge" atop conning towers of** *LSM(R)s 196* **through** *199.* **Gunnery officers had custody of a Safety Plug Type B (Department of the Navy, Bureau of Ordnance,** *Missile Launchers and Related Equipment Catalog OP 1855,* **1 June 1953, page 324).** *Bottom:* **Plan view of typical Mark 51 Rocket Launcher arrangements on "Spinner"** *LSM(R)s 196* **through** *199* **(used with permission from John C. MacKay).**

unloaded was 230 lb. Launchers were manufactured by Consolidated Steel Corporation and provided by the Bureau of Ordnance.

Mark 51 launchers were arranged in varying banks and rows in relation to ship's centerline, and conformed to the deck and superstructure for safe firing clearances and access for loading and maintenance. Insulated electrical leads connected the launchers to the Firing Panel Mark 19 Mod 0 mounted in the LSM(R) conning tower.

Twelve spin-stabilized rockets were loaded manually into each launcher, and stacked atop one another into two adjacent magazines holding six rounds each. As rockets fired, the next upper round dropped down in the magazine by gravity feed through a gate, where a reel alternately aligned each successive round into firing position guides and electrical contact.

Each "Spinner" LSM(R) could launch a maximum deck load of 1,020 SSRs between 45 and 60 seconds.[110] The Mark 51 launcher could ripple fire 12 spin-stabilized rockets in 4.5 seconds.[111] The first manual reload required 45–60 minutes, while subsequent reloads took up to 2 hours requiring all hands.[112]

5.0-inch Spin-stabilized Rocket (SSR)

The 5.0-inch Spin-stabilized Rocket (SSR) Mark 10 Mod 0 averaged 32 inches long and weighed about 50 pounds. HCSRs (High Capacity Spin-stabilized Rockets) were designed for ranges of 5,000 yards, 2,500 yards, and 1,250 yards at 45° quadrant elevation (QE).[113] The approximate velocity was 790 feet per second with a 129 rate of spin per second (rps). Nominal dispersion, or rocket scatter at the impact point, was less than 10 mils and ranged upwards of 20 mils due to sea, atmospheric and other conditions. (One mil approximates a 1-yard deflection in 1,000 yards).[114]

The primary components consisted of a Rocket Head, Rocket Motor, and Nose Fuse:

- The Rocket Head Mark 10 (a 5.0-inch Mark 1 AR Head) was approximately 18 inches long and weighed about 28 pounds containing over nine pounds of TNT;
- The Rocket Motor Mark 4 was 5.0-inches diameter over 15 inches long and weighed about 22 pounds;
- The Mark 30 Mod 3 Nose Fuse was point-detonating and modified from the US Army M48 fuse.[115]

Rounds were stored in ships' magazines fully assembled (motors plus bodies), less fuses stowed separately. Fuses were installed prior to manual loading into the launchers.[116]

For transport, SSRs were packaged as sub-assemblies: 5.0-inch Rocket Heads and 5.0-inch Rocket Motors shipped together unassembled in a rocket box, while the 5.0-inch Rocket Nose Fuses were shipped in separate containers.

LSM(R)s 196 through *199* rocket stowage capacity was 7,000 Spin-stabilized Rockets (SSR) per ship.[117] Caltech scientists and engineers often referred to these rockets as "Spinners."

Mark 51 Launcher Problems

Caltech scientists, engineers, and Navy inspectors began testing production line models of newly-manufactured Mark 51 Launchers at California proving grounds at Inyokern, Camp

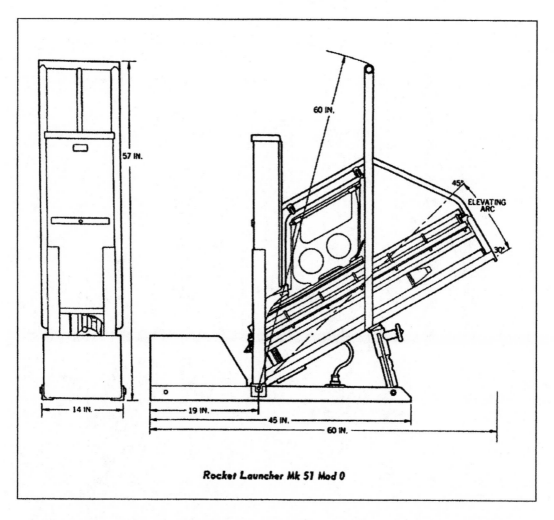

Rocket Launcher Mk 51 Mod 0

Eighty-five Mark 51 Mod 0 Rocket Launcher banks were mounted on "Interim" *LSM(R)s 196 through 199*. Launchers were fixed for train and set at nominal 45° quadrant elevation (QE). Behind each launcher, a concave deflector channeled rocket blasts upward and aft (Department of the Navy, Bureau of Ordnance, *Missile Launchers and Related Equipment Catalog OP 1855*, 1 June 1953, page 170).

Pendleton, Goldstone Range, and Eaton Canyon. These were samples from among the launchers quickly contracted by BuOrd in a crash building program with Consolidated Steel Corporation in Orange, Texas.[118] But tests revealed launcher malfunctions: working parts were not manufactured to design tolerances, and clearance problems caused rocket jams.[119]

The Bureau of Ordnance in Washington, D.C., received this unsettling news from Cal-Tech late in November; but it was a week later when these problems were brought to the attention of Charleston Navy Yard. Once informed of the potential launcher problems, during the night of 1 December, the shipyard made a test gauge and spot-checked their first 25 Mark 51 launchers: each was found defective and failed inspection. The following day, the shipyard contacted BuOrd for further instructions, asking the Navy "to advise the Yard whether the correction is vital and whether or not a simple method of correction can be developed."[120]

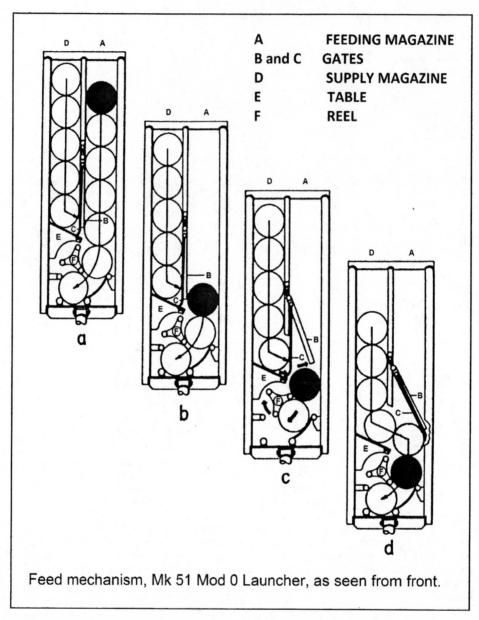

A   FEEDING MAGAZINE
B and C   GATES
D   SUPPLY MAGAZINE
E   TABLE
F   REEL

Feed mechanism, Mk 51 Mod 0 Launcher, as seen from front.

Spin-stabilized Rockets (SSRs) were gravity-fed in the Mark 51 Mod 0 Rocket Launchers from the upper feeding and supply magazines to the bottom firing magazine. Misfires were less than 10 percent, usually caused by a faulty round, poor electrical contacts, or improper feeding in the launcher (adapted from Paul E. Lloyd, ed., *Rocket Launchers for Surface Use*, **Pasadena: California Institute of Technology, 1946, Figure 4, page 16).**

By late November, the first Mark 51 launchers mounted on *LSM(R) 196* were ready for preliminary evaluation by representatives from BuOrd and BuShips. Overall, the inspectors were satisfied with the progress of the ship, although none of the new launchers had yet been test-fired. But a clearance problem was found, whereby the projected rocket flight paths from two launchers were obstructed by the bow 40-mm gun tub and structures forward of the

Top: Mark 51 Rocket Launchers being assembled and mounted near the forecastle of a "Spinner" LSM(R) during sea trials off Charleston, South Carolina, circa late 1944. *Bottom:* Work party painting, greasing, assembling, and mounting Mark 51 Rocket Launchers on a "Spinner" LSM(R) near Charleston Navy Yard, Charleston, South Carolina, circa late 1944 (official U.S. Navy photograph).

Conn if the launchers were set at angles less than 45°. BuOrd desired that all launchers remain adjustable and fire at all elevations, so recommended that either the two launchers be relocated, or locked in position to fire only at 45°. The Navy inspectors advised Charleston Navy Yard to devise a solution.[121]

Meanwhile, *LSM(R)s 196* and *197* were nearing Builder's and Acceptance Trials, followed by pre-commissioning inspections.[122] To the chagrin of the prospective rocketship skippers, however, only a small number of the expected increased crew complement for the LSM(R)s had reported for duty. Moreover, much shipyard work remained, including replacements of the original SO-8 radar gear with the SU-1 radar system, mounting all the Mark 51 launchers on the rocket decks, and other outfitting.[123]

Commissionings for *LSM(R)s 196* and *197* on 8 December 1944, and for *LSM(R)s 198* and *199* on 12 December 1944, were brief occasions with little fanfare. Soon afterwards, work parties resumed loading supplies and provisions while shipyard welders, fitters, and inspectors finalized work.[124]

One other problem arose as the last four LSM(R)s were hurriedly outfitted: no SSRs were yet available from the Charleston Naval Ammunition Depot. Consequently, *LSM(R)s 196* and *197* performed structural firing tests of only conventional ordnance before leaving the shipyard. In fact, the two rocketships' Mark 51 launchers would not be rehabilitated, much less field tested, for weeks hereafter, and it was anyone's guess if they would even work.

LSM(R)s 198 *and* 199 *Structural Firing Tests:* 16 *December 1944*

Before departing South Carolinian waters, *LSM(R)s 198* and *199* conducted structural testing of conventional ordnance and limited, improvised tests of their new Mark 51 rocket launchers on 16 December 1944.[125]

At the firing practice area, a U.S. Navy blimp was on hand, this time, to observe the test firings with a photographer and liaison officer aloft. But concern arose about rockets damaging the blimp, because of the limited target testing area. Given the rocket trajectories and distances, moreover, in the slightly rough seas with wind gusts up to 18 knots, the two rocketships had trouble maintaining a satisfactory range heading for adequate observation from above.

The rocketships first fired familiarization rounds from their 20mm, 40mm, and 5"/38 guns; in *LSM(R) 199*, however, the blast concussions from her fantail 5-inch gun broke a salt water pipe, and knocked out light bulbs in the engine room and in an adjacent passageway.

Fifty rockets were provided to each rocketship for test firing by the Bureau of Ordnance from a batch manufactured by Caltech in Pasadena, California. But stowage in the rocket storage bins presented a problem: the rockets on hand were the 10,000-yard HVSRs (High Velocity Spin-stabilized Rockets), with a motor some eight inches longer than the 5,000-yard HCSRs (High Capacity Spin-stabilized Rockets), actually intended for the LSM(R)s.

Due to the limited numbers of rockets on hand, the plan was to load one or more rockets in only those launcher banks which would test each of the eight firing circuits. En route to the firing area, launcher electrical contact surfaces were all scraped clean of paint and corrosion. But because of hurried and limited re-work of the launchers at the Charleston Navy Yard, Lt. Henry G. Carrison, Jr., Operations and Gunnery Officer of LSM Flotilla Nine, later

Top: LSM(R) 196 was the first "Spinner" rocketship fitted with Mark 51 Rocket Launchers and designated the LSM(R) 196 Class. *Bottom:* Mark 51 Rocket Launchers being serviced on a "Spinner" LSM(R) in Charleston Navy Yard, Charleston, South Carolina, circa late 1944. A conventional LSM is tied alongside to the right of the photograph (official U.S. Navy photograph).

advised in his report, "Note: Due to various reasons beyond control, all of the launchers were not in conditions to fire and the launchers that did fire were prepared for firing on very short notice."[126]

In the early afternoon, *LSM(R) 199* fired the first salvos. Sixteen rockets misfired from five launchers: 12 rockets failed to launch because seawater leaked into a Mark 51 launcher's wiring box; three rockets jammed in their launchers; and one misfired from inadequately cleaned electrical contact points. During the cease fire, the misfires were reloaded into other launchers for another launch attempt; this time only six rockets fired, leaving ten unfired rockets jammed in their launchers, which were unloaded, disassembled and stowed for future training exercises.

An hour later, *LSM(R) 198* fired her first salvos, with all but five rockets launching due to poor electrical contacts and jamming in launchers. The five were re-loaded into another launcher, and all fired properly in the second attempt.

Reports submitted by each LSM(R) gunnery officer and the flotilla gunnery officer noted the launcher jams and electrical contact problems. All assured that rocket exhaust blasts and heat did not affect the ships' rocket decks, nor was vibration from the launchings noticeable. The officers admonished Charleston Navy Yard to check all dimensions and working parts of the launchers and incorporate modifications; one other recommendation was to test fire rockets from each launcher before tactical use to insure good working order. Finally, in light of the high maintenance demanded by the Mark 51 launchers, training and drills were strongly urged to achieve proficiency and efficiency.[127]

Several weeks later, a handwritten, initialed note on the routing slip attached to the three officers' reports commented: "Remembering that the HV [high velocity] ammunition was not intended for use on the LSMs [*sic*], and that it is known not to function properly, the performance (90%) obtained here is unusually good. It entirely justifies the risks taken in providing these launchers before they were fully developed."[128]

By happenstance, the twelve "Interim" LSM(R)s evolved into two distinct classes of rocketships. All were originally conceived with aviation-type rockets and launchers, later designated the *LSM(R) 188* Class. When finless, spinning rockets with specialized launchers became available, these were quickly outfitted on the latter four rocketships to configure the *LSM(R) 196* Class. Thereafter, these two new classes of "Interim" LSM(R)s posed the greatest concentrated striking power of the U.S. Navy's wartime Amphibious Force. Yet as one skipper later reflected, "even then I wasn't sure what a weapon we were riding and its firepower."[129]

CHAPTER 2

Forward Routing

The LSM(R) flotilla was to transit the Panama Canal Zone, then sail directly to Pearl Harbor, Hawaii, two months in advance of the Iwo Jima operation.[1] Anticipating the extended passage, water ballast tanks were filled with additional diesel fuel.[2]

The twelve LSM(R)s departed Charleston Navy Yard, South Carolina among four task units:

30 November 1944: *LSM(R)s 188, 189, 190, 191*[3];
4 December 1944: *LSM(R)s 192, 193, 194, 195*[4];
15 December 1944: *LSM(R)s 196, 197*[5];
18 December 1944: *LSM(R)s 198, 199.*[6]

Passing through the Gulf of Mexico, crews drilled as rocketships practiced tactical maneuvers and simulated attacks at battle stations; gunners fired at target sleeves and tows; launchers were tested and rockets fired. Many sailors also experienced rough waters and sea sickness for the first time. But especially memorable to Storekeeper Robert W. Landis in *LSM(R) 192* was "the ever-present stink of diesel fuel oil on the LSM(R). That stink was always there and everywhere on the ship. And then there was the incessant vibration of the diesel engines. There were times, when possible, I would go up to the bow 40mm to inhale fresh air…."[7]

In Panama, crews enjoyed short-lived liberty ashore, if at all. *LSM(R) 199* was delayed at Coco Solo Naval Base in Panama, however, for prolonged repairs below her 5"/38 gun mount for a severely leaking port bulkhead, separated welds in the aft steering boxes around the propellers, and testing of ships control and navigation equipment.[8] Upon leaving the Panama Canal Zone, a Japanese submarine reportedly monitored the rocketships entering the Pacific Ocean.[9]

But storms were treacherous in the Gulf of Tehuantepec[10] off western Mexico. "Four months before reaching Okinawa there were 2 days of terrible hazard and sheer terror that could have cost even more lives than the battles," recalled Laurie R. Russell, Gunnery Officer in *LSM(R) 191*.

At that time there were westerly gale force winds and rougher seas than any of us had ever seen anywhere. The seas were so heavy that at times we'd lose sight of each other behind 100 ft. waves. And the rolling was something fierce. When the ship rolled to starboard, the wind was so strong from port that the ship seemed to hang there forever moaning and shuddering—then slowly struggle to right herself. I was so seasick that I mentally gave up and did not think we would survive this storm—and so sick that I didn't care. I'm pretty sure most of us felt the same. If any of the engines failed, I'm sure we would have capsized.[11]

Ships suffered split seams and cracked welds causing hull and compartment leaks, engine breakdowns, power failures, and ammunition damages. Numerous side-mounted Mark 30 rocket launchers on the Finner rocketships were damaged or broken off and lost. Diversion of the entire flotilla to San Diego Naval Repair Base became unavoidable.[12]

"As we entered the Pacific, the commander, who had been radioing messages frantically in order to get permission to proceed straight to Pearl Harbor from Balboa [Panama], reluctantly announced that we would head up the coast for San Diego," explained Paul S. Vaitses, Jr., Executive Officer of *LSM(R) 193*. "This news raised morale considerably in the flotilla, because it meant that Christmas, and probably New Year's, would be spent in the States."[13] The four LSM(R) task units reached San Diego Naval Repair Base between 22 December 1944 and 9 January 1945.

Finners in San Diego

LSM(R)s 188, 189, 190 and *191* reached San Diego, California on 22 December 1944, and *LSM(R)s 192, 193, 194* and *195* arrived in San Diego on 24 December 1944.

Each rocketship underwent an Arrival Inspection by a team of nine Navy officers from the Ship Inspection Board of the Training Command, Pacific Fleet Amphibious Forces.[14] Inspectors queried and observed personnel, scrutinized log books, and assessed seaworthiness and combat readiness. Material conditions of the eight Finner rocketships ranged from "fair" to "good." Numerous discrepancies were cited, on the other hand, and recommended correctives included extensive dry dock repairs in some cases.

During Christmas Eve, the American Red Cross delivered gifts to ship-bound, homesick sailors. Liberty was granted infrequently and often limited to half of a ship's crew at any given time, known in Navy parlance as "port" and "starboard" sections. After Christmas, repairs and inspections resumed, while gun crews attended anti-aircraft gunnery school ashore, and damage control personnel reported for practical firefighting training.

San Clemente Island, California: 29 December 1944 to 1 January 1945

The eight Finner rocketships conducted gunnery exercises with an airplane-towed sleeve, and rocket firings at a target range on San Clemente Island, California, about 75 miles northwest of San Diego. Here concrete reinforced pillboxes and other structures simulated Japanese gun emplacements.[15] *LSM(R)s 191, 193, 195* shoved off early in the morning of 29 December, followed the next day by *LSM(R)s 188, 189, 192*; arriving lastly on New Year's Eve were *LSM(R)s 190* and *194*.

Lt. Neal B. Hadsell, commanding *LSM(R) 192*, recalled, "When we got through the Panama Canal and wound up in San Diego, there was some delay because a few of the ships needed more time for repairs than others."

Well, those ships which got repaired early were just sitting around, but our good officers of the Flotilla staff decided that sitting around was not a good thing. So, they made arrangements for us to do firing practice with rockets on a little island out and away from San Diego. We got a whole "armload" of instructions about what to do, how many rockets to fire, and what we were supposed to aim at. We each were to take a turn and fire—it was only a few rockets in number—and then we were to move out of the way for the next LSM(R).[16]

LSM(R)s launched rockets at night for the first time, but it proved harrowing for *LSM(R) 193*. Executive Officer Lt.(jg) Paul S. Vaitses, Jr., recalled a rocket exploded prematurely near the conning tower and showered fragments of shrapnel on the bridge. "I was in the pilot house, plotting our run by radar ranges and bearings when the explosion took place. Receiving no answers to my anxious calls through the speaking tube, I rushed to the bridge expecting the worst. Luckily, I found the commander, skipper, and the enlisted men stunned, but unharmed. It was indeed miraculous that we suffered no casualties."

That same night, XO Vaitses continued, "Having fired our deckload of rockets, we had turned and were coming away from the firing line. Suddenly a lone rocket took off wildly from the deck of the nearest ship and screamed over our forecastle, plunging into the water a few feet off our port bow." As a result, "These two incidents brought us to the sober realization that even practice with this new type of ammunition was extremely hazardous, but of course no one talked about it."[17]

In sister ship *LSM(R) 192*, Lt. Hadsell added, "The rockets were so sensitive that static electricity could cause them to fire. This would have been disastrous to the two [men] loading the rocket as well as any crew members adjacent on either side." Moreover, "The one weak link in the whole process was the fins. They did not always stabilize the flight of the rocket, [and were] always providing some wobble at takeoff."[18]

Exercises were concluded mid-afternoon 31 December, and the LSM(R)s returned to San Diego to anchor outside the harbor until morning. But especially noteworthy this last day of 1944 was formal hoisting of the command pennant for LSM(R) Group 27 under Lieutenant Commander John H. Fulweiler, USNR.[19]

Preparations intensified over the coming days and nights. Repairs continued, crews and yard workers loaded fresh and dry food provisions, cleaned and painted, and loaded ammunition and rockets. Some lucky gobs also hit the beach on Liberty.[20]

On 3 January, the Navy Ship Inspection Board revisited the Finner rocketships for Departure Inspections, but examined much more rigorously this time. (*LSM(R) 194* was inspected on 5 January). Particular emphases were proper allotments of equipment and spares; orderliness and cleanliness within departments; and material conditions of the ships, As before, the Engineering, Ordnance, and Construction and Repair departments were scrutinized.[21]

Inspections revealed the general material conditions of the ships and appearances of their crews ranged from fair to good. Only four Finner LSM(R)s had satisfactory sanitary conditions, two were rated fair, and two rated poor. *LSM(R) 189* was cited for 250 fully assembled AR rockets[22] while in port; *LSM(R) 191* was missing wiring for nine Mark 36 rocket launcher rails; and *LSM(R) 194* failed to be dry docked for needed repairs. Lesser problems included missing spares, damage control equipment and towing gear; dirty, rusty or unpainted compartments; some Mark 30 launchers still remained bent out of shape; life rafts improperly stowed; hatches failed water tight condition with minor leaks; and some rocket launchers were mounted too close to fuel oil tank vents and overflow pipes.

On 5 January 1945, the LSM(R)s cast off lines and steamed out of San Diego Harbor in convoy accompanied by *LSM 90* with *LSM 186*,[23] the latter as temporary flagship embarking Commander Francis as acting OTC.[24] By coincidence, the eight Finners passed the Spinner

LSM(R)s 196 and 197, standing by awaiting permission to enter San Diego Naval Repair Base.[25]

Spinners in San Diego

LSM(R)s 196 and 197 moored in San Diego Naval Repair Base on 5 January 1945, and were immediately swarmed by activity. "Any ideas of good Liberty soon vanished," later wrote Ensigns Jack Shedd and David Mallery, Engineering and Communications officers respectively aboard LSM(R) 196, "as they were in a hurry for these ships...."[26] Signalman Leonard A. VanOteghem also remarked in his diary: "Repairs were expedited on both the 196 and 197. The 197 had a split seam in the hull. Also a tremendous amount of provisions were taken aboard both ships. We had highest priorities for everything."[27]

The following day, both vessels underwent Departure Inspections by the Ship Inspection Board. Material conditions were favorable overall, crews' appearances were considered fair, and sanitary conditions good. Minor discrepancies included inadequate damage control equipment. LSM(R) 197 required miscellaneous welding and her radar was inoperative, and LSM(R) 196 suffered a bulkhead leak. The report further noted, however, that neither ship carried rockets on board, nor 5"/38 star shells, nor even shotgun shells. Navy inspectors also cited water collected in rocket launcher electrical firing boxes and circuitry whenever launchers were left uncovered, a problem first reported at Charleston Navy Yard.

Besides repairs, refueling, and reprovisioning, both rocketships received their first allotments of 5.0-inch Spin-stabilized rocket bodies and motors before leaving San Diego. Neither vessel had yet test-fired a single rocket from their launchers, in part because of stateside shortages, since SSR rockets were rushed to forward units and bases overseas. Consequently, each rocketship received only fifty Mark 10 rocket bodies and Mark 4 rocket motors—and only "dummy" practice rounds at that.

After only 48 hours in San Diego, LSM(R)s 196 and 197 cast off mid-afternoon of 7 January 1945, and set sail for Pearl Harbor per orders via the 11th Naval District.[28]

LSM(R) 198 and LSM 102, meanwhile, reached San Diego Naval Repair Base the evening of 6 January 1945.

With strained patience, Commander Francis reported, "The LSM(R)s 198 and 199 have been routed forward with less shakedown training than any of the previous eight (8) ships of Group Twenty-seven. In as much as they are moving in pairs or by single ships, any comprehensive training program will not be possible. It is believed that until these ships have had at least two (2) weeks of supervised training at a training base, they will not be ready for duty in forward areas."[29]

The next morning, the Ship Inspection Board's Arrival Inspection rated LSM(R) 198 in fair condition materially and crew appearance good. But radar equipment operated "erratically," the signaling department reflected "poor maintenance," and sanitary conditions were fair. Engineering spaces were "clean and in good order," but found a "small split in seams, port and starboard," in the after steering room.

Discrepancies within the Ordnance department were unusually extensive, however. The Navy inspectors noted "rocket launchers are out of alignment to the extent that the last rocket in the launcher [sic] does not seat in the launching rails." Rocket fuses had no separate fuse locker or magazine, so they were stowed in the original wooden shipping boxes in the rocket ready service rooms; and canvas covers were needed for the rocket launchers. The 40mms, 20mms and 5"/38 guns all required adjustments, alignments, and spare parts.

Within an hour of the Navy team's inspection, a tug towed *LSM(R) 198* into dry dock. Over the next 24 hours, shipyard workers repaired the split seams in her hull, radar equipment was tested, and supplies and ammunition brought aboard. The following day, the rocketship was towed out of dry dock and refueled; by late evening of 8 January, *LSM(R) 198* shoved off from San Diego, accompanied only by *LSM 221*, en route Pearl Harbor.

The next morning of 9 January 1945, *LSM(R) 199* arrived outside San Diego Harbor, covered by extremely heavy fog.

Due to shortages of 5.0-inch Spin-stabilized Rockets, *LSM(R) 199* was the sole Spinner rocketship carrying SSRs, and this only because ten out of 50 rockets had failed to fire during sea trials off Charleston Harbor, South Carolina on 16 December 1944. En route San Diego after transiting the Panama Canal Zone, on 5 January eight SSRs were assembled and loaded into launchers: first, only four fired off successfully, then the other four fired in a second attempt. "...we got very few rockets when we left the states," recalled Lt.(jg) George Passey, Executive Officer of *LSM(R) 199*, "and our firings off the coast of Charleston revealed problems with the launchers. When we got to Panama, we found that it would be necessary to go to the West coast to get them repaired. We first went to San Diego, then to Los Angeles to get the work done."[30] (Present at both of the rocket test firings by *LSM(R) 199*, coincidentally, were Lt. Henry G. Carrison, Jr., the Flotilla Nine Staff Gunnery Officer and acting OTC, and Ensign C.A. Sanders, from the Bureau of Ordnance in Washington, D.C.).[31]

The Mark 51 rocket launchers were closely scrutinized on 10 January by numerous naval officers and civilians alike. Over the next two days in San Diego, other work on the *LSM(R) 199* included inspection and repairs to the gyrocompass, re-working piping in the engine room, and repairs to the electrical wiring and alignment of the 5"/38 gun with the Mark 51 gun director.

One of the civilians was Robert E. Sears, a Caltech research staff member of the Office of Scientific Research and Development (OSRD) for the Land/Amphibious Launcher Group, Design and Development Section. While an engineering student, Sears had joined the OSRD Launcher Group in 1944, then became a consultant for Consolidated Steel Corporation in Orange, Texas—the same manufacturer that built the Mark 51 rocket launchers. Now, Sears was tasked with troubleshooting and supervising repairs to the faulty launchers.[32]

Sears learned that the Mk 51 launchers mounted on the four Spinner LSM(R)s at Charleston Navy Yard were among the initial allotments manufactured by Consolidated Steel Corporation. In fact, Caltech engineers first became aware of rocket "hang-ups" during proof-testing of eight sample launchers provided by the manufacturer. However, before Caltech had determined the recommended corrections, defective production line launchers had been hurriedly mounted on *LSM(R)s 196* thru *199*.[33]

The Port Director ordered a delay of departure when *LSM(R) 199* prepared to cast off from San Diego for Pearl Harbor shortly after noon on 11 January 1945.[34] Some two hours later, a civilian and two naval officers embarked to inspect the rocket launchers once again and to check firing circuits. While *LSM(R) 199* remained in San Diego another full day, albeit for minor repairs on her radio equipment, Caltech scientists and senior naval echelons, including the Bureau of Ordnance, discussed whether the rocketship's departure could be delayed to replace the launchers.

Early Saturday morning on 13 January, Sears and a civilian associate embarked *LSM(R) 199* to inspect and work on the rocket launchers once more. Within the hour, the rocketship cast off from San Diego and entered Roosevelt Base, San Pedro, California eight hours later. Here, the launchers were more accessible for Caltech scientists and engineers in Pasadena, as well as to shipyard workers and civilian contractors from local machine shops.[35]

Replacing all 85 Mark 51 launchers was not possible since time was prohibitive. So, the worst launchers were replaced with 14 BuOrd launchers, 10 experimental launchers from Caltech, and eight other launchers from San Diego, and the replaced launchers were kept aboard for rework as spares. Stabilizing tie rods connecting the launchers were added, and waterproof canvas covers for the launcher banks were provided. Work began in earnest on 16 January and was more or less completed by 18 January.

After a final Departure Inspection by the Ship Inspection Board,[36] *LSM(R) 199* set sail the morning of 19 January for another test fire, including a group of workers and observers. Some 20 miles north of Santa Barbara and Santa Catalina islands, General Quarters sounded at 1340 and "Condition R-1" set. A hundred HCSR 5.0-inch Spin-stabilized Rockets were fired in salvoes from 1412 to 1419, with just one misfire that was successfully fired after a second try.[37]

Two other ships soon rendezvoused, all passengers were transferred, then *LSM(R) 199* fell astern *LSM 326* en route for Pearl Harbor.

San Diego to Pearl Harbor

Shipyard work at San Diego Naval Repair Base brought the LSM(R)s to adequate states of readiness and seaworthiness, given the limited time, and allowed the rocketships to proceed onward to Pearl Harbor. Yet the flotilla was hardly a cohesive fighting unit, for insufficient training and persistent material problems nagged the rocketships.[38]

The LSM(R) flotilla sailed in four task units from San Diego to Pearl Harbor:

5–14 January 1945: *LSM(R)s 188* thru *195* with *LSMs 90* and *186*;
7–15 January 1945: *LSM(R)s 196* and *197*;
8–17 January 1945: *LSM(R) 198* and *LSM 221*;
19–28 January 1945: *LSM(R) 199* and *LSM 326*.

En route, the task units conducted shipboard drills, gunnery exercises, and tactical maneuvers. Finner rocketships practiced rocket run formations and fired un-fused rockets. Although some Spinner rocketships acquired limited numbers of practice or "dummy" rockets, none was fired.

Pearl Harbor, Territory of Hawaii

Upon arriving in Pearl Harbor, Territory of Hawaii, the LSM(R) flotilla underwent intense remedial training, replenished supplies and provisions, re-fueled and repaired between Middle Loch, West Loch, and Waipio Point. New radio gear was installed by yard workers at Waipio Amphibious Operating Base, though proving laborious and time-consuming. Here, some LSM(R) gunnery officers adopted pedestal-type .50-caliber machine guns, some including protective splinter shields, to enhance defensive firepower.[39] Meanwhile, liberty was granted only occasionally, limited in part because some sailors considered Honolulu the last place to raise hell before leaving for the great unknown.[40]

At Pearl Harbor, half of the LSM(R)s[41] were dry docked for hull and structural repairs, some unexpectedly. In one instance, *LSM(R) 196* backed into *LSM(R)s 191* and *192* in Middle Loch on 21 January, although no one was injured. *LSM(R) 191*'s stern anchor cradle was bent with broken welds; *LSM(R) 192* suffered a fifteen-inch crack in her after steering compartment below the waterline, requiring a submersible pump to prevent flooding. *LSM(R) 196*, in turn, discovered water seeping into her after steering compartment and needed two submersible pumps.[42]

LSM(R) 199, meanwhile, reached Pearl Harbor on 28 January, and two days later, all ammunition was completely unloaded from her magazines for anticipated internal repairs. Indeed, water seeping through the split seam in after steering was pumped out hourly or as needed. But it was another week before she finally entered floating dry dock *ARDC 3* from 7 to 8 February.

Mark 51 Launcher Rework: 22–30 January 1945

On an emergency request from BuOrd, Caltech engineer R. E. Sears flew from California to Pearl Harbor on 20 January to supervise remedial repairs on the LSM(R)s' Mark 51 launchers.[43]

Launcher inspections of *LSM(R)s 196* thru *198* revealed the same defects suffered by *LSM(R) 199*'s launchers, "partially, if not wholly inoperative,"[44] due to any or all of three independent causes:

1. Defective launcher construction;
2. Improper wiring;
3. Improper Installation and provisions for adequate maintenance.[45]

All launchers were removed from the three Spinner rocketships from 23 to 30 January for crash rework ashore at several facilities around Pearl Harbor. Most were satisfactorily repaired and remounted, including those of dubious readiness.[46]

Finners at Kahoolawe Island: 24–28 January 1945

From 24–28 January, *LSM(R)s 188, 190* and *193*, with Lt. Comdr. John Fulweiler embarked in *LSM(R) 194* as OTC, commenced tactical training maneuvers[47] in international waters, including towing, gunnery, and general shipboard drills. The following day entailed ship handling maneuvers, more towing exercises, and re-fueling at sea. The remaining two days and nights honed rocket run and beach bombardment techniques at Kahoolawe Island's naval gunnery target areas.[48]

But the combined concussive effects from firing the 20mms, 40mms, and 5"/38 guns took tolls on ships' structures. A seam split open in the aft port side of *LSM(R) 188* ("due to strain of engine [*sic*] and gun firing"), requiring shoring and pumps to limit flooding, exacerbated by fire sprinklers leaking in two magazines. Similarly, *LSM(R) 194* suffered a split seam in her port side in the after steering flat near frame 33. Afterwards, *LSM(R)s 188* and *190* were both sent to dry dock for repairs and repainting from 30 January to 3 February.

Spinners at Kahoolawe Island: 4–5 February 1945

From 4 to 5 February, *LSM(R) 197* accompanied *LSM(R) 196* embarking Comdr. Francis as OTC for training exercises off Kahoolawe Island. Drills included ship handling and maneuvers, smoke screens, and daylight and nighttime firing practices.

For the first time, both rocketships trained under live rocket-fire conditions, which also tested the recently reworked Mark 51 rocket launchers. *LSM(R) 196* acquired 150 SSRs from *LSM(R) 198*, and *LSM(R) 197* obtained 300 SSR rocket bodies, rocket motors, and point detonator fuses from Naval Ammunition Depot Oahu. "Dry firing rocket runs" employed shore approach plans, radar fixes and visual bearings, and calculated attack points by firing preliminary ranging "spotter" or "spotting" rockets.[49] Some rockets failed to launch, but *LSM(R) 196* successfully fired 115 out of 121 rockets, and *LSM(R) 197* fired 252 out of 268 rockets.[50] However, *LSM(R) 196* suffered a hull crack with subsequent seawater leaks in her after damage control compartment, though of undetermined cause.

Upon retiring from Kahoolawe Island, the two Spinner rocketships moored at the Pearl Harbor naval base for continued radio upgrades, refueling, reprovisioning, and repairs.

The LCTs

After mid–January 1945, LSM(R) Flotilla Nine was withheld from the Iwo Jima operation.[51] The LSM(R)s would still deploy across the Pacific, to be sure, but with time on their hands before the next operation, senior commanders seized a unique opportunity.

LCTs[52] were urgently needed in forward areas of the western Pacific theatre. But large LSTs and LSDs were not available to transport the increasing numbers of LCTs arriving at Pearl Harbor. But LSM(R)s could escort or tow these LCTs, instead.

The LCT(6), or Landing Craft, Tank (Mark 6), was almost 120 feet long with a 32-foot beam, the smallest amphibious landing craft with crews living aboard, berthing a junior officer and 10 to 12 enlisted men. LCTs were constructed in three watertight sections, transported aboard larger ships either in sections or fully assembled. Thus an LST, or Landing Ship, Tank, could either carry five LCT sections, or transport a complete LCT that could be launched over the side on rails. An LSD, or Landing Ship, Dock, could transport three assembled combat loaded LCTs in its hold.[53]

On 28 January, LCT Flotilla Twenty-Three had five days to make ready 36 LCTs for sea,[54] and secret movement orders were issued the following day.[55] *LSM(R)s 189, 191, 193* and *194* with *LCSs 24, 37, 38, 39, 40, 44* and *57* with *SCs 1028* and *1311* would escort the LCTs from Pearl Harbor to Eniwetok, via Johnston Island and Majuro Atoll, on a journey of 3,000 miles, after which the LCT flotilla would proceed independently to Guam and forward areas.[56]

The diminutive LCT was not designed nor intended for ocean travel or heavy seas. This first convoy, an historic milestone, would prove these hardy amphibious landing craft and their stalwart sailors could successfully navigate the briny deep, indeed.[57]

The First LCT Convoy

LSM(R)s 189, 191, 192, 193, 194, 195
Task Unit 13.12.1
Pearl Harbor to Johnston Island, Majuro Atoll, and Eniwetok Atoll
3–25 February 1945
Landing Craft Overseas Convoy Task Group 13.12
CTG 13.12 Captain E. Friedrick, USN (Ret)
Task Group Escort Unit
CTU 13.12.1 Lt. Comdr. John H. Fulweiler, USNR
Task Unit 13.12.1—LSM(R) Group Twenty-Seven
CTU 13.12.2 Lt. Comdr. A. L. Jones, USNR
Task Unit 13.12.2—LCT Flotilla Twenty-Three, Groups 67, 68, 69

On 2 February 1945, Convoy Commodore Captain Friedrick (CTG 13.12) established his quarters and staff aboard *LSM(R) 189* for his temporary flagship as SOPA. This same day, Escort Commander Lt. Comdr. Fulweiler (CTU 13.12.1) assumed *LSM(R) 193* as his flagship for LSM(R) Group 27. 36 LCTs of LCT Flotilla Twenty-Three,[58] under Lt. Comdr. A. L. Jones (CTU 13.12.2), reported ready for sea as directed.[59]

Each LCT carried an LCVP (Landing Craft Vehicle, Personnel) lashed on deck, plus several tons of staff gear and drums of lube oil. Three LCT guide ships were issued a complete set of navigation charts. The journey was additionally burdensome for LCT officers because Conns had to be manned at all times, so watches were stood four hours on and four hours off, around the clock. LCT staff, officers and enlisted, were dispersed as passengers among the escorting LSM(R)s and LCSs. An exception was Lt. Comdr. Jones, who shared the hardships of his men, stowing his seabag alongside his bunk aboard the "Lucky Thirteen," *LCT 1313*.

At 0600 of 3 February 1945, the Landing Craft Overseas Convoy wended a long, slow column through the harbor channel and over anti-submarine nets guarding the entrance to Pearl Harbor. The convoy formed up by late morning and got underway for the first leg of the voyage to Johnston Island, six days or 715 miles southwest of Hawaii.

As convoy guide, *LSM(R) 189* set course and speed, while *LSM(R) 193* as station guide stood to port of the formation (*LSM(R)s 192* and *195* were delayed, but caught up with the convoy the next morning). The 36 LCTs formed six columns with six abreast: Group 67 in the center, Group 68 to port, and Group 69 to starboard. The two subchasers proceeded a thousand yards ahead of the convoy, port and starboard, using underwater sound gear to detect Japanese submarines. But because the convoy proceeded unusually slow due to the LCTs—five to six knots—the LSM(R)s steamed either at one-third or two-thirds speed between port and starboard engines. En route, LCSs alternated with LSM(R)s as column leaders and radar guards. In addition to radar, station keeping was aided by yellow and blue signal lights, especially helpful at night.

In days, ideal weather and seas turned sour. Choppy waters, ocean swells, and intermittent rains disrupted station-keeping and hampered visibility. Convoy wartime protocol required all lights turned off at night for concealment from the enemy, but an exception was made with side lights turned on during an especially stormy passage. The "Five flag" was broken out frequently, warning of emergency mechanical or electrical troubles, as some ships fell out of formation for repairs. POSIT signals requested ship handling positions and alerted those straying from stations. Luckily, occasional rammings and collisions caused little harm in all but one instance, prompting LCT skipper Lt. Jack E. Johnson to quip, "The damage was noticeable but nothing that a few women welders couldn't repair back home in the states."[60]

Shipboard drills and gunnery exercises resumed as weather improved. *LSM(R) 193* released helium balloons for 20mm and 40mm target practice, while *LSM(R) 194* tested her newly-acquired .50 caliber machineguns. But with reports of Japanese subs in the area, the convoy commodore repositioned the LSM(R)s and LCSs for greater protection on the flanks and rear.

The morning of 9 February, Johnston Island's 200-foot radar tower loomed into view just as fresh provisions were running out for the LCT crews. Johnston Island is a raised coral atoll 3,000 feet by 600 feet and barely above sea level with a single peak rising to 44 feet. Storekeeper 1c Robert W. Landis in *LSM(R) 192* keenly described it as "a hot, dry rock with no vegetation in the middle of the Pacific."[61] A landing field took almost the full length of the island, and after the Japanese surprise attack at Pearl Harbor, Johnston Island was among a handful of strategically located Pacific islands still in Allied hands, serving as a ferrying point for aircraft from the United States and as a naval fueling and minor repair station.[62]

The six LSM(R)s anchored southeast of the island for replenishing and immediate repairs, and the dozens of LCTs dropped anchors nearby on the south side, because they would have overwhelmed the anchorage otherwise. Ships allowed passage into the anchorage soon jammed together, however, and several rammed and collided with minor damages. The convoy commodore set foot ashore for only an hour, then re-embarked *LSM(R) 189*. After a six-hour layover, the task group weighed anchors and departed Johnston Island under light rain showers.

SC 1028 suffered serious engine problems, however, and she drifted behind the convoy while her crew struggled with repairs. An hour after leaving Johnston Island, *LSM(R) 194* was ordered to tow the disabled subchaser. Heaving and fastening lines tore off the subchaser's jackstaff at one point, and another towline became fouled in the rocketship's port screw. Finally a towing cable from the rocket ship was wrapped around the subchaser's forward 40mm gun mount, and the tow got slowly underway by evening. Despite both engines out of commission, *SC 1028* powered an auxiliary generator for underwater sonar and surface radar through the night from astern *LSM(R) 194*, though now trailing some 14 to 20 miles behind the convoy.[63] By noontime the next day, the stragglers were shadowing the convoy about 400 yards astern, when the disabled craft lit off a repaired engine and began trial runs. Tow lines were cast off early afternoon, and the subchaser resumed her screening position abreast *SC 1311* some 2000 yards ahead of the task group.

Two days later, an LCS struggled to tow an LCT with engine problems, but they fell further behind formation. *LSM(R) 193* took over towing the small landing craft and caught up with the convoy that evening, then cast off the tow by dawn next morning.

LSM(R) 189 suffered navigational breakdowns and radar failure, forcing her to leave the convoy guide position to go alongside *LSM(R) 193* to transfer a radar technician for repairs. Next day in the early hours of 13 February, a coxswain fell overboard from *LSM(R) 189* while assisting transfer of the radar technician to *LSM(R) 192*; a life preserver was quickly thrown over the side and the sailor was rescued unharmed.

(14 February 1945 was omitted from all records when the convoy crossed the International Date Line).

The task group commander dispatched *LSM(R) 194* to steam ahead with all due haste to Majuro Atoll. The rocketship was to advise the port director of the impending arrival of the task group within forty-eight hours, and to make ready for logistics replenishment, ship repairs, and night entry.

Entering Majuro on 19 February, the subchasers, LCSs and LSM(R)s stood aside as convoy flagship *LSM(R) 189* led long lines of LCTs through channel waters, sheltered by the large natural breakwater formed by surrounding coral reefs and shore.[64]

This same day, the invasion of Iwo Jima, which had been anticipated for over a week, commenced. Many in the convoy listened to ships' radios for news, some with family or friends in harm's way.

After payday for all hands, alternating liberty sections went ashore for swimming parties, exercise, and relaxation in the fresh west wind and clear skies. "Arrived Majuro Atoll, Marshall Islands," wrote Storekeeper Robert Landis in his diary on 20 February 1945 on the *LSM(R) 192*. "First mail call in twenty days. Beer party. Went ashore the next day on the main island. Saw first movie since leaving San Diego. It was shown outdoors in the evening."[65]

The convoy departed Majuro's anchorage before 0600 of 21 February, but left an LCS behind for further duty. In a couple hours, the task unit was heading northwesterly on the trek six hundred miles to Eniwetok Atoll. Upon departure, Storekeeper Landis jotted in his diary: "Departed Majuro Atoll, most beautiful island of the Marshall group for little fighting was required to take it from the Japanese. Destination unknown. Again in the convoy. Tokyo Rose heard for the first time on our ship's radio receiver, she claims the Japanese forces are aware of the advancing LSM rocket ships and they are prepared to deal with us."[66]

An LCT fell behind the convoy because an engine was being changed, so *LSM(R) 195* doubled back to take her under tow, and eventually caught up with the convoy that evening.

Frantic shouts alerted a man had fallen overboard from *LSM(R) 194*, F1c Charles "A" Casey. At 1630 hours of 21 February, the signalman quickly broke out the 5 Flag at the dip, the ship's whistle sounded five short blasts, and a life ring was dropped with smoke pots marking the area.[67] The radioman alerted convoy guide *LSM(R) 189* and the entire task group of the emergency, and the column following astern turned to starboard. The "Williamson's Turn" emergency maneuver was executed, designed to rapidly return a ship or ships to the same area of water, and *LSM(R) 193* with two LCSs joined *LSM(R) 194* in the recovery efforts.[68]

One account recalled the lost sailor had been ill for some days, and his skipper planned to transfer the man ashore for treatment. But that fateful day, the sickly tar went topside, leaned against the lifelines, then lost his grip and fell as the rocketship pitched and rolled in choppy seas.[69]

The LCT task unit maintained formation at ½ speed, or about three knots, while the search ships crisscrossed and circled the ocean.[70] At nightfall, rescue operations reluctantly ceased, and the task group re-formed. The convoy commodore ordered all vessels to lower ensigns at half-mast over the next twenty-four hours in respect for their missing shipmate.

At dawn of 22 February, the other task unit with *LSM(R)s 188, 190, 196, 197, 198* and *199* under Comdr. Dennis L. Francis, also en route Eniwetok, overtook and passed the larger but slower LCT convoy.

That morning, *LSM(R) 195* finally cast off tow lines from the LCT, which resolved her engine problems since leaving Majuro. But a few hours later, the small landing craft was in distress again, so at noontime *LSM(R) 193* took the LCT under tow. Buffeted by broadside winds, however, the towing gear broke at one point, and towing lines once became fouled in two of the LCT's three screws.

Before noon of 23 February, *LSM(R) 192* was dispatched ahead to Eniwetok Atoll to make preliminary arrangements for the approaching convoy.

Lookouts sighted lights from Eniwetok before dawn of 25 February, and by 0900, *LSM(R) 192* rejoined the formation bringing guard mail with entry and logistics schedules. The atoll was clearly visible by 1030, and naval vessels of all shapes and kinds seemed everywhere. While the convoy formed into a long column outside the atoll, *LSM(R)s 189, 191, 192, 193, 194* and *195* anchored apart in "Charlie" anchorage.

From Eniwetok, most of the LCTs would continue onward to Guam, and others forwarded to Ulithi Atoll and the Philippines. Before Task Group 13.12 was formally dissolved, the convoy commodore sent a congratulatory message praising commanders and crews:

TASK GROUP 13.12

25 February, 1945.

FROM: TASK GROUP COMMANDER.
TO: COMMANDING OFFICERS.

As I was saying when so rudely interrupted by Captain Stewart's bell—having arrived at the end of this part of the voyage the TGC [Task Group Commander] wishes to express to all hands his appreciation for the fine way in which they got their ships ready for the trip—and for the good seamanship and hard work that has enabled the group to arrive here this morning—exactly on schedule.

My particular thanks go to the Engineers, and the Motor Machinist's Mates—headed by Persons, Crofts, Hall, Foster and Korri—for their fine attention to duty, hard work and skill, which have kept the engines running in top form. Also thanks to Farrara for his good work in keeping those damn sleep-disturbing gadgets in good adjustment. And a word in memory of a shipmate: Charles A. Casey, F1c, who unfortunately was lost overboard from LSM(R) 194 on the afternoon of 22 February.[71] We mourn his loss but bend to the Will of Almighty God. May his soul rest in peace.

Lieut. Comdr. Fulweiler
Lieut. Comdr. Jones
Lieutenant's Thirkield, Johnson, Sommerhalter and McNeill and all of your officer's and men of this group:

I am proud of you and your work on this voyage, and I feel it a privilege to have been associated with you in this enterprise. Thank you again for your fine work, co-operation and your loyal support of my efforts as T.G.C.

My best wishes go with you for your continued success—and an early end to the dirty job on hand. Good luck to all hands—and may God be with you in all your undertakings.

E. Friedrick
Captain, U.S. Navy
Commander
Task Group 13.12[72]

The Second LCT Convoy

LSM(R)s 188, 190, 196, 197, 198, 199
Task Unit 13.11.14
Pearl Harbor to Majuro Atoll and Eniwetok Atoll
8 to 24 February 1945

The second LCT convoy[73] was very different from the first LCT convoy. "LCTs are required for combat and base service duty in the forward Central Pacific Area in quantities greater than can be transported on LSTs and other shipping," explained AdComPhibsPac. "The decision has been made to sail LCT(6)s under tow and under their own power to the Forward Central Pacific Area, escorted by suitable small craft. [But] The LSM(R)s will not be available for towing beyond Majuro owing to the necessity of meeting operational requirements at Leyte."[74] Towing the LCTs in convoy, therefore, was seen as increasing speed and saving time.

On the afternoon of 8 February 1945, *LSM(R)s 188, 190, 196, 197* and *198* steamed out of the Pearl Harbor channel to rendezvous with five awaiting LCTs. As formation guide, Commander Dennis L. Francis was OTC in *LSM(R) 196*, the flotilla's temporary flagship since 30 January. This second convoy would bypass Johnston Island, and instead proceed directly to Majuro Atoll, Marshall Islands, a journey of 2,280 miles. Fortunately, the weather was mild and seas calm for much of the 12-day journey.

Each LCT made fast their towing bridle to a cable from LSM(R) stern anchor windlasses. As LCT engines churned forward, the LSM(R)s pulled slowly ahead, drawing the cables taught, then gradually increasing the scope from 300 feet to well over 600 feet. Tension and stress was distributed thereafter by drawing in or paying out the scope by a foot at a time.[75] During daylight hours, optimal convoy speeds rose above 8 knots; overnight, the task unit strove for a nominal 6 knots.

Each day was taxing, nevertheless, as cables parted and towing gear broke under the strains. Accidental collisions and hull damages occurred when coming too close aboard, usually while heaving lines or making transfers. Despite breakdowns, the convoy moved onward, even as one or more paired rocketship and landing craft stopped for repairs or re-secured cables and bridles. Distances between the convoy and stricken vessels could thus stretch beyond the horizon at times, even beyond radio or radar contact, in which case one or more LSM(R)-LCT teams would fall back to intermediate positions to act as communication relays. On occasions, LCTs were switched among LSM(R)s when towing gear broke, or was lost, or otherwise malfunctioned.

From Pearl Harbor, the task unit set course due south in Formation DOG with two columns abreast. *LSM(R) 199* joined the convoy that evening, due to last-minute dry dock repairs at Pearl Harbor from 7–8 February and from replenishing supplies and ammunition, although rockets were conspicuously absent from the inventory. In the early morning hours of 9 February, the convoy turned southwest. By 10 February, the OTC ordered the convoy to Formation YOKE as three columns abreast for the balance of the journey.

Despite rigors and frustration, training persisted with tactical ship handling, dry rocket runs, target-firing practice, smoke screen exercises, and never-ending drills.[76]

About midway on 16 February, Radioman Clyde Blue in *LSM(R) 197* wrote, "On watch right now. Had a sub scare last night but nothing to it. Going to Marshall Islands to dump off the LCT. Sure a long trip, as we have to go so slow with the LCT behind us. Will get there in two or three days. I had the "Hit Parade"[77] on last night. Number One was "Accentuate the Positive," Number Two was "Don't Fence Me In," and Number Three was "There Goes That Song Again." The number one song sure sounds funny to me. First time I had heard it."[78]

(18 February 1945 was omitted from all official records as the convoy crossed the International Date Line).

A collision at sea was barely averted on 19 February, when *LSM(R) 198* suddenly lost steering control and veered to port toward *LSM(R) 196*, who reacted quickly by also veering to port. *LSM(R) 197*, immediately astern, also turned to avoid collision, but the sudden movements strained and broke the towing gear with her LCT. Falling behind formation, *LSM(R) 197's* towing cable and *LSM(R) 198's* malfunctioning rudder controls were repaired, then rejoined the convoy hours later.

By 21 February, the formation assumed FORM 18, a single-file column guided by OTC flagship *LSM(R) 196*, because radar picked up a land mass in the morning darkness, thought to be Arno Atoll in the Marshall Islands. In hours, the convoy reached Majuro Atoll where the task unit was dissolved, and the LCTs cast off for onward routing to Guam and other forward areas in the central Pacific.

Proceeding with haste through the anchorage, each rocketship moored alongside oil tankers with only enough time to replenish drained fuel tanks and get mail. In four short hours, the LSM(R)s set sail—sans LCTs—on the 680-mile "hop" to Eniwetok Atoll: the rendezvous point for the divided LSM(R) flotilla upon release from their two respective LCT convoys. No longer burdened by bucking tows, the half dozen LSM(R)s easily steamed flank speed averaging 10 knots.

Only hours later, however, a fire broke out in *LSM(R) 188* from the starboard generator in the engine room, but beyond repair by ship's force. Almost the same time, *LSM(R) 198* lost all electrical operations to bridge steering controls, forcing her to steer by the "trick wheel," manned deep within the after steering station in the fantail via voice commands from the Conn. Meantime, the convoy advanced steadily, and *LSM(R) 197* was dispatched ahead of the formation to act as a picket ship for the morrow's scheduled radar drills and tactical maneuvers.

At dawn of 22 February, the half-dozen LSM(R)s overtook and passed the larger but slower convoy of 36 LCTs escorted by their six LSM(R) brethren, still en route Eniwetok under Lt. Comdr. John H. Fulweiler.

Commanding officers now informed their crews about their future mission, as Clyde Blue noted in his diary: "The old man called the crew together and said that we would be in an invasion within the next 6 weeks. Also said it would be within 450 miles of Japan. Formosa is my guess or maybe along the China coast but I doubt the latter. We pick up our rockets at the next island after Eniwetok."[79]

LSM(R)s 188, 190, 196, 197, 198 and *199* dropped anchors outside Eniwetok Atoll before midnight of 23 February, a full day ahead of the other convoy of six rocketships.

Island Hopping

The rendezvous in Eniwetok marked a singular milestone never to be repeated. All 12 rocketships were united operationally for the first time on 24 February, and the entire flotilla would sail together over the next four weeks until reaching Okinawa on 26 March.

Originally, LSM Flotilla Nine, LSM(R) Group 27, was to proceed from Eniwetok to Ulithi Atoll for ammunition and logistics, then sail directly onward to Leyte, Philippines, to arrive by 6 March 1945 for "operational requirements," that is, to prepare for the invasion of Okinawa, Operation Iceberg. Revised orders, however, delayed departure from Eniwetok until 28 February and added one more "island hop" after Ulithi: Kossol Roads, Palau, in the western Caroline Islands. There, the 12 rocketships would rendezvous with the flotilla's new headquarters command flagship in a fortnight, then on to the Philippines.[80]

Eniwetok Atoll became an important Micronesian staging point for the U.S. Navy since its capture from the Japanese the year before. Located about 670 miles WNW from Majuro, a thousand miles from Guam, and 330 nautical miles NE of Kwajalein, this large, round atoll is a circular reef of intermittent islets surrounding an enormous, protective lagoon of about 388 square miles. Three of the atoll's islands—Engebi to the north, and Parry and namesake Eniwetok to the south-southeast—were developed to limited extent by the Japanese during the war. Eniwetok became a valuable forward outpost, with American airfields on the three islands and a seaplane base, for air searches and neutralizing Japanese activities between the bypassed enemy islands in the U.S. Pacific drive to Japan.[81]

As ships re-provisioned and refueled, liberty parties went ashore for recreation. *LSM(R) 198* scored 70 cases of Pepsi-Cola, and transferred two .50 caliber air-cooled machineguns with mounts and ammunition to sister ship *LSM(R) 199* for field modifications. In *LSM(R) 188*, men from a repair ship fixed a hole in the ship's side and repaired a generator. But the malfunctioning salt water evaporator produced insufficient fresh water, so orders forbade showers and clothes washing until further notice.[82]

"LSM(R), Eniwetok, 2/24/45, Marshall Is." Lawrence J. Low, untitled unpublished diary, notebook and sketches.

Heavy sea swells and winds pushed, pitched, and rolled the high-sided and flat-bottomed rocket ships, placing heavy strains upon already doubled-up mooring lines. *LSM(R) 189* suffered a damaged outboard Mark 30 rocket launcher when winds set her against *LSM(R) 193*, and the next day she also lost a launcher torn off completely by an LCT coming alongside. *LSM(R) 198* was damaged with splits in welded seams and pipe fenders at Frame 13, and her deck was buckled while negotiating choppy waters that carried her stern into the moored *LSM(R) 190*. As necessary, many of the rocketships cast off lines to moor or anchor independently to avoid further damages or injuries.

Practically from dawn to dusk, meanwhile, the four Spinner LSM(R)s simulated rocket runs within the Eniwetok chain near the small atoll of Rigili. *LSM(R)s 196, 197, 198* and *199* approached the island in pairs on attack runs, then veered off on opposing sides, as the next pair following astern commenced attack runs in turn.[83]

Eniwetok to Ulithi: 28 February 1945 to 6 March 1945

Mid-afternoon of 28 February, skies were clear but seas were heavy when the LSM(R) flotilla departed Eniwetok. The Port Director issued supplemental orders in a conference of all commanding officers, directing the twelve rocketships to proceed in convoy with twenty other ships[84] to Ulithi Atoll, a major Navy forward staging base. Ulithi was also important to *LSM(R)s 196, 197, 198* and *199* for finally supplying 5-inch Spin-stabilized Rockets.[85]

Repair ship *Oahu ARG 5* was convoy OTC of Task Unit 96.3.22, with *LSM(R) 196* as temporary LSM Flotilla Nine flagship for Commander Dennis L. Francis, and *LSM(R) 193* as LSM(R) Group 27 group flagship for Lieutenant Commander John H. Fulweiler. After clearing Eniwetok, the convoy practiced anti-aircraft gunnery at target sleeves towed behind two planes.

The twelve rocketships steamed independently from the large convoy at times to practice ship handling and tactical maneuvers. LSM(R)s simulated rocket runs signaled by red and green shells fired by Very's pistols.

En route, *LSM(R) 191* had an engine breakdown on 2 March, and fell three miles behind the convoy until repaired a day later. Late that same night, *LSM(R) 198* discovered a leak in her after steering compartment with water rising to 18 inches. Despite pumping, the source of the leak could not be located or repaired. The evaporators aboard *LSM(R) 188* still remained secured, which forced the rocketship to take on fresh water through hoses while underway alongside convoy ships.

But the weather and seas grew rougher than ever for the convoy. In churning seas, two of the rocketships lost directional control, because master gyro or gyro repeaters were in error or otherwise malfunctioned; another LSM(R) lost her radar; and still another lost a locker of smoke pots overboard when a retaining cable snapped. As a result, the flotilla's OTC ordered casualty drills in addition to routine shipboard exercises.[86]

That evening of 3 March, a "man overboard" distress call went out by voice radio at 2015 from *Oahu*, the convoy's guideship. Dark, overcast, and rough seas reduced visibility from 1 to 1½ miles as lookouts strained to see any signs of the missing sailor. Soon rain squalls passed over, making searches all but impossible, until the man was finally presumed lost. Nearly an hour later, almost mystically, a rare nighttime rainbow appeared dead ahead as the rains let up, with its spectral colors in the light cast from the rising moon.[87]

The following day, the rocketships continued tactical maneuvers and gunnery exercises. The *LSM(R) 198* captain, however, sent a message to the flotilla commander and "requested permission to not fire [the] five-inch gun due to leaks in after steering." The commander shot back: "Request denied." Obeying orders, *LSM(R) 198* fired a single round then secured the big gun.[88]

The night before reaching Ulithi, *LSM(R) 189* lost all power and lights. Plunged in darkness for three long minutes, they discovered an engine's generator oil filter had clogged.

Ulithi Atoll: 6–8 March 1945

On 6 March the convoy entered Ulithi Atoll, a major hub of naval activity in the Pacific theatre. Tars quipped that the U.S. Navy had so many ships at Ulithi, a sailor could walk across the harbor stepping one ship to the next without ever getting wet. Indeed, the twelve rocketships shrank in comparison to the enormity of the war effort. "Arrived Ulithi at about 10:30 a.m. Boy, is there ever a lot of warships here," remarked awe-struck *LSM(R) 197* Radioman Clyde Blue. "There are about 15 carriers here. We start loading rockets this afternoon...."[89] Another sailor in *LSM(R) 188* added, with equal amazement, "Harbor is crowded with every type of ship the Navy has. At least 15 carriers. Must be at least 1000 ships in all."[90]

Ulithi was on a pivot point, lying 3,660 miles from Pearl Harbor, about 360 miles between Guam and Peleliu, 900 miles from Leyte, and equidistant from Okinawa and Lingayen Gulf along a 1,200-mile arc. Its lagoon was nearly as hospitable to naval vessels as that of Eniwetok, but offered more land areas in her surrounding islets for air bases. Earlier in the war, the Japanese utilized the atoll for a radio and weather station, including some use as an anchorage and seaplane base, but they determined Ulithi was of no long-term value by 1944. When the Americans took over, they estimated the lagoon could accommodate over 700 naval vessels, and, in fact, some 617 U.S. Navy ships were actually anchored at Ulithi at the height of preparations for the Okinawa operation.[91]

The LSM(R)s entered Ulithi's Mugai Channel to the east, where a boat closed alongside each vessel to distribute anchorage charts and instructions from the Port Director's office. Half the rocketships proceeded to the southern lagoon anchorage, between the islets of Mangejang, Lolang, Songetigech, and Fassarai, while *LSM(R)s 188* and *193* accompanied the four Spinner rocketships to the northern anchorage near Asor and Falalop islets. Meantime, armed lookouts occasionally fired a rifle or handgun at suspicious floating objects in adjacent waters, purportedly as precautions against enemy swimmers.

The Spinner rocketships nested alongside cargo ship *Pitt APA 223*, and took on 5-inch HCSR (High Capacity Spin-stabilized Rocket) rocket bodies, motors, and fuses, passed by a human chain to the rocket assembly rooms for magazine stowage.[92]

"Up at 7 a.m. and started loading again at 8 a.m.," wrote Clyde Blue on 7 March in *LSM(R) 197*. "We worked all day long to just now and it's four o'clock. We are shoving off for Kossol in the Palau group today. We loaded 1500 rockets and same amount of fuses. I am tired as hell and have the 12 to 4 watch tonight."[93] Loading finally finished early evening, and the actual numbers of rocket bodies, motors, and fuses loaded aboard each Spinner LSM(R) exceeded 4400. Unfortunately, an LCT could not take all the discarded wooden rocket boxes and packing materials, so much of it was tossed into the waters and created a mess.[94]

LSM(R) 188 still rationed water due to the still-inoperative evaporator, so she tied along-side *Baham AG 71* for 4,000 gallons of fresh water while the crew embarked the auxiliary ship for hot showers and a movie.[95] The next day, the rocketship took on another 400 gallons of fresh water from *Oahu*.

To Kossol Roads: 8–10 March 1945

Under secret orders, a 16-ship convoy departed Ulithi for Kossol Roads, "when in all respects ready for sea about 2200 ZEBRA 7 March."[96] The LSM(R)s weighed anchors by 0800 of 8 March, and assembled in the southern Ulithi anchorage. After heading east through the Mugai Channel entrance, the convoy rounded the atoll's southern shoreline and steamed westward.

Upon open seas, the convoy formed up with guideship *Lyra AK 101* escorted on the flanks by three minesweepers. The Ulithi Port Director cautioned that the western Caroline Islands were enemy-held, except Ulithi, Anguar, Peleliu and Kossol, and warned that mines drifted in the shipping lanes. Therefore, they advised, "ships operating in adjacent waters keep sharp lookout and destroy any mines sighted."[97]

The two-day, eight-knot, three-hundred mile journey from Ulithi to the Palau Group was only marred by a collision, when *LSM(R) 190* suffered a punctured hole in her hull, while passing mail underway, after drifting into the port quarter of *LSM(R) 189*. That same morning, *LSM(R) 192* lost wheelhouse control and shifted to emergency steering, but the steering gear and rudder indicator box were soon repaired.

The rocketships practiced more rocket runs, cued by red and green flares, for approaches to firing lines and simulated rocket attacks while also generating billows of oil-burning "fog." Ensigns David Mallery and Jack Shedd aboard *LSM(R) 196* observed, "by this time, the crew began to take this constant underway program for granted. It felt more natural to be underway than it did to be anchored…."[98] But such sentiments were not shared by everyone. "Will reach Kossol tomorrow morning some time," Radioman Clyde Blue noted in his diary; "Had maneuvers all day long. Bunch of crap if you ask me…"[99]

Kossol Roads: 10–13 March 1945

On 10 March, the convoy arrived at the east entrance to the ten-mile-wide strait of Kossol Passage in the Palau Islands, also known as Kossol Roads or Kossol Roadstead. Lying fewer than 600 miles east of Leyte, Fleet Admiral Nimitz believed these islands were needed as staging points for the future Philippine operations, while Admiral Halsey recommended by-passing the Palaus altogether.

Kossol Roads remained a staging point for ships and aircraft during the war, although its anchorage offered no protection from foul weather. Moderately rough swells, in fact, caused *LSM(R) 198* to ram *LSM(R) 194*, leaving a hole in the latter's starboard side.

The Palau group is westernmost of the Caroline Islands, extending about 110 miles north-south and surrounded by coral reef. The Palau invasions of Peleliu and Anguar were notable for ferocious fighting from September 1944 until secured November 1944. It was here that the Japanese strategy set the pattern for the bitter struggles over Iwo Jima and Okinawa by protracting the American amphibious assaults.

Because the Japanese still controlled nearby Babelthuap Island, round-the-clock armed guards were posted fore, aft and atop the conns. Enemy suicide swimmers were also a threat to American ships and crews, capable of detonating explosives attached to hulls, or stealing aboard for hand-to-hand killing sprees. "These islands are still partially Jap-held," commented a sailor on *LSM(R) 188*. "Five men are on watch topside with rifles 24 hours per day and have orders to shoot at any objects in the water. Japs swim out to boats under boxes or any other object to float and come in close enough to bomb the ships. We're taking no chances."[100] Storekeeper Robert W. Landis added from *LSM(R) 192*, "Laying off about ten miles in protection of coral reefs. During the evening US Marine Hellcats and Corsairs attacked Japanese positions on the islands."[101]

Recreational activities were limited to swimming parties, watched over by armed guards, and Hollywood movies. "Back in Honolulu we had purchased a 16mm movie projector from contributions from each man in the crew," recalled *LSM(R) 196* Ensign David Mallery, and "during these short stops we would show films topside, providing the main recreational aspect during the next five months."[102]

On 11 March, Lt. Comdr. Fulweiler, Commander LSM(R) Group 27, embarked the *Ozark LSV 2* for advance passage to Leyte. There, he would confer on the coming operations and greet the flotilla's arrival in San Pedro Bay, Leyte Island, Philippines. Meanwhile, the LSM(R) departure from Kossol Roads was delayed to await the flotilla's new headquarters command flagship.

USS LC(FF) 535

USS *LC(FF) 535*[103] steamed into Kossol Passage late morning of 12 March, and tied alongside *LSM(R) 196*, Commander Francis' temporary flagship. "The day before my birthday, LSM Flotilla Nine staff reported aboard and assumed operational control," recalled Harold J. Ball, then a Lieutenant (Junior Grade) in the naval reserves and Executive Officer of Landing Craft, Flotilla Flagship 535. But, emphasized Ball, "that means that they assumed control of the Flotilla, not of our ship."[104] At 1900 hours of 12 March 1945, the LSM Flotilla Nine command pennant was officially hoisted aloft.

Nevertheless, command responsibilities between Commander Francis and the ship's Commanding Officer, Lieutenant Himus S. Sims, remained distinct, explained Lt. (jg) Ball. "The parameters of command are different for a 'visitor' such as a Flotilla Commander and the responsibilities which rest with the Captain of a ship or his representative; that is, the officer having the watch. The Captain is responsible for the safety of the ship—the Flotilla Commander is accountable for the functions and movements of the ships in his command, i.e., Flotilla Nine."[105]

USS *LCI(L) 535* was commissioned 15 January 1944 at New Jersey Shipbuilding Corporation, Barber, NJ, and served as a training ship at the Amphibious Training Base, Solomons, Maryland. The landing craft, infantry was ordered to Norfolk Navy Yard, Virginia, for conversion and reclassification as Force Flagship on 31 December 1944. "We kept the same hull number but were now the "USS *LC(FF) 535*,"" said Ball.

LCI(L) 535 was converted to a force flagship and re-designated LC(FF) 535, which became the LSM Flotilla Nine headquarters ship under Commander Dennis L. Francis for the Okinawa operation (official U.S. Navy photograph).

At Norfolk, the ship was almost gutted below. That area which previously was designed to hold landing troops was converted into quarters for a flotilla commander and his staff. Numerous new types and numbers of radio equipment were added so that, to the best of my recollection, we had as much radio communication gear as that of a cruiser. Various types of antennae now surrounded the conning tower, a new flotilla radio shack was added below decks, mounts for holding ranging rockets were placed where the old landing ramps were located, the engines were overhauled, et cetera. Except for the basic hull design, we had a new ship.[106]

Armaments were only five single 20mm guns. Six pairs of Mark 51 rocket launchers, spares from Spinner LSM(R)s, were subsequently mounted on the flagship while at Leyte, Philippines.

Once at Kossol Roads, Harold Ball continued,

The chief island of the Palau group was Peleliu, an island which was considered necessary to hold as an advanced base for attacking the Philippines. The island was never entirely secured by reason of the fact that it wasn't worth the cost of lives that would be involved taking the island. Enough of the island was secured to provide a bomber strip and provide landing facilities for several squadrons of search and rescue aircraft, primarily PBM units. During our stay at Kossol Passage it was essential to keep men on deck night and day as Japanese remaining would swim out—usually hiding under floating debris—and attempt to attach explosives to some part of the hull. Frequently, during the night I would hear small arms fire or hand grenades explode in the water because crew members on watch were attempting to prevent Japanese swimmers from damaging our ship. I think the crew had a "lot of fun" shooting at whatever in the water might conceal an enemy swimmer; [but] it was good to leave and get underway again.[107]

To Leyte, Philippines: 13–16 March 1945

The day after *LC(FF) 535* arrived in Kossol Roads, the LSM(R) flotilla weighed anchors at 0900 of 13 March and formed up with a 27-ship convoy. The Convoy Commodore was embarked in transport *Allendale APA 127*, the Escort Commander in minesweeper *Hazard AM 240*, and Commander Francis was designated Convoy Vice-Commodore in *LC(FF) 535*. Orders prescribed ocean routes at convoy speeds of 9 knots and to "maintain strict radio silence except in emergency."[108]

In between heavy rain squalls, severe lightning storms, choppy seas, and even a large waterspout that some thought was a tornado, the LSM(R)s conducted tactical maneuvers and exercises with their new flotilla flagship. Meanwhile, numerous net buoys, or perhaps Japanese floating mines, were sighted and fired on en route. Before reaching the Philippines, the escorting minesweepers dropped depth charges on one, or possibly more, suspected enemy submarines.[109]

San Pedro Bay, Leyte, Philippines: 16–19 March 1945

By noontime of 16 March, the flagship *LC(FF) 535* of LSM Flotilla Nine veered from convoy formation into San Pedro Bay, Leyte, Philippine Islands. A small control craft scurried from ship to ship, distributing navigation charts and anchoring instructions. Natives in outrigger canoes, called "bum boats," also greeted the new arrivals to trade and barter. Meanwhile, the rocketships took turns topping off fuel tanks alongside merchant oiler SS *Hanging Rock*. Lt. Comdr. Fulweiler, already in Leyte for advance briefings, resumed his quarters aboard *LSM(R) 193* as LSM(R) Group 27 flagship.

CONVOY TO LEYTE

"Convoy to Leyte." Lawrence J. Low, untitled unpublished diary, notebook and sketches.

Leyte, Philippines, was the assembly, loading, and jumping off point for the Western Islands Attack Group (TG 51.1), under Rear Admiral Ingolf N. Kiland. The Western Islands Attack Group would assault and capture the Kerama Retto islands beginning 26 March 1945, prior to the primary invasion of Okinawa on 1 April 1945.

Commander Francis reported in person to Adm. Kiland aboard headquarters ship *Mount McKinley AGC 7*, then reported to Captain Theodore W. Rimer (ComLCI(L)Flot14) in *LC(FF) 657*, commanding the Western Islands Support Craft Flotilla (CTU 51.1.16). Francis also reported via dispatch to Rear Admiral John L. Hall, Jr., in headquarters ship *Teton AGC 14*, who, as Senior Officer Present, Amphibious Forces Pacific Fleet at Leyte, coordinated logistics for the Okinawa operation. For the assault and capture of Okinawa beginning 1 April 1945, Admiral Hall was commander of the Southern Attack Force (Task Force 55), in coordination with the Northern Attack Force (Task Force 53) under Rear Admiral Lawrence F. Reifsnider.

Back-breaking work began for all hands the morning of 17 March. Two LSM(R)s, as intermediaries, loaded extra supplies of fresh, dry, and frozen provisions from large supply vessels, then distributed the stock to the other rocketships of the flotilla. Meanwhile, Spinner rocketships took SSRs from attack transport *Pitt APA 223*. "We loaded about 2,000 rockets today," wrote Radioman-diarist Clyde Blue in *LSM(R) 197*. "Got up at 5 a.m. and started. Loaded fresh food tonight. Oranges, apples, grapefruit and lemons. I stole some of everything, ha-ha! Guess we load dry provisions some time tonight also. They told us our mail was not here. What a knock that was. I got some of my letters mailed, though. I have the 12 to 4 watch tonight. I am dirty as hell and no hopes for a shower. Heard an old 'Hit Parade' today. 1. Trolley Song. 2. I'm Making Believe. 3. Don't Fence Me In."[110]

Admiral Kiland convened a conference aboard his command ship with the LSM(R) captains the afternoon of 17 March. As Ensigns Mallery and Shedd on *LSM(R) 196* recalled, "our Captain went to a special briefing aboard an operations flagship in Leyte Gulf, where he was informed that we would be there for only 48 hours. Wild scuttlebutt rushed around the ship: bad guesses as well as what turned out to be good guesses were a 'dime a dozen.'"[111]

Comdr. Francis and Lt. Comdr. Fulweiler also held a final conference of LSM(R) commanding officers aboard *LC(FF) 535*; that evening, five photographers from CINCPAC reported aboard the flotilla flagship to photograph and film the Okinawa invasion.

LCI(R)s at Leyte

After midnight of 19 March, *LSM(R)s 196, 197, 198* and *199* were inexplicably swarmed by gunboats from LCI(R) Flotilla 16 seeking 5.0-inch SSRs.

The LSM(R)s obliged at first and transferred untold numbers of rockets to the eager LCI(R)s. But confusion (and resentment) arose upon questioning whether authorization had been granted to distribute the rockets. Indeed, one LSM(R) skipper flat out refused to give any rockets to the LCI(R)s until orders were clarified. In another instance, an LCI(R) even bartered over rockets in exchange for gasoline.

Transfers were halted after investigation, because, as one OOD reported, "each LCI wants 1000 rounds of rockets but [we] have received no such order from Commander LSM Flotilla Nine."[112] But orders remained muddled, for even after the message from the flotilla flagship "to not deliver rockets to any ship until further notice,"[113] some LSM(R)s continued transferring rockets to various LCI(R)s regardless. Finally, Commander Francis sent a directive at 0500 allowing each Spinner LSM(R) to proceed with the rocket transfers, but to retain a minimum of 5,400 SSRs on board. Not all were pleased, however, about being rocket supply ships, as *LSM(R) 197*'s Radioman Clyde Blue commented in his diary: "Went outside the bay and dropped the hook. Gave some LCIs about 1000 of our rockets. We load them and give them to someone else. Some deal."[114]

Stormy Weather

As work reached a crescendo in San Pedro harbor, seas became increasingly choppy, which made ship-to-ship transfers difficult, dangerous, and sometimes impossible. Aerological reports indicated a tropical storm was developing in the vicinity of Ulithi Atoll, and would become a cyclone of typhoon intensity over the coming week as it moved slowly toward the Philippines. At one point, *LSM(R) 189* rolled so hard while alongside *LSM(R) 191*, that every one of her remaining portside Mark 30 outboard rocket launchers was severely damaged, and a hole was punctured in her hull below the superstructure deck.

But Admiral Kiland was neither pleased with the weather nor the readiness of his Western Islands Attack Group. Training at Leyte for individual ships and units was scheduled for 9–11 March, and coordinated exercises were planned from 13–15 March, but heavy swells, winds, and prolonged rains hindered rehearsals or forced postponements. The value of the training was further diminished, moreover, because as many as 65 vessels did not report on time for either some, or any, of the rehearsals. Tardy ships ranged the gamut from LCIs and LSTs to destroyers and an aircraft carrier—and the LSM(R)s, which arrived ten days late to Leyte on 16 March. Thus, concluded Kiland, "Considering the complexity of the operation and the relative inexperience of naval personnel involved, the curtailment of these exercises by weather conditions made the training provided entirely inadequate."[115]

CHAPTER 3

The Kerama Rettos
26 March 1945–1 April 1945

The "Interim" LSM(R)s were among the vanguard of Operation Iceberg, spearheaded by the Western Islands Attack Group of the Amphibious Support Force, in the Kerama Retto invasion west of Okinawa beginning 26 March 1945.

The LSM(R) Group (Task Group 52.21) comprised two units under Commander Dennis L. Francis (Commander LSM Flotilla Nine) and Lieutenant Commander John H. Fulweiler (Commander LSM(R) Group 27):

LSM(R) Unit One (Task Unit 52.21.1)
LSM(R)s 188, 189, 190, 191, 192, and *LSM(R) 193* as LSM(R) Group 27 flagship;
LSM(R) Unit Two (Task Unit 52.21.2)
LSM(R)s 194, 195, 196, 197, 198, 199, and *LC(FF) 535* as LSM Flotilla Nine flagship.

The Amphibious Support Force (Task Force 52), under Rear Admiral W. H. P. Blandy (CTF 52), was charged with preparatory minesweeping, underwater demolitions, surface and air bombardments, and neutralizing Japanese forces in the Kerama Retto islands and on Okinawa from 24 March up to the main assault day on 1 April 1945. Component elements assembled at Ulithi advance naval base and departed for Okinawa in echelons.[1]

The Western Islands Attack Group (Task Group 51.1), under Rear Admiral Ingolf N. Kiland (CTG 51.1), was charged with the capture and defense of the Kerama Retto island group; establishing an anchorage for fleet logistical support and a seaplane base within the Kerama Rettos; and capture of Keise Shima for mounting two battalions of long range artillery preceding the Okinawa invasion on 1 April 1945. An admiring Adm. Kiland remarked, "The idea of capturing these islands and having the base actively functioning as such before the main assault was a bold conception."[2]

Under the Amphibious Support Force, the LSM(R) Group was assigned to the Advance Support Craft (TG 52.25) commanded by Captain Theodore W. Rimer (Commander LCI(L) Flotilla Fourteen). For the Kerama Retto operation only, Adm. Blandy assigned Capt. Rimer and his Advance Support Craft to Adm. Kiland and additionally designated the Western Islands Support Craft Flotilla (Task Unit 51.1.16).

As the Okinawa operation unfolded, the LSM(R)s would be assigned to various task forces, task groups, and task units.

Once Vice Admiral Richmond Kelly Turner (CTF 51) reached Okinawa with the main

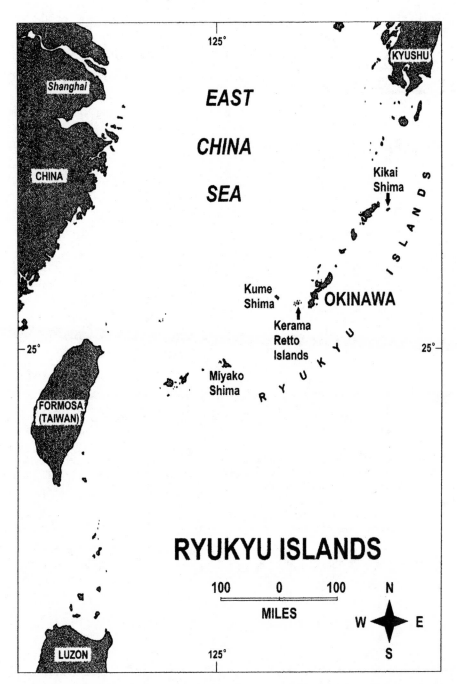

The Ryukyu Islands form a natural barrier between the East China Sea and North Pacific, extending from Japanese-held Formosa (modern Taiwan) to the southern Japanese home island, Kyushu. U.S. seizure of Okinawa, the central link in the island chain, would effectively cut Japanese lines of communication and sea lanes with their southwestern conquests for vital war-making resources such as oil. Okinawa would also provide American forces with airfields, bases, and anchorages to carry the war to the very heart of Imperial Japan (adapted from Roy E. Appleman et al., *Okinawa: The Last Battle*, The War in the Pacific, United States Army in World War II, Washington, D.C.: U.S. Government Printing Office, 1948, Map No. 1, page 5).

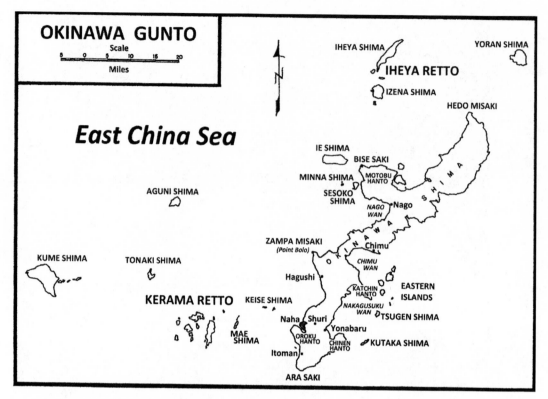

The Okinawa archipelago. More than 100,000 men of the Japanese 32nd Army, including naval, air force, and island Home Guard units, were entrenched in southern Okinawa. The Japanese high command realized they could not defeat the invading U.S. forces; instead, they sought a prolonged battle in depth and at length to maximize American casualties (adapted from Chas. S. Nichols, Jr., Major, USMC, and Henry I. Shaw, *Okinawa: Victory in the Pacific* Historical Branch, G-3 Division, Headquarters, U.S. Marine Corps, Washington, D.C.: U.S. Government Printing Office, 1955, Map 2, page 3).

Joint Expeditionary Force (Task Force 51) on 1 April 1945, he would assume direct command of all amphibious operations and thereupon subsume Adm. Blandy's Amphibious Support Force. Senior naval commander of Operation Iceberg was Admiral Raymond A. Spruance (CTF 50), Commander U.S. Fifth Fleet.

Three Convoys

The Western Islands Attack Group lifted the Western Islands Landing Force (TG 56.4) of the U.S. Army's 77th Infantry Division (reinforced) under Major General A. D. Bruce, USA, and a Marine Reconnaissance Battalion (less one company) commanded by Major James L. Jones, USMC, of the Fleet Marine Force.

Three convoys, two slow tractor groups and a fast transport group,[3] sailed in echelon from Leyte, Philippines to the Kerama Retto islands of Okinawa.

On 19 March 1945, Western Islands Tractor Group GEORGE (TU 51.7.1) was the first convoy to depart Leyte, commanded by Captain Richard C. Webb (ComLSTFlot16) as OTC in force flagship *LC(FF) 783*. The 107 ships required a full week's passage averaging 9 knots to arrive southwest of Okinawa by 25 March. The main body was two dozen LSTs, flanked by two score LCIs of various types, and a couple LSMs. Following astern was the LSM(R) flotilla forming four columns of three rocketships each. Trailing the convoy was a group of net tenders, minesweepers, and two cargo ships, while a destroyer with destroyer escorts provided screening protection around the convoy.

Two days later on 21 March, the second, faster convoy Transport Group FOX (TU 51.1.1) steamed from Leyte with Rear Admiral Kiland as OTC embarked in his amphibious headquarters ship *Mount McKinley AGC 7* and Captain Frederick Moosbrugger, Screen Commander, embarked in *Biscayne AGC 18*. The 39 ships were largely attack cargo ships, with destroyers and destroyer escorts, and a few support craft. Following astern was Support Carrier Unit Four under Rear Admiral Felix Stump as OTC with three escort aircraft carriers, two destroyers and six destroyer escorts providing anti-submarine screen and combat air patrol coverage.

The third and final convoy was Western Islands Tractor Group HOW (TU 51.7.9) sailing on 24 March with Commander Ellsworth D. McEathron as OTC embarked in *Bouyant AM*

LSM(R) 193, flagship of LSM(R) Group 27 under Lieutenant Commander John H. Fulweiler, in convoy en route to Okinawa from Leyte, Philippines, circa 19 to 25 March 1945. In rough seas, the blunt bow plowed the water while the flat bottom bucked the swells. Ship handling became difficult and arduous for the crew. The *LC(FF) 535* stern is seen at lower right (official U.S. Navy photograph).

153. The 23 ships comprised 7 LSTs and 9 LSMs with attached screens until final approach of the Kerama Retto islands on 31 March.

All three convoys encountered stormy weather en route, so preferred routes were adjusted to coordinate approaches to the Kerama Rettos. Heavy seas, strong headwinds and drifting made transit difficult from the outset. The pitching, tossing and pounding from churning seas posed challenges for flat-bottomed and high-sided LSM(R)s, LSMs, and LCIs alike. "Getting rougher all the time," wrote Radioman Clyde Blue in his diary in *LSM(R) 197*. "Roughest seas we have been in yet. Ship is taking a beating. Hope it can take it. We are going to hit Kerama Retto on the 26th at 8 a.m. with 700 rockets."[4] The next day Blue added, "Awfully rough out. [You] lay in your sack and fly right off of it when the ship hits a wave."[5] One other account[6] clocked a declination roll angle of almost 55°.

But weather and sea conditions did not entirely curtail shipboard activities, as the LSM(R)s held rocket assembly drills, simulated rocket firing exercises, and tested alarm circuits. Many ships practiced anti-aircraft tracking, fired at a target sleeve from a tow plane, or conducted individual gunnery exercises. More mundane activities included routine passing of guard mails between ships, officers holding disciplinary deck courts, aircraft recognition classes, and instruction on the enemy's submarines and new midget subs.

LSM(R) 193 passing guard mail attached to a line with *LC(FF) 535* while in convoy en route to Okinawa from Leyte, Philippines, circa 19 to 25 March 1945. Note the pipe rail limit stops attached to the 40mm gun tubs, which block the gun barrels from aiming into the ship (official U.S. Navy photograph).

LSM(R)s, among other ships, contended with occasional mechanical and electrical breakdowns, such as malfunctioning radar units, cracked engine cylinder liners, stuck rudders, gyro compass errors, and sundry lesser difficulties. A recurring problem with LSM-types was the sudden loss of electrical steering controls in the wheelhouse. This emergency required a man to manually steer the ship using the "trick wheel" located in the after steering compartment. From within the lowest level of the fantail, he would communicate with the bridge via sound-powered headphones and microphone until ships control was restored.

Once underway, the following message was dispatched among the rocketship flotilla:

TO ALL HANDS:

> The Group Commander wishes to commend all hands for the excellent manner in which the backbreaking lot of loading supplies and ammunition was carried through at Leyte. We can use every thing we got at the next stop—.

JOHN H. FULWEILER
Lieut. Comdr., USNR
COMDR. LSM(R) Grp. 27[7]

Nighttime Chaos: 20–21 March 1945

Convoy emergency turns or zigzags were *de rigueur* during GQ alerts for enemy submarines or floating mines. But late night of 20 March, chaos suddenly broke out within the convoy's formation, and could have ended disastrously. Despite squally weather, visibility was good enough this evening with the aid of the light of a half moon peering through broken clouds. Without warning, however, at 2317 *LSM(R) 193* veered to avoid colliding with an LST dead ahead, suffering steering problems during a convoy maneuver. Minutes later, *LSM(R) 192* reported at 2320:

> Last LSM(R) in starboard column swung to port, passed astern of this ship and proceeded to pass close aboard on port side. Reason unknown. It was observed that *LSM(R) 191* has simultaneously swung across our bow, and appeared to be lying dead in the water. Ship ahead of [*LSM(R)*] *191* appeared to have swung to port and to be maneuvering without signal. This ship changed speed from standard to all back ⅔. Entire convoy appeared to be in disorder as appearing on radar screen. Reason unknown. Minelayer came dangerously close to this ship.

By 2330, *LSM(R) 191* reported hearing three short whistle blasts from an unidentified ship ahead, then observed an "unknown LSM(R) crossed 200 yards ahead of the bow of this vessel followed closely by an unknown LST. LST circled and again crossed bow of this vessel." By the time *LSM(R) 192* returned to her convoy position astern *LSM(R) 191*, the "Position of various ships appeared disorganized but some resemblance of order returning gradually."

Final Preparations

After several days at sea, officers began briefing crews on the top secret orders of their missions and about the Japanese forces lying ahead at Kerama Retto and Okinawa. Hereafter, shipboard drills took on added urgency with the sobering realization of entering Japanese home waters where an enemy was ready to strike and kill at any moment. Apprehension, although understated, can be sensed from Clyde Blue's diary entry from aboard *LSM(R) 197*, yet undoubtedly shared by many. "I am wondering about the invasion. The 'Retto' is a small one, but the one on April 1st is going to be a big one. I have got all my gear ready in case I have to go over the side."[8]

The afternoon of 22 March, *LCI(G) 560* suffered engine troubles and fell out of formation. Despite being towed by *LCI(M) 755*, however, the hapless vessels lagged increasingly behind in restless seas and squalls. By direction of the convoy's OTC, the LSM(R) flotilla commander dispatched *LSM(R) 199* to take over towing. Closing more than seven miles to rejoin the convoy formation hours later, the rocketship continued towing the gunboat by stern anchor cable for two more days until the smaller landing craft could sail under her own power. Unfortunately for *LSM(R) 199*, she lost her stern anchor to Davy Jones' Locker when it dislodged from its fantail cradle.

The sense of entering a war zone grew increasingly evident by 24 March: floating debris, an oil slick, green marker dye, an oil-smeared kapok life jacket. Planes, thought to be friendly, appeared more frequently in the skies passing the convoys, while others—possibly enemy "snoopers" or reconnaissance aircraft—lingered on the distant horizon. "Had aircraft alerts this morning," recalled *LSM(R) 197* Radioman Clyde Blue. "No planes, though. We [will] assemble 400 rockets and put them in the ready racks tomorrow."[9] "General Quarters," Storekeeper Robert W. Landis also wrote in his diary in *LSM(R) 192*. "Two enemy aircraft approaching. Reported by escorting destroyers. No contact. Aircraft turned back. We are now entering East China Sea skirting northern Formosa. General Quarters is now in full battle gear."[10] A sub alert that morning caused the convoy to emergency zigzag, the sluggish mass of warships first turning 45° to starboard, then turning 45° back to port a quarter-hour later. No submarines were ever confirmed, however, but nerves grew tenser nonetheless.

The afternoon of 25 March, LSM(R) crews assembled rockets, tested alarms and launcher electrical firing circuits, stowed assembled rockets in ready service magazines, and loaded rockets into launchers. Rocket run instructions drafted by the flotilla's officers and staff were distributed. The four Spinner ships loaded 700 rockets in Mark 51 launchers, which took up to 2 hours. The eight Finner ships loaded 300 rockets in the inboard Mark 36 launchers only, which varied between 90 minutes and almost 3 hours; the outboard Mark 30 rocket launchers, on the other hand, were not loaded and remained empty.

Love Minus Six (L-6) Day: 26 March 1945

After midnight of 25–26 March, the first two echelons of the Western Islands Attack Group converged due West of the Kerama Retto island group. Transports and warships organized under cover of darkness for the morning's assaults of 26 March 1945, designated L-6 or Love-minus-Six Day.

At 0330, the LSM(R) Group deployed from the convoy and reformed as two units. By 0600, the LSM(R)s steamed eastward, skirting the southern periphery of the Kerama Retto islands, and timed their approach by adjusting courses and speeds. This was the last time the twelve "Interim" LSM(R)s sailed as a flotilla.

In morning twilight, the islands grew visible under heavy AA fire some 15 miles away. Japanese air attacks against American naval forces around the Kerama Rettos were only sporadic at first and without discernible organization, but soon enemy aircraft began swarming the islands. "Two Zeros flew around the outer part of the convoy this morning," observed Clyde Blue from *LSM(R) 197*, "and some DEs knocked one down. We opened fire on three planes and they turned out to be our own."[11]

"That morning before daylight," recalled *LSM(R) 196* Quartermaster-striker Bruce McDaniel, "blue flames were seen streaking down toward the islands, which turned out to be the exhausts from the engines of American carrier planes as they were attacking."[12] Gunners from at least one rocketship tracked planes with their guns, apparently without regard to enemy or friendly, until a 5"/38 round discharged at a passing TBF Avenger. The American fighter-bomber was not hit, fortunately, but an irate captain in *LSM(R) 189* immediately forbade his gun crews from tracking planes until further orders.

Until Okinawa airfields were captured, carrier planes supporting the invasion forces were dispatched from Admiral Blandy's flagship *Estes AGC 12* until 0600 of Love Day.[13] Meanwhile, cruisers and destroyers pounded the islands with heavy preliminary bombardment. Target priorities were enemy aircraft, amphibious tanks, and small boats. Primary targets among the islands included coastal defense guns and field artillery, anti-aircraft guns, floating mines, communication facilities, and barracked areas.[14]

The Kerama Retto assaults were assigned to U.S. Army Battalion Landing Teams (BLTs) of the 77th Division, famously known as "The Statue of Liberty" Division. During 26 March, troops would land on Geruma, Aka, Zamami, Hokaji, and Yakabi islands. On 27 March, troops would assault Tokashiki, Kuba, and Amuro islands, while smaller islands would be scouted and secured as soon as possible. By 31 March, troops would take Keise and Nagunnu islands.[15] The LSM(R)s were assigned fire support at Aka Shima, Zamami Shima, Tokashiki Shima, and Keise Shima.

Each army beach assault was assigned a naval gunfire unit comprising a destroyer supported by combinations of LCI(G)s, LCI(M)s, and LSM(R)s under a Support Team Commander[16] who, explained Adm. Kiland, "is responsible for the coordination of the effort of the different elements of the support team attacking on his beach. He must insure that rocket, mortar, and machine gun fire from support craft do not seriously endanger our own forces; and he must take action to adjust timing of fires with respect to the scheduled landing hour if the boat waves are markedly early or late."[17]

"Inasmuch as the plan involved the simultaneous assault of six islands [*sic*], it was of necessity unusually complex," Kiland later reported. "The location of the beaches, and of the transport and launching areas, required in all cases an irregular approach, with several large changes of direction. Physical limitations also precluded the use of the conventional line of departure 3–4000 yards off shore. In general only the final 1000 to 1500 yards of each approach could be made directly and on a straight course."[18]

On 26 March 1945, morning skies were sunny and clear with good visibility and calm waters. "The weather was especially suited to our invasion forces" remarked Commander Francis. "There were very light winds and the sea gave very little swell…. The temperature was mild at all times, averaging about 72 degrees Fahrenheit throughout the entire period." At 0500, Admiral Kiland gave the order to commence the Kerama Retto assaults in Phase One of Operation Iceberg.[19]

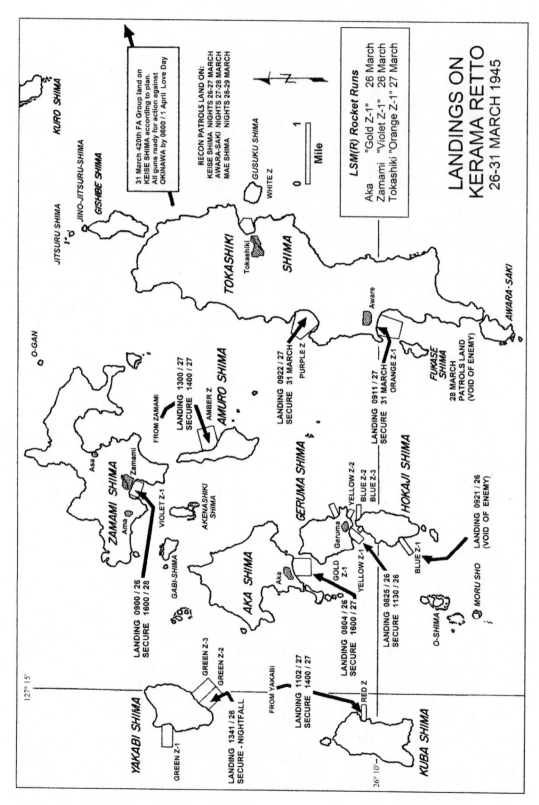

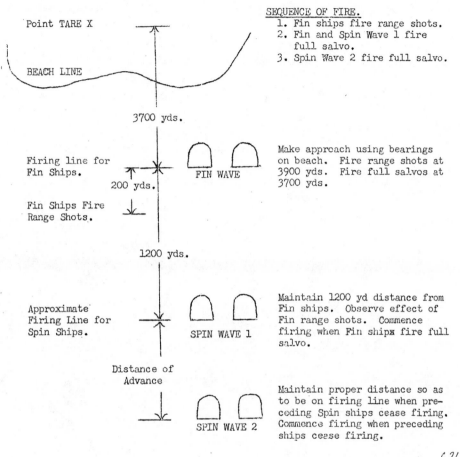

HEAVY CONCENTRATION TARGET APPROACH FORMATION
(to be used when firing time is less than ten (10) minutes)

Point TARE X

BEACH LINE

3700 yds.

Firing line for
Fin Ships.

200 yds.

Fin Ships Fire
Range Shots.

1200 yds.

Approximate
Firing Line for
Spin Ships.

Distance of
Advance

FIN WAVE

SPIN WAVE 1

SPIN WAVE 2

SEQUENCE OF FIRE.
1. Fin ships fire range shots.
2. Fin and Spin Wave 1 fire full salvo.
3. Spin Wave 2 fire full salvo.

Make approach using bearings on beach. Fire range shots at 3900 yds. Fire full salvos at 3700 yds.

Maintain 1200 yd distance from Fin ships. Observe effect of Fin range shots. Commence firing when Fin ships fire full salvo.

Maintain proper distance so as to be on firing line when preceding Spin ships cease firing. Commence firing when preceding ships cease firing.

LSM(R) commanders formulated a protocol for rocket runs during the Okinawa operation, adaptable for any number and combination of Finner and Spinner rocketships (from Commander, LSM Flotilla Nine, Action Report—Ie Shima and Southeastern Okinawa, 2 April through 20 April 1945, Serial 0010, 21 April 1945, Enclosure [F], New Attack Formations).

Opposite: The Kerama Retto islands lay about 15 miles due west from southern Okinawa. The island group was lightly defended and the U.S. invasion caught the Japanese commanders by surprise. American forces discovered more than 350 small explosive speedboats dispersed and hidden among the Kerama Rettos, intended for suicide crashes against the main American naval forces invading Okinawa proper (adapted from Commander in Chief, U.S. Pacific Fleet and Pacific Ocean Areas, Operations in the Pacific Ocean Areas during the Month of April 1945, Plate V).

Aka Shima: "Gold Z-1" 26 March 1945

LSM(R)s 196, 197, 198 and *199* under Commander Dennis L. Francis in LSM Flotilla Nine flagship *LC(FF) 535* of LSM(R) Unit Two (TU 52.21.2)[20] were the first LSM(R)s to fire rockets in anger. Aka Shima beachhead, designated "Gold Z-1," was among several Kerama Retto island assaults the morning of 26 March 1945.

Comdr. Francis (CTG 52.21) was Support Team Commander of "Support Team Gold," including *LCI(M)s 805, 806* and *807* for pre-landing, close-in fire support with the four LSM(R)s. Simultaneously, waves of amphibious tracked landing vehicles lifting U.S. Army 3rd BLT of the 305th Regimental Combat Team (RCT) would converge from south-southwest for landings beginning at 0800, codenamed M-Hour or "Mike Hour." Francis therefore emphasized, "Commanding Officers are responsible that no rockets are fired over boats."[21]

Aka Shima is an irregular-shaped island, resembling a misshapen sting ray flying northward, about 3,400 by 3,000 yards with two peaks of 539 and 635 feet. Its southern seaport village of Aka rests above a sandy beach, code-named "Gold Z-1," that gently curves outward

LSM(R) 196 crewmen pass and carry assembled 5-inch Spin-stabilized Rockets (SSRs) to the rocket deck for manual loading into Mark 51 Rocket Launchers. Note protective canvas covers still draping many of the launchers (official U.S. Navy photograph).

S1c Joseph Clapaftis carefully loads a 5-inch Spin-stabilized Rocket into a Mark 51 Rocket Launcher on *LSM(R) 196* (official U.S. Navy photograph).

some 500 yards both directions, opening a shoreline of occasional coral fringes just below the surf. Immediately southwest of Aka village, four rocky volcanic islets taper to form a "tail" stretching about a thousand yards southward.

The mission was to destroy Aka village and reduce adjacent enemy defenses, which U.S. Intelligence identified as a pillbox, 11 vehicles (possibly amphibious tanks), 21 caves and two tombs.[22] Particular attention was given to areas beyond the beaches, suitable for enemy mortar locations against landing American troops.[23]

The rocket run on Aka village would commence at 0746, or M-14, fourteen minutes before 0800. Each Spinner rocketship loaded 700 SSRs in their Mark 51 rocket launchers, and the schedule of fire allotted two minutes to lay down rocket salvos for a 600-yard depth of pattern (DOP) by 600 yards wide. Course adjustments south of Aka Shima were plotted from radar fixes and visual bearings: to the left, Moru Sho called "Mole Rock," a small but prominent rocky formation; farther north, the uninhabited islet O-Shima (or Ono Shima); to the right, Mukaraku Jima, a small, uninhabited islet south of islands Hokaji Shima and Geruma Shima. The final approach landmark was the southern-most rocky islet at the tip of Aka Shima's "tail."

Timing and alertness were critical. Immediately southeast of Aka Shima, other gunfire support craft and Army landing vehicles would converge for simultaneous landings on Geruma Shima, "Yellow Z-1," and might cross into the LSM(R)s' line-of-fire. So, cautioned Admiral Kiland, "At this [Aka Shima] beach careful coordination is required of the Support

LSM(R) 196 crewmen load 5-inch Spin-stabilized Rockets into Mark 51 Rocket Launchers while anchored among the Kerama Retto islands circa late March 1945. Note the .50 caliber machine gun mounted on a support stand on the rocket deck in the left foreground (official U.S. Navy photograph).

Team Commander in order that rockets may be fired as late as possible and still not be fired over either of the column of LVTs and boats proceeding to Gold Z-1 and Yellow Z-1."[24]

LSM(R)s sounded General Quarters and set Condition One Roger, calling all hands to clear the rocket decks, then gunnery officers energized launcher circuits from atop "Flying Bridges." Except for ships' control in the Conn, all sailors disappeared below decks to escape the rockets' searing exhaust blasts of toxic fumes, noise, and turbulent debris. An additional danger was the potential misfire of the highly explosive projectiles. Only gun crews shielded within the 5-inch fantail gun mounts remained at battle stations for counter-battery fire.

Destroyer *William D. Porter DD 579* closed from the south-southeast, firing 5-inch guns at targets of opportunity and poised for counter-battery fire. Three LCI(M)s stood some 2000 yards due east of Aka village, ready with 4.2-inch mortars for heavy saturation and suppressing fire following the LSM(R)s' attack up the middle. (An LCI[M] skipper later complained the "LSM[R]s astern were crowding" and making firing more difficult within the congested area.)[25] Aircraft also sortied for pre-landing strikes.

LSM(R)s 196, 197, 198 and *199* launch rockets in line abreast at Aka Shima preceding the U.S. amphibious invasion of the Kerama Retto islands on 26 March 1945. The islet Moru Sho, called Mole Rock, is in the background. This dramatic photograph is among the most iconic images from the Second World War (official U.S. Navy photograph).

Bearing due north on their final approach and true line of fire, the four LSM(R)s formed line abreast in a single wave, advancing 6 knots or about 200 yards/minute. Some 5,000 yards south of Aka village, the firing point was "Mole Rock" when bearing 270° relative, simultaneous with the visual flag hoist signal from guide ship *LSM(R) 196*, at which two initial range rockets were launched.

Suddenly, premature volleys of rockets streaked upwards from one or more LSM(R)s, though no one knew (or would say) for sure from where. Tensions were running high during this first wartime engagement, to be sure, and the ranging rockets were mistaken for commencing the actual rocket attack.

Despite confusion, all rocketships followed suit with repeated salvos. Dozens of rockets landed in the waters short of the shoreline, however, and detonated among coral reefs while marching inland across the sandy beachhead into Aka township and beyond. The barrage lasted forty-one seconds: *LSM(R) 196* fired 696 rockets with four misfires, while *LSM(R)s 197, 198, 199* and *LC(FF) 535* launched all rockets without reported misfires.[26] "Made the beachhead at 0730 and fired our rockets," wrote Radioman Clyde Blue in *LSM(R) 197*. "We fired at a fishing village but couldn't see what we did because of the smoke."[27] The four Spinners then turned from Aka Shima to rendezvous with the flagship for further orders, steering clear of troop-laden amphibious assault vehicles that landed at 0804.[28]

LSM(R) 196 Ensign David Mallery explained, "On signal we fired our first rockets onto our target. Up on the conn, we all crouched over just before the Captain gave the signal to fire, because of the heat and flying particles accompanying the firing. This was our first big moment as a ship."[29] Standing nearby was Quartermaster-striker Bruce A. McDaniel: "We came in close to the fishing village, and one could see villagers walking amid the ruins. There must have been civilian casualties, if they had not fled into the hills before dawn. There did not seem to be fires in the buildings, but some napalm had been dropped around by carrier planes, and what appeared to be some phosphorous."[30]

Ensign Mallery continued, "We had just stuck our heads up and out to watch the rockets hit the beach and watch the last explosion when the Flotilla Commander's radio message came. This moment was made immeasurably bigger by the Commander calling us on the radio and giving our ship a 'well done.' We were suddenly aware of each other again, and all eyes were toward the skipper. The look on his face was worth the rewards of our paydays."[31]

Cameras were also rolling from *LC(FF) 535* pacing abreast the rocketships. Navy combat photographers CPhoM Leif Erickson and Sp(P)2c William Loewe captured dramatic black-and-white motion pictures and still photographs, famously framing the four rocket-firing LSM(R)s, and arguably among the most iconic images from the Second World War. "Leif Erickson, a former Hollywood actor, was aboard our ship and took considerable footage of all the activity in the area," recalled Harold J. Ball, Executive Officer of *LC(FF) 535*. "Leif Erickson was married to Frances Farmer, a Hollywood actress.... I ran out of film for my 35mm and I asked Leif for enough film to load several cassettes. He gave me a hundred-foot roll of film which I used to load my own cassettes in my cabin, late at night when conditions allowed. Great man and good shipmate for some time."[32]

Afterwards, Commander Francis put his best foot forward. "At 0738 LSMRs [*sic*] of Unit Two fired rockets on town of Aka with many rockets short in range due to premature firing by two ships. Second salvo, however, landed directly on objective. At 0746 rocket firing was completed by this unit."[33] Later, Francis offered additional details: "The rocket attack ceased at 0748 with approximately 2200 rockets expended. About 50% of the rockets fired landed in the target area, resulting in the destruction of numerous village huts and partial destruction of others. The remaining rockets landed in the water just off the beach and destroyed coral heads in the shallow water, facilitating the beaching of small landing craft. This latter fact was attested to by Major Patrick Crafton of the US Army." But, Comdr. Francis conceded, "Flag hoists in connection with rocket runs were far less effective than the paralleling voice circuit."[34] Admiral Ingolf I. Kiland, on the other hand, tempered his assessment: "The 5" rocket impacts were effective and provided complete neutralization of areas hit to the satisfaction of the assault troops. [However] The number of 'shorts' can be reduced by placing greater reliance on the careful use of ranging shots."[35]

Zamami Shima: "Violet Z-1" 26 March 1945

LSM(R)s 188, 189, 190, 191 and *192* under Lieutenant Commander John H. Fulweiler in LSM(R) Group 27 flagship *LSM(R) 193* of LSM(R) Unit One (TU 52.21.1) were accompanied by *LSM(R)s 194* and *195* cross-assigned from LSM(R) Unit Two (TU 52.21.2). Zamami Shima beachhead, designated "Violet Z-1," was among several Kerama Retto island assaults the morning of 26 March 1945.

Captain Theodore Rimer (CTG 52.25/CTU 51.1.16), in flagship *LC(FF) 657*, was Support Team Commander of "Support Team Violet," including *LCI(M)s 801, 802, 803* and *804* for pre-landing, close-in fire support with the eight LSM(R)s. Simultaneously, waves of amphibious tracked landing vehicles lifting U.S. Army 1st BLT of the 305th Regimental Combat Team (RCT) would converge from west-northwest, then turn left oblique for landings beginning at 0830, codenamed M+30 or M-Hour-plus-30. Fulweiler therefore emphasized, "The responsibility for controlling fire so that it will not endanger LVTs rests on each Commanding Officer."[36]

Zamami Shima is the northernmost island of the Kerama Retto group, once described as an ungainly, "two-legged, humpbacked island."[37] Stretching approximately 5,500 yards east-to-west and 400 yards at its narrowest, forested hills rise over 400 feet with a few flatlands along the southern coast. Zamami village faces south from a beach guarded by a man-made harbor sea wall lining its U-shaped bay.

The mission was to destroy Zamami village and reduce adjacent enemy defenses, which U.S. Intelligence identified as fourteen camouflaged vehicles, dozens of machine guns and tombs, and fishing vessels.[38] Defenders included a company of Japanese troops with about 300 Korean laborers, and the harbor seawall posed an additional defense against invasion assault vehicles. Here, advised Admiral Kiland, "Protect [US Army] boat waves during their approach as practicable with deliberate machine gun fire."[39] Aircraft also supported the pre-landing bombardments.

"Went to GQ at 4 a.m. after brief breakfast," *LSM(R) 192*'s Storekeeper Robert W. Landis scribbled in his diary. "Ready for the assault. About 5:45 still dark, we moved toward the beachhead. With the dawn came the Japanese aircraft squadrons. We are firing 40 mm's and 20 mm's. This is heavy action. The sky is filled with tracers and anti-aircraft shell bursts. The noise is deafening. An enemy suicide pilot attempted to hit a destroyer on our starboard side but missed and plunged into the sea."[40]

The rocket runs on Zamami village would commence at 0800, designated M-Hour or "Mike Hour." Each Finner rocketship loaded 300 ARs in their inboard Mark 36 rocket launchers only, and the schedule of fire allotted two minutes to lay down rocket salvos for an 800-yard depth of pattern by 800 yards wide. Course adjustments south of Zamami Shima were plotted from radar fixes and visual bearings to the left on Hanta Saki, Aka Shima's prominent southeastern cape. The final approach landmark was the small island Akenashiki Shima, west of the entrance to Zamami Bay.

LSM(R)s sounded General Quarters and set Condition One Roger, calling all hands to clear the decks, and gunnery officers energized rocket launcher circuits from atop "Flying Bridges." Except for ships' control in the conn, all sailors disappeared below decks to escape the rockets' hazardous exhaust blasts, noise and debris. Only gun crews shielded within the 5-inch gun mounts on the fantails remained at battle stations for counter-battery fire.

Destroyer *Isherwood DD 520* closed from the southeast for targets of opportunity and poised for counter-battery fire. The four LCI(M)s stood some 2000 yards southwest of Zamami village, covering the flank with 4.2-inch mortar rounds of heavy saturation fire and suppressing gunfire as the LSM(R)s attacked up the middle. "Mortar craft may maneuver at will near areas assigned but must keep clear of line of fire of [LSM(R)] rocket craft during scheduled rocket fire," warned Adm. Kiland.[41] Moreover, advised Fulweiler, "A number of Gun Boats will be in the area. Use caution and common sense when approaching firing point. Pass astern [original emphasis] of all Mortar Ships and Gun Boats firing on Aka Shima."[42] Nevertheless, Kiland emphasized once more, "Support Team Commander [must] watch approach of boat waves and ensure that rocket fire is delivered as late as practicable without firing rockets over the boats."[43]

At 0805, Captain Rimer signaled the initial wave to commence their rocket run, and Lt. Comdr. Fulweiler would signal all subsequent waves.

The original Rocket Firing Plan[44] organized the eight rocketships in two waves of four ships line abreast:

> 1st Wave: Division One—LSM(R)s 193, 192, 191, 194;
> 2nd Wave: Division Two—LSM(R)s 190, 189, 188, 195.

Prior to the rocket runs on Zamami Shima, the rocket firing plan was modified, that much is certain, but official reports and eyewitness accounts remain at odds or ambiguous on the final rocketship attack formations.

The first LSM(R)s advanced at 7 knots (235 yards/minute) on course 003° True and took final radar and visual bearings on a prominent hill left of Zamami village. About 4,000 yards from Beach Violet Z-1, rocket salvos were launched in four-second intervals.

As the rocketships retired, sailors donning helmets, lifejackets, and battle gear rushed topside to man 20mm and 40mm guns as 5-inch/38s returned fire against enemy mortars and machineguns.

The rocket barrages lasted from 0807 to 0812: LSM(R)s 191 and 193 reported no rocket misfires; LSM(R) 192 suffered 5 misfires out of 284 rockets; and LSM(R) 194 reported 299 rockets fired, although hot exhaust cinders ignited a small fire, damaging flags and pennants in the auxiliary flagbag.[45]

Lt. Comdr. Fulweiler cancelled further rocket runs. Zamami was shrouded in smoke and dust after intense explosions and burning, and troop-carrying LVTs were approaching the firing zone and would soon foul the range.[46]

Storekeeper Robert W. Landis resumed his diary in LSM(R) 192: "At 8:30 a.m. under the cover of [US naval gunfire] barrages, eight rocket ships approached the beach in a column of two's. Within 500 yards of the beach we released the rockets, quickly turned 180 degrees and retreated to open seas. Looking back the beach was obscured by smoke. Troops went ashore."[47]

Ensign John P. Wickser aboard LSM(R) 194 later commented, "we certainly made an enormous mess of the beaches, and there was some relief of tension, after all those months, in actually carrying out a mission for which we were designed and firing our first shots in anger. We reported our 'mission completed' in code to Admiral Blandy's flagship, the USS Estes, which lay off Okinawa, and were ordered to cruise around the islands and report any enemy activities which seemed to be taking place. This took up most of the day and our apprehension increased somewhat when we saw many floating contact mines in the waters nearby."[48]

Admiral Kiland, however, was less than enthusiastic with the initial performances of the LSM(R)s:

Support rendered by LCI(G)s as compared to LSM(R)s was superior because of the lesser ranges involved in such support, the resultant lesser effect of atmospheric conditions on the trajectory of the smaller rocket and the greater experience of these craft. LSM(R)s were used for the first time in this operation. Although many of the LSM(R) rockets fell short, it is pointed out that this was their first assault against enemy territory and they did not arrive from the rear area in time to take part in the rehearsal for the operation. [Nevertheless] The Army reported rocket fire from the LSM(R)s to be very effective.[49]

Night Patrols: 26–27 March 1945

Immediately after the rocket runs against Aka and Zamami islands, during the next week, the LSM(R)s and flotilla flagship were assigned nighttime coastal patrols. Patrol areas were among the Kerama Retto islands initially, then expanded to Okinawa's western shoreline. Tasks included interdiction of enemy barges and boat traffic, harassing fire of Japanese troops, and destruction of targets of opportunity, such as gun emplacements, supply depots, transportation and communication networks, caves, and the like. Most LSM(R)s also patrolled with deck loads of rockets, although rarely fired.

Patrols against Japanese speedy suicide boats in particular were soon called "Flycatchers," coined after Vice Admiral Turner once cautioned, "be particularly alert as this looks like a fine night to catch flies."[50] "Skunks" was another name American sailors gave to enemy small boats, thus such assignments were also known as "Skunk Patrols."

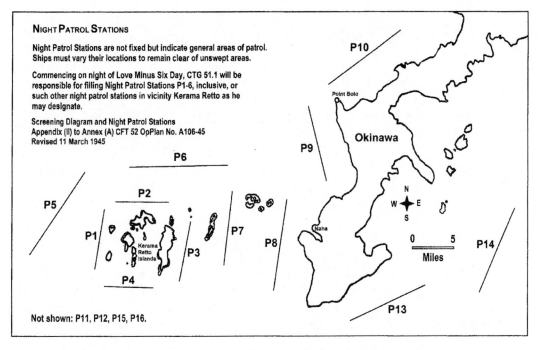

LSM(R)s, gunboats and destroyer-types patrolled Night Patrol Stations P1 through P16 among the Kerama Retto island group and off the Okinawa coastline beginning 26 March 1945. Patrols varied with local commanders and tactical requirements (adapted from Commander, Amphibious Group One [Task Force 52], Operation Plan No. A106–45, Serial 00032, 5 March 1945, Screening Diagram and Night Patrol Stations, Appendix [II] to Annex [A], revised 11 March 1945).

Beginning the afternoon of 26 March, rocketships initially patrolled enemy-held Tokashiki Shima. *LSM(R)s 193, 194,* and *195* screened the island's entire southern tip, and *LSM(R)s 188, 189,* and *192* screened the northern tip.

Most enemy return fire from the islands was light and sporadic, but, as Storekeeper Robert W. Landis recalled aboard *LSM(R) 192,* "There was continuous enemy air action on and off all day. We remained at General Quarters for twelve hours. Also assembled and loaded more rockets while patrolling close to shore. Now firing 5 inch gun into caves along the shore. Occasionally we take small arms fire."[51]

Patrols were often methodical. "Made systematic search for enemy installations and small boats, and destroyed many of these targets," reported Lt. (jg) Courtlyn H. Jorgensen from *LSM(R) 192.* "Particular attention was paid to caves where small boats could be hid and later launched. Destroyed buildings and possible artillery installations." His skipper Lt. Neal B. Hadsell added, "Fired at all targets of suspicious nature with particular attention given to possible hiding places of small boats."[52] Indeed, Commander Francis later commended the rocketship:

> On 26 March 1945, during the course of a night patrol you were able to achieve considerable damage to enemy facilities and material. This destruction included four small boats on the beach, one PT boat, one defense position, one building completely burned and two others partially demolished. For this series of accomplishment during one evening, you are hereby commended as well as your officers and entire ship's personnel. Well done. D. L. Francis LT. COMDR., [sic] USN.[53]

Finner *LSM(R)s 190* and *191* supplemented the screen of the four Spinner *LSM(R)s 196, 197, 198* and *199* generally south and west of Zamami Shima. Flagship *LC(FF) 535* briefly accompanied the rocketships, ranging south of Aka Shima to north of Zamami Shima.

"The first night," recalled Ensigns Mallery and Shedd in *LSM(R) 196,* "we were sent on patrol against suicide boats, against which we had been fully warned, and against small boats used for commuting from one of the small islands to another."[54] *LSM(R) 197,* during another offensive action, fired upon an enemy gasoline dump on the coast of Yakabi Shima, resulting in its complete destruction by fire.[55] Still, grumbled Clyde Blue, the rocketship's Radioman, "We patrolled all night about 300 yards off of shore…. Did not see a thing all night. We really gave the Japs plenty of hell. There are a lot of our ships here, and more coming."[56]

That evening, *LSM(R)s 189, 190, 191, 192* and *193* ceased night patrols and *LC(FF) 535* guided them southward from the Kerama Retto islands. Here they rendezvoused with scores of converging ships then sailed southeast for night retirement. Ensign Victor Anderson was OOD in *LSM(R) 192* and reported, "in vicinity area south of Kerama Retto … convoy consists of LSTs, LCIs, Minelayers, Patrol Craft, and LSM(R)s. Formation guide for LSM(R)s is *LCI 535.* Speed varies, but is averaging all ahead two. Course of formation describes a large circle, and is not constant, circle is clockwise."[57]

Under a clear, moonlit sky, the remaining rocketships continued nighttime patrols where their screen formed a sweeping arc: *LSM(R) 197* between Yakabi Shima and Aka Shima; *LSM(R) 196* west of Zamami Shima; *LSM(R)s 198* and *199* north of Zamami Shima; and *LSM(R)s 188, 194* and *195* east of Tokashiki Shima.

Loss of USS Halligan

Late afternoon of 26 March 1945, about eight miles west of Okinawa, *LSM(R)s 194* and *195* manned General Quarters on lookout for surfaced enemy mines. Both armed with deck loads of rockets in their launchers, *LSM(R) 194* was lying with no way on some 400 yards astern sister ship *LSM(R) 195*. In Area B5, the southern leg of patrol station P7, or "Peter 7," the rocketships were roughly halfway between Okinawa and Tokashiki Shima. A couple miles to the south, three small patrol craft stood by, firing into the seas to explode floating mines.[58]

Ensign John P. Wickser doubled as 1st Lieutenant and Communications Officer for *LSM(R) 194*. "Later that day we were ordered to proceed to the southern end of the main island of Okinawa, about twenty miles away, and join a destroyer on patrol at a certain rendezvous point. Our arrival at Okinawa, I might add, had already been noted by 'Tokyo Rose,' who ominously predicted in her broadcasts our imminent destruction by the Imperial Japanese Navy."

"I remember when we hove into sight of the destroyer," Wickser continued. "I was watch officer and it was a lovely calm evening. At about 6 p.m. the [USS *Halligan DD 584*][59] sent us a voice message indicating that we should approach to within about a thousand yards of her, and follow a zig-zag patrol pattern designed to avoid the possibility of being too easy a target for enemy submarine torpedoes." About three quarters of a mile away, *Halligan* passed the port beams of the two LSM(R)s, then made a complete turn about one and one half miles off the rocketships' port bows.

The destroyer was returning on a reciprocal course about a mile away when at 1840, recalled Ensign Wickser, "Suddenly, at a distance of about 1500 yards ahead of us, an enormous explosion occurred on board the *Halligan*, one of such force that some of her crew were hurled into the air almost as far back as half the distance between us. Huge bursts of flame and smoke billowed from the stricken ship and soon the waters around her, which were covered with oil, were also flaming. I, of course, immediately sounded the General Quarters alarm and the Captain, Lt. Allan M. Hirshberg, came on the bridge on the double and took command."

The column of smoke and flames shot up several hundred yards into the air. As the plume began clearing the destroyer seemed to be afloat but was only slowly moving forward while turning wearily. "Viewing intently through our binoculars, we were able to determine that the entire bow of the destroyer had been blown away right back to the first stack," said Wickser. "Our Captain promptly ordered a course directly through the flames to pick up survivors and assist the stricken ship. I attempted to point out to him that—should we run through the flaming oil with the full deckload of rockets we had armed—this might very well cost the Navy two ships instead of one. He curtly dismissed my craven objections, however, by informing me he intended to fire all of the rockets out to sea, if necessary ($40,000 worth) and, in any event, what did I expect he should do—let those men on board die?"

LSM(R) 194 swung about full speed toward the burning destroyer. Meanwhile, survivors were spotted in the waters about a half mile to starboard, and sister ship *LSM(R) 195*, skippered by Lt. William E. Woodson, moved quickly in their direction. Miles away, two of the patrol craft, *PCs 584 and 1128*, also sailed for the stricken destroyer. The other patrol craft, *PC 1598*, was ordered to continue seeking and destroying floating mines in the vicinity of *LSM(R) 195*.

"We broke out our fire hoses and played water from the bow of our ship over the flaming oil," explained Wickser, "working our way finally alongside what remained of the destroyer. The scene was truly one of carnage. Men lay all about the deck literally in pieces, moaning and crying out in pain. We took as many of the wounded on board as we were able to find, after ascertaining from an officer, the only officer in evidence[60] that the entire officer complement of the destroyer other than himself, 22 men, had been either in the wardroom or on the bridge and were all killed."

Daylight was fading as *LSM(R) 194* tied up alongside the destroyer's starboard side, about ten minutes after the initial explosion. The rocketship's Pharmacists Mate 2c Daniel W. Styles assisted two other pharmacists mates from the *Halligan* and directed the evacuation of the injured. As casualties were being assembled on the destroyer's fantail, near a rigged signal light, the senior surviving officer ordered his crew to abandon ship.

At the same time, *PC 584* tied alongside the destroyer's port side and aided the rescue and evacuation of wounded. *PC 1128*, coming close aboard, signaled *Halligan* to set all her depth charges on safe; then, on the chance that the explosion might have been caused by a submarine torpedo, the patrol craft circled the group of ships on a sonar search but without underwater contacts. Further sonar searches were abandoned, since depths were less than fifty fathoms, and circumstances were suggesting a moored or floating mine had detonated.

The bright, rising moon helped illuminate the sea for careful visual searches until the last survivors were picked up about an hour later. *LSM(R) 194* took 72 men from the *Halligan* and *LSM(R) 195* picked up two survivors from the sea. A patrol craft also took aboard a number of destroyer men.

"She had hit a mine and her ammunition magazines went up, too," said Harold Catchpole, the Yeoman aboard *LSM(R) 195*. "The ship broke in half and the forward section sank. The stern section floated listlessly away. We found two oil-covered young boys in the water. That night, Navy minesweepers came in and swept the waters. We spent the entire night with long wooden poles pushing away mines that floated to the surface away from the ship. The loss of life on the destroyer was very heavy."[61]

About 1900, after Lt. Hirshberg reported the disaster to Admiral Kiland, "We were instructed to go aboard the *Halligan* and destroy all Top Secret equipment—this job falling to me as communications officer," said Ens. Wickser. "I went aboard but could not seem to find any secret equipment, [not] even the electric coding machine, but the destroyer's officer assured me it had been destroyed by the blast.[62] He also explained what had happened—the *Halligan* had taken a mine right under her starboard bow which exploded the ammunition handling room of the forward 5-inch gun mount. Needless to say, she appeared certain to sink."

"We were next ordered to direct the surviving officer to stay on board, evacuate all personnel except an emergency crew, bring the wounded to a hospital ship which was anchored off Okinawa in Buckner Bay, and await further instructions," Wickser continued. The one surviving officer of the *Halligan* remained on board with a party of men in order to cut into the C.I.C. room: it was thought that the Executive Officer or others might be trapped inside. "This, of course, assumed that the *Halligan*'s hull was somewhat seaworthy, and miraculously enough, this seemed to be the case," added Wickser.

About 1910, *LSM(R) 194* cast off all lines from the *Halligan* and proceeded in search of a hospital ship while *PC 584* remained tied to the destroyer. Meanwhile, *LSM(R) 195* continued patrolling the immediate area, with the two *Halligan* survivors still aboard, and assisted the other two PCs with finding and destroying floating mines. Later that evening, around 2155, two Japanese "snooper" reconnaissance planes began probing the area, which *LSM(R) 195* fired on and probably damaged.[63]

"Our return trip seemed an eternity, as we carried wounded men," said Wickser, "doing our best to minister to their condition with our limited amount of medical supplies and morphine under the direction of our pharmacist's mate. War was no longer an abstract concept to us." While plasma transfusions were given to one of her wounded men, *Halligan*'s survivors reported that the destroyer had been at General Quarters at the time of the explosion, and the mine had been spotted beforehand and the ship was attempting to turn out of the way.[64]

The minesweepers *Impeccable AM 320* and *Spear AM 322* were dispatched and stood by to render assistance. Many survivors were transferred to the minelayer *Breese DM 18*, which had a larger sickbay with additional medical staff.

About 2330, CTF 51 instructed *LSM(R) 194* by radio to turn over survivors to the *Biscayne AGC 18*. The rocketship tied up alongside the amphibious headquarters ship by 0250 of 27 March and transferred survivors over the next forty minutes. One of the men had also retrieved four confidential manuals on the destroyer's classified radar and RCM, or radar counter measures. After departing *Biscayne*, *LSM(R) 194* returned to her original patrol area. "Early that morning at dawn," added Wickser, "we sighted the hull of the *Halligan*, beached on the East Side of Tokashiki Jima."

LSM(R) 195 patrolled throughout the night, meanwhile, then was ordered to rendezvous with the casualty evacuation transport ship *Rixey APH 3* next morning, when the two survivors were transferred via small boat by 1130 of 27 March.[65]

Commander Francis reported soon afterwards:

> The Commanding Officer and entire ship's company of the USS *LSM(R) 194* are deserving of Unit Citation for their joint act of heroism in connection with rescue work on the USS *Halligan* (*DD 584*) on 26 March 1945. Noting the latter to be in distress with flames covering her deck, the *LSM(R) 194* despite the fact that her rocket racks were loaded, proceeded alongside the *Halligan*. Turning her hoses on the flames she extinguished them and at the same time took aboard 72 survivors, caring for same until they were delivered aboard the USS *Biscayne*, some hours later. For this action, which was over and above the call of duty, this command feels the ship's company of the *LSM(R) 194* to be worthy of special commendation.[66]

Years after the war, Allan M. Hirshberg reflected upon that day as Commanding Officer of USS *LSM(R) 194*: "The thing in retrospect that I was most proud of was the action of the crew of the *LSM(R) 194* in rescuing the survivors of the *Halligan* (*DD 584*), after she struck a mine over her forward magazine in a mine field. The crew of our ship manned our hoses, fought the fire on the destroyer and rescued all the available survivors, with our deck loaded with rockets in the middle of a mine field. This crew evolved into a proud fighting ship, and to the man they knew it, and did it in the best traditions of the Navy."[67]

Tokashiki Shima: "Orange Z-1" 27 March 1945

*LSM(R)*s 188, 189, 190, 191 and 192 under Lieutenant Commander John H. Fulweiler[68] in LSM(R) Group 27 flagship *LSM(R) 193* of LSM(R) Unit One (TU 52.21.1) were accompanied once more by *LSM(R)*s 194 and 195, cross-assigned from LSM(R) Unit Two (TU 52.21.2) (though not included in the original Rocket Firing Plans). Tokashiki Shima beachhead, designated "Orange Z-1,"[69] was among two of the island's simultaneous assaults the morning of 27 March 1945.

Captain Theodore Rimer (CTU 51.1.16), in flagship *LC(FF) 657*, was Support Team

Commander of "Support Team Violet," including *LCI(M)s 801, 802, 803* and *804* for pre-landing, close-in fire support with the eight LSM(R)s, and reprised the team color designator from the Zamami Shima assault of 26 March. Simultaneously, amphibious tracked landing vehicles lifting U.S. Army 2nd BLT of the 306th Regimental Combat Team would converge from the west-northwest, then turn sharply left for final approaches and landings set for 0900, codenamed J-Hour or "Jig Hour." Lt. Comdr. Fulweiler therefore emphasized, "The responsibility for controlling fire so it will not endanger LVTs rests with each Commanding Officer."[70]

Tokashiki Shima, the largest and eastern-most island of the Kerama Rettos, has an irregular coastline roughly six miles long north-south and approximately one mile wide. From narrow shores, cliffs and steep hills rise over 600 feet in the central areas and the island's northern and southern tips. The southwestern seaport village of Aware, codenamed "Orange Z-1," rests above a shallow bay called Aware Ko and sheltered to seaward by the small isle of Fukase Shima.[71]

The mission was to destroy Aware village and reduce adjacent enemy defenses. U.S. Intelligence estimated Tokashiki Shima was well fortified, including artillery positions, camouflaged and tracked vehicles, pillboxes, barracks, and numerous machinegun and rifle pits.[72]

The rocket runs on Aware village would commence J-Hour-minus-30 (J–30), or 0830, thirty minutes prior to the first American landings. Each Finner rocketship loaded 300 AR Fin-stabilized rockets in their inboard Mark 36 launchers only. The schedule of fire allotted each wave two minutes to lay down rocket salvoes with 700 yards depth of pattern (DOP) by 800 yards wide. Course adjustments south of Tokashiki Shima were plotted from radar fixes and visual bearings on the southern-most tip of Tokashiki island and Fukase Shima, an islet of rock, coral and reef lying seaward of Aware bay, which in turn narrows the sea lane to Aware village.

Destroyer *Isherwood DD 520* was stationed south-southwest of Orange Z-1 for counter-battery fire and targets of opportunity. The four LCI(M)s stood some 2,000 yards southwest of Aware village covering the flank with 4.2-inch mortar rounds of heavy saturation fire and suppressing gunfire as the LSM(R)s attacked parallel with the western coastline. Aircraft also supported pre-landing bombardments.

Gunnery officers energized rocket launcher circuits from atop "Flying Bridges" as the LSM(R)s sounded GQ setting Condition One Roger calling all hands to clear the decks. Except for ships' control in the conn, all sailors disappeared below decks to avoid the rockets' hazardous exhaust blasts, noise and debris. Only gun crews shielded within the five-inch gun mounts on the fantails of the LSM(R)s remained at battle stations for counter-battery fire.

The LSM(R)s assumed close order formation in four pairs of sister ships abreast: *LSM(R)s 193* and *192*; *LSM(R)s 190* and *191*; *LSM(R)s 189* and *188*; and *LSM(R)s 194* and *195*. Their line of fire was 17° True at 9 knots speed of advance (300 yards/minute), firing rocket salvos at 2-second intervals. (En route to the firing point, *LSM(R) 190* collided with *LSM(R) 191* port amidships, scarring both rocketships' hulls and tearing off two unloaded outboard Mark 30 rocket launchers from the latter. The OOD in *LSM(R) 189* also complained *LSM(R) 188* collided with the former after swerving from her proper station, although damage was not reported).

Meanwhile, flotilla flagship *LC(FF) 535* stood some 2000 yards from shore, providing CINCPAC staff photographers[73] CPhoM Leif Erickson and Sp(P)2c William Loewe another opportunity to capture motion and still pictures of rocket runs and amphibious landings.

On signal from Capt. Rimer, at 0839, 0846 and 0848, three successive waves of LSM(R)s unleashed deckloads of rockets upon Aware village, adjacent defenses and obstacles to landings, about 3800 yards from the beachhead. "Barrage is very heavy and beach is totally obscured by smoke," reported Rimer. Enemy resistance and counter-battery fire was light to negligible.

LSM(R)s 194 and *195* were about to begin the fourth and final attack wave when the OTC ordered them to hold fire: the assault LVTs were arriving ahead of schedule and fouling the range, and, more seriously, friendly fire was reported falling around their line of departure. After confusion and delay, the amphibious tracked landing vehicles resumed advances and hit "Orange Z-1" beach by 0916.[74] Maintaining steerageway to other landing craft and nearby ships, LSM(R)s returned small arms counter-fire at the beaches as they retired southward, and rendezvoused some 2 miles south-southwest of Tokashiki Island.

"About 95% of the rockets fired landed effectively," reported Commander Francis, some 1700 rockets all told, "resulting in almost complete obliteration of the entire village. The remaining rockets landed in the water off the beach."[75] Admiral Kiland praised the rocketships. "This was the first use of LSM(R)s in an amphibious assault operation. Their employment was successful and they proved to be a very definite asset…. The relatively long rocket range, great versatility, and high firepower of the LSM(R) as compared to other types of support craft proved it to be a highly successful addition in amphibious operations."[76]

Night Patrols: 27–28 March 1945

During 27 March, stormy weather curtailed enemy air activities, as clouds and rains decreased visibility markedly, and choppy seas tossed ships and craft. During daytime replenishment, *LSM(R) 197* suffered scraped strakes and bent stanchions while alongside a cargo ship. *LSM(R) 188*, close aboard transport *Suffolk AKA 69*, rolled and pitched so heavily that her starboard bow lifted into the larger vessel. Resulting damage included a six-inch hole puncturing the rocketship's hull, a three-foot long gouge bashed in her conn, and a crushed bulkhead that trapped her signalman in the wheelhouse. Fortunately, the sailor was soon rescued, treated for shock, and returned to duty.

LSM(R) overnight screening assignments from 27 to 28 March resumed among the Kerama Retto islands but extended hereafter to include Okinawan shores. Sister ships *LSM(R)s 196* and *197* patrolled station P8, called "Peter 8," a ten-mile course several miles off southwestern Naha and Oroku peninsula. In *LSM(R) 196*, Ensigns David Mallery and Jack Shedd remembered, "The second night provided a few more hazards and considerably more excitement on a patrol three miles off the coast of Okinawa, whose attack day was to come in a few days. Our mission was to provide harassing gun fire on and over the airport [Naha Airfield] to prevent their rebuilding at night what had been destroyed by fleet and air bombardment in the daytime. The results of this were not known to us."[77] Signalman Leonard VanOteghem also added in his diary, "We left Aka Shima to patrol off southern Okinawa. Fired 40mms on airstrip to harass the enemy. Expected suicide attacks but weather was in our favor."[78]

LSM(R)s 198 and *199* patrolled station P9, or "Peter 9," a 12-mile course several miles off the southwest coast of Okinawa and paralleling the Hagushi beaches. Just after midnight of 27–28 March, *LSM(R) 199* sighted tracer fire in the distance which her radar reported about 23 miles away. At 0455, radio alerted that an unknown number of enemy planes were approaching, but none closed.

The eight Finner LSM(R)s were assigned nighttime patrols along a low, sweeping southern arc from Kerama Retto to Okinawa: *LSM(R)s 192* and *193* south of the Kerama Islands; *LSM(R)s 188* and *189* off the southern tip of Tokashiki Shima; *LSM(R)s 190* and *191* east of Tokashiki Shima; and *LSM(R)s 194* and *195* only miles off southeastern Okinawa. The flotilla's flagship *LC(FF) 535* meanwhile pulled patrol duty first off Aka Shima then night patrols west of Yakabi Shima.

"While patrolling along shore we grounded on a reef, but were able to back off," recalled Robert Landis on *LSM(R) 192*, then noted, "Later we snared a submarine net but broke loose."[79] In fact, the rocketship accidentally crossed over a LISP-2 anti-submarine net stretching between Kerama Retto islands that enclosed the anchorage and seaplane base. and emitted eerie screeches and reverberations from metal rasping against metal, as recalled Radarman 2c Ronald R. "Railroad" MacKay:

> The night was as black as the inside of my hat. I was down below in my bunk, and I could get the full effect of that scraping noise from the bottom of the hull. I was certainly glad that we had a flat bottom! A minesweeper was flashing her signal lanterns for us to get the hell out of the area because it hadn't been swept, and they certainly didn't want any of us to get caught in something like that. It made a temporary Christian out of me! We slowly got the thing turned around—you know, you just don't turn those ships around right away—and passed back over those nets and the noises going by again from the bow to the stern. A ship like ours couldn't take anything like a mine, we barely had enough of a hull to be seaworthy. Even something as big as a battleship can't take very much from mines.[80]

Perhaps not entirely coincidental, next morning Admiral Kiland warned all ships of Task Group 51.1 to "take every precaution to keep clear of nets being laid in Kerama Retto."[81]

Overnight, Leonard VanOteghem listened to an "Intercepted message over radio that one of our destroyer minesweepers about 15 miles north of us was under attack by eight motor torpedo boats. We didn't hear the results."[82]

Night Patrols: 28–29 March 1945

At sunrise of 28 March, LSM(R)s were ordered to cease nighttime patrol assignments, rendezvous north of Kuba Shima, then retire within anchorages for rest and general logistics. The day was completely overcast with periodic showers and winds veering an average of 25 to 30 knots. Visibility gradually decreased from 6–8 miles to one mile or less through the day.

"Today we're taking it kind of easy," remarked a sailor aboard *LSM(R) 188*. "Tonight we have to patrol the island of Okinawa Shima. This is one of the main islands of the Jap Homeland. If we take it, it will mean a lot in making the end of this war closer. There are three big airfields and a big radio station on this island. It is about 60 miles long and about 10 miles wide. [At] 1300 we leave the mooring in Kerama Retto to go to our patrolling station."[83] Clyde Blue of *LSM(R) 197* also commented in his diary: "Haven't done anything all day long. We have been roaming all over the ocean today. We patrol off of Kerama Retto tonight. I have the 2 to 4 watch tonight."[84]

Nighttime patrol assignments were issued in the afternoon. But before Commander Francis' flagship departed to anchor off the west coast of Geruma Shima for the night, *LC(FF)*

535 rendezvoused with *LSM(R) 196* to transfer the two CINCPAC photographers, "Erickson, L., CPHoM, 632-01-30; and Loewe, W. C., Sp(P)2c, 726-08-25."[85] Thereafter, *LSM(R) 196* was dispatched to patrol independently between Kuba Shima and Aka Shima overnight.

Five rocketships were assigned nighttime patrol stations surrounding Tokashiki Shima: *LSM(R) 194* off the west coast; *LSM(R)s 195* and *198* on the north-northeastern tip; and *LSM(R)s 197* and *199* off the east coast. Action was light. An empty raft and suspicious objects in the waters were shot at, all potential shields for enemy swimmers. Only two air raid alerts warned of unidentified airplanes in the area; meanwhile, the rocketships made occasional smoke cover from fog generators.

LSM(R)s 190 and *191* reported to station P7, or "Peter 7," assigned harassing patrols off the southern tip of Okinawa. Hundreds of 20mm, 40mm, and 5" rounds struck beach targets. Just after midnight near Mae Shima, *LSM(R) 190* drove off an attack from a suspected suicide boat, inflicting damage but failing to destroy it. Other small boats were found and fired at along the shores, but darkness and distance made it impossible to tell if any had been hit. Between midnight and 0300, the two rocketships with *LCI(G) 751* and *Twiggs DD 591* were attacked seven times by enemy planes east of Tokashiki Shima, where they shot down a Betty twin-engine bomber.[86]

LSM(R)s 192 and *193* patrolled off the southeastern tip of Okinawa. Twice this evening, the latter rocketship and a nearby destroyer fired starshells at beaches to illuminate the shoreline, while the former rocketship opened with harassing 5"/38 and 40mm fires.

Just before midnight of 28–29 March, a Val Japanese dive bomber flew low and astern the *LSM(R)s 192* and *193*. In the darkness, an object was seen falling into the waters off their bows, thought to be a bomb. The 20mm gunners fired at the plane, but it escaped and no hits were observed. Another Val passed over both rocketships at half past midnight; this time, all guns opened up, but this plane also escaped with unobserved damage. At about 0245, a destroyer dead ahead of *LSM(R)s 192* and *193* shot down an enemy airplane, which burst into flames and crashed into the sea. The trio scoured the crash site, but neither the plane, survivors, or bodies were found. Finally, shortly before daybreak of 29 March, yet another Val dived toward *LSM(R) 192*'s starboard and dropped a bomb, which narrowly missed. Despite all guns firing, this dive bomber, too, escaped without visible damage.

Speed Boat Attacks: 28–29 March 1945

The afternoon of 28 March 1945, *LSM(R)s 188* and *189* were ordered to patrol station P9, or "Peter 9," off western Okinawa. This NNW-SSE course was some three miles long and varied upwards of a mile from shore, tracking parallel with the northern Hagushi coastline from the Bishi Gawa river to Zampa Mizaki, or "Point Bolo." In days, the Hagushi beachhead would bear the main assault landings of Operation Iceberg on 1 April 1945. Once on station, the rocketships were often several miles apart, with *LSM(R) 188* patrolling the northern sector, and sister ship *LSM(R) 189* patrolling the southern sector.

In the evening dusk, *LSM(R) 189* was about 3000 yards off Okinawa when lookouts spotted an enemy plane ashore that appeared to be a Judy,[87] a single-engine divebomber. Permission to open fire was requested, but while awaiting reply, the plane was lost from view in the growing darkness.

JAPANESE SUICIDE BOAT
(WITHOUT DEPTH CHARGE) LENGTH: 18'

"Japanese Suicide Boat." Lawrence J. Low, untitled unpublished diary, notebook and sketches.

About midnight of 28–29 March, destroyer *Barton DD 722* arrived and advised *LSM(R) 189* to keep station a thousand yards east or inshore of the destroyer's north-south patrol courses. Not long after, the rocketship's gunnery officer Ensign F. Donald Moore witnessed this first of many close calls this morning: "About 0130 a Jap bomber flew within 400 yards of us. Thank God he didn't see us."[88]

About 0300, the gunboat *LCI(G) 560* was attacked by a small speedboat that dropped a depth charge close aboard. All nearby ships were alerted and went to General Quarters. Some six minutes later, *LSM(R) 189*'s radar picked up what was believed to be the attacking boat. Underway to investigate the target, within minutes the rocketship spotted the Japanese boat dead ahead and opened fire with both 40mms. The boat sped toward the rocketship and dropped a depth charge, which exploded in front of the ship but no damage was evident. "Bow seemed to lift out of the water. Conn was covered with water. Boat passed along port side within ten feet of ship," jotted down Ensign Moore, ships gunnery officer.[89] As the enemy boat sped astern, *LSM(R) 189* tracked it, and as her automatic weapons riddled the escaping craft, the fantail 5"/38 dual purpose gun blew it apart with a direct hit.

But the melees had only begun. At 0318, radar identified a second surface target, so *LSM(R) 189* circled the area to contain it, then lost contact. Six minutes later, radar picked up the target again, and when lookouts spotted the boat, it sped evasively as the rocketship's guns opened fire.

In minutes, radar identified a third small boat, which *LSM(R) 189* spotted off her port quarter. The rocketship opened fire with all available guns, but the boat moved too quickly as it attacked. Dropping its depth charge, the explosion only sprayed water onto the ship as the small craft sped toward shore. Tracking the fleeing boat, *LSM(R) 189* finally trapped it near the beach. Guns scored many hits, but a round from the bow 40mm finally demolished it.

LSM(R) 188, meanwhile, was patrolling north of the speedboat fray. "We stayed at battle stations all night," recalled MoMM3c Burton E. Weed. "We took turns with breaks after awhile—lying on deck or sitting and resting our eyes. (Using your night vision—staring, and staring, and staring at the darkness looking for boats or anything is tough on your eyes.) You can't see anything and need a break to rest your eyes. The cooks would bring coffee and things up to us once in a while. The night seemed extra dark...."[90]

But a "friendly fire" incident occurred that remains disputed. *LSM(R) 188* took an agile speedboat under attack off the rocketship's port bow, but fire had to be lifted when *Henry A. Wiley DM 29* crossed into the line of fire[91] while shelling Japanese shore targets. According to the destroyer-minelayer's skipper, "Intermittent harassing fire was conducted until 0355 when mistaken identity resulted in the *Wiley's* bridge getting hit by 40mm fire from *LSM188* [*sic*] which did not respond to our "Emergency Cease Fire" order.

> It was most impressive to see those golden tracers gracefully arc their way toward us. I immediately ordered "Emergency Full Speed Ahead." A fire had been started on the 40mm ready ammunitions which was quickly extinguished and three men suffered minor injuries. At 0401 a "Jake" passed directly overhead and dropped a bomb (150–200 lbs.) which fell in our wake about 70 yards astern. (Reason for the miss was probably the acceleration just taking effect from the "Emergency Full Speed Ahead" ordered six minutes before.) It was believed that the "Jake" had been attracted by the flames. He was fired at by the 40mm, but with no apparent results.[92]

About the same time, sister ship *LSM(R) 189* picked up a bogie on radar as AA fire was observed dead ahead. The enemy plane came into view a moment later, identified as a Rufe— a seaplane version of the Japanese Zero fighter—and shot down by the rocketship's 20mm gunners with assisting fire from other ships.

In twenty minutes, the rocketship's radar picked up yet another target off the starboard quarter. Lookouts spotted an enemy boat and commenced automatic weapons fire. The boat then approached at high speed, evidently targeting the ship's vulnerable stern. As the speedboat closed 75 feet astern and prepared to let go of its depth charge, the ship's fantail 5"/38 gun registered a direct hit, virtually at point-blank range, and completely destroyed the craft. By 0500, word was passed to stand easy from GQ Condition One, and *LSM(R) 189* circled to examine the scattered debris and search for survivors, but none was found.

"The boats attacking us," explained Lt. James M. Stewart, Commanding Officer of *LSM(R) 189*, "were contacted by radar at 1200 to 1500 yards and sighted at 500 to 600 yards. They did not appear to be suicide boats as they returned to attack their objective. The boats were relatively high-powered for they made over 15 knots and appeared to be twenty-five to thirty-five feet long, looking much like our Higgens Boats in type. The personnel manning them seemed to vary. One boat reported by our look-outs had a crew of four, and as to the others, no estimate can be made. It was very dark and there were so many explosions, covering this ship with water, that it was difficult to get a detailed description."[93] Lt. Stewart was later summoned to report his account of the enemy speed boats to Admiral Kiland in headquarters ship *Mount McKinley*.

Commander Francis later commended USS *LSM(R) 189*:

> On 28 March 1945, while proceeding on night patrol, your ship underwent attack three (3) times by Japanese suicide boats, which dropped depth charges and strafed the ship. The same evening you were attacked by an enemy plane and strafed by same. Your accomplishment in sinking all three suicide boats and emerging from those attacks with no personnel casualties or significant damage to your ship is deserving of the highest praise. You and your officers as well as all personnel aboard your ship are hereby commended. Well done. D. L. Francis.[94]

Keise Shima: 29 March 1945

In the early morning of 29 March 1945, LSM(R) Unit Two (TU 52.21.2) was dispatched to support an underwater demolition team encountering enemy resistance at Keise Shima.[95]

Departing Kerama Retto armed with rockets, the Finner *LSM(R)s 194* and *195* accompanied the Spinner *LSM(R)s 196, 197, 198* and *199* with flagship *LC(FF) 535* at full speed, reaching the small island group by 1111. Two naval officers, dispatched from *LCI(R) 783* by small boat, embarked *LSM(R) 199* for observation purposes.

Unexpected sniper fire had wounded a UDT officer during reconnaissance and demolition surveys at Keise Shima. Nevertheless, their commander reported that LSM(R) support was now no longer required, so only ten minutes after arriving, the two observers were disembarked and the seven rocketships returned to Kerama Retto anchorage.

Dawn Attack on LSM(R) 188

By 0430 of 29 March 1945, *LSM(R) 188* stood down from General Quarters to Condition One-Easy and resumed north-south reciprocating patrols on station P9, or "Peter 9," in Area C2 off western Okinawa.[96] But full General Quarters sounded again at 0540 as AA crossfire was seen and heard from nearby ships. Three or four enemy planes closed, so the rocketship increased speed to flank and her 5"/38 gun assisted with downing one of the planes about 0555.

Just then a second plane, possibly a Val, came in low and began strafing *LSM(R) 188* on her starboard. Gunners opened fire from the two forward 40mms and starboard amidships 20mm as the attacker flew by. The plane, now burning and smoking, veered off in a right turn away from the rocketship, but unexpectedly winged over to the left, arced across the ship's bow, then circled back toward *LSM(R) 188*. Radioman 3c Harold Franssen, LSM(R) Group 27 Staff, was leaning against the conn having a cigarette when he saw the enemy plane dive about 45° off the port beam and aiming abaft the conning tower.[97]

Gunners struck the attacker from several hundred yards away, but were unable to stop the plunging aircraft. At 0602,[98] the plane's wing crashed into the Mark 51 gun director and carried the tower over the side, taking three sailors inside the gun tub. Six men firing the port and starboard aft 20mm guns were killed instantly as the plane's 100 kg bomb exploded above the rocket deck, blasting a 14-foot by 9-foot hole. Two gunners inside the 5"/38 mount were killed with others wounded from hot, penetrating shrapnel that ignited gunpowder cans.[99] Although the bomb's explosive force also pressed slightly downward, the hull's integrity, unknown at that moment, remained remarkably intact. Radioman Franssen, still topside, remembers the tremendous explosion knocked him down onto the slippery, oil-soaked deck, where he cut his thumb on a jagged piece of metal. The Japanese plane crashed into the sea off the starboard beam about 75 yards and burned on the surface until sinking minutes later.[100]

A near-simultaneous secondary blast erupted next, pushing upward and outward from inside *LSM(R) 188*. Rocket bodies and motors exploded from ready service racks and within the after magazine, and airborne shrapnel pierced the circular conning tower, killing two radiomen, a signalman, and the pharmacists mate.[101] Radar and radio were knocked out, electrical wiring and cabling were severed, and internal phone connections cut off to some parts of the ship. Bulkheads were dished from the explosion, and one compartment door was completely blown off. Compressed air was lost to the main engines, and the starboard engine was shut down because its leaking fuel oil line posed an immediate fire threat. More than half of the rocket launchers were either missing or damaged; luckily, none were loaded with rockets.

LSM(R) 188 in Kerama Retto anchorage after a Japanese airplane crash and bomb explosion the morning of 29 March 1945 on Night Patrol Station P9 off western Okinawa (official U.S. Navy photograph).

Not least, the national ensign and signal flags fell to the deck when flying splinters sliced halyard lines.

Fires were immediately put out due in large part to the internal flooding from the ruptured fire mains. But rising water trapped in lower compartments caused the stern to settle dangerously low in the water with little freeboard.

As enemy planes circled for strafing runs, *LSM(R) 188*'s forward gun crews continued to fight off air attacks with assists from nearby ships. Able-bodied men, including many of the wounded, aided injured shipmates. Radioman Harold Franssen recalled the gruesomeness of recovering the scattered, dismembered remains of seven dead crewmen onto a single stretcher.[102]

LSM(R) 189 first steamed flank speed to aid the closer *LCI(G) 560* after its brush with a crash-diving plane, but when the gunboat signaled that conditions were under control, the rocketship changed course and sped to assist her sister ship. But before *LSM(R) 189* arrived, the fires on *LSM(R) 188* appeared to be extinguished by 0607 and was already retiring full speed for Kerama Retto.

But MoMM3c Burton E. Weed recalled the captain first ordering a course for the Okinawa shoreline.

At this point the Captain panicked or temporarily cracked. We were sinking and he wanted to run it onto the beach. We would have been mincemeat if he did ... there wouldn't be anyone there but Japs. We could see the beach and trees real well, so I figure that we must have been about one-half mile from the beach before other officers took command and turned toward other islands. Even then, while we were going full speed to get back to safety the Captain is hollering to "Drop the anchor!" which, if we did and the anchor grabbed the bottom, we could have rolled over.[103]

Several ships converged on the stricken rocketship to render aid. *LCI(G) 452* hailed *LSM(R) 188* by signal light to finally stop then transferred her pharmacists mate at 0650. About 0715, a medical officer and pharmacists mate with a salvage party with Handy Billies also embarked from the fast transport *Loy APD 56*.

By 0830, battleship *Arkansas BB 33* advised Admiral Kiland that *LSM(R) 188* was sinking and requested immediate tug support. Meanwhile, both *Arkansas* and heavy cruiser *Indianapolis CA 35* escorted the diminutive rocketship en route. As "Motor Mac" Burton E. Weed recalled, "All of a sudden we looked up at this great big ship pulling alongside of us. It was the battleship *Arkansas*. They lowered portable pumps down to us and hoses to help keep us afloat. Also a doctor and a couple of pharmacists mates. They then followed us the rest of the way back. The pumps helped to pump us out and they found that the hull wasn't ruptured. It was all the broken water lines filling us up with water."[104]

Soon, the Service and Salvage unit at Kerama Retto dispatched repair ship *Clamp ARS 33*, which towed *LSM(R) 188* into the anchorage. MoMM3c Weed continued, "We got back in the middle of the rest of the ships [at Kerama Retto]. A landing craft came alongside and we climbed down to it and they took us over to the hospital ship. They took the Captain over to an LST which they called 'Section 8.' That was for fellows that cracked or had breakdowns. We had to lay in wire baskets which they hooked on a boom and raised us up on the hospital ship. It sure felt terrific to be back to safety."[105]

Another sailor on *LSM(R) 188* also recalled:

There were so many broken fire mains that we had to secure our pumps to keep from sinking, and used fire extinguishers on the magazine. Out of 79 men, there were 34 of us unhurt. 14 killed instantly and 3 died later. Our pharmacists mate was killed so we had to get Doc's from some other ships. The battleship, *Arkansas*, and the cruiser, *Indianapolis*, and some 'cans' [destroyers] came out from Kerama Retto to escort us to the mooring and to take off our wounded. All together we got six Jap planes this a.m., but we paid a hell of a price for them. We tied up alongside the *ARL 8* [USS *Egeria*] this morning. A repair ship and spent the night aboard it. This has been a day I'd like to forget, but know I never will.[106]

USS *LSM(R) 188* lost 17 killed and 32 wounded in action.[107] The dead were interred on Tokashiki Shima. At 1315 of 29 March 1945, colors were lowered to half-mast.

Lieutenant Harold A. Bowman, USNR, commended his men:

The Commanding Officer is full of pride to be serving with a crew, which acted so rapidly and so correctly in an emergency. From a glance at the Personnel Casualty reports, it is obvious that many of our key petty officers were put out of action. However many men, with their blood running freely, carried on their regular duties, and also duties of their comrades-at-arms who had been killed or knocked unconscious. It was due entirely to the quick thinking and steadfastness of purpose of the Executive Officer, the Junior Officer, and the individual members of the crew that the ship was able to remain afloat. The Commanding Officer has the deepest of respect and admiration for each officer and man aboard. They all acted in the manner of the highest traditions of our Navy. To cite any man or group of men would work the greatest of injustice to the other members of the crew. Team work and coordination of action among the Officers and crew were perfect. In view of the above, the ship as a whole should be commended—an honor which may be shared equally by all hands.[108]

LSM(R) 188 **lost 17 men and suffered 32 wounded from the Japanese airplane crash and bomb explosion off western Okinawa on 29 March 1945 (official U.S. Navy photograph).**

Word quickly spread about the attack on *LSM(R) 188* as the flotilla's rocketships returned from either Keise Shima or overnight patrols to anchor in the transport area between Kuba Shima and Aka Shima. "This was the first shock we had as a unit," recalled Ensigns David Mallery and Jack Shedd of *LSM(R) 196*, "and knocked the false confidence out of us that had sprung from the strange non-resistance policy we had [met] at the Kerama's. Obviously, any thought of another patrol for us in that area was not too appealing."[109] Commander Francis, back in the anchorage by 1355 after UDT support at Keise Shima, embarked *LSM(R) 188* to assess the damages and casualties; after a forty minute investigation, Francis returned to his flagship *LC(FF) 535* to file his report.[110]

The death and destruction suffered by *LSM(R) 188* deeply affected the psyche of all LSM(R) sailors. Its impact, then and years after the war, remains difficult to overstate.

Seaman 1c Lawrence Willison from *LSM(R) 197* recalled, "On March 31 a request was made for 5 volunteers to board her and assist in clean-up. I was one of the 5 men who volunteered." He continued,

> Upon coming aboard the *LSM(R) 188* it was hard to believe that this ship had survived the attack. The superstructure, 5-inch gun director, and control tower had been torn off. There was a jagged hole through the deck midway between the conn and the port side 10–12 feet in diameter. Through this hole one could see a pile of 5-inch projectiles, some of which were flattened as if placed under a press. It was a miracle that these did not explode and sink the ship.

The clean-up began by using brooms to sweep remaining debris over the side, much of which consisted of body parts. The worse area was around the port side 20mm gun mount. After cleaning the deck and surrounding areas as good as possible, we waited until the ship was moved out to deep water where we could dispose of the damaged projectiles. These were passed from man to man through the hole in the deck and tossed overboard. When they reached a certain depth the pressure of the water caused them to explode.

I talked to a crew member who had been in a repair party. He said that when he came up from mid-ship the first thing he saw was the head of his friend which was severed from the body, laying looking up at him. He remembered screaming until someone shook and slapped him...

This is something that I will never forget. I thank God that the crew of the *LSM(R) 197* never had to go through what the *LSM(R) 188* crew experienced.[111]

"Men who go to war expect to witness wholesale death and destruction," philosophized Paul S. Vaitses, Jr., Executive Officer of *LSM(R) 193*, recalling the reaction to the *LSM(R) 188* attack. Yet, he added,

They also know in the back of their minds that they themselves risk injury and death. So it is only human that they erect mental barriers to such realizations in order to enable them to carry on with peace of mind.

But to a crew as young as ours, this first experience with violent death was a cruel jolt. You could just feel the emotional impact on these lads as they struggled to rationalize such an awful scene.

But if the sight of death made a lasting impression on all of us, the smell of death was even worse. As a youngster I can remember reading stories of the Civil War, and I recall that the authors frequently mentioned how the 'stench of death' hung over the battlefields. In my naiveté, I wondered if perhaps they were not guilty of sensationalism or exaggeration. That day aboard the *188* I learned the horrible full meaning of their phrase, and I learned that those words or any other words are wholly inadequate to describe the ghastly odor. It is a penetrating odor that permeates everything—your papers, your clothing, your hair, and even your skin. That day it filled the entire ship and the atmosphere around it. There was no escaping it.[112]

Robert W. Landis, Storekeeper from *LSM(R) 192*, added, "When our crew went aboard the [*LSM(R)*] *188* to remove ammunition, I also went aboard to assist the *188* Supply Officer with some matters needing attention (their Storekeeper was either killed or wounded during the bombing). At that time I had the opportunity to examine the damage, the extent of which was far more devastating than I had expected to see. Although the deck had been hosed down, there was some remaining evidence of the carnage left on vertical surfaces of the Conning Tower, gun tubs, etc. That [*LSM(R) 188*] Skipper was responsible for the lives of his crew, as all Skippers are, and I can understand how shaken he must have been..."[113]

Night Patrols: 29–30 March 1945

Just after noontime of 29 March, Captain Moosbrugger assigned half the LSM(R)s to night patrols near Okinawa, while Captain Rimer ordered the remaining rocketships to night patrols around the Kerama Retto islands, where Commander Francis in flagship *LC(FF) 535* would also remain anchored overnight. Enemy activities were only sporadic, however, and other tasks included making smoke, firing illumination shells, and harassing gunfire.

Off Okinawa, *LSM(R)s 190* and *191* patrolled area P9, or "Peter Nine," along the Hagushi coast. During midwatch from 0000 to 0400, an undetermined number of Japanese speedboats approached from the north; in the melee, one boat was sunk and another possibly destroyed, but the remainder fled. *LSM(R) 190* also sank a sampan this night.[114] *LSM(R)s 194* and *195* patrolled the southeast coastline accompanied by a destroyer and three LCIs, where *LSM(R)* *195* sank an abandoned small craft. *LSM(R)s 198* and *199* destroyed two floating mines off Okinawa.

At Kerama Retto, *LSM(R) 192* screened the northern anchorage entrance between Tokashiki Shima and Zamami Shima as minesweepers stood by. Accompanied by other amphibious vessels encircling Tokashiki Shima, *LSM(R) 189* patrolled the northeastern coast; *LSM(R)s 193* and *197* watched sectors along the eastern shoreline; and *LSM(R) 196* screened the southeastern corner of the island.

Good Friday: 30 March 1945

By 30 March 1945, the Kerama Retto island group was under American control. Combat elements of the 77th Infantry Division had made 15 separate landings, including ship-to-shore and shore-to-shore assaults, yet casualties had been low despite the complexity of the maneuvers. At 1030, Admiral Kiland sent a message to all commands congratulating the officers and men of TG 51.1 on capturing the islands.

LSM(R) Conference

The afternoon of 30 March 1945, Commander Francis and Lieutenant Commander Fulweiler convened a conference aboard flagship *LC(FF) 535* with LSM(R) commanding officers to review experiences gained and problems encountered during the Kerama Retto operation.

Most agreed, because of the premature rocket fire during the Aka Shima attack, that flag hoists were less effective for signaling or coordinating rocket runs than using parallel voice circuits among the LSM(R)s. Some questioned the usefulness of the Mark 51 Mod 3 fire control director for the 5"/38, because its short operating range, fragility, and difficulty of repair diminished its value. The LSM(R) CICs (Command in Control) were inadequate and required improved equipment close at hand adjacent the radar in the pilot house. And, LSM(R)s had insufficient ammunition stowage for the 5"/38 and rocket white phosphorous ammunition in the magazines below decks.

The commanding officers emphasized several points regarding anti-small boat patrols. A consensus agreed that LSM(R)s should patrol at only one third speed with one engine at 350 rpm; because the rocketships do not give much of a silhouette at night, it would be harder for the enemy to spot the ships if the screws did not splash and create a wake that revealed ship's position. Next, the rocketship captains contended that patrolling ships should not fire on targets until definitely identified as enemy, in order to avoid revealing their presence or position until the last possible moment. Finally, the LSM(R) skippers found that a number of Japanese small surface craft were not necessarily suicide boats *per se*, because in many instances enemy speedboats attacked close aboard to release depth charges, then tried to escape, rather than suicide crash.[115]

Night Patrols: 30–31 March 1945

Overnight among the Kerama Rettos, *LSM(R) 196* screened the eastern coast of Tokashiki Shima, where *LSM(R)s 198* and *199* also patrolled as a team. *LSM(R) 197* made smoke screens in the anchorage between Kuba and Aka islands (until the fog generator broke down). *LSM(R) 193* stood south of Aka Shima and due west of Geruma Shima, southwest from where flotilla flagship *LC(FF) 535* occasionally generated fog oil smoke screens for Admiral Turner's headquarters ship *Eldorado AGC 11*.

Off Okinawa, *LSM(R)s 190* and *191* patrolled area P9, or "Peter Nine," along the northern Hagushi coastline. About 0220, small enemy surface craft attacked and one boat was sunk.

Immediately south of the Hagushi beaches, *LSM(R)s 189* and *192* patrolled station P8, or "Peter Eight," near Naha. The latter rocketship screened the northern sector with *Twiggs DD 591* and two LCIs; the former rocketship took the southern sector, closing beaches at irregular intervals for 40mm harassing fire. Illuminating Starshells were fired over suspected Japanese positions on a small island lying off Sakihara Saki peninsula, which only revealed empty small boats along the shores, but soon destroyed by ships' gunfire.

South of Naha, guide ship *LSM(R) 194*, followed by *LSM(R) 195* and three LCIs, laced the shoreline with harassing gunfire and rockets, but targets and results of the attacks are unknown.

Return to Keise Shima: "Black Z-3" 31 March 1945

LSM(R)s 189, 190, 191 and *192*, under Lieutenant Commander John H. Fulweiler in LSM(R) Group 27 flagship *LSM(R) 193* of LSM(R) Unit One (TU 52.21.1), reached Keise Shima at 0600 of 31 March 1945. Kamiyama Shima beachhead, designated "Black Beach Z-3," was the primary island assault target.

Captain Theodore Rimer (CTU 51.1.16), in flagship *LC(FF) 657*, was Support Team Commander of "Support Team Violet," once more reprising the team color designation from the Zamami Shima assault of 26 March and Tokashiki Shima assault of 27 March.

For Keise Shima alone, a Landing Craft Support Unit comprised LCI Mortar Support Division Six, LCI Mortar Support Division Eight plus *LCI(M)s 805* and *806*, and LCI Gunboat Support Division One. Captain Richard C. Webb (ComLSTFlot16), in flagship *LC(FF) 783*, commanded the Keise Shima operation as Commander Western Islands Tractor Flotilla (CTU 51.1.6).[116]

Keise Shima is actually a group of four small islands, about eight miles northeast of Tokashiki Shima of the Kerama Retto islands, and five miles northwest of Naha, Okinawa's capitol city and seaport. Beachheads on Nagannu Shima, Keupu (or Keufu) Shima, Kamiyama Shima (West) and Kamiyama Shima (East) were designated "Black Beach Z-1" through "Black Beach Z-4," respectively.

Western Kamiyama Shima is about 900 yards by 300 yards, relatively flat with inland vegetation and two small huts, but surrounded by a prohibitive barrier reef that only allowed landings on the south side.[117] A single assault by U.S. Army 2nd BLT of the 306th Regimental Combat Team (RCT) was set for 0830, codenamed M2 or "Mike Two Hour." Support Team Violet deployed 3000 yards off beaches Black Z-1, Black Z-3 and Black Z-4, but advised to hold fire and conserve ammunition until called by the Army 77th Infantry Division. Auxiliary elements from Tractor Group HOW arrived from Leyte to support the landings as well.

Visibility was low, from 2 to 4 miles, though slowly increasing as troops hit the beach ahead of schedule at 0757 without opposition (although several boat patrols reported friendly fire). Keise Shima was declared secure by 1015, and before noon, amphibious transports unloaded twelve "Long Tom" heavy 155mm guns of the 420th Field Artillery. The artillery batteries would begin registration fire on enemy defenses near Naha that evening. Marine Air Warning Squadron Eight (AWS-8) landed on Nagannu Shima beachhead, "Black Z-1," to set up an early warning radar site.[118]

But an oversight almost caused a disaster, as Support Team Violet stood off Keise Shima through the afternoon awaiting orders. The gunnery officer in *LSM(R) 193* was testing electrical circuits from the conn, but had overlooked the small, removable safety plug inserted in the firing panel that fully energized the rocket launchers. When he pressed the firing button, rockets suddenly launched. "As they arched in their lofty trajectory they barely missed two carrier-based fighters which happened to be overhead," recalled Ensign Paul S. Vaitses, Jr., the Executive Officer. "Then they fell into the sea two miles ahead of us, straddling a small AP(D) [*sic*] as they hit the water. Immediately we anticipated stern radio warnings from our Flotilla Commander, the two fighter pilots, and the skipper of the AP(D)."

The rocket firings apparently went unnoticed except by those on *LSM(R) 193*; fortunately, only one man was standing near the launchers at that moment, and he escaped unscathed except for a temporary hearing loss from the rocket blasts. According to Ens. Vaitses, however, the mistake shook the skipper's faith, so he decided to replace the gunnery officer with "a more seasoned and experienced man," if the opportunity arose. A week later, gunnery officers were exchanged between *LSM(R) 193* and *LSM(R) 188*.[119]

Assessing the rocketships at Kerama Retto, Captain Rimer remarked, "The LSM(R) units proved themselves an invaluable adjunct to assault operations. In addition to other missions, the armament of one 5"-38 makes them an excellent patrol unit for destruction of suicide craft during daylight hours," and concluded, "The performance of LSM(R) units on every mission was excellent and highly commendable."[120]

Patrols: 31 March 1945 to 1 April 1945

By 1600 of 31 March, *LSM(R)s 189, 190, 191, 192* and *193* were relieved from duty off Keise Shima, but dispatched only miles southeast to patrol the Mae Shima island group of namesake Mae Shima, Naku Shima, Hate Shima, and a small unnamed island. The rocketships patrolled independently where they fired into camouflaged caves protecting small boats, shot at floating mines, and strafed cliffs and beaches at will with 40mms and 5"/38s. Although *LSM(R) 192* ran aground at Hate Shima and damaged her port screw, she pulled off to deeper waters and resumed patrols.

Departing Mae Shima before sunset, the five Finners rendezvoused again near Keise Shima, then patrolled southwestern Okinawa in column at 800-yard intervals. Meanwhile, each rocketship loaded 440 aircraft rockets into its launchers for the 1 April 1945 invasion of Okinawa.

The four Spinner LSM(R)s, on the other hand, remained within the Kerama Retto anchorage the entire day for replenishment. "We patrolled inside nets last night and nothing happened," remarked Clyde Blue in *LSM(R) 197*. "We loaded rockets all day long, also 40mm stuff for some LCIs. We have a full load for tomorrow. The battleships *Texas, Tennessee* and one other pounded Okinawa all day long. Also cruisers and cans. We put a 5-man working party on the *LSM(R) 188* to help clean it up. I guess she won't be with us for quite a while. Too much damage. Beans tonight for supper. Ham cooked with them. What a chow. We patrol off 'Oki' tonight where the [*LSM(R)*] *188* got hit. I have the 12 to 4 [watch] tonight. I got a crew cut and Mom and everyone would sure laugh if they could see me now. Ha ha! No hair and a big mustache with the ends curled up. Wild Ben Blue. Ha ha!"[121]

The other Finners, *LSM(R)s 194* and *195*, also remained within the anchorage this day for logistical tasks which also took them alongside battleships *Tennessee* and *Idaho*. Early that afternoon, *LSM(R) 188* sailed out of the Kerama Retto anchorage to jettison battle debris and damaged ammunition from her magazines.

The latter six rocketships were finally dispatched as pairs for the night's patrols— *LSM(R)s 194* and *195* to "Peter 13"; *LSM(R)s 196* and *197* to "Peter 8"; and *LSM(R)s 198* and *199* to "Peter 7." Patrols were reciprocating courses along the southwestern coast of Okinawa, from Naha to the southern tip of the island, including harassing beach fire at varying distances and irregular intervals. Concentrated return fire from Japanese shore batteries, however, forced the patrolling rocketships to retire out of range.

Midnight Attack on LSM(R) 196

The evening of 31 March 1945, *LSM(R) 196* patrolled off southwestern Okinawa near Naha on Station P8, or "Peter 8," followed by sister ship *LSM(R) 197* some 500 yards astern. The rocketships were at readiness Condition Two, so half their crews were standing watches at battle stations. But, opined Quartermaster-striker Bruce A. McDaniel in *LSM(R) 196*,

> The harassing patrol off the airfield was on a night operation that was ill-conceived. From the Marine Corps' account, the Japanese shore guns were operated by some Japanese Navy personnel. Our object was to fire armor-piercing 40mm shells across the area to keep any repairs being made on the [Machinato] field at night. My duty that night on the Conn was to relay orders to the gun tubs to commence firing. This was done on the half-hour after reversing course and returning to the same firing area: we maintained our distance from shore and this timing and distance gave the shore gunners their range and expected time.[122]

About 0040 of 1 April 1945, McDaniel stepped out from the wheelhouse to get a cup of hot cocoa, and while standing on the flag deck, he looked ashore and saw a spout of water, then heard the distinctive crackling sound of a shell coming in. He instinctively crouched down as the conn was suddenly hit, and small pieces of hot shrapnel tore his jacket and bloodied his head and back, while severed halyards with flags from the mast fell around him. Another shell struck lower in the superstructure, just missing a sailor in the crew's head where he was about to shave after taking a shower. Shrapnel shattered the mirror and wash basin before him, and splinters riddled the shower and deck with holes.

Signalman Leonard VanOteghem recalled,

> The explosion was terrific…. It split the seam around the Conn about three feet, three bolts were sheared off on a bracket that held a steel box on the bulkhead in which we kept confidential material, knocked off four welded buttons that our battle telephone box was bolted to, and knocked the compass out of its stand. The shrapnel from it literally mangled anything in its way. It went through as many as three thicknesses of steel plating, mangled our starboard running light, life jackets, flag bag, severed all out flag hoisting lines except one, and there were about seven of them strung over an area of about ten feet, so you can get an idea how thick the pieces of shrapnel were in order to catch all these small lines.[123]

The national ensign also fell to the deck, but someone returned it aloft on the single remaining halyard.

"Immediately I noticed the Flag Bag was smoldering," McDaniel continued. "I clawed open the hatch down to the radio shack where I burst in to see the radioman looking wide-eyed at me, draped with flag halyards. Captain O'Callaghan was bunked in the radio shack to be on hand during any action, and was sitting up when I came in. He said, 'What's going on, McDaniel?' I remember I calmly said in an obvious way, 'The enemy is firing on us.'"[124] The two rocketships immediately stood away from shore.

Six crewmen were wounded, but a shell struck and instantly killed Gunners Mate 1c Joseph A. Staum, who was topside on the starboard bow between the .50 caliber gun and bow 40mm gun. Twelve rocket launchers and about 15 Spin-stabilized rockets were superficially damaged by flying shrapnel, but no rockets misfired, so those with damage were thrown overboard.[125]

"We had a naval photographer aboard at this time, as he was going to take some pictures of the invasion of Okinawa in the morning," continued Leonard VanOteghem. "He was as scared as anyone could be, and said he never was so glad to get off of a ship as he was to get off of this one when he got transferred. His name was Leif Erickson. He was a movie actor before entering the service." Bruce McDaniel also remembered the actor-turned-combat photographer, adding, "Leif Erickson's camera equipment in the radio shack got riddled full of tiny shrapnel holes, and his helmet was riddled like a sieve."[126]

CHAPTER 4

Okinawa and Patrols

1–13 April 1945

Under a waning moon, eleven "Interim" LSM(R)s and flagship *LC(FF) 535* formed into LSM(R) Unit One and LSM(R) Unit Two in the early hours of 1 April 1945 for the L-Day or "Love Day" invasion of Okinawa, Operation Iceberg.

Never had greater numbers of warships assembled over such vast distances for an invasion, nor were so many types of ships and craft ever available to any naval commander.[1] Over 1200 ships and almost a half-million men under arms converged from the U.S. West Coast and Hawaiian, Southwest Pacific, Marshall, Caroline, and Philippine islands. As Commander Expeditionary Force and Commander Task Force 51 (CTF 51), Vice Admiral Richmond Kelly Turner wielded this unprecedented projection of American power: "The Amphibious Operations for the capture of Okinawa Gunto in terms of ships employed, naval gunfire delivered, naval air support conducted and the magnitude of the logistic [*sic*] problems and distances involved may well be considered the largest single naval operation in the history of Pacific Ocean warfare."[2] Turner's counterpart, Lieutenant General Simon Bolivar Buckner, Jr., would command all U.S. Army and Marine forces at Okinawa as Commander Expeditionary Troops, Commander Task Force 56 (CTF 56), and Commanding General Tenth Army.

The scheduled landings of American infantry and marines across the eight miles of Hagushi beaches on western Okinawa were confirmed for 0830 at H-Hour or "How Hour." The Bishi Gawa (river) was the geographical midpoint separating the northern U.S. Marine landings and the southern U.S. Army landings.

Rear Admiral John L. Hall, Jr., as Commander Task Force 55 (CTF 55) would oversee the entire Hagushi assault and direct the Southern Attack Force supporting Army landings of southern Hagushi. Rear Admiral Lawrence F. Reifsnider as Commander Task Force 53 (CTF 53) would direct the Northern Attack Force supporting Marine landings of northern Hagushi. The Amphibious Support Force (TF 52) would provide carrier air support and gunboats, and the Gunfire and Covering Force (TF 54) would provide heavy surface gunfire. Other supporting forces included a transport screen, service and salvage group, area and floating reserves, and demonstration group.

LSM(R) Unit One: Gusukuma

For the Love Day assault, LSM(R) Unit One comprised *LSM(R)s 189, 190, 191* and *192*, with *LSM(R) 193* as LSM(R) Group 27 flagship embarking Lieutenant Commander

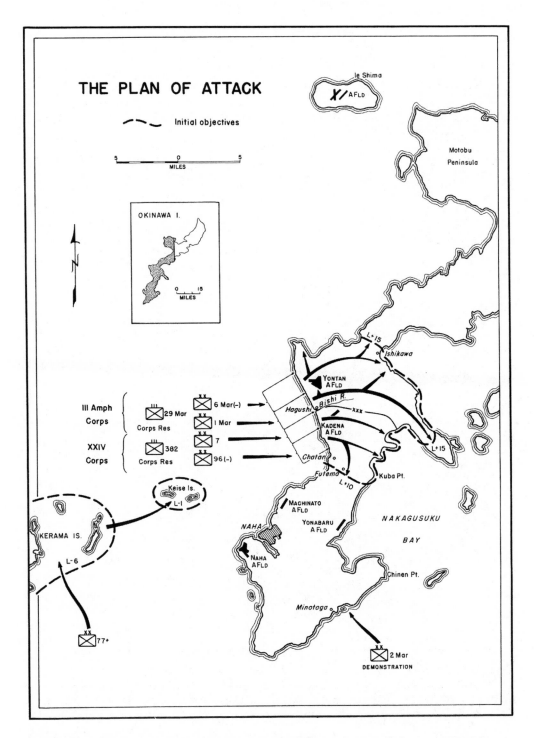

The U.S. Tenth Army, comprising the Marine III Amphibious Corps and the Army XXIV Corps, landed across the Hagushi beachhead of western Okinawa on 1 April 1945. The Bishi River was the geographical centerline separating the northern Marine and southern Army assaults. As U.S. forces drove across the Okinawa isthmus to divide and isolate the Japanese defenders, III Amphibious Corps turned north and XXIV Corps turned south (adapted from Roy E. Appleman, et al., *Okinawa: The Last Battle*, The War in the Pacific, United States Army in World War II, Washington, D.C.: U.S. Government Printing Office, 1948, Map No. 3, page 30).

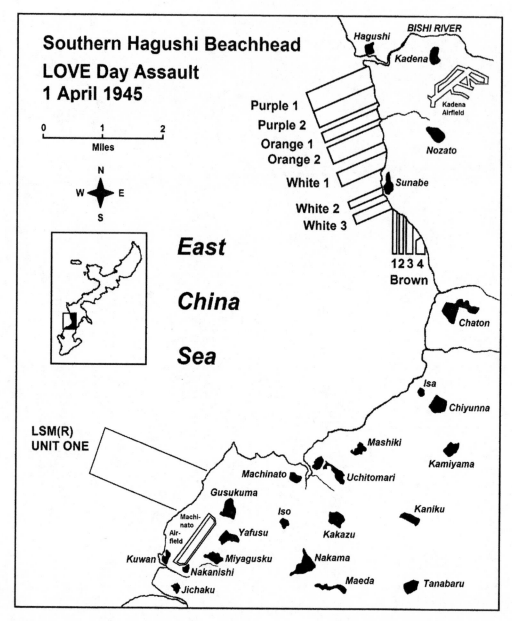

Southern Hagushi Beachhead
LOVE Day Assault
1 April 1945

East

China

Sea

On 1 April 1945, Unit One *LSM(R)s 189, 190, 191* and *192* with LSM(R) Group 27 flagship *LSM(R) 193* attacked Japanese positions in and around Gusukuma village northeast of Machinato Airfield (adapted from Roy E. Appleman, et al., *Okinawa: The Last Battle*, The War in the Pacific, United States Army in World War II, Washington, D.C.: U.S. Government Printing Office, 1948, Map No. V and Map No. XXVIII).

John H. Fulweiler, who reported on station under nominal command of Captain Theodore C. Aylward (CTG 55.11), Commander Southern Support Craft of the Southern Attack Force (TF 55). The southern staging point, designated "Area Sugar," was some three miles north of Keise Shima and about five miles from the Hagushi coastline.

The Southern Support Craft (assigned from TF 52) stood line abreast south of the Bishi

River from Purple Beach 1 to Brown Beach 4 with LCS(L) Division 2, LCI(M) Division 1, LCI(G) Division 1, LCI(G) Division 2, LCI(M) Division 2, LCI(M) Division 3, and LCS(L) Division 5, respectively. LCI(R)(3RCM) Divisions 1 and 2 and LSM(R) Unit One stood at the southern-most flanks of the Hagushi landing beaches. (Direct heavy naval gunfire support included 3 battleships, 4 cruisers, and 7 destroyers).[3]

LSM(R) Unit One's point of attack was the village of Gusukuma.[4] The mission was clear: "Purpose of fire is to prevent reinforcement of main beaches from the south by destroying rail road, highways and troop movements," ordered Commander Francis. "This area is heavily defended. Be prepared to fire 5" [*sic*] and to knock out emplacements."[5]

The strategic and tactical values of Gusukuma village offered the enemy advantages against beach landings or attacks from the north. Lying immediately north of the Machinato Airfield and less than a mile from shore, Japanese troops and conscripted Okinawan laborers had bored networks of tunnels for living quarters and aid stations months beforehand. Occupying this area were two infantry companies, an antitank company, a machine gun company, and parts of antiaircraft, artillery, and mortar units, reinforced by several hundred Okinawans. Within a fortnight, stubborn Japanese resistance surrounding Gusukuma would come to be known as the battle for "Item Pocket."[6]

Since Gusukuma was south of the main landing beaches, the LSM(R)s had little to fear of their rockets flying over or errantly falling onto friendly forces. But low-level American aircraft posed a very real hazard. Comdr. Francis thus warned, "In regard to air strike[s] from H-7 [H-minus-seven, or 0823] to H-2 [H-minus-two, or 0828], Commanding Officers will note that [instructions] appear to be at variance. It is not likely that planes will be over our target, however do not endanger them under any circumstances."[7]

The LSM(R)s took bearings on a small peninsular outcropping south of the Hagushi beaches called Kezu Saki. Their line of fire would be 111° True, an acute ESE heading, while steaming 9 knots (300 yards/minute). The rocket depth of pattern (DOP) would be 1900 yards and width of target area 1400 yards, with each rocketship selecting a relative point of aim 400 yards inboard from the outer edge. Only 200 rockets were allotted per ship on the initial rocket run; if necessary, another hundred rockets would be allowed for a follow-up attack. Salvos would be every nine seconds, or at such intervals to fire their allotment of 5-inch Fin-stabilized AR rockets within 4½ minutes.

"Our rocket ship group was assigned the task of cutting off the highway and railroad which ran north along the western shore from Naha," explained Ensign Paul S. Vaitses, Jr., Executive Officer of *LSM(R) 193*. "We were to lay down a hail of rockets which would disrupt the road, tear up the railroad, and make nearby Machinato airstrip inoperable. This would prevent Jap supplies and reinforcements from arriving via that route, temporarily at least."[8]

The Hagushi beaches took poundings from battleships, cruisers, and destroyers, then carrier planes struck targets inland. Explosions, dust and debris rose high in the air.

By 0800, the five rocketships formed three waves: Unit Guide *LSM(R) 193* assumed lead ship with *LSM(R) 192* starboard abreast, followed by paired *LSM(R)s 190* and *191*, and *LSM(R) 189* last. Standing at General Quarters, warning horns cleared all unnecessary topside personnel as launcher circuits were energized by gunnery officers atop conning towers.

The first wave loosed their rockets at Gusukuma on schedule, but the distance from shore was too great: the opening salvos fell in the water followed by others exploding on the beaches, far short of their intended target. To compensate, *LSM(R)s 192* and *193* ceased fire

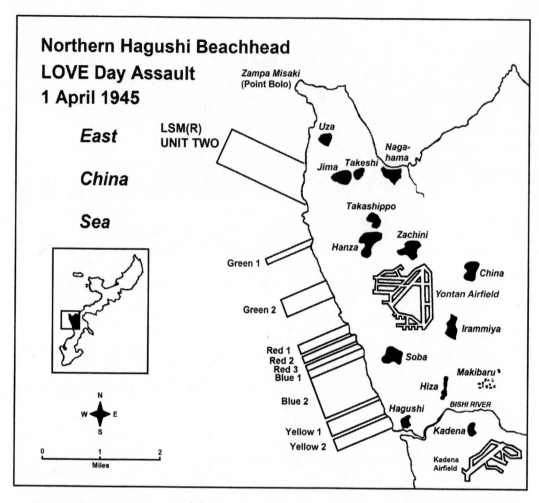

On 1 April 1945, Unit Two *LSM(R)s 194, 195, 196, 197, 198* and *199* with LSM Flotilla Nine flagship *LC(FF) 535* attacked Japanese positions in and around Takashippo village northwest of Yontan Airfield (adapted from Roy E. Appleman, et al., *Okinawa: The Last Battle*, The War in the Pacific, United States Army in World War II, Washington, D.C.: U.S. Government Printing Office, 1948, Map No. V).

until closing range, then resumed successive rocket salvos. From *LSM(R) 192*, Storekeeper Robert W. Landis wrote in his diary, "This is Love Day. Invasion of Okinawa. A vast operation. We made our run to the beach at 8:30 a.m. Continuous air action overhead. The beach is ablaze. Troops are ashore."[9]

After a ten-minute pause, the second wave with *LSM(R)s 190* and *191* fired rocket salvos next, followed ten minutes later by *LSM(R) 189*. "*BB* [45] *Colorado* on our starboard side firing salvos in 3-second intervals to cover rocket attack," noted Ensign F. Donald Moore, Gunnery Officer in *LSM(R) 189*.[10] Most of the rockets launched successfully, although a few misfired due to faulty electrical connections.

All rocketships retired seaward except *LSM(R) 193*, from which Lt. Comdr. Fulweiler scanned the results of the rocket attacks. Comdr. Francis reported afterwards, "The rocket attack ceased at 0840 with approximately 1500 rockets expended. About 75% of the rockets landed in the target area, resulting in destruction of about 200 yards of railroad and primary highway and almost complete obliteration of the town proper. The remaining rockets dispersed laterally on either side of the town, resulting in possible destruction of local defenses and troop concentrations."[11] The rocketships braced for aggressive enemy counter battery fire, and cargo nets were rigged over gunwales for emergencies.

Immediately after the Love Day assault, LSM(R) Unit One reported to Commander L.M. Bailliere (CTG 52.23) in *LC(FF) 679*, Commander Southern Support Gunboats (CTU 52.9.4). Upon return to "Area Sugar" north of Keise Shima, the rocketship sailors assembled and reloaded rockets in launchers while awaiting further orders.

LSM(R) Unit Two: Takashippo

For the Love Day assault, LSM(R) Unit Two comprised *LSM(R)s 194, 195, 196, 197, 198* and *199* with LSM Flotilla Nine flagship *LC(FF) 535* embarking Commander Dennis L. Francis, who reported on station directly to Commander Northern Attack Force (CTF 53), although under nominal command of the Northern Support Craft (TG 53.11). The northern staging point, designated "Area Roger," was about six miles due west of cape Zampa Misaki, or "Point Bolo."

The Northern Support Craft (assigned from TF 52) stood line abreast north of the Bishi River from Green Beach 1 to Yellow Beach 3 with LCI(M) Division 8, LCI(G) Division 4, LCI(M) Division 6, LCS(L) Division 4, LCI(M) Division 7, and LCS(L) Division 3, respectively. LCI(R)(3RCM) Divisions 4, 5 and 6 and LSM(R) Unit Two stood at the northernmost flanks of the Hagushi landing beaches. (Direct heavy naval gunfire support included 4 battleships, 4 cruisers, and 8 destroyers.[12])

LSM(R) Unit Two's point of attack was the village of Takashippo. The mission was "to destroy the town of Takushippo [*sic*] and to disrupt transportation facilities nearby," ordered Commander Francis.[13] Lying a mile or so inland from the Hagushi beaches and about 4 miles south of Zampa Misaki, Takashippo was one of six small villages scattered around the outskirts of Yonton (or Yontan) Airfield. American forces were intent on capturing the airfield quickly, so all Japanese resistance in adjacent areas was to be neutralized.

Just after 0800, the six LSM(R)s and flotilla force flagship shoved off the departure line on a southeasterly course toward "Black Beach," which extended approximately 2000 yards south from Zampa Misaki, or "Point Bolo." No amphibious landings were assigned this northern beachhead, which eliminated concerns of rockets flying over marines in landing craft. The approach was adjusted by radar fixes for range and visual bearings for tangent on Zampa Misaki. Their line of fire would be 114° True, an acute ESE heading, while steaming 6 knots (200 yards/minute). The rocket depth of pattern (DOP) and width of target area would each be a thousand yards, with succeeding waves alternating between two points of fire to achieve a thousand-yard dispersion.

The six LSM(R)s and flotilla flagship assumed attack formation "Uncle 3": four waves led by *LSM(R)s 194* and *195*, followed by *LSM(R)s 196* and *197*, then *LC(FF) 535* and lastly *LSM(R)s 198* and *199*. The order to commence the rocket run was by voice command via radio from Commander Francis in *LC(FF) 535* to unit guide ship *LSM(R) 196*. Should the rocket run be canceled, lookouts stationed topside from each LSM(R) were to watch for the

LSM(R) 194 off Okinawa on 1 April 1945 with rockets loaded in all launchers. Nearby is sister ship *LSM(R) 195*, also loaded with rockets and sporting a unique "scalloped" camouflage pattern (official U.S. Navy photograph).

cease fire signal flag, "Negat Dog," if hoisted aloft the flotilla flagship. "Commanding Officers are responsible that firing stops <u>immediately</u> [original emphasis] upon sighting signal," warned Francis.[14]

About a mile south, a vast line of amphibious gunboats began moving forward in line abreast toward the Hagushi beachhead; dust and debris rose in billows from intense naval and air bombardments, virtually obscuring the entire shoreline, leaving a filmy haze above the landing beaches.

LSM(R) Unit Two had assembled rockets and loaded launchers the day before: the two "Finner" *LSM(R)s 194* and *195* each loaded 450 Fin-stabilized AR rockets, while the four "Spinner" *LSM(R)s 196, 197, 198* and *199* each loaded 500 Spin-stabilized SSR rockets.[15] After each ship completed rocket runs, General Quarters would sound once more, recalling gunners to resume topside battle stations to man the 40mms and 20mms, and in some ships, .50 caliber machineguns.

LSM(R)s 194 and *195* advanced 1400 yards and launched Fin-stabilized rockets in salvos toward the center of Takashippo town. After turning hard right, the two rocketships returned to the rendezvous area at flank speed. Ensign John P. Wickser in *LSM(R) 194* recalled, "On that occasion I might add that we did receive a good deal of return fire from the shore, including mortars which again placed us in considerable peril when our ship ran aground due to inaccurate charts of the coastal waters. Fortunately we were able to free ourselves before suffering any damage."[16]

Four minutes later, *LSM(R)s 196* and *197* aimed toward the left of Takashippo at a small

U.S.S. LSM(R) 197 firing at Okinawa 1 April, 1945

From U.S. Navy Photo

"USS *LSM(R) 197* firing at Okinawa 1 April 1945." Lawrence J. Low, untitled unpublished diary, notebook and sketches.

but prominent hill. After firing a couple of ranging rockets, salvos were launched at ten-second intervals totaling 470 and 483 Spin-stabilized rockets, respectively. David Mallery and Jack Shedd, both Ensigns aboard *LSM(R) 196*, recalled how this attack affected their ship at a gut level. "Thirty minutes before the H-hour, we carried out our mission. The *LSM(R)s 194* and *195* went in first, we followed with the *197*, our faithful partner, then the *198* and *199* together. Just before we fired off our load of rockets, someone noticed—written in chalk on one of the rocket's body in the launcher—'This is for Joe.' That was the whole crew's message to the enemy who had cost them one life the night before."[17]

In a lone rocket run, flotilla flagship *LC(FF) 535* followed seven minutes later, launching 132 SSRs aiming for the center of the village, divided by a country road. Pausing another eight minutes, *LSM(R)s 198* and *199* made 400-yard rocket runs in unison abreast, striking a hill to the left of Takashippo town about 3000 yards from the beach.

Comdr. Francis reported a total of 900 ARs and 2100 SSRs fired. "About 60% of the rockets fired landed in the town of Takushippo, resulting in almost complete obliteration to several communes and heavy destruction to the remainder. Approximately 85% of the rockets landed in the assigned target area, thus neutralizing local defenses and transportation facilities in addition to the destruction of the town proper. The balance of the rockets landed to the south and southeast of the target area causing some damage to the town of Hanza and nearby vicinity."[18]

During rocket runs, the LSM(R)'s commanding officer, gunnery officer, quartermaster, signalman and phone talker crouched atop the Conn to shield themselves from swirling hot cinders and debris from the rockets' exhaust (official U.S. Navy photograph).

Immediately after the Love Day assault, LSM(R) Unit Two returned to "Area Roger" north of the Hagushi transport area. Here, the rocketships reported to Captain Theodore W. Rimer (CTG 52.24) in *LC(FF) 657*, who assumed command of the Northern Support Gunboats (TU 52.9.3).

Days later, Francis led an inspection team ashore to examine and document the rocket destruction of Takashippo. Thousands of craters ranged 4 to 6 feet in diameter and 3 to 5 feet deep. "Several communes of huts had been almost completely obliterated by rocket hits. Stone walls were crumbling and contained large gaps and crevices. Parts of trees had been sheared. Throughout, heavy concentration of rocket fins and shrapnel were evident." Presumably, the town had been evacuated beforehand since no human remains were evident, but dead animals were found, including a horse.[19]

Among Commander Francis' entourage was Robert W. Cox, Pharmacists Mate in flotilla flagship *LC(FF) 535*. "I don't know why it was but I was always picked for something or other." He continued,

After the invasion I went ashore with the Exec Officer to see what kind of damage we did after firing our rockets. The target that was given us looked like some kind of fortification from our vantage point [at

LC(FF) 535, flagship of LSM Flotilla Nine, also mounted Mark 51 Mod 0 Rocket Launchers from spares among the Spinner LSM(R)s. LSM(R) 194 is seen off the starboard bow, circa early April 1945 (official U.S. Navy photograph).

sea]. When I went ashore to look at the damage we did, the target was anything but fortifications. We couldn't really figure it out. Plenty of damage was done. Someone said it was a burial ground or a terraced rice patty. I'm still not sure today what we blew apart. It looked something like a terrace located on the side of a hill.[20]

"The damage inflicted by the rocket fire was thorough," assured Ensigns Mallery and Shedd from *LSM(R) 196*, "and later on personal inspection by our flotilla commander was described as accurate and extensive. Much of it was apparent even to us in the distance at the time. This was tangible, if inadequate, return for the night before and for the crew a grim satisfaction of having made their answer to the Japs."[21]

"Very Little for Us to Do"

Following the massive naval assault of Okinawa on 1 April 1945, with the exception of the Ie Shima operation two weeks hence, the LSM(R)s and other amphibious fire support ships were suddenly out of work. Most of the fighting had moved inland, so battleships, cruisers, and destroyers took over deep naval gunfire support for the army and marines.

"We laid off 'Oki' all day long awaiting assignment," commented a bored Clyde Blue, Radioman in *LSM(R) 197*. Ensign John P. Wickser added from *LSM(R) 194*, "After the actual invasion of Okinawa took place on April 1st, however, and we had discharged our rockets at the appointed landing area, there was really very little for us to do."[22]

Vice Admiral Turner had already reached the same conclusion. "No support tasks were performed after Love Day until 14 May due to navigational limitations in the southern sector and the lack of concentrated defenses in the northern portions of the island."[23]

Moreover, Turner continued, "After zero hour, these craft had little employment as support craft, due to the rapid movement of troops and the tendency of the enemy to avoid shore areas. However, some specific tasks [were found] and all of these types proved of great value as smokers, inshore screening and flak vessels, RCM ships, anti-suicide-boat pickets, and dispatch boats."[24]

The LSM(R)s were thus soon released, albeit "for duty temporarily,"[25] to Captain (soon Commodore) Frederick Moosbrugger, Screen Commander, Task Group 51.5.

Patrols, Air Attacks and Repairs: 1–13 April 1945

The first two evenings in April, Screen Commander Capt. Frederick Moosbrugger dispatched eight LSM(R)s on overnight patrols along the eight-mile Hagushi coastline. Some patrolled as close as 600 yards to the Okinawa beaches, while others anchored on station some 3,000 to 8,000 yards off shore, and still other rocketships stood guard off the Keise islands Nagunna and Kamiyama. Small, speedy enemy boats with explosives were known to operate around the Naha area for suicide crashes into American ships. The remaining LSM(R)s stood in or near transports to generate smoke screens during air raids, and guard against enemy swimmers, small craft, and airplanes. Comdr. Francis' flagship *LC(FF) 535*, meanwhile, provided nighttime smoke screening for *Eldorado*, Adm. Turner's headquarters ship, anchored in Dodger Area, Hagushi Anchorage.

At daylight of 2 April, the CINCPAC staff photographers hitching rides with the LSM(R) flotilla bade farewell and reported for more accommodating quarters aboard battleship *Nevada BB 36*.[26] Meantime, daytime hours were occupied with refueling, resupplying, and repairs—except for two rocketships with pressing matters.

The previous evening, *LSM(R) 196* had sought hospital ship *Solace AH 5* on procedural disposition of their deceased shipmate. Now, after a two-hour journey to Kerama Retto, the rocketship anchored off Zamami Shima near cargo ship *Pitt APA 223*. A small boat transported the body of Joseph Anthony Staum, escorted by a small group of his shipmates as pallbearers, for processing by Graves Registration.

That same evening, a sailor aboard sister ship *LSM(R) 197* needed intense medical care for severe burns from a fire that erupted from the ship's fog generator. "We pulled alongside the *Comfort* [AH 6] which is a hospital ship," explained Radioman Clyde Blue. "We sent [the sailor with burns] aboard her. We saw our first white women. They were the nurses aboard it. Did they ever look good. The whole crew was up topside looking at them. Ha ha! I was on watch in the [radio] shack and it sure didn't take me long to get out to look them over. Ha ha! Still a wolf, I guess!"[27]

Meanwhile, Japanese air attacks spread during 2–3 April from the ships on the distant radar picket stations to the Hagushi and Kerama Retto anchorages. From midnight to 0700, about sixty enemy planes in eleven raids approached Okinawa from the north and southwest.[28]

Protective smoke screens over the transport areas, however, hampered friendly as well enemy forces. Nighttime visibility dropped to about 100 yards, further reduced by a waning moon, and prompted a rocketship's OOD to remark in his log entry, "on patrol station smoke laying too thick to maneuver."[29] Indeed, *LSM(R) 189* was struck by an unidentified LST, which collided into the rocketship's port quarter at the stern anchor winch flat. Damage if any to the larger ship was unknown. As Commander Francis explained, "The collision occurred during an air alert and a dense smoke screen had been laid. Subject ship received a 'V' shaped hole on her port side between frames 38 and 40. The hole was six feet across at the top and two feet at the bottom. Vertically it extended from the sheer strake to the water line."[30]

In the early morning of 3 April, only fifteen minutes after the highest air raid alert "Flash Red—Control Green" was set, a bogie[31] was sighted at 0245 off *LSM(R) 196*'s port beam, skimming about 100 feet over the water. As Ensigns David Mallery and Jack Shedd related, "Subsequent days were spent in Hagushi Anchorage, off Okinawa, followed by night screening patrol outside the anchorage."

Smoke screens effectively concealed American ships from enemy air attacks. Mechanical smoke generators vaporized a heated mixture of water and fog oil, which condensed into microscopic droplets, or "smoke," upon contact with the cooler outside atmosphere (official U.S. Navy photograph).

On one of the patrols shortly after L-Day a two-engined Jap bomber came in low across our fantail. Our 20mms got hits on it. It burst into flames and crashed into the water between the two ships off our starboard quarter. We were credited with our first plane as of that night, and we painted one Jap flag on our conning tower when the official credit was given.[32]

Quartermaster-striker Bruce McDaniel added,

It was a night with low overcast, and no moon or stars were visible. As I came up from below running across the deck to my battle station on the Conn, I noticed George Lee Wilson—the Stewards Mate—was already manning the 20mm gun aft of the life raft behind the Conn on the starboard side. George was a likable young fellow, often practicing boxing with one of those pear-shaped balls dangling under the 40mm gun mount…. I had reached the flag deck when I looked aft and saw a twin engine Betty coming in very low toward the aft starboard quarter. Wilson began firing and I could clearly see the tracers going into the greenhouse in the nose of the plane. For some reason—considering the aggressiveness of Japanese pilots—maybe they were surprised to find us there—which seems unlikely—it immediately banked to its right heading away over the sea in the direction of the DD. When the first five-inch round was fired it burst short, but a second fused round burst under the plane when the plane landed flat on the sea where it began to burn briefly. No effort was made to find the wreckage or look for survivors in the darkness.

Shortly after the DD queried us, "Did you see a plane go down?" We replied that we had shot one down, to which the destroyer communicated to the headquarters ship, "One of our little fellows has splashed a bogey."[33]

LSM(R) 188 *and Rocket Launchers*

Early 3 April, *LSM(R) 192* shoved off for Kerama Retto, which Storekeeper Robert W. Landis noted in his diary: "On patrol off the coast of Okinawa. Enemy air action during the night as well as day now. We tied up alongside the *LSM(R) 188*. We took off the ammunition then assisted in clean up to enable the *188* to return to Pearl. I spent two days aboard the *188* to assist their supply officer with paperwork. They lost their storekeeper; he was one of the casualties…."[34]

LSM(R) 192 pumped fresh water over to the crippled *LSM(R) 188* while transferring 5"/38 AA Common rounds from the latter; an ammunition ship and *LSM(R) 189* also removed Fin-stabilized rockets and rocket motors per orders from CTG 51.1, SOPA of the Kerama Retto anchorage.[35] *LSM(R) 188* then moved alongside *Gunston Hall LSD 5* for intense repairs.

That afternoon, Lt.(jg) William H. Turner, *LSM(R) 188*'s Executive Officer since the ship left San Diego in January, assumed command in an hour-long ceremony attended by Commander Francis. The rocketship would remain in Kerama Retto until 14 April, after which she sailed for the Ulithi advanced fleet base, lay over from 23 April until 19 May, then steam into Pearl Harbor by 7 June.

"We finished the clean up on the [*LSM(R) 188*] today," Storekeeper Landis continued in his diary on 4 April, "and then proceeded to an LSD dry dock to repair damage to the screws caused by the earlier grounding on a reef. We also removed all the outboard rocket launchers which had become a major source of shrapnel and caused so many casualties on the *188*."[36]

Here, Lt. Neal B. Hadsell, Commanding Officer of *LSM(R) 192*, seized the initiative to also rid his ship of the Mark 30 rocket launchers—that is, those not already lost in past months due to damages—and the bane of the Finner rocketships.

Mark 30 Rocket Launchers, mounted along the gunwales of the Finner rocketships, were occasionally damaged while alongside docks and other ships, and some were bent and even broken off from the whiplash of stormy seas. These outboard launchers were removed at Okinawa during the first week of April 1945. Another LSM(R) is seen in the distance (official U.S. Navy photograph).

"With regard to the outboard rocket launchers," Hadsell later recalled,

they were a pain. I can remember ours very well because of the inconvenience of loading them and the unexpected damage to them when we moored alongside another ship.... They had to be swung inboard to load the rockets. Every time we tied up anywhere, we lost one or two, they being mashed as we rode whatever sea there was at that location. We finally cut them all off and forgot them.

The decision to cut off the remaining outboard launchers was not a flotilla order. Our Flot commander was one to do things by the book. He had had some kind of difficulty earlier in the Navy and was not about to do anything that would jeopardize his retirement. I got so fed up with our own experience with them that I just gave the order to cut off the few remaining ones that were functional. I never reported this to the Flot commander and nothing was ever said about it from above. C.O.s had some autonomy, particularly on detached duty. So we got some necessary things done in spite of the system.[37]

Working parties passed the outboard launchers across to the *LSM(R) 188* for temporary storage. Meanwhile, workers from *Gunston Hall* fitted, welded, and rigged new lifeline stanchions along the open areas of the gunwales where the launchers once stood. Days later, *LSM(R) 189*, while awaiting hull and rocket firing control repairs in Kerama Retto, also transferred her dismantled outboard launchers to sister ship *LSM(R) 188* as well.

Months afterwards, *LSM(R) 192* Gunnery Officer Ensign Thomas Boak wrote about some of these experiences in a letter to his wife Helen:

> The *188* did not participate in the Okinawa strike because she was hit by a suicide plane ("One Drive Charlie") on the 29th [of March]. Between the plane and the bombs she carried, her fantail was torn to pieces. The Gunnery Officer [of the *LSM(R) 188*] was slightly injured by shrapnel but he rushed the 5" handling room and rescued a boy who was pinned. So he has been recommended for a medal. The ship was so badly damaged that she was patched up to make her seaworthy and sent back to the states. All of our outboards [i.e., Mark 30 launchers] were sent back with her. The other [LSM(R)s] had so much trouble with the electrical circuits and keeping them in adjustment that the Commodore ordered them removed.[38]

By 5 April, none other than Vice Admiral Turner sanctioned removal of the troublesome launchers: "*LSM(R)s 188* through *193* inclusive [*sic*]" were to "demount" all Mark 30 side-mounted rocket launchers for transfer to cargo ships *Laurens APA 153* and *Appling APA 58* for return to the United States.[39] More importantly, the launcher removals cleared lines of fire for the two portside 20mms. That very morning, *LSM(R) 191* removed 35 outboard launchers, including spares, and passed them to *Laurens*, along with six Mark 36 exhaust deflection grates. The other Finner rocketships soon followed suit.[40]

Denouement

By late 3 April, Captain Moosbrugger assumed formal authority of the LSM(R)s. Over the next several days, however, the rocketships remained on standby near the transport area off the coast of Okinawa near Keise Shima. Ships' maintenance and logistics were the main activities, other than making smoke and manning battle stations during air alerts.

But the Japanese withheld most of their air forces as weather worsened at Okinawa. Between 0200 and 0750 of 4 April, enemy planes made only intermittent air attacks in small groups from the north.[41] The balance of the day, under overcast skies, scattered rains and lowered visibility, remained largely free from Japanese air raids. Between 1700 and 1745, bogies approached from the southwest, closing 60 miles of Okinawa, but retired to the west. CAP planes gave chase, but no contacts were made and no enemy planes destroyed.[42] Late that night, storm warnings were radioed to ships in the Kerama Retto and Hagushi anchorages.

Skies and seas grew increasingly foul the morning of 5 April. Ships tied close aboard sustained damage to and from one another as lines parted under the strains. Personnel were also at risk doing any but the most essential tasks. During the day, only a single air alert was signaled, while evening air activity was practically nil, save for a Val from the north, which was quickly shot down.

But as weather and flying conditions improved, the tempo of enemy air attacks escalated with a vengeance. During 6–7 April, the Japanese army and navy air forces launched the first in a series of massive air attacks against U.S. naval forces at Okinawa and Kerama Retto, called Operation *Ten-Go* (Heavenly Operation). An estimated 20 air raids,[43] with hundreds of aircraft, were unleashed on American ships patrolling the outer radar picket lines and those anchored in the transport areas.

As a precursor, between midnight and 0800, about 35 enemy planes swarmed from the north and northeast.[44] Among those closing Okinawa, lookouts in *LSM(R)s 198* and *199* heard and then spotted an unidentified plane to the north, flying low over the transport area about 0545. Presumed enemy, both ships opened fire with 40mm, 20mm, and .50 caliber, but the aircraft apparently escaped harm.

In the evening of 6 April, the four Spinner LSM(R)s anchored on stations along the western Hagushi coastline screening the Inner Transport Area. *LSM(R) 196* sounded alarm at 1610 when lookouts spotted an Oscar fighter plane crossing overhead. Gunners got off just 15 rounds from their 40mm guns when the plane was hit by gunfire from nearby ships and splashed. Signalman Leonard VanOteghem was monitoring the ship's radio and tallied enemy planes shot down, and noted in his diary: "At anchor off Okinawa. Air attacks at 4:15, one plane down; 4:28, two planes down; 5:15, seven planes down."[45]

In minutes, sister ship *LSM(R) 197* took another plane under fire at 1617. "We had an air alert this afternoon and a Jap Oscar flew over," Radioman Clyde Blue wrote in his diary. "Everyone started shooting and it came our way. We opened up just as it started to make a suicide dive on the BB *New Mexico*. We hit it with our 40mm and it crashed about 1000 yards off starboard side. It sure made us feel good. Two other Japs and two US planes were shot down by the ships here."[46] The ship's Gunnery Officer, Ensign Lawrence J. Low, also noted this attack: "On 6 April during air raid on anchorage, shot down Jap Oscar with 40mm guns, while in dive attack on USS *West Virginia* (*BB 48*)."[47] Commander Francis later submitted a commendation crediting *LSM(R) 197* for the splash. "Well done.... You are entitled to paint one Japanese flag emblem on your conning tower ... as credit for the disposal of this plane."[48]

By 1640, the Combat Information Center (CIC) in Admiral Turner's headquarters ship *Eldorado* reported 12 more incoming enemy air raids, and at dusk still more bogies were closing on radar.

In Hagushi Anchorage, *LSM(R) 191* tracked an unidentified plane at 1715 and opened fire as it passed forward of the *LSM(R) 194*, but falling rounds—assumed from the enemy plane, but possibly from friendly fire—struck the latter rocketship and injured her damage control officer. "Fortunately, [with] a rugged build, [he] had been a member of the Green Bay Packers professional football team, [but] suffered a serious wound when a 20mm shell went through his groin as we were rushing up the bridge to General Quarters," recalled Ensign John P. Wickser, the rocketship's Communications Officer.[49]

A few minutes later, at 1723, the flotilla flagship *LC(FF) 535* also spotted an enemy plane 800 yards off her starboard bow, identified as a Zero fighter. The ship's gunners commenced firing until it crashed into the sea about 200 yards off the port beam.

At 1740, *LSM(R) 198* fired four rounds from her 5"/38 gun at yet another unidentified plane, but failed to knock it down.

In the wake of the intense Japanese air raids of 6 April, that evening Moosbrugger hurriedly selected LSM(R)s for coastal patrols and distant radar picket supports. From 7 April through the next few days, *LSM(R)s 196, 197, 198* and *199* actively patrolled between the Hagushi beachhead and the "Easy Fox" Inner Transport Area. Along this coastline, LCS(L)s, LCIs, destroyers, and cruisers also sought and destroyed enemy suicide boats and disrupted coastal activities. Japanese movements ashore appeared to be increasing,[50] so *LSM(R) 193* was ordered to assist the four Spinner rocket ships with these "Skunk" and "Flycatcher" patrols.

Admiral Turner later explained, "Elaborate precautions and very effective work by screening vessels prevented the suicide boats from becoming as destructive as anticipated.

It was soon deduced that remaining suicide boats on the West side of Okinawa were based near Naha [and] a 'Flycatcher Detail' was organized each night to cope with them."[51]

By the end of the first week in April 1945, enemy shoreline activities seemed well-suppressed, so the LSM(R)s saw little action along the western Okinawa coast. Now, the larger threat was the heavy Japanese air attacks, against which the rocketships were increasingly dispatched to the far radar picket stations, often only returning long enough for refueling, resupplying, and repairs, then sent back out again. Thus, by 9–10 April, LSM(R)s 193 and 196 alone remained on anti–small boat patrols. The only notable incident was recovery of the body of a Japanese airman from the waters north of Naha off Brown Beach. After a search for personal effects and intelligence, the aviator was relinquished to the sea with military rites.

A brief exception was 11–12 April, when LSM(R)s 191 and 192 returned from the picket lines due to radar malfunctions and joined the other two rocketships on overnight coastal patrols. From LSM(R) 192, Storekeeper Robert W. Landis noted in his diary, "Have developed a problem with our radar and we are leaving the Picket line. Now anchored off the coast of Okinawa awaiting repairs of the radar."[52] The rocketship also brought back a secret code book for U.S. naval intelligence, found on the body of a Japanese aviator recovered from the sea while on picket duty.[53]

Here, too, General Quarters suddenly sounded early 12 April at 0345, while LSM(R)s 191, 192, 193 and patrol leader LSM(R) 196 steamed slowly in column. The CIC in Eldorado picked up four raiding aircraft, and in minutes the "Flash Red–Control Yellow" alert was signaled to U.S. ships around the Hagushi transport area. An AA barrage with tracers soon rose in the darkness as gunners aimed skyward, where lookouts from LSM(R) 196 saw a plane burst into flames and crash into the water.

This scene repeated itself about two hours later, when heavy ack-ack covered the transport area once more—arcing over and above the four patrolling rocketships—tracking incoming enemy planes. Several men on LSM(R) 192 were wounded from errant friendly fire, however, as Robert Landis noted in his diary. "Enemy aircraft overhead. We took a strafing hit on the bow 40mm causing a clip burst, which injured four gunners. These are the first wounded on our ship. I assisted our Pharmacists Mate with treatment of the wounded."[54] The casualty report concluded, however, that bursting shrapnel from a 20mm round fired from an adjacent ship had set off the powder charge, exploding a 40mm shell in the #1 forward gun mount. Luckily, injuries were limited to powder burns and minor lacerations to hands, arms and faces.[55]

After sunrise, the four LSM(R)s secured from patrols and returned to the Hagushi anchorage for repairs and to await further orders. A medical officer was sent to LSM(R) 192 via small boat from Crescent City APA 21 to examine the injuries of the four gunners, two of whom were taken off the ship with the doctor for further treatment.

At nightfall from 12–13 April, LSM(R)s 191 and 193 resumed coastal patrols, but the former was dispatched to the radar picket lines. The latter patrolled alone until released next day by the Screen Commander for the Ie Shima operation.

CHAPTER 5

The Radar Picket Lines
7–30 April 1945

The LSM(R)s acquitted themselves during the Kerama Retto operation and Love Day assault of Okinawa. But because no fire support missions were immediately foreseen after 1 April 1945, the rocketships were temporarily assigned to Captain Frederick Moosbrugger on 2 April,[1] and as Screen Commander, he dispatched them on coastal patrols and transport screening. The next day, Moosbrugger assumed formal command of the LSM(R)s after Captain Theodore Rimer[2] and Commander Lawrence Bailliere[3] relinquished their respective commands of LSM(R) Unit Two and LSM(R) Unit One.

Captain Frederick Moosbrugger, Screen Commander

Captain Frederick Moosbrugger (CTG 51.5) was directly accountable to Admiral Turner as Screen Commander for the Okinawa operation. Foremost responsibilities were maintaining and controlling the objective area's anti-submarine (A/S) and anti-aircraft (A/A) screen, the radar pickets and support vessels, local hunter-killer groups, and anti–small craft and suicide boat screen ("Flycatchers" or "Skunks"). Moosbrugger also coordinated rescue missions, convoy escort assignments and typhoon deployments. Further duties entailed the logistics of fueling, rearming, and provisioning the screening vessels as well as maintaining records of the materiel and maintenance conditions of each unit. The Screen Commander was additionally required to make recommendations and arrangements for emergency repairs or tender availability; provisions for "at anchor" availability for upkeep; installation of fighter direction equipment in destroyers; and daily delivery of mail to screening units on station.[4]

Perhaps as early as 2 April, but certainly by 5 April, Admiral Turner and Captain Moosbrugger effected what may be among their most fateful decisions: ordering the LSM(R)s to the Radar Picket Stations. Presaging what lay ahead, Turner ordered removal of the Mark 30 launchers on the Finner LSM(R)s to clear portside 20mm lines of fire; and Moosbrugger alerted the LSM(R) commanders to "complete repairs and logistics and prepare for sea."[5] This cryptic warning is more understandable in light of recent postwar historical research, for U.S. intelligence was monitoring and deciphering Japanese internal military and diplomatic communications more closely than heretofore disclosed. This, in turn, allowed Admiral Nimitz to forewarn his senior commanders of impending Japanese attacks at Okinawa.[6]

The next morning, Captain Moosbrugger summoned Commander Dennis L. Francis and Lieutenant Commander John H. Fulweiler to headquarters ship *Biscayne AGC 18*.[7] Details of this lengthy 6 April conference are lost to history. Moosbrugger doubtless advised the two commanders that Japanese air attacks were fraying the radar picket lines. Insufficient numbers of destroyers and support ships, furthermore, were staggering under murderous Kamikaze attacks, and more losses were certain. Uppermost, until sufficient land-based radar units were established around Okinawa, sustaining the radar picket lines against enemy air raids was imperative to the success of the operation.[8]

Thus, as Admiral Turner later explained, "It soon became necessary to augment [the Radar Picket Stations] with gunboats (LCS) and later LSM(R) types in order to add fire power and provide immediate assistance for stricken ships. The gunboat types proved valuable additions by their AA armament, and by the fact that they are a difficult target to hit.... The LSM(R) types were detailed for their ability to tow damaged ships until tugs could reach and relieve them."[9] Curiously, destroyer escorts were deemed inadequate in firepower and therefore rarely deployed, yet smaller, lighter-armed PGM gunboats were dispatched to radar picket patrols.[10]

Excluding rocketships requiring urgent repairs, Captain Moosbrugger initially assigned LSM(R) Unit One to the Radar Picket Stations and LSM(R) Unit Two to the Hagushi Inner Transport Screens and to coastal anti-small craft patrols. Over the coming week, however, the rocketships were gradually withdrawn from coastal patrols and sent increasingly to the distant radar picket stations.

A fortnight later, effective 26 April, the LSM(R)s were folded organizationally into the Gunboats and Mortar Support Flotillas under Captain T. C. Aylward, CTG 52.9 of LCS(L) Flotilla Three. Commander Francis would continue as CTG 52.21 of LSM Flotilla Nine, but additionally assigned as CTU 52.9.12 of the LSM(R) Picket Supports, under which the LSM(R)s were designated Picket Support Gunboats of TU 52.9.1. An administrative arrangement was further reached whereby Capt. Moosbrugger, as CTG 51.5 Screen Commander, would no longer directly assign LSM(R)s to screening stations, but instead submit *pro forma* requests directly through Comdr. Francis.[11]

The Radar Picket Stations (RPS)

While planning Operation Iceberg, Admiral Turner conceived a distant, early-warning defense perimeter of fifteen Radar Picket Stations (RPS) surrounding Okinawa. Ships patrolling these picket stations would provide continuous radar and visual searches against enemy air and surface forces attacking from Kyushu, Korea and Formosa. Turner prescribed a single Fighter Director (FD) destroyer, embarked with a Fighter Director Operator (FIDO) team to vector CAP fighters, accompanied by two LCS-type Picket Support Gunboats. Ironically, destroyermen often disdained the slower, lighter-armed picket support gunboats, mocking such "little boys" as "pallbearers," "meat wagons," and the like.[12]

"Pickets are primarily radar guard ships," continued Turner. "They have been so spaced that contacts may be passed from one Radar Picket to another without losing contact, thereby facilitating fighter direction."[13] Picket locations ranged from 18 miles to almost 100 miles from the Hagushi transport area, although the most frequently patrolled RPSs averaged

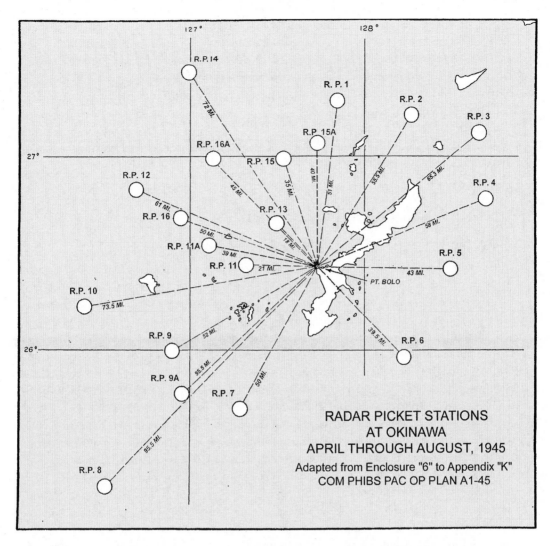

RADAR PICKET STATIONS
AT OKINAWA
APRIL THROUGH AUGUST, 1945
Adapted from Enclosure "6" to Appendix "K"
COM PHIBS PAC OP PLAN A1-45

LSM(R)s, LCSs, and destroyer-types patrolled the Radar Picket Stations (RPSs) around Okinawa to warn American forces of Japanese air and surface attacks from Kyushu and Formosa. At most ten, but often far fewer, RPSs were ever actively patrolled at any given time during the operation (adapted from Commander, Amphibious Forces, U.S. Pacific Fleet [ComPhibsPac], Operation Plan No. A1–45 [OpPlan No. A1–45], Serial 000120, 9 February 1945, Enclosure "G" to Appendix II to Annex "K." Reprinted with permission from Robin L. Rielly, *American Amphibious Gunboats in World War II*, Jefferson, NC: McFarland, 2013, page 307).

between 50 and 70 miles from Okinawa. Each RPS prescribed a 5000-yard patrol radius and assigned a theoretical latitude, longitude and distance from Zampa (Cape) Misaki codenamed "Point Bolo," the primary geo-operational reference point at the tip of the prominent western peninsula north of the Hagushi beaches.

Until land-based radar units were established to expand coverage, Radar Picket Stations were variously activated, deactivated, modified, or increased during the Okinawa campaign. The numbers of RPSs reached more than twenty in addition to several unnumbered intermediate stations, but no more than ten were operational at any one time between March and June 1945.

Above all else, emphasized Admiral Turner, "The primary idea in any amphibious operation is that the most important task of all forces involved is the support of the troops that are trying to capture the position. No other consideration should ever over-ride that idea. On the other hand," he continued, "all must recognize that, in order to maintain effective support of the troops, we must provide adequate protection for the most vulnerable elements of the expedition, which are the ships."[14]

Turner anticipated additional ships and ship types would supplement the outer and inner defense screens off Okinawa. However, LSM(R)s were never considered for the Radar Picket Stations before April 1945.[15]

Operation Ten-Go and the Kikusui

Not since the surprise attack on Pearl Harbor on 7 December 1941 had the Japanese amassed greater air power prior to launching Operation *Ten-Go* (Heavenly Operation) against American forces at Okinawa during 6–7 April 1945. "Leave nothing to be desired in order to fulfill the operation with hard struggle by all our forces," exhorted Emperor Hirohito, "because *Ten* [-Go] No. 1 will decide the fate of our Empire."[16]

Operation *Ten-Go* was a series of ten air raids between April and June 1945 filling the skies with hundreds of bombers and fighters including the "Special Attack Corps," squadrons flown by volunteer Kamikaze pilots known as the *Kikusui* (Floating Chrysanthemum). The Japanese first exploited organized suicidal crash-dive tactics during air battles late in 1944 in the Philippines, deploying small units of Kamikaze planes to avoid detection yet strike quickly. At Okinawa, a bold, expanded strategy would coordinate Japanese navy and army air forces flying from airfields in Kyushu and Formosa with waves of Kamikaze planes among conventional raiding aircraft escorted by protective fighter cover.[17] Additional raiders not associated with Operation *Ten-Go* also targeted radar picket ships and Okinawa anchorages.

Initial targets were American aircraft carriers and battleships, but the Japanese quickly learned such large battle groups were heavily defended and difficult to reach. But in order to directly attack and destroy the U.S. forces invading Okinawa, the exposed ships on the Radar Picket Stations—the outer early warning system defending the American anchorages and ground forces—soon became the targets of the Kamikazes.

The Japanese *Ten-Go* plans were readied by late March 1945, but U.S. carrier air and land-based long range bomber strikes on Kyushu and Formosa airfields hindered gathering planes for concerted attacks. Also essential for success was favorable weather for navigation, not only because of the distances and hours of flying, but for accurately pinpointing American targets as well.

The morning of 6 April 1945, Admiral Turner forewarned his naval forces of impending enemy air attacks "in force,"[18] garnered from U.S. intelligence monitoring Japanese communications.[19] By mid-afternoon, the first enemy planes reached American naval forces at Okinawa after avoiding or otherwise attacking and penetrating the outer Radar Picket Stations and Combat Air Patrols. Ships on RPSs 1 and 2 were hit hard. An estimated 700 enemy planes were sortied, including 355 Kamikaze airplanes, of which about fifteen percent scored direct or indirect hits against American ships.[20] The total numbers of raiding aircraft in *Kikusui* Raid No. 1 during 6–7 April remain uncertain, however, and may never be known.[21]

The U.S. Navy was stunned. "During the past 24 hours we have been hit badly by enemy aircraft," admitted Turner, which caused reassessments of the Radar Picket Stations.[22] Nineteen ships were damaged and six sunk, and over a thousand American sailors were killed, wounded, or missing.[23]

LSM(R)s on the Radar Picket Stations: April 1945

By 0900 of 7 April, five LSM(R)s were en route Radar Picket Stations 1, 10 and 14, and soon other rocketships were sent to RPSs 2 and 3; before the month was over, the LSM(R)s would also patrol RPSs 4 and 12.

The LSM(R)s saw little action during their first week on RPS patrols, other than occasional but distant enemy "snoopers," or fast, high-flying reconnaissance planes. At sea, the rocketships kept watch for enemy floating mines, tell-tale debris, and oil slicks, while bodies of Japanese were recovered from the waters for identification and documents useful to U.S. intelligence.[24]

Inexplicably, LSM(R)s often patrolled the radar picket lines with armed rockets in launchers, though none was ever fired against Japanese aircraft.[25] Seaman 1c Lawrence Willison on *LSM(R) 197* recalled, moreover, "The Captain at no time explained to us why we were being used for this duty. I think everyone knew we were not suited for this kind of service, but we all did the best we could to do our part with this assignment."[26]

Rumors claimed (or blamed) Commander Francis and Lieutenant Commander Fulweiler as favoring LSM(R) deployments to the radar picket stations. According to former *LSM(R) 197* Ensign and Gunnery Officer Lawrence J. Low, "I distinctly remember scuttlebutt among the LSM(R) officers that Francis was so hot to make a name for himself and gain a promotion that he'd have us attack the *Yamato* [Japanese battleship] in the East China Sea. [But] This may be doing the old boy an injustice...."[27] That view mirrors an anecdotal conversation with Lt. Comdr. Fulweiler, related by Ensign Paul S. Vaitses, Jr., Gunnery Officer on *LSM(R) 193*. "...[Lieutenant] Commander Fulweiler hurried aboard. Smiling broadly and rubbing his hands together in obvious delight, he greeted us warmly. 'Well, boys, I've got great news for you. We've landed a real job for the rocket fleet this time.' 'Yeah, what's that?' scowled the [*LSM(R) 193*] skipper unappreciatively. 'You're going out on the radar picket lines!' responded the Commander enthusiastically." But, continued Vaitses, "The events of the next few weeks would prove to be quite a damper on the Commander's enthusiasm."[28]

On the other hand, a contrary perspective was offered by Signalman Leonard Van-Oteghem on *LSM(R) 196*. "All during our RP patrols, our flotilla commander was trying to get us relieved of such hazardous duty, as we were not designed for such as we carried too much explosives. He even went to the extent of writing to Washington, D.C., and finally after the unit was so badly beaten up, they relieved us of such duty. These patrol assignments were not much less than suicide to go on. Every time an assignment would come up, we would wonder if this was it..."[29]

Former Ensign John P. Wickser from *LSM(R) 194*, however, contended his ship's daring rescue of the crippled destroyer *Halligan* first planted the idea. "It was this incident which prompted Admiral Blandy, and later Admiral Richmond Turner, to decide that our group would make excellent support ships to assist the destroyers on picket patrol. Considering we were practically floating ammunition lockers limited to a top speed of 12 knots, we regarded this as a very unfortunate decision."[30]

Kikusui *Raid No. 2*

Under Operation *Ten-Go*, *Kikusui* Raid No. 2 was launched 12–13 April 1945, and sortied at least 380 Japanese army and navy aircraft with 185 Kamikaze planes, including twin-engine bombers carrying *Oka* (Cherry Blossom) manned rockets. Waves of air attacks struck the radar picket stations and Okinawa. Seventeen U.S. ships were damaged and two sunk, and 700 American sailors were killed, wounded or missing.[31]

Forewarning the onslaught, Vice Admiral Turner alerted his task force at 0940 of 11 April 1945: "Indications are that 12 April will be good weather and the enemy air will attack very strongly from Japan and Formosa. Be ready. Don't let any get back home."[32]

RPS 2: 12 April 1945

At Radar Picket Station 2 on 12 April 1945, USS *LSM(R) 198* (Lt. George B. Timmerman, Jr., USNR) was column guide for USS *LSM(R) 197* (Lt. John M. Cooper, USN), and *LCS 32* was column guide for *LCSs 51* and *116* about 4–5 miles abeam to port. Stationed between the columns were destroyers *Stanly DD 478* followed by *Lang DD 399* as OTC. The 3-column formation patrolled parallel courses, alternating directions northwest and southeast.

Weather was sunny with clear skies, light winds, and occasional broken clouds.

At 1313, a bogie was picked up on air search radar, possibly a Japanese "snooper" reconnaissance plane. General Quarters was sounded and the picket support ships began closing for mutual fire support. The destroyers maneuvered independently around the smaller ships at increased speeds, although their evasive actions disrupted the formation. Earlier, *LSM(R) 198*'s skipper had wisely ordered all rockets removed from launchers, disassembled, and stowed below deck.

Picket ships patrolling around Okinawa were warned of enemy air raids approaching from three different bearings. By 1340, *LSM(R) 197* was first to open fire and drove a plane away, possibly damaged. As Radioman Clyde Blue recalled, "a Val came in and flew around us and we fired everything we had at him, but none of the ships hit him. He dropped a bomb off the DD *Lang*'s stern but it was a miss. He then went out of sight and we had a let up of about 15 minutes or so."[33]

Stanly, meanwhile, was ordered to assist *Cassin Young DD 793* under heavy air attack in adjacent RPS 1. Steaming flank speed, the destroyer was attacked en route by a handful of planes, but *Lang* and *Stanly* fended them off beyond gun ranges.

According to one estimate, ten enemy planes, some flying in pairs, approached within 15 miles between 1400 and 1520. Some used scattered clouds as cover while others were lost from view at higher altitudes. About eight miles north and northwest, meanwhile, Japanese aircraft were dropping "Window," batches of thin foil metal strips to confuse American radar signals.

At 1404, a raid of 5 to 7 aircraft was picked up 8 miles away and quickly closed from the east. Two minutes later, a single plane attacked *LSM(R) 198* and dropped a bomb while strafing the entire length of the ship as it flew by. The bomb overshot the rocketship, however, and fell in the water about 50 yards off her starboard quarter.

Watching from *LSM(R) 197*, Clyde Blue continued, "eight Hellcats came flying by over us and made a circle and ran right into two Vals. They had a dogfight and shot one down. Then 4 of them chased the other one all over the place and finally shot it down."[34] Shipmate and Signalman Karl Matchett added, "They were in time to save us, and shot down the Vals in the prettiest 'dog fight' you'd ever see."[35]

Stanly's orders to RPS 1 were rescinded in transit at 1418, and she immediately turned back. En route, the destroyer was attacked once again, and combined batteries from *Lang* and *Stanley* downed one Val and fended off another that dropped a bomb just missing *Lang*.

Just then, *LSM(R) 198* nearly met disaster from the strangest foe: "A missile, appearing to be a buzz bomb, fell on our port side about 100 yards out, ricocheted and dived under [the] ship, evidently passing clear," noted the rocketship's watch officer.[36] This so-called missile, however, was an *Oka*, a rocket-powered suicide plane that Americans sarcastically dubbed *Baka*, meaning "fool" or "idiot" in Japanese. The rocket plane exploded underwater but knocked out the ship's rudder angle indicator and forced *LSM(R) 198* to shift ship's control from the wheelhouse to after steering.

From *LSM(R) 197*, Gunnery Officer Lawrence J. Low observed the rocket plane dead ahead about 75 feet above the water, "and he was screaming." Skipper Lt. John Cooper added that the craft was "so fast we could not train on it before it crashed. This was a new type of plane with twin tails and pilot controlled." Ensign Low jotted in his notes, "Bomb passed *LSM(R) 197* on a parallel (reciprocal) course—400 yards on starboard side and crashed into water about 700 yards off bow of *LSM(R) 198*."[37] Radioman Blue also witnessed this bizarre attack and added, "an aircraft glided by us and hit the water and exploded. It wasn't a real plane but as far as we can figure out it was a Japanese Buzz bomb flown by a suicide pilot. It came by us so fast it was almost a blur."[38]

The *Oka* Mark 11 was the most widely employed type and attained speeds of 550–600 miles per hour. Essentially a glider with three rocket boosters, the first booster was fired to free itself of its mother craft and the other two boosters were used as necessary during its final, full-speed death plunge. Released from 15,000 feet, the *Oka* was typically launched only miles away from the point of attack because of its limited 15-mile cruising range. An *Oka* was carried under a two-engine bomber, usually a Betty or Frances, and often escorted by fighters en route from airfields in Japan. Because the added weight slowed air speed and maneuverability, many of these attack formations were picked up on American radar during approach and intercepted by Combat Air Patrols (CAP).[39]

Ensign Low immediately sketched his recollection of the strange craft on paper, and radioed his observations to *Lang* for further routing to Naval Intelligence. The destroyer's OTC soon responded:

> Refer NR h615 which describes suicide buzzbomb found on Okinawa. This craft rocket propelled guided by suicide pilot 12 foot wing spread with twin tail carrying approximately 1000 lb. warhead painted silver color. This fits what we saw in four instances today. Would like your sketch for report and will pick it up tomorrow.[40]

Lt. Cooper submitted a memorandum eleven days later describing the *Oka* and its attack on 12 April. "As observed by Commanding Officer and others aboard this vessel, subject

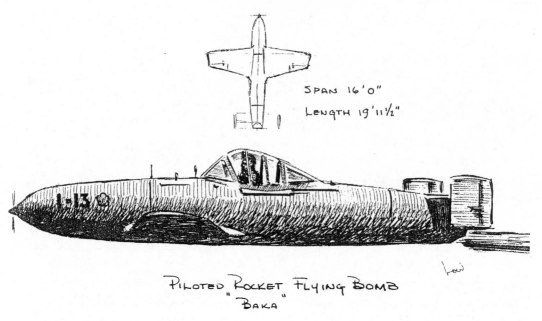

"Piloted Rocket Flying Bomb 'Baka.'" Lawrence J. Low, untitled unpublished diary, notebook and sketches.

aircraft was quite long, with a sharp tapering nose, bulky underbody and pronounced canopy. Wings were short and stubby, the profile not being observed. The tail assembly was of the double type, being of a squarely built box kite arrangement … the color of the body or fuselage was a dirty yellowish brown."

> This craft was first observed by us at a distance of about 1,000 to 1,200 yards, 75 feet above the water and approaching at an apparent speed of several hundred miles per hour. As it passed there was a distinct buzzing sound which might have been made by either internal combustion engines or rocket or jet propulsion motors.
>
> The craft passed us about 400 yards on our starboard side, crashing into the water about 800 yards off our starboard quarter. From [the] time we first sighted it until it crashed, we hardly had more than about 20 seconds in which to observe.
>
> Enclosure (A) is a rough sketch by Ensign L. J. Low, USNR, former aircraft engineer and flyer, from his own observations and those of the Commanding Officer and other bridge personnel. It is hoped that this description and sketch may prove of material value in the development of a defense against these craft.[41]

Among the estimated 185 Kamikaze planes of *Kikusui* Raid No. 2, eight were dual engine bombers each laden with an *Oka*, six of which were successfully launched according to Japanese accounts. "As the result of the scarcity of small type suicide planes, we were compelled to use the *Oka* in order to make our attack effective," noted the Fifth Air Fleet operations log. "On this day the weather conditions were favorable for a high altitude surprise attack therefore *Oka*s were employed."[42] Precise numbers of *Oka*s launched against the Radar Picket Stations throughout the Okinawa campaign may never be fully known, however, because *Oka* attacks occurred quickly amidst simultaneous attacks by conventional enemy planes. And like other Kamikaze attacks, some *Oka*s missed their targets entirely while others were shot down with their mother craft by American fighters before launchings.[43]

Moments after the *Oka* attack on *LSM(R) 198*, around 1434 *Lang* witnessed a second

Oka crashing in the water 500 yards off her port beam, which failed to explode. Then a third *Oka* closed *Stanly*'s starboard bow fast and low over the water about 1449. This human-guided rocket hit the destroyer just above the waterline, blew out the port side, then crashed into the sea and exploded, engulfing *Stanly* in smoke. *Stanly* suffered 6 casualties and the explosion's concussion blew two sailors overboard. "Thursday the 12th of April 1945 was a day that will not soon be forgotten by all the officers and men aboard the USS *Stanly*," her commander later confided.[44]

About 1500, *LSM(R) 198* found *Stanly*'s missing men, one floating in the water and the other in a life raft. Enemy aircraft hampered rescue efforts, but several sailors from the rocketship paddled in a life raft to recover one of the men regardless. Ensign George M. Addison, Jr., Executive Officer on *LSM(R) 198*, sensed the other survivor was in danger of drowning, however, so he jumped overboard and kept the man afloat. Both destroyer sailors were soon safely recovered aboard the rocketship.

Minutes after the *Oka* hit *Stanly*, *Lang* tracked a fourth *Oka* at 1456 and opened fire as it crossed her bow. The suicide rocket plane passed between *Stanly*'s two smoke stacks, swerved to its right presumably for another attack run, but lost control and crashed. *Lang* soon reported a fifth *Oka* skimming past her at 1504, but it too crashed in the sea. Air attacks over RPS 2 ended about 1615, and GQ was secured forty-five minutes later.

The next day, before the two rocketships departed picket patrols, Commander W. T. McGarry, USN, Commander Destroyer Division Four, radioed appreciation from USS *Lang*:

> Following message sent to USS *LSM(R) 197* and USS *LSM(R) 198* on being relieved of Radar Picket duty on 13 April 1945: …your performance of duty and cooperation has been outstanding while working with me in an isolated and hazardous Radar Picket Station for the period eight dash twelve April. Well Done.[45]

RPS 14: 12 April 1945

At Radar Picket Station 14 on 12 April 1945, USS *LSM(R) 189* (Lt. James M. Stewart, USNR) and USS *LSM(R) 190* (Lt. Richard H. Saunders, USNR) were stationed about a mile starboard and port abeam of destroyer *Mannert L. Abele DD 733*, respectively. The trio patrolled a large figure-eight course along a northwest-southeast axis.

Visibility was excellent with a calm sea and light winds from the north.

In early afternoon, *Abele*'s CIC radar picked up bogies about 60 miles north-northeast. When the enemy planes closed twenty miles, the destroyer sounded General Quarters about 1330 and ordered the two LSM(R)s to cease picket patrols and follow the destroyer's movements. As planes neared six to eight thousand yards, *Abele* accelerated and maneuvered radically to keep the aircraft abeam while remaining between the rocketships for mutual fire support.

Three Val dive bombers, two abreast with the third trailing slightly higher, flew in tight formation about 500 feet on westerly to southwesterly courses. At about 5 miles, the destroyer commenced fire until the three Vals broke off southward or southeastward. *Abele* tracked two planes flying about 20 miles south where they orbited out of range, but the other turned back until almost abeam of the picket ships and increased speed for an attack run from the south. The destroyer resumed heavy AA fire assisted by *LSM(R) 189*, now directly in the line of fire between *Abele* and the attacking plane.

Intense ships' gunfire set the Val afire as it swerved and aimed directly astern of *LSM(R) 189*. The plane strafed the rocketship as it dropped its bomb, which fell in the water some 75 yards off the starboard bow. At that same moment, the skipper ordered hard right rudder and flank speed, and the smoking plane passed low over the port side. The rocketship's two aft 20mm gun crews made direct hits before the Val careened into the sea just off the port bow about 1335.

Abele warned the LSM(R)s that more enemy planes were approaching RPS 14, and the three picket ships were soon surrounded as aircraft feigned attacks yet remained beyond gun ranges. About 1400, the destroyer advised the two rocketships that a Combat Air Patrol was on its way from escort carrier *Petrof Bay CVE 80*; unfortunately, the American fighters were vectored to another ship instead, and subsequent requests for air cover were unavailing.

A Lily twin-engine light bomber broke off from a group of four bombers, then flew low over the water to cross the bow of the *Abele*, apparently attempting to get around to the other side for a pincer attack. But AA fire may have damaged the plane, because it continued flying south and beyond range with the others.

About 1430, concerted air attacks began in earnest against Radar Picket Station 14. Seven or eight planes closed from about 20 miles northeast, and two groups of two to four planes orbiting 16 miles north and east came in low and fast.

By 1434, three aircraft approached low on the horizon, the two leading planes practically wingtip to wingtip and the third close behind. As they aimed for *Abele*, the trailing plane, a Kate carrier bomber, broke off and circled back, then swept almost full around until bearing upon *LSM(R) 189*'s starboard bow. The rocketship's 5"/38 gun made direct hits and knocked a wing off, causing the bomber to erupt in flames and crash into the sea about 500 yards astern at 1442. As the Kate was shot down, an approaching Val dive bomber veered off.

The other two planes, both fighters, continued past *LSM(R) 189* and targeted the destroyer. *Abele* hit one of the Zekes with heavy AA fire, causing it to wing over sharply and trail smoke until crashing in the sea. Ship's batteries continued firing at the remaining attacker, but at 1445 the lone fighter with its bomb crashed into the *Abele*'s starboard side, about level with the main deck, and penetrated the after fireroom, causing a terrific explosion.

Ship's control was lost and the *Abele* began to lose way rapidly; though not fully realized at that moment, the destroyer's keel and forward engine shaft had been broken. Internal communications were intact, but power was disrupted to ordnance, ammo hoists and fire directors, which required gunners to switch to local manual controls for tracking, train and elevation. Repair parties sought to save their ship and aid casualties.

Little more than a minute later, the enemy unleashed their fantastic new weapon—an *Oka*. Only moments beforehand, lookouts watched the "mother craft" launch her rocket-propelled progeny, which the destroyer's captain described as "a small, mid-wing job with no projections, large fuselage, stubby wings and painted light blue-grey or aluminum."[46]

"It is difficult to say what it was that hit the *DD 733*," reported Lt. James M. Stewart, skipper of *LSM(R) 189*. "This officer personally saw what appeared to be two (2) planes orbiting in a northerly direction from the *DD 733* and then suddenly, what appeared to be one plane, accelerated at a terrific rate, too fast for us to fire at. This plane dove at an angle approximately 30 degrees, starting at about four miles away. Since we had no air search radar, the above statements are merely my own conclusions.... What it was that had such acceleration as the craft which hit the DD, has never before been observed by this officer."[47]

Stewart recalled the strange craft "proceeded in undulating spurts"[48] during its fatal run. About 1446, the *Oka* hit the destroyer at the waterline, abreast the number one fireroom, and caused a powerful explosion. The shock jolted the *Abele* and she buckled when her keel separated. The destroyer rapidly broke in half, her bow section listing to port on parting from her stern section. The midship next settled in the water as the tips of her bow and stern rose skyward. Less than two minutes after the *Oka*'s crash, the destroyer disappeared below the waves with scores of her crew trapped inside and many more left struggling on the ocean's surface. USS *Mannert L. Abele* lost 79 killed and 35 wounded.

As the destroyer sank, *LSM(R)s* 189 and 190 proceeded full speed to assist her survivors. Enemy planes, meanwhile, pressed attacks on the two rocketships as some strafed the desperate men in the water, many clinging to rafts and wreckage.

At 1502, another Kate dive-bomber approached low over the water from the north, and *LSM(R)* 189's gunners fired as the plane swung right to left across her bow. Once abeam, the plane winged over on its left in a dive and commenced strafing. Despite heavy AA fire, the plane's momentum brought it crashing abaft the rocketship's conning tower, where it carried away the flagbag and all ladders to the Conn, ruptured fire mains, and tore up eight loaded rocket launchers amidships.

"Just prior to the plane crash, when it was inevitable that we were going to be hit, the order was given to 'hit the deck'" recalled Lt. Stewart. "This order probably led to saving many personnel as they were able to avoid flying shrapnel." Continuing, "When we went to general quarters we had several fire hoses running and playing on the deck. The plane that crashed us dumped her entire gas tank on the deck and severed quite a number of our electric wiring circuits. It is considered quite a 'lucky break' that no fire developed and the gasoline was washed off immediately."[49] *LSM(R)* 189 had a full deckload of assembled and fused rockets, among which sixteen rocket launchers were damaged and ten rockets clipped and dislodged. Rockets were also drenched with the plane's gasoline but none caught fire or detonated.[50] Two men were blown into the water and rescued, and two other sailors reported to the Pharmacist's Mate with shrapnel wounds and possible internal injuries. Also recovered from the sea was the body of the Japanese airman who flew his plane into the rocketship.

At 1513, a Val next commenced a suicide dive on *LSM(R)* 190. Both rocketships put up heavy AA fire and shared knocking the plane down, causing it to barely miss its target. All told, the gunners aboard *LSM(R)* 190 were credited with downing two and a half planes.[51]

As soon as skies over RPS 14 seemed clear of Japanese planes, *LSM(R)s* 189 and 190 resumed full speeds to where the *Abele* had sunk. Rescue efforts were twice interrupted, nevertheless, by probing Japanese aircraft. "Underway on zigzag course as enemy plane closes, opened fire with all guns," noted Ensign F. Donald Moore, *LSM(R)* 189 Gunnery Officer. "Plane veered away from heavy AA (ours & *LSM(R)* 190). Guns all on extreme alert because we do not have air search radar."[52] By 1530, some forty-five minutes after *Abele* went down, oil-soaked men began to be lifted from the sea, and would continue to be over the following two hours. The sheer numbers overwhelmed the two rocket ships. An estimated 150 men, including the destroyer's captain and medical officer, were brought aboard *LSM(R)* 189, and 108 men were recovered by *LSM(R)* 190.

Those needing emergency medical care severely taxed ships' resources. The stock of ten complete sets of landing party clothing were depleted quickly, as well as blankets, long underwear, and Red Cross survivor kits from ship's supply. Their Sick Bays' medical supplies were practically exhausted, too. The rocketships' officers and men gave freely from their sea bags and ditty bags, meanwhile, although much was ruined by the bunker oil that soaked the survivors.

Emphasizing this problem, Lieutenant Commander John H. Fulweiler, Commander LSM(R) Group 27, commented days later,

The rescue of survivors as detailed in this [Lt. Stewart's] report, is the fourth such rescue of more than seventy-five (75) men that ships of this Group have carried out since 26 March 1945. In each instance the lack of adequate clothing for the survivors proved a real hardship. It is therefore recommended that LSM(R)s be each provided with 100 sets of survivors clothing—coveralls, underwear, socks and shoes are minimum requirements. The present allowance of clothing in the landing force equipment is inadequate for this purpose.[53]

On behalf of his ship and crew, Commander Parker wrote letters of appreciation to the LSM(R)s' skippers. "Dear Captain: I want to thank you, your officers, and crew for the splendid job of fishing us out of the water, and the care you gave us while aboard. It was with great pride as we watched your performance during the attack. All of the *Abele* are proud to have worked with you. Best of luck and warmest personal regards to yourself, your officers and crew. Sincerely, Allen B. Parker, Commander."[54]

In his final official report, the destroyer commander underscored his gratitude as a metaphor, widely quoted[55] since: "It is also the opinion of this officer that the small LSM(R)s are literally worth their weight in gold as support vessels...,"[56] and added, "There is no doubt in my mind that the LSM(R)s are excellent support vessels. I wish we had had more."[57]

Lt. Stewart also praised his officers and men. "I can truthfully say that I am, indeed, proud of this crew and their complete disregard of self interest in order to take care of a job at hand."

When we arrived at the place where the survivors from the *DD 733* were, all hands not directly on battle stations rigged cargo nets, accommodation ladders, Jacob's ladders, and life rings and pulled in survivors from 1527 until 1645. All men stayed on their battle stations and kept the most vigilant lookout and had their guns firing whenever enemy planes closed in. The crew realized throughout the entire action that their primary mission was to stay on the battle stations and keep the guns firing. It was a real tribute to the men, the way they stayed there when their humanitarian interest drew them toward the rescue of survivors.[58]

Commander Dennis L. Francis, Commander LSM Flotilla Nine, cited, "On 12 April 1945 while on patrol with *LSM(R) 190* and *DD 733*, you shot down three (3) Japanese planes and assisted in destroying another. The planes were identified as (1) VAL and (2) KATES. The plane you assisted the *190* in destroying was (1) VAL. You are hereby commended. Well done. You are entitled ... to paint three and one half (3½) Japanese flag emblems on your conning tower as credit for destruction of these planes."[59]

Commodore Frederick Moosbrugger also remarked, "The performance of the *LSM(R) 189*, as described in this excellent report, is an example of the courageous and efficient support and rescue service being rendered by vessels of that type on the Radar Picket Stations. The Commanding Officer, *LSM(R) 189*, is commended on the Combat Efficiency of his ship and on its outstanding service in rescuing the survivors of the *Mannert L. Abele*."[60]

Lieutenant James M. Stewart was awarded the Silver Star Medal.[61]

USS *LSM(R) 189* was awarded the Navy Unit Commendation,

For outstanding heroism in action against enemy Japanese aircraft and suicide boats. While on an aggressive patrol off Okinawa, she engaged and destroyed three enemy suicide boats and assisted other vessels in repelling a determined air attack. Later, while on a radar picket station engaged in a task far exceeding her designed employment, while in company with a destroyer and another LSM(R), without air coverage, she successfully brought down three of eight attacking planes. When the accompanying destroyer was violently attacked and sunk within two minutes, the *LSM(R) 189* proceeded at full speed to pick up survivors. While courageously fighting off further attacks during which she herself was hit by a suicide plane, she courageously rescued one hundred and fifty men of the destroyer's crew. Her courageous determination and effort were in keeping with the highest traditions of the United States Naval Service.[62]

Kikusui *Raid No.* 3

Asserting air control over the American forces was the prime objective of the third *Kikusui* attack of Operation *Ten-Go*, comprising more than 400 aircraft during 15–16 April, 1945. Planes of various types including 160 Special Attack or Kamikaze fighters and bombers sought U.S. carrier forces while other smaller units of planes were sent to attack airfields on Okinawa. But the largest numbers of Special Attack planes by far were those specifically designated to strike the Radar Picket ships. Escorted by a handful of fighters, virtually all others were suicide planes. "With air superiority attained," asserted the Japanese Fifth Air Fleet, "the way was now clear to carry out *Kikusui* Raid No. 3 and the annihilation of enemy ships off Okinawa, and to carry on further, the anti-task force attack."[63] Fourteen U.S. ships were damaged and one sunk, causing over 600 American sailors killed, wounded and missing.[64]

RPS 14: 16 April 1945

At Radar Picket Station 14 on 16 April 1945, picket supports USS *LSM(R) 191* (Lt. John W. Loyer, USNR) and *LCS 34*, with destroyers *Pringle DD 477* and *Hobson DMS 26* as OTC, patrolled in a box formation, turning counter-clockwise every half-hour on the intercardinal points.

The morning was bright and sunny, an almost cloudless blue sky, and a windless calm sea.

About 0815, *Pringle's* radar tracked several groups of aircraft to the north and northwest, and *Hobson* identified two other bogies about 20 miles away to the northeast. However, despite requests to the fighter director team on *Eldorado AGC 11* in Hagushi Anchorage, no CAP coverage seemed in prospect.

LSM(R) 191 and *LCS 34* went to General Quarters by 0830, and *Hobson* ordered the two support ships to take cover about ten miles away in light haze southwest of RPS 14, with instructions to act at their own discretion. For the next hour, the two amphibians could only watch from afar, helplessly, as a fateful drama unfolded. *Hobson* and *Pringle*, meanwhile, assumed column formation and increased speeds to 20 knots and radioed tactical maneuvers over TBS (Talk Between Ships).

By 0840, *Hobson* reported two large bogie raids approaching from the northwest at 40 miles and again requested fighter cover. In minutes, the two enemy groups split up and began circling the picket station, later estimated between ten and fifteen aircraft. *Hobson* renewed her call for CAP, but none was forthcoming.

At 0851, the destroyers' combined fire downed the first attacker, then drove off a Val about 0905. Ships' CICs now plotted five separate enemy raids from the north, four within 15 miles and the other closing at about 25 miles.

As Japanese planes circled RPS 14, three Vals were seen about 8000 yards to the east, but variously closing and opening ranges. Coyly, the trio weaved in the distance as if taunting the destroyers, yet effectively tiring ships' gunners who repeatedly checked fire.

When the three planes finally veered to attack, the trailing and lowest Val flew into a 5-inch shell burst, causing it to spin and crash. The two other Vals stayed on course, then one climbed to about 1000 feet while the other descended low over the water. The higher Val started a shallow suicide glide, estimated at 175 knots, and pursued *Pringle* despite evasive maneuvers and intense AA fire. The enemy bomber rapidly plunged into the destroyer about 0920, causing a violent explosion that buckled her keel, covered the ship in smoke, and sank the *Pringle* within five minutes.

Another Val approached *Hobson* from dead ahead, then circled *Pringle*'s survivors as if it wanted to strafe the water-borne sailors, but heavy AA fire drove it and one other attacker away. Once again, *Hobson* requested CAP cover, but no fighters seemed available.

Still some ten miles on the horizon, *LSM(R) 191* and *LCS 34* were ignored or overlooked by friends and foes alike, but they now rang up flank speeds to rescue survivors.

The Val that was driven away from strafing *Pringle*'s survivors is believed to be the same bomber that made the attack run on *Hobson* at 0945. Diving at the destroyer, it missed and splashed close aboard, but its bomb let loose and penetrated the main deck to explode in the forward engine room. The plane's forward momentum also carried its separated engine into the *Hobson* to lodge in her deckhouse amidships. *Hobson* radioed *Eldorado* about *Pringle*'s loss and her own damages, and requested support to aid survivors and casualties.

Over the next several minutes, 6 more enemy planes were counted orbiting *Hobson*, identified as a twin-engine Betty bomber among Val dive bombers, but all were either driven off by gunfire or remained out of range. From among these half-dozen Japanese bombers, however, may have been the 3 Vals that next intercepted *LSM(R) 191* and *LCS 34* with separate attack runs beginning 0945.

"Doc" Joe B. Smith, the Pharmacists Mate 2c in *LSM(R) 191* recalled, "As we were going, full speed, one Kamikaze spotted us and came straight for us, and every gun we had was pouring lead into him, and he just kept coming. I had a full view of this because my assignment for General Quarters was with the Forward Damage Control party just behind the 40mm gun tub, on the bow of the ship." He continued,

> ... our 1c Gunners Mate was also assigned to this station, and they had installed a .50 caliber machine gun on a port stanchion for him to use. He had never had an opportunity to use it, but I always told him that if and when he did, I would be his ammunition man. (He never needed one because if I remember, the ammunition was belted and came out of a box on the deck). But, anyway, I was at his side watching them pouring lead into that plane until it got so close that I was sure he was going to hit us, and I made a dive for cover (crouched down on the deck behind the forward gun tub), but [he] didn't waver.[65]

The gunners on the rocketship's bow single 40mm were also ducking for cover, expecting a fatal Kamikaze crash at any moment—except S2c Roy Moceri. "I was practically paralyzed," he recalled, sitting behind his single-barreled, anti-aircraft Bofors gun. As he tracked the Japanese plane in his line of sight flying about 50 feet above the water, he knew only two clips were loaded in his gun for a total of eight rounds. "I give the utmost credit to Roy Moceri's quick thinking," affirmed Lt. (jg) Laurie R. Russell, the Gunnery Officer for *LSM(R) 191*.

> Roy told me just after the incident that as round after round was hitting the Val's engine, he could see that this was not going to divert the planes' path. So, in his words, 'I just cranked the gun control a little to the

left to direct the shots to the right wing.' His action broke off the right wing, flipping the plane over and probably saving the *191*. I saw no flame on the Val, which hit the sea hard aport. As we passed the plane [in the water], I could see the pilot from my excellent vantage point on the port side of the upper deck of the conning tower. He was wearing a parachute which opened partially in the water.[66]

The plane's starboard wing was seen crumpling perhaps 1200 yards away or even closer. As gunfire riddled the plane's fuselage, some recalled seeing the plane explode after taking rounds near its gasoline tank. *LSM(R) 191*'s skipper succinctly noted in his report: "While proceeding to pick up survivors, this ship shot down one Val which approached from dead ahead in a suicide dive, and landed fifteen yards off the port beam."[67] Official credit for splashing this plane was given to the gunners of *LSM(R) 191*.[68] Seaman 2c Roy Moceri was later awarded the Commendation Ribbon, citing him in part for "Demonstrating outstanding skill and courage in the face of extended enemy strafing and suicide plane attacks, he caused an accurate and effective fire to be directed onto an attacking suicide plane until it was destroyed."[69]

Ten minutes later, the next Val approached low off the port quarter and closed to about 2500 yards. "[We] opened fire with 5" gun on second Val attacking from astern [and] scored possible hits," continued Lt. Loyer. Trailing smoke, the Val broke off the attack by veering off and last observed slowly losing altitude then disappearing over the horizon. This plane was credited as a "probable" kill, while a third Val attack was subsequently repulsed.[70]

At 1000, *Hobson* commenced generating smoke at the request of a friendly plane attempting to identify the destroyer, but smoke was soon shut down when several enemy planes closed, instead. By 1025, *Hobson*'s skipper finally declared, "All enemy planes have departed area."

About 1045, the three picket ships slowly moved toward *Pringle*'s survivors, whose commanding officer, executive officer, and medical officer were among those rescued by *LCS 34*. Numerous life rafts were deployed as a pair of sharks was seen heading toward men in the water, but rescue work continued until every possible survivor was recovered. *LSM(R) 191* picked up 28 men from *Pringle* and 4 men from *Hobson*; *LCS 34* in turn recovered 87 men from *Pringle*. All told, 258 officers and men were finally rescued.

"The day of April 16, 1945 was a terrible day for me," confided "Doc" Joe B. Smith, the Pharmacists Mate on *LSM(R) 191*.

> We had been up and down to General Quarters most of the night. Even though we were on the same Station with the *Hobson* and *Pringle*, we were not real close to them, but over the horizon from them.
>
> Of course, we were called to General Quarters when these planes were coming in, and we were on our way toward the *Pringle* and *Hobson* when we got the word that the *Pringle* had been sunk and that survivors were in the water. We soon arrived at the site where the survivors were and started getting them aboard.
>
> The *Hobson* was sitting dead in the water, I think, but the *LCS 34* was there picking up survivors also. The first ones we brought aboard had been blown over the side of the *Hobson*…. The rest of the day was like a nightmare for me … everyone yelling for the Doc, and I really wasn't ready for anything like this. I spent quite a bit of time with a sailor that was severely burned, arms looked like he had been scalded. I gave him a shot of morphine and tried to get him wrapped in Vaseline gauze. Many were in shock. The whole crew pitched in and helped as much as they could, but I was sure relieved when that PCE came alongside that afternoon to pick up all the casualties to transport to a hospital ship. I'll never forget the inadequacy I felt that day. We really should have had a Doctor aboard.[71]

Ocean sweeps were made for drifting sailors, and destroyer *Isherwood DD 520* joined the search.

"Five survivors from the sunken *Pringle* swim toward *LSM(R) 191* on 16 April 1945 after Japanese air attacks on RPS 14 (U.S. Navy photograph by Lt. [jg] Laurie R. Russell).

By 1130, *Hobson* departed RPS 14 followed in column astern by *LSM(R) 191* and *LCS 34*. *Isherwood* also joined the trio, and just-arriving *J. William Ditter DM 31* fell in to provide additional gunfire support in transit. For a time, two friendly fighter planes circled overhead as the vessels steamed with survivors toward the Hagushi transport area.

Two days later, *Hobson* sent a secret message to CTF 51 recapping the air attacks on RPS 14, and added, "Performance by gunboats outstanding in defending themselves and rescuing survivors."[72]

Afterwards, in remarks assessing *Hobson*'s performance, the Commander of Mine Division 58 sternly rebuked the destroyer's commanding officer: "For the air action of 16 April 1945, it is considered that the additional gun power of *LSM(R) 191* and *LCS(G) 34* [*sic*] was too lightly regarded and that they should have been retained in the immediate vicinity and disposed for the best mutual gun support. They were apparently dispensed with because of speed limitations. It is considered that a speed in excess of that necessary to keep the battery unmasked is useless and that high-speed violent evasion maneuvers are futile in avoiding suicide plane attacks."[73]

At the very height of the 16 April Japanese air attacks, at 0945 Vice Admiral Turner radioed a fleet wide message praising the radar picket ships at Okinawa:

> This dispatch is for the purpose of giving special honor to the ships who are and have been on radar picket duty. DD types, DEs, LSMs and LCS types are all on this distant guard whose work is doing so much to help our troops make this operation a success. We are very proud of the magnificent courage and effectiveness with which these vessels have discharged their difficult and hazardous tasks…. Pass this on

***Hobson, LCS 34,* and *LSM(R) 191* search for *Pringle* survivors on 16 April 1945 after Japanese air attacks on RPS 14 (the original photograph is blurry) (U.S. Navy photograph by Lt. [jg] Laurie R. Russell).**

to captains whose ships have been sunk in this service…. Lt. Gen. Buckner joins VAdm. Turner in this tribute.[74]

RPS 10: 18 April 1945

At Radar Picket Station 10 on 18 April 1945, picket supports USS *LSM(R) 194* (Lt. Allan M. Hirshberg, USNR) and USS *LSM(R) 195* (Lt. William E. Woodson, USNR) patrolled with destroyer *Morrison DD 560.*

All ships' logs were lost when these three ships were subsequently sunk in early May 1945, but Commander Francis twice reported an otherwise unknown and un-credited air attack this day: "18 April 1945, while on radar picket station 10 right, *LSM(R) 194* opened fire at 1914 on a low flying Betty. The plane crashed into sea a few seconds later"; and, "*LSM(R) 194* while patrolling at RPS 10 on 18 April 1945, fired on a Betty with 5"/38 and observed the plane going down in flames."[75]

Lt. Hirshberg later commented, however, "Fire control of weapons aboard the USS *LSM(R) 194* was found inadequate for night firing to a degree which made the ship practically defenseless in darkness or in conditions of low visibility. If rocket ships are to be used for patrol or escort missions as in the past a system of radar fire control will be advisable."[76]

Intermediate Radar Picket Stations

Beginning 20 April 1945, Screen Commander Commodore Moosbrugger[77] assigned LSM(R)s and LCSs as supplemental "Radar Relay Ships" or "Linking Ships," stationed ⅔ distances from Point Bolo to Radar Picket Stations 1, 2, 3, 4, and 14. Ships patrolling these unnumbered, intermediate picket stations were to track, interdict, and warn of enemy planes breaking through the outer radar picket lines en route Okinawa. LCSs were withdrawn before the end of the month, but LSM(R)s continued these patrols albeit re-designated "Survivors and Medical Ships" on 30 April. Foreseen embarking medical officers under Commander Francis' new Operation Plan #2103–45,[78] this plan was only tentatively implemented[79] when these intermediate stations were deactivated after 2 May 1945.

2/3 RPS 14: 20 April 1945

At 2/3 Radar Picket Station 14 on 20 April 1945, USS *LSM(R) 199* (Lt. Charles D. Cobb, USNR) was the lone "radar relay ship" patrolling about 50 miles from Point Bolo. The rocketship steamed a box-like course, turning on each intercardinal compass point NW-NE-SE-SW every thirty minutes.

At 1815, ship's radar picked up a bogie approaching from due west, and 45 minutes later a lone bomber was sighted. *LSM(R) 199* immediately changed speed to standard and opened fire on the plane at 1858. The rocketship's watch officer reported, "[A] Jap torpedo bomber launched a torpedo which crossed ship's bow."[80] The plane's torpedo missed its mark as did the ship's 20mm, 40mm, and 5-inch gunfire as the bomber flew by.

Commander Francis later noted, "At 1915 *LSM(R) 199* reported being attacked by a single HAP [*sic*] that dropped a torpedo or 'Buzz' bomb while on station. Reported no damage or casualties." Lieutenant Commander Fulweiler noted elsewhere, "On arriving at station [*LSM(R)*] *199* was attacked by a Betty which released a *Baka* that missed the ship."[81] During this twenty-four hour period, reports warned the Japanese were launching concerted torpedo attacks on U.S. ships around Okinawa.[82]

Radar Picket Station Objections

A fortnight after the LSM(R)s began patrolling the radar picket stations, Commander Francis formally objected.

> LSM(R)s of this command have been assigned to act as radar picket fire support ships during the period of time covered by this report. It is believed that these ships are not particularly suited for this duty. Since their primary function is to deliver rockets during invasion operations, it seems feasible that subjecting them to continual air attack will allow a secondary duty to seriously effect [*sic*] their ability to perform their primary function due to mechanical damage. They have no great value in combating enemy air craft due to the absence of air search radar, adequate director control for the 5"/38 main battery, and director control for the 40 MM single guns. The fact that they carry a considerable quantity of high explosive rockets in their magazines presents another hazard. In general, it is believed that assigning them to this duty should be avoided since it means risking the operation of a limited number of specialized landing craft whose primary function is more closely coincident with screening operations.

In the same report, Comdr. Francis reiterated, "Against aircraft, the LSM(R) is well suited to care for itself against occasional attack only. The fire control and amount and type of automatic weapons present is not satisfactory to counteract continual heavy air attack." Underscoring his point a final time, "LSM(R)s should be used more frequently for rocket harassing and close patrol of enemy beaches, prior to an attack. LSM(R)s should not be used as fire support ships for radar pickets against enemy aircraft."[83]

RPS 14: 22 April 1945

At Radar Picket Station 14 on 22 April 1945, USS *LSM(R) 195* (Lt. William E. Woodson, USNR) was patrol guide in the center of a large 3000-yard circular formation steaming 10 knots. Destroyer *Wickes DD 578* and *LCS 83* were stationed off the port and starboard bow respectively; *LCS 15* stood off the port beam; destroyer *Van Valkenburgh DD 656* as OTC alternated between the starboard beam and quarter; and *LCS 37* trailed almost directly astern. Visibility was almost unlimited with calm seas, light winds, and billows of high cumulus clouds.

CTF 51 in *Eldorado AGC 11* warned of a probable air attack and General Quarters was sounded at 1620. By 1745, *Wickes* vectored a ten-plane Combat Air Patrol toward an estimated 9–10 enemy planes coming from the northeast. Over the next 15 minutes or so, Marine fighters engaged the Japanese in dogfights and broke up all but two of the raiders—both Val dive bombers—which burst through the melee. Heavy ships' AA fire drove one Val off, but the other enemy bomber pressed its attack until it started smoking, then tried to escape eastward as the CAP chased it down.

By 1820, the formation of picket ships resumed their northwesterly base course en route nighttime RPS 14, but eight minutes later a lone bogie also penetrated the CAP fighter screen. Ships' radars picked up the raider less than ten miles away to the west-northwest, and virtually every gun commenced firing on the plane, variously identified as a Nate or a Val.

Approaching from the setting sun, the Japanese dive bomber made a gliding run from 3000 feet at an estimated speed of 165 knots. Seeking the closest American target, 40mm rounds were seen bursting along its fuselage as the plane crashed into *LCS 15*'s port side after the superstructure, at about 1831. One or more bombs carried by the aircraft exploded and blew holes in both the port and starboard sides of the ship, above and below the waterline. Due to overwhelming burning and flooding, the ship listed rapidly to starboard with no chance to save her. At 1832, her captain passed the word for all hands to abandon ship. Thirty seconds later she capsized, and in two minutes the gunboat sank stern first. *LCS 15* lost 15 killed and eleven wounded.

Wickes commenced circling the area to ward off further air or sea attacks while the other picket ships turned to rescue and recovery. The sun had set when all the survivors that could be found were recovered, after which *LCSs 37* and *83* closed alongside *Van Valkenburgh* to transfer the men for medical care and rest. With increasing twilight, however, it was imperative to blackout all ships' lights, so *LSM(R) 195* retained the recovered officer and twelve enlisted men until later transfer.

Commanding Officer of USS *LCS(L)(3) 15* wrote a letter thanking USS *LSM(R) 195*:

The officers and crew of my command wish to extend you, your officers and crew our most sincere thanks. The prompt rescue and wonderful treatment given all hands, both wounded and otherwise, will always be a comforting thought. Again our thanks, appreciation and the best of luck to you and your ship. N. H. Brower, Lieut., USNR, Commanding.[84]

RPS 10: 22 April 1945

At Radar Picket Station 10 on 22 April 1945, USS *LSM(R) 193* (Lt. Donald E. Boynton, USNR) and *LCS 34* were stationed 7 miles north and south of destroyer *Wadsworth DD 516*, respectively, patrolling various courses and speeds. Skies were partly cloudy throughout the day, with light winds and calm seas.

About 1813, a group of bogies was picked up on radar 42 miles due west and approaching rapidly. *Wadsworth* remained 6 miles away while *LSM(R) 193* and *LCS 34* closed in column formation for mutual fire support. "We looked like easy pickings," later remarked Ensign Paul S. Vaitses, Jr., *LSM(R) 193*'s Executive Officer.

Three planes closed the picket ships, variously identified as Val or Judy single engine bombers.[85] The destroyer shot down one plane about 1830, and the others split up: one headed for *LSM(R) 193*, and the other for *Wadsworth*. "Circling out of range, he disappeared momentarily in the evening dusk," continued Ens. Vaitses. "An instant later, he appeared directly astern and high above us bearing in for the kill."

At 1835, "On orders from the skipper, our 5" mount hammered determinedly at the Jap. The first couple of fuze settings were excellent," added Vaitses. Firing 9 rounds, the bomber retired in a northerly direction, last observed smoking and considered damaged. "As he fled through our farewell barrage, our gun crews and topside personnel broke into a lusty cheer."[86]

The other plane, meanwhile, sped southwest, climbed, and then returned, aiming directly abaft the destroyer. As it passed over *Wadsworth*'s stern, the plane's momentum caused it to crash in the water nearby with a tremendous explosion.[87]

RPS 2: 24 April 1945

At nighttime RPS 2 on 24 April 1945, USS *LSM(R) 189* (Lt. James M. Stewart, USNR) was followed a thousand yards astern by USS *LSM(R) 194* (Lt. Allan M. Hirschberg, USNR), and *LCSs 25, 61,* and *87* patrolled in column a thousand yards to the west. Destroyers *Bennion DD 662* and *Russell DD 414*, meanwhile, steamed in column on a box patrol around the picket support ships. The formation patrolled on courses NW-SE, changing direction every 20 minutes.

That evening at 1944, *LSM(R) 189* picked up an unidentified target on her radar at 900 yards north-northwest. Sounding General Quarters, the rocketship changed course and moved toward the object, now lying dead ahead, but in moments it suddenly disappeared. Perplexed, patrols resumed when, ten minutes later, her radar picked up another target, this time 1400 yards due north. Changing course once more, the rocketship made a run at the object and closed 1200 yards when the mysterious target altered course, opened distance, then disappeared from radar entirely. Twice confounded, *LSM(R) 189* secured from GQ by 2035. Unknowingly, they had encountered the legendary apparition known as "The Galloping Ghost of Nansei Shoto," an erratic radar mirage induced by unique topographical and atmospheric phenomena.[88]

Kikusui *Raid No. 4*

From 27–28 April 1945, *Kikusui* Raid No. 4 of Operation *Ten-Go* comprised as many as 318 aircraft of all types, including 165 army and navy Kamikazes.[89] Japanese air attacks damaged ten U.S. ships and caused 200 American sailors killed, wounded, and missing.[90]

RPS 10: 27 April 1945

At Radar Picket Station 10 on 27 April 1945, USS *LSM(R) 193* (Lt. Donald E. Boynton, USNR) and USS *LSM(R) 195* (Lt. William E. Woodson, USNR) patrolled astern the column guide *Macomb DMS 23* with *J. William Ditter DM 31* as OTC. Column intervals ranged from 500 to 1000 yards while patrolling a box-like course at ten knots, making counterclockwise turns on compass cardinal points North-West-South-East.

In the morning twilight, predawn visibility was poor under low overcast skies. Seas were choppy but with light winds.

Before sunrise, radar picked up a bogie just after 0500 about 30 miles northwest. In 15 minutes, the picket ships went to General Quarters as three or four aircraft closed and then split up about ten miles away. One plane, possibly a Kate or Jill, dropped radar-interfering chaff or "Window," and was thought to be the control aircraft with air-borne radar.

Their attack commenced about 0525, when a Val dove in a steep glide at *Macomb*, but missed and crashed in her wake. Ships' anti-aircraft fire destroyed one other Val that burst into flames and fell to the sea.

"That left one more to be accounted for," recalled Ensign Paul S. Vaitses, Jr., Executive Officer in *LSM(R) 193*. "There he was, way up, flitting in and out among the clouds. He had obviously seen his two companions go down to death in their futile missions. He was evidently trying to decide if this was the time and place for him to make his sacrifice." With the rising sun, this Kate or Val was shot down after five-inch tracers burst behind and beneath the plane, causing it to turn over in a steep spiral into the water at 0555.[91] One other orbiting plane was seen retiring to the south, but it was apparently shot down later by the CAP.

LSM(R) 193 was credited with one of the splashes, cited by Lieutenant Commander John H. Fulweiler, Commander LSM(R) Group Twenty-Seven. "While on patrol on the morning of April 28th [*sic*], [*LSM(R)*] *193* was attacked by two Vals and one Kate which came in from 10,000 feet. The ship succeeded in shooting down one Val and escaping injury."[92]

RPS 14: 28 April 1945

At nighttime Radar Picket Station 14 on 28 April 1945, USS *LSM(R) 196* (Lt. Dennis D. O'Callaghan, USNR) was guide ship followed in column astern by *LCSs 62* and *64*. Destroyers *Bache DD 470* and *Irwin DD 794* as OTC were stationed some 2000 yards off the column's port and starboard flanks, respectively. Patrol courses alternated northeast and southwest each half hour.

Weather was ideal with moderate seas, brilliant moonlight, and clear skies.

At 0035, *Irwin*'s radar detected bogies orbiting 16 miles to the east, while *Bache* picked up bogies 38 miles to the south. General Quarters sounded, and in about thirty minutes the OTC identified what appeared to be two or three Betty bombers dropping "Window" anti-radar chaff. Ships' AA fire commenced when the enemy planes closed to four miles. *LSM(R) 196* fired on a twin-engine bomber that passed low over her bow, although no damage was observed. Fire ceased at 0112 as the Japanese aircraft escaped southward.

Picket patrols resumed, but GQ sounded once more about 0330 as two bogies closed, one 12 miles south and the other nine miles southeast. In twenty minutes, *LSM(R) 196* opened fire on a low-flying plane coming from astern. *Irwin* reported it was a Betty bomber by its reflection in the moonlight, but it disappeared to the northwest regardless. Signalman Leonard VanOteghem wrote in his diary afterwards, "Attacked by two Jap Sallys [and] believed to have crippled one."[93]

2/3 RPS 4: 28 April 1945

At 2/3 Radar Picket Station 4 on 28 April 1945, USS *LSM(R) 197* (Lt. John M. Cooper, USN) was detached as the radar relay "linking ship" this morning, about twelve to fourteen miles southwest of RPS 4 proper. While returning to Hagushi Anchorage, the rocketship's skipper described encountering heavy air attacks.

> At 1820, an enemy plane which had apparently picked us as his target, and was preparing to make a howling dive, was splashed by friendly fighters about 600 yards off our port bow. This was about five (5) miles north of Ie Shima. We were unable to fire without endangering our planes.
> At about 1850 an enemy plane made a suicide dive at a destroyer going on a reciprocal course bearing 230 relative, three (3) miles from us and crashing. No hit was made; again we could not fire without endangering our own forces.
> At about 1900 three (3) low flying enemy planes attacked a destroyer, at 055 relative, six (6) miles and were shot down by the destroyer. The distance was too great for us to fire.[94]

Radioman Clyde Blue in *LSM(R) 197* offered another perspective:

> Have had Bogies around all day. This afternoon we had orders to report back to Oki. On our way back, we had five Jap planes shot down around us. We didn't fire a shot at them. We sure are lucky. One Oscar glided right across our fantail and tried a suicide crash on a "Can." It just ticked one of its stacks and caused very little damage. I don't see how they miss in these dives but very few of them ever hit one of the "Cans." Every Jap plane is a suicide plane now. We have some Japs flying over us now and are shooting at them [but] we haven't hit any of them yet.[95]

RPS 10: 28 April 1945

At Radar Picket Station 10 on 28 April 1945, USS *LSM(R) 195* (Lt. William E. Woodson, USNR) was guide ship ("Fleet Center") of the "Able Victor" anti-aircraft defense cruising formation, and *LCS 53* followed two thousand yards astern at ten knots. Leading the large "Y" formation, destroyers *J. William Ditter DM 31* and *Brown DD 546* as OTC were stationed port and starboard, respectively.

Weather offered good visibility under scattered but low stratocumulus clouds, and seas were calm with light winds.

After CAP fighters returned to base about 1700, reports warned of Japanese raids approaching from the north, west, and southwest. Sunset was 1904, and at dusk four groups of 3–4 planes neared RPS 10 from the north and another group closed from the northwest. The destroyers took evasive actions and fired on a plane that crashed about 1936, but the other aircraft opened distances beyond range. Soon afterwards, a full moon rose at 1943.

Around 2030, another group of 4 to 6 bogies closed RPS 10, but variously reported to the south, west, and northwest at differing ranges and altitudes. At first, the planes circled the picket ships in apparent attempts to draw and divide fire, then finally pressed attacks between 2055 and 2151. All picket ships commenced firing while taking evasive maneuvers, with lines of fire crisscrossing and shells falling in threatening patterns amongst one another. Torpedoes were launched as well, but all missed their targets. More enemy planes approached the picket station, which made tracking and identification difficult during the melees. One plane dove close aboard the *Ditter* into the sea, another barely missed *LCS 53*, and one more faded from radar. The remainder were thought to be splashed, however.

Afterwards, Lieutenant Commander John H. Fulweiler, Commander LSM(R) Group Twenty-Seven, cited, "In the evening of the 29th [*sic*], *LSM(R) 195* was attacked by suicide planes (2 Vals and 2 Kates) at very low level, she escaped damage."[96]

RPS 12: 28 April 1945

At Radar Picket Station 12 on 28 April 1945, USS *LSM(R) 192* (Lt. Neal B. Hadsell, USNR) was followed in column astern by USS *LSM(R) 190* (Lt. Richard H. Saunders, USNR), and both ordered to maintain close distances with destroyer *Wadsworth DD 516* as OTC.

The evening's weather was partly cloudy with light winds and a moderate sea. A full moon rose some 45 minutes after sunset. At dusk, two Vals closing the picket station were shot down by CAP fighters.

About 2007, two bogies closed the picket ships, then split right and left after taking fire. *LSM(R) 190* was nearest a Kate sweeping right, and commenced firing as the bomber attempted to turn and press his attack run on the starboard quarter. The rocketship's Executive Officer Lt.(jg) George T. Harmon recalled, "…we were attacked, but this time we put a five inch shell into the bomber that was diving at us. He exploded in mid-air and fell into the water about 150 feet off our bow."[97] *Wadsworth* confirmed, "This maneuver brought him in close vicinity of *LSM190* [*sic*], where he was seen to splash in flames."[98] The other bomber, possibly a single engine Myrt, dropped a torpedo that missed *Wadsworth*. It dove at the destroyer but glanced into the sea, causing only minor damage and no casualties.

Over the next 90 minutes, *Wadsworth* maneuvered radically against several more, albeit intermittent, air attacks of one or two planes at a time. However, the destroyer ranged far from the mutual fire support of the two rocketships until finally ceasing fire by 2136.[99]

Storekeeper Robert W. Landis in *LSM(R) 192* wrote in his diary that evening, "Frequent nuisance raids keep us at GQ. The destroyer has been taking many strafing attacks. The *LSM(R) 190* shot one out of the sky. The pilot tried to crash us as he came down but he missed and went into the water just off our stern."[100]

2/3 RPS 14: 30 April 1945

At 2/3 Radar Picket Station 14 on 30 April 1945, USS *LSM(R) 196* (Lt. Dennis D. O'Callaghan, USNR) patrolled alone as a nighttime "radar relay" picket ship.

Ensigns David Mallery and Jack Shedd, respective Communications and Engineering Officers, described a surprise:

> On the night of April 30th about 0300, amid several contacts reported by radio from the destroyer in charge, a large Jap bomber, most likely a Betty, was suddenly spotted veering in from astern, flying almost low enough to scrape our conn. Then, it banked sharply away from us and headed straight abeam from us. Before it was a mile away, our five inch gun got some solid hits and the plane was seen to shatter into flaming fragments and crash into the sea.[101]

Signalman Leonard VanOteghem also recorded in his diary, "April 30, 1945—Patrol at RP 14, 3 a.m. in the morning a Jap twin engined bomber, believed to be a Sally, closed in on us and Eddie Shaeffer S2c brought it down with his 20mm. This was the second plane we were credited with."[102] Ammunition expended during the attack was five rounds of 40mm, 60 rounds of 20mm, and three rounds of 5"/38.

The Cruelest Month

Before April 1945 ended, Vice Admiral Richmond Kelly Turner forwarded the following dispatch:

To: *Bennion, Allen, Brown, Cowell, Daly, Hudson, J. W. Ditter, R. H. Smith, Twiggs, Wadsworth, Wickes, Van Valkenburgh, Bache, H. F. Bauer; LCSs 23, 61, 81–83, 21, 31, 11, 87, 110, 52, 54, 109, 13, 16, 53, 62, 64; lsm(r)s 194, 198, 189, 199, 195, 190, 192, 196:* MY HEARTY CONGRATULATIONS TO ALL PILOTS AND RADAR PICKET GROUPS CONCERNED IN YESTERDAYS' SUPERB DEFENSE OF OUR SURFACE FORCES IN THE OKINAWA AREA X WELL DONE.[103]

Fleet Admiral Nimitz agreed, and added,

The Commander in Chief Pacific Fleet shares with the entire Navy the admiration expressed [by] CTF 51 [Turner] for the valor and gallantry of the resolute ships on Radar Picket duty who are contributing so magnificently to the successes being achieved by the current campaign.[104]

The radar picket ships were hit hard during the first full month of Operation Iceberg. By 30 April 1945, Japanese air attacks sank six ships and damaged 26 more. Over 400 American sailors were killed with more than 500 wounded and missing.[105] In contrast, the first four *Kikusui* "Floating Chrysanthemum" air attacks of Operation *Ten-Go* expended more than a thousand aircraft against American forces, including almost 600 suicide planes, which lost an estimated 820 Japanese airmen.[106]

CHAPTER 6

Ie Shima

13–18 April 1945

The morning of 13 April 1945, Commander Francis was summoned for a conference with Rear Admiral Lawrence F. Reifsnider aboard headquarters flagship *Panamint AGC 13* to quickly finalize LSM(R) assignments for the Ie Shima operation. Adm. Reifsnider had requested a unit of LSM(R)s only the day before, which Vice Admiral Turner (CTF 51) immediately authorized: *LSM(R)s 192, 193, 196, 197, 198,* and *199* with LSM Flotilla Nine flagship *LC(FF) 535* were ordered to report no later than 1500 the next day.[1] Indeed, with little time to waste, pre-assault deployments would commence this very evening and up to the 16 April 1945 amphibious landings on Ie Shima, designated "William Day" or "W-Day." The first American troops would land at 0800 on "Sugar Hour" or "S-Hour."

"On William minus 4 [12 April]," explained Adm. Reifsnider, "an LSM(R) Group consisting of six ships were made available to Commander Ie Shima Attack Group. They were assigned missions, during the preliminary bombardment period, consisting of harassing fires and night illumination from William minus 3 to William Day. Each ship was assigned an area of responsibility during the night and so stationed as to serve the additional purpose of patrol, preventing any enemy movement of small boats from the island..."[2] The LSM(R)s and flotilla flagship would be a temporary contingent of the Support Craft Group that included two gunboat divisions and five mortar divisions, comprising ten LCI(G)s, 21 LCI(M)s and two LC(FF)s.[3]

Originally, the amphibious assaults of both Ie Shima and Motobu Peninsula were planned under "Phase II" of the Okinawa operation, tentatively scheduled for L-Day-plus-30 or 1 May 1945.[4] However, due to the unexpectedly rapid progress of III Amphibious Corps into northern Okinawa and the early capture of Motobu, Adm. Turner saw a strategic opportunity by 10 April, and ordered Adm. Reifsnider to commence planning the assault, capture, and defense of Ie Shima. Turner added, "It was further foreseen that if during Phase I adequate airfields had not been captured at an early date, the capture of Ie Shima might have to take place during the so-called Phase I."[5]

By happenstance, amphibious gunfire support ships were in abundance after the 1 April 1945 Okinawa landings, because many like the LSM(R)s had little to do. Much of the ground fighting had moved inland and away from the coastlines, so larger fleet ships took over supporting fire assignments. An added impetus for the seizure of Ie Shima, moreover, was the massive Japanese *Kikusui* air attacks of 6–7 April, causing over a thousand American casualties

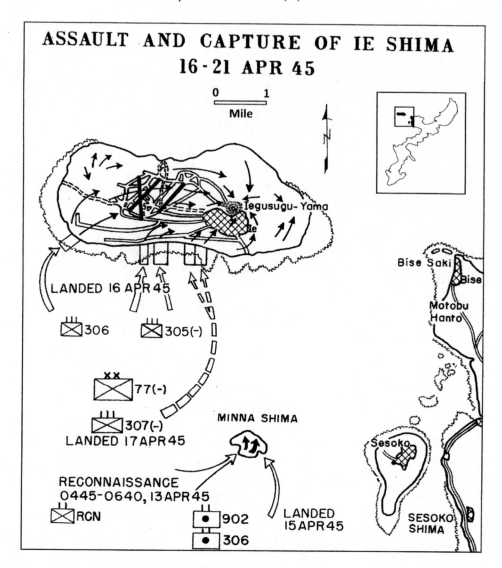

LSM(R)s 192, 193, 196, 197, 198 and 199 with flotilla flagship LC(FF) 535 supported the Ie Shima operation from 13–18 April 1945 (Adapted from Chas. S. Nichols, Jr., Major, USMC, and Henry I. Shaw, *Okinawa: Victory in the Pacific*. Historical Branch, G-3 Division, Headquarters, U.S. Marine Corps, Washington, D.C.: U.S. Government Printing Office, 1955, Map 17, page 113).

and scores of wrecked or sunken ships. And while captured Okinawa airfields were being put to rapid use, Ie Shima offered an ideal forward base for American fighter planes to intercept incoming enemy air raids and for land-based radar units to help relieve the radar picket ships.

Ie Shima and "The Pinnacle"

Ie Shima is a small, oval island, about two miles wide north-south and five miles long east-west. Isolated by the Ie Strait, it lies about three miles from Okinawa's Motobu Peninsula, and roughly 20 miles north of the Hagushi beaches. On clear days, Ie Shima is visible from the northern tip of Zampa Misaki peninsula. Some 7,000 Japanese military and civilian conscripts heavily defended the island in well-camouflaged firing positions, and in bunkers connected by networks of tunnels and caves. The Japanese built three airfields about mid-island which greatly increased its strategic value, so much so that "Ie Shima resembled a huge, immovable aircraft carrier."[6]

Entirely ringed by coral reefs, Ie Shima's north and northwest coasts rise with steep sea cliffs, but its southern coastline has gentle sandy beaches ideal for amphibious landings. Most of the interior is plateau about 165 feet above sea level, and small clumps of scrub trees spot the island with areas of knee-high grass and cultivated fields. The most distinctive feature of Ie Shima is Iegusugu Yama (Mountain), rising over 600 feet center-east of the island. American soldiers would call this mountain "the Pinnacle," below which spread the southern town of Ie.

LSM(R) Tactical Plans

The LSM(R)s were designated the "Night Patrol Group," variously supported by either a destroyer or destroyer escort, beginning the night of 13 April or "William minus 3" (annotated W–3 Day) through 15 April or W–1 Day. The LSM(R) unit was charged with nighttime offensive patrols and harassing bombardments of Ie Shima from sunset to sunrise.

During daylight hours, the rocketships would retire at anchor to allow crews to rest while logistics and maintenance carried on. An hour before sunset, the LSM(R)s would rendezvous with flagship *LC(FF) 535* for briefings and orders, then report on station by sunset. Harassing fire was to commence at 1930, and continue throughout the night until ceasing at 0530. At sunrise, the LSM(R)s would rendezvous once more with *LC(FF) 535* for debriefings and orders, then retire at anchor. This cycle repeated until the morning of 16 April, "William Day." In reality, however, wartime necessities and unforeseen circumstances often interfered with such fastidious planning.[7]

Ie Shima was divided into Patrol Sectors I through VI, numbered counterclockwise. Each sector was assigned a baseline coordinate for rocket mean points of impact (MPI).[8] Originally, each LSM(R) was to patrol a single sector that alternated on succeeding nights, but this plan was soon modified, so rocketships operated in pairs covering two sectors each night instead. As a result, Finner and Spinner LSM(R)s were frequently paired for combined Fin- and Spin-stabilized rocket fires.[9]

Chronic shortages of 5-inch SSR and AR rockets were a problem, however, long before the start of the Okinawa campaign.[10] Consequently, rocket allowances and targeting were stringent and conservative. Finner and Spinner LSM(R)s were to only expend up to 100 ARs and 200 SSRs per ship per night, respectively. Rates of fire were further parceled from 12 to 25 rockets per hour per sector. Moreover, nightly rocket runs were limited to six specific island targets, or one MPI per sector.

"Ships assigned to sectors will make every effort to keep their rockets in [the] area designated," advised Comdr. Francis, and "Ships will so patrol their stations that at some point in their track they will be in a position to launch rockets in designated areas. A figure eight track which will give two opportunities to be in firing position to cover target area would be

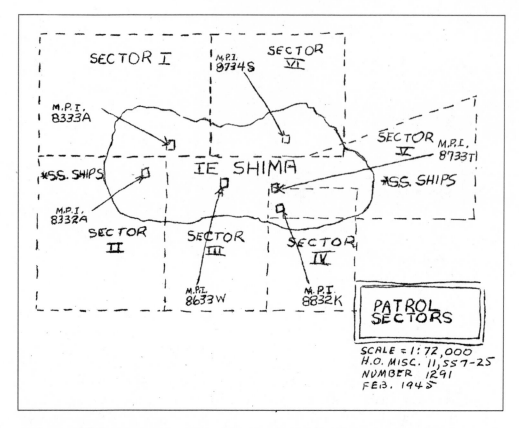

Ie Shima LSM(R) Patrol Sectors. Each sector was assigned an MPI or mean point of impact for rocket attacks. "*S.S. Ships" denotes Spin-stabilized rocket-firing LSM(R)s 196 through 199 (from Commander, LSM Flotilla Nine, Rockets for harassing fire—use on Ie Shima and recommendations regarding future employment, Serial 008, 19 April 1945, [a], CTG 52.21 OpPlan 2101–45, Serial 006, 13 April 1945, Enclosure [A]).

most desirable." According to Francis, LSM(R)s would be poised in rocket firing positions off Ie Shima at least ten times each night, but, "Each C.O. will fire rockets at odd times during each hour in order to confuse the enemy and maintain the harassment."[11]

By far, the LSM(R)s' primary harassing weapon of choice was their 40mm guns, fired in irregular but frequent bursts to prevent enemy work on beach defenses. Six hundred 40mm rounds were allowed per ship per night. On occasions when the rocketships were close to shore, their 20mms (and .50 calibers, if available) guns would supplement gunfire.

On the other hand, the LSM(R)s' most potent ordnance, the 5"/38 dual purpose gun, was to be used only as counter battery to enemy shore fires, with an allowance of a mere 5 rounds "as needed." Instructions for 5"/38 nighttime illumination fires were even more detailed. LSM(R)s patrolling Sector II and Sector V—southwestern and eastern Ie Shima, respectively—were to fire one star shell every 10 minutes. A maximum of 50 star shells was allowed per night, with bursts set for 1500 feet but coordinated so ships did not illuminate beaches simultaneously. A destroyer-type would also supplement night illuminations, circling the island at 10 knots and firing a five-inch star shell every ten minutes, and covered by harassing or counter battery fires.

"The harassing assignment was particularly valuable to this command primarily to provide more training in performance of rocket attacks," added Commander Francis. Commanding officers were challenged to draw up individual rocket attack plans and depend upon their respective ship's internal organizations to fulfill the pre–William Day missions. Furthermore, each night's sector assignments were changed and thus offered variations in the selection of targets, navigational approaches and reference points on land, with and without radar plotting. "In effect," proclaimed Francis, "this assignment provided the individual LSM(R)s with much more actual combat rocket attack experience than the large scale phase operations previously encountered."[12]

"William Minus Three": 13 April 1945

At mid-morning of 13 April, Commander Francis in LSM Flotilla Nine's flagship *LC(FF) 535*, and Lieutenant Commander Fulweiler in LSM(R) Group Twenty-Seven's flagship *LSM(R) 193*, rendezvoused in the Hagushi transport area with *LSM(R) 196*, then steamed full speed for Ie Shima. En route, the trio intercepted *LSM(R)s 197* and *198* returning from patrols on Radar Picket Station 2, and *LSM(R) 199* relieved from patrols on Radar Picket Station 3. *LSM(R) 192*, however, remained behind in Hagushi as an ersatz supply ship, loading extra allotments of ordnance for later unit distribution, so she would report to Ie Shima about midnight.

After briefings, Radioman Clyde Blue from *LSM(R) 197* summarized the coming days in his personal diary: "Well, today at noon we were ordered back to the Transport area. We almost got there when we met the *LCI 535* [*sic*] who is our Commander, and we turned back and laid off Ie Shima, which is a small island off Oki about 5 miles. We are going to throw 200 rockets every night until the 16th of this month. The 77th Infantry is going to invade. We also will fire our 40mm at the beach."[13]

Robert W. Landis, Storekeeper for *LSM(R) 192*, also noted in his diary,

Today [13 April 1945] we learned of the death of President Roosevelt. I was able to get a good supply of provisions today from a supply ship. Among other things I got two crates of oranges to the delight of the crew. We are under constant air attacks. Many aircraft being shot down, U.S. as well as Japanese. We have been assigned to a new mission. We've been temporarily assigned to the US Army, to cruise along the Okinawa shoreline and assault enemy gun positions with our five inch gun. An Army officer and two GI's came aboard to spot the positions for us.[14]

Ships' deck forces busied with the sundry tasks, meanwhile: scrapping rust and oversprayed paint off electrical contact surfaces, assembling rockets below decks, then passing the projectiles bucket-brigade-style up ladders to the rocket decks. Spinners loaded only 200 SSRs (although *LSM(R) 197* actually loaded 240 rockets), while Finners loaded only 100 ARs. Flagship *LC(FF) 535* also readied 5-inch SSRs in her launchers.

About an hour before sunset of 13 April, the five rocketships (less *LSM(R) 192*) rendezvoused southwest of Ie Shima with *LC(FF) 535* for final instructions. During night patrols, the ships would close the Ie Shima coastline from 3000 to 5000 yards.

Departing first were *LSM(R)s 196* and *199* for Patrol Sectors V and VI in east and northeast Ie Shima. Their assigned targets included an extensive underground network, an 800-yard fire trench, heavy machinegun positions, an ammunition storage site, three blockhouses, and 18 Pillboxes.[15] On schedule, *LSM(R) 196* was the first rocket ship to commence fire, raking the eastern beachhead with 40mm harassing gunfire followed by 5-inch starshells and rockets. Signalman Leonard VanOteghem jotted in his diary,

> Special Mission. We had to soften up Ie Shima by rocket bombardment three nights in succession prior to the invasion and also beach harassing with our 20 and 40mm guns to prevent the enemy from setting up beach mortars and various other installations to prevent our invasion. We fired 200 rockets each night for three consecutive nights totaling 600 from about 6 rocket ships, plus 5" star shells for illuminating purposes and countless 20 and 40mm shells on the beaches.[16]

LSM(R)s 197 and *198* steamed to Patrol Sectors III and IV in south central and southeast Ie Shima. The Japanese had fire trenches, three underground trenches, four anti-aircraft gun sites, a radio unit, two heavy machinegun positions, and 13 Pillboxes.

After a final conference with Comdr. Francis, Lt. Comdr. Fulweiler in *LSM(R) 193* stood off Patrol Sectors I and II in northwest and southwest Ie Shima. Intelligence identified a lighthouse, two fire trenches, two "Auto-Matic" AA sites, and ten pillboxes.

Before midnight, however, LSM Flotilla Nine's flagship struck a coral reef and became firmly lodged. Not far away, the patrolling *LSM(R)s 197* and *198* lent a hand. But despite best efforts to break free, the tide was ebbing, unfortunately, so Commander Francis and his landing craft were stuck until morning's rising tides. "The embarrassment in all of this, of course," later explained Lawrence J. Low, Ensign and Gunnery Officer in *LSM(R) 197*, "was that Navy ships were never, never, never supposed to run aground. Least of all, flotilla flagships."[17] Also stranded in *LC(FF) 535*, Pharmacists Mate "Doc" Robert W. Cox added:

> I also remember going aground at Ie Shima.... If the Japanese had any big guns ashore we were an easy target. We tried all kinds of tactics to get unstuck. Other ships trying to pull us off weren't too effective. I really don't remember how we got off the reef but after a lot of maneuvering we finally did. Maybe the tide changed. I was glad to get the hell out of there. We were so close to shore I remember seeing a lot of horses running all over the place. Not much else.[18]

LSM(R) 192 arrived off Ie Shima after midnight, meanwhile, and began lone patrols along the southern coastline. This first night, however, her launchers remained empty of rockets and she refrained from harassing shore fire, since Japanese counter fire could set off the exposed stockpiles of ammunition topside.

"William Minus Two": 14 April 1945

During the morning of 14 April, as the six LSM(R)s rendezvoused with the now-freed *LC(FF) 535*, messages flashed around the world about the death of President Franklin Delano Roosevelt. Commencing with Colors at 0800, all National Ensigns were ordered lowered to half-mast for 30 days in mourning and respect.

The rocketships and flotilla flagship retired off southeastern Ie Shima and away from the daytime naval gunfire zones of bombarding battleships, cruisers, and destroyers. "[Overnight] we fired our 200 rockets and sure made some noise around here," commented Clyde Blue, *LSM(R) 197* Radioman. "During the day we just laid off, loading up again for the night's raid. We fire the same amount again tonight."[19]

Commander Francis' flagship stood off Ie Shima for observation during roving patrols and occasionally fired at beach targets. *LSM(R)s 196* and *198* briefly returned to Hagushi

Anchorage for logistics; meanwhile, the remaining rocket ships partook 5"/38 Star Shells, AA Common, and powder cases from *LSM(R) 192*.

From 1700 to 1800, the half dozen rocketships sailed either alone or in pairs for their respective patrols around Ie Shima while assembling and loading rockets into launchers. The first rocket attack this evening commenced at 1715, and 40mms and 20mms strafed beaches in bursts.

In Patrol Sectors I and II, *LSM(R) 192* had only 90 Finner rockets, while *LSM(R) 199* loaded 203 Spinner rockets. During the half-dozen nighttime rocket runs, salvos varied from about a dozen rockets to as many as 40.

In Patrol Sectors III and IV, *LSM(R) 193* made a dozen rocket runs, firing small clusters of rockets; *LSM(R) 197*, with 252 rockets in her launchers, made seven rocket runs, firing between 16 and 45 rockets per salvo. In morning's twilight before dawn, she launched a final barrage of 95 rockets. Harassing fires included irregular shelling by 5"/38 guns.

In Patrol Sectors V and VI, *LSM(R) 196* made five rocket runs, launching between 24 and 48 SSRs with each attack. *LSM(R) 198* fired star shells every 10 minutes and 25 rockets each hour.

"William Minus One": 15 April 1945

Nighttime patrols around Ie Shima ceased after dawn of 15 April. "We fired rockets again [last night]," Radioman Clyde Blue noted in his diary, "and tonight we load 804 rockets. Planes from carriers have rocket bombed and strafed the island all day long."[20]

Now, however, the LSM(R) crews began working virtually 'round the clock, for by 0917, Admiral Reifsnider intensified patrols throughout 15 April.[21] Upon his withdrawal of battleships, cruisers, and destroyers from Ie Shima, the LSM(R)s and other amphibious fire supports took over.[22]

Commander Francis initially dispatched *LSM(R)s 193, 196, 197,* and *199* on patrols to observe enemy activities on Sesoko Shima and Menna (or Minna) Shima. (*LSM(R)s 192* and *198*, meanwhile, stood off the attack transport *Montrose APA 212*, where small LCMs transported injured or ill sailors requiring a medical officer). These patrols lasted but a few hours at most and proved uneventful.

Under new orders by noontime, the LSM(R)s resumed sector patrols around Ie Shima. *LSM(R)s 196* and *197* assumed Patrol Sectors II and III about a thousand yards off the south-southwestern beachhead. *LSM(R)s 198* and *199* took Patrol Sectors IV and V off the east-southeast coastline, where *LSM(R)s 192* and *193* also paired-up in Patrol Sector IV.

Harassing fire was only occasional, for targets were limited: *LSM(R) 192* fired on a small boat on a beach, and *LSM(R) 199* shelled a barricaded cave near shore.

In midafternoon, the half dozen rocketships ceased island patrols and rendezvoused with LSM Flotilla Nine's flagship for updated operation orders. Here, Commander Francis and the flotilla's intelligence officer embarked *LSM(R) 199*, then patrolled southern Ie Shima for almost three hours, "firing at any and all targets,"[23] while gathering intelligence. "One attack on the afternoon of W-1 Day," Comdr. Francis later reported, "produced three fires in the grid area 8633 [Sector III] which burned from 1730 until 2300 and spread to area 8533Q."[24]

Meanwhile, *LC(FF) 535* methodically moored alongside and then cast off from each of the five LSM(R)s, briefing officers on the latest orders. Thereafter, the rocketships sailed independently toward Ie Shima for nighttime disruptive and destructive fire on beach targets. Among other tasks, deck forces also assembled and loaded rockets into the launchers in the remaining daylight—and many more than any of the previous nights.

LSM(R)s 196 and *199* assumed Patrol Sectors I and II, the western one-third of Ie Shima. Harassing gunfire commenced after twilight as the latter rocketship fired a Star Shell every twenty minutes to illuminate beaches. They made four and five rocket runs some 3500 yards offshore, respectively: *LSM(R) 196* fired 48 SSRs each time, while *LSM(R) 199* launched salvos ranging from 25 to 76 rockets.

LSM(R)s 192 and *193* took Patrol Sectors III and IV along the mid-southern and south-eastern coastlines. Disruptive gunfire was timed to commence not before sunset at 1852, after which topside 40mms and 20mms randomly opened up at shore targets. (A half-hour before midnight, however, *LSM(R) 192* ran aground on a sandbar about 1200 yards off Ie Shima. Luckily, she pulled herself off by her own power almost instantly, and doubly lucky to escape damages to her hull and screws.) After midnight, the former made 15 rocket runs before dawn, while the latter sister ship made seven runs of 3 to 7 rockets per salvo. (The rocket failure rate was startlingly high for *LSM(R) 192*, which reported nine misfires out of 29.)

LSM(R)s 197 and *198* staked out Patrol Sectors V and VI on the eastern and northeastern third of the island. 40mms, 20mms and .50 caliber machineguns fired bursts at irregular intervals, and *LSM(R) 197* skipper Lt. John Cooper reported that "several houses were destroyed and two apparently defended caves were neutralized by 5-inch fire." After nightfall, Star Shells were fired every ten minutes. Before midnight, *LSM(R) 198* commenced rocket runs on Ie Shima, launching five rocket salvos of a score or more at a time. *LSM(R) 197*, in turn, delivered three consecutive barrages of 51, 78, and 80 rockets, although eight of her firing circuits energized an actual total of 804 SSRs.[25] As recalled by Radioman Clyde Blue, "This afternoon we shelled the island with our 5-inch. The [*LSM(R)*] *199* also fired about 200 rockets up on a ridge in the middle of the island. We sure have pounded the island. It's 5 miles in length and 3 across so we can really rake it. Tomorrow we invade."[26]

The flotilla's flagship *LC(FF) 535* also fired rockets intermittently at Ie Shima between patrols about a mile offshore.

Commander Francis summarized the three days of pre-assault harassment operations at Ie Shima by first declaring, "a new function was discovered for the LSM(R)s."

> It is believed that harassing by rocket fire is a very effective method of keeping relatively large areas neutralized by the use of comparatively few rocket craft, as substantiated by the fact that Ie Shima, an area of approximately 8 square miles, was kept under continuous attack three nights by using only six LSM(R)s.
>
> The rapidity of recurrence of the rocket attacks (six ships gave an average of one attack every ten minutes), combined with irregular star shell and 40MM fire, produced the psychological effect necessary to successful harassing. The concurrent destruction of enemy installations whose grid locations are available for rocket plot is an equally desirable advantage. It is further believed that LSM(R)s are well suited for such rocket harassing due to their ability to produce illumination, 5" counter battery if necessary and 40 or 20 MM fire against possible beach reinforcement. In this particular assignment, 20 MM fire proved satisfactory for setting beach fires and destroying huts by daylight.[27]

During 51 hours of harassing fires, the LSM(R)s launched 183 separate rocket missions into nine target areas, according to Francis. "Each attack produced at least one fire, some as many as five fires…. No less than two large oil fires were ignited each night," he added.

Commander Francis insisted the LSM(R)s had not yet reached their full potential, because they were limited to repeatedly attacking a small group of pre-assigned target areas. Yet despite such mission limitations, the Ie Shima operation actually proved beneficial for the young crews as training grounds to hone naval skills.

The inaccuracy of the individual ship's adherence to the prescribed plotted attack, due wholly to lack of experience, produced a much wider coverage of rocket fire than would normally be present…. It is firmly believed that this practice has so improved the individual ship's ability to carry out the plotted attack according to plan that for future harassing assignments a different mean point of impact could be assigned for each run, resulting in the desired combination of harassing while destroying or neutralizing important enemy positions as given by latest intelligence reports.[28]

Concluding his report, Francis made a final pitch, conceivably parrying (albeit subtly) the concurrent radar picket assignments: "Considering the extreme value as a training aid to ships of this command, and the offensive value of the results produced in comparison with the forces involved, it is recommended that LSM(R)s be used extensively for future day and night harassing assignments."[29]

Rear Admiral Reifsnider concurred, stating, "The LSM(R) proved valuable for night harassing fires and are capable of keeping comparatively large areas neutralized with a minimum use of ammunition. LSM(R)s were employed with good result in the pre-bombardment of Ie Shima. They have the advantage of a 5" gun for counterbattery and illumination enabling them to supply their own protection, and in addition, have a large ammunition capacity. It is recommended their use be expanded and developed for future operations."[30]

"William Day": 16 April 1945

Minutes before sunrise on 16 April, the six LSM(R)s ceased nighttime harassing patrols and rendezvoused south of Ie Shima. U.S. landings were set for 0800, designated "S Hour" (or "Sugar" Hour). The crisp morning air promised clear, sunny skies and moderate sea. At 0534, Rear Admiral Reifsnider gave the traditional order, "Land the Landing Force."

Heavy pre-landing air strikes and naval bombardments created enormous clouds of smoke and dust over the small island. Explosions from enemy ammunition dumps and gasoline stores erupted in huge black and white billows. At moments, Ie Shima disappeared from view. When air and naval gunfire moved inland, LCI gun- and mortar-boats preceded the assault waves with suppressive fires. As the amphibious tanks and tractors neared the landing beaches, the small gunboats sustained flanking fire.

Until the Ie Shima operation, the LSM(R) flotilla had had no formal protocol for rocket runs: rocketship formations and attack procedures were crafted contingent to the given requirements of each mission. Here for the first time an LSM(R) tactical rocket attack plan was formally promulgated. Its strengths were simplicity and adaptability, by assimilating the unique characteristics of Finner (AR) and Spinner (SSR) rockets to deliver heavy concentrations of rockets efficiently. The plan itself was confined to six LSM(R)s in three waves, but its versatility could easily accommodate greater or fewer numbers of rocketships.[31] (See "Heavy Concentration Target Approach Formation," page 81.)

For "William Day," the LSM(R)s' line of fire would bear north-northeast with an attack speed of about 11 knots, or approximately 370 yards per minute. The barrage would begin at the shoreline and "walk" into the town of Ie—the target, or "Point Tare"—and culminate at the peak of "the Pinnacle," the island's prominent mountain Iegusugu Yama. The entire target area was 1200 yards wide by 1800 yards deep. From his flotilla flagship off shore, Commander Francis would signal when to commence rocket fires, during which time the three waves of paired LSM(R)s had exactly ten minutes.

At 0715, the LSM(R)s departed the rendezvous area, passed through and emerged from the gathered armada, wove northeast then turned left onto course 310° True. Visual bearings were taken on Iegusugu Mountain, and radar bearings plotted from a point of land on Ie Shima called Hama Zaki.

LSM(R)s 192 and 193 led the first wave of rocket runs. Several ranging rockets were launched about 3900 yards from the target. A minute later, when the two ships passed over the theoretical firing line—3700 yards from Point Tare for Finners—full rocket salvos were launched on schedule at 0745. Remarkably, only one misfire was reported.

LSM(R)s 196 and 197 followed by about 1200 yards. Reaching the firing line at 0750–4900 yards from Point Tare for Spinners—they too loosed rocket salvos.

The last advancing wave of LSM(R)s 198 and 199, cautioned to "maintain proper distance," launched the final rocket salvos upon crossing the firing line—also 4900 yards from Point Tare—although exceeding the unit's allotted ten-minute time frame.

"Approximately 2600 rockets were fired into a target area," reported Comdr. Francis, "composed principally of the South Eastern sector of the town of Ie and the Eastern and South Eastern vicinities of Iegusugu Yama. These areas contained considerable lightly constructed revetments, fire trenches, and possible troop concentrations."[32]

Aboard LSM(R) 197, Radioman Clyde Blue later wrote in his diary,

Well, we fired a few rockets last night but our radar went out so we could not fire very many. This morning it opened up with airplanes and battleships, cruisers, destroyers shelling Ie Island. Then we came in for our own run and let loose 500 rockets or more. We aimed just before a knob of land that sticks up 500 feet in the air [i.e., Iegusugu Yama]. We really threw the lead at that knob. All of us except the LSM(R)s 192 and 193 fired 500 or more rockets. They can only fire 400 at a time. They have a different kind of rocket than we have. After all the rockets we fired we could not even see the island for dust.[33]

As the last rockets fell on Ie Town and Iegusugu Yama, a mile west, the first wave of assault troops landed on Red Beach 1 and Red Beach 2. Soon, seven U.S. carrier fighters dropped napalm on Iegusugu Yama, and four more carrier fighters and ten attack bombers reported on station to support the landings. The Americans found little resistance initially, as succeeding waves of amphibious vehicles ran up on the beachheads and troops actually advanced standing upright. At 0802, Rear Admiral Reifsnider sent a brief signal to Vice Admiral Turner: "Assault landing on schedule." Soon, waves of American troops hit the southwestern corner of the island, Green Beach 1, followed by supporting assault vehicles. Six minutes after "Sugar Hour," all of the initial waves had landed.

Following their rocket runs, the LSM(R)s continued on an easterly course to retire between Ie Shima and Motobu Peninsula. Standing by at General Quarters awaiting further orders, Material Condition "Baker" and Readiness I were set as the deck forces assembled several hundred more rockets and loaded launchers for more rocket runs, but scrubbed two hours later. "A second fire mission for this unit was contemplated either in [the same] target area 8733, or in the woods and high ground to the north," according to Reifsnider. "However, the low ordinate required by Air Support to complete their missions prevented further 5" rocket fire."[34]

Air Attacks

"This is W-Day (Wilco Day) [*sic*]," wrote Robert W. Landis, Storekeeper on *LSM(R) 192*, updating his personal diary. "Invasion of Ie Shima. After two nights of rocket runs to the beach and strafing of the beach with 40's and 20's, Ie Shima was invaded. There was little resistance until an hour later when a large force of enemy aircraft arrived on the scene. This became an intense air-to-ship battle. An enemy Val crashed into a DD [likely destroyer escort *Bowers DE 637*] along our port side. The DD remained afloat. We did not take any damage but it certainly was intense for about 30 minutes."[35]

Coinciding with the Ie Shima operation, the third major Japanese air attack under Operation *Ten-Go*, *Kikusui* Raid No. 3, began 15 April and continued the next day. Little was felt at Ie Shima before dawn of 16 April, however, because few enemy air attacks successfully penetrated the operations area. "This [16 April] attack followed the general pattern of those on 6 and 12 April," added Rear Admiral Reifsnider. Most raiders were destroyed or driven off by a combination of CAP fighters, radar picket ships, and other screening vessels 25 to 40 miles north and northwest of Ie Shima. Seven enemy planes that did break through were shot down by ships' AA gunfire, none harming the Ie Shima Attack Group. "Fortunately," continued Reifsnider, "the raids arrived in the Ie Shima Area after the troops had landed and, therefore, did not interfere appreciably with air or gunfire support at the time of the initial landing [*sic*]."[36]

By 1004, Reifsnider further updated Turner: "Landing proceeding per schedule at 1000/Item. Resistance slight. Four enemy planes attacking Transport Area [were] splashed. No damage." The follow on landings with munitions, rations, and other essential supplies had progressed rapidly, and in another hour the assault phase would be declared completed on all beaches. But Turner immediately shot back: "Form your ships for repulsing air attacks. Modify assignments [of] gunfire support ships."[37]

The LSM(R)s returned to the transport area south of Ie Shima, and Commander Francis ordered the rocketships to screen 1000 yards south of the large supply and troop ships against enemy air attacks. Here Clyde Blue caught up his diary in *LSM(R) 197*:

> We are now patrolling around the LSTs and transports that brought the Doggies up.
> We had a suicide plane dive on a destroyer and it looked like it sank out quite a ways from us.
> The *LSM(R) 189* shot down two suicide planes and the third one hit it in the Conn and killed or wounded a radioman and a Quartermaster. That's three LSM(R)s that's been hit so far since we went into operations March 26th.
> We heard about Roosevelt dying and it kind of made us all feel funny inside. We could hardly believe it until we got the story by the press over the radio. That sure is tough luck for us. I hope old Truman carries on pretty good.
> We have no idea when we will get any mail or be able to get down to where the outgoing mail ship is. I started a letter to Mom on the 12th but the air attacks broke that up and I don't have much time to write anymore. I will try and finish it one of these days.
> The war in Europe looks like it was coming to a close pretty soon. I sure hope so... [38]

Interdiction Patrols: 16–18 April 1945

New orders in mid-afternoon of 16 April sent the LSM(R)s to support nighttime interdiction patrols of the three to five mile strait between Ie Shima and Okinawa's Motobu Peninsula.[39] Preceding the Ie Shima invasion, Captain T. W. Rimer (CTG 52.24) deployed destroyer types and gunboats to guard against transiting enemy craft, swimmers, and mine-laying.[40]

Uncharted reefs posed continuing threats as well. *LSM(R)s 198* and *199* both ran aground that night: the former dislodged using her rudders and engines, but the latter remained firmly stuck until rising tides lifted her off. Luckily, they escaped damage and enemy attention.

By 17 April, however, only *LSM(R)s 196* and *197* remained patrolling Ie Strait. "Well, we just patrolled off Ie Shima all night long to see that no Jap swimmers or small boats get off and over to Oki," wrote Clyde Blue. "Nothing has happened all day and I guess we patrol in the same place tonight."[41]

In the meantime, *LSM(R)s 192, 198* and *199* steamed in the wake of *LSM(R) 193* en route Nago Wan Anchorage lying in the southern crux of Motobu peninsula. But at 1818, the guide ship suddenly slowed then stopped altogether after hitting a reef. A six-foot by two-inch hole was ripped in the bottom near the centerline between frames 21 and 22. Her engine room began flooding and damage control parties broke out shoring and pumps.

LC(FF) 535 went to assist due to her shallower draft. A cable was rigged and, with the help of rising tides, about ninety minutes later the flagship towed the rocket ship off the reef to deeper water. The two landing ships remained tied for buoyancy and stability as the smaller craft's engines aided maneuvering. Several hours later, the fleet tug *Tawakoni ATF 114* came alongside to pump out the flooded engine room.[42] That night, the four rocketships and flagship remained anchored in Nago Wan, and made smoke from fog generators to cover the anchorage.

Patrols in Ie Strait proved uneventful for *LSM(R)s 196* and *197* until the morning of 18 April. Lt. John M. Cooper, commanding *LSM(R) 197*, reported, "While on interdiction patrol off eastern end of Ie Shima in company with *LSM(R) 196*, both ships fired on several rafts, and floats made of inner tubes, destroying enemy personnel attached thereto. The total of enemy destroyed is estimated at between nine (9) and fifteen (15)."[43]

Here, Bruce McDaniel, Quartermaster-striker on *LSM(R) 196*, witnessed the darkest nature of men at war. "We were patrolling back and forth between Ie Shima and the main island of Okinawa to prevent people from leaving. It was early in the morning, and my Watch was dogged so I could go down to breakfast; it was daylight by then and I had just begun to eat when I heard gunfire.

I went up to the foredeck to discover that they had been shooting a 20mm and small arms at some Japanese that were in the water that had tied airplane inner tubes together and had tried to swim across the long strait of water. But adverse currents and the fatigue of such an effort caught them barely halfway across. They had all been shot to death. I noticed one floating with his head down as if playing dead, and I suggested that we take him prisoner, but one of our Gunners Mate's with a Thompson machine gun fired a burst at his head.

The ship maneuvered close and a grappling hook was used to hook a leg and pull him aboard. Laying the body on the deck on his back, he had a very strong build, black hair graying at the temples, his skull split open like a book from the forehead back onto the deck. Someone tore open his tunic; he was dressed in what seemed like white silk underwear, an olive green cloth band was around his waist, which had on it hand-sewn Japanese characters in red thread. His shoes were the kind with the big toe divided from the rest. Someone pulled out his gold teeth, another pulled out a bunch of papers, which were like thin tissues and threw them on the deck and the wind blew them across the deck into the sea—they could have been important.

The whole thing was sickening; I remember I got a sweet taste in my mouth. Someone said they would have done the same to you, to which I said at the time: "So!" They could have been taken prisoner, but at the time there was a feverish anger at the Japanese. Much later that Gunners Mate, when we were sitting by ourselves, said with tears in his eyes, "Those guys weren't given a chance." The man's body was dumped over the side, where it sank out of sight.[44]

By 0800 of 18 April, the two Spinner LSM(R)s ceased patrols and returned full speed to the Hagushi transport area.

Earlier that morning in Nago Wan Anchorage, Lt. Comdr. Fulweiler and his LSM(R) Group 27 staff transferred temporarily from the patched-up *LSM(R) 193* to Commander Francis' flotilla flagship. The column formation of *LC(FF) 535* and *LSM(R)s 192, 193, 198* and *199* proceeded south over the 20-odd miles to the Hagushi Anchorage, where a repair ship was sought for the damaged rocketship and supply ships with fuel and provisions for the unit.

Demonstration Landing: 19 April 1945

Ensigns David Mallery and Jack Shedd on *LSM(R) 196*, meanwhile, speculated on a new assignment: "We were ordered back to Hagushi Anchorage where our Captain was briefed on the rather strange mission of a mock invasion of the southern tip of Okinawa. The best reason we could imagine for this at the time was to draw enemy troops south, away from an almost deadlocked area in the center of the fighting."[45]

Rear Admiral Reifsnider summoned Commander Francis for a briefing in the *Panamint*, while the LSM(R) flotilla's Intelligence Officer spent several hours aboard Vice Admiral Turner's headquarters ship *Eldorado*. As work parties took on fuel, fog oil, and provisions, Comdr. Francis and Lt. Comdr. Fulweiler with five LSM(R) commanding officers embarked Rear Admiral Blandy's flagship *Estes* for a high-level conference on the Demonstration Landing off southeastern Okinawa next morning.

A feigned American amphibious landing on the southeastern shores of Okinawa was being planned even as plans evolved for the Ie Shima operation. As early as 10 April, the U.S. Army foresaw a tactical usefulness of diversionary maneuver to confuse, disrupt, and divert Japanese ground forces in southern Okinawa. Vice Admiral Turner promised every available naval resource to embellish this fiction.

No such task group existed, however, so everything had to be improvised, and quickly. To make this façade believable, a credible assemblage of ships was needed to impress the ever-watchful but suspicious Japanese army. Carrier support, battleships, cruisers, destroyers, transports, gunboats, amphibious tractors, and auxiliaries were scoured for immediate availability. Many were already or soon to be engaged in important missions and could not be spared. Almost every area naval commander was requested (or expected) to ante up support for this mock invasion. Admiral Mitscher loaned fast aircraft carriers, and Commodore Moosbrugger relieved screening ships. Turner even dispatched a message to Reifsnider, anticipating the Ie Shima Attack Group might release troop transports and control-type vessels.

By the morning of 17 April, Adm. Turner designated Rear Admiral W. H. P. Blandy to lead the Demonstration Landing as Commander Task Group 51.23. Subordinate naval commanders were chosen that afternoon, followed by conferences and dispatches to arrange details. That evening, Blandy's staff released his formal Operations Order A108–45, drawing heavily from existing operations plans of the two earlier Demonstration Landings off the same beaches during 1–2 April 1945. Staffs literally "burned the midnight oil," piecing together disparate naval units to resemble a cohesive force. Approach routes, target assignments, naval bombardment and air strike schedules were but some of the minutia to be worked out, as well.[46]

The afternoon of 18 April, five LSM(R)s rendezvoused within the Hagushi Anchorage, where the flotilla flagship passed guard mail. *LC(FF) 535* then led the column of rocketships on a southerly course at full speed, while deck forces assembled and loaded rockets into launchers.

After rounding the southern tip of Okinawa, Commander Francis relinquished command of the unit to Lieutenant Commander Fulweiler, embarked in temporary flagship *LSM(R) 192*. Before sunset, the LSM(R)s began overnight "passive patrols" about five miles offshore along the ten-mile coastline of southeastern Okinawa up to Chinen Peninsula. *LC(FF) 535* stood alone to the northeast near Kutaka Shima. "We are now patrolling off the southern tip of 'Oki,'" noted diarist Clyde Blue in *LSM(R) 197*. "We loaded a deckload of rockets and I guess we are going to fire them at something in the morning. The southern part of 'Oki' is where all the fighting is and they really light the place up at night." As for the seas, he added, "It's rougher than hell out."[47]

Indeed, weather conditions had soured over the past 24 hours. Falling barometric pressure was drawing a cold front from across China's Yellow Sea. Winds shifted and rose from 10, to 18, to as high as 30 knots, while high clouds and scattered showers compounded rising ocean swells.

19 April 1945

The proximate center of the Demonstration landing beaches was the small harbor village of Minatoga and nearby island O Shima. The American "landings" would spread about 1500 yards east of O Shima, designated Green Beach, to about 3000 yards west of O Shima, code-named White Beach.

Overnight, the *Estes* steamed from Hagushi Anchorage with transport ships and control and screening vessels to southeastern Okinawa. An hour before sunrise, battleships and destroyers commenced slow, deliberate fire from the southeast, while the U.S. Army's XXIV Corps artillery opened a simultaneous barrage from the north against the Japanese positions in Shuri Castle. By some accounts, the combined ground, naval and air bombardments were the single largest coordinated attacks of the Pacific war.[48]

The LSM(R)s were two units in the Demonstration Landing of 19 April: Unit One—Lieutenant Commander Fulweiler (CTU 52.21.1) in temporary flagship *LSM(R) 192* with *LSM(R)s 198* and *199*; and Unit Two—Commander Francis (CTU 52.21.2) in flagship *LC(FF) 535* with *LSM(R)s 196* and *197*.

At dawn, the five LSM(R)s ceased passive patrols of the southeastern beaches and stood seaward of the line of departure. The order to commence rocket runs with deliberate neutralizing fire would come from Admiral Blandy (CTG 51.23), from 0730 until 0745.

LSM(R) 192, the lone Finner, was allotted 300 Fin-stabilized (AR) rockets for a single targeted area on the beach, visible from sea. Her line of fire (LOF) was 330° True at minimum speed, target width was 800 yards, and depth of pattern (DOP) 600 yards. She would have only five minutes—0730 to 0735—for her rocket run.

The four Spinners were given coordinates for longer-range, inland rocket attacks. *LSM(R)s 196* and *197* were each to launch 500 Spin-stabilized (SSR) rockets, paired as a single wave on the same target. Their LOF was 320° True at minimum speed, a target width of 500 yards, and DOP of 1000 yards. Starting 0730, the two ships were given a full fifteen minutes to accomplish their rocket runs, after which they were to stand by for a possible secondary mission.

LSM(R)s 198 and *199* were each to fire 500 Spin-stabilized rockets on two adjacent shore targets, sharing rocket run characteristics of 340° degree True LOF at minimum speeds, with 500-yard widths of targets and 700-yard DOP. If ordered afterwards, these two Spinners were to pair up as a single wave on a secondary target after 0800 at six knots and each fire 500 SSRs on a LOF of 000° True, both covering thousand-yard widths of target and depths of pattern.

About 0730, carrier air strikes lifted and the signal to commence rocket runs was expected any moment. But nothing happened. The officer of the deck in *LSM(R) 192* simply (if incorrectly) noted in the ship's log: "0730: Fire postponed, waiting for orders."

As the LSM(R)s stood by, the Demonstration Landing continued on schedule regardless. Commencing 0742, LCI-type gunboats stepped off the line of departure ahead of the first wave of LVTs. "During the movement of boats toward the shore, beach neutralization fires were delivered by advancing LCI(G)s and LCI(M)s," noted Rear Admiral Blandy. "The LCI(M)s delivered early heavy fire on O Shima and in the vicinity of Minatoga Town. The LCI(G)s fired rockets and 40mm as the [infantry assault] boats advanced."[49] Assault boats transporting infantry formed "V" formations and headed toward the beaches while guns of the fleet pounded the shore. By 0758, the leading boat waves were returning seaward along the flanks of the assault beaches to the line of departure. In another 19 minutes, the last boat waves returned, and heavy naval gunfire ships resumed deliberate destructive fire as troops re-embarked their respective transports.

What went wrong? Reporting the operation, Rear Admiral Blandy commented, "The LSM(R)s were scheduled at the same time [as the LCIs] to deliver heavy long range rocket fire on several areas of suspected military activity. However, they did not get the word to commence firing, transmitted after the completion of the pre-landing airstrike. Their fires were delivered later."[50]

This was clearly an embarrassment for Commander Francis, whose explanation expanded upon Adm. Blandy's.

> Communications as a whole worked effectively between 1 April and 20 April, with one exception. On 19 April in the demonstration attack on Southeastern Okinawa, an order to fire was not received by this command. This order was addressed from the headquarters ship [*Estes*] to the Task Unit to which this Command was assigned and called for execution of prior written instructions, which we held. A succeeding order addressed specifically to this Command enabled us to proceed with our mission.[51]

Perhaps better late than never, LSM(R) rocket runs were re-scheduled two hours later. At 0940, the five rocketships commenced slow beach attacks on their originally designated targets: *LSM(R) 192* launched 284 rockets with two misfires, three Spinner ships fired 500 rockets, and *LSM(R) 198* launched 480 rockets.

Commander Francis summarized, "approximately 2300 rockets were fired into four different target areas selected because of their important enemy installation contents,"[52] where "numerous fires were started, one resulting in destruction of a small ammunition dump, but full extent of damage remains unknown."[53]

Overlooking the faux pas, Ensigns Mallery and Shedd in *LSM(R) 196* later recalled, "The night of April 18th we patrolled off southern Okinawa and the following morning—with our fellow LSM(R)s—we fired our rocket salvos on our various targets. The entire little operation was a complete job of deception for the enemy. After the shore bombardment, masses of transports, standing by, even began to lower their personnel in boats with every apparent intention of landing them. The feint was over before noon…"[54]

The Demonstration Landing concluded by late morning, so Adm. Blandy began releasing various units of the Demonstration Group to return to their parent task organizations for further assignments. At 1216, Blandy reported to Vice Admiral Turner that the feint was completed, and while enemy mortar fire was observed, no ships were hit.[55] Oddly enough, Turner's estimation was uncharacteristically equivocal. "As in the case of previous demonstrations, results are difficult to evaluate, although the net result of the 'all-out' attack was an advance not as great as had been hoped for."[56] Others, however, were blunt with their assessment: "The big attack of 19 April had failed. At no point had there been a breakthrough. Everywhere the Japanese had held and turned back the American attack."[57]

That afternoon, *Estes* departed southeastern Okinawa for the Hagushi Anchorage, then sailed the following day for Saipan, where Rear Admiral Blandy would help plan the invasion of Imperial Japan.

CHAPTER 7

The Radar Picket Lines
1–21 May 1945

The LSM(R)s began patrolling Radar Picket Stations (RPS) as "Radar Support Ships" on 7 April 1945. These distant patrols continued the following month until 21 May 1945, including RPSs 1, 2, 3, 4, 5, 7, 9, 10, 11A, 12, 14, 15, and 16. On 20 April, LSM(R)s were assigned additional solitary patrols stationed two-thirds distances from Point Bolo to RPSs 1, 2, 3, 4, and 14. Informally called "Radar Relay" or "Linking" ships, the LSM(R)s served as intermediate defensive air guards, emergency rescue vessels, and communications relays between Okinawa and the picket ships patrolling their respective distant RPSs. By 30 April, LSM(R)s patrolling these intermediate picket stations were re-designated "Survivors and Medical Ships," but such patrols ceased after 2 May 1945 when the intermediate stations were deactivated.

Kikusui *Raid No. 5*

In May 1945, the Japanese navy and army air forces continued attacks *en masse* under Operation *Ten-Go*. During 3–4 May, *Kikusui* Raid No. 5 sent an estimated 350 aircraft including 125 "Special Attack" suicide planes. Many enemy aircraft not attached to *Ten-Go* also sortied from Japan, Korea, and Formosa and attacked radar picket ships and American forces at Okinawa as well. Japanese air attacks sank or damaged some 22 U.S. ships and caused over thirteen hundred American sailors killed, wounded and missing.[1]

RPS 10: 3 May 1945

At Radar Picket Station 10 on the evening of 3 May 1945, USS *LSM(R) 195* (Lt. William E. Woodson, Jr., USNR) was tactical guide ship to *LCSs 14, 83* and *25*, stationed about 25 miles SSW of the prominent Japanese-held island Kume Shima. The four amphibians[2] patrolled a clockwise, box-like course called "Corpen 9" that turned right each half-hour, bearing on the four cardinal compass points. Destroyers *Aaron Ward DM 34* as OTC and *Little DD 803* patrolled beyond the horizon some 17 miles northeast.

Weather and seas were calm for the first time in days. Clouds broke up into patches, rains gave way to sunshine and blue skies, and a light breeze smoothed the seas and cleared the horizon.

LSM(R) 195 had already patrolled a full week on this distant picket station, yet she still mounted a full deckload of rockets useless against enemy aircraft. "As ordered, this ship had 300 5" Fin Stabilized Rockets loaded topside and 386 Fin Stabilized Rockets assembled in ready service racks...," noted Lt. Woodson. Devoid of irony, the captain coolly added, "After this experience, we recommend that assembled rockets never be stowed in ready service racks or loaded on launchers while on any duties that do not require the use of rockets."[3]

During enemy air attacks, the Fighter Director Officer (FIDO) in *Aaron Ward* would vector the Combat Air Patrol as the destroyers increased speeds and closed the smaller support craft for mutual gunfire support. Should bogies approach from multiple directions simultaneously, *Aaron Ward* was responsible for tracking northerly targets and *Little* for southerly targets. If, or when, Japanese planes came within extremely close range, each picket ship was to maneuver at will and fire as necessary for self-defense, while keeping vigilant against collisions.[4] Fatefully, "Communications with OTC were not swift enough to enable us [the picket support ships] properly to prepare for oncoming enemy planes," said Lt. Woodson.

About 1813, destroyers' radars detected two large groups[5] of aircraft approaching from the west and southwest, likely from Formosa, which formed four raids that divided into flights of 5 to 6 planes each, then divided into smaller units as they closed. At least 25 Japanese planes would hit RPS 10.

The destroyers signaled the highest air raid alert warning, "Flash Red–Control Green," about 1815, and ordered *LSM(R) 195* and *LCS*s 14, 25 and 83 to close the formation. "It is believed that the Japs may have homed in from Kume Shima," asserted *Little*'s commander. "From that island the Japs were in a position to observe not only ship movements but also CAP strength and movements."[6]

From 1840 to about 1845, enemy raiders overwhelmed the four Combat Air Patrol fighters and swarmed the two destroyers. Kamikaze crashes into *Aaron Ward* caused loss of all steering control and locked the destroyer's rudders into a hard-left position, which forced the ship to circle wildly to port as fires raged. *Little* was hit in rapid succession, which left her powerless, burning, and dead in the water.

The four amphibians, far south of the destroyers, were helpless onlookers to the unfolding devastation, and ranges were too great for their guns to have any effect against the circling Japanese aircraft. Guide ship *LSM(R) 195* directed all support ships to proceed independently at flank speed to assist the destroyers as enemy planes approached. But the rocketship's starboard engine suddenly broke down en route and had to be secured, so *LSM(R) 195* slowly fell behind and became increasingly isolated from the others still steaming to aid *Little* and *Aaron Ward*.

Both destroyers were burning out of control. The *Little* was broken amidships, and as she sank, her captain ordered all hands to abandon ship. About 1855, the destroyer slipped into 850 fathoms of water as depth charges exploded within. The sun was setting as enemy planes now pressed their attacks against the crippled *Aaron Ward* and the four amphibious support ships.

About 1904, two twin-engine planes approached the lone *LSM(R) 195* on her stern and port quarter, "one surely identified as a Nick, the other probably a Nick or a Dinah," recalled Lt. Woodson. The planes split up: one circled off the starboard beam about 500 feet above the water, and the other veered slightly left at very low altitude while still approaching the port quarter, "using fast evasive tactics." *LSM(R) 195* and *LCS 83* both opened fire on the aircraft but with no apparent affects.

The attack revealed a skillful pincer movement dividing the rocketship's defensive anti-aircraft fires. "The 5"/38 was able to keep the first aircraft away with help from the 40 mm when [the] aircraft came within their firing area on the starboard side," said Lt. Woodson, but this plane may have been a decoy to draw fire. "The second, very low-flying aircraft approaching on the port quarter had to be stopped by the two 20 mm guns on the port side"—one gun opposite the conning tower, the other gun adjacent the five-inch gunmount—"since time did not permit the 5"/38 to shift targets and the pipe rail limit stops on the 40 mm guns would have prevented these guns from getting on target. The outboard [rocket] launchers had been removed and 20 mm cams re-cut previously, otherwise the two 20 mm guns could not have trained on the very low-flying aircraft." Chance thus favored the enemy, explained Lt. Woodson, since "the armament for protecting that portion of the ship against suicide aircraft was inadequate."[7]

And all hell broke loose.

Yeoman 2c Harold Catchpole was a Phone Talker on the Conn:

> We were already at battle stations and commenced firing at the planes high in the sky. I don't know how many planes were up there. Our radar could "see" much further but our eye contact was only about 11 miles to the horizon. While we were shooting high, a bogie came over the horizon about 40 feet above the water towards us. We turned our guns on him but it was too late and he hit the main deck just below the Conning Tower where Captain Woodson, the gunnery officer, [Terence W.] Listen the Signalman, and me were at the open top of the tower. The Radar and Radio men were also in the Tower in rooms below us. We had a full load of rockets on the main deck and many ignited and exploded when the plane hit. It appeared that the plane was sinking down through the ship amid all the flames and exploding ammunition.[8]

Signalman Frank Pizur next faced a fateful choice:

> I watched one of them come at us low on the water at full speed, directly at the spot where I was standing. I had to make a quick decision: either stand there and die instantly, or dive overboard and see how long before the sharks got me. I decided to give the sharks a chance and leaped overboard a split second before the Kamikaze crashed. I was knocked unconscious, and when I came to, realized I was in the churn and only inches from the ship's screws which were turning full speed ahead. I must have been pulled under the ship and I sort of glanced off the side edge of the screw and was pushed aside and backwards of the ship, otherwise I would have been pulled into it and sliced to pieces.[9]

Strafing on its approach from 240° relative, "the plane dived into Frame 17, port side of USS *LSM(R) 195*, ripping rocket launchers from [the] deck," described Lt. Woodson.

> After smoke had cleared away, the plane appeared to have landed in the midship and forward rocket magazines and forward crews quarters. An unusual amount of shrapnel resulted from burning rockets which were loaded topside. These burning rockets were propelled only short distances from the ship with numerous hits about the deck, lighting small fires and causing additional amounts of shrapnel.... The assembled rockets without nose fuses in the ready service and the rockets with shorting out clips intact loaded on all of the inboard launchers proved to be a definite hazard to the ship and its personnel. After the suicide aircraft hit the ship, the flames from the aircraft ignited the ballistite in the motors which caused the rockets to leave the rails and land on the ship and around the ship in the water. From limited observation, none of the rockets seemed to travel very far. The crew received a considerable amount of shrapnel from the explosion [*sic*] of the rockets loaded on the topside.... Order was given to fight the fire and turn on [the] sprinkler system [but] it was discovered that both the fire main and auxiliary pumps were broken and inoperative.[10]

The crash caused a gaping hole in the port side amidships, and internal explosions erupted upward through the rocket deck between the Conn and bow. The dual-engine plane's ruptured fuel tanks splashed aviation gas that quickly ignited, burning men and ship alike. "It could have been me, too," reflected Harold Catchpole, "if the pilot had just pulled up a little bit coming in. The whole Conning Tower would have went. He hit the ship in the port side and settled in the main deck just below the Conning Tower. The rockets in the racks [launchers] were blowing up all over the place."[11]

Still more Japanese planes attacked *Aaron Ward* to finish off the burning destroyer. She wouldn't sink, but *Aaron Ward* lost 45 killed and 49 wounded. *LCS 14* moved alongside to fight the blazing fires while rescuing men from the waters. *LCSs 83* and *25*—the latter was crashed close aboard en route by a Kamikaze that killed one and caused numerous casualties—reached the site of the lost *Little* to recover survivors. *Little* lost 30 killed and 79 wounded.

LSM(R) 195 burned furiously in the evening twilight amidst internal explosions, which forced her captain to make his gravest decision as Commanding Officer. "When it seemed that nothing could be done with the fire, and loaded and ready service rockets were hitting all parts of the ship, the order was given (at approximately 1920) to abandon ship," said Lt. Woodson.

"After a few minutes," continued Yeoman Catchpole,

> the Captain (knowing the ship was mortally wounded) gave the order to all crew to go to the stern and prepare to abandon ship. Most of us left the ship by jumping into the water or going down the fantail ladder into the water. All life rafts had been released into the water. We all had life jackets on with a small waterproof flashlight pinned to them. I am pretty sure that Captain Woodson was the last to leave his ship climbing down the fantail ladder into the water. Some crewmen were in the rafts and others clung to the ropes strung on the rafts. Still others were floating by themselves in the sea.[12]

Despite extraordinary efforts to save *LSM(R) 195*, explained her captain, "Ten to fifteen minutes later, the ship after numerous explosions went down bow first. Two life rafts had been put over with almost 20 men on each (the Commanding Officer in the water). Shortly thereafter tremendous explosions from the 5" powder magazine occurred underwater."[13]

Trying to escape the threatening undertow of their sinking rocketship, Harold Catchpole recalled only hearing and feeling the final throes of his dying ship in the surrounding darkness. "The first ½ hour we were in the water, there were two tremendous explosions and we knew the 195 was gone."[14] "The ship sank within three or four minutes while exploding like the Fourth of July," said Signalman Frank Pizur. "I had the feeling of bubbles going up my spine from the concussions in the water. It was around 2000 hours, and I could see Kume Island about 5 miles away. Before I could decide to swim for it, it was already dark and I lost sight of it."[15]

"As darkness descended, it was a sight to see all the lights over the water," remembered Catchpole,

> We were afraid the Japs would see them and strafe us in the water. I believe, counting the wounded, there were 70 men in the water. Inasmuch as all of the ships in Picket Station 10 were damaged heavily, we had to stay in the water for 3 to 4 hours until a destroyer came over from the next Picket Station to pick us up.
> I don't know the name of the destroyer that picked us up, but it was damaged by a bogie that just missed. I am pretty sure that Captain Woodson was on that destroyer, too, as I recall he had the crew list from his waterproof flashlight and was checking to see who was there and whether we had seen any others alive, dead or wounded.[16]

"Some of us survivors grouped together (8 or 16 men, I'm not sure)," added Signalman Pizur, "and I began sending S.O.S. signals with my flashlight until we were picked up by the destroyer USS *Bache*, about 0100 hours."[17]

Destroyer *Bache DD 470* reached RPS 10 at 2040 from adjacent RPS 9, and destroyer-minelayer *Shannon DM 25* rendezvoused with *Aaron Ward* about the same time. *Bache* commenced the search for survivors from the *Little* and *LSM(R) 195* when lookouts spotted blinking white lights among the waters from the flashlights of men from the sunken rocketship. Two whale boats were immediately lowered, and by 2145, all the survivors in the immediate area appeared to be recovered. Searches continued until 2313, when *Bache* ceased further efforts: "Completed search for survivors, having rescued 5 officers, 69 enlisted men and one dog from *LSM(R) 195*."[18]

Most of the men from *LSM(R) 195* were transported to the receiving ship *Lauderdale APA 179*, then briefly transferred to the transport *Karnes APA 175*, before returning to the United States. A small group remained aboard hospital evacuation ship *Crescent City APA 21* for medical attention, while a half dozen men were cared for aboard hospital ship *Solace AH 5* before going home.[19]

"The performance of all hands was exemplary," lauded Lieutenant William E. Woodson, Jr., who was awarded the Silver Star Medal.[20]

Lt. Comdr. John H. Fulweiler, Commander LSM(R) Group Twenty-Seven, cited, "This command particularly wishes to commend the bravery and coolness of the Commanding Officer of the *LSM(R) 195*, Lt. W. E. Woodson. In the face of the enemy he fought his ship to its utmost limit, and upon its loss he rallied his men together and maintained them as a unit in the early hours of the night until rescue ships picked them up. To his coolness, gallantry, and disregard for his personal safety, many of his men owe their lives." Commander Dennis L. Francis, Commander LSM Flotilla Nine, added, "The *LSM(R) 195* has an excellent record of performance in the combat area as indicated in action reports of this command."[21]

USS *LSM(R) 195* lost 9 killed,[22] 16 wounded, and 6 missing.

RPS 1: 4 May 1945

At Radar Picket Station 1 on the morning of 4 May 1945, *LCSs 31* and *23* led the patrol formation in Station 1000, a thousand yards dead ahead of *LCS 21* and USS *LSM(R) 194* (Lt. Allan M. Hirshberg, USNR) in Station 1180. On opposing sides of the column, two destroyers varied their speeds and distances: to the left in Station 1270 was *Ingraham DD 694* as OTC; to the right in Station 1090 was *Morrison DD 560*. Patrol courses alternated NW-SE at 10 knots and changed direction each half-hour.

Weather was clear and sunny, with unlimited visibility and smooth seas.

Bogeys sporadically heckled the formation before dawn. After 0810, however, increasing numbers of enemy planes began to overwhelm the Combat Air Patrol, so the Fighter Director in *Morrison* requested reinforcements. "At this time the sky appeared to be filled with enemy planes, circling the formation. Most of them were tied up by the CAP in dogfights. Japs appeared to be attempting to break away to attack our ships from all directions," explained *Ingraham*.[23] Estimates varied on the final numbers of Japanese planes that descended upon Radar Picket Station 1, ranging from 35 to 50 enemy aircraft or possibly more. Destroyer protocol was to maneuver independently at high speeds during air attacks, but remain close enough to the amphibious picket support ships for mutual fire support.[24]

John P. Wickser, an Ensign aboard *LSM(R) 194*, later reflected upon being the target of a Kamikaze attack:

> Watching a raid descend upon you from the bridge as the destroyers put up their barrage of anti-aircraft fire and the Jap pilots attempting to dive the ships in desperate maneuvers had all the gruesome fascination of being tied to a railroad track with an express descending on you. From a distance it was almost like watching some sort of deadly ball game—as they say, war is, after all, man's greatest game—and each time the destroyers scored a hit our crew would burst into cheers. But all too often, we found ourselves required to pick up survivors and render such assistance as we could.[25]

The picket formation was steaming northwesterly when the first air attacks focused relentlessly on the destroyers about 0815. *Ingraham* fought off numerous attackers, but was hit by a fighter plane whose bomb exploded, killing 14 and wounding 37. *Morrison* struggled against repeated air attacks and evaded several near misses, but was finally hit by two Zekes, one whose bomb exploded. The CAP helped down many of the Japanese raiders, but many broke through the gauntlet and overwhelmed the ships. *LCS 31* was attacked by several enemy fighters which either crashed close aboard or glanced off, killing 5 and wounding 2. Two float planes stealthily tracked the *Morrison*, then crashed into her and set off such devastating explosions abaft that the destroyer's captain had to order the crew to abandon ship. *Morrison* finally sank about 1836, losing 159 men and suffering 102 casualties. But because the Japanese air attacks were too intense to safely render aid, *Ingraham* maneuvered to a mutually supporting position with the *LCS*s.

A bogie got past the CAP and made a run on the *LCS(L) 21*, then continued towards *LSM(R) 194* using evasive maneuvers until closing within a thousand yards off the starboard beam. The rocketship opened fire with her 40mms and 5"/38, but the latter gun checked fire to avoid hitting *LCS 21*. Gunners of the two single 40mms scored hits but failed to sufficiently damage the plane; then men on a 20mm and a .50 caliber machinegun opened up.

"In our frantic attempts to zig-zag, our gunnery was more inaccurate than usual, I suppose," reflected John P. Wickser. "But in any events, we brought everything to bear we had—our 40 and 20 millimeters—even our 5 inch—practically shooting side arms at the descending planes." Ultimately, concluded Lt. Allan M. Hirshberg, "[The] armament aboard the USS *LSM(R) 194* proved inadequate to protect the ship from a low-flying ramming plane."[26]

At 0838, AA fire struck the closest aircraft—identified as a Tony fighter[27]—causing it to burst into flame, but it quickly swerved and plunged into *LSM(R) 194* at the water line between the 5"/38 gun mount and the fire director tower at Frame 27. The bomb it carried exploded, which started fires in aft steering and the engine room, caused the boiler to blow up and spread flames through the aft handling room. The explosion also ruptured the ship's fire and flushing system and killed men in the after repair party.

"The ship was shaken by a stunning blast," recalled Wickser, and "I thought, 'This is it.'"

> I flung open the door of the radio shack and stood out on the deck, and on the afterdeck I saw a frightening sight. A flaming Japanese plane had crashed into us just above the waterline at the starboard quarter, penetrating into the 5-inch handling room—the flash fire instantly killing all personnel there. Live ammunition and rockets were exposed and why we did not explode right then and there, I will never know. I stood almost paralyzed as I saw the flames belching out of a giant hole literally large enough to drive a truck through as the remains of the Japanese plane flamed away. All I could think of was, "Well, this is it for me and for all of us." For an instant, the thought [also] ran through me, "I've got about a minute or

two at the most to make up my mind whether to stand on this deck and attempt to do my duty or jump overboard before the entire ship explodes."[28]

Men in the after damage control party were all badly burned, so the forward damage control party was called aft to take over. But before hoses could be rigged for pumping, the ship immediately started to settle by the stern and listed to starboard, with water washing up on the after rocketdeck. "All direct communication to the bridge was cut off," explained former Ensign Wickser, "but I shouted to the best of my ability to get the Captain's attention. I heard him frantically giving orders on a battery-operated bullhorn, when I observed the hatch which led from our radio shack to the deck below [was] opening."

> I could see flames coming through and heard screams and moans as half a dozen men struggled their way out of the engine room and after steering compartment up through the radio shack, covered with oil—their hands and faces having been exposed to flash fire, they looked as if they were draped in wet Kleenex. This brought me to my senses, I suppose. I tried to assist and calm them. We called frantically for our pharmacist's mate but he was still at his battle station.
>
> One of my duties was that of assistant damage control officer, a field about which I knew very little, having been rather busy with my own duties.... A chief warrant officer appeared on deck, a man who never particularly liked me, as he was a "regular Navy" type who resented Reserve Officers as well as amphibious duty, and asked me for instructions as to what damage control measures should be taken. I could not contact the Captain effectively, so I said I thought we should flood the magazines. This you accomplished by breaking a glass cover over a little box with a hammer and pulling a lever which sets off an auxiliary power pump and floods water into the ammunition lockers—practically the entire central part of the ship. He asked, "Was this an order?" and I replied, "Yes." I am convinced this order had a great deal to do with the sinking of our ship, although I suppose one will never know whether had we not flooded the magazines, we would have blown up.[29] Finally, after what seemed an interminable period of time, the Captain called down through a megaphone and directed me to take my division over the side and abandon ship. I have never heard more welcome words.

In the meantime, Lt. Hirshberg ordered the two 40mm gun crews to man their guns to fend-off enemy air attacks until all hands evacuated.

Only three life rafts could be deployed from *LSM(R) 194* because fire had damaged the others. "Most of my division had assembled and were on the deck as the Japs could see we were sinking and we had given up any attempts to fire our guns at this point," explained John Wickser.

> On receiving the order to abandon ship, I attempted to get the wounded men in my division, and any others that were nearby, into the few life rafts we had. The combination of the intense burns and salt water would have been excruciating to them had they had to jump over the side. Actually, nobody had to jump much of anywhere, because by this time you could almost step off the stern of the ship, so badly was she listing."
>
> Getting my division into the water, I jumped in and shouted as loudly as I could to stay on their backs. Underwater explosive force from exploding depth charges or other explosives on sinking ships is extremely intensified as opposed to concussive force in the air because water is not compressible, and we had been warned if you are on your back [then] you have a better chance of surviving its force. A great many of the men were in a state of shock. Also, some panicked, but I kept shouting to them and swimming on hopefully getting far enough away before the ship sunk to avoid the anticipated usual suction.
>
> As I swam on my back and saw our ship listing further and further until it finally rose at an angle of about 75 degrees in the water, like a giant leviathan or a vision of the *Titanic*, or so it seemed to me at the time, tears came to my eyes. I could think, strangely enough, of nothing but how terrible it was, what a terrible loss it was—to lose all of the extra equipment I had secured on board through stealth and trickery from supply bases—such as extra binoculars, typewriters—everything tumbling about the deck—but as far as I could ascertain, just about everyone had abandoned ship: that is to say, those that were still alive.[30]

LCS 21 was standing by the sinking rocketship to give assistance, while the captain of the *Ingraham* watched from afar as the proud rocketship "went down with her guns still firing."[31] Finally, the 40mm gun crews were ordered to abandon ship and were followed by the commanding officer. USS *LSM(R) 194* settled straight down, stern first. "I do remember observing my Captain virtually perched at the top of the conning tower over the bridge," said Wickser, "and true to the dictates of tradition, he indeed must have been the last man to leave the ship. Later he valiantly attempted to save others in the water, towing rafts by fastening lines around his shoulders, and as I have said, performing acts which won him the Navy's highest award."[32]

"This was a very traumatic period in this campaign," explained Allan M. Hirshberg, captain of USS *LSM(R) 194*:

> ... the Kamikazes were attempting a mass penetration of the screen. After the station destroyers were hit or sunk, our ship came under attack and was hit by a suicide plane right at the water line, exploding internally into the engine room compartment. Within a very short time it became apparent [that] the ship could not be saved, and I called for "Abandon Ship." The command was duly executed. All life rafts were released, those surviving abandoned ship while myself and some gun crews remained to give cover to those in the water. I left the ship from the conning tower with most of the ship awash. I believe that within minutes the entire ship was gone. We attempted to move as far from the scene as possible, but either heat or pressure set off a terrible explosion of all the ammo that was stored aboard. Many members of the crew and officers received intestinal perforation and bleeding from the explosion. We lost a considerable number of men who were killed aboard and some from the explosion.[33]

Many years passed before Lieutenant Hirshberg could share his innermost thoughts and feelings. "I have spent almost fifty years blotting out my own painful memories of the Pacific war, especially the Okinawa Campaign. To do so was my own way of healing myself..."[34]

Time and space compressed on Radar Picket Station 1. "About ten minutes after our ship disappeared in a final great rush, or so it seems to me now although my sense of time was confused," then-Ensign John P. Wickser admitted, "a tremendous explosion took place as all our rockets detonated underwater. I can best describe it by saying that it felt as if you had suddenly been kicked in the back by twenty mules. I have very little recollection of this experience except a brief glimpse of a vast mushroom of water, under which I was thrust up, and later descending into the water again where I guess I must have floated partially unconscious."[35]

LCS(L) 21 was en route to pick up survivors of *LSM(R) 194* when she noted the rocketship exploding at 0854. The sheer power and intensity was staggering: "Magazine of LSM [*sic*] exploded underwater with this ship approximately 300 yards from area. Our gyrocompass was burned out, water mains were sprung, generator burned out, and several seams split."[36]

Wickser continued,

> When I came to my senses, I noticed my shoes were blown off my feet, as I had loosened them in an attempt to remove them; my life jacket was blown partially off, my helmet gone and a shock-proof wristwatch my father had given me was without crystal and hands. I must have been stunned for some time, and having received one of the granddaddys of all high-colonics ever administered, was bleeding internally and in some pain. I noted vaguely that the Marines had arrived overhead and were driving off the remaining Jap planes who were attempting to strafe the survivors in the water. After some time I found myself on the decks of the LCI [*sic*] which was literally awash with the blood of the survivors packed aboard from the three sunken ships. What happened after that is another tale....[37]

As *Morrison* and *LSM(R) 194* went down, the enemy redoubled attacks on the *Ingraham*. "During this period, [my] remembrance of which is hazy because of the complexity of the situation and the volume of attacks, *Ingraham* shot down four more planes and was hit by a fifth," recalled the destroyer's captain. "It is estimated that the CAP splashed ten (10) and that the LCSs shot down numerous attackers. In reconstructing this phase of the action, which lasted only about two (2) minutes, it has been established that *Ingraham* was under coordinated suicide attack by at least five Nips, that other enemy planes were seen crashing amongst the small support craft and that our courageous CAP tied up more potential attackers, many of them overhead ... but the CAP was still operating in superb fashion overhead, driving off all attacks and repeatedly scoring kills."[38]

By 0900, *Ingraham* directed the three LCSs to fan the waters for survivors of the *LSM(R) 194* and *Morrison*. While *LCS 21* rescued sailors, her damage control party was also busy repairing damage incurred by the underwater explosion from the sinking rocketship. *LCS 23* recovered one officer and 19 enlisted men from the *LSM(R) 194*; *LCS 21* picked up the commanding officer of *LSM(R) 194* and 50 of his crew plus 187 men from *Morrison*. Among the recovered were two doctors and several pharmacists mates, who provided valuable aid with the overwhelming numbers of casualties.

Once back at Okinawa, fourteen *LSM(R) 194* survivors were transported to hospital ship *Relief AH 1* and four were transferred to *Solace AH 5* for medical care.

Lt. Comdr. John H. Fulweiler, Commander LSM(R) Group Twenty-Seven, cited, "This command wishes particularly to commend the performance of the Commanding Officer of *LSM(R) 194*, Lt. Allan M. Hirshberg, for his coolness, judgment and bravery in the face of the most hazardous circumstances. All reports agree, that many men owe their lives to his cool gallant example."[39]

Lieutenant Allan M. Hirshberg was awarded the Permanent Citation for the Navy Cross.

USS *LSM(R) 194* was awarded the Navy Unit Commendation,

> For outstanding heroism in action against enemy Japanese Kamikaze aircraft. Operating in the advanced flank at Okinawa on Radar Picket Station, she heroically repelled numerous suicide attacks being responsible for the destruction of several enemy aircraft. When finally succumbing to a Kamikaze attack, she fought gallantly with intrepidity until she sank. Her courageous determination and effort were in keeping with the highest traditions of the United States Naval Service.

USS *LSM(R) 194* lost 14 killed[40] and 23 wounded.

RPS 12: 4 May 1945

At Radar Picket Station 12 on the morning of 4 May 1945, USS *LSM(R) 190* (Lt. Richard H. Saunders, USNR) was acting OTC for *LCSs 81, 84* and *118*. The four picket support ships were stationed among the four corners of a large box-like patrol formation surrounding destroyer *Luce DD 522*[41] in tactical center. East-West courses alternated every 5 miles at 8– 10 knots.

Weather was sunny and mild with light winds, limited cirrocumulus clouds, and ten miles' visibility.

At 0750, *Luce* reported enemy planes approaching from the north at 20 miles and sounded General Quarters, then fired to port on the first wave of attackers. "We had been under heavy attacks all the night before," later recalled Lt. (jg) Gordon Etter, *LSM(R) 190*

Engineering Officer. Now, "The Japs brought over 18 planes. Then our Corsairs came in dog-fighting over us. The Japs began making dives at us, coming in over us with their guns blasting away."[42] The Combat Air Patrol splashed several planes, but bogies were still piercing the American fighter screen.

"At this time two planes attacked the *Luce*," explained Lt.(jg) George T. Harmon, Executive Officer of *LSM(R) 190*, "the first coming from high out of the clouds, the second flying low over the water. This latter plane crashed the destroyer amidships leaving her in a sinking condition. The *LSM(R) 190* reported by radio that the *Luce* had been hit. Meanwhile, *LCS 118*, having been previously ordered by this ship to investigate an object to Port, was some distance astern."[43]

Attackers broke through the CAP around 0808 and streaked toward the destroyer from opposing directions. *Luce* took five violent suicider crashes in rapid succession which caused her to burn and flood rapidly. The destroyer's stern was going underwater at 0814 when her captain ordered abandon ship and the Japanese turned attention to nearby *LSM(R) 190*.

"The attack on the *LSM(R) 190* began with a Dinah flying in over the stern and dropping a bomb which missed," continued Lt. (jg) Harmon. "This plane was hit by our automatic weapons. Thereupon the plane turned over, returned and dived into the 5"/38 mount, setting it on fire."[44] Later, Harmon offered additional details during a newspaper interview: "One plane crossed our bow and dropped a bomb which barely missed, although it did shake us up considerably. Our gunners hit him several times and set the plane on fire. He then banked and dived straight for us, hitting the *190* in the stern and setting it on fire."[45]

"Shrapnel resulting from the plane crash severely injured the Commanding Officer," said Lt. (jg) Harmon, "rendering him prostrate and immediately killed the Gunnery Officer," Ensign Stuart C. Bjorklund. At the time of this first attack, Harmon was on the main deck directing Damage Control Parties and unaware of his captain's injuries and the death of the gunnery officer. "Severely wounded in the first five minutes of action, the Commanding Officer lay on his back in the Conn, and though unconscious from time to time, nevertheless roused himself to approve or direct the handling of the ship by his juniors."[46]

As their wounded skipper slipped in and out of consciousness, the rocketship continued steaming under the last order given to the helm prior to the crash—full right rudder at flank speed. Reacting quickly, Radioman William J. Nuber, standing Phone Talker watch on the bridge, took over the Wheelhouse and conned the ship until relieved by wounded Communications Officer Ensign Lyle Tennis. Lt. (jg) Harmon later praised Ensign Tennis in his final report for "His calm, cool and efficient handling of the ship despite shrapnel wounds [and] was largely responsible for the minimum number of casualties suffered during the continuing attacks."

The 5"/38 mount, said Mr. Harmon, "was practically knocked off its foundation and set on fire that spread to the Handling Room and After Stowage Space.... The sprinkler system to the 5"/38 magazines and the after rocket assembly room were ordered turned on and fire hoses broken out from amidships and played on the 5"/38 mount." Harmon added, "However, as fire mains had been ruptured, pressure was negligible, and the Damage Control Parties commenced breaking out lines from the auxiliary fire pump."[47]

The rocketship was bearing due north when a second kamikaze attacker approached low above the water from the port beam, then crashed into the upper level of the engine room. "Wreckage of this plane remained stuck into the side of the ship," reported Harmon.

Fires broke out in the engine room and the crash disabled the auxiliary fire pump; soon, "smoke was so thick that is was impossible to see the controls." Engineering Officer Gordon Etter remained in the engine room as fires turned it into a virtual blast furnace. When permission was finally granted to abandon the engine room, Lt. (jg) Etter supervised its orderly evacuation and then reported to the Conn to assist Mr. Tennis.[48]

A third Japanese plane, identified as another Dinah, came after *LSM(R) 190* about 0824, and the rocketship attempted evasive maneuvers and zigzagging at flank speed. As the twin engine fighter crossed from port to starboard about masthead height, it dropped a bomb that missed widely by some 700 yards. By now the rocketship was all but defenseless with every gun out of action except the starboard abaft 20mm.

Two minutes later, resumed Lt. (jg) Harmon, "A fourth plane attacked in 'sneak' fashion releasing a bomb which hit in the area of the Mk. 51 Director tub. A fifth plane, a Val, dove from considerable height pursued by Corsairs of the CAP which had arrived on the scene at 0815. This plane crossed from port aft of the Starboard 20mm [but] causing no damage."[49]

Some four miles from *LSM(R) 190*, *Luce* suffered its final death throes as her stern lifted high in the air then plunged below the surface with an underwater explosion erupting from her innards. USS *Luce* suffered 149 killed or missing and 96 wounded. *LCS 81* proceeded toward the survivors some two miles off her port beam, and was joined by *LCS 118*.

LSM(R) 190 was still underway as wild flames and smoke clouds billowed from her stern. Tennis continued manning the Conn as Etter and Ensign Benner, the ship's Sixth Officer, organized working parties dropping cargo nets over the side. "As the fires were now beyond control and the ship had developed a decided port list," said Lt. (jg) Harmon, "it was decided to prepare to abandon ship." The body of Ensign Bjorklund and the wounded commanding officer were carried down from the Conn by officers Tennis and Etter. Mr. Harmon reported to the skipper that fires had spread throughout the 5" magazine, the aft stowage space, and the engine room; the auxiliary fire pump was inoperative, all power was lost. He advised the captain to order abandon ship, so "this was carried out at about 0830."[50]

Ensign Tennis remained behind with two wounded enlisted men to cut free the life rafts, which they lashed together and in which they placed their weakened commanding officer and other wounded. "Twenty minutes later (0850 approx.)," said Mr. Harmon, "the ship went down and forty minutes thereafter the *LCS 84* started to pick up survivors...."[51] As the abandoned, burning *LSM(R) 190* sank beneath the waves, even those aboard *LCSs 81* and *84* felt the violent underwater explosions from the rocketship. (Much later, *LCS 84*'s commanding officer leveled a caustic reproach: "In the action of 4 May 1945 the destroyer and LSM(R) were sunk without any of the LCSs being able to fire a shot in their defense because they insisted on cruising at a distance of about four or five miles from us."[52])

Destroyer-minelayer *Henry A. Wiley DM 29* reached RPS 12 about 0933, and immediately commenced lifesaving operations where the *Luce* had sunk. A dozen minutes later, *LCS 118* steamed at flank speed to "Dodger Area," Hagushi Anchorage, but was recalled to transfer badly wounded to the *Wiley*, then cast off once more for Okinawa. Meanwhile, *LCS 84* picked up 6 officers and 47 enlisted survivors from *LSM(R) 190*, 12 of whom were stretcher cases, and *LCS 81* recovered a badly wounded survivor at 1000.

After the survivors' medical and physical conditions were assessed, the LCSs transferred the recovered men among the *Wiley*, rescue vessel *PCE(R) 852*, and high speed transport *Kilty APD 15*. (As *PCE[R] 852* approached within visual contact of the ships at RPS 12, lookouts sighted a man in the waters 500 yards off the starboard bow; it proved to be a Japanese airman upon rescue.) Fleet tug *Cree ATF 84* also arrived and was laying to, but, finding her services were no longer needed, the tug and *PCE(R) 852* both set courses for Okinawa and were followed by *Kilty* about forty-five minutes later. Most survivors were subsequently transferred to *Lauderdale APA 179* for medical treatment and some to hospital ship *Mercy AH 8* for intensive care.

By 6 May 1945, many men were transferred to *Karnes APA 175* for transportation to the Receiving Station at Treasure Island, San Francisco, a journey of three weeks. Once stateside, they were granted thirty days' survivor's leave. En route, *LSM(R) 190*'s officers Harmon and Etter, accompanied by Yeoman 1c Frank Gosnell, disembarked at Saipan and were flown ahead to the United States via Naval Air Transport Service (NATS) in a PB4Y. The trio proceeded from the West Coast to Washington, D.C., for duty with the Navy Annex of the Bureau of Naval Personnel, where *LSM(R) 190*'s official records were compiled, updated, and closed out. Completing their assignment by mid–June, they too were granted one month's survivor's leave.[53]

USS *LSM(R) 190* was awarded the Navy Unit Commendation,

For meritorious service in action against enemy Japanese Kamikaze aircraft. Operating on the advanced flank at Okinawa on radar picket stations, the USS *LSM(R) 190* heroically repelled numerous suicide attacks, being responsible singly for the destruction of several enemy aircraft. The USS *LSM(R) 190* participated in the rescue of survivors from sinking ships to a total of one hundred eighty. When finally succumbing to four Kamikaze attacks, three of which directly hit the ship, the USS *LSM(R) 190* fought gallantly until she sank. Her courageous determination and effort were in keeping with the highest traditions of the United States Naval Service.[54]

USS *LSM(R) 190* lost 14 killed[55] and 18 wounded.

RPS 10: 4 May 1945

At Radar Picket Station 10 on the evening of 4 May 1945, guideship USS *LSM(R) 192* (Lt. Neal B. Hadsell, USNR) led the picket patrol column followed by *LCSs 110, 55* and *54* about five miles southwest of Japanese-held Kume Shima. Stationed some five miles west-southwest were destroyers *Cowell DD 547* as OTC and *Gwin DM 33*. The picket support ships and destroyers steamed at 8 to 10 knots on courses reciprocating NW and SE each half-hour.

Weather and seas were ideal.

Cowell set General Quarters at sunset about 1914, then minutes later, her radar picked up a target closing from the southwest. The Japanese favored air attacks during the dusky twilights of mornings and evenings, which American sailors called "Bogie Hour," when the blurring between lightness and darkness deceives and conceals. The destroyer's OTC, however, failed to warn the LSM(R) and three LCSs, which were caught by surprise by the fast, low-flying raiders. Hence, enemy estimates (4 to 10 planes), aircraft identifications (Vals, Oscars, Judys, Zekes, a twin engine bomber), and descriptions of flight paths varied widely among the ships' official reports and eyewitness recollections. Some accounts also traced enemy planes flying either from or escaping to the protective cover of nearby Kume Shima to the east-northeast.

"General quarters was sounded on this ship as soon as the planes were spotted," reported

Lt. Hadsell, "but action was so fast that War Cruising gun crews remained at the ship's guns."[56] Russell Wydeen, an Ensign and Engineering Officer in *LSM(R) 192*, added, "We were eating when GQ was sounded and we could hear our guns firing as we left the wardroom on our way to Battle Stations. We were in a state of reduced gun watch at that time with one 20 mm and two 40 mm manned. I came through the radio shack on the rocket deck headed toward the fantail to check our readiness with the damage control crew who were stationed at the rear of the ship."[57]

"The original attack was made on the *Cowell* and the *Gwin*," explained Lt. Hadsell. "[But] as soon as these ships opened fire, two of the planes diverted their attacks to the remaining four ships. One headed for the LCS(L)s and the other for the *LSM(R) 192*." One plane crashed *Gwin*'s after deck, killing 2 and wounding nine. *Cowell* fought off several other attackers, some strafing and crashing in the water close aboard, but she suffered no casualties. The destroyers and LCSs claimed credit for downing and assisting splashes of as many raiders as had attacked, although one or more enemy planes may have escaped toward Kume Shima.[58] Afterwards, the picket ships would search the waters overnight into the next morning for missing men and survivors.

Hadsell continued, "The attack was made from dead ahead at an altitude of approximately 40 feet. It is estimated that the bow 40 mm gun opened fire at 4000 yards. The forward port 20 mm and the amidships 40 mm guns joined in the defense. All three guns observed their tracers striking the target." The rocketship's gunners identified the attacking plane as an Oscar fighter, but it could not be stopped.[59]

Ensign Russell Wydeen was topside during the attack on *LSM(R) 192*:

> ... the Kamikaze passed down the ship from bow to stern on the port side, tearing up some rocket launchers, bounced off the deck aft of the 5" mount and crashed into the sea astern of us. The plane passed about 20 feet from me. Our 20 mm gun crew aft of the radio shack were firing at a plane off to our starboard which was attacking the minelayer, I believe. Then it was over—quickly. We strung new wire cable lines to replace those torn off by the plane, washed down the deck to get rid of fuel which had been spilled on the deck. The damage to rocket launchers from the wing of the plane was not too extensive and the steel shield around the port 20 mm was torn up. We were fortunate in that that gun was not manned when the attack started. Only one man had arrived on station and he was placing a 20 mm drum in the gun. He said he saw the plane coming over the bow and dropped to the deck behind the shield just in time. He had a broken finger when the deck was torn up a bit.[60]

Radarman Ronald MacKay added, "There was a crunching noise—just so fast, you know—and a bunch of stuff [airplane debris] coming down from the opening where the anchor engine was located ... and I walked over and picked up some of it because the plane had just hit and gone off into the water."[61]

The plane's left wing struck three outer banks of rocket launchers ("P, Q, and R"), just forward of the 5" gun's director tower, and knocked off barrels of fog oil. Aft portside damages included an air blower and the 20mm gun, gun tub and splinter shield. Some claimed seeing a parachute just before the plane hit the water, but neither chute nor pilot was recovered. "The enemy's intentions were not clear," concluded the rocketship's skipper. "He did not strafe the ship even though he had ammunition, for both A.P. [anti-personnel] and H.E. [high explosive] 20 mm shells were found on the deck; though his attack was of the suicide type, he appeared to swing wide of the conn possibly in order to hit the 5"/38 director and mount. If the latter was true, then his attempt was thwarted by his wing striking the rocket launchers."[62]

Years after the war, former *LSM(R) 192* skipper Neal Hadsell reflected:

With regard to the Radar Picket Station incident, there was a definite plan and a good one: the five planes came in very low behind the island [Kume Shima] so that they could not be detected until the very last minute. They came close to accomplishing their goal for the tin can and the minelayer were badly damaged. The two that came our way could have very easily disposed of the rest of the ships assigned to the Station with a bit different happening. We had a theory that the pilot that engaged us may have misjudged, being fooled by the wake of our ship. Being shallow-draft, we kicked up as much wake as a tin can even though our speed at best was 10 to 12 knots. I had kicked up the speed to full ahead so that we had a bit more maneuverability, even though it was poor at best. We did not maneuver with the plane coming directly head on…. This was about the best we could have done even had we had time to plan the response. This all happened so fast that there wasn't time to think about the potential.[63]

Lt. Comdr. John H. Fulweiler, Commander LSM(R) Group Twenty-Seven, cited, "The alert performance of the War Cruising Gun Crews, appears to have contributed largely to this Ship's successful escape from severe damage…. The fine devotion to duty of this Ship and LSM(R)s as a Group under the most hazardous circumstances on Radar Picket Assignments is to be highly commended. Recommendations for awards and commendations, will be forwarded separately by this Command in conjunction with LSM Flotilla Nine."[64]

Kikusui *Raid No. 6*

From 10 to 11 May 1945, Japanese Operation *Ten-Go* launched *Kikusui* Raid No. 6, dispatching over 200 aircraft including 150 Kamikazes. A half-dozen U.S. ships were damaged and caused over 800 American sailors killed, wounded and missing.[65]

RPS 16: 10 May 1945

At Radar Picket Station 16 on 10 May 1945, USS *LSM(R) 191* (Lt. John W. Loyer, USNR) was unit guide of the picket support ships followed in column astern by *LCSs 55, 110* and *54*. Destroyer *Lowry DD 770* was OTC and the column's leader followed by destroyer-minelayer *Henry A. Wiley DM 29*. Patrol courses alternated East-West at 8 knots about 5 miles north of Tori Shima.

Seas were calm and visibility was good with scattered clouds.

An hour before sunset, *LSM(R) 191* left formation to investigate an object spotted in the water. Once retrieved aboard, they guessed it to be the landing gear strut and wheel from a twin-engine Japanese Betty bomber. One of the crew took snapshots as shipmates posed with their prize.

About 1918, only minutes after sunset, a single-engine Japanese bomber, variously identified as either a Kate or Jill, suddenly broke out of a cloud to the south over Tori Shima. Possibly homing from the larger Japanese-held island Kume Shima 15 miles farther south, the plane closed low over the water and caught the westward column of picket ships by surprise. The bomber crossed over the bow of *LSM(R) 191*, whose alert gunners were among the few from any of the picket ships to open fire. Aiming for *Lowry*, the plane launched a torpedo, then turned away to the south to escape until a Combat Air Patrol F4U Corsair shot it down. *Lowry* took evasive actions, but the torpedo was launched from too great a distance, so it passed between the two destroyers and exploded harmlessly at the end of its run.[66]

RPS 15: 11 May 1945

At Radar Picket Station 15 on 11 May 1945, USS *LSM(R) 193* (Lt. Donald E. Boynton, USNR) was guideship of a large diamond formation within a thousand-yard diameter. Following off her port and starboard quarters were *LCSs 82* and *83*, respectively, while *LCS 84* trailed a thousand yards dead astern. Steaming ten knots, their northeast-southwest patrols reversed direction each half-hour. Meanwhile destroyers *Hugh W. Hadley DD 774* as OTC and *Evans DD 552* patrolled clockwise around the smaller picket ships about fifteen knots.

Seas were unusually calm and flat with light variable winds. Visibility was uneven as morning skies slowly cleared north and east, but misty haze lingered over the western horizon.

LSM(R) 193 had already patrolled a full week on radar picket stations when *Hadley* and *Evans* arrived on 10 May. As recalled by the rocketship's Executive Officer, Ensign Paul S. Vaitses, Jr., "Among the orders we received was a new air-attack formation which we were to assume automatically upon the approach of enemy planes. The small ships were to stay to one side, while the two destroyers raced ahead in column at flank speed. It sounded suspiciously like every man for himself to us." But, he added, "The self-assured newcomers were not long in receiving their baptism of fire."[67]

LSM(R) 193's skipper noted that "Enemy action during the night [10–11 May] had been light and spasmodic with very few alerts and no planes sighted since the preceding evening."[68] Probing Japanese "snooper" aircraft caused the men on the radar picket ships to stand prolonged periods at General Quarters, nevertheless.

In the morning of 11 May, a Combat Air Patrol responded to bogies reported to the northeast about 0740. They splashed a high-altitude reconnaissance plane, identified as a Frances, and suspected in hindsight as the control aircraft spearheading the subsequent attacks on RPS 15. Acting on intelligence reports, Commander Fifth Fleet warned U.S. naval forces at Okinawa that heavy enemy air attacks were expected for 11 May.[69]

The formation was nearing the bottom leg of their southwesterly course when raiders came in on their port quarter, catching the smaller picket ships by surprise: *LSM(R) 193* sounded General Quarters quite literally at the last minute, reacting to "two low-flying bogies who had made an undetected approach from the North." The leading aircraft was actually a seaplane emerging from the morning mist at an estimated 180 knots and about 150 feet above the water. The second, trailing aircraft was unidentified but possibly another seaplane. An F4U Corsair splashed the first plane, its gas-filled pontoons erupting in flames and smoke as it crashed into the sea between the destroyers. Contact was lost with the second plane, however, which apparently broke off attack and was assumed shot down.

Between 0755 and 0830, ships' radars discerned five large raids coming from the north and north-northwest with 156 aircraft: Raid One with 36 planes; Raid Two with 50 planes; Raid Three with 20 planes; Raid Four estimated between 20 and 30 planes; and Raid Five with another 20 planes. Vectored CAP fighters would expend enormous amounts of ammunition against the overwhelming numbers of Japanese aircraft. After running out of ammo, Corsair pilots fearlessly chased enemy planes away from the picket ships and physically forced attackers into the sea.

As raiders closed, at 0829 the OTC in *Hadley* directed the entire picket formation to turn on a southeasterly heading of 140° True, thus placing the enemy relative astern. *LSM(R)*

193's 5"/38 dual purpose gun was now fully unmasked, but this advantage faded as bogies fanned out on all sides of RPS 15. Immediately, the six picket ships began fighting off aggressive, continuous attacks as seen in the rocketship's running account:

> At 0832 the *Hadley* again began firing and reported bogies in the area. The planes (Bettys) were sighted on each quarter, distance about 6000 yards flying parallel to formation. One made a low level bomb run from the port quarter of *Evans*. This one did not attempt to crash dive, but was shot down and settled into the water. This ship fired 5" VT [Variable Timed] and fuzed alternately but observed no hits. The two planes to starboard retired without making a serious attack when taken under fire by our 5" and the 40MM of the LCSs.
>
> At 0845 another plane (Kate) made a dive bombing attack on *Evans*, missing. This plane also did not try to crash dive but pulled out and veered toward this vessel. He was splashed by 40MM and/or 5" fire from this ship.
>
> At 0847 two F4U Corsairs appeared from cloud cover on starboard bow and were fired upon until recognized.[70]

From 0852 to 0855, the diamond formation of four picket support ships changed course, making a wide right turn to bring them bearing due South. Meanwhile, the two destroyers shifted east of the support ships by evasive and often independent maneuvers against the Japanese air attackers. The relentless air attacks further diminished mutually supportive anti-aircraft fire, not only by separating the destroyers from the slower amphibious ships, but by isolating *Evans* from *Hadley* as well. *LSM(R) 193*'s captain continued:

> At 0858 both destroyers began firing on two more low flying planes (Kates?) from astern. This ship also opened fire with 5" but at 0859 shifted targets to a Kate attempting to gain altitude for a dive from starboard. Several 40mm hits and one 5" hit were observed before this ship did a wing-over and spun into the water, barely missing *LCS 84*. It is believed that this plane intended crashing this ship. At this point *LCS 83* splashed a plane (Hamp) which was making an attack on him from dead ahead.[71]

The Japanese pilots now stalked the isolated destroyers, each forced to fend almost entirely for herself. By 0900, the support ships' diamond formation had lost cohesion entirely while they maneuvered independently to repel the smothering air attacks. With her guide ship role all but over now, *LSM(R) 193* rang up all-ahead flank speed for evasive action: "At 0907 two bogies approached the DDs from their port side (Northeast), and one was sighted attacking this ship almost overhead. At this point so many enemy planes were in view that an accurate chronological narrative would be impossible."[72]

Enemy planes dived at the destroyers in rapid succession. From 0905 to 0910, *Hadley* was crashed by three suicide planes, and from 0907 to 0913, *Evans* was struck by four Kamikaze crashes. Both destroyers were left dead in the water impotent amidst horrific carnage and severe damages. The smaller amphibious ships struggled to fight off the remaining attackers until the close of action about 0925. *Hadley* lost 28 killed and 67 wounded; *Evans* lost 30 killed and 29 wounded.

Evans lost power and communications. Heavy fires raged from amidships to the bridge as bucket brigades bailed seawater, portable Handy Billy pumps suctioned flooded compartments, and men tossed excess weight over the sides to keep afloat.

Hadley began settling astern in the water and rapidly listed five degrees to starboard. A fire raged aft and facing imminent danger of capsizing, the commanding officer ordered "Prepare to abandon ship." About fifty determined men remained aboard, "organized to make a last fight to save the ship."[73] All available fire equipment was brought to bear on the fires, water was pumped over the side, and weight was jettisoned overboard to lighten the ship.

By 0918 the support ships started converging on the crippled destroyers. *LCSs 82* and *84* rang up maximum speed to aid *Evans*, which last reported abandoning ship before losing radio communications. *LSM(R) 193* and *LCS 83* sailed all-ahead full and reached the *Hadley* by 0924.

About half of *Hadley*'s crew was in the surrounding waters, recounted Ensign Paul S. Vaitses, Jr., in *LSM(R) 193*. "'We've got to move through these men in the water to get alongside,' reported the skipper to me through the battle-phones. 'Pick up as many as possible, but we can't stop.' 'Better launch the wherry to round up some of those drifting away,' I suggested. The skipper agreed." Vaitses continued,

> The next few minutes were wild confusion. We were torn between the desire to aid the men in the water and the duty of trying to save the *Hadley*. Most of the men in the water were suffering from burns and shock. They did not respond logically to directions. Our ship was so highsided that it was extremely difficult to haul them up on deck. Some of them, in a half-mad frenzy, almost swamped the wherry we had launched to help rescue them. Others cursed at us because we continued to proceed alongside their ship rather than stop completely while we got them out of the water.[74]

"When interrogated via SCR [Signal Corps Radio], *Hadley* said she was abandoning ship," reported Lt. Boynton. "This vessel and *LCS 83* stood by to pick-up survivors. About eighty survivors were rescued this time."

LSM(R) 193 recovering *Hadley* **crewmen after Japanese air attacks at RPS 15 on 11 May 1945 (U.S. Navy photograph by Ensign Wallace E. Kendall. Used with permission from Douglas G. Aitken, Captain, USN [Ret.]).**

Since many personnel, including wounded, were still aboard, this ship [LSM(R) 193] went alongside to port at 0933 leaving LCS 83 to pick-up wounded. At this time Hadley had a fire below decks apparently in the Engine Room and had lost all propulsive and electrical power except for the auxiliary diesel generator. Many minor explosions, apparently of 40mm ammunition were occurring. Transfer of wounded men and ship's records as well as intensive fire fighting measures were undertaken immediately. Eleven hoses were put on the fire, the first at 0935. The wherry was put over to gather survivors. Also foam, fire axes, two handy billies, and three submersible pumps as well as several working parties to handle lines and help control damage. At 0944 LCS 83 came alongside to starboard assisting in a similar manner.[75]

Cargo nets and lines were rigged over the high-sided LSM(R) 193 to allow able-bodied survivors to climb up. About 175 survivors were brought aboard the rocketship, where wounded and exhausted crowded the deck.

Meanwhile, LSM(R) 193 and LCS 83 tied fast to Hadley's port amidships and starboard quarter respectively to buoy the sinking, burning destroyer. Together, the two smaller ships played 7 hoses on fires and brought under control by 0945, though not entirely extinguished until some 45 minutes later. LCS 83 administered first aid in the meantime, while assisting transfers of official records from Hadley.

"At 1024," said Lt. Boynton, with "the fire being out and pumping operations well underway, this ship cast off and picked up approximately ninety-five more survivors still in the water. Survivors were cared for and given dry clothing and casualties were cared for by this ship's and the Hadley's Pharmacist's Mates, and Hadley's Medical Officer. It was necessary to organize medical treatment on a mass production basis using several crew members."[76]

Ensign Vaitses continued, "Our own crewmen certainly acquitted themselves in heroic fashion that day, too."

Fully realizing that at any moment they might be blown to pieces if the Hadley had exploded, they calmly went about their appointed tasks of fighting her fires and rescuing her crew. When called upon to give first aid to the burned and maimed, they never once visibly flinched at the sickening sights. Every member of our crew, without exception, had some part in the rescue and salvage operations, and some of the hitherto most uncooperative crew members rose to the occasion with laudable displays of courage, self-sacrifice, and human understanding.[77]

LSM(R) 193 screened the waters in various directions between 1037 and 1109, repeatedly stopping and restarting her engines as needed to rescue drifting survivors. (Unnoticed, a hole was discovered in her forward compartment on the starboard side a foot below water line from undetermined cause but was deemed "negligible.")

Shortly after 1100, a flurry of warships streamed to RPS 15 to support recovery operations and to reinforce the picket station's defense perimeter. Wadsworth DD 516 closed Hadley and rescued two sailors blown overboard, while Harry E. Hubbard DD 748 aided the Evans with assistance from LCSs 82 and 84. Fleet tugboats Arikara ATF 98 and Cree ATF 84 arrived to assist and tow Evans about 1300 and 1450, respectively, followed by Ringness APD 100, LSM(R) 199, PCE(R) 855, Snyder DE 745 and Walke DD 723.

"At 1125, no survivors being left in the water, this vessel again went alongside Hadley and prepared to tow alongside," reported the rocketship's skipper. "At this time all uninjured and slightly injured survivors were transferred back to the USS Hadley. Towing commenced at 1146, LSM(R) 193 towing on port side of Hadley and LCS 83 on starboard."[78] The destroyer's commander added, "It was believed that the buoyancy of these two ships would aid in preventing the Hadley from capsizing."[79] Hadley's executive officer commended in turn,

"These two ships did a remarkable job in caring for the wounded, expediting the fighting of the fire, and later towing."[80]

The trio got underway from 38 miles north-northeast of Point Bolo, bearing almost due south at speeds beginning all ahead one-third and gradually increased to all ahead two-thirds. At half-past noon, the vessels stopped all engines when met by the high-speed transport *Barber APD 57*, who first tied alongside *LSM(R) 193* to take aboard 32 seriously injured, then closed *LCS 83* for 29 more casualties. *Barber* cast off all lines by 1335 and set sail for advanced treatment facilities and medical staffs aboard hospital ships *Hope AH 7* and *Crescent City APA 21* off Okinawa.

Just then, fleet tug *Tawakoni ATF 114* rendezvoused, so *LSM(R) 193* cast off all lines as the tugboat closed the destroyer to assist pumping operations and sent a salvage crew aboard to control the tow. The rocketship then attached a bridle with chain to the wire cable from her stern anchor winch and rigged it to

LSM(R) 193 standing off the *Hadley* after Japanese air attacks at RPS 15 on 11 May 1945 (U.S. Navy photograph by Ensign Wallace E. Kendall. Used with permission from Douglas G. Aitken, Captain, USN [Ret.]).

Hadley's bow, while *Tawakoni* and *LCS 83* tied securely alongside the destroyer's port and starboard respectively. Towing recommenced at 1401 as *Hadley* relayed instructions plotting a course for the Kerama Retto anchorage, which traced a sweeping arc west to south. Destroyer *Evans*, meanwhile, would be towed and escorted directly to the Ie Shima anchorage, instead.

Progress was slow, usually making four but occasionally six or seven knots. *Tawakoni* and *LCS 83* continued pumping water from *Hadley*, and *LSM(R) 193* frequently adjusted engine speeds attending to the tensions playing on the more than 200-yard towline. Wide, easy turns finally brought the ships bearing due south by 1540, where their positions plotted some eleven miles northwest of Ie Shima. Here, revised instructions were passed by *Tawakoni* that belayed the journey to Kerama Retto with new orders for the Ie Shima anchorage. The four vessels swung slowly around to a southeasterly course, and an hour later they were about five miles southeast of Ie Shima. *LCS 83* was relieved by salvage tug *Deliver ARS 23*, who assumed towing and pumping after sending a damage control crew aboard *Hadley*.

LSM(R) 193 continued towing *Hugh W. Hadley* for two more hours, supported by *Tawakoni* and *Deliver*, to the lee of Ie Shima anchorage until a suitable berthing space was found. Once the destroyer was anchored in berth M-15, in 20 fathoms of water among various other naval and merchant ships, *LSM(R) 193* cast off the towline at 1841 and immediately proceeded to Hagushi Anchorage.

Lt. Boynton concluded his report, "In addition to the above, it is felt that the unified efforts of the officers and men of this ship constituted distinguished and meritorious service sufficient to justify the award of the Navy Unit Commendation."[81]

Lt. Comdr. John H. Fulweiler, Commander LSM(R) Group Twenty-Seven, cited,

> The report on subject action demonstrates again the value of the 5"/38 Gun and V.T. Fuzes on this type vessel not only as a weapon to destroy suicide planes but as a weapon to drive off such attacks.... This command particularly desires to commend the Commanding Officer of *LSM(R) 193*, Lieutenant Donald E. Boynton, D 107613, USNR, for his fine leadership, courage, coolness and seamanship. He successfully fought his own ship and by his prompt and positive action contributed very largely to saving the USS *Hugh W. Hadley* (DD774) and a majority of the personnel.[82]

Commander Dennis L. Francis, Commander LSM Flotilla Nine, further cited,

> This action report, portrays one of the outstanding rescues of the present operation. The cool, daring, and expert shiphandling displayed by the commanding officer, Lt. D. E. Boynton was directly responsible for the saving of the *Hadley*. The ship had been abandoned by more than two-thirds of its crew. It had been afire for fifteen minutes. 40 mm ammunition was exploding. In spite of these disadvantages and obvious hazards the commanding officer put his ship alongside, landed his hoses and supervised the firefighting until the fire was extinguished. In addition, he proceeded with the towing of the disabled ship, and was successful in towing until relieved by salvage tugs.[83]

Commodore Frederick Moosbrugger added, "The courage and efficiency of the USS *LSM(R) 193* in action, and in assisting the *Hadley*, is noted with pride."[84]

Lieutenant Donald E. Boynton was awarded the Silver Star Medal.

USS *LSM(R) 193* was awarded the Presidential Unit Citation,

> For extraordinary heroism against enemy Japanese aircraft in one of the most outstanding actions of World War II. While on Radar Picket Station Fifteen off Okinawa, engaged in a task far exceeding that for which she was designed, as a member of a task unit composed of the destroyers, USS *H. W. Hadley* and USS *Evans*, and the LCS(L) 82, 83, and 84, she contributed greatly in repelling the overwhelming onslaught of one hundred and fifty-six Japanese suicide planes, all of which were destroyed; the *LSM(R) 193* destroyed eight by her individual action. When the USS *H. W. Hadley* had been overwhelmed by enemy planes, abandoned by more than two-thirds of her crew and had been burning fiercely and exploding for fifteen minutes with complete loss of power, the *LSM(R) 193*, disregarding all hazards, courageously went alongside and saved this destroyer by putting out the fire, and in addition, rescued the majority of the crew and towed the stricken ship safely to port. Her courageous determination and effort added to and were in keeping with the highest traditions of the United States Naval Service.[85]

RPS 9: 13 May 1945

At Radar Picket Station 9 on 13 May 1945, USS *LSM(R) 197* (Lt. Henry O. Bergkamp, USNR) was OTC of the picket support ships including LCSs 23, 56 and 87 in column formation, assigned radar observation, fire support, and casualty rescue. Patrols alternated northwest and southeast each half hour at 7–9 knots. Patrolling independently, *Cowell DD 547* was OTC of the picket station followed astern by *Bache DD 470*.

The afternoon's weather was pleasant with a calm sea, moderate swell and light breeze. Visibility was almost unlimited except for high broken clouds.

During enemy air raids, standing orders called the four amphibious ships to close a thousand yards of the destroyers. "The general practice of the support groups at radar picket stations is to maneuver independently with speed and heavy rudder in close support of each other during periods of attack," explained Lt. Bergkamp.[86]

At 1800, *Bache* detected about a dozen bogies approaching on radar bearing fifteen miles west-southwest, identified as Vals and possibly including Zekes and a Betty, followed by three or more slower biplanes with pontoon floats. The picket ships braced to repel air attacks as CAP splashed some of these planes ten miles west. "Not having air search radar, we received our first reports of planes from the USS *Cowell*," said Bergkamp; in the meantime, "We made use of the "SU" radar for station keeping and navigating to cover our assigned area."

Then, continued Lt. Bergkamp, "we received word at 1815 (Item Time) that a flash blue condition ["Air attack probable"] was put into effect by the USS *Cowell*. The fire support craft were in column formation on 220 degrees heading; the destroyers in column on a near reciprocal course about two (2) miles on our port quarter."[87]

In about thirty minutes, lookouts on *Cowell* spotted planes low over the water eight miles northwest, which *LSM(R) 197* identified as Val carrier dive bombers. A radio alert also warned that enemy planes were seen coming from Kume Shima, the large Japanese-held island north of RPS 9.

Commencing high-speed maneuvers, the destroyers moved southwest to unmask batteries to repel what seemed a well-coordinated attack. As acting OTC, *LSM(R) 197* dissolved the column formation at 1845 and ordered the picket support ships to maneuver independently while closing *Bache* and *Cowell*. "It was after this series of engagements on 13 May," later remarked Lawrence J. Low, Ensign and Gunnery Officer in *LSM(R) 197*, "that I learned from the Motor Machinist Mates in the engine room that the progressive firing of smaller caliber AA guns during an air attack was the only way they could figure out how hot it was getting topside. When the 20mm guns opened up, it was time to think about escape routes."[88] As the destroyers and picket supports closed to a half-mile or so west and east respectively, friendly F4U Corsairs circled the radar picket station.

Vals[89] closed the *Bache* off her port bow: the first turned to attack and was shot down, the second was shot down passing to port, but the third broke off and veered away. "The destroyers and *LSM(R) 197* opened fire on the planes with 5" guns," reported Bergkamp, using half VT proximity fuses and half mechanically-timed fuses. "The planes separated and we continued fire on one (1) plane. On the thirteenth (13) round we scored a hit (confirmed by USS *Cowell*), the plane burst into flames and plunged into the water. During this period all ships were maneuvering on various headings closing the destroyers."[90]

LSM(R) 197's Radioman Clyde Blue recalled the attacks in his diary, adding: "The "Cans" opened up with their 5-inch and so did we. We then had another [Val] come in on us from the starboard side. 4 Corsairs forced him right down into the water without firing a shot. The other Val came in and we got a direct hit with the 5-inch and blew him to pieces."[91] Credit for the splash was subsequently verified by the captain of *LCS 87*: "This will confirm the destruction of one (1) Japanese Val by you while on patrol on 13 May 1945. Five inch gun fire was observed to hit the plane."[92]

The third Val that had veered away from *Bache*, however, continued turning in a low, wide arc abaft the ship until returning for another run, aiming at the destroyer's port beam.[93] Although followed by a CAP fighter braving the AA flak, the Japanese plane climbed rapidly then nosed down in a 60° dive toward the centerline of the *Bache*. At 1850, its wing struck a smoke stack, then plunged into the main deck starboard amidships where its bomb exploded. Clyde Blue added, "Afterwards, they [*Bache*'s gunners] said that they thought it was a Corsair coming at them … when they come in like they do in that long low glide."[94] "[We] Opened fire," tersely reported *Cowell*'s commander, "but could not stop him."

Among other attackers, "a biplane (Nakajima 95) [code-name Dave, a reconnaissance seaplane] was seen to be approaching low on our starboard hand," reported *LSM(R) 197*'s skipper. "We immediately took her under fire with two (2) 40MM guns and 5" gun. The order to cease fire was given when it was noted that our air cover was diving through our tracer to attack. The air cover quickly destroyed the plane."[95] Former Ensign and Gunnery Officer Lawrence J. Low noted later, "If I remember correctly, we got one Val flying from west to east past us towards the *Bache*. Another, older single float bi-plane that I called a Dave … was engaged flying at low level towards us out of the west. We could not hit it with our 5" or 40mm and in fact were shooting at it with 20mm when 3 or 4 CAP Corsairs roared right over our ship with all guns blazing. We ceased firing and the bi-plane folded its wings and hit the water."[96]

U.S.S. "BACHE" STRUCK BY KAMEKAZI.
OFF KUME SHIMA   13 MAY 1945 (R.P.S)

"U.S.S. *Bache* Struck by Kamikazi Off Kume Shima 13 May 1945 (R.P.S.)" Lawrence J. Low, untitled unpublished diary, notebook and sketches.

The four amphibious support ships then converged on the burning destroyer. *LSM(R) 197* and *LCS 87* came along her port side as *LCS 56* moored to her starboard. Pharmacists mates embarked to aid casualties as fire equipment was rigged and seven hoses were played on the fires. Other sailors jettisoned ammunition and fired off torpedoes posing danger of exploding due to the flames and heat. Men wearing oxygen breathing apparatus probed inside the wreckage for trapped sailors and casualties. *Bache* lost 41 killed and 32 wounded.

The battle of RPS 9 was all but over by 1857 when a twin engine bomber—variously identified as a Frances, Dinah, Betty, and Sally—closed the picket ships on a bombing run. "Another (or same bombing plane) was sighted falling into the water in flames," recalled Lt. Bergkamp, however, "We did not have the plane under fire and cannot state whether she was hit by AA or fire from our aircraft."[97]

"Support craft meanwhile had been rendering assistance, two alongside supplying water, one putting tow line over to hold *Bache* into wind and the fourth standing by, circling *Bache*," noted the *Cowell*. "All support craft deserve a 'Well Done' for the expeditious manner in which they went to assistance of *Bache*."[98] *Cowell* stood clear and commenced defensive patrols upon reports of approaching enemy aircraft, and circled the rescue operation while critically wounded attended by medical officers and corpsmen were transferred among the smaller amphibious ships. All fire was suppressed by 1923, and *LCS 56* rigged the crippled destroyer for towing.

By 2130, relief ships reached RPS 9 from Okinawa. Rescue patrol craft *PCE(R) 855* took aboard casualties, while high speed transport *Sims APD 50* with destroyers *Sproston DD 577* and *Van Valkenburgh DD 656* searched the waters for survivors, and fleet tug *Lipan ATF 85* assumed towing *Bache* to Kerama Retto. Through the night, remaining ships formed lines abreast and crisscrossed RPS 9 until recovery efforts were abandoned next morning about 0430. *Van Valkenburgh*, however, would resume search efforts through dawn into early 14 May.

Commander Dennis L. Francis, Commander LSM Flotilla Nine cited, "In this action the commanding officer of the USS *LSM(R) 197* has displayed the conspicuous gallantry and intrepidity in action deserving of the award of a Silver Star Medal."[99]

RPS 9: 14 May 1945

At Radar Picket Station 9 on 14 May 1945, USS *LSM(R) 197* (Lt. Henry O. Bergkamp, USNR) followed last in the column formation of picket support ships led by guide *LCS 66* with *LCSs 65* and *67*. Patrols were 5 miles long at 9 knots on base courses alternating northwest and southeast. Patrolling parallel courses about 1000–1500 yards to the southwest were destroyers *Cowell DD 547* as OTC and *Van Valkenburgh DD 656*.

The clear, sunny weather turned completely overcast by afternoon, with low cumulonimbus clouds, showers, and decreasing visibility. Winds were about ten knots with seas of low swells.

At 1758, *Van Valkenburgh* detected unidentified aircraft in the vicinity and went to General Quarters, but nothing more developed. A half-hour later, *Cowell* also sounded GQ, but for the wartime twilight alert called "Bogie Hour" by American sailors. By 1852, the CAP fighter cover departed for base because clouds and rains had severely lowered visibility to some 300–400 yards.

Suddenly, reported the captain of *LSM(R) 197*, "While steaming in light rain with poor visibility, General Quarters for a flash red condition was called at 1910 on 14 May 1945. One plane was sighted about 1915 heading for the column of gun support ships. All ships in the column fired but she crossed ahead of the leading ship and disappeared in the clouds without receiving a hit."[100] Possibly a twin engine Betty bomber, it made no attempt to attack and continued on a northeasterly course. Ship's Radioman Clyde Blue recalled, "Just before dark it started raining, but about 7:30 a bogie came in and we took him under fire but he kept right on going. We only got about 50 rounds of 40 MM out at him before he was out of site [*sic*] in the rain and haze." Blue added, "It rained all night and can't see very far in front. It may clear up later on. We should get released tomorrow as we usually stay out 4 days and then rest 4 days but then we might stay out a full week."[101]

Cowell's commander, however, offered an unsettling explanation for being caught by surprise. "[The] plane was not detected by radar, probably because he was very low and the surface radar scope was cluttered up with sea return and side lobes. [And] The presence of Kume Shima to the north still gave us trouble with the air search radar."[102]

RPS 7: 16 May 1945

At Radar Picket Station 7 on 16 May 1945, *LCS 117* was guide of the patrol column followed astern by USS *LSM(R) 192* (Lt. Neal B. Hadsell, USNR) and *LCSs 118* and *12*. Destroyers *Bradford DD 545* and *Walke DD 723* as OTC patrolled in column and orbited the four picket support ships.

General Quarters sounded at evening twilight upon a report of enemy aircraft closing RPS 7. Ensign Thomas D. Boak later wrote in a letter to his wife, "[W]e were tensely following a bogey report when all of a sudden the LCS directly astern of us opened up with a twin 40 mm just missing our fantail." The gunnery officer of the *LSM(R) 192* continued, "I had been standing on my seat for better visibility. Boy, with the first shot, I went straight down into the conn—but did keep my eyes above the coaming (side). [Lt.] Neal [Hadsell] thought I was going to land right in his lap. The LCS hastily apologized. Their mount captain was merely switching from local to director control and forgot to train his mount away from our direction. Nice guys!"[103]

Finale

21 May 1945 was the last day LSM(R)s patrolled on Radar Picket Stations, and four days later the Screen Commander formally released all LSM(R)s from Radar Picket duty.[104]

"It was now apparent," reflected Ensign Paul S. Vaitses, Jr., "that our LSM(R) Flotilla faced almost certain annihilation if the radar picket station assignments continued. Even though we on the [*LSM(R)*] *193* felt proud of our recent showing, we had no illusions as to our fate had the battle been much more prolonged."[105]

Admiral Turner, after leaving Okinawa in late May 1945 for his new assignment planning the invasion of Imperial Japan, summarized his *raison de guerre* in what he called the "Baptism of the LSM(R)s":

LSM(R)s were assigned to Radar Picket Stations as supporting ships to protect DDs carrying Fighter Director Teams, to tow them, to pick up survivors, and to render medical assistance when necessary. Though their performance was noteworthy, they are not well suited to such assignment due to lack of sufficient anti-aircraft armament. In carrying out these duties, four of the twelve LSM(R)s were sunk or badly damaged due to enemy suicide aircraft. They were used because they were the best type available for the above purposes.

The LSM(R) [sic] turned in an altogether creditable performance and is considered here to stay. New LSM(R) will be equipped in a much better fashion to fulfill their mission [sic] and eventually the interim type used at Okinawa will be utilized as ammunition carriers. Their capacious magazines, well insulated and ventilated, should make them ideal for this purpose.[106]

Commodore Moosbrugger further commended the rocketships' unsung intrepidity:

The LSM(R)s of Flotilla Nine, who have been under the operational control of CTG 51.5 while serving as support vessels on Radar Picket Stations, have performed outstanding service and contributed materially to the successes of the Okinawa operation.

While agreeing with Commander LSM Flotilla Nine that these ships are not ideally suited for anti-aircraft duty, they have pitched in with what they had and backed up the line where help was needed most.

Every destroyer who has had Radar Picket duty in this operation will long remember the LSM(R) as one of his best friends. F. Moosbrugger.[107]

"Towing and Medical Ships": 30 April 1945–28 May 1945

In late April 1945, *LSMs 14, 82, 167, 222, 228* and *279* were designated "Towing and Medical Ships,"[108] in response to the U.S. Navy's mounting loss of ships and rising casualties from relentless Japanese air attacks and horrific Kamikaze suicide crashes. Rapidly fitted out as emergency rescue vessels embarking medical officers, Commander Dennis L. Francis, Commanding Officer of LSM Flotilla Nine, was additionally charged with implementing these new LSM operations beginning May 1945.

Earlier, Comdr. Francis raised the problems of inadequate care for sailors whose ships were damaged or sunk on the Radar Picket Stations. "*LSM(R) 189, 190, 191, 194, 197* and *198,* have rescued survivors. In every case, it was necessary to supply clothing."

Individual men in these ships supplied the clothing from their personal lockers. There appears to be no way in which these individuals can be re-imbursed, except through their own ship's welfare fund.... There is every reason to believe that LSM(R)s will be continued on patrol duty which will inevitably involve further expenditures of personal clothing.... It is urgently recommended that this Command be authorized to procure sufficient survivors clothing to supply ships on patrol for this emergency.[109]

Initial planning[110] sought ten conventional LSMs with each embarking a physician, but settled upon 6 LSMs and ten Navy doctors[111] distributed among the LSMs and LSM(R)s.[112] Nine medical officers reported for duty, and a tenth doctor was already assigned as group staff in *LSM 14.* Fundamentally, explained Francis, "The duties of the LSMs were to immediately go to vessels requiring assistance from enemy aerial attack and to provide medical and towing facilities as required."[113]

Commander Francis detailed forthcoming LSM and LSM(R) assignments in his Operation Plan #2103-45 of 30 April 1945 that outlined three defensive screens off Okinawa:

- LSMs designated "Towing and Medical Ships" stationed one-third distance to RPSs 3, 7, 9, 10, and 12. "Each ship must carry a Medical Officer before reporting on station.... These ships will defend when attacked and be prepared to go immediately to vessels requiring assistance."
- LSM(R)s designated "Survivors and Medical Ships" stationed two-thirds distance to RPSs 3, 7, 9, 10, and 12. "Each ship must carry a Medical Officer before reporting on station.... These ships will defend when attacked, furnish medical aid, and aid in survivor rescue work to all ships in area."
- LSM(R)s designated "Radar Support Ships" stationed on RPSs 2, 3, 4, 9, and 14, but "they will not carry a Medical Officer except when LSM(R) 190 is assigned one of these stations.... These ships will assist and support Radar Picket vessel [sic] in charge on RP stations."[114]

Upon activation, the six LSM "Towing and Medical Ships" conformed closely with Commander Francis' OpPlan #2103–45 during operations from 30 April 1945 until 28 May 1945. LSM(R) operations were only partially implemented as Francis conceived, however, and often modified or superseded altogether due to exigencies.[115]

On station, each LSM embarked a medical officer while the remaining pool of doctors was distributed among LSM(R)s. The medium landing ships were stationed close-in along a sweeping defensive western screen, from north between Ie Shima and northwestern Motobu peninsula, to south between the Kerama Rettos and southwestern tip of Okinawa. No more than 5 medium landing ships stood patrols at any given time, allowing rotation of the sixth LSM to Hagushi Anchorage for logistics and repairs. During relief at sea, the Navy doctors were usually transferred with baggage and medical supplies via wherry between ships.

Lt. Paul M. Jones commanding *LSM 279* reported,

> The mission of this ship was to furnish medical aid, towing, and rescue service to Radar Picket Ships in the Ryukyu Area. Towing gear was continuously rigged, as were davits and lines for picking up survivors. The after troop compartment was converted into a temporary sick bay and plans to handle patients were set up.... It is thought that LSMs might be put to a very profitable use as rescue and towing ships. The after troop quarters can be easily converted into a temporary sick bay and they can tow a comparatively large ship at about five knots. The amount of fire fighting equipment on board could be a great help to ships on fire, and due to their maneuverability positions can be held where other ships might find it impossible.[116]

None of the LSMs suffered casualties or battle damages from enemy actions, although *LSM 279* had a close call before noontime of 25 May, when a diving Japanese plane aimed for the ship's fantail but crashed into the sea a mere twenty feet away. Yet as Lt. John R. Pahmeyer of *LSM 167* suggested, "All duty and action was considered routine and no claim is made for awards or citations. [But] After about five (5) days and nights of continuous patrol plus many hours at General Quarters, the result of fatigue on the crew is noticeable. It is felt some special mention should be made of this type of duty in view of its hazardous nature."[117]

Factors of time and distance diminished the Towing and Medical Ships' effectiveness, however, since the LSMs were stationed many miles away from the distant radar picket stations that suffered most from the heaviest enemy air attacks. Timely assistance to damaged ships and casualties was often hindered, more to the point, simply because the medium landing ships could only muster a dozen or so knots en route.

On the other hand, Lt. Frederic S. Dean, Jr., skipper of *LSM 82* insisted, "The lack of personal action during the subject period is in no way considered a waste of time by this command. More than once, nearby ships avoided damage only by a very narrow margin. In less fortunate circumstances, the services of an LSM for towing and fire fighting should be of high value."[118]

Comdr. Francis praised the service of the "Towing and Medical Ships." "The performance of the LSMs during this duty was very satisfactory. Although it was not necessary for any LSM to exercise his function to great extent, they were always ready if needed. On several occasions LSMs proceeded to assist injured vessels and stood by until it was ascertained that their help was not required. At all times, they operated so effectively that they were able to obtain complete logistics in the necessarily short periods allowed...."[119]

Evolving tactical circumstances at Okinawa during May 1945 ultimately eclipsed the interim missions given the half-dozen LSMs. The network of ground-based early warning radars expanded, and fighter protection increased over the radar picket stations, which in turn allowed the Navy to withdraw ships from harm's way. The active radar picket stations declined from nine RPSs on 30 April to five RPSs after the first week in May. Thus, with each passing week, medical officers were gradually transferred (less *LSM 14*) until the last doctor finally disembarked on 21 May. The following week, the 6 LSMs were detached in pairs from Commander Francis and LSM Flotilla Nine between 26 and 28 May 1945, after which the "Towing and Medical Ships" unit was deactivated.

CHAPTER 8

The Finners

Naval Gunfire Support,
21 May 1945–2 June 1945

From 21 May 1945 into the first days of June 1945 the four Finner rocketships were assigned naval gunfire (NGF) support missions in southern Okinawa. *LSM(R)s 192* and *193* supported the Army's XXIV Corps, units primarily of the 7th Infantry Division along the southeastern coast; *LSM(R)s 189* and *191* supported the Marines' III Amphibious Corps, principally elements of the 6th Marine Division along the southwestern coast. "Each ship," added Lieutenant Commander Fulweiler, Commanding Officer of LSM(R) Group Twenty-Seven, "reported with 3,000 Fin Stabilized Rockets aboard."[1]

The American Tenth Army's general scheme of maneuver was a pincer movement upon the heavily fortified headquarters at Shuri Castle, where Lieutenant General Mitsuru Ushijima's main army forces of an estimated 30,000 men were concentrated on Okinawa. In the U.S. drives southward, the eastern Army and western Marine ground forces were to put pressure toward the middle, envelop the Shuri fortress, then destroy the Japanese forces therein. The weather, initially favoring the Americans from 13–22 May, would severely hamper battle plans thereafter, however, with heavy rains causing ubiquitous mud and runoffs that sometimes ground the frontlines to a standstill. Cunningly, Ushijima and most of his forces in the Shuri stronghold would exploit the oppressive weather and battlefield conditions, often under cover of nightfall, to elude Lieutenant General Simon Buckner's tightening noose by withdrawing to southern Okinawa during May's closing days.[2]

From mid–May 1945 onward, amphibious gunboats increasingly supported U.S. ground forces during the fighting along the southeastern and southwestern coastlines until Okinawa was declared secured six weeks later. And the Army and Marine responses were gratifying: "Small boats [*sic*] were first used as a continuous support weapon under division control on 16 May by the III Phib Corps. The craft used were mortar-equipped LCIs. This support was received enthusiastically by the troops. From this date, various support craft were used, such as LSM(R) and LCI(R), as well as the mortar craft. They proved to be of great help not only with their rockets and mortars but also with their 40mm and 20mm fire."[3]

Naval Gunfire Control at Okinawa

On 17 May 1945, Vice Admiral Hill relieved Vice Admiral Turner to assume the mantle of Commander Task Force 51 (CTF 51, later CTF 31) as Joint Expeditionary Force Commander

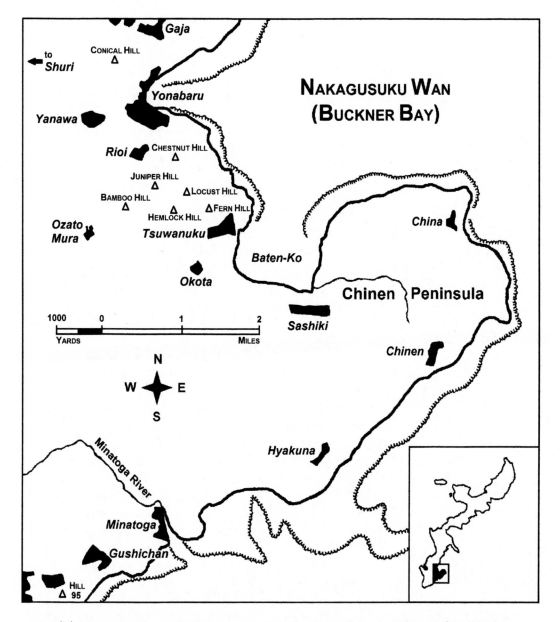

LSM(R)s 192 and 193 supported U.S. Army operations in southeastern Okinawa from 22 May to 1 June 1945 (adapted from Roy E. Appleman, et al., *Okinawa: The Last Battle*, The War in the Pacific, United States Army in World War II, Washington, D.C.: U.S. Government Printing Office, 1948, Map No. XLVI).

and as Commander, Amphibious Support Force (CTF 52, later CTF 32), with overall command of naval gunfire support at Okinawa. In general,

> Fire support ships of TF 32 were at all times assigned to one of the following Task Groups: Western Fire Support Group, Covering and Standby Fire Support Group, Logistics Group, and Eastern Fire Support Group. CTG [*sic*] 51/31 made assignments to these groups twice daily (night assignments on the preceding morning and day assignments on the preceding evening) based on the number of ships available for

Fire Support and the request received from the troops ashore. After the ships were assigned respective groups, the command in control of close support fire made direct assignments of ships to specific units ashore.[4]

Rear Admiral John L. Hall, Jr., as CTG 51.22, directly coordinated NGF support for the Army XXIV Corps and Marine III Amphibious Corps on the east and west coasts of southern Okinawa, respectively.[5]

Southeastern Okinawa: USS LSM(R) 192 and USS LSM(R) 193

At noon of 21 May 1945 Vice Admiral Harry W. Hill (CTF 51) ordered USS *LSM(R) 192* and USS *LSM(R) 193* to proceed from Hagushi Anchorage to Nakagusuku Wan, Okinawa's large southeastern bay. The two Finners reported to Rear Admiral C. Turner Joy, SOPA Eastern Okinawa (CTG 51.19) in flagship *San Francisco CA 38*, for further assignment as naval gunfire support.[6]

Nakagusuku Wan (Bay) was an anchorage under development as a naval base. "In addition to fire support ships, there were numerous other naval ships and small craft, as well as merchant vessels, in the area, for the security and general administration of which S.O.P.A. Eastern Okinawa was responsible."[7] Following the sudden combat death of the Tenth Army's Commanding General Simon B. Buckner, Jr., killed 18 June, Americans renamed the anchorage "Buckner Bay" in his honor.

One or more Shore Fire-Control Parties (SFCP), codenamed "Oboe," directed and coordinated naval gunfire support with American ground units, and, of equal importance, assure that NGF did not endanger friendly forces.[8] Initially, explained Admiral Joy, "a division of LCI(R)s was made available to an oboe ashore for continuing support in order to fire on targets theretofore difficult to reach such as reverse slopes and in ravines to the south of Yonabaru Town. The enthusiasm of the oboe increased the demand for rocket craft. Later two LSM(R)s were sent to the area to meet requirements."[9] Thereafter, XXIV Army Corps was furnished day and night with "Call fires, and fire at designated targets delivered by the heavy ships and destroyers augmented from time to time by 40 M.M. fire from LCSs and by rockets from LCI(R)s and LSM(R)s."[10]

Admiral Joy directed the two rocketships report to Commander Lawrence M. Bailliere in *LC(FF) 679*, Commander LCI Flotilla Twenty-One, Eastern Gunboats (CTU 52.9.7)[11] for fire support assignments with the U.S. Army.[12] Comdr. Bailliere served under Captain Aylward (CTG 52.9), who commanded LCS(L) Flotilla Three and the Gunboat and Mortar Support Flotillas from his force flagship *LC(FF) 988*.[13] Capt. Aylward oversaw some 200 LCS(L)s, LCI(G)s, LCI(R)s, and LCI(M)s[14]—and LSM(R)s after 26 April.[15]

The U.S. Army

Major General John R. Hodge, USA, XXIV Corps commander, planned a two-phase strategy to assault the heavily-defended Japanese stronghold in Shuri Castle. First, seize the coastal township of Yonabaru on Nakagusuku Wan and take the southern high ground of the

Ozato Hills (sometimes referred to as the Ozato-Mura Hill Mass). From this area, the army would isolate, destroy, and defend against local enemy forces, including any attempting to enter or leave Chinen Peninsula on the left (East) flank. Next, troops positioned in the Ozato Hills would cover the main attack force of the 7th Infantry Division as it pivoted westward from Yonabaru to close Shuri from the east-southeast on the road to Naha.

The initial phase was spearheaded by the 184th Infantry Regiment jumping off at 0200 of 22 May. Upon securing Yonabaru, troops pushed south about a thousand yards to take the first major highpoint in the Ozato Hills, called Chestnut Hill, then assaulted neighboring hills codenamed Bamboo, Juniper, and Locust. Units soon probed further east-southeast toward Baten Ko [Harbor] and into the Chinen Peninsula for build-ups of Japanese units.

But steady rainfall grew increasingly heavy through the day as infantry and vehicles passed through the village of Yonabaru. Before long, roads washed out, hampering battle plans and ground attacks as transports, tanks, and heavy equipment bogged in rivers of mud. Since poor weather also often hindered air support, troops would depend upon supporting fire from land-based artillery and seaborne forces.[16]

22 May 1945

In Nakagusuku Wan[17] the morning of 22 May, all hands in *LSM(R)*s *192* and *193*[18] assembled and loaded rockets in launchers as armed lookouts stood topside watches on bows, sterns, and conns. This day the two rocketships would coordinate naval gunfire support with cruiser *Portland CA 33*, designated O-840.[19]

Naval gunfire, scheduled in advance to soften enemy positions, shifted southward preceding the infantry's forward progress, then was supplanted by artillery fires.[20] The LSM(R)s' target areas were the rising hills north-northwest of the Okinawan seaside village of Tsuwanuku, about one and a half miles southeast of Yonabaru, overlooking the western beaches of Baten Ko in the crux of Chinen Peninsula.[21] Both rocketships made two rocket runs. The first attack was in unison between 1240 and 1248, after which they retired to central Nakagusuku Wan Anchorage to reload. The second attack was in succession, led by *LSM(R) 193* firing from 1452 to 1505, then *LSM(R) 192* fired from 1523 to 1543.

Afterwards, 7th Infantry Division Headquarters contacted the two LSM(R)s:

THANK YOU LOTS. YOUR ROCKETS HIT HOME, AND WE DON'T KNOW HOW TO EXPRESS OUR SATISFACTION. IF WE WERE A NAVY MAN WE WOULD BE ABLE TO SAY "WELL DONE" BUT BEING THAT WE ARE GI'S, WE DON'T KNOW HOW TO EXPRESS OUR SATISFACTION. WE ALL THANK YOU FROM THE DOGFACES UP TO THE GOLD AND BRASS. THANK YOU FOR YOUR SPLENDID COOPERATION. THAT COMPLETES OUR MISSION FOR TODAY, AND YOU MAY HEAD HOME.[22]

Admiral Joy later summarized, "*LSM(R) 192* and *193* have been made available for close support work in Eastern Okinawa, and worked with O-840 [*Portland*]. They rocketed and destroyed mortar positions in TAs 8968, 8468, and 8268[23] which had been firing on our troops."[24] Lt. Comdr. Fulweiler added, "[*LSM(R)*s *192* and *193*] Delivered 1200 Rockets in assigned Target Areas on Southeastern Okinawa. Some light enemy mortar and machine gun fire experienced."[25]

Storekeeper Robert Landis on *LSM(R) 192* wrote in his diary, "We have skirted around Okinawa to the city of [Yonabaru]. The *193* is with us. We made two runs to the beach. On the second run we took mortar fire but no hits. Once again we've been assigned to the Army, the Seventh Infantry Division of the Tenth Army."[26]

Retiring once more to northern Nakagusuku Wan Anchorage, deck forces again assembled and loaded rockets in launchers. Dropping anchors in Berth B-170, the rocketships made smoke intermittently from twilight to midnight.

23 May 1945

Naval gunfire targets scrutinized throughout 23 May included a supply dump, a sealed cave housing a five-inch gun, storage sheds, troop concentrations, ridges and trenches, and origins of enemy anti-aircraft fire. However, "Low visibility again hampered firing and assessment," reported Admiral Joy as CTG 51.19. "Visibility during the day and early evening was limited, with low overcast and rain squalls."[27]

LSM(R) 193 rendezvoused near Baten Ko by 0845 to coordinate gunfire with Rooks DD 804, designated C-842.[28] Along the southeast slope of Chestnut Hill, the 3rd Battalion of the 32nd Infantry had been drawing enemy heavy machine-gun fire from caves.[29] Setting General Quarters, LSM(R) 193 fired 300 rockets from 1036 to 1059, once again targeting the hills north-northwest of the Okinawan seaside village of Tsuwanuku.[30] Following her rocket run, LSM(R) 193 secured from GQ, reloaded launchers, and returned to the Nakagusuku Wan Anchorage.[31]

By 0853, meanwhile, sister ship LSM(R) 192 was standing off Yonabaru Beach paired with St. Louis CL 49, designated O-810.[32] At GQ, the rocketship approached the firing line and launched 12 rocket salvos from 1119 to 1123; taking a new position, she loosed more rockets from 1145 to 1149.[33] All told, the two Finners launched 600 rockets against enemy positions this day.[34]

LSM(R) 192 remained off the Yonabaru beaches through noontime and fired at shore targets from 1225 to 1235 with guns 1, 2, 3 and 5. "This morning," wrote Robert Landis, Storekeeper on LSM(R) 192, "under the direction of the Seventh Infantry, the 192 and 193 made one rocket run against enemy positions outside [Yonabaru],[35] then strafed the shoreline with 20's and 40 mm's."[36] The rocket ship thereafter rejoined her sister ship to retire in the Nakagusuku Wan for the night.

Afterwards HQ 7th Infantry Division sent the following message to the LSM(R)s:

> THIS MISSION IS COMPLETED. YOU DID A GOOD JOB. THERE WERE QUITE A FEW JAPS THERE LAST NIGHT, BUT YOU SEEM TO HAVE CLEANED THEM OUT PRETTY WELL. THANKS FOR YOUR WORK TODAY. YOU DID A SWELL JOB.[37]

The 184th Infantry Regiment had struggled against Japanese long-range fire, accurate machine-gun fire, and grenade battles for command of Bamboo, Juniper, and Locust Hills south of Yonabaru, roughly along an east-west line from Baten Ko. By evening, however, American troops were firmly established and able to defend the southern flank of the 7th Infantry Division's western drive to envelop and destroy the enemy in Shuri Castle.[38]

24 May 1945

Rains had stopped the morning of 24 May when the two sister rocketships reported to the operations area in Baten Ko harbor. Headquarters 7th Infantry Division sent orders to *LSM(R) 193*, relayed in turn to *LSM(R) 192*, directing daytime support of SFCP spotters.[39]

A morning airstrike at 0700 presaged the Army's attack on Locust Hill, a key summit located a thousand yards from the western shore of Baten Ko and about a half-mile southeast of Yonabaru. The hill was a steeply rising escarpment of black coral and rock, and infantrymen faced little choice but to climb its sheer two-hundred-thirty-foot walls. In recent days, *LSM(R)*s 192 and 193 including other gunfire support ships had rocketed and shelled this hilly area. Now, in unison with Army suppressing fires from neighboring Juniper and Chestnut Hills, the two rocketships would target Locust Hill again in preparation of the 184th Infantry's struggle against the Japanese defenders.[40]

LSM(R) 193 made the first attack, firing 300 rockets not far off from Tsuwanuku village[41] from 0820 to 0830, then turned from the beach while her crew reloaded rockets in launchers. Next, *LSM(R) 192* made her rocket run from 0855 to 0900 and moments later she, too, turned away as all hands reloaded rockets.

After the rocket attacks, the two Finners stood off shore for harassing fires over the coming eight hours. The watch officer aboard *LSM(R) 193* reported, "Steaming close to beach to strafe area of activity and possible gun positions using all guns."[42] From 0908 to 0950, *LSM(R) 192* fired at will to flush out enemy positions with 20mms, 40mms, and the 5"/38 gun, then took new targets and suspicious objects under fire by direction of shore spotters from 1019 until 1034.

Fighting for Locust Hill proved difficult. The first units of the 184th Infantry approached the summit around 0930. Japanese, scattered among the crags and crevices of the hill, delivered accurate fire causing casualties and firefights throughout the day. At one point, American troops discovered a well-concealed enemy command post that had eluded detection, including field telephones, radios, beddings, mortars and other equipment.[43]

At 1100, the deck officer in *LSM(R) 192* noted, "*LSM(R) 193* reported sighting enemy troop activity on ridge. Army shore spotter advised opening fire."[44] Soon, both rocketships commenced heavy fires from 1115 to 1140, the results of which were considered satisfactory.

Harassing patrols ceased about noontime as the rocketships laid off Yonabaru beach. But *LSM(R) 192* soon resumed fire at suspicious shore targets, then retired from the beach fifteen minutes later to assemble and load rockets. Meanwhile, *LSM(R) 193* "commenced firing all guns at enemy patrols, possible gun positions and troop concentrations. Observed some counter fire but no hits were observed."[45] *LSM(R) 192* finished reloading rockets by 1431, and upon closing *LSM(R) 193*, both sister ships continued sporadic firing at beach targets for the next three hours.

Late afternoon, the rocketships ceased harassing fires to prepare for rocket runs. At 1829, from the firing line in Baten Ko, *LSM(R) 193* loosed 200 rockets against counterattacking Japanese units among hills and ridges south of Locust Hill, some fifteen-hundred yards southwest of Tsuwanuku near Okota village.[46] Next, *LSM(R) 192* maneuvered to the firing point and launched rocket salvos from 1902 until 1920.[47] Firing was briefly held up, however, while a blaze was extinguished in some cargo netting, ignited from rockets' exhausts.

Minutes after sunset, the two rocketships ceased rocket fires and retired from the area in the evening twilight to anchor in Nakagusuku Wan.[48] "Still with the Army," wrote Storekeeper Robert Landis in his diary. "We made two more rocket runs against Japanese troops now retreating along the shoreline. We are taking mortar fire but no hits."[49]

During 24 May, the two rocketships expended 1100 rockets, 400 rounds of 5"/38 AAC, and 2700 rounds of 40mm.[50] Summarizing actions covering 22 to 24 May, Commander Bailliere (CTU 52.9.7) noted briefly, "*LSM(R) 192* and *193* operated with the Army giving call fire. The Headquarters XXIV Army Corps reported that the firing mission [*sic*] proved very effective in clearing out enemy mortar positions that artillery could not reach. The LSMs [*sic*] used rocket fire."[51] Additional enemy targets struck by the LSM(R)s and other naval gunfire support ships this day were several camouflaged buildings, an enemy strongpoint, two medium artillery pieces, and a five-inch gun that had been firing on U.S. lines. Mortar and gun emplacements and a dual-purpose gun were neutralized, troops were killed or dispersed, one tank was demolished while three others were damaged, two blockhouses were destroyed, one of which contained a medium caliber gun. Fifteen to 20 suicide boats were also discovered in a revetment, all of which had been completely destroyed or riddled by previous firings.[52]

Despite little rainfall, visibility was poor during the day, so no enemy aircraft had been detected until after 1900, when planes approached in coordinated attacks from the west, northwest, north, and north-northeast."[53] Indeed, the Japanese, in support of their counterattacks on the 7th Infantry Division, dispatched combined Kamikaze-airborne squadrons against Okinawa.[54] Smoke was thus ordered over the Nakagusuku Wan Anchorage at 2022 with few breaks before midnight.

25 May 1945

The Japanese air raids that began in the evening twilight of 24 May continued throughout the night and into the morning of 25 May. Accordingly, "All small craft," said Commander Bailliere, "were instructed not to nest together."[55]

"A few minutes after midnight," reported Admiral Joy, "new raids were picked up to the north and northeast and at 0010, one raid had closed to within ten miles of Nakagusuku Wan. Thereafter, three other raids, of one or two planes each, closed the anchorage. At 0050, several planes, pursued by nightfighters, dropped flares in vicinity of Tsugen Shima and then retired to the southeast...." Over the next hour, ships on Radar Picket Station 5, some thirty miles to the east, reported air attacks as well.[56]

At 0225, anti-aircraft fire was seen near Katchin Wan, followed by a large burst of flames from a Jill crashing into the sea. The bomber's pilot was picked up as a prisoner of war, "apparently in fair condition."[57]

General Quarters sounded again at 0255 in Nakagusuku Wan as enemy planes circled the anchorage. About 0300, a Navy minesweeper saw a low-flying plane drop a bomb three thousand yards away, then at 0310, *LSM(R) 192*'s No. 1 and No. 2 single forty millimeter guns fired 9 and 3 rounds, respectively, at an unidentified enemy plane passing on her starboard side.

By 0353, the air attacks finally abated, so ships were ordered to cease making smoke for the anchorage. Yet, at 0520, nearby ships took a plane under fire until it crashed.

LSM(R) 193 was anchored off Yonabaru, then got underway after sunrise to take on ammunition, and *LSM(R) 192* followed thirty minutes later. Mooring to opposite sides of *LSM 83*, the Finners took on rockets until an air alert signal at 0800 warned of enemy aircraft to the north and east. A half-hour later, loading resumed after GQ was secured.

Vicksburg CL 86 was the designated fighter director ship this day,[58] and reported that a four-plane Combat Air Patrol was on station about ten miles southeast of Nakagusuku Wan. The fighters were vectored several times, but failed to intercept Japanese aircraft, "probably due to the extremely poor visibility," reasoned Admiral Joy. "Visibility at this time was spotty," he continued, "but in general it was poor with very low overcast, mist and rain squalls."[59] Throughout the morning, reports indicated that enemy fighters and bombers were still closing, encircling, and penetrating the Nakagusuku anchorage, some splashed and others escaping.

General Quarters suddenly sounded again at 0910 on *LSM(R) 192* as her lookouts sighted an approaching enemy plane thought to be an Oscar. Over the next two minutes, the rocketship's gunners opened fire and believed they fatally hit the fighter with the #1 bow 40mm gun, causing the plane to crash and explode in the water beyond other ships lying in the anchorage.[60] GQ was secured soon after, and ammunition loading resumed throughout the rest of the morning into early afternoon.

Japanese aircraft continued attacking the anchorage until late morning, when the all clear "Flash White" was finally signaled at 1148. "There were no further enemy air attacks during the day," reported CTG 51.19. "It is believed that a minimum of nine planes were shot down in Nakagusuku Wan and Katchin Wan during the day."[61]

LSM(R) 193 ceased taking on ammunition at 1300, and cast off for the target area while her crew reloaded rocket launchers. By 1511, the rocketship "Commenced harassing patrol of beach area near Baten Ko, working with spotters from 184th Infantry, US Army and firing in cooperation with them."[62] The only American advance in the area this day was in taking Fern Hill, east of Locust Hill. Otherwise, the infantry spent the afternoon consolidating positions, evacuating casualties, and mopping up remnants of the enemy.[63]

LSM(R) 192 finished loading ammunition by 1415, taking aboard 900 rocket motors, 901 rocket bodies, 864 nose fuses, and 400 rounds of 40mm.[64] The deck force reloaded rockets into her launchers, meanwhile, as she steamed for Yonabaru Beach. There she awaited instructions until about 1740, when, instead of launching rockets, the rocketship fired 18 rounds from her fantail 5"/38, shelling shore targets near Yonabaru.

Around 1700, *LSM(R) 193* came under enemy mortar fire near the southern beach of Baten Ko, but escaped damage. Returning two hours later that evening, the rocketship's 5"/38 shelled a probable enemy mortar position west of Sashiki village.[65]

Although naval gunfire support was limited to harassing fire due to poor visibility during 25 May, it was thought to have thoroughly covered areas of reported enemy activity. "It was reported," added Admiral Joy, "that reverse slope rocket firing of LSM(R) [*sic*] had destroyed one pillbox and gun positions in TA 7367M,[66] fired ammunition dump and knocked out two mortar positions in TA 8766A [east of Sashiki village]."[67]

That evening, the two rocketships were relieved from gunfire support missions, and they departed the operations areas to return to Nakagusuku Wan Anchorage in grid area 9274Q. Here *LSM(R) 192* came alongside *LSM(R) 193* for 5"/38 ammo,[68] then cast off to anchor independently off Yonabaru for the night.

26 May 1945

Quite unlike the previous twenty-four hours, noted Admiral Joy, "The night of 25/26 May passed without any enemy aircraft being reported." But once again, weather conditions inhibited operations during 26 May. "Poor visibility prevented accurate spot and observation. Harassing and interdiction fire were carried out in assigned areas."[69]

LSM(R)s 192 and 193 anchored separately overnight off Yonabaru and in Nakagusuku Wan Anchorage, respectively, until dawn of 26 May. Weighing anchors to rendezvous, they proceeded in column to an operational area about twenty-five hundred yards off Yonabaru[70] in support of the 7th Infantry Division.[71]

LSM(R) 192 maintained steerageway off Yonabaru, scanning for enemy shore activities while awaiting specific target assignments. Sister ship LSM(R) 193 steamed south to a firing area off the eastern beaches of Baten Ko[72] when she suddenly ran aground. The shoal was shallow, fortunately, and the rocketship worked herself free minutes later and got underway.

For the next couple of hours, LSM(R) 193 engaged in harassing fire on Japanese troops and patrols observed inland along the eastern shore of Baten Ko.[73] The rocketship ceased fire at 1100, however, and proceeded northward for a conference with the destroyer Paul Hamilton DD 590, designated as C-842, and spotters for the U.S. Army 184th Infantry.[74] Stopping all engines, she stood several thousand yards east of Yonabaru[75] until 1245, then got underway towards the beach to pick up an Army unit of four. Embarking the soldiers an hour later, the rocketship set sail by 1348 to the designated operations area in Baten Ko, but it was still two more hours before spotters directed 40mm gunfire to bear on enemy troops west-southwest of Tsuwanuku village.[76]

Indeed, reported Vice Admiral Hill, "About mid-afternoon air observers discovered a general southerly movement of enemy troops. The movement extended nearly across the island and was estimated variously up to 4000 troops in groups varying from 50 to 900. For the remainder of the day, fire support ships,[77] artillery and planes shelled, bombed and strafed troops and vehicles. A number of tanks towing artillery [were also] seen moving south. One column of enemy troops estimated from road space observations to be a regiment was seen near Ozato headed North [sic]."[78] However, American intelligence was uncertain whether these enemy troops were signs of redeployments, reinforcements, or withdrawals.

LSM(R) 192 was also closely observing mainland areas for suspicious movements[79] when a "Flash Red—Control Green" air raid warning was signaled at 1600. Only half an hour earlier, two Japanese Tony fighters attacked U.S. ships off eastern Okinawa to the north in Chimmu Wan, which, CTG 51.19 admitted, "was a complete surprise." At that moment, the all clear "Condition White–Control Green" was set on both sides of the island, so the undetected enemy planes caught the Americans off guard.[80]

That afternoon, General Quarters sounded once more at 1712 over the LSM(R)s' public address (PA) speakers warning of imminent rocket runs. At 1742, LSM(R) 193 was first to launch rocket salvos before evening, firing 300 projectiles on a concentration of 500 enemy troops.[81] These may have been the Japanese force that had left Shuri Castle the day before and marched southeast to strengthen the enemy's covering and holding force against the 7th Infantry Division's thrust toward Shuri.

LSM(R) 192 stood by with her target pinpointed off Yonabaru Beach,[82] and by 1820 commenced her rocket run to launch 300 AR rockets at Japanese troops ashore, as well. By 1905, the rocketship was released from further assignment and retired to Yonabaru Anchorage.

The 184th Infantry found only light resistance to probing patrols pushing southward,[83] so LSM(R) 193 was also released from gunfire support. She disembarked the four Army spotters by 1923, and then anchored in northeastern Nakagusuku Wan Anchorage overnight.[84] For 26 May, noted Lt. Comdr. Fulweiler very briefly, "[*LSM(R)*s] *192* and *193* delivered 500 [*sic*] Rockets in assigned areas for 184th Infantry."[85]

27 May 1945

Reveille sounded at 0525 in *LSM(R) 192*. Her deck force began assembling and loading rockets into launchers by 0610 before shoving off. *LSM(R) 193* got underway by 0631 to the operating area and was joined twenty minutes later by her sister ship, who fell astern on course 225° T. The rocketships arrived in Baten Ko at 0710, and resumed daylight harassing coastal patrols. *LSM(R) 193* immediately opened fire with both her 40mm guns while *LSM(R) 192* finished loading rocket launchers.

Soon a "Flash Red—Control Green" signal warned of an air raid. "This was the beginning of another day of intensive air attacks," explained Admiral Joy. The first enemy aircraft were picked up 30 miles to the northeast, with "raids continuing at intervals until 0830 the next morning. Over a hundred enemy planes were reported shot down by CAP and ships' gunfire in the Okinawa area during this period."[86]

Enemy planes failed to interfere with the gunfire support operations,[87] so by 0800 *LSM(R) 192* contacted American army patrols ashore, and throughout the morning both rocketships carried out harassing patrols and spotted enemy movements with the Army. *LSM(R) 193* strafed suspicious areas east of Sashiki village on the eastern shore of Baten Ko[88] with automatic weapons fire, and later *LSM(R) 192* fired both 40mms at shore targets and reported, "Results good."[89]

The 184th Infantry was penetrating further south and southeast of Yonabaru and effectively interdicting enemy movements to and from Chinen Peninsula. Now the rocketships began searching for Japanese troops, equipment, vehicles and installations on the peninsula and the southeastern coastline of Okinawa. Seventh Infantry Division's commanders were concerned about the enemy's strength on Chinen Peninsula; one estimate believed some five thousand troops with artillery and antiaircraft pieces defended this general region. Accordingly, American commanders sought to completely isolate the peninsula in order to prevent Japanese troops from reinforcing the Shuri defenses, and, in turn, block Chinen Peninsula as a refuge for enemy forces escaping from Shuri.[90]

Over noontime, *LSM(R) 193* stood guard offshore while *LSM(R) 192* fired her 5"/38 at caves and suspicious targets, expending 101 rounds of AA Common. Unexpectedly, the latter rocketship ran aground on an uncharted mud flat at 1250, but because of her shallow draft and flat bottom, she soon cleared and was underway again.

Early that afternoon, *LSM(R) 192* investigated a Japanese dugout canoe, and an armed lookout shot 15 rounds from a carbine rifle at its possible contents. Meanwhile, the *LSM(R) 193* went alongside a pier in Baten Ko near the seaside fishing village of Tsuwanuku.[91] Here, a junior naval officer and radar technician from LSM(R) Group 27 Staff disembarked, while two Army observers came aboard at 1410. Departing on an additional observation mission, the rocketship resumed harassing and interdiction patrols in coordination with Army units ashore.

A scout with the 7th Infantry Division sent a message via headquarters on the results of the LSM(R)s' rocket runs:

I AM NOW PASSING THROUGH THE ROCKET AREA. THE EFFECT OF THE ROCKETS IS DEVASTATING. SOME WERE DIRECTLY ON ENEMY POSITIONS WHEN THEY DID [sic] THE POSITIONS WERE DEMOL- ISHED. NO PLACE THROUGHOUT HERE SEEMS TO BE IMMUNE TO A ROCKET. I FOUND ONE DUD. TAIL FINS ARE SCATTERED EVERYWHERE. THIS WAS A VERY STRONG ENEMY POSITION. THE EFFECT OF THE ROCKETS IS ENCOURAGING TO ME. (FROM OUR REPRESENTATIVE YP FRONT ON PATROL).[92]

The two rocketships patrolled independently that afternoon. *LSM(R) 192's* 40mm gunners fired at targets on the beaches and hilly ridges lying beyond. Meanwhile, *LSM(R) 193* skirted the eastern shores of rugged Chinen Peninsula where she shelled a highlands cave[93] with her 5"/38 and opened 40mm fire at enemy personnel near the peninsular village of China.[94] Retracing the coastline back to Baten Ko, the rocketship renewed automatic weapons fire at Japanese troops east and west of Sashiki village.[95]

Admiral Joy later reported, "LSM(R) [sic] delivered supporting fire on southern and eastern slopes in advance of our lines. Casualties were noted in TA 8565DE [near Sashiki] where [enemy] troops were taken under fire. ComGen7thInf reported that the LSM(R) had kept down troop movements along the shore and furnished him with valuable reconnaissance information."[96] On the other hand, Vice Admiral Hill added, "Rain and mud with consequent supply difficulties prevented any large scale offensive operation [sic]. However, patrols probed the entire front to determine whether enemy was withdrawing under cover of bad weather…. Patrols from 7th Inf. Div. working well south of the left flank encountered many dead Japs and found several wrecked barges along the coast…."[97]

At 1200 on 27 May, Rear Admiral C. Turner Joy was relieved by Rear Admiral I.C. Sowell (Commander Battleship Division Four) in *West Virginia BB 48*, who assumed command as CTG 31.19 and SOPA Eastern Okinawa. Among his first reports, Adm. Sowell noted, "Rocket *LMS* [sic] *192* and *193* in close support for Headquarters 7th Infantry gave satisfactory area coverage in Target Area 8766 and 9067 [near Sashiki and China villages] causing several enemy casualties."[98] But before departing, Adm. Joy praised the LSM(R)s as the culmination of naval gunfire support built upon the experiences gained from preceding LCSs and LCI(R)s. "The results were most gratifying. Unfortunately, a shortage of rocket ammunition made it necessary to restrict call fires somewhat."[99]

Around 1900, the rocketships were released from gunfire assignments at sunset. *LSM(R) 192* soon anchored off Yonabaru, where she made smoke that evening for the anchorage, while *LSM(R) 193* continued onward to anchor in Nakagusuku Wan overnight.[100]

28 May 1945

During the night of 27–28 May, the constant rains gave way, however briefly, to clear skies and moonlight that invited renewed Japanese air attacks.[101]

At 0651, *LSM(R) 193* got underway and was soon followed astern by *LSM(R) 192*, setting course 250° T, speed 1/3, to the beach area in Baten Ko to continue call fire support.[102] En route, General Quarters sounded at 0722 due to Japanese aircraft in the area, and six minutes later an enemy plane was splashed close aboard a battleship anchored in the bay.

During 28 May, reported Admiral Sowell, "Bombardment [was] curtailed because of operations of friendly advance patrols and low visibility. [Nonetheless,] Considerable harassing fire [was] delivered…."[103] Japanese troop activities, however, continued to puzzle the Americans. "Considerable enemy movement on roads was again taken under fire by artillery, naval gunfire and air support planes," said Vice Admiral Hill, now designated CTF 31 under Halsey's Third Fleet. "Considerable destruction of enemy equipment and personnel was effected. Movement reported as mostly southwesterly but without definite pattern to indicate enemy's intention."[104]

By 0740, *LSM(R) 192* was lying off Baten Ko Beach, watching for enemy activity, while *LSM(R) 193* closed the shoreline and embarked five Army observers an hour later.

LSM(R) 192 stood guard while *LSM(R) 193* commenced harassing fire, beginning in the Baten Ko area then continuing after rounding Chinen Hanto (Peninsula). Through mid-morning, the rocketship poured 5"/38 and 40mm fires into areas south of China village, noting several successful hits that included a nearby cave.[105]

LSM(R) 192 remained in the area of Baten Ko harbor but, at 1030, *LSM(R) 193* set course 150° T at ⅔ speed to patrol the southeastern coastline of Okinawa. In twenty minutes, the rocketship passed through Kutaku Kuchi,[106] then changed course to 260° PGC (per gyro compass).

At 1135, she came under fire from unidentified beach points. Going to battle stations, the rocketship sought the source of the enemy attacks, and by 1152 she opened fire on suspicious activity ashore. Within thirty minutes, however, *LSM(R) 193* changed course again to 178° T to retire from the beach area and secured from General Quarters.

In early afternoon, *LSM(R) 193* made a rocket run firing 300 rockets[107] against a bridge, road, and fortifications around Minatoga[108] at 1450, followed by shelling the same targets with her 5"/38 fifteen minutes later. Retiring by 1520 to begin an observation patrol, in minutes the rocketship changed course for return to Baten Ko, instead, to disembark the Army personnel by 1650.

The two rocketships retired northeast to anchor in berth B-183 near Tsuken (or Tsugen) Shima. After transferring 5"/38 projectiles between ships, *LSM(R) 192* re-anchored off Yonabaru by 2030.

29 May 1945

LSM(R) 192 got underway at 0637 of 29 May, leaving Yonabaru Anchorage en route to Baten Ko for reconnaissance with Army observers.[109] But as Admiral Sowell noted, sour weather hampered assignments once again, and "Poor visibility limited fire support to harassing fire...."[110] *LSM(R) 193* remained behind this time, and closed the *Lindenwald LSD 6* by 0900 in Berth B-180 in Tsugen Shima Anchorage for overdue repairs. The rocketship eased into the repair ship's well deck and was firmly secured in dry dock by 1350.

By mid-morning of 29 May, the Marines were first to enter Shuri Castle, breaking through the remnants of Japanese troops holding the fortress' perimeter. Despite this hard-fought triumph, however, American commanders now slowly realized that most of General Ushijima's forces had evacuated Shuri to southern Okinawa between 22 May and that very day.[111]

In Baten Ko, *LSM(R) 192* closed the beach to exchange Army fire coordinators via wherry.[112] "I well remember the first day an Army officer and two GI's came aboard the *192*," recalled Robert Landis, the ship's Storekeeper.

> They, as you might suspect, were unshaven, muddied and tired-looking. I remember how grateful they were to get a hot meal in our mess. I remember noting the GI's kept their rifles at their sides at all times:

in the mess hall, in the head or wherever. They also expressed concern as to where do you take cover on the deck of this ship if strafed by enemy aircraft. You can guess what they had been exposed to ashore. As we cruised the shoreline they directed our gunners to a number of targets which were pounded with five inch, 40mm and 20mm fire. That was a very interesting experience.[113]

With Army spotters embarked, the rocketship patrolled off the southeastern coast of Okinawa. But *LSM(R) 192* inauspiciously ran aground by striking a reef off Chinen Mura. Held fast on its starboard side amidships, she was now a sitting duck to enemy fire. Resorting to various combinations of the ship's engines and rudders, the rocketship finally broke free after five long minutes—and was doubly lucky to escape without hull damage.

Ten minutes after getting underway, *LSM(R) 192* opened fire against Japanese targets on Chinen Mura with her #2 40mm gun; sounding General Quarters at 0945, fifteen minutes later her 5"/38 also commenced fire. Rounding the southeast peninsula of Chinen Hanto, at 1045 she opened 40mm gunfire on Japanese soldiers on the beach near Chinen Misaki and employed her 5"/38 gun against other targets ashore.

It may have been here where the *LSM(R) 192* rounded a rocky promontory for a chance encounter with a Japanese soldier—wearing only skivvie shorts while washing his laundry among enormous rocks along the beach. "We did daytime coast patrol and close-in support as required," recalled Radarman 2c Ronald R. MacKay. "We were generally scouting for trouble, or any reinforcement or other seaborne activity, when we kind-of rounded a coastal salient and there among those big boulders was the little Jap." The OOD ordered the 40mm gun crews to open fire, but the gunners were reluctant and slow to bring their guns around, so the officer angrily threatened courts martial if they failed to obey. Radarman MacKay continued, "He was as startled as we were until he saw our guns swing around in his direction—then he hauled ass." Responding to orders, the gun crews deliberately fired wide-ranging salvos that bounced off the large boulders—some as big as a house—as the enemy soldier scrambled away.[114]

Battle stations were secured by 1119 as patrols continued, but General Quarters was set once again at 1240—albeit quietly by "passing the word." Closing the shoreline for closer observation, at 1255 the rocketship's 40mms opened fire at suspicious movements on a road, possibly a truck and Japanese troops.

After another twenty minutes of observation, *LSM(R) 192* patrolled down along the coast over the next hour, headed toward the southern tip of Okinawa, then reversed course at 1435 and returned northward. Securing from General Quarters an hour later, the rocketship returned to Baten Ko where she tied up to the pier and disembarked the Army personnel. About this same time, the OOD received intelligence concerning Japanese gun positions. Resuming her search for the enemy, the rocketship discovered the targets, and from 1800 to 1845, *LSM(R) 192* shelled enemy emplacements with her 5"/38, expending 25 rounds.

Released thereafter from further assignments, the Finner retired to drop anchor in the Katchin Wan Anchorage by sunset. Wearily, gun crews frequently manned their guns overnight due to repeated air raid alerts.

30 May 1945

Because sister ship *LSM(R) 193* remained in dry dock in *Lindenwald* for ongoing repairs, *LSM(R) 192* resumed independent patrols during 30 May. The Finner got underway from

Yonabaru Anchorage at 0655 and was standing in Baten Ko within thirty minutes.[115] The ship's wherry was lowered over the side at 0830 and dispatched to shore with a coxswain, and upon return, three Army observers embarked with their equipment. The small boat departed once more and returned with two more Army soldiers by 0905.

Finally assigned a target, the rocketship poised for a rocket run, but the attack was called off about 1000 because of nearby friendly Army patrols. Instead, *LSM(R) 192* patrolled the Baten Ko beaches for enemy activity. "On the east flank of 7th Div.," explained Vice Admiral Hill, "only moderate resistance was encountered as the lines advanced to hill which furnishes commanding view across the shoulder of Chinen Peninsula. 7th Rcn Troop [sic] patrols in Chinen Peninsula met and reduced scattered pockets of enemy. Jap movement southward under cover of bad weather was discovered and artillery broke up several groups each estimated from 100 to 200...."[116]

Admiral Sowell later noted that "Ship [sic] furnished little fire support because of dense fog which made spotting impossible.... Bombardment limited due to poor visibility and no results were observed."[117] Nevertheless, the go-ahead for another rocket run assignment came through in mid afternoon, so GQ sounded as *LSM(R) 192* maneuvered to the firing line. First firing two ranging salvos, the rockets soared far beyond the target area. After maneuvering to adjust for the proper distance, all banks of rockets were launched between 1515 and 1520.[118]

After the rocket run, the rocketship returned near the pier at Baten Ko, and the Army observers were returned to the beach via ship's wherry. *LSM(R) 192* then got underway thereafter for Katchin Wan, where she dispatched a group of sailors for medical care at a nearby transport ship, and anchored from the stern for the day.

By mid-afternoon, meanwhile, repairs were completed on sister ship *LSM(R) 193*, so she backed out of dry dock from the *Lindenwald* in Isuken Anchorage, then anchored in the transport area of Lauhen [sic] Anchorage.[119] The rocketship took on supplies from an LST, then dropped anchor in Berth 154 in Nakagusuku Wan by sunset.

31 May 1945

LSM(R) 193 got underway about an hour after sunrise and moored a short time later portside to *LSM(R) 192*, then cast off for Baten Ko. Once the latter rocketship got underway, she first closed an LST for provisions through mid morning, then reported to Baten Ko.[120]

During 31 May, reported Admiral Sowell, "*LSM(R) 192* and *193* operated in close support of Headquarters 7th Infantry patrols, obtaining valuable reconnaissance information and inflicting casualties on the enemy." The admiral further noted that "Slightly improved weather permitted some observation," but "Fog caused cancellation of most naval gunfire support scheduled during the afternoon."[121] Vice Admiral Hill added, "The southern portion of the 7th Div. made no advance but sent out strong patrols which penetrated 1½ miles finding little enemy activity.... Heavy enemy artillery concentrations in the early morning in 7th Div. zone and several infiltration attempts were the only night activities."[122]

A group of U.S. Army spotters from the 184th Infantry embarked *LSM(R) 193*, then the rocketship shoved off by 0930 to observe enemy movements off the southern coastline of Okinawa.

Before noon, *LSM(R) 192* stood off a Baten Ko pier and also embarked a group of Army observers while all hands assembled and loaded 298 rockets in the launchers. The rocketship then patrolled beach areas, but soon returned to Baten Ko about 1500. While the Army observers disembarked, *LSM(R) 192* provided covering fire, shelling a shore target with 91 rounds from her bow 40mm.

LSM(R) 192 thereafter steamed eastward around the Chinen Peninsula until standing off China Saki at 1600 and watched for enemy activity. Ten minutes later, the #1 40mm bow gun opened fire, but jammed. Taking over, her #2 40mm gun, forward of the conn, shelled what looked like a stone hut on a hill. But, because no appreciable damage was observed, the target was believed to be some kind of reinforced pillbox. Thereafter, *LSM(R) 192* set sail for northwest of China Saki to observe further enemy movements, where her repaired forward 40mm fired at a cave with 222 rounds from 1720 to 1754. Summarizing the action, Lt. Comdr. Fulweiler briefly noted, "[*LSM(R)s*] 192 and 193 strafed beach targets, and were taken under fire by enemy beach emplacements. No damage."[123]

At dusk, *LSM(R) 192* was released from further assignments and anchored off White Beach in Nakagusuku Wan by 2010. *LSM(R) 193* also retired from Baten Ko, and dropped anchor a couple miles northeast of Yonabaru[124] for the night.

Before midnight of 31 May, *LSM(R) 193*'s captain was unable to decode an encrypted message, so he called upon *LSM(R) 192* for assistance. Due to heavy fog, however, nighttime visibility was especially poor, so navigating the anchorage depended upon the radarman taking bearings from the SU-1 radar. Easing through Nakagusuku Wan, she finally secured lines with *LSM(R) 193* at 0011 of 1 June. After huddling for some forty-five minutes, *LSM(R) 192* cast off to anchor nearby through the remainder of the morning.[125]

1 June 1945

About an hour after sunrise, *LSM(R) 192* set sail from Nakagusuku Wan at 0622 of 1 June. But because of the continuing dense morning fog, she used radar to maneuver various courses and speeds en route to Hagushi Anchorage in western Okinawa. *LSM(R) 193* also weighed anchor some thirty minutes later, but first sought *Endymion ARL 9* to pick up propellers, then set sail for Hagushi as well.

Reflecting on his recent experiences in *LSM(R) 192*, Storekeeper Robert Landis wrote in his diary,

> We have been assigned to the Army for the past nine days. Each day we made one or more rocket runs and continued strafing the shoreline. Occasionally we would take artillery fire, more often mortars and small arms fire, but no serious damage. Many near misses, however. For two of those days we had Army spotters aboard, two officers and 4 enlisted men. They liked our hot food and showers but when a Jap Zero circled us they were distressed when they couldn't take refuge in a fox hole. In the end, they said they preferred to be ashore. Later this day we were released by the Army. Okinawa is now considered secured.[126]

LSM(R) 192 rounded the southern tip of Okinawa by 0800 and entered Hagushi anchorage before 1100, followed by *LSM(R) 193* just after noontime. Awaiting further orders, the two rocketships would soon leave Okinawa behind.

Rear Admiral Sowell commended the fire support gunboats serving in eastern Okinawa, noting, "The use of rocket equipped LSMs and LCIs was found to be extremely valuable to

Army Division Headquarters in: (a) providing close-in support for advance patrols; (b) quickly destroying small pockets of enemy resistance; (c) destroying mortar emplacements on reverse slopes and, (d) providing valuable reconnaissance for Army observers."[127]

Southwestern Okinawa: USS LSM(R) 189 and USS LSM(R) 191

At noon of 21 May, Vice Admiral Harry W. Hill (CTF 51) ordered USS *LSM(R) 189* and USS *LSM(R) 191* to report to Rear Admiral J. L. Hall, Jr., SOPA Hagushi (CTG 51.22) in headquarters flagship *Teton AGC 14*, for further assignment as naval gunfire support.[128]

Besides the two LSM(R)s, Sixth Marine Division naval gunfire support requirements from mid May into early June averaged eight heavy warships, including battleships, cruisers, and destroyers. Assignments for both the west and east coasts of Okinawa were issued twice daily by CTF 51: night assignments were made the preceding morning, and day assignments on the preceding evening, based on the number of ships available for Fire Support and the request received from the troops ashore. "While the heavy ships were available if needed," explained Admiral Hill, "they were brought into the anchorage at night to avoid needless exposure to torpedo plane or suicide plane attack."[129] Air support for spotting naval gunfire included some half-dozen VOF observation planes until Okinawa was secured.

Admiral Hall added, "During the weeks immediately following Love Day gunfire support craft were not used in the Southern Attack Force except for smoke protection. This was due principally to the prohibitive width of the fringing reef for almost the entire length of the southwest coast. As the Sixth Marine Division approached Naha, however, an opportunity for exploiting the capabilities of these craft arose" after mid–May.[130]

Upon reporting to Adm. Hall, the two rocketships were directed to report to Commander Clarence E. Coffin, Jr., (CTG 52.20) in *LC(FF) 370*, Commander LCI Flotilla Sixteen, Southern Support Gunboats (CTU 52.9.4),[131] for fire support assignments with the U.S. Marines. Comdr. Coffin served under Captain T.C. Aylward (CTG 52.9) commanding LCS(L) Flotilla Three and the Gunboat and Mortar Support Flotillas from his force flagship *LC(FF) 988*.[132] Under Aylward at Okinawa were some two hundred LCS(L)s, LCI(G)s, LCI(R)s, and LCI(M)s[133]—including LSM(R)s after 26 April.[134]

But Commander Coffin disputed Admiral Hall's (and Adm. Turner's[135]) contention that gunfire support craft had little tactical value during the six weeks following the invasion on 1 April 1945. Coffin believed a lack of information—even misinformation—and an absence of "salesmanship" had failed to promote rocket-firing gunboats. "Conversation [*sic*] with Army and Marine personnel indicated that much earlier use would have been made of the LCI(R)s had more information been available as to their capabilities and had they been made available for fire support missions," Coffin argued. Indeed, "Army and Marine Units unfamiliar with 5" rockets apparently cannot visualize their effectiveness and consequently did not request their use at first. However, after they had seen the LCI(R)s work, they were full of praise for them and regretted that they had not been used before."[136] Commander Coffin's argument applied equally to Commander Francis and his LSM(R)s.

LSM(R) fire support orders from the Marines were not soon forthcoming, however, so the two rocket ships remained on standby in Hagushi anchorage for several days, while

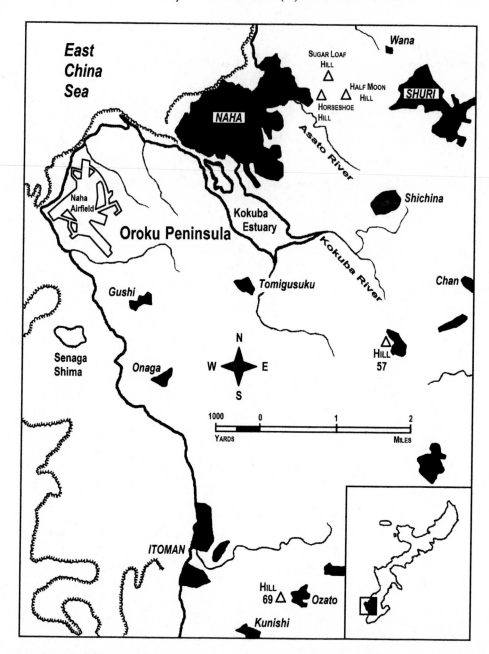

LSM(R)s 189 and *191* supported U.S. Marine operations in southwestern Okinawa from 26 May to 1 June 1945 (adapted from Roy E. Appleman et al., *Okinawa: The Last Battle*, The War in the Pacific, United States Army in World War II, Washington, D.C.: U.S. Government Printing Office, 1948, Map No. XLVI).

otherwise attending to maintenance and logistics, or manning battle stations and making smoke during air raid alerts. Notably, Commodore Moosbrugger, the Screen Commander at Okinawa, forwarded a belated message to LSM Flotilla Nine on 25 May: "By dispatch CTG 51.5 released all LSM(R)s from Radar Picket Duty."[137]

The U.S. Marines

Beginning the second week of May, the Sixth Marine Division was charged with pushing south along the western coast of Okinawa, then moving southeast in a pincer movement to envelop the Shuri Castle stronghold and destroy Lieutenant General Mitsuru Ushijima's main army forces of about 30,000 men. However, progress was slow after almost two weeks of fierce fighting against Japanese defending the notorious Sugar Loaf complex—Sugar Loaf Hill, Half Moon Hill (also known as Crescent Hill), and Horseshoe Hill—and later considered the costliest fighting in Marine Corps history. Here heavy rains and muddy battlefields also effectively slowed the Sixth Marine Division and compounded efforts to exploit a southeastward thrust toward Shuri.

By the third week of May, the division's commander, Major General Lemuel C. Shepherd, Jr., USMC, decided to also push south and southwest toward Naha and the Kokuba River, then turn east to attempt a southwestern encirclement of the fortified Shuri Castle. Until now, the razed capital city of Okinawa had not been their primary objective.[138] But from 24 to 28 May, Marines gained control over most of the devastated and largely deserted city, roughly bifurcated by the Asato River, finding scattered civilians hiding amidst the rubble while encountering occasional sniper fire. Beyond Naha, however, the Marines faced increasingly heavy Japanese resistance.[139]

26 May 1945

For 26 May, a battleship, cruiser and three destroyers were among the designated NGF support of the Marines on the western coast of Okinawa.[140] "Throughout the night," explained Admiral Hill, Commander, Task Force 51, "heavy ships operating to seaward of the small craft furnished illumination along the beaches and delivered harassing fires on possible hiding places for suicide boats. The small craft kept close lookouts for possible enemy movements and adjusted the illumination as necessary."[141] "Special Assignments" as "Flycatchers" and harassing missions also supported the III Amphibious Corps.[142]

At 0100, *LSM(R) 189*, dubbed "Miss Rocket," tested her launcher electrical circuits, then set Condition One Roger at 0440 as all hands began loading Fin-stabilized Aircraft Rockets (AR) into launchers. She weighed anchor an hour later and proceeded along a generally southwesterly course. "Underway to area south of Naha," noted Gunnery Officer Ensign F. Donald Moore.[143] All rocket launchers were full by 0655, and minutes later *LSM(R) 189* reported ready for duty to the Sixth Marine Division. Half an hour later, the rocketship entered the designated rendezvous area off the northwestern tip of Oroku Peninsula,[144] where she cruised on station awaiting further instructions.

At 0600, meanwhile, her partner *LSM(R) 191*, called "The Dragon Lady," also loaded rockets in launchers, then got underway by 0732 as her deck force finished fusing the 300 ARs. An hour later she rendezvoused with *LSM(R) 189* west of Naha, and both were standing on station by 0930. The alert calling for gunfire support finally arrived in early afternoon and set a rocket attack for 1430 in northern and northeastern Oroku Peninsula.[145]

The LSM(R)s' attack sectors in northern Oroku Peninsula were high grounds overlooking Naha. Naha Airfield on the peninsula's northwestern coast was defended by the Imperial

Japanese Navy's Okinawa Base Force of some 10,000 men under Rear Admiral Minoru Ota. By May 1945, however, this force was no longer a naval organization *per se*, but an amalgam of navy personnel reinforced by Home Guard soldiers and conscripted civilians.[146]

Not yet known by American commanders, the Okinawa Base Force was defending Oroku as a holding action while General Ushijima's main army units stealthily evacuated Shuri Castle. Then, Admiral Ota's navy force would withdraw to join Ushijima in southern Okinawa by 28 May. The new Japanese defensive ramparts would thus stretch across Okinawa from Itoman on the west coast to Minatoga on the east coast.[147] But, a misunderstanding of a secret communiqué led Ota to order all weapons destroyed that could not be carried, and he commenced early evacuation of Oroku Peninsula on 26 May, two days ahead of Ushijima's original plan.[148] Upon discovering their mistake, two days later Ota's force returned to resume defensive positions on the peninsula.

By 1350, both rocketships sounded General Quarters and set Condition One Roger while maneuvering into positions. Leading the initial rocket run, *LSM(R) 189* loosed successive salvos on northern Oroku from 1437 to 1455 as 212 Fin-stabilized rockets launched without failures. After her last volley, *LSM(R) 189* maneuvered away from the reef and sent men topside to battle stations while *LSM(R) 191* aligned perpendicular to the coastline. Ensign F. Donald Moore observed her beginning her rocket run at 1500, from afar: "*LSM(R) 191* now going in on run. Target area is north end of Naha airport."[149] In twenty minutes the rocket ship launched[150] 200 rockets at the enemy airfield.

Lt. James M. Stewart, commanding USS *LSM(R) 189*, later reported: "All rockets with few exceptions hit target areas. Barrage was requested to extend over one hour periods. Both ships closed to within 500 yards of harbor entrance to city of Naha. *LSM(R) 189* made first run with *LSM(R) 191* covering her approach, then the *LSM(R) 189* covered the approach of *LSM(R) 191*."[151] While departing the target area, *LSM(R) 189* shelled what appeared to be an enemy field gun; but after expending four 5-inch rounds on the target, a renewed examination concluded it was probably a wrecked plane.

After Marine headquarters was advised the assigned mission was completed, Gunnery Officer Ensign Moore noted at 1545, "Ordered to stand by for further orders. Working with 6th Marine Division–Bastille 8."[152] "Bastille 8" was code name for the Naval Gunfire Liaison Officer (NGF O) Major E. W. Gardner, USMC, coordinating Sixth Marine Division NGF requirements with the senior naval gunfire support vessel designated "Bastille," which for 26 May was battleship *Idaho BB 42*.[153] As Bastille 8, Maj. Gardner also coordinated air spotting, typically by radio from aboard whichever ship was designated "Bastille" that given day, although he embarked other ships and craft as warranted.

The next rocket attack assignment came in mid-afternoon: "Ordered by 6th Marine Division to make another run on same target," noted Ensign Moore,[154] and *LSM(R) 189* set Condition One Roger at 1730. Target areas were sectors located midway down the southwestern coast of Oroku Peninsula, near the seaside town of Gushi and neighboring village of Onaga,[155] which face the rocky island of Senaga Shima.[156]

This time, *LSM(R) 191* led the attack, beginning her rocket run at 1820 and launching a hundred rockets from 1831 to 1849. Overlapping this barrage, *LSM(R) 189* plotted course 094° T. toward the firing point and, moments after launching a ranging rocket, she unleashed rocket salvos timed at five-second intervals. Afterwards, Ens. Moore summarized, "1846 Completed run. 122 rounds expended, no casualties."[157]

"On retirement," explained Lt. Stewart, "Senaga Shima was subjected to harassing fire. The *LSM(R) 189* fired 100 rounds of 40mm and five rounds of 5"/38. The *LSM(R) 191* fired 39 rounds of 40mm, 50 rounds of 20mm and five rounds of 5"/38 along with 818 rounds of 50 caliber."[158] Before clearing the area, however, the fantail smoke generator on *LSM(R) 191* caught fire from the blasts from her 5"/38, but was quickly extinguished.

By 1900, the rocketships secured from General Quarters and "Bastille advised no further duties for day."[159] Two hundred and twelve rockets were fired,[160] yet, Lt. Stewart concluded, "No destruction could be observed and no opposition was encountered on day's bombardment."[161] Comdr. Coffin instructed *LSM(R)s 189* and *191* to return to Dodger Area,[162] and an hour later the two Finners entered a darkened Hagushi Anchorage, "determined by Radar bearings,"[163] to anchor and make smoke that night.

27 May 1945

Before dawn in Hagushi Anchorage, *LSM(R) 191*'s deck force began assembling and loading rockets into launchers at 0430 under Condition One Roger. By 0546, all hands in *LSM(R) 189* commenced loading rockets as well,[164] even as the rocketship shoved off at 0630. Setting course 220° True at standard speed, Gunnery Officer Ensign F. Donald Moore noted they were "underway to area off Naha to await orders for day."[165] *LSM(R) 191* followed suit by getting underway at 0648 at full speed on course 225° True. Besides the two rocketships, NGF support on the southwestern coast of Okinawa included *Tuscaloosa CA 37*—designated "Bastille" this day—with two other cruisers, two battleships, and four destroyers.[166]

Continuous rains hampered offensive ground operations during 27 May, so Marine patrols probed to determine whether the Japanese were attempting withdrawals or reinforcements under cover of the bad weather. "Ground conditions grew steadily worse during the day," said Vice Admiral Hill, "and many emergency measures were initiated to get supplies through the mud to the troops. Amtracs and weasels were used extensively for supply, supplemented by hand carrying by troops."[167]

LSM(R) 189 reached the staging area about four thousand yards off Naha[168] at 0715, and *LSM(R) 191* joined her five minutes later, then "advised Bastille we were ready for fire support," reported Ensign Moore.[169] As before, the Marine Corps liaison officer was Maj. Gardner as "Bastille 8,"[170] now embarked in *Tuscaloosa*. The two rocketships, while awaiting orders from the Sixth Marine Division, paced northeast-southwest courses at various speeds off western Okinawa as ships' deck forces finished loading rocket launchers.

At mid-morning, "The Dragon Lady" was assigned an NLO (Naval Liaison Officer) in the area of Naha[171] operating with destroyers, and their mission was area fire support for a Marine patrol. Here Ensign Edward Bowden, 1st Lieutenant in *LSM(R) 191*, and Gunnery Officer Lt.(jg) Laurie R. Russell, plotted the Marine and Japanese positions and gained permission to lay down 5" fire. Ens. Bowden recalled the enemy responded with large caliber mortar fire that was well-directed.[172] At "0845 *LSM(R) 191*, under orders from Sixth Marine Division, furnished support to 0222 patrol on Red Oak [fire support station], with her 40mm guns, expending 575 rounds of ammunition. She carried out a very difficult assignment of call fire, which necessitated her staying in a hazardous, exposed position for approximately seven hours, close in to shore, surrounded by reefs, with small opportunity to maneuver."[173]

The Sixth Marine Division's naval gunfire officer[174] pronounced the results "good" as the rock-etship stood close offshore with her deck load of rockets through the afternoon awaiting further orders.

"Miss Rocket," meanwhile, was ordered to rendezvous near the Hagushi Anchorage[175] with Commander LSM Flotilla Nine's flagship *LC(FF) 535*. Mooring alongside by 1115, officers and enlisted staff of LSM(R) Group Twenty-Seven, including Lt. Comdr. Fulweiler, transferred to *LSM(R) 189* for temporary duty.[176]

Returning to the operations area in early afternoon, the two Finners' gunfire assignments were similar to those of the previous day: patrols and fire support along the southwestern coast of Oroku Peninsula in sectors around Gushi and Onaga villages and Senaga Shima.[177]

Making final course corrections, *LSM(R) 189* fired ranging rockets on course 087° T. at 1428. But within the next sixty seconds, she made literal, last-minute course adjustments to her rocket run, and settled upon course 080° T., firing her first rocket salvos about 1429. Quickly swinging about to bear on target again, "Miss Rocket" was suddenly ordered to cease fire because low-flying friendly planes were strafing the target area.

No more than ten minutes passed when Ensign Moore noted, "Observed large fire started by rockets."[178] Skies were clear of American planes by 1436, and *LSM(R) 189* resumed rocket salvos on various bearings between 087° T. and 110° T. until 1454. "Completed run," continued her gunnery officer; "146 rounds expended, no casualties. [Now] Taking Senaga Shima under fire."[179] Targeting the island once again, the rocketship expended 114 rounds of 40mm harassing fire, while *Tuscaloosa* stood by to provide cover fire for small craft protection and counterbattery.[180] Lookouts also spotted a building still standing near Gushi village,[181] so *LSM(R) 189*'s 5"/38 demolished the structure with five rounds.

Departing the target areas, *LSM(R) 189* secured General Quarters at 1515 as "two large fires [were] observed which were started by rockets." Notifying the Sixth Marine Division that they were ready for their next assignment, the rocket ship set Condition One Roger and "commenced reloading rockets," wrote Ensign Moore, while "cruising off Naha awaiting further orders."[182]

Morning through afternoon, *LSM(R) 191* stood off Naha supporting a Marine patrol by strafing enemy positions with hundreds of rounds of 40mm. Ceasing fire and securing GQ by 1631, she got underway on various courses to rendezvous with *LSM(R) 189* for an assignment south of the Oroku Peninsula. Indeed, after advising "Bastille" they were standing by, at "1645 Ordered in to another target," penned Ensign Moore. "Proceeding to new target (Itoman). *LSM(R) 191*, who gave harassing fire in Naha during morning, is to join us on this run."[183]

Forty-five minutes later, General Quarters sounded again with "*LSM(R) 191* and us maneuvering into position for run," said Ensign Moore. Bearing on course 088° T., *LSM(R) 189* commenced the first rocket run on Itoman, launching 299 Fin-stabilized Aircraft Rockets from 1753 to 1757, although one rocket failed to ignite and was quickly jettisoned overboard. "Many cook-offs observed," continued Ens. Moore, and "large fire started, possibly ammo or fuel dump," then he added, "all target area now smoldering amid wreckage."[184]

While *LSM(R) 189* stood off the target area, *LSM(R) 191* made her rocket run on Itoman village from 1804 to 1814, firing 300 rockets and then shelling the beach with her fantail 5"/38 gun.[185] Gunnery Officer Moore concluded afterwards: "Completed run. Target area appears to be demolished."[186]

LSM(R) 189 notified Marine headquarters that their mission was completed, and "reported to Bastille that target area was destroyed and in flames," said Ensign Moore.[187] The ship's OOD noted in the logbook, "6th Marine Division advised that they had no more assignments for that day and commended ships on fine work."[188] Lt. Comdr. Fulweiler later summarized their day's accomplishments: "On detached duty [*LSM(R)*] *189* delivered 147 Rockets, 5 inch and automatic weapon [*sic*] fire in assigned area. [*LSM(R)*] *191* on a particularly exposed mission delivered 7 hours of call fire, 575 rounds of 40mm. At 1800 both Ships fired total of 600 Rockets in assigned area."[189]

Securing from GQ, the two rocketships retired for the Hagushi Anchorage. En route, *LSM(R) 189* set Condition One Roger as her deck force assembled 188 rockets and loaded them into empty rocket launchers. By 1901, finally, "Secured from loading rockets. ½ deck loaded," noted Gunnery Officer Ensign F. Donald Moore.[190]

28 May 1945

Overnight 27–28 May, constant heavy rains gave way briefly to clear weather and moonlight. At half-past midnight, *LSM(R) 189* began making smoke screen in Hagushi Anchorage, as enemy aircraft grew active in the darkness overhead. At 0155, Ensign Moore observed an "AA barrage overhead," then "more AA fire" at 0225, and then at 0315: "More AA fire. Bomb dropped on airfield."[191]

After sunrise, *LSM(R) 189* set sail for Naha[192] as all hands in *LSM(R) 191* assembled and loaded rockets into launchers. The latter weighed anchor and then followed, bearing 240° True, in remarkably clear weather. Throughout the morning, both rocketships stood off Naha awaiting orders, as the deck force on *LSM(R) 189*, meanwhile, finished loading rockets.

During 28 May, NGF support for the Marines on the southwestern coast of Okinawa were cruiser *Tuscaloosa*—once more codenamed "Bastille"—with two other cruisers, two battleships, and three destroyers including a VOF spotter plane.[193] *Picking DD 685* also reported for harassing assignments with III Amphibious Corps.[194]

Admiral Ota's Okinawa Base Force had resumed defensive positions on Oroku Peninsula by 28 May, after prematurely evacuating two days earlier.[195] Yet the Americans remained puzzled whether the Japanese were redeploying forces or withdrawing. "Considerable enemy movement on roads was again taken under fire by artillery, naval gunfire and air support planes," said Vice Admiral Hill. "Movement reported as mostly southwesterly but without definite pattern to indicate enemy's intention."[196]

Meanwhile, the two Finners were ordered southward to begin the day's fire support.

After skirting the Oroku Peninsula, the assigned target—Gushi village[197]—appeared off their port beams at half past noon. Setting General Quarters, *LSM(R) 189* led the first rocket run, swinging to course 090° T. then firing 300 rockets with "no casualties" (i.e., no rocket misfires).[198] *LSM(R) 191* immediately followed with her rocket attack, also launching 300 rockets into the target areas.[199]

During withdrawal, a large fire blazed near Gushi.[200] "Completed run. Entire area smoldering, target demolished," reported Ens. Moore, noting the time at 1258.[201] As *LSM(R) 189* retired, her 40mm gunners strafed Senaga Shima.

The rocketships notified Sixth Marine Division Headquarters via *Tuscaloosa* that the mission was completed, and at "1302 Bastille advised to reload immediately," jotted Ensign Moore.[202] New instructions assigned "Miss Rocket" and "The Dragon Lady" rocket attacks south of the Naha airfield on northwestern Oroku Peninsula, then to neutralize enemy emplacements on Senaga Shima using 40mms once more.[203]

In thirty minutes, the pair arrived in the target area and all hands went to GQ before the rocket runs. *LSM(R) 191* closed the firing line as *LSM(R) 189* first loosed 300 rockets from 1520 to 1524, then opened 40mm harassing gunfire while passing Japanese batteries concealed on Senaga Shima. In turn, *LSM(R) 189* stood off Senaga Shima providing cover as *LSM(R) 191* launched 200 rockets from 1532 to 1545.[204] The next half-hour, the two rocketships shelled the enemy-held island with 40mms.

Upon retiring, *LSM(R) 189* informed Marine Headquarters the mission was completed, after which the two rocketships were released from further assignments. Between them, 1100 rockets had been launched during 28 May.[205] Once in Hagushi Anchorage, S1c Theodore Hall reported aboard *LSM(R) 189* that evening, following his hospital care and recuperation from injuries suffered during the enemy air attacks on 12 April.[206]

29 May 1945

The Sixth Marine Division continued pressing south into Naha and southeast along the Kokuba estuary, but they would not assault the Oroku Peninsula *per se* until a week later. Japanese peninsular forces nevertheless threatened the Marines' southern, or right, flank during its eastward drive toward Shuri.

After 0800 of 29 May, *LSM(R)s 189* and *191* were at Condition One Roger as their deck forces began assembling and loading rockets. Once on station off Naha, the two Finners steamed alternating courses of 200° and 020° T., awaiting instructions. By 0930, all rocket launchers were fully loaded.

On 29 May, NGF support for the Marines on southwestern Okinawa comprised *Tuscaloosa*, reprising codename "Bastille,"[207] with another cruiser, two battleships, and three destroyers reporting to III Amphibious Corps.[208]

The fire support assignment issued at 1000 ordered a strike on a fortified ridge,[209] where a road linked the towns of Onaga and Itoman along the southwestern coast of Okinawa.[210] Both rocketships sounded General Quarters and set Condition One Roger as they proceeded southward to the target area.

The first rocket run began at 1050, but was checked by nearby friendly aircraft: "Withholding fire until air activity in target area is finished," noted the deck officer on *LSM(R) 189*. In minutes the skies were clear, so at 1107, "Miss Rocket" launched ranging salvos on course 080° T., some 3200 yards from the beach. Firing rockets in earnest by 1109, she retired from the beach after a three-minute barrage. Next, "[at] 1123 *LSM(R) 191* commenced firing," observed Ensign Moore,[211] and "The Dragon Lady" completed her rocket run by 1129.

As the two Finners secured from battle stations, *LSM(R) 189* radioed a disappointing assessment of the rocket runs to the Sixth Marine Division: "Notified Bastille 8 that rockets may have fallen short of target but that we couldn't go any closer."[212] On the other hand, the Naval Gunfire Liaison Officer, Major E. W. Gardner, USMC, considered the results satisfactory:

"[TA 7365] Area coverage—rounds landed in area—[TA 7364] good coverage—600 Rds 5" Rockets."[213]

Standing by for the next assignment, *LSM(R) 189* reset Condition One Roger at 1245 and commenced reloading rockets, while also securing her port engine to repair a problematic fuel line. Upon securing from Condition 1-R by 1402, her gunnery officer reported, "All launchers loaded" with 300 rockets.[214] No more than fifteen minutes passed, however, when the Sixth Marine Division ordered the Finners to strike areas around Gushi village once more.[215]

Steadying on course 090° T. by 1454, *LSM(R) 191* stood by as cover while *LSM(R) 189* loosed rockets, beginning 3300 yards until ceasing 2800 yards from the beach. "1502 Commenced firing. Fired at 2 sec intervals—many cook-off's," observed Gunnery Officer Moore.[216] By 1505, all rockets had landed in the target area except a single misfire, which was removed from its launcher and thrown overboard. Major Gardner noted the results of the attack in his naval gunfire report: "[TA 7167]—Area coverage—no results observed—[TA 7267] good coverage—300 Rds 5" Rockets."[217] Altogether this day, the two rocketships had fired some 900 Fin-stabilized ARs.[218]

By 1530, *LSM(R) 191* was advised "mission completed," and released from further fire support of the Sixth Marine Division, so she set sail to retire in Hagushi Anchorage.[219]

Meanwhile, *LSM(R) 189* got underway for the *Tuscaloosa* to embark an important passenger. Mooring alongside the heavy cruiser by 1607, "Major Gardner USMC (Bastille 8) came aboard from *Tuscaloosa*," recorded Ensign F. Donald Moore.[220] After casting off, the rocketship steamed for Dodger Area. While en route, however, the Sixth Marine Division requested Maj. Gardner transported to the vicinity of Machinato Airfield, instead. Changing course, Ensign Moore noted about an hour later, "Standing off northern Naha. Amphibious tank came out and Major Gardner boarded it."[221] Bidding one another good luck, the rocketship resumed her trek to Hagushi Anchorage for the night.

30 to 31 May 1945

From 30 to 31 May, *LSM(R)*s *189* and *191* continued to stand by as fire support for the Sixth Marine Division, but remained within the Hagushi anchorage, "Taking on provisions and supplies," recounted Ensign Moore,[222] and manning battle stations and making smoke during air alerts.

1 June 1945

*LSM(R)*s *189* and *191* were still attached to the Sixth Marine Division for fire support missions off southwestern Okinawa,[223] but the Marines issued no gunfire assignments for the first day of June 1945, so the rocketships remained moored in Hagushi.

The same morning of 1 June, *LSM(R)*s *192* and *193* were relieved from fire support missions with the U.S. Army off southeastern Okinawa, so each rocket ship steamed independently, circumnavigating the southern tip of the island from east to west, and returned to Hagushi Anchorage by midday.

Earlier this morning, *LC(FF) 535* and *LSM(R)s 196, 197, 198* and *199* with Task Group 31.25 had also returned to Hagushi, but only because the Iheya Shima operation was postponed due to foul weather.

Before noon, *LSM(R) 192* moored alongside the flotilla's flagship, and the rocketship's skipper Lt. Neal B. Hadsell reported to Commander Francis for a brief conference and orders. Thereafter, the Finner ship's deck force unloaded rockets from launchers and stowed the projectiles in magazines below deck. *LSM(R) 192* also took on 25 rounds of 5" AA Common from *LSM(R) 189*, and refilled fresh water tanks from a tanker before anchoring with sister ship *LSM(R) 193* for the night. However, the operational status of the Finners remained uncertain, cautioned Lt. Comdr. Fulweiler, with "*LSM(R)s 189, 191, 192* and *193* at Hagushi, Okinawa awaiting orders from CTF 31."[224]

2 June 1945

In the morning twilight of 2 June, *LSM(R) 189* set Condition One Roger to reload rocket launchers, then got underway by 0554 to an area off Naha to support the Marines on Okinawa.[225] *LSM(R) 191* next set sail out of Hagushi while also loading rocket launchers, and joined *LSM(R) 189*, who reported on station to Sixth Marine Division Headquarters by 0725. While awaiting orders, the two Finner rocketships moved about a mile northwest of Naha,[226] but by 1145, they were relieved from Naval Gunfire Support altogether by Rear Admiral Hall (CTG 31.22). Instructed to return to Dodger Area, *LSM(R)s 189* and *191* unloaded rockets from launchers and stowed the projectiles in magazines below decks.

Within twenty-four hours, the four Finner rocketships would take leave of Okinawa, first to the Philippines and then to Pearl Harbor, for shipyard conversions into Ammo Carriers for the invasions of Imperial Japan.[227]

CHAPTER 9

Iheya Shima and Aguni Shima

30 May 1945–11 June 1945

LSM(R) 199 was the last rocketship relieved from radar picket patrols, and upon her arrival in Hagushi Anchorage at midnight of 21–22 May, all four Spinners were reunited for the first time in a month.

Yet Radioman Clyde Blue in *LSM(R) 197* sensed something afoot. "It looks like we are going to go on an invasion somewhere. An awful lot of ships around here."[1] Indeed, earlier this month three of the Spinners were dry-docked in *Oak Hill LSD 7*, with the fourth tied alongside *Achelous ARL 1*, all for overdue repairs. And Blue's hunch paid off, as he wrote in his diary the next day: "Today we loaded 1000 rockets, so now I am sure that we are going to hit some place. I think it will be one of those islands just north of Okinawa here. It will probably be the end of the month or near there. Otherwise we haven't been doing much."[2]

A week after the main "Love Day" invasion of Okinawa on 1 April 1945, the LSM(R)s were ordered to the distant radar picket lines, although some were briefly withdrawn mid–April for the Ie Shima operation and the feigning Demonstration Landing off southern Okinawa.[3] Meanwhile, most amphibious rocket, mortar and gunships usually drew such ancillary assignments as mail distribution, transportation runs, smoke and anti-aircraft screens, coastal interdictions and anti-suicide boat patrols.[4]

But 14 May 1945 was a signal turning point when amphibious warships would assume greater fire support roles at Okinawa. That morning, Vice Admiral Turner sent a secret "warning order" designating Rear Admiral Lawrence F. Reifsnider as the commander of naval and marine forces to assault, capture, and defend the islands of Iheya Shima and Aguni Shima.[5] LSM(R)s and other close-in naval gunfire support would be essential. The two operations would establish additional American air warning radar and fighter director stations ten days hence, and Turner was optimistic: "Objectives will be taken preferably first commencing about 24 May."[6]

Notwithstanding crash planning and preparations, the target date of 24 May came and went. That evening, however, the Japanese came close to disrupting the gathering American naval forces. Although fog generators blanketed Hagushi Anchorage with dense smoke cover, Clyde Blue wrote the next day from *LSM(R) 197*, "Well there were a lot of bogies around and we fired on them last night. Too high to hit so they didn't bother much. 60 or 70 of them were shot down."[7] Signalman Leonard VanOteghem in *LSM(R) 196* also recorded in his diary: "Tied up alongside of repair ship getting our holes patched up from the hits we received

April 1 off southern Okinawa. Bomber flew over and we opened up on it with our 20mm on the port side but it was too short-ranged and we didn't get in any hits. It flew overhead and guns all over the anchorage were blazing away at him. Shrapnel was falling on our deck. As far as we know, the plane escaped."[8] The danger of friendly fire falling upon U.S. forces became so ominous, in fact, that Vice Admiral Hill (CTF 51) directed ships covered by smoke not to open fire regardless of the air alert color control.[9]

Finally, "On May 29th we were briefed for the Iheya-Aguni Shima operations," recalled Ensigns David Mallery and Jack Shedd in *LSM(R) 196*. "The assaults on those two islands were considered as one operation although in completely different regions. We were part of a gunboat support unit, acting as anti-aircraft protection during the days for the LSTs assigned to the operation and as smoke cover during the nights...."[10]

Commander Dennis L. Francis was designated Commander Gunboat Support Unit (CTU 31.25.4) for both the Iheya and Aguni operations in which he would command LCS(L)s and LCI(M)s in addition to the LSM(R)s:

> All commanding officers and unit commanders to Gunboat Support Unit reported aboard the *LC(FF) 535* for a conference and briefing. Each unit was briefed on the operations plan as set forth by [CTG] 31.25 [Rear Admiral Reifsnider] and the attack order as set forth by [CTU] 31.25.4. Briefing covered all phases of role [*sic*] to be played by Gunboats in Iheya Jima attack. Special notice was given to the screening operations, which was to be the primary responsibility of the Gunboat Support Unit except during attack phases. All commanding officers were thoroughly briefed in anti-aircraft screen procedure and also in the smoke screen plan as drawn up and developed by C.T.U. 31.25.4.[11]

But misjudgments, allegations, and indifference would mar these two otherwise successful amphibious operations.

Outlying Islands

The Iheya Shima and Aguni Shima operations were responses to the heavy Japanese air attacks of April-May 1945. Their tolls on U.S. ships and sailors increased pressure on American commanders to expedite Phase III[12] plans of Operation Iceberg to capture outlying islands for additional distant radar and fighter director stations. Phase II had ended by 21 April with the rapid seizures of Ie Shima and northern Okinawa, but American forces would continue wresting control of Okinawa proper under the broader Phase I plan.

Phase III originally foresaw seizing the outer islands of Okino Daito Shima, Kume Shima, Miyako Shima, Kikai Shima, and Tokuno Shima. Activation of this third phase was contingent upon whether Admiral Nimitz deemed it essential for further strategic developments against Imperial Japan.[13] But most of these islands were determined inadequate or non-essential for operational purposes, thus assault plans were either postponed or cancelled.[14]

In early May, however, Admiral Turner requested General Buckner to reassess prospective outlying islands and submit recommendations on their capture. "After breakfast," the general wrote in his diary on 4 May, "I had a staff meeting and gave out decisions regarding the capture of neighboring islands for radar stations to control planes. Adm. Turner is impatient about this...."[15] Gen. Buckner's review subsequently recommended seizing the islands of Tori, Aguni, Iheya and Kume in succession.[16]

The following week, in fact, Marines established shore-based radar sites that were operational by 10 May in the Eastern Islands of Okinawa.[17] On 12 May, a special Army landing force captured Tori Shima where Marines set up another radar station that was operational the next day.[18] Plans were also reactivated for Kume Shima, lone among the original Phase III islands, where Marines would land by 26 June.

At the same time, one other original Phase III island, Kikai (or Kikaiga) Shima, code-named "Friction," was studied. Prospective naval commanders were Rear Admirals Hall (ComPhibGrp12) and Kiland (ComPhibGrp7).[19] Gen. Buckner's planning staff submitted Tentative Operations Order No. 11–45, which included a request for the two LSM(R) units as amphibious gunfire support during the main assault landings. Although an alert order issued on 6 May was downgraded four days later, the Kikai Shima operation remained viable until canceled altogether after mid–July.[20]

Planning: 14 to 28 May 1945

Planning for the Iheya and Aguni operations started from scratch. Although it proceeded at breakneck speed, Admiral Turner's preferred invasion date of 24 May proved impracticable: that day, in fact, was the very soonest the designated landing force, 8th Combat Team, 2nd Marine Division, could be readied to mount out from Saipan for the six days' passage to Okinawa. Navy and Marine commanders and their subordinates, meanwhile, attended innumerable conferences reviewing intelligence, organizing units, and developing operational and contingency plans. Preliminary orders were issued while staffers flew between Saipan and Okinawa via Guam to coordinate with higher echelons. "A minimum of time was available for the planning period," recalled Colonel Clarence R. Wallace, USMC, commander of the landing force, and "lack of time precluded holding a rehearsal for the Iheya-Aguni Operations."[21] The commanding general of the two operations, Brigadier General LeRoy P. Hunt, USMC, added, "Planning was complicated by the necessity for speed and the distance (Okinawa-Saipan) between RCT 8 and the Naval Attack Group Commander. Considering the difficulties encountered, the operation was executed extremely well."[22]

As overall commander of the Iheya Shima and Aguni Shima operations, Rear Admiral Reifsnider issued operation alerts on 22 May at the same time Vice Admiral Hill submitted his Force Operation Order A210–45. Vice Adm. Hill, as Commander Fifth Amphibious Force, had earlier relieved Vice Admiral Turner, Commander Amphibious Forces, U.S. Pacific Fleet and CTF 51 at Okinawa on 17 May. Ten days later on 27 May, Admiral Halsey as Commander Third Fleet relieved Admiral Spruance, Commander Fifth Fleet, which changed all task organizations to Third Fleet numerations, thus Vice Admiral Hill became CTF 31. Adm. Reifsnider' formal Operation Order A408–45 would not be ready until 26 May, however, two days after his secret despatch to Adm. Hill and subsidiary commands advising his tentative recommendation of 1 June as the D–Day assault on Iheya Shima.[23]

Once the Marine landing force arrived at Okinawa on 30 May, they staged with the balance of Reifsnider's Attack Group presently assembled in the Hagushi Anchorage.

Later, war correspondent and historian Robert Sherrod leveled scathing criticism for what he viewed as irresponsible delinquency:

> There was no valid reason why the 77th Infantry Division or the 2nd MarDiv—which had been sent back to Saipan—could not have seized the outlying islands of Iheya and Aguni before 3 June and 9 June,

respectively. It turned out that no enemy troops were there, anyway. A long-range early-warning radar set of AWS-1 was sent to Iheya and began operating 9 July; AWS-1 and AWS-8 sent detachments and equipment to Aguni 29 June and 3 July. If Iheya—20 miles north of Ie [Shima]—had been able to start operating six weeks earlier, when Ie went on the air, it is a safe guess that many picket ships might have been spared loss or heavy damage. It is true that the 2nd MarDiv was originally scheduled to capture Kikai Jima in July, but the failure to provide substitutes for the picket ships (which stood just off Iheya at Roger Peter One) was a costly omission.[24]

Gunboat Support

At 1100 of 30 May, Commander Francis in *LC(FF) 535*, as Commander Gunboat Support (CTU 31.25.4), reported for duty to Rear Admiral Reifsnider (CTG 31.25) in headquarters ship *Biscayne AGC 18*. Under Comdr. Francis were LSM(R) Unit 2 with *LSM(R)s 196, 197, 198, 199*; LCS Division 8 (*LCSs 68, 69, 91, 95, 120, 124*); LCI(M) Division 3 (*LCI(M)s 351, 352, 353, 354, 355, 356*); and LCI(M) Division 7 (*LCI(M)s 807, 808, 809, 810, 1088, 1089*) with force flagship *LC(FF) 1079*.

"Duties assigned were twofold," explained Comdr. Francis, "namely to provide protection through action as inner AA Screen, Smoke Screen, Flycatcher, support patrol, and to provide fire support prior to the landings." While staging at Okinawa, ships assigned to antiaircraft stations ringed the northern, southern and eastern edges of what was designated "Block Anchorage, Hagushi," per Francis' highly-detailed Support Gunboat Plan # 2540–45 of 26 May 1945. In addition, "This period allowed the screening ships to train their complements in efficient, rapid, and accurate application of screening doctrine."[25]

"At sunset," Francis continued, "all gunboat support units upped anchor. Upon order from OTC, 'Take Smoke Stations,' all units moved smartly into the smoke screen formation and were anchored on station. All units upped anchor at 1 hour before sunrise each morning in preparation for order from OTC to 'Take AA Screen Stations.'"[26] Although braced for air attacks, very few Japanese planes actually approached this staging area.

The Jump-Off: 31 May 1945

The morning of 31 May, staff from Adm. Reifsnider's Amphibious Group Four convened a conference on board Commander Francis' flotilla flagship *LC(FF) 535*, including Support Gunboat units commanders, for what was described as a "full and explicit briefing."[27] Returning to their ships before noontime, the gunboat skippers made final preparations for the Iheya Shima invasion.

"Anchored off Okinawa, assembled and loaded 1000 rockets," wrote diarist Leonard VanOteghem, Signalman on *LSM(R) 196*.[28] Clyde Blue in sister ship *LSM(R) 197* added in turn, "We were here at midnight for the operation and [will] loose 500 rockets tomorrow morning at 8:20 a.m." But, the Radioman surmised, "we don't look for much resistance from shore batteries or the likes of that. We may have some more suicide planes around but guess we can take care of them."[29] Ensign Lawrence J. Low, Gunnery Officer for *LSM(R) 197*, only jotted tersely, "Acting as smoke screen and AA support ships for convoy gathering in Hagushi Anchorage in preparation for invasion of Iheya Retto."[30]

By 2330 of 31 May, the four Spinner rocketships restarted main engines, heaved 'round their anchors, and steamed various courses and speeds through the Hagushi Anchorage. With running lights turned on, the LSM(R)s sortied with the Iheya Attack Group at 2345, which would set sail in just minutes before midnight.

The Iheya Attack Group TG 31.25

Once Rear Admiral Reifsnider was designated naval commander of the forthcoming Iheya and Aguni Shima operations, he temporarily transferred his command flag from erstwhile headquarters ship *Panamint AGC 13* to *Biscayne AGC 18*.[31]

The Iheya Attack Group, designated Task Group 31.25, comprised 27 LSTs, 4 LC(FF)s, 1 LSD, 1 PCE(R), 7 PCs, 1 ATF, 1 APD with UDT embarked, 8 DDs, 3 DEs, 4 LSM(R)s, 6 LCS(L)s, 12 LCI(M)s, 1 AGC, and 1 LCT. Assault troops were Regimental Combat Team (RCT) 8 (reinforced), from the 2nd Marine Division, and air support aircraft were provided through CTF 31.[32] Reifsnider's sortie and movement orders directed cruising disposition at eight knots, forming on *LST(H) 951* displaying a red guidon truck light. "If not under air raid condition Blue or Red," advised Reifsnider, all task group ships will "turn on anchor lights ten minutes before getting underway and show running lights when underway and forming up until directed by OTC to darken ship."[33]

Forming an AA cruising screen, Commander Francis in *LC(FF) 535* took station to the right flank of the convoy 1700 yards off the starboard quarter of Adm. Reifsnider's *Biscayne*. Lt. Dennis D. O'Callaghan in *LSM(R) 196* was Unit Commander of the Unit 2 LSM(R)s, designated Task Unit 31.25.44, and maneuvered astern of Comdr. Francis' flotilla flagship with *LSM(R)s 197, 198* and *199*. Here they formed a column at 400-yard intervals while maintaining 500 yards distance starboard of the convoy's right hand transport column. Meanwhile, *LC(FF) 1079* with LCS Division 8 formed to the left flank of the convoy, and LCI(M) Divisions 7 and 3 screened the convoy's left and right rear, respectively.[34]

"Request for Tomorrow"

Almost six hours before the Iheya Task Group weighed anchors from Okinawa, however, Rear Admiral Reifsnider sought postponement of the Iheya Shima landings, codenamed HOW or H-Hour, in a visual signal to Vice Admiral Hill (CTF 31) at 1807 of 31 May: REQUEST HOW HOUR FOR TOMORROW.[35] Threatening weather favored delay, but Commander Task Force 31 hoped sea and weather conditions might clear en route, so he withheld a final decision for nearly eight hours as Task Group 31.25 sailed for Iheya Shima.

In the days leading up to the Iheya jump-off date, a low-pressure system passed 200 miles to the north. Stormy weather saw heavy rains with gusty winds up to 30 knots and fearsome lightning. "Great concern was felt over the possibility of typhoon damage to ships in the Okinawa area," explained Vice Admiral Hill, "and comprehensive plans were issued in the initial Operation Plan in order to minimize this danger...."[36] One other ominous sign late 31 May was the descending cloud ceiling from 8000 feet to zero—just as the convoy was underway and threatened air support—which only lifted by 0500 of 1 June.[37]

Marine General Hunt, on the other hand, later suggested the Japanese had actually stalled the mission. "After proceeding nearly to the objective, D–Day, scheduled for 1 June, 1945, was postponed due to enemy air activity. The task group returned to its original anchorage at Okinawa."[38] Whatever the reason, the critical element of surprise was lost.[39]

"Operations Postponed": 1 June 1945

The Iheya Task Group was in full view of Iheya Shima when, at 0257 of 1 June 1945, Vice Admiral Hill, Commander Task Force 31, granted Rear Admiral Reifsnider's request via secret message: OPERATIONS POSTPONED X RETURN THIS ANCHORAGE IMMEDIATELY X ADVISE YOUR DM'S AND DMS'S ALSO.

Reifsnider quickly relayed the following dispatch to his task group at 0304: OPERATION POSTPONED X WILL REVERSE COURSE BY 45 DEGREE CHANGES TO LEFT X STANDBY TO COMPLY.[40]

After recalling and diverting the minesweeper unit to Kerama Retto, the task group commenced immediate return to Okinawa. *LC(FF) 535* noted at 0310, "Began reversing course by 45° Corpen 'Q' movement to the left," then, from 0400–0800, "Underway to Hagushi Anchorage, steaming in formation guiding on *AGC 18* by radar on various courses and speeds pertaining to the task group. Heavy fog, visibility 50 yards." The OOD standing watch in *LSM(R) 199* echoed, "Visibility very poor due to thick fog." By 0745, the four Spinner rocketships were lying off Point Bolo north of Hagushi, yet only forty-five minutes later the *LSM(R) 199* watch officer reported, "Fog lifted, visibility good. Point Bolo bearing 090 T., distance 6 miles. Proceeding to Hagushi Anchorage."

Ensign Lawrence J. Low, Gunnery Officer in *LSM(R) 197* noted, "Night of 31 May, invasion forces set out for Iheya Retto with LSM(R)s as gun boats—Task Group 51.25 [*sic*]. Off Ie Shima, operation is reported postponed, presumably due to bad weather and convoy returns to Hagushi Anchorage."[41] Aboard *LSM(R) 196*, Signalman Leonard VanOteghem also recalled, "1230 in the morning [1 June] we set out with a convoy of ships for the invasion of Iheya Shima. After being underway a short while, the invasion was postponed. We returned to the anchorage and set up smoke and anti-aircraft stations."[42] In turn, Radioman Clyde Blue from *LSM(R) 197* summarized, "Well, we left at midnight and got halfway up to Iheya and they called the invasion off. So we came back to the anchorage. We may go tomorrow."[43]

Shortly after noontime of 1 June, Vice Admiral Hill signaled Admiral Reifsnider that the D-Day date for Iheya Shima was reset for 2 June. He followed with another message in mid-afternoon setting HOW Hour for 0900, but "to be confirmed prior to landing." Sea and weather conditions remained a major concern, however, so Adm. Hill scrubbed these revisions that evening and reset the operation for 3 June with H-Hour at 1045.[44] Indeed, under overcast skies of 2 June, heavy squalls drenched the ships in Hagushi as 15-knot winds shifted dramatically from south to north.[45] As the task group's gunboats resumed screening stations in and around Block Anchorage, Clyde Blue observed from *LSM(R) 197*, "Well we never went last night and we might go tonight but I doubt it. Raining like mad out...."[46]

The Iheya Shima Operation: 3 June 1945

At 0050 of 3 June 1945, Commander Francis was alerted to prepare for getting underway: Admiral Reifsnider affirmed the HOW Hour assault for Iheya Shima was on.[47]

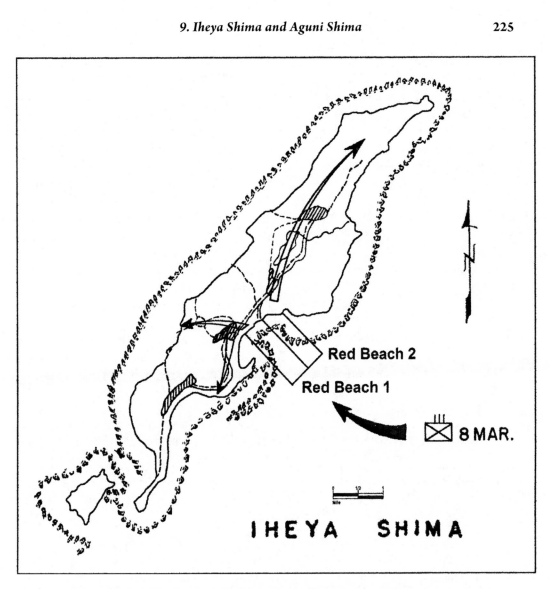

Red Beach 2

Red Beach 1

8 MAR.

IHEYA SHIMA

LSM(R)s 196, 197, 198 **and** *199* **with flotilla flagship** *LC(FF) 535* **supported the Iheya Shima operation on 3 June 1945. Marines landed on Red Beach 1 and Red Beach 2 (adapted from Tenth Army Action Report, Ryukyus, 26 March to 30 June 1945, 3 September 1945, Chapter 7, Section IV, Tenth Army Situation Map, Iheya Shima, April 1945).**

The 77 ships and craft of the Iheya Attack Group 31.25 shoved off under radio silence, guarding limited communications and signals. As before, *LC(FF) 535* led *LSM(R)s 196, 197, 198* and *199* stationed in the convoy's starboard column off guide ship *LST 957* steaming 8 knots in cruising disposition 5A.[48]

Transit to Iheya Shima plotted due North from Hagushi and passed a half-dozen or so miles west of Ie Shima. After a gentle right turn bearing due east, a final left turn brought the convoy on a north-northwest course, targeting the southeastern coast of Iheya Shima. Passage would take about eight hours at eight knots.

Iheya Retto is a group of islands encircled by fringing or barrier coastal reefs and lying about 15 nautical miles northwest of Hedo Misaki, the northernmost tip of Okinawa. Iheya

Shima is the largest island, about 7½ miles long northeast-southwest with a maximum width of 1½ miles and a high, terraced central area rising to 965 feet elevation in the south. A long, curving, but shallow beachhead along the lower southeast half of the island was assigned adjacent amphibious landing sites designated Red Beach 1 and Red Beach 2. Nearby Izena Shima is the only other significant island, pentagonal in shape, about 2½ miles across. American intelligence believed a diminished Japanese garrison force of less than a thousand defenders remained on the main island Iheya Shima, manning observation posts, radio and radar installations. Many enemy military personnel, however, were believed transferred to Okinawa prior to the U.S. invasion on 1 April. Photographic interpretation did not show explicit defenses, although strong points and caves in mountainous areas suggested "such positions would be excellent for suicidal delaying actions."[49]

Biscayne signaled Flash Red–Control Green at 0223 warning of an imminent air raid, and ordered destroyers and destroyer escorts of the Gunfire Support and Screening Unit to equalize the screen around the transports. But, cautioned Reifsnider, "do not fire unless directly under attack and the planes are visible."[50] As the admiral later explained, "During the early morning [of 3 June], several small raids closed the Hagushi area, passing over or near the Iheya-Aguni Attack Group in the Iheya Area; however, no damage was reported."[51] As a further precaution during morning twilight, destroyers and destroyer escorts formed a close anti-aircraft circular screen around the transports, and the transports in turn closed distances and intervals between ships.

The press was also on hand:

> The Iheya Landing Operation was well covered by civilian and service correspondents. Representatives of the United Press, Associated Press, Herald Tribune, and Boston Herald landed on D–Day at about 1300 to cover the spot news. A Marine Public Relations Officer (PRO), four combat correspondents, five combat photographers, and one combat radio correspondent covered the landing and the subsequent action with emphases on personal experiences of hometown interest. A Navy photographic team of one officer and two enlisted men also covered the operation.[52]

Lt. Colonel R. W. Hayward, USMC, commanding the First Battalion, 8th Marines also noted, "Two (2) enlisted personnel were attached to the S-2 section…. They were given complete freedom to photograph and interview. The results indicate only human interest articles and pictures were obtained."[53]

After sunrise, "the LSTs moved into the transport area, Iheya at 0700 [*sic*, 0800], 3 June 1945," said Colonel Wallace of Combat Team Eight, Second Marine Division, and "The closest LSTs were 1,000 yards from the line of departure."[54] Brigadier General Hunt succinctly added: "The task group left for the objective about 0130 3 June and the landing ship flotilla arrived in position at H-75 minutes."[55]

Here Adm. Reifsnider sent yet another warning message to all ships at 0807:

> PREPARE TO REPEL ENEMY AIR ATTACKS ON PLANES POSITIVELY IDENTIFIED AS ENEMY X MANY FRIENDLY PLANES ARE IN THE AREA X PREVENT FIRING TOWARD OWN SHIPS.[56]

Meanwhile, tactical command of the amphibious assault on Iheya Shima passed to Captain James S. Laidlaw (Commander, LST Flotilla Six) in *LC(FF) 1080*, heretofore commanding the Landing Ship Flotilla (TU 31.25.1).

Pre-HOW Hour Naval Gunfire and Air Support

Admiral Reifsnider lifted radio silence around 0815 and signaled CARRY OUT THE SCHEDULE to Captain T.B. Dugan's Screening Unit (TU 31.25.32), whose five destroyers commenced pre–HOW-Hour bombardment of the beaches immediately following completion of exploratory mine sweeping.

"On D–Day," explained Colonel Wallace, "Naval pre-bombardment began at H-150 minutes [0815] and continued until approximately H plus 60 minutes [1145]. In general, naval gunfire covered all probable gun emplacements and enemy activities with special emphasis being placed on the beach area, the high ground flanking the beaches and the high ground inland of the beaches. In addition, concentrated naval gunfire was placed on all probable enemy coast defense positions."[57] The intense shelling created billowing clouds of smoke and dust that hampered visibility of targets by spotters, and destroyers had to check fires on occasions due to low-flying friendly aircraft.

Col. Wallace added, "During D–Day, four VOF [Navy observation fighter planes] were on station working with Battalion Shore Fire Control Parties and firing ships. From time to time front line positions and intelligence data concerning the situation ashore were furnished to Regiment over the Naval Gunfire Command Net."[58]

By 0956 of 3 June 1945, Rear Admiral Reifsnider formally affirmed the HOW Hour landings for 1045, and "Pre-HOW Hour bombardment was commenced by naval support aircraft striking shore and inland positions using napalm, rockets and strafing against possible observation posts and potential firing posts overlooking boat lanes and landing beaches."[59] Flying from Yontan airfield on Okinawa, fourteen Corsair fighter-bombers from Marine Fighting Squadrons VMF 311 and VMF 441 of Marine Aircraft Group 31 (MAG 31) pounded the landing beaches respectively from 0745 to 1030 and from 0945 to 1145. However, "The extent of damage caused was unobserved due to smoke," reported VMF 441.[60]

"On D–Day," continued Col. Wallace,

air support operations began at H-50 minutes [0955] with VF [fighter planes] dropping napalm bombs on the high ground on both flanks of the landing beaches. Other napalm bombing was concentrated on the three high peaks immediately to the west of the landing beaches. This bombing ceased at H-20 minutes [1025].
... At H-5 minutes [1040] the beaches and ground to the immediate rear of the beaches were strafed by machine gun and rockets, this fire lifting just before H-Hour.... Although eight VFs were on station for airstrikes during the daylight hours, no strikes were called during the operation.... An air observer was on station during D–Day and the early part of D plus one. Inclement weather necessitated the securing of aircraft at about 1200 of D plus two. The air observer was able to give an accurate account of the advance of our troops during the two days of the operation.[61]

"Land the Landing Force"

The Central Control officer reported at 0848 that surf conditions for the landings were good this morning, with slight breaking surf along the southern reefs, and occasional breaking surf of one to two feet along the northern beaches.[62] So far, weather was low overcast with intermittent light rains and a northeast wind at 12 knots.[63]

Rear Admiral Reifsnider thus signaled at 0910, LAND THE LANDING FORCE, which

Colonel Wallace tactically summarized: "The general scheme of maneuver was to quickly cut the island in two, landing with two battalions abreast. Thus it was planned to divide the enemy and destroy him in detail....["]64 By H-75 Hour or 0930, the LSTs disgorged LVTs loaded with Marines that streamed toward the line of departure 4,000 yards from the beachhead. After drawing parallel with the shoreline, the amphibious tanks formed in waves of two landing teams abreast for simultaneous assaults on Beaches Red 1 and Red 2.[65]

The Support Gunboats

The Support Gunboats of Task Unit 31.25.4 arrived with the main body of the Iheya Task Group at 0800 and assumed protective anti-aircraft screening while transports and landing craft positioned for the amphibious landings. At 0900, the LSM(R)s, LCS(L)s and LCI(M)s were released from AA screens and maneuvered to their respective units' fire support stations. By 1007, Commander Francis reported to Admiral Reifsnider the gunboats were in position and ready.[66] As the waves of landing forces formed and approached the Iheya beachhead, Francis' flagship LC(FF) 535 stood 5,000 yards off the island's southeastern tip, monitoring his Support Gunboats throughout the assault. Visibility was moderate under overcast skies with a light breeze[67] and a calm sea that offered greater gunfire accuracy.[68]

LCS Division 8 led the first boat wave toward the beaches and fired 40mm at shoreline targets. Once inshore of the fire support destroyers, the LCSs split into two sections to the right and left of the boat lanes and launched full salvos of rockets at flanking positions. LCI(M) Division 3 and LCI(M) Division 7 stood to the right and left flanks of the boat lanes, respectively, and fired 40mm at shore targets, then "walked" mortar fires inland.

"LSM(R) Unit 2," reported Comdr. Francis,

composed of 4 LSM(R)s, when released from the Sortie screen, proceeded to individual stations, located east of north-east from the landing beaches, and prepared to deliver rocket fire.

The LSM(R)s 197 and 199 each delivered approximately 500 5.0" spin stabilized rockets on a high hillside, running roughly east and west, and located on the right flank of the landing beaches and boat lane. The LSM(R) 198 delivered approximately 1000 5.0" spin stabilized rockets into high defensive positions located about 1000 yards inland and to the north west of the landing beaches. The LSM(R) 196 delivered approximately 1000 5.0" spin stabilized rockets into low and high positions of suspected enemy defense located west and north west of the landing beaches. Upon completion of the rocket fire the LSM(R)s lay to, awaiting screen assignments.[69]

However, "One rocket motor exploded on deck," noted the skipper of LSM(R) 198,

damaging its rocket launcher beyond repair, and causing several small fires on the rocket and superstructure deck [sic], which were quickly extinguished by damage control. The rocket body, containing the high explosive, is believed to have been hurled into the water several hundreds of yards ahead of the ship during the explosion. No damage was caused to the ship. Fortunately this explosion occurred in a launcher forward of the Conning Tower, thus reducing the possibility of the body striking any parties of the ship during its flight.[70]

Commander Francis advised Admiral Reifsnider once all gunfire support missions were completed, and reaffirmed the lines of fire had cleared as scheduled. "A complete report was made are [sic] target destruction and ammunition expended, from [CTU] 31.25.4 to [CTG] 31.25," added Comdr. Francis, and ordered all subordinate gunboat units to submit full reports directly to Adm. Reifsnider.[71]

Assessing the effectiveness of the Support Gunboats at Iheya Shima, Commander Francis commented, "the assigned targets were neutralized by all units. A few early mortar shorts were observed falling in the water due to the advanced range of LCI(M) Division Seven.... Early 40 MM fire was more inquisitive that [*sic*] actually directed at visible enemy forces. Small revetments and possible positions of enemy forces were penetrated by this fire. The mortar fire against the beach areas was effective and well dispersed inland." As for LSM(R) Unit 2, "The barrage rocket fire, except for the shorts previously mentioned, fell in the assigned target areas, producing a few small fires, large amounts of shrapnel, and large craters,"[72] yet causing "the destruction of no targets other than scheduled" from the "2700 rockets expended with no casualties and damage unobserved."[73]

"Undetermined Friendly Fire"

During the first critical minutes after Marines had landed, Admiral Reifsnider was alerted, "1052—LVT on shore hit by undetermined friendly fire—1 KIA, 1 WIA."[74] Reports would be forthcoming of many more Marines killed and wounded caused by errant fire suspected from the Support Gunboats.

Two days after the Iheya Shima landings, Rear Admiral Reifsnider initiated an inquiry into the non-battle casualties from the "friendly fire" that killed and wounded Marines.[75] On 5 June, Reifsnider dispatched a visual message addressed to ComDesDiv46 (Commander H. H. McIlhenny, Commander Gunfire Support Unit, CTU 31.25.31) and to destroyers *Converse*, *Beale*, *Paul Hamilton*, and *Daly* (curiously, *Twiggs* was overlooked or omitted): REPORT DETAILS TIME AND TYPE OF ANY FIRE YOU MAY HAVE OBSERVED FALLING ON OR NEAR OWN TROOPS ON 3 JUNE.[76]

Admiral Reifsnider documented the following responses:

ComDesDiv46: "About 1040/I [I or Item, the local time zone identifier] 3 June observed what appeared to be salvo of rockets land just ahead and near right hand sector of first wave."
Converse: "With first wave about 200 yards from beach (about 1043/I) observed salvo of about 10 rockets fall in water just in front of first wave."
Beale: "At 1042/I observed 5 inch projectiles and rockets landing in water close vicinity troops approaching beach. At 1048/I observed 5 inch projectiles landing on beach close proximity troops landing."
Paul Hamilton: "Observed 2 air bursts height about 75 feet and 50 yards in front of LCI(G)s as they proceeded first wave. When first waves within shoal area of beaches observed splashes thought to be rockets hitting in vicinity of amphtracks. Rockets not from aircraft. No hits observed."[77]

Although Reifsnider did not record a response (if any) from *Daly*, the destroyer reported elsewhere, "First wave hit the beach at 1045 without opposition. However, several casualties were suffered by assault troops from a stray rocket and a 'short.' *Daly* was not firing in the area at time of accident."[78]

Adm. Reifsnider also noted receipt of an unsolicited message from Captain Beverly M. Coleman of the Control, Beach and Hydrographic Parties (CTU 31.25.2):

Attention Gunnery Officer. LVT(A) commander reports that on last run rockets to the number of 2 salvos fell in water considerably short of beach and just ahead of and alongside LVT(A)s blowing one clear out of water though no casualties sustained. Request rocket ships be informed and first wave carefully watched on next run to prevent recurrence.[79]

Two months later, however, Rear Admiral Reifsnider's findings remained inconclusive:

During the attack on Iheya Shima, shortly after HOW hour, two members of the Landing Force were killed and several wounded by explosive missiles striking an LVT on the beach at TA 0571C and a house about 200 yards inland at TA 0572S. The Attack Group Commander investigated the circumstances in connection with these incidents but was unable to determine the sources of the missiles other than that they probably were fired by our own forces.[80]

For now, the initial reports indicting Commander Francis' Support Gunboats for the friendly fire incidents at Iheya Shima went unchallenged.[81]

Friendly Fire: Red Beach One[82]

The Marine 2nd Amphibian Tractor Battalion landed Marine BLT 3/8 on Red Beach One at 1042, three minutes before H-Hour.[83] Lieutenant Colonel Paul E. Wallace, USMC, commanded the Third Battalion, Combat Team Eight at Red Beach One (not to be confused with Colonel Clarence R. Wallace, USMC, Commander, Combat Team Eight). "Air Support was used only in the general preparation during and immediately after H-Hour. No missions were called for by this BLT after landing. This Battalion suffered six (6) wounded as a result of a plane or planes loosing a barrage of rockets that hit the beach after the first wave had moved inland and as the second wave disembarked from the LVTs. One LVT was hit direct and other rockets burst on the beach."[84]

Lt. Col. Wallace continued: "The Battalion Aid Section landed in the fourth wave of the assault without opposition. The initial Battalion Aid Station was set up in a revetment just beyond the beach. Four casualties from an LVT were treated on the beach and evacuated by LVT to an LST-H. The remainder of casualties were evacuated through the regimental Aid Station."[85] BLT 3/8 finally listed thirteen wounded but none killed or missing in action.[86]

Friendly Fire: Red Beach Two[87]

The Army 726th Amphibian Tractor Battalion landed Marine BLT 2/8 on Red Beach Two some two minutes behind schedule at 1047.[88]

Lieutenant Colonel Harry A. Waldorf, commanding the Marine Second Battalion, Combat Team Eight at Red Beach Two observed, "The Army wave guides did excellent work in landing the assault waves of the LT [Landing Team]. The 1st wave landed on the beach at the appointed time, as did each succeeding wave. The proficiency of the Navy guide boat officers was excellent."[89]

Lt. Col. H. C. Switzer, USA, commanding the Amphibian Tractor Group added, "Firing from the first waves of troop carrying LVT's was very limited," and "Troops were debarked immediately on the beach near a road running parallel to the beach."[90]

As BLT 2/8 moved ashore, Company "D," 3rd Provisional Armored Amphibian Battalion, provided supporting fire but was ordered not to move inland beyond 200 yards.[91] However, "The Amphibian Tractors continued firing their 50 cal weapons after the 1st wave advanced inland, thereby endangering the 1st wave of assault troops," said Lt. Col. Waldorf. "Evidently there was a severe lack of fire discipline and control on the part of the Amphibian Tractor Crews." All told, Marine casualties were one killed and four wounded, but none reported caused by errant naval or air support fire at Red Beach Two.[92]

Accounting Marine Casualties

Inexplicably, Brigadier General LeRoy Hunt, USMC, Commanding General of the Iheya and Aguni Landing Forces, offered no accounting in his report about the friendly fire that killed and wounded his Marines, but he merely summarized the casualties: KIA—2, WIA—16, MIA—0, NBC—6.[93] To the contrary, General Hunt chose to emphasize operational successes, instead. "The landing was made on schedule as planned. There was no opposition encountered. The ship-to-shore movement was executed very smoothly and unloading progressed rapidly," and "no naval gunfire or air support were used other than was planned supporting fire for the landing." In sum, the general viewed the Iheya-Aguni operations "of inestimable value as training for the elements of the Division engaged," yet "of minor importance."[94]

On the other hand, Colonel Clarence Wallace, USMC, Commander Combat Team Eight, assessed a higher tally of casualties in his report while also noting those claimed from friendly fire:

Our Losses—

a. Killed in action—2 *
b. Wounded in action—16 *
Injured in action—2
c. Missing in action—0
d. Non-battle losses—14
*Short rounds from naval gunfire and air rockets.[95]

Like General Hunt, Colonel Wallace made no specific comments about the non-battle Marine casualties at Iheya Shima, but one of his recommendations hinted otherwise: "S-3—When LVT(A)(4)s are used in the first wave of the assault, naval gunfire and air support on the landing beaches need not be as close as that used in this operation. Since the LVT(A)(4)s carry 75mm guns a heavy fire may be delivered by them on the beach up until the time of landing, and thus avoid the dangers inherent in too close air and naval support."[96]

The proximate causes of the friendly fires killing and wounding U.S. Marines at Iheya Shima on 3 June 1945 were misguided rockets, bombs, and strafing from one or more U.S. Marine fighter-bombers, and reckless ground fire from amongst the U.S. Marine landing forces themselves. Although errant rounds from one or more U.S. destroyers may have contributed to casualties, official records remain ambiguous. Beyond dispute, Commander Francis' Support Gunboats caused none of the U.S. Marine casualties at Iheya Shima on 3 June 1945.

Action and Reaction

In the wake of Vice Admiral Reifsnider's investigation of friendly fires at Iheya Shima, the admiral's staff convened a conference including Commander Francis on 6 June. Although Reifsnider mentions nothing of this meeting, and Francis only notes it in passing, the conference almost certainly reviewed the Support Gunboats' gunfire roles at Iheya Shima to refine tactical rules of engagement for the upcoming Aguni Shima operation. The outcome of the meeting was a memorandum[97] issued by Commander Francis on 7 June, followed by a briefing he convened later that day with his Support Gunboat unit commanders emphasizing operational safety precautions.

Anti-Aircraft Screens, Smoke Screens and Flycatcher Patrols

As the Marines seized Iheya Shima on 3 June, the Support Gunboats returned seaward awaiting further assignments. Before noontime, the LSM(R)s took anti-aircraft stations, and soon the LCS(L)s and LCI(M)s also reported on AA screening stations around the transport anchorage or were dispatched as fighter direction supports per Commander Francis' Op Plan 2540–45.[98] Meanwhile, Francis' flagship *LC(FF)* 535 either patrolled or stood off the southeastern coast of Iheya Shima overseeing the defensive screens of Task Group 31.25.

Suddenly, "At 1230 heavy raids developed," noted Admiral Reifsnider. "These raids, 12 in all, consisting of groups of four or more planes, closed from the Northern Sector," and many were downed by CAP fighters and radar picket ships. But he also sent a cautionary warning to his ships' gunners: FLASH RED CONTROL GREEN X FIRE ONLY AT PLANES IDENTIFIED AS ENEMY X THERE ARE MANY FRIENDLIES IN THE AREA.[99]

"About 1530," said Reifsnider, "the situation cleared and the remainder of the day was spent in routine patrols."[100]

"Well," wrote diarist Clyde Blue aboard *LSM(R)* 197,

> we left at 1 a.m. and got here at Iheya Shima around 8 a.m. We fired our rockets around 10 o'clock and then the doggies went in. We fired 500 rockets, also so did the *196–198–199* and some other LCI rocket ships. Haven't seen much fighting or heard much shooting or think so [but] I don't think that they are meeting much resistance. There were Jap planes all around but none came around us. Three were shot down with American markings on them. I have been on watch all day since last night at 11:30 p.m., 18 hours total. Getting pretty sleepy now...[101]

Also on *LSM(R)* 197, Ensign Lawrence J. Low recorded in his notebook, "Took positions in anchorage as AA Screen ships (LSM(R)s). Air raid in late afternoon. Vals and Kates shot down by CAP (Corsairs) were reported to have US insignia painted on wings and fuselage."[102]

Here, however, Bruce McDaniel, a Quartermaster-striker aboard *LSM(R)* 196, recalled watching a peculiar incident unfold ashore:

> A young boy began running along a long spur of sand to our left, [and] a soldier (Japanese) was chasing him but soon gave up as the boy ran out to the end of the sand and stood there. It may have been that the boy was driven by fear even though the soldier was trying to get him together with the villagers. I distinctly remember that the Japanese soldiers had herded the whole inhabitants of that small island down to the sea wall where they were waving white flags and troops landed unopposed. We were close into shore and able to see this clearly and I have no recollection of standing off the limit of our trajectory range to fire rockets.[103]

LSM(R) 198, meanwhile, came under sudden gunfire. "During the afternoon of this day," reported Lt. George B. Timmerman, Jr., "while anchored on AA station between the transport area and the beach, a number of shots were fired from a hillside, left of the landing beach, which were heard as they passed by at the Conn and on the superstructure deck below. One bullet struck the splinter shield around the forward 40MM gun platform, a few feet from one of the 40MM ready gun crew members, leaving a deep mark on the shield where it struck. This fire is believed to have come from our own troops strafing the hillside in question."[104]

Japanese air raids proved infrequent though not entirely absent during the Iheya operation. "The task group was not attacked by enemy planes," later commented Commander Francis, although "There were a number of flash reds and blues each day but no planes approached the ships screened by the gunboats."[105]

That evening, CTG 31.25 signaled a Flash Red–Control Green air raid warning and repeated to all ships gunners, "Do not fire on friendly planes in the vicinity."[106] Lt. Timmerman in *LSM(R) 198* noted the heightened alert lasted from 1805 to 1840: "General Quarters—enemy aircraft reported in vicinity. The sky was overcast with low clouds, light breeze, visibility moderate. AA bursts were observed toward the west at about five miles distance. No enemy planes were seen and no action was taken."[107]

Commander Francis assigned *LSM(R)s 196, 197* and *198* to smoke screen stations around the transport anchorage against possible enemy air attacks overnight. *LSM(R) 199*, on the other hand, was designated a "Flycatcher" to patrol the Northern flank of the transport area through the night with two LCSs, while two other LCSs also stood "Skunk" patrols along the Southern flank. Their tasks, as described by Lieutenant Commander Joseph A. Dodson, Jr., (CTU 31.25.41), were to "Intercept and destroy any enemy small boats or swimmers attempting infiltration of transport area, or landing craft attempting to land reinforcements."[108]

Typhoon Plan "William": 4 to 5 June 1945

At 0250 of 4 June, *Biscayne* re-enciphered a CINCPAC storm warning of a tropical weather disturbance several hundred miles southwest of Okinawa. Before sunrise, Vice Admiral Hill (CTF 31) advised Admiral Reifsnider to expect a typhoon-intensity storm, then warned all units at 0846: PREPARE TO EXECUTE PLAN WILLIAM.[109] Concern over the approaching typhoon all but overshadowed the Marines' concurrent declaration of the cessation of hostilities on Iheya Shima.[110]

By 1100, Reifsnider decided to withdraw his task group from Iheya Shima and shelter his ships among Okinawa's two northwestern peninsular harbors of Obaru Wan and Nago Wan.[111]

Under Rear Admiral Reifsnider in *Biscayne*, the Landing Ship Flotilla (TU 31.25.1) and Gunfire Support and Screening Unit (TU 31.25.3) took refuge in Obaru Wan. Units anchored in the crux of northern Motobu Peninsula by 1742 and set a circular AA screen during passage of the typhoon.[112]

Transit to Nago Wan took about five hours for the Support Gunboats (TU 31.25.4) and the Control, Beach and Hydrographic Parties (TU 31.25.2), as LSM(R)s, LCI(M)s, and LCS(L)s formed column astern *LC(FF) 535*. "Unit commanders of TU 31.25.4 told to take charge of their units and anchor in company," said Commander Francis, "and dispose to provide smoke screen if required." Since the storm precluded posting picket patrols, at nightfall Francis directed all gunboats to be prepared to get underway on short notice in case of air attacks.[113] "Well," wrote Clyde Blue from aboard *LSM(R) 197*, "we had reports that a typhoon was coming our way so it looks like we may have a rough time of it. We are going to hug the coast of Okinawa tonight."[114]

Overnight, an updated weather report forecast that the typhoon would pass about a hundred miles east of Okinawa and estimated the residual tropical disturbance would diminish by 0300. Soon, Admiral Reifsnider ordered the separate elements in Obaru Wan and Nago Wan to get underway for return to Iheya Shima: STORM DANGER OVER X REVERT TO NORMAL.[115] Upon returning to the Iheya anchorage, Commander Francis delegated gunboat unit commanders to resume AA screens around the LST transport area.

But the emergency withdrawal from Iheya Shima proved precipitous and unnecessary, according to Rear Admiral J. L. Hall, Jr., (CTF 35/CTG 31.22), who lamented the inadequate weather collection and reporting system at Okinawa. "During the critical day of June 4, when there was considerable doubt as to the exact location and movement of the storm center, there was a noticeable scarcity of reliable reports from the general area of the storm."[116]

Standing Down at Iheya Shima: 5 to 7 June 1945

On 5 June, Task Group 31.25 systematically stood down as individual naval elements retired to the Hagushi anchorage at Okinawa to prepare for the forthcoming operation at Aguni Shima. Late that morning, Vice Admiral Hill (CTF 31) commended the success at Iheya Shima in a message via Rear Admiral Reifsnider, Brigadier General Hunt and Colonel Wallace at 1127: "WELL DONE X CONGRATULATIONS FOR EFFICIENCY WITH WHICH YOUR OPERATION WAS ACCOMPLISHED."[117] By evening, Adm. Reifsnider set the tentative date and time for the next assault: "8 June designated as Able-Day for attack on Aguni [Shima]. H-Hour 0600 to be confirmed before landing."[118]

By 1300 Reifsnider assigned the four Spinner LSM(R)s to escort a convoy departing Iheya Shima for Hagushi by 1600, which also released LSM(R) 199 from northern island "Flycatcher" duty.[119] Radioman Clyde Blue caught up his diary in LSM(R) 197: "Well we escorted a convoy of LSTs back to the Anchorage. We got here too late to get our mail so we will probably get that tomorrow. We were supposed to go back up to Iheya Shima but we just got a message telling us not to so I don't know what we will do now." The next day, he added, "There is a lot of scuttlebutt about going back to Leyte."[120]

Commander Francis in LC(FF) 535 remained behind at Iheya Shima with dwindling numbers of Support Gunboats. "The number of gunboats available for the A.A. screen varied because as many as 2 to 6 ships were provided in screening LSTs coming to and leaving the Iheya Shima area," explained Francis, continuing:

> During the nights of the 3rd, 5th, and 6th of June, a protective smoke was provided at Iheya Shima. ... Some modification of the formation as used at Block Anchorage were necessary due to absence of from 2 to 6 of the smokers who were away on temporary screening duty. However, at all times there were sufficient ships to provide adequate and effective smoke. No smoke was provided on the night of June 4 as all gunboat support units were detached from Iheya Shima to seek shelter in the Nago Wan Anchorage from the impending typhoon.[121]

Finally, on 7 June, Comdr. Francis departed Iheya Shima in his flotilla flagship with a large convoy to Okinawa. "From 7 June to 8 June an A.A. screen was provided for the LSTs at Block Anchorage, Hagushi," said Francis. "As the number of ships to be protected had diminished doing the job with less gunboats was no problem."[122] By midnight, Rear Admiral Reifsnider formally pronounced: "2400—Naval Phase of Iheya Shima Operation declared terminated as of this time with the withdrawal of all Naval Units of TG 31.25."[123]

Memoranda and Addenda

Mid-afternoon of 7 June, Signalman Leonard VanOteghem on *LSM(R) 196* observed, "Anchored at Okinawa, assembled and loaded 1000 rockets for the invasion of Aguni Shima,"[124] and Radioman Clyde Blue in *LSM(R) 197* added, "Well we loaded 500 more rockets today so I guess we will go up to Aguni Shima in the next few days. Don't know when as yet," but "we got some mail yesterday…."[125] The OOD in *LSM(R) 199* also reported at 1548, "All hands manned their R-2 [*sic*] stations to assemble rockets and load all the launchers,"[126] while *LSM(R) 198* finished loading 1,020 rockets in her launchers by 1645.

Meanwhile, the Support Gunboats' skippers met with Commander Francis in his flagship *LC(FF) 535*, where "All ships' captains and unit commanders under this command attended a briefing conference on Aguni Jima objective."[127] Here Comdr. Francis reviewed his "Memorandum to Support Gunboat Plan # 2540–45" and outlined his new "Addendum to Support Gunboat Plan #2540–45 for Phase II [*sic*], Aguni Shima," underscoring gunfire assignments and safety precautions.[128]

The Aguni Attack Group TG 31.25

Task Group 31.25 for the Aguni Shima Operation had far fewer LST transports than at Iheya Shima, but the composition otherwise remained similar: 7 LSTS, 4 LC(FF)s, 1 LSD, 1 PCE(R), 5 patrol craft, 1 ATF, 1 APD with UDT embarked, 7 Destroyers, 3 Destroyer Escorts, 16 Support Gunboats, and 1 AGC. Assault troops comprised BLT 1/8 from RCT 8, reinforced, from the 2nd Marine Division, with air support aircraft provided as before by CTF 31.[129]

Commander Francis' Support Gunboats (Task Unit 31.25.4) also deployed fewer ships, now comprising LSM(R) Unit 2 with *LSM(R)s 196, 197, 198, 199*, LCS Division 8 (*LCSs 68, 69, 91, 95, 120, 124*), and LCI(M) Division 3 (*LCI(M)s 351, 352, 353, 354, 355, 356*).[130]

"Invasion Postponed": 7 to 8 June 1945

While *LC(FF) 535* generally patrolled among the ships assembled for Task Group 31.25,[131] "On the nights of 7 and 8 June 1945 smoke screen was provided at Block Anchorage, Hagushi with some modifications of the original plan," said Commander Francis.[132]

Air alerts sounded due to hecklers that evening in Hagushi, which Lt. Timmerman of *LSM(R) 198* noted from 1915 to 1943: "General Quarters—enemy aircraft reported in vicinity. Cloudy, light breeze, visibility good. Several enemy planes reported splashed from 20 to 50 miles out. No enemy planes observed."[133]

That evening, however, the "Able Day" assault on Aguni Shima was delayed due to heavy swells over the island's reefs.[134] As Gunnery Officer Ensign Lawrence J. Low on *LSM(R) 197* noted, "Preparing for assault on Aguni Jima scheduled for 8 June. Invasion postponed to 9 June. Acting as smoke screen and AA support ship for invasion convoy in Hagushi Anchorage."[135]

Anti-Aircraft and Smoke Screening Stations: 8 June 1945

With improving weather, Japanese aircraft grew active over Okinawa and the Hagushi anchorage the night of 7 to 8 June, and ships repeatedly generated clouds of protective smoke.

Before dawn of 8 June, General Quarters sounded at 0050, 0200, and 0400 as fourteen raids came from the north and two others from the southwest. *LSM(R) 198* noted between 0053 and 0123, "General Quarters—enemy aircraft reported in vicinity. None observed. Visibility good, cloudy, light breeze."[136] The gunboats stood by their smoke sectors until morning's twilight, then dispatched to anti-aircraft stations around Block Anchorage about 0730.

Vice Admiral Hill commented, "Good weather brought [an] estimated sixty to seventy enemy aircraft into the area for a total of thirty-seven raids,"[137] which continued well after daybreak until noon.[138] *LSM(R) 198* reported on one such raid between 0814 and 0836: "General Quarters—enemy aircraft reported closing from north and west. Weather conditions same as above. Planes closed to about 15 miles, but none observed. Several planes reported splashed from 15 to 20 miles out," then further noted from 0850 to 0856: "General Quarters—enemy planes reported closing from north. Weather same. Enemy planes reported splashed. None seen visually."[139] The Japanese air raids finally ceased by midday and would not resume until evening dusk.

"Well we leave tonight somewhere after midnight for Aguni Shima," commented Clyde Blue, Radioman aboard *LSM(R) 197*. "Don't know much about it as yet. I guess we are to fire a full deckload of rockets. Aguni is north of Kerama Retto and west of Okinawa. I guess they have Iheya Shima all secured already. The sun shone all day. Got out in the sun for the first time in quite awhile."[140]

That evening at 1945, Comdr. Francis later reported, "...on the 8th June 1945, smoke screen was positioned so as to facilitate impending sortie movement. LSM(R)s were positioned across north side of transport anchorage. LCI(M) Div. 3 was stationed on the east side. The LCS Div. 8 took station on the south side of anchorage. The bearing of the wind was 010° T at 1900, and shifting to 090° T at 2400 thus allowing adequate coverage with the smoke screen in this position."[141]

Soon after assuming nighttime stations, Japanese aircraft approached Okinawa in the evening twilight. "A series of raids commenced which lasted until 0430 on 9 June," said Vice Admiral Hill. "From 1935 to 0000 ten raids all from the north were over the area. During the day CAP splashed twelve Nips and ships Anti-aircraft fire accounted for three more,"[142] and additional nighttime raids struck at 1959, 2220 and 2350.[143]

LSM(R) 198 noted from 2020 to 2034, "General Quarters—enemy planes reported closing from north at about 20 miles. Weather same as above. No enemy aircraft observed," then between 2110 and 2128: "General Quarters—AA fire observed to the west of us that appeared to be 40mm and 5"38 [*sic*] gun fire, distance about six to ten miles."[144] Meanwhile, *LSM(R) 197*'s OOD dutifully recorded the recurring demands for protective smoke cover in the ship's log: "2127 Ceased making smoke. 2144 Make smoke. 2205 Ceased making smoke. 2217 Make smoke. 2230 Ceased making smoke. 2330 Make smoke."[145]

LC(FF) 535 witnessed an unusual spectacle when Japanese aircraft dropped a series of five parachute flares about 5000 yards off her starboard quarter. *LSM(R) 198* also observed these or similar incidents between 2213 and 2230: "General Quarters—enemy planes reported closing at 18 miles. Flares were dropped, apparently from enemy planes, about two to five miles north of us. Plane [*sic*] could not be picked up visually."[146]

The Aguni Shima Operation: 9 June 1945

The Support Gunboats secured making smoke around Block Anchorage in northern Hagushi at 2230 of 8 June, and upped anchors by midnight while awaiting the Aguni Attack Group TG 31.25 to form up.[147] Even so, weather and sea conditions still seemed doubtful for the jump-off when Rear Admiral Reifsnider noted, "Task Group 31.25 at anchor off Hagushi beaches, waiting moderation of swell."[148]

In the meantime, a lull in Japanese air activity became apparent after midnight, so at 0035 Admiral Reifsnider ordered: DO NOT MAKE SMOKE AGAIN UNLESS ORDERED BY CTG 31.25 X THIS MESSAGE APPLIES ONLY TO TG 31.25.[149]

But only minutes later, Reifsnider signaled an all clear by 0043, in part to reduce night-time navigating hazards for his task group, and in other part to steady the nerves of tense sailors and marines.

Finally, "At 0100, 9 June 1945," reported Commander Francis, "TU 31.25.4 sortied with TG 31.25 forming A.A. Screen about transport formation and got under way for Aguni Shima. LC(FF) 535 in the lead with LSM(R) unit #2 astern formed A.A. screen 500 yards on the right flank of transport formation. LCS Div 8 formed left flank screen and LCI(M) Div 3 formed a screen to the rear of the transports. Arrived Aguni Shima 0500, 9 June 1945 without having contacted any enemy units."[150] Passage was plotted directly west-northwest from northern Hagushi anchorage, a four-hour transit.[151]

Aguni Shima lies approximately 30 nautical miles west of Okinawa. Appearing gently

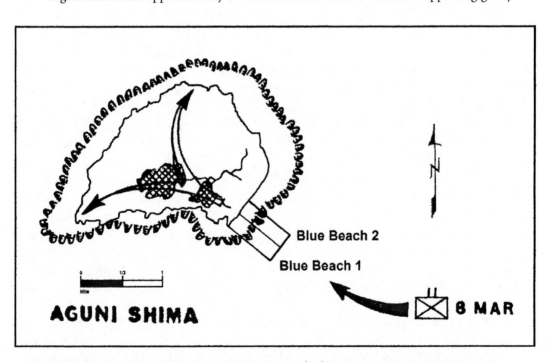

LSM(R)s *196, 197, 198* and *199* with flotilla flagship *LC(FF) 535* supported the Aguni Shima operation on 9 June 1945. Marines landed on Blue Beach 2 (adapted from Tenth Army Action Report, Ryukyus, 26 March to 30 June 1945, 3 September 1945, Chapter 7, Section IV, Tenth Army Situation Map, Aguni Shima, April 1945).

triangular, the island is about 2½ miles long northeast-southwest, 1¾ miles at its widest, and rises to 308 feet. Surrounded by uplifted coral formations and fringing reef, a narrow southeastern beachhead was suitable for amphibious landings and designated Blue Beach 1 and Blue Beach 2. Pre-assault estimates placed enemy strength at 150 troops deployed as a Home Guard unit.[152]

En route, ten Japanese raids approached Okinawa from the north between 0050 and 0430.[153] Commander C. E. Perkins, the Navy's Commander Air Support Control Unit (CASCU) for Amphibious Group Four in *Biscayne*, also noted: "At 0300 and again at 0500, single enemy planes flew over TG 51.25 [*sic*] (while enroute to Aguni) at very high altitudes, heading for Zampa Misaki. Neither of these planes made any attempt to attack this group."[154]

Although the convoy made no direct contact with the enemy en route to Aguni Shima, Signalman Leonard VanOteghem recalled a "white-knuckler" in *LSM(R) 196*:

> Left at 0130 on the morning with task force of about 30 ships for the invasion of Aguni Shima. This was about a 40-mile trip. After being underway for a short while, we commenced getting reports of air raids over Okinawa again. In the distance we could see the AA fire from our gun batteries and ships back there. Everything was blacked out. Not a light could be seen in our convoy any place and all ships had strict orders not to fire on anything unless you were actually being attacked by it as this would give up the task force position, and possibly stop the capture of Aguni Shima for a period. A few moments after the sighting of the AA fire back at the anchorage, we could hear a roar of engines. Closer and closer it came, and we knew it wasn't our aircraft as it had no running lights on. It kept closing on us and we still couldn't see it. In a matter of seconds it zoomed close by our port side and over the bow. It was a twin engine bomber and we never fired a shot because of the orders. From the way it was closing on us we felt sure it was going to hit us, but cleared by a matter of a few feet we judged. This was our closest call by a plane and it left all of us on the conn shaking in our shoes. A few hours later we came in sight of Aguni. Preparations were made for the invasion....[155]

Unlike the Iheya Shima operation, Colonel Clarence R. Wallace noted that no civilian newsmen were present to chronicle this invasion. "At Aguni only Marine PRO [Public Relations Officer] personnel covered the operation. There were one PRO, one radio combat correspondent, two combat correspondents, and two photographers."[156] Lt. Col. Richard W. Hayward, commanding the First Battalion, Eighth Marines added, "The Division Public Relations Officer and his group accompanied the LT [Landing Team]. They were equipped with motion and still photographic equipment, radio recording equipment, and reporters. The unit was prepared to cover any outcome of this landing."[157]

"Land the Landing Force"

Rear Admiral Reifsnider signaled LAND THE LANDING FORCE in the morning darkness of 9 June.[158] As Col. Wallace explained, "CT-8 as part of the Iheya-Aguni Landing Force was ordered to capture, occupy, defend, and develop Aguni in order to establish radar stations thereon, employing LT ⅛ for this purpose."[159] Construction of an airstrip for U.S. aircraft would be expedited as well.

By 0445, LST transports disgorged LVT amphibious tractors which "proceeded in column to the line of departure along the right flank," said Major Fenlon A. Durand, USMC, "until they were one-hundred and fifty (150) yards behind the right flank control vessel. At this point they executed a column left and came across the rear of the line of departure to the left flank control vessel where they executed "boats right" and came to the line of departure abreast."[160]

Pre-HOW Hour Naval Gunfire and Air Support

The Gunfire Support Unit destroyers were *Beale, Converse, Daly*, and *Paul Hamilton*. "During the approach to Aguni Shima and just prior to scheduled commencement of bombardment enemy aircraft were reported in the area," said Rear Admiral Reifsnider. "Orders were issued for Fire Support Units to hold fire until further notice. Upon arrival of fighter cover on station, about HOW minus 60, the bombardment was ordered to commence. Two destroyers with VOF planes were assigned in direct support of the landing force. The preparation fires were carried out as scheduled with no request for call fires."[161]

Due to the lack of opposition during the assault on Iheya Shima, estimates of the enemy forces at Aguni Shima were revised and air support implemented changes "in the interest of conservatism," according to Commander Perkins of the Air Support Control Unit. With safety of the Marines in mind, "all runs were made parallel to the beach, and the point of aim was moved inland 1000 yards when the first boat wave was 400 yards from shore."[162] Flying from Yontan airfield on Okinawa, 22 fighter-bombers from Marine Fighting Squadrons VMF 311 and VMF 441 of Marine Aircraft Group 31 (MAG 31) supported pre-landing bombardments, although "Results were unobserved because of smoke and fire."[163]

Lt. Comdr. J. A. Dodson, Jr., commanding LCS Division 8 (TU 31.25.41) added, "At 0515 the action was opened by Fire Support Destroyers opening fire on designated targets and areas on the beach. From 0515 until 0535 own aircraft bombed beach with napalm and bombs," then, "...From 0605 until 0613 (H-Hour was 0610) friendly F4Us and TBMs made strafing and rocket firing runs on beach area, and areas directly behind landing beaches. Upon conclusion [of] beach bombardments, the action was terminated."[164]

Memoranda and Addenda: Shadows of Iheya Shima

Because of the Marine casualties at Iheya Shima on 3 June 1945, and the subsequent meeting on 6 June with Adm. Reifsnider's staff over operational safety, Commander Francis' instructions for his Support Gunboats were unusually detailed and the most exacting of the entire Okinawa operation.

For Able Day, the amphibious assault on Aguni Shima, each unit commander would station a safety observer to note the results of fire from all the gunboats. Afterwards, the observers were to submit reports to the OTC over the Naval Gunfire Control circuit. "If the fire was performed safely," added Comdr. Francis, "the report will state, 'SAFETY OBSERVER REPORTS THAT NO FIRE ENDANGERED OWN TROOPS [original emphasis].'"[165]

Ordnance was to fall only in the targeted zones inland from the water's edge, said Commander Francis, then he warned, "Ranging rockets and mortars may land in the water, but salvos shall not be fired until it is ascertained that shorts falling in the water will not occur."

Furthermore, all gunboats would cease firing immediately when the first boat wave was 700 yards from the beach. "Even though the entire allowance of ammunition has not been delivered, the position of the first boat wave is the governing factor for ceasing fire. If in doubt as to the boat wave's position, cease fire," emphasized the commander.[166]

Specifically, the six gunboats of LCS Division 8, while preceding the first boat wave toward shore, will cease all forty- and twenty-millimeter gunfire when landing craft were 700 yards from the beach, reiterated Commander Francis, with only limited exceptions for emergencies. "The emergency condition prevails when: (1) Enemy troops definitely visible. (2) There is a need for them to be fired upon. (3) Our own forces will not be endangered in any way." All rocket bombardments will also cease when the first wave reached the 700 yards line, regardless of the numbers of projectiles remaining in launchers. Regardless, "No rockets will be fired over friendly boats at any time."[167]

The six gunboats of LCI(M) Division 3, in turn, were to conform with the current beach neutralization doctrine, where "...the shortest falling mortars will be on the beach line at 'Commence Firing' and the fire will 'walk' inland as firing progresses." Such mortar fire shall have reached 500 yards inland by the time the "Cease Fire" order is signaled the moment the leading boat wave was 700 yards from shore. "Definite steps shall be taken to cease fire if the firing ship swings off course any appreciable amount," asserted Comdr. Francis.[168]

Finally, the four Spinner rocketships of LSM(R) Unit 2 would also conform to the preceding instructions, assured Commander Francis, but cautioned, "It is permissible to fire ranging rockets only as necessary in the water. [However,] Firing [is] to be completed as soon after H-10 as possible and not in any case to continue after H-5 regardless of the number of rockets fired. Ranging rockets may be fired shortly before H-10."[169]

The Support Gunboats

As the Marine landing force prepared to assault Aguni Shima, the Support Gunboats were released from anti-aircraft screening of the transports. By 0500, LCI(M) Division 3, LCS Division 8, and LSM(R) Unit 2 formally reported to fire support stations at the same time Commander Francis' flagship LC(FF) 535 maneuvered to monitor the naval gunfire support.[170]

LCI(M) Division 3 divided into two sections of three ships each, where Section I took station to the right flank of the boat lanes east of the landing beaches and fired mortars, while Section II assumed a secondary station launching mortars at the southwestern corner of the island. LCS(L) Division 8 with flagship led the boat waves to the landing beach firing 4.5" rockets, then split to the right and left flanks to stand by for call fire as the landing boats passed.

"LSM(R) Unit 2," explained Comdr. Francis, "composed of 4 LSM(R)s, when released from Sortie screen, proceeded to rocket firing stations on the southern side of the island, located roughly south of southeast and southeast from the landing beach."

The LSM(R) 196[171] delivered approximately 1000 5.0" spin stabilized rockets into the town of Aguni. The LSM(R) 199[172] fired approximately 1000 5.0" spin stabilized rockets along a high, possibly defended, ridge, running northeast-southwest and located about 1500 yards inland of the landing beach. The LSM(R)s 197 and 199[173] each delivered 500 5.0" spin stabilized rockets into possible enemy emplacements on the south western corner of the island. Upon completion of firing, the LSM(R)s returned to the vicinity of the anchorage and awaited screening assignment.[174]

"No enemy activity was encountered," reported Lt. Timmerman of LSM(R) 198, however, his ship was "forced to cease firing in middle of first salvo to avoid friendly aircraft which flew past in vicinity of rocket trajectory, but completed run on schedule."[175] Altogether, the four Spinner LSM(R)s of Task Unit 31.25.44 fired 2,834 rockets at Aguni Shima.[176]

Assessing the effectiveness of the Support Gunboats, Commander Francis commented,

> At Aguni Shima, the assigned targets were neutralized by all units except for the immediate terrain on the water's edge. No mortar or rocket "shorts" were observed to fall into the water. The target areas assigned the LCS(L)s and LCI(M)s were thoroughly covered, producing many small craters, heavy shrapnel, and minor fires throughout. The town of Aguni was about 50% demolished, with the inland portion being most heavily hit. The ridge covered by the *LSM(R) 199* was heavily hit causing heavy fires over the entire length. All rockets fired by the *LSM(R)s 197* and *199* fell into the suspected enemy emplacement areas, neutralizing them effectively.[177]

Blue Beach Two

The weather for the Aguni Shima assault on 9 June 1945 was overcast with winds east-northeast at 12 knots.[178] "Visibility good, light air, partly cloudy," remarked one LSM(R) commander.[179] At 0530, however, the H-Hour landing time on Blue Beach Two was delayed ten minutes and reset for 0610 (Blue Beach One was not assaulted).

Major F. A. Durand, USMC, commanding the Marine Second Amphibian Tractor Battalion reported,

> Plans were made to have thirty-five LVT(4)s and fourteen LVT(2)s for transporting LT 1/8 in the assault. The above includes two LVT(4)s as free tractors for the infantry LT Commander and the LT Executive Officer.... It was planned to have three waves of twelve LVTs each and one wave of eleven LVTs, with the two free tractors landing behind the first wave and the fourth wave. In addition, [plans included] one platoon (six LVT(A)4s) on each flank of the first wave in an inverted "V" formation....[180]

Maj. Durand added, "Time interval between waves was to be five minutes between the first and second waves and ten minutes between each successive wave...."[181]

"Particular attention was paid to radar tracking in each landing," explained Admiral Reifsnider: "At Aguni the support gunboats just ahead of the first wave were tracked from ABLE Control Vessel, radio communication being maintained between radar operators and leading wave guide. While tracking was reasonably successful, it was not felt that this method had any positive effect in correcting the minor discrepancies that occurred between scheduled and actual progress."[182]

For Blue Beach Two, the first wave crossed the LD (Line of Departure) at 0542 and hit the beach at 0613.[183] But the approaches got off track from the start, as Major Durand continued:

> Each wave was guided from the line of departure to the beach by an LCVP which carried a Naval Wave Guide Officer and an LVT Officer. [But] Control vessels marking the LD were not directly opposite the landing beach. Their positions (approximately 500 yards too far south) resulted in the LVTs having to approach the beach at a slight angle. With this angle of approach three LVT(4)s landed to the left of the landing beach."[184]

According to Lt. Col. Hayward, "Control boats governing flow of LVT's to and from beach were issuing conflicting statements. One control vessel should have [communications] channel control."[185]

Fog of War Redux

Despite stringent precautions to avoid repetition of the friendly fire that occurred at Iheya Shima on 3 June 1945, the First Battalion, Eighth Marines reported falling fire at Aguni Shima on 9 June 1945 nonetheless: "The spotting Officer was on the NGF Control Net on a TCS [radio] set in his LVT on the way to the beach. One (1) round HE fell between the first and second waves as they approached the beach, and the Spotting Officer was able to report it on the NGF Control Net immediately."[186] The Marine Second Amphibian Tractor Battalion also reported falling fire during the assault. "During the landing on Aguni, several rockets from supporting craft fell in and around the first and second waves. Luckily, none of the LVTs were hit and no personnel casualties resulted. However, such rocket fire should be so timed and directed that it be imperative that it should be lifted from the immediate area of the landing beach when the first wave is five-hundred (500) yards from the beach."[187]

The two reported incidents of falling fires transpired approximately within a twenty-four-minute timeframe, between 0549 when the second boat wave began advancing from the Line of Departure and 0613 when the first boat wave hit Blue Beach Two. The First Battalion, Eighth Marines did not suggest a source for the errant HE round, but the Marine Second Amphibian Tractor Battalion clearly cast responsibility on the Support Gunboats—"supporting craft"—for misguided rockets. Rear Admiral Reifsnider did not indicate whether he was aware of these reports, however. Nevertheless, given the heightened awareness and precautions to prevent falling friendly fires at Aguni Shima, and given the Support Gunboats commenced fires preceding the assault boats and from the flanks facing away from the assault boat lanes, the origin or origins of the misguided round and rockets are conundrums that may never be resolved with certainty.

Anti-Aircraft Screens, Smoke Screens and More Friendly Fire

In *LSM(R) 197*, Radioman Clyde Blue reviewed his day at Aguni Shima:

We left Okinawa at 1 a.m. and arrived off of Aguni about 5:10 a.m. We fired about 500 rockets as did also the [LSM(R)s] 6–8–9. Planes dropped fire bombs on it and planes rocket bombed it. Well they went ashore at about 6:10 and had it secured at 12:30 p.m. They had very few casualties. Guess there were not many troops on the island.... We probably will go back to the Anchorage tomorrow some time.[188]

Immediately after the Aguni landings, Commander Francis dispatched the Support Gunboats to anchor on transport AA screening stations. By noon, Admiral Reifsnider declared, "The island was reported secured at 1200/I without opposition."[189] General Hunt was unimpressed, on the other hand, "since this operation was of minor importance and unopposed...."[190]

In early afternoon, CTG 31.25 signaled the day's first Flash Red—Control Green air raid alert of single raids of Japanese aircraft.[191] Lt. Timmerman, captain of *LSM(R) 198*, noted from 1415 to 1435, "General Quarters—enemy aircraft reported approaching area from northeast. Enemy aircraft reported at 10 miles. A plane was picked up visually on reported bearing, but was identified as a TBF. Later, another plane was reported to the east of us at 10 miles.

A plane was picked up visually on this bearing and was believed to have been a PBM. No identified enemy aircraft were picked up visually."[192]

That evening, Admiral Reifsnider sent another Flash Red–Control Green warning at 1922 as more raids of single enemy planes closed but now from the west.[193] About this time Bruce McDaniel, Quartermaster-striker aboard *LSM(R) 196*, recalled a fortuitous friendly fire near miss at Aguni Shima:

> The landing was more or less uneventful except some almost laughable mistake. It was almost completely overcast with low clouds when a Navy plane flew low from the south across the front of the beach landing area parallel to the beach, when from above through the clouds tracers could be seen coming down at the plane splattering on the sea. The plane proceeded on a leisurely course on out of sight. Immediately another Navy plane came down through the overcast flying along the same course as the first plane, rocking its wings from side to side apparently looking for its quarry. At this point some guy on the can [destroyer] next to us, who probably never took an aircraft identification class, opened up on the second plane with a stream of tracers which signaled other ships to commence firing (except ours). There was a mass of tracers floating like red hot Ping-Pong balls, like the Fourth of July toward this low flying slow plane that flew on and out of sight unscathed, ending a comedy in mistaken identity.[194]

Clyde Blue in *LSM(R) 197* also remembered the confusion:

> We had several air alerts and one just before dark a Hellcat made a enemy run on the ships around us and we all opened fire on him. He was hit but I guess he didn't crash. The ships on patrol fire on any plane that makes a direct approach on them flying real low. So many ships have mistaken a Jap Val for a Corsair and have been hit that they aren't taking any chances any more....[195]

Vice Admiral Hill later explained, "the dusk CAP shot down a friendly night fighter and fired on another VF pilot who evaded the attacking Corsair and then received friendly AA resulting in wounds in hands and legs. 4 Corsairs returning to base from dusk CAP with IFF on and recognition lights also received friendly AA but were unharmed...."[196]

Another series of single enemy air raids were tracked coming from the north between 2100 and 2140[197] with a Flash Red—Control Green warning once more with the familiar orders, "Make Smoke."

Smoke and smoke screens, called obscurants, were often thick and effective. Mechanical smoke generators vaporized a mixture of water and fog oil, and these hot vapors condense into minute liquid droplets upon contact with the cooler, outside air. Smoke generators, however, were known to flare up and burst into flames at times, causing severe burns to nearby personnel. But, said Commander Francis, "the greatest difficulties in making smoke was that the oil smoke generators could not be completely relied upon to do the job. There were many smoke generator breakdowns but all ships had ample supplies of smoke pots and smoke floats which were immediately substituted when the occasion demanded."[198] And *LSM(R) 197* Radioman Clyde Blue learned firsthand that this smoke can be overwhelming: "We laid down a smoke screen tonight and it was so thick in the [radio] shack here that you couldn't see two feet in front of you. You almost choked to death trying to get your breath. My throat is all sore from it."[199]

Late evening of 9 June, still more raiders came from the northwest from 2220 to 2250,[200] causing CTG 31.25 to again signal "Flash Red–Control Green" followed by another order for smoke cover. "Starting at dusk and continuing throughout the night," reported Commander Perkins, the ASCU Commander for Amphibious Group Four, "several raids consisting of from one to three planes approached the Aguni Area. These planes were heckling raids and in one instance dropped flares close to the anchorage. No night fighters were controlled by our Task Group and no damage was reported."[201]

By midnight of 9–10 June, Admiral Reifsnider finally signaled the all clear "Flash White– Control Green" and ordered "Stop Smoke." But two more air alerts would sound before day- break of 10 June, from 0352 to 0409 and 0503 to 0509, although no intruding enemy aircraft were reported in the Aguni Shima area.

Standing Down at Aguni Shima: 10 June 1945

Like Iheya Shima, Americans discovered evidence of the Japanese military on Aguni Shima. "Two enemy radio sets were captured," said Lt. Col. Hayward.[202] "Prior to landing the enemy removed a transmitter of sufficient size to contact Japan. This is indicated by the dam- aged power supply which was left. It consists of a three (3) KW Motor generator and a large wet battery—both damaged beyond repair."[203]

"At this time 1658 civilians [are] interned," Adm. Reifsnider further noted, but "No POWs. Indications are that there are more civilians still at large. One case of suicide among the natives. Some natives appear reluctant to surrender. One non-battle casualty reported. Eight civilian dead...."[204]

On 10 June, under continuous overcast and east-southeast winds of 14 knots,[205] naval elements of Task Group 31.25 retired from Aguni Shima. By 1330, *LC(FF)* 535 and LSM(R) Unit 2 sortied with a formation of six LSTs and other ships en route to Hagushi Anchorage. The convoy arrived off Okinawa by mid-afternoon,[206] and the four Spinner rocketships stood by as anti-aircraft screens until relieved by Rear Admiral Reifsnider at 1645.[207]

That evening, Radioman Clyde Blue jotted a few notes in his diary.

> Well we had air alerts all night long but nothing came of it. We got mail today.... We got our mail at Aguni and left there around 1 p.m. We got back to the Anchorage around 5:30 p.m. On the way back we unloaded what rockets we never fired and put them below. I guess we will lay around until the next inva- sion. I hope we lay around. We may get some more mail today. Well I guess I will close for now. Hit Parade of June 9th, 1945:
>
> 1. Laura
> 2. Dreams
> 3. Sentimental Journey
> 4. All My Life
> 5. Just a Prayer Away
> 6. Candy
> 7. I Should Care
> 8. My Dreams are Getting Better All the Time.[208]

Vice Admiral Hill (CTF 31) released Commander Francis and his Support Gunboat unit from the Iheya-Aguni Attack Group the next day at 1100 of 11 June,[209] just hours before he formally dissolved Task Group 31.25 at 1400.[210]

"High Standard of Performance"

Following the Iheya-Aguni operations, Rear Admiral Lawrence F. Reifsnider offered measured acknowledgment of Commander Dennis L. Francis' unit: "The Support Gunboats efficiently performed their assigned tasks throughout the operations covered by the attached report."[211] Some recalled elsewhere, however, the admiral proffered a more traditional Navy commendation: "The performance of your gunboats during the operations for the capture of Iheya and Aguni has been outstanding. Well done."[212]

Commander Francis generally praised his Support Gunboat commanders. "While there was no particular instance of outstanding achievement by any individual there was a high standard of performance throughout the operation." Nevertheless, "the Unit Commanders are particularly cited for their uniform high standard of performance, their alertness, and the alacrity with which orders were executed."[213] Furthermore, he continued,

> It is felt that the communications during the operation were the most effective and the most facile that this command has yet encountered. The success of radio communications was due largely to the fact that this command held and monitored on individual voice circuit. With this advantage, units taking station in anti-aircraft screens and smoke screens as well as those units in preliminary bombardments could be maneuvered in an extremely expeditious manner.[214]

"The results of the fire delivered by these units is satisfactory to this command," added Commander Francis. "Had enemy garrisons been present in force, it is believed that the positions bombarded by mortar and rocket fire would have been rendered useless and neutralization would have been complete." Between the Iheya and Aguni operations, he estimated the rockets, mortars, and ammunition expended by the Support Gunboats totaling 2100 4.5-inch Barrage Rockets; 5600 5.0-inch Spin Stabilized Rockets; 2100 4.2-inch Mortars; and 400 rounds of 40mm.[215] Yet, as Commanding Officer of LSM Flotilla Nine, his attention focused primarily on the LSM(R)s. "The performance of both rockets and launchers were satisfactory and the amount of misfires and jams encountered indicates that steady maintenance improvement is present." Overall, 2720 rockets were fired at Iheya Shima and 2820 rockets fired at Aguni Shima, but, "not enough use was made of the 5"/38 or automatic weapons to make particular comment. No jams or misfires were encountered."[216] "Gunnery personnel performed in their customary excellent manner," concluded Comdr. Francis, and "Overall loading and firing operations were very satisfactory. No enemy aerial opposition was encountered so comment cannot be made on automatic weapons. The little shore bombardment with 40 MM guns was well controlled and highly adequate."[217]

Finally, Commander Francis offered a frank appraisal of the rocketships:

> A. LSM(R)s [are] not particularly suited as A.A. Screen ships because the 5"/38 and 2 40 MM guns have not adequate fire control mechanisms and only 3 20 MMs are present.
>
> B. LSM(R)s are very well suited to act as individuals in destroying or neutralizing enemy positions. Their use as a wave seems a waste if enough other targets are present to use them singly.
>
> C. LSM(R)s [are] well suited as screening ships against surface targets. The 5"/38 is a formidable weapon and the 40 MMs are enough to destroy small boats. Their radar is good allowing effective station keeping on night patrols. In general [LSM(R)s are] better suited as flycatchers than smokers. They can [also] provide their own illumination.[218]

CHAPTER 10

The Spinners

Naval Gunfire Support,
11–18 June 1945

After the Iheya-Aguni operations, the return of the four LSM(R)s and flotilla flagship to Hagushi Anchorage on 10 June 1945 coincided with the final, fateful struggle for Okinawa. U.S. Army and Marine forces launched concentrated drives southward along the entire length of the Japanese front lines that penetrated the enemy's western and eastern flanks defending the Kiyan (or Kiyamu) Peninsula, the southern-most tip of Okinawa below the coastal villages of Itoman to the west and Minatoga to the east. *LSM(R)s 196, 197, 198* and *199*, after brief replenishment in Hagushi, were called to support this final push south against the Imperial Japanese Army.

Scuttlebutt swirled after an 11 June LSM(R) captains' conference with Commander Francis. "Well," began Clyde Blue, writing in his diary in *LSM(R) 197*, "we are back at the Anchorage again. We never did nothing but lay at anchor all day.… There is a lot to talk of us going on a 5-day operation. Some say to throw a lot of rockets on southern Okinawa at the Japs pinned along the coast…"[1] But the lull was only temporary, as Radioman Blue added the next day on 12 June: "Did not do nothing today. We are going to fire rockets at the southern tip of Okinawa for the next few days. I think we are supposed to do a lot of heavy firing down there. We got mail today."[2]

As plans unfolded to deploy the LSM(R)s once more, during the ten days from 11 June until Okinawa was declared secured on 21 June 1945, Vice Admiral Hill (CTF 31)[3] delegated duties of the Amphibious Support Force to Vice Admiral Jesse B. Oldendorf (ComBat-RonOne) as CTF 32[4] in flagship *Tennessee BB 43*. Oldendorf exercised direct control of all naval gunfire support on both sides of the island for III Amphibious Corps and XXIV Army Corps.[5] Accordingly, *LSM(R)s 197* and *198* would soon operate under the Eastern Fire Support Group CTG 32.14 with the Army, and *LSM(R)s 196* and *199* would operate under the Western Fire Support Group CTG 32.11 with the Marines.

Although the four Spinners were divided between Army and Marines, on occasions the rocketships would be assigned similar or overlapping targets and tactical areas (TA) by the 7th Infantry Division and 1st Marine Division as battle lines narrowed southward into Okinawa's Kiyan Peninsula. During the three days from 13 to 15 June 1945, the LSM(R)s attacked Japanese troop concentrations, outposts, gun positions, supply dumps, vehicles, caves, and reverse slopes as the Spinner rocketships' last and greatest onslaught of the war.

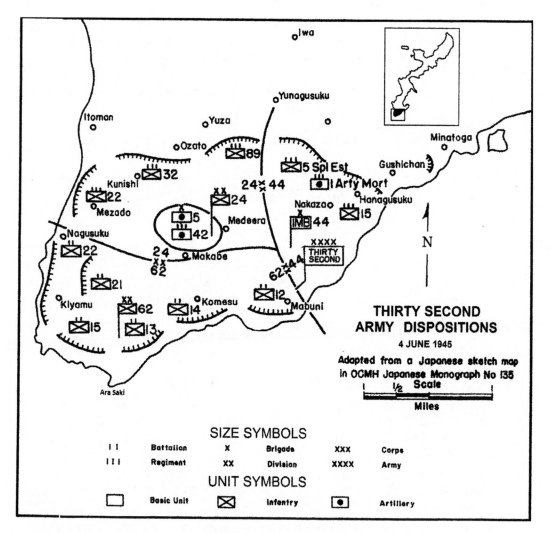

Remnants of the Japanese 32nd Army fought its last stand after 3 June 1945 with an estimated total strength of about 30,000 men within 20 square miles of southern Okinawa. U.S. ground, air, and naval forces pounded the enemy until Okinawa was declared secure on 21 June 1945 (adapted from Chas. S. Nichols, Jr., Major, USMC, and Henry I. Shaw, *Okinawa: Victory in the Pacific*. Historical Branch, G-3 Division, Headquarters, U.S. Marine Corps, Washington, D.C.: U.S. Government Printing Office, 1955, Map 33, page 216).

Southeastern Okinawa: USS LSM(R) 197 and USS LSM(R) 198

13 June 1945[6]

On 13 June 1945, *LSM(R)s 197* and *198* reported to the Eastern Fire Support Group (CTG 32.14) and temporarily attached to LCI(R) Flotilla Sixteen (Task Group 32.20) under Commander C. E. Coffin, Jr., whose units had provided continuous fire support for HQ 7th Infantry Division, Tenth Army since the first of the month.

Lt. Henry O. Bergkamp, skipper of *LSM(R) 197* explained, "This vessel proceeded under tactical command of CTU 32.20.4 to station off Southern Okinawa for rocket bombardment and in-shore patrol in support of US Army and Marine forces ashore."[7]

Captain of *LSM(R) 198* Lt. George B. Timmerman, Jr., added, "this vessel was assigned to support the Seventh Infantry Division by making rocket runs against designated targets and by making a close inshore patrol prior to sunset and at sunrise to locate and take under fire with automatic weapons any enemy activity observed."[8]

Assembling and loading rockets into launchers en route, the two Spinners steamed various courses and speeds rounding the southern tip of Okinawa and laid off the southeastern coastline by 0815. On station about a mile off shore from the town of Mabuni,[9] they reported to a staging area several miles due south[10] and stood by for orders from the U.S. Army. Here, several LCSs preparing to make rocket attacks were "called off due to the arrival of 2 LSM(R)s in area to fire rockets."

In addition to *LSM(R)s 197* and *198*, a half-dozen LCI(R)s under Comdr. Coffin were providing fire support to the Seventh Infantry Division, Tenth Army.[11] In direct tactical command was Lt. Comdr. Henry T. McKnight (CTU 32.20.4)[12] in *LCI(R) 648*, codenamed "Hotel," who dispatched the day's general orders that included the two LSM(R)s, coded "Alberts," and rockets called "Peerless":

WE WILL CARRY ON SAME ACT TODAY X ALBERTS 197 AND 198 AGAIN TO FIRE PEERLESS X ARMY GROUND COMMANDER STATES YESTERDAYS PEERLESS FIRE VERY EFFECTIVE AND HOTEL THANKS FOR GOOD WORK X ... ALBERTS REPORT WHEN READY TO FIRE PEERLESS ...[13]

Shortly after 0900, 7th Infantry Division Headquarters transmitted orders to *LSM(R)s 197* and *198* to bombard hills and seaside cliffs south and northeast of Mabuni.[14] In caves deep under adjacent Hill 89 was General Ushijima's headquarters and final command post for his Thirty-second Army. Setting General Quarters and securing topsides automatic weapons, the two rocketships initially commenced tandem rocket runs from 0941–42 launching scores of Spin-stabilized Rockets (SSRs). The Army thereafter requested additional barrages over the Mabuni area this morning, and the two rocketships attacked either as pairs or singly for a dozen rocket runs before noon.[15] However, explained Lt. Timmerman of *LSM(R) 198*, "On the first day, after each run, misfired rockets were transferred to other launchers in an effort to expend them. This accounts for the large number of misfires, many of them being the same rockets that previously misfired, as is indicated by the total of 1856 having been expended out of a total of 1880 loaded."[16]

By noontime, the rocketships stood down and had steamed about four miles due south of the Mabuni beaches[17] when the Army dispatched *LSM(R)s 197* and *198* to resume assaults in the Mabuni area[18] with another half-dozen rocket attacks through the afternoon from 1345 to 1611.[19] "No casualties were experienced during these runs," said Lt. Timmerman, "except at 1345 on 13 June 1945, one rocket landed on deck a few feet in front of its launcher, circled around several times and finally went off our port quarter and landed in the water about two hundred yards out...."[20] *LSM(R) 198*'s Radioman Louis Gobeille recalled, "When we were shooting our rockets off one time, one of the rockets misfired and landed on our deck. We were very fortunate, because it swerved around the deck a few times and went over the side without exploding...."[21]

An hour later, *LSM(R) 197* also reported a rocket misfire in a launcher, but no damage was suffered here, either, while at this same moment *LSM(R) 198* was forced to check fire in the midst of her rocket attack at 1446, "Unable to complete run due to friendly planes in line of fire." Later, a cartridge exploded in a .50 caliber machinegun on *LSM(R) 198* that blew the barrel over the side, but no injuries were reported.

After rocketing the hilly, rocky areas of Komesu village from 1607 to 1611, targeting areas held by the Japanese 14th Infantry Battalion, the two rocketships stood by off shore again awaiting further orders. That afternoon the Army advised that rocket assignments were concluded for the day, so remaining rockets were removed from launchers and stowed below decks as *LSM(R) 199* briefly came alongside her sister ship *LSM(R) 198* to pass guard mail at 1726.

The U.S. Army soon requested the LSM(R)s to commence evening patrols with orders to fire on likely targets ashore. By 1830 the two rocketships reported on station patrolling the shorelines between Komesu and Mabuni,[22] intermittently firing automatic weapons at caves, rocks and wooded areas.[23] "During the evening and morning patrols," said Timmerman, "this vessel operated a few hundred yards off the beach. Areas in which enemy activity was observed were taken under fire. On 13 June evening patrol, Japs were observed in grid area 7757 [east of Komesu] and one Jap was seen in grid area 7455 [Ara Saki, the southern-most tip of Okinawa] ..."[24]

The rocketships ceased patrols by 1945 and nested in an anchorage overnight lying off Gushichan and Minatoga villages on the southeast coast.[25] Ammunition expended that evening by *LSM(R) 197* was 80 rounds of 40mm and 60 rounds of 20mm; and 77 rounds of 40mm and 1,806 .50 caliber rounds fired by *LSM(R) 198*.[26] "LSM(R)s' fire was tremendously effective," remarked Lt. Comdr. McKnight, LCI(R) commander. "The volume of fire and the accuracy achieved was outstanding."[27]

"Well we left the Anchorage around 4:30 a.m. for the southern part of Okinawa," wrote Clyde Blue in his diary from *LSM(R) 197*, continuing,

> We are to be down there for 5 days firing rockets but as we only have 3800 rockets I don't think we will be down there that long. On the way down we loaded a deckload. [The *LSM(R)s*] *196–8–9* are with us also. *198* is working with us. We fire our rockets at a target given to us by the Army and fire about 100 rockets at a run. We fired all our rockets and then fired at the beach with 20 mm and 40 mm. The day was just right for this kind of work. The Army men said we were doing a good job. They have about 40,000 Japs cornered on the southern tip of the island so that's a lot of Japs in a real small area.[28]

14 June 1945[29]

LSM(R)s 197 and *198* weighed anchors and got underway by 0500 of 14 June and set General Quarters en route for patrols on the southeastern coastline of Okinawa,[30] for "close support with automatic weapons, fires on targets of opportunity, call and harassing fires," explained Comdr. Coffin.[31]

Before sunrise, skipper of the *LSM(R) 197* Lt. Henry O. Bergkamp noted, "On in-shore patrol from 7756M to 7956D [between Komesu and Mabuni]. Fired 164 rounds 40MM and 120 rounds 20MM at enemy personnel spotted emerging from caves in grid areas 7956 and 7856 [rocky sea cliffs and hills south of Mabuni]."[32] Lt. George B. Timmerman, Jr., captaining *LSM(R) 198* added, "On 14 June morning patrol, Japs were observed in grid areas 7656 [south of Komesu], 7355 [southeast of Kiyamu] and a probable gun emplacement was observed in 7455 [southern tip of Okinawa] ...."[33] His ship's gunners also strafed the enemy-held beaches expending in turn 242 rounds 40mm, 20 rounds 20mm, and 380 rounds .50 caliber, after which both Spinners secured from GQ about 0700.

While lying to about a mile off southeastern Okinawa, ships' deck forces began assembling and loading rockets into launchers. By 0855, loading was complete on *LSM(R) 198*, but launchers on *LSM(R) 197* were only full by 0930.

Morning rocket attacks concentrated on targets in the Mabuni area,[34] the command post of the remnant Japanese Thirty-second Army and nearby 12th Infantry Battalion. Both rocketships launched four salvos between 0936 and 1115, with each rocket barrage either in approximate unison or succession. *LSM(R)s 197* and *198* each made four rocket runs from 0936 to 0946, 1028 to 1030, 1040 to 1054, and 1114 to 1115,[35] and launched 100/88, 100/79, 112/95, and 204/84 SSRs respectively.[36]

By 1125, the two rocketships laid to off the target area awaiting further orders when sister ship *LSM(R) 199* came alongside *LSM(R) 198* briefly to deliver personal mail this time. Soon afterwards, the latter warship launched another salvo of 88 rockets at 1148: "All rockets were fired on target areas designated by the Army off southeastern end of Okinawa," noted the OOD.[37]

Thereafter, the two Spinners resumed attacks in the Mabuni area[38] with an irregular series of rocket runs from high noon through mid afternoon. *LSM(R) 198* launched 104 rockets at 1202, while the deck force on *LSM(R) 197* finished reloading her rocket launchers by 1245, pausing only long enough to pass mail from 1230 to 1235. The first of nine afternoon assaults thus began at 1312 and, as in the morning's rocket runs, the two rocketships varied attacks by firing singly or in unison to saturate the Mabuni complex.[39] In succession, *LSM(R) 197* launched 100, 112, 96, 84 and 100 spin-stabilized rockets[40] while *LSM(R) 198* fired 94, 87, 73 and 84 SSRs.[41]

Afterwards, the rocketships stood by off the target areas through late afternoon until the Army directed *LSM(R) 198* to pound the Mabuni area once again. Commencing her rocket run at 1710, she launched a barrage of 69 rockets from 1734 to 1735 then repositioned for another strike of 22 rockets at 1743. By this time, however, *LSM(R) 198* had depleted most of her SSRs, as her OOD noted: "Total rounds of rockets expended this date is 972, leaving 8 rounds on board."[42]

But *LSM(R) 197* still had 700 SSRs readied in her launchers. So once the Army designated a new target area by 1736, the village of Komesu[43] and elements of the Japanese 14th Infantry Battalion nearby, she loosed 96 rockets.[44]

Immediately after the last rockets had fallen, the Army released the two Spinners from gunfire support and ordered to commence evening coastal patrols ranging from the southern tip of Okinawa to Mabuni.[45] Setting General Quarters by 1845, the rocketships strafed the beach where Japanese troops were spotted south of Komesu,[46] and raked caves and wooded areas with automatic weapons fire.[47] South of Mabuni,[48] possible mortar emplacements were also taken under fire. "On 14 June evening patrol," noted Timmerman, "Japs were observed in grid area 7656 [south of Komesu] and one or more snipers were believed to be in the vicinity of grid area 7555 ABCFG and 7556 UVWX [southwest of Komesu]...."[49] Total ammunition expended this evening by *LSM(R 197* was 232 rounds of 40mm and 540 rounds of 20mm; *LSM(R) 198* fired 490 rounds of 40mm, 690 rounds of 20mm, and 1480 rounds of .50 caliber.

"Well today we started loading at about 7 a.m. and started firing around 10:30 a.m.," recalled Clyde Blue from his station in the radio shack in *LSM(R) 197*:

We fired all day and then we had to reload again with what rockets we had left. We only had around 800 but it sure is hell loading them. We made one reload out there and are going to fire the rest tomorrow. We went in close to the beach and fired our 20's and 40 mm again. We spotted about 40 Japs just in off the beach in some trees and bushes. We opened up on them but don't know how many we got. I would sure like to know how many we have gotten so far. There is a lot of talk going around that we are going back to Guam or Leyte. The fin ships have gone back some place but don't know where as yet. It sure has been hot here today. Also all night. I am writing this on the 12 to 4 midnight watch. Well I hope we do go back to some base but it will probably be so dam hot we wont be able to stand it.[50]

Ceasing fire by 1948, both rocketships secured from evening patrols and returned to the anchorage near Gushichan and Minatoga off southeastern Okinawa[51] for the night. "Today the Army observers ashore advised that [LSM(R)] rocket fire was achieving outstanding results," reviewed Lt. Comdr. McKnight, the LCI(R) commander. "LSMs [*sic*] remained on patrol in area during the night with *LCI(R)s 647* and *764.*"[52]

15 June 1945[53]

Shortly after 0500 of 15 June, the two rocketships got underway on orders from CTU 32.20.4[54] for daylight patrols, often just 200 yards from the shoreline ranging between Mabuni and the southern tip of Okinawa.[55]

Between 0540 and 0715, reported Lt. Bergkamp of *LSM(R) 197,* "While patrolling beach from grid area 7454 to 7855 [southern tip of Okinawa to approximately Komesu village], fired 397 rounds 40MM and 60 rounds 20MM at enemy pillbox and troops in grid area 7856 [south of Mabuni] .... Results of beach strafing," he continued, were "one pillbox opened by 40MM fire and possibly 20 enemy casualties caused by firing into personnel concentrations. Many small brush fires started and many hits scored on caves which might have been used to conceal the enemy."[56] *LSM(R) 198* also opened fire at the same time, strafing the beach with automatic weapons.

By 0700, however, an Army Piper Cub *Grasshopper* observation plane directed *LSM(R) 198* westward of the assigned patrol areas. According to skipper Lt. Timmerman, "On 15 June morning patrol, Japs were observed in grid areas 7756 [between Komesu and Mabuni], 7455 and 7555 [southern tip Okinawa]. During this latter patrol, area 7255 CDEHIJ [south of Kiyamu] was taken under fire at request of a friendly plane, who reported a concentration of troops in that area. These troops could not be seen from this vessel but the pilot of the plane indicated by signs that he was pleased with the results."[57] These sightings were likely holdouts of the Japanese 14th and 15th Infantry Battalions.

LSM(R) 198's Radioman Louis Gobeille recalled that *Grasshopper* spotter:

One day when we were patrolling the shoreline of Okinawa, an American plane came swooping down to our ship, [and] one of the men aboard the plane pointed to us to observe their flight as they flew a short distance from the shore and pointed at a specific area, then came back and asked us to fire some rockets in that area. Our captain obliged and we did fire directly where they asked us to. We apparently hit the target, because they came back, swooped down close to us again and the American stuck out his hands and arms in a motion to acknowledge that we hit the target, he thanked us then flew away.[58]

Reports of observed enemy activity were made to "Cliffdweller Four," codename for the naval gunfire liaison officer, but fire was ceased a half-hour later and General Quarters secured. The morning's total ammunition expenditures came to 301 rounds of 40mm, 480 rounds of 20mm, and 1440 rounds of .50 caliber. The two Spinners were released from the harassment and interdiction patrols by 0730, and rendezvoused off the southern tip of Okinawa some 5,000 yards south of Kiyamu village[59] to await further orders.

The day before, however, *LSM(R) 198* virtually exhausted her magazines of SSRs. "Additional runs could have been made on the [*sic*] 15 June 1945, except for the fact that our supply of rockets had been expended," explained Lt. Timmerman. He added, "While the destruction inflicted on the designated target areas could not be observed from this vessel, a number of commendatory messages were received from Cliffdweller 4, who designated our targets and from Headquarters Seventh Infantry Division, which indicated that the rocket bombardment produced the desired results."[60]

LSM(R) 197, meanwhile, commenced her first rocket run this day at 0850, but checked her attack just seven minutes into the run when an intruding LCI fouled the line of fire. Standing by until 0915, the rocketship made another attempt and launched salvos of 108 rockets from 0922 to 0925 south of Mabuni,[61] followed by a second run at 0947 firing 96 SSRs,[62] and a third attack at 1005 launching 108 rockets.[63]

After 1023, *LSM(R) 197* stood off southern Okinawa by the target area awaiting further orders until noon. Meantime, *LSM(R) 199* came alongside from 1100–1105 to pick up 150 rocket fuses.

The respite ended when *LSM(R) 197* resumed attacks on Mabuni at 1216 by firing a salvo of 96 SSRs.[64] The rocketship struck again with a barrage of 108 rockets at 1243 and once more at 1352 with 62 rockets, then finally exhausted her last ten rounds of SSRs on board with a concluding rocket run at 1400.[65] *LSM(R) 197* radioed results of the day's assignments, including a reference to "Hupmobile," codename for 40mm gunfire:

ENEMY OBSERVED IN CONCENTRATION IN AREAS 7656 AB 7756 GHIJ 7856 FG X INDIVIDUALS SEEN IN AREAS 7856 J X PILLBOX IN 7856 K X RESULTS OF FIRE POSSIBLY 20 NIPS HIT AND PILLBOX DEFINITELY OPENED UP X AMMO EXPENDED 629 ROUNDS HUPMOBILE AND 600 ROUNDS 20 MM BT K.[66]

Ensign Lawrence Low, Gunnery Officer on *LSM(R) 197*, briefly outlined their three days supporting American ground forces:

13 June–15 June: Rocket bombardment of enemy troop concentrations, headquarters and gun-mortar emplacements on southern Okinawa. Three day continuous daylight bombardment. Under (*LSM(R)*s *196, 197, 198, 199*) direction of the 7th and 77th Infantry Divisions. Army very enthusiastic over results and deeply appreciative. Jap headquarters ("Park Avenue" district) subjected to three day bombardment by *LSM(R) 197*—2,800 rockets fired in salvos of 108–96. Dawn and dusk in-shore patrols, sweeping enemy troop concentrations and pillboxes with 40MM and 20MM fire. Troops observed moving on slopes and in vicinity of caves. Mortars and small arms returned fire from beach, but ineffectively.[67]

Ens. Low also noted two messages of appreciation sent from HQ Seventh Infantry Division, and Lt. Comdr. McKnight, Commander of Rocket and RCM Division Four:

ALBERT 197 & ALBERT 198 •CLIFFDWELLER 4 Ø515
YOU ARE RELEASED FROM THIS DUTY X RETURN TO YOUR PASTURE AS YOU HAVE BEEN OTHERWISE DIRECTED X THANK YOU FOR YOUR COOPERATION X YOUR WORK HAS BEEN EXCELLENT X BEFORE YOU SECURE THIS NET WILL YOU SUBMIT AMMO EXPENDITURE REPORT FOR TODAY X THANK YOU AGAIN AND GOOD LUCK. BT.

And:

ALBERT 197—ALBERT 198 •HOTEL Ø549 15 Ø549 BT
I WANT TO ADD ADDITIONAL WORD TO CLIFFDWELLER 4'S TRANSMISSION X YOU HAVE

DONE A MAGNIFICENT JOB WITH YOUR PEERLESS X I WANT TO THANK YOU FOR ALL THE DOUGHBOYS. BY OVER.[68]

During the attacks on southern Okinawa from 13 to 15 June 1945, USS *LSM(R) 197* exhausted her entire allotment of 2712 Spin-stabilized Rockets (HCSR) and expended 873 40mm HEITSD, 260 20mm HET, and 520 20mm HEI rounds of ammunition. "The performance of rockets, launchers and automatic weapons was completely satisfactory to this command," reported Lt. Bergkamp. "A total of 21 rocket misfires and jams occurred in the three (3) days of firing and action is being taken to prevent their reoccurrence."[69] In contrast, USS *LSM(R) 198* practically depleted her magazines of SSRs after the second day. Nevertheless, noted Lt. Timmerman, "A total of 1856 rockets were fired, out of 1880, during a total of twenty-two firing runs against designated target areas during the morning and afternoon of 13 and 14 June 1945 [although] twenty-four misfires and sixteen jams were experienced.... A total of 1,110 rounds of 40MM, 2,049 rounds of 20MM and 5,106 rounds of 50 Calibre [*sic*] ammunition were expended during the above mentioned patrols...."[70] Lt. Bergkamp summarized in conclusion, "Both CTU 32.20.4 and Headquarters 7th Infantry Division reported that rocket bombardment in assigned areas was most effective. Practically all rockets were observed to land on targets assigned," and "personnel performance was highly commendable in the execution of this duty."[71]

Southwestern Okinawa: USS LSM(R) 196 and USS LSM(R) 199

13 June 1945[72]

On 13 June 1945, *LSM(R)*s *196* and *199* reported to the Western Fire Support Group (CTG 32.11) to support HQ 1st Marine Division, III Amphibious Corps.

"This vessel proceeded under tactical command of CTF 32 to station off southern Okinawa for rocket firing in support of US Army and Marine forces ashore," noted Lt. Dennis D. O'Callaghan, commanding USS *LSM(R) 196*.[73] Lt. Charles D. Cobb, skipper of USS *LSM(R) 199*,[74] further added, "At 0602 13 June 1945 proceeded from Hagushi Anchorage to southern Okinawa to standby for orders to fire rockets. Our mission was to fire rockets onto targets on southern Okinawa. Targets to be designated by Headquarters First Marine Division.... Senior in tactical command was CTF 32."[75]

Before sunrise, *LSM(R) 196* and *LSM(R) 199* sailed south from Hagushi anchorage along the Okinawa coastline until stopping all engines just after 0800 to assemble and load launchers with Spin-stabilized Rockets (SSRs).[76] By 0920 the two rocketships reported to firing stations off southwestern Okinawa per orders transmitted via CTU 32.11, with observation spot by the First Marine Division.[77]

"For our last rocket assignment," explained Ensigns David Mallery and Jack Shedd aboard *LSM(R) 196*,

we were sent down to the southern tip of Okinawa, where the last ditch resistance of the beaten enemy was raging at its fiercest. The Marines, by radio, spotted for us and assigned targets by grid position on charts. In many ways this period was our most successful as a rocket ship. The four rocket ships involved succeeded in getting accuracy previously considered impossible for our equipment. At the end of the three day bombardment, our unit of four received very rewarding congratulations from the Marine head-quarters. Perhaps our favorite comment about this operation came from a task unit commander in charge of a unit of LCI(G)s near the southern tip, addressed by radio to the Marine headquarters on the beach: "Get more targets for those rocket fellows, they can put 'em in a bucket."[78]

The two Spinner rocketships alternated attacks throughout the day. "On 13 June 1945 at 1100," reported Lt. Cobb of *LSM(R) 199*, "fired rockets on town of Nagusuku.[79] Repeated firing as stated above at following times: 1120, 1159 and 1235,"[80] launching 96, 94, 100, and 115 SSRs respectively. Meanwhile, in two attacks, *LSM(R) 196* launched 202 rockets at 1100 and 190 rockets at 1153 against Nagusuku,[81] where the Japanese 22nd Infantry Battalion was poised against U.S. forces.

Over noontime, First Marine Division Headquarters shifted targets toward Makabe vil-lage, but weather and seas posed challenges. "Clear and hot weather," noted Lt. Cobb, and "gusty winds with short chopping sea. Due to wind and sea this vessel experienced difficulty in maintaining proper firing station when firing speed was zero. If it had been necessary to fire at a definite time this vessel would probably have been unable to fire on more than one occasion."[82] Near Makabe, the Japanese held their 22nd Regiment in reserve adjacent to their 42nd Artillery Regiment.

LSM(R) 196 launched 194 rockets from 1346 to 1350,[83] while *LSM(R) 199* fired 200 SSRs.[84] Following a brief lull, the latter rocketed Makabe again with 186 SSRs at 1423,[85] after which the former struck again with 140 rockets from 1451 to 1500.[86] *LSM(R) 199* concluded with an attack on a new target. "At 1537 fired rockets onto town of Komesu," said Lt. Cobb. "Left hand edge of town was used as point of aim. Fired on course of 308° T. when 4300 yards from beach."[87]

Major General Pedro A. del Valle, USMC, later commented, "Naval gunfire added the fire of two LSM(R)s to its usual striking power, with the rocket-launching craft moving into position off the southern tip of the island to rake reverse slope defenses. More than 800 5" rockets were hurled into the village [sic] of Makabe and Komesu alone."[88]

Awaiting further orders,[89] by 1640 CTG 32.11 released the two Spinners from further call fire assignments.[90] After the ships exchanged official guard mail, *LSM(R) 199* set sail at full speed for the Hagushi Anchorage, passed Cham Zaki (the southwestern tip of Okinawa) starboard abeam at 4000 yards by 1805, and arrived in the transport area by 1920. Here she closed the LSM Flotilla Nine flagship, USS *LC(FF) 535*, in berth H-12 to receive personal mail for later distribution to the other rocketships, then dropped anchor for the night.

LSM(R) 196, meanwhile, remained standing off southern Okinawa until 2100, when she got underway to commence nighttime patrols of the coastline. Maintaining 5000 yards off shore, the rocketship steamed at one-third speed on reciprocal courses of 060° and 240° True (T.), alternating direction every ten minutes.

14 June 1945[91]

Next morning, *LSM(R) 199* returned to southern Okinawa and rendezvoused with *LSM(R) 196* at 0630.[92] "On 14 and 15 June," reported Lt. Cobb in *LSM(R) 199*, the two Spin-ners "fired on [the] same targets as on 13 June, and on various other targets."[93]

Once on the firing line, *LSM(R) 196* commenced rocket runs at 0702, sending scores of rockets against Japanese ground forces hunkering between the towns of Kunishi, Nagusuku, and Makabe until 0750.[94] *LSM(R) 199* reinforced these barrages by launching 75 rockets into the same areas at 0725.[95]

Orders soon directed the two rocketships to strike a road connecting Nagusuku and Komesu.[96] At 0845 *LSM(R) 196* fired 120 rockets, then stood by for further orders, while at 0854 *LSM(R) 199* launched 275 rocket rounds 2500 yards inshore.[97] The Japanese 22nd Infantry held ground in Nagusuku while their 14th Infantry Battalion stood west of Komesu.

Standing by once more, the next attack order was a "newly assigned target, inland on southern Okinawa," where *LSM(R) 196* fired 130 rockets at 1010.[98] The Spinner ship also loosed 220 rockets into the hills northwest of Komesu at 1032,[99] then fired 70 rockets on the same target[100] two minutes later.

Around noontime, Commander Francis' flagship *LC(FF) 535* arrived with a Marine Corps Public Relations party, an officer and three enlisted men, "to observe [the] rocket fire of LSM(R) Unit 2."[101]

LSM(R) 199 commenced a rocket run at 1226 steaming 000° T. at one-third speed about 3600 yards from the beach, firing 108 rockets between the villages of Kiyamu and Komesu.[102] Another barrage of 98 rockets followed a dozen minutes later. "The only damage observed was on the town of Komesu on 14 June 1945," noted Lt. Cobb. "This vessel's rocket fire caused an explosion and started a fire in the center of the town. This fact was confirmed by Headquarters First Marine Division's observer in a plane over the target."[103]

Afterwards, *LSM(R) 199* moored alongside the flotilla's flagship to embark the four Marines at 1248,[104] after which *LC(FF) 535* departed for Hagushi Anchorage.

Years after the war, Robert W. Cox, the Pharmacists Mate on *LC(FF) 535* recalled, "I happened to tune in to the 'Travel Channel' on TV. The program that was on at the time was about Okinawa. One of the sequences shown was about the tunnels the Japanese constructed. It was amazing to see this. The work involved must have been tremendous. The narrator also mentioned that 4,000 men committed suicide inside the tunnels. Also shown were the cliffs where others committed suicide. This I witnessed first hand …."[105]

"Doc" Cox continued, "I also was a witness to a very horrible sight which we had no control over. We were patrolling along the southern part of Okinawa at the time. A lot of the natives with their children were jumping off the cliffs, killing themselves. We all felt helpless, unable to do anything about it."[106]

LSM(R) 196 ran low of rockets, however, so after taking on 195 rocket motors and 150 fuses from *LSM(R) 199*, Marine headquarters assigned a single rocket run to the latter rocketship targeting the town of Kiyamu. Positioned nearby was the Japanese 15th Infantry Battalion, and at 1429, *LSM(R) 199* launched 210 rockets while some 3800 yards from the beach.[107]

By 1600, the Marines renewed target areas with Japanese troop concentrations between Makabe and Komesu,[108] where *LSM(R) 199* fired 185 SSRs, then, after immediately repositioning for another rocket run, launched 230 SSRs on the same target by 1620, then departed on course 180° T. at full speed.

With evening darkness, the two rocketships laid to off southern Okinawa maintaining 7000 to 5500 yards from shore until around 2100, when the Marine Corps requested unusual evening naval gunfire support. By 2130, *LSM(R) 199* launched 101 rockets between Nagusuku and Kiyamu,[109] and at 2145, *LSM(R) 196* fired a hundred rockets as well.[110] Thereafter, the two rocketships secured from further call fire support but remained off the southern Okinawa coast overnight.[111]

15 June 1945[112]

During midwatch from 14–15 June, the Officer of the Deck on *LSM(R) 199* noted, "CTG 32.11 has secured us from firing rockets and we are standing by awaiting further orders from CTG 32.11 as to the time we are to again commence firing rockets."[113] When orders finally arrived by mid-morning, the two Spinners got underway but with differing assignments.

LSM(R) 199 sailed seaward and rendezvoused with the fast transport *Scribner APD 122* by 1040, and disembarked the four-man Marine Corps Public Relations party.[114] The rocketship shoved off to moor alongside *LSM(R) 197* to take aboard 150 rocket fuses, then cast off by 1105 to lay off southern Okinawa through noontime awaiting further orders.

LSM(R) 196, meanwhile, proceeded to firing station at 0953, sounded General Quarters at 1025, and launched 117 rockets from 1037 to 1057. SSRs struck target areas that included a road network running west-northwest from Komesu to Nagusuku.[115] This attack would be her final rocket run of the war.

Lt. O'Callaghan summarized his ship's performance off southern Okinawa:

> Results of rocket firing reported to this command by HQ 1st Marine Division were extremely effective. All fire was reported on target causing very effective results…. The performance of both rockets and launchers [were] completely satisfactory to this command. Causes for the few misfires and jams have been determined and action is being taken to prevent reoccurrence. Ammunition expended: 5" Spin stabilized rockets—1607.

The *LSM(R) 196* skipper concluded, "Performance of ships company in execution of this duty is highly commendable."[116]

Leonard VanOteghem, *LSM(R) 196* Signalman, reflected on the past several days in his diary:

> Proceeded with orders to southern Okinawa with *LSM(R)*s *197, 198,* and *199.* We were to operate with the Army artillery and reconnaissance planes. They radioed various targets to us where the Japs were dug in and we threw rockets into them. God only knows how many Japs we killed in this operation. In our operations down here, we fired approximately 1600 rockets in three days. It was extremely successful. A commander in charge of a group of ships in our area said, "Get more targets for these fellows, they can put them in a bucket." Late June 15 we returned to the anchorage.[117]

For *LSM(R) 199*, however, a new gunfire request called for rocket runs aimed between Kiyamu and Komesu villages,[118] where, at 1312, she launched 250 SSRs against enemy infantry positions and followed ten minutes later by a second barrage of 271 rockets.

While *LSM(R) 199* stood by for gunfire support, mid-afternoon orders directed *LSM(R)*s *196, 197* and *198* to retire to Hagushi Anchorage, "Dodger Area," off western Okinawa. Fittingly, as the last of the original class of twelve "Interim" rocketships, fate destined *LSM(R) 199* the last to fire rockets at Okinawa.

LSM(R) 199 resumed rocket attacks on southern Okinawa with orders first directing strikes between Makabe and Medeera,[119] firing 96 then 104 SSRs at 1429 and 1445, respectively. At 1519, she launched a hundred SSRs on a target area bearing 340° T., range 3400 yards,[120] then loosed 148 rockets in areas north-northwest of Komesu and south of Makabe[121] by 1534. After firing another rocket salvo north of Makabe at 1553,[122] USS *LSM(R) 199* struck Okinawa for the last time at 1611 with 108 SSRs falling southwest of Komesu.[123] This final series of far-ranging rocket attacks was also notable for striking an array of enemy ground forces: at Makabe, the 22nd Regiment and 42nd Artillery Regiment; at Madeera, the 24th Infantry Division Headquarters; at Komesu, the 14th Infantry Battalion.

Running low on rockets, the "Forward and midships rocket magazines are empty," noted the ship's log, while the "Aft rocket magazine contains 170 rocket motors and 33 rocket bodies."[124] During the three-day mission from 13 to 15 June, she had expended 3,262 Spin-stabilized Rockets. *LSM(R) 199* now departed southern Okinawa for Hagushi, where she anchored near her three Spinner sister ships by late afternoon.

"Performance of ordnance material was satisfactory" reported Lt. Cobb, and "Performance of personnel was excellent. There were no personnel casualties."[125] The *LSM(R) 199* skipper added, "Headquarters First Marine Division reported that all rocket fire was very effective." Indeed, the Marines themselves testified, "Support craft was [*sic*] employed very effectively during the period. LSM(R)s flattened the town [*sic*] of Makabe and Komesu as well as other small villages in the area."[126]

That evening, Radioman Clyde Blue in *LSM(R) 197* wrote in his diary, "Well we saw more Japs this morning and cut loose at them. We fired the rest of our rockets and came back to the Anchorage about 5 p.m. Never got no mail but heard that we leave Monday for some place. I hope so."[127]

Last Days at Okinawa

After the four Spinners were released from naval gunfire support of U.S. ground forces,[128] 16 June was devoted to repairs and logistics replenishment. "Well," summarized diarist Clyde Blue, "today we loaded stores and took on fuel. We got for the shack cans of fruit juice, pineapple and cherries. The officers get all of that stuff so I guess we might just as well have it as them. No mail again today. Tomorrow's Sunday and I believe Holiday Routine. There aren't as many ships here as there use to be. A couple battleships are sitting off our stern aways."[129]

Early next morning of 17 June,[130] *LSM(R)s 198* and *199* weighed anchor and rendezvoused six miles north of "Point Sexton" with a convoy designated Task Unit 31.29.10/Task Unit 96.5.9 that set sail for Leyte, Philippine Islands.

Meanwhile, Ensign Lawrence Low, Gunnery Officer on *LSM(R) 197*, noted the latest news in his diary. "17 June: All Jap resistance on Okinawa suddenly reported crumbling. Officers are committing suicide and men are surrendering in the greatest numbers ever experienced in the Pacific war. Many are blowing themselves to bits with grenades while others are burying themselves in mud."[131]

They also got some hopeful if not curious news. "Well today was Sunday and I slept all day long. Ha ha," wrote Clyde Blue from *LSM(R) 197*. "We leave tomorrow morning for Saipan. Then I think right on to Pearl Harbor…. I think we are going to leave our rocket launchers there and at Pearl I think we are going to be made into a straight LSM. If that's so, there will be quite a few of the boys transferred. I haven't been writing any letters as we couldn't get them off the ship…. I have the mid watch tonight. We have been copying code for the flagship for the last two days but are secured now."[132]

Preparing to leave Okinawa, Ensign Low added in his diary, "*LSM(R) 197* standing by in Hagushi Anchorage prior to getting underway for Saipan, Marianas Islands at 1000, 18 June 1945."[133] His rocketship soon joined sister ship *LSM(R) 196* and flotilla flagship *LC(FF) 535* to rendezvous with a convoy designated Task Unit 31.29.12. En route, Signalman Leonard

VanOteghem on *LSM(R) 196* took a final look back. "Departed from Okinawa. This was three days before the island was completely secured, and all that was left was just the mopping up. We had been here since 6 days before the invasion, totaling 84 days in the campaign. We went to GQ 117 times, and spent 103 hours at our battle stations. We were now headed for Saipan with a convoy of about 35 ships including our escorts."[134]

CHAPTER 11

Return to Pearl Harbor

Upon release from fire support missions, the LSM(R)s departed Okinawa for Pearl Harbor in task units among three convoys on 3 June, 17 June, and 18 June 1945.

The First LSM(R) Convoy: 3 June 1945 to 7 July 1945

On 1 June 1945, *LSM(R) 192* and *LSM(R) 193* were relieved from close fire support for HQ 7th Infantry Division, and on 2 June 1945 *LSM(R) 189* and *LSM(R) 191* were relieved from close fire support for Sixth Marine Division. The four Finner rocketships remained in the Hagushi Anchorage to take on provisions and refuel as new orders were rapidly forthcoming. "Group Commander received CTF 31's 311315, 011430 and 020605 Secret Dispatches," explained Lieutenant Commander John H. Fulweiler, "directing *LSM(R)s 189, 191, 192* and *193* with 8 LSMs and 2 LSDs to proceed 3 June to Leyte for availability. ComLSM(R)Group27 OTC until *LSD 8* joins convoy."[1] Lt. Comdr. Fulweiler would be embarked in *LSM(R) 193* and the estimated arrival in the Philippines was 8 June.[2]

By 0730 of 3 June, the four rocketships departed Hagushi to converge with other ships north of Keise Shima in accordance with CTG 51.22,[3] then were "Underway to rendezvous point south of Kerama Retto where convoy will form up," noted Ensign F. Donald Moore on *LSM(R) 189*.[4] On departing Okinawa, Storekeeper Robert W. Landis in *LSM(R) 192* remarked, "Today we learned we would return to Pearl [Harbor] with the *189, 191* and the *193* for repairs and preparations for the big invasion of Japan..."[5]

Task Unit 31.29.23 set course due south at 9 knots assuming 600-yard distances between columns and 300-yard intervals between ships in each column.[6] As OTC, *LSM(R) 193* was guide of the starboard column followed astern by *LSM(R)s 192, 191*, and *189*. Guided at first by a DE flanked by SCs and AMs, *White Marsh LSD 8* then assumed convoy guide on the starboard column, while *Casa Grande LSD 13* assumed guide of the port column. "Disposition is two columns of LSMs and one of LSM(R)s. LSD guides for columns one and three. Screen deployed by Escort Commanders," duly recorded Lt. Comdr. Fulweiler.[7] Secret dispatch ComPhibPac 020526 further advised Fulweiler of "granting six days availability on reporting to ComServronTen [Commander, Service Squadron Ten] at Leyte. Relayed message to all LSM(R)s and LSMs."[8]

The convoy zigzagged briefly then continued due south. That evening the weather turned so sour with heavy rains that the LSM(R)s depended on radars for station keeping.

259

By 0700 of 4 June the convoy altered direction: "Changed course to 090°—attempting to miss typhoon," observed Ensign F. Donald Moore, then added, "Ship pitching and rolling heavily. Sea rough with moderate swells."[9] After passing the typhoon's track, the convoy resumed its southward course that evening.

On 6 June at 1730, floating mines were sighted 450–500 yards to port and starboard of the convoy, for which the destroyer escort left formation to investigate and destroy.

In mid-afternoon of 7 June, *LSM(R) 192* left formation to test pyrotechnics at the rear of the starboard column. Upon conclusion of the test firing, the ship returned to her convoy position by 1515, when the OOD Ensign Victor C. Anderson cryptically noted in the ship's log, "Discovered some damage through water." Equally mysterious was a green flare observed 090° relative at 2125 that evening, although its origin could not be determined.

By 0530 of 8 June, the convoy entered Leyte Gulf, Philippines, and soon passed net buoys marking the harbor entrance. Forming a column, the ships followed the channel to San Pedro Bay, where the four LSM(R)s left formation and moored together off the town of Tacloban by noontime.

Lt. Comdr. Fulweiler went ashore from 1240 to 1720, and upon his return the four rock-etships were relocated to another berth to anchor for the night. "Group commander [Ful-weiler] reported to ComServronTen and four LSM(R)s ordered to *Vulcan AR5* at berth 71 Leyte for at anchor availability. Group Commander and Group Engineer reported with work requests to Repair Officer on *Vulcan*."[10] Movies were shown this evening aboard *LSM(R)s 191* and *193*.

While at Leyte from 9 to16 June, liberty parties went ashore to the Fleet Recreation Center each day. The four LSM(R)s underwent rework alongside the *Vulcan* repairship, which was tied adjacent to the damaged battleship *New Mexico BB 40*. In one instance, *LSM(R) 192*'s lifeline stanchions were re-welded on the port side of the fantail, repairing remnants of the damage from the Kamikaze crash of 4 May at Okinawa. In other work, explained OOD Ensign J. R. Thompson, fitters and welders "commenced cutting away protruding angle irons on main deck. Vestiges of side launchers," referring to the Mark 30 rocket launchers removed in early April at Okinawa.

After repairs and rework, each rocketship re-fueled from oilers and loaded provisions and ammunition, including rockets from transport and cargo ships. *LSM(R) 189* reported taking 2500 rocket motors, 2282 nose fuses, and 2500 rocket bodies, while *LSM(R) 192* took aboard 1140 rocket bodies and 888 rocket motors.

The evening of 15 June, ComPhibsPac directed via secret dispatch 140720 that the LSM(R)s report to the Port Director for onward routing to Pearl Harbor. After a captains conference next morning, the *LSM(R) 192* watch officer reported, "Crew jubilant about returning to Pearl Harbor. All convinced we are heading for the States with 30-day leaves in prospect."

From late morning though evening of 16 June, *LSM(R)s 189, 191* and *192* beached and retracted off the nearby Naval Refuse Dump, Samar, Philippine Islands. "Ship beached for first time in its career," noted *LSM(R) 192*'s OOD Ensign Thomas D. Boak in the ship's log. Work parties threw empty wood ammunition crates over the sides and discarded spent 5-inch brass shell casings for the dump.

After a departure conference of commanding officers aboard *LSM(R) 193*, in early after-noon of 17 June the four LSM(R)s set sail from Leyte to Eniwetok Atoll. The ships formed

in open numerical order—*LSM(R)*s *193* (OTC), *192*, *191* and *189*—in Dog Cruising formation at convoy speed of 10 knots. The next day, however, "Main gusts from northeast [made
it] impossible to see the other ships in group except in lightning flashes," noted one ship's
watch officer, and radio messages relayed typhoon advisories.

Allied ships and aircraft occasionally passed the task unit, but Japanese submarines were
also on the prowl. "Due to numerous submarine reports [we] have set special watch on 5"/38,"
reported Lt. Comdr. Fulweiler on 19 June. Two days later on 21 June, *LSM(R) 189* "took
extra precautions against submarines, when notified by *LSM(R) 193* of three recent torpedo
messages." Another interest to enemy subs was Ulithi Atoll, a major hub of American naval
activity, which the convoy passed this same day in mid-morning 18 miles to starboard.

Activities at sea were otherwise routine: passing guard mail and movie reels, firing practices and tactical maneuvers, signal flag hoist exercises, and emergency drills. Interestingly,
from 0130 to 0445 of 26 June *LSM(R) 189* noted the earth's eclipse of the moon that resulted
in a near-total, albeit brief, lunar black out.

Before dawn of 27 June, lights were sighted from Eniwetok Atoll in the Marshall Islands.
The ships entered the harbor after 0800 and soon tied up alongside yard oilers for re-fueling
until noontime; afterwards, the four LSM(R)s nested together. Here a seaman reported for
duty aboard *LSM(R) 189*, returning since his transfer for medical treatment at a naval hospital
after the radar picket station air attacks at Okinawa on 12 April 1945.

The following day on 28 June, the four rocketships cast off, sortied and departed Eniwetok in column formation for Pearl Harbor, Territory of Hawaii. "In accordance with Com-
PhibsPac's 140720 and Routing Instructions of Port Director Eniwetok, Unit designated as
96.5.17–ComLSM(R)Group27 in *LSM(R) 193* C.T.U.," noted Lt. Comdr. Fulweiler.[ll]

En route, ships' forces contended with sporadic steering problems, engine breakdowns,
and inexplicable damage. The afternoon of 30 June, *LSM(R) 191* suddenly lost power,
sounded two warning blasts, broke out the breakdown flag, and swung to port across the formation's axis as steering gear repairs were made; yet ten minutes later the rocketship returned
to formation. The next day, *LSM(R) 189* discovered a split in her bilge about 3" long in the
after steering flat, and flooding and further damage was controlled by shoring. On 3 and 4
July, respectively, *LSM(R) 193* suffered a faulty rudder angle indicator and then an inoperative
gyro compass, which swung her off course and forced the helm to steer by magnetic compass
until fixed. A day later, a sudden power failure in *LSM(R) 192* shut down her gyro and radar
equipment for a time.

Because erstwhile guide and OTC *LSM(R) 193* fell astern with persistent steering problems, *LSM(R) 192* assumed guide of the open order formation, followed in turn by *LSM(R)*s
191 and *189*. Meanwhile, activities included firing exercises by the gun crews; the occasional
passing of guard mail; exchanging movies, and sharing a film projector for crew entertainment
as the task unit quietly crossed the International Date Line on 2 July. The rocketships' signalmen even competed with one another during flag hoist drills, prompting Gunnery Officer
Ensign Thomas Boak to proclaim in the ship's log, "*LSM(R) 192* definitely superior."

During the evening of 6 July, now only a half-day's journey away from Pearl Harbor, an
unidentified transport ship cut through the convoy. Ships' radars had tracked the cargo vessel
for hours while still miles ahead on the horizon, but it continued headlong toward the four
rocketships regardless. Ensign Victor C. Anderson explained while standing OOD watch,
"Above target is merchant ship bearing down on this formation on our port bow. At 2000

yards she suddenly changed her course and is cutting across our bow. This ship gave 3 blasts and backed down full. Merchant ship passed from port to starboard ahead of this ship. Merchant ship showing range lights, also running lights and stern wake light. *LSM(R) 193* changed course slightly when this ship backed down."

Near 0800 of 7 July 1945, the four Finner rocketships arrived in Pearl Harbor and proceeded to George Berths in Middle Lock; soon, Lt. Comdr. Fulweiler reported to Commander, Administrative Command, Amphibious Forces, U.S. Pacific Fleet. As liberty parties went ashore, they were greeted by new instructions: "*LSM(R)s 189, 191, 192, 193* with *188* ordered to Navy Yard for conversion to Ammunition Carriers."[12]

The Second LSM(R) Convoy: 17 June 1945 to 25 July 1945

On 15 June 1945, *LSM(R) 198* and *LSM(R) 199* were relieved from close fire support for HQ 7th Infantry Division and HQ 1st Marine Division, respectively. Both Spinners remained in the Hagushi anchorage to take on provisions and refuel while awaiting further orders. Within days, new orders directed both rocketships to join convoy Task Unit 31.29.10 departing Okinawa on 17 June en route Leyte, Philippines. The convoy, composed of 19 LSMs, included an LC(FF) flagship, a destroyer escort, one rescue tugboat, a minelayer, and two subchasers. The estimated arrival in Leyte was 22 June.[13]

The two rocketships rendezvoused with the other warships before 0800 of 17 June, northeast of the Kerama Retto islands. *LSM(R)s 198* and *199* assumed convoy position as the third and fourth ships in the fourth column, respectively, and about an hour later the task unit set course south at 9 knots.

During the passage, *LSM(R) 198* repaired a broken fuel line on 18 June; the next day she went alongside both *LSM(R) 199* and *LSM 235* for cylinder heads to repair her port engine. On 20 June, both rocketships commenced firing practice of their 40mm guns; then later that day the convoy commander designated *LSM(R) 199* as radar guide for the convoy from sunset to sunrise.

Early in the morning of 22 June, the convoy stood outside Leyte Gulf and entered the channel to northern San Pedro Bay. En route, an alert lookout in *LSM(R) 199* spotted a frantic, dog-paddling pooch in the waters and warned "dog overboard." The canine proved to be "Bill the Dog," a Chesapeake Retriever and beloved mascot of USS *LSM(R) 198*. Bill's owner was Executive Officer Lt. (jg) George M. Addison, Jr., since before the rocketship had been commissioned. Bill had somehow slipped over the side, but he was soon rescued and happily returned to his grateful master.[14]

By 1200, the two rocketships were anchored and tied alongside for ten days' availability in the shipyard under ComServRon 10. Shipyard activities at Leyte included replenishment, working parties, and repairs facilitated by the repair ship *Cebu ARG 6*. Meanwhile, mail call was held and liberty parties sent ashore.

A shipyard officer inspected the Mark 51 rocket launchers on both rocketships on 24 June, and two days later an eight-man working party from *Cebu*, comprising four shipfitters and four electricians, disconnected cables and fittings and cut loose all launchers from the decks. Finished by midday, the two rocketships shifted moorage near *YF-732* floating crane, where all rocket launchers with firing and warning apparatus were removed and placed in a nearby barge.

*LSM(R)*s *198* and *199* were ordered onward to Guam and departed San Pedro Bay and Leyte, Philippines the afternoon of 2 July. The five-day journey was uneventful and the ships arrived at Apra Harbor, Guam, the morning of 7 July. The rocketships moored in a nest of LSMs along the southern side of the breakwater at Luminar Reef, where they received supplies, repairs, fuel and mail over the next two days.

On 9 July, the two rocketships set course with orders to Eniwetok Atoll, arriving mid-morning of 14 July for re-fueling; however, engine repairs in *LSM(R) 199* delayed departure from Eniwetok until the afternoon of 15 July.

With new orders to Pearl Harbor, both rocketships set sail from Eniwetok accompanied astern by *LCS 88* as Task Unit 96.5.9 with CTU and guide in *LSM(R) 198*. The seas were heavy with frequent rain squalls; en route, *LSM(R) 199* reported two small yet persistent leaks in her after steering compartment. After crossing the International Date Line on 20 July, *LSM(R) 198* suffered intermittent breakdowns with her steering gear, rudder indicator, and an engine fuel line, while *LSM(R) 199* also lost operation of her SU-1 radar.

After dawn of 25 July, land was sighted and by mid-morning the task unit was lying outside the channel entrance to Pearl Harbor; by noon, the two rocketships were moored together in George Berth, Middle Lock, Pearl Harbor Navy Yard. Here, "*LSM(R)*s *198* and *199* reported to Commander, Administrative Command, Amphibious Forces, US Pacific Fleet for conversion" to Ammunition Carriers, noted Lt. Cmdr. Fulweiler, and that evening a work party commenced unloading ammunition to a barge.[15]

The Third LSM(R) Convoy: 18 June 1945 to 11 July 1945

On 15 June 1945, *LSM(R) 196* was relieved from close fire support for HQ 1st Marine Division; and *LSM(R) 197* was relieved from close fire support for HQ 7th Infantry Division. Taking on provisions and fuel in the Hagushi anchorage, the two rocketships and LSM Flotilla Nine's flagship *LC(FF) 535* were directed to join Task Unit 31.29.12 sailing from Okinawa on 18 June en route to Saipan. The convoy comprised a cargo transport,[16] one other LC(FF) flagship, a destroyer, four minesweepers, 21 LSTs, 10 LSMs, and a repair ship for an estimated arrival on 24 June.[17]

Over noontime, *LSM(R)*s *196* and *197* heaved to about two miles northeast of Kerama Retto, and *LC(FF) 535* passed mail and transferred passengers among several LSMs. Around 1300 the three ships fell into convoy position as *LSM(R) 196* assumed lead ship of the sixth of seven divisions, and *LSM(R) 197* followed 300 yards astern. *LC(FF) 1080* was OTC and *LST 923* served as formation guide ship, setting an initial base course due south at six knots, then increasing to standard convoy speed of nine knots.

On *LSM(R) 197*, Radioman Clyde Blue wrote in his diary,

We left for Saipan around 8:30 this morning and are to arrive on the 24th or near there. Then we are supposed to go on to the Pearl Harbor. We are with a group of LSMs and LSTs. About 25 of us altogether. We have had bogie reports all night but none have came very close to us. I don't know if we will stay very long at Saipan or not. We may stop in the Marshall Islands again on the way back. It takes about 22 days for a LST to make it from Saipan to P. H. What a trip that would be.[18]

Signalman Leonard VanOteghem in *LSM(R) 196* added to his journal, "We were going to be converted into rocket carriers for the new LSM(R)s that were coming out. Our days as a rocket ship were over."[19]

As the convoy proceeded onward, General Quarters was routinely sounded at dawn, then secured about an hour later. On the first morning at sea, the convoy veered course when a floating mine was sighted ahead 300 yards to starboard. Several days later in the early hours of 22 June, the convoy's screen warned of a submarine contact and the formation responded with zigzag maneuvers and executed emergency turns intermittently in the days ahead. The passage was otherwise uneventful, as routine reports on fuel and water levels were relayed by flaghoist and ships occasionally closed alongside to pass mail and engine parts, but more often exchanged movies, film projectors, and even a film splicer.

"At 1320 radar picks up land at 56 miles, dead ahead," noted *LSM(R) 197*'s OOD Ensign Lawrence J. Low, as the convoy neared Saipan on 24 June. Then, two hours later, "LSMs and LSM(R)s separated from main body on signal and proceeded ahead of convoy under ComLSMFlot13 in USS *LSM 372*," explained Ensign David Mallery, OOD aboard *LSM(R) 196*, to which Ensign Low added: "At 1525 changed speed to full 13 knots (710 rpm). At 1534 changed speed to flank, 740 rpm."[20] By late afternoon, *LC(FF) 535* with *LSM(R)s 196* and *197* were berthed in "L" or Love Anchorage, Naval Base Saipan.

The brief layover in Saipan allowed just enough time to take on fuel, fresh water, and provisions. Here *LSM(R) 197* also unloaded 190 cases of 40mm HEIT to a naval base boat, while *LC(FF) 535* transferred 18 Mark V smoke pots and 36 Mark IV smoke pots to another flotilla flagship. By 0800 of 26 June, the three amphibians weighed anchors and were underway at 11 knots from Saipan's harbor to Pearl Harbor, with *LSM(R) 196* as acting OTC followed astern by *LSM(R) 197* and *LC(FF) 535*.

Upon leaving Saipan, however, both *LSM(R) 197* and *LC(FF) 535* developed engine problems, and the latter requested the OTC at one point to reduce speed to 8 knots while undergoing repairs. Although convoy speed was resumed soon thereafter, engine troubles plagued Commander Francis' flotilla flagship.

At 1630 of 28 June, lookouts in *LSM(R) 196* warned of a solitary hull approaching on the horizon, and in half an hour a U.S. destroyer closed on the three amphibians. "Sighted *DD 577* off starboard bow," reported Ensign David Mallery as OOD, which he identified as the *Sproston*, the very same destroyer that so easily passed them earlier this morning. After immediately establishing visual contact when in range, the destroyer abruptly assumed temporary tactical command of the amphibious trio[21] to support ASW (Anti-Submarine Warfare) sweeps. Sounding General Quarters, Ens. Mallery recorded in the ship's log, "Course diverted for these three ships to join *DD 577* in search of two submarines known to be in area and to have been damaged by gunfire from *DD 577* several hours before."[22]

Earlier that afternoon, *Antares AKS 3* had radioed distress signals as her crew bravely returned fire under heavy attacks by Japanese submarines. Only *Sproston*'s fortuitous intercession saved the large cargo ship from further harm. (By coincidence, *Antares* had also sailed in the convoy from Okinawa to Saipan with *LSM(R)s 196, 197* and *LC(FF) 535*.) For nearly three hours, the lone destroyer made repeated hunter-killer counterattacks, including ramming, gunfire, and sustained depth charging until entirely expended. But *Sproston* lost visual and sonar contacts with the enemy subs by 1656, so the destroyer cast a wider dragnet for what was learned much later to be the Imperial Japanese Navy's *I-36* submarine and her smaller *Kaiten* ("Heaven Shaker") offspring.

IJN Lieutenant Commander Sugamasa Tetsuaki commanded the HIJMS *I-36*, a Type B1 fast, long-range submarine modified to carry six *Kaiten* midget subs on her back. *Kaiten* were the Imperial Japanese Navy's sea-going kamikazes: manned torpedoes guided to crash into their targets. The week before, the "mother" submarine had deployed two *Kaiten* in a combined attack on shipping in Saipan Harbor on 21 June, but both midget subs malfunctioned. The *I-36* skipper was nonetheless persistent, and before slipping away he torpedoed the anchored repair ship *Endymion ARL 9*.[23]

A week after the Saipan Harbor attack, at midday of 28 June 1945 the *I-36* was some 400 nautical miles NNE of Truk Island and stalking the *Antares*. After launching a *Kaiten*, it and the larger submarine commenced joint attacks about 1330, and over the next thirty minutes the cargo ship evaded at least one torpedo and sank the midget sub with gunfire. When USS *Sproston* interceded about 1400, the mother Japanese sub launched more *Kaitens*, but one was sunk by the destroyer's gunfire while the *I-36* sustained damage from repeated depth charging. Yet the enemy submarine evaded pursuit, so *Sproston* radioed a fleetwide alert:

QNL—A—D577–280900 00 GR54
BT SPROSTON WENT TO ASSIST ANTARES UNDER SUB ATTACK X LARGE SUB SIGHTED VISUALLY IN CLEAR WATER ON FIRST ATTACK X ATTACKS REPEATED BY SONAR X ALL DEPTH CHARGES EXPENDED X TWO TORPEDOES FIRED AT SPROSTON X MIDGET SUB SIGHTED AWASH X ATTACKED BY GUN FIRE X BOTH SUBS BELIEVED DAMAGED X OIL SLICK IN AREA SPROSTON BT.[24]

By 1747, the Fletcher-class destroyer assumed column guide ship with *LSM(R)s 196* and *197* with *LC(FF) 535* forming astern on course 090° True (T.). Steaming East and maintaining 2000-yard intervals between ships, distances were increased to 4000 yards some thirty minutes later. Speeds, however, were limited to about nine knots because the flotilla flagship was operating on only one engine.[25]

A PBM patrol seaplane arrived overhead to join the ASW screen around 1817. Meanwhile, the destroyer designated *LSM(R) 197* as the new formation guide, and *Sproston* fell astern followed by *LSM(R) 196* and *LC(FF) 535*. After thirty minutes, the column executed ships right, bearing South at 180° True, and swept areas of previous submarine contacts, then twenty minutes later the formation turned right again to bear West at 270° T. At 2000 the column turned once more to form a line of bearing 000° T. due North, then after twenty-five minutes, the formation executed ships left bearing West again on course 270° True. Soon, a second PBM arrived over the area to expand the sub hunt.

Sproston began picking up a surface radar contact at fifteen miles, although not a definite pip, bearing SSW at 188° True. At 2052, the column executed ships left to turn south toward the unknown target and the destroyer retook formation guide. Soon *Sproston* got a more definite radar contact and sent a PBM to investigate, but the seaplane reported back, "no contact, weather." Undeterred, at 2105 the destroyer commander ordered the column to execute ships right bearing West once more on course 270° T.

By 2145, *Sproston* ordered intervals between ships opened to three miles, although the destroyer commander sensed something didn't add up: "Radar contact obviously not weather and tracking had obtained course of 290° T. speed 18–20 knots. PBM sent to investigate again reported 'no contact.'"[26]

In the next twenty-five minutes, *LC(FF) 535* reported sighting an unidentified ship through the darkness but moving in the opposite direction about six miles north, while at this same time *Sproston* tracked a surface contact at 13 miles bearing 237° True. "Landing craft reported radar surface contact to northward," noted the destroyer's commander, however, "None of the above contacts answered to challenges on voice radio. *Sproston* proceeded to investigate contact now to WSW and landing craft in charge of *LSM 196* [*sic*] directed to investigate contact to north."[27] The destroyer quickly left formation at 2215 and steamed southwesterly as the three amphibians sounded General Quarters once more and came right on course 000° due North.

Meanwhile, visual contact of the northerly target was lost in the darkness, last reported at 2210 bearing 028° T. at 5 and a half miles' distance. But another mysterious sighting was made about 2255,[28] and tension mounted. What followed was a near-fatal encounter, recalled in remarkable detail by Quartermaster-striker Bruce McDaniel in *LSM(R) 196*:

> I was on the conn through that whole event, where as during general quarters [Engineering Officer] Shedd was usually in the engine room and Mallery being the Communications Officer would usually be in the radio compartment. The usual people on deck at night were lookouts in the 40mm gun tubs and during GQ hatches were dogged down and the only personnel on deck were the gun crews and those on the open conn.
>
> It was late in the day and was soon dark, lookouts were on the alert and I began to see what could be the conning tower of a sub about fifteen degrees off the starboard bow, at some considerable distance of a few miles. I had become cautious about reporting what I saw as [Commanding Officer] O'Callaghan had made a dig about what I saw. After a bit, I think it was Mallery on watch, I told him what I saw, to which he asked how long I had been watching it, I said about fifteen minutes, he said, FIFTEEN MINUTES?
>
> At any rate, General Quarters was sounded and I was told to report the object's bearings. There was a certain advantage to being higher up than the other lookouts in the gun tubs had been. O'Callaghan called down the tube asking radar if anything had been detected, saying there is a man up here who says there is an object out there. Radar man's answer was negative....
>
> The Captain ordered all ahead full, even at that we hardly seemed to be closing the distance as the quarry seem to be moving pretty fast. They were unaware of us. After some time, radar finally had a blip on the screen and could not get a response on the grass, the IFF, a bar graph in green looking like grass that could give corresponding elevations in the (grass) in code response or Identification Friend or Foe. Mine sweepers being mostly wood explains to some degree why radar was not able to pick up on it right away.
>
> The Captain tells [S2c Edwin C.] Schaefer (I think he was the Signalman) to use the infra red lamp on them (a hand held lamp with a red lens that always smelled like iodine), there was no reply, the target (by now) was finally on radar, held its course steady and we could barely close with it.
>
> Finally the Captain ordered star shells from the five inch to be fired over the ship. None of these worked, just a little spark then nothing but a faint smoke trail as it descended, by then we were following at top speed in the wake of the ship which had long revealed to not be a sub ... some claimed we had got the [star] shells from the [*LSM(R)*] *188* and that is why they didn't work. Finally I could see a thin sliver of light coming from a crack in a hatch. At this time every gun including the five inch were trained point blank at the ship, everyone with itchy fingers.
>
> So a top secret code book with a yellow cover was consulted for the light sequence arrangement identification friend or foe but had not received a response. When the mast head yard signal was lit the ship being pursued returned the signal on its yard but it was the wrong one for that day.
>
> The Captain says to the Signalman, signal them with an open light, which he did, we got an immediate response. "This is the US minesweeper so and so" at the time we were ready to blow him out of the water, before he finally woke up to our presence fast astern, not much to say for their observance.[29]

Radioman Clyde Blue in *LSM(R) 197* noted this incident in his diary as well.

We got a contact about 10 p.m. and it kept closing us so we went to GQ and the *196* and LCI and us went to investigate. We intercepted it and challenged it but no answer. We then challenged it by radio and no answer. We fired 4 star shells over it and finally it blinked back the wrong signal. Then it came back with the right one. We still were not sure of it and blinked again…. Then it came up on the radio and I sure thought he was a dead duck when he couldn't answer the signals. He sure was a dumb one.[30]

Once contact was finally established after exchanging proper recognition signals the mystery ship identified herself as *YMS 268*,[31] one of three Navy minesweepers[32] responding to earlier emergency radio messages that Japanese submarines were attacking *Antares* and *Sproston*. Now the minesweeping trio prepared to assist the sub hunt utilizing sonar.

Securing from General Quarters, the three amphibious landing ships resumed their anti-submarine screen, maneuvering various courses and speeds. *LSM(R) 196* continued as column guide and remained OTC because *LC(FF) 535* still had engine troubles and was lagging behind.

By half-past midnight, *Sproston* returned after investigating the unknown surface contact. Despite incorrect responses to challenges, the target was eventually identified as friendly and appeared to be a large XAK transport, thought a Victory Ship.[33] Soon, destroyer-escorts *Parks DE 165* and *Levy DE 162* also reported for anti-submarine patrols, so with additional screening ships at hand, *Sproston* released command of the three amphibious landing ships by 0123 of 29 June 1945 to proceed onward and carry out previous orders.

(Despite thorough Hunter-Killer sweeps overnight from 28–29 June, the *I-36* Japanese submarine escaped, although she sustained a leak in her torpedo room and a damaged rudder from numerous depth charge explosions. The sub and her crew survived the war, in fact, albeit narrowly escaping an attacking American patrol plane and evading torpedoes from a U.S. submarine while returning to her naval base at Kure, Japan, by 6 July 1945. After the war ended, *I-36* was surrendered and later scuttled in deep Japanese waters by the U.S. Navy on 1 April 1946.)[34]

LSM(R) 196, setting course once more for Pearl Harbor, resumed OTC and column guide bearing 105° T. at nine knots, while *LSM(R) 197* and *LC(FF) 535* formed astern at 300-yards intervals (although the flotilla flagship would continue to suffer persistent engine breakdowns, occasional mechanical or electrical steering failures, and even a contaminated fuel problem). For the balance of the journey, the ships exchanged mail, movies, and spare parts, and drilled at burst firing practices of the 5"/38, 40mm, 20mm, .50 caliber, and small arms fire. On 6 July, the three amphibians crossed the International Dateline. Only days before reaching Pearl Harbor, *LSM(R) 196* also developed engine troubles, which at one point forced her to fall astern briefly for repairs as *LSM(R) 197* assumed temporary formation guide.

By mid-afternoon of 11 July, the three landing ships approached Pearl Harbor and entered the channel entrance, when OOD Ensign Lawrence J. Low noted in *LSM(R) 197*'s log, "At 1500 blinker from ashore, 'Welcome to Pearl Harbor after your recent support of operations.'" Signalman Leonard VanOteghem in *LSM(R) 196* also remarked in his diary, "Upon arrival, we got a message from the tower, welcoming us back to Pearl from a job well done. This made us all feel good."[35] Another Signalman, Karl G. Matchett in *LSM(R) 197* added to his journal that day, "It surely looks good to us! … Got 23 letters and 2 packages today. Things have changed a lot since we were here in January. Not quite so crowded."[36]

Soon after mooring in Middle Lock, "*LSM(R)s 196* and *197* reported to Commander, Administrative Command, Amphibious Forces, US Pacific Fleet for conversion" to Ammunition Carriers.[37]

CHAPTER 12

Ammunition Carriers

"I guess we will be here [in Pearl Harbor] until August some time. Then back out to the Pacific again," Radioman Clyde Blue confided in his diary aboard *LSM(R) 197*. The next day he added, "We are supposed to be converted to a ammunition ship and carry rockets. They say we will be here until August 15 at least. I sure hope so. There is a possibility that we may go to the states to get our rockets."[1] Still, shipmate Signalman Karl Matchett was cautious: "Lots of 'scuttlebutt' aboard…"[2]

Speculation about the futures of the "Interim" LSM(R)s was nothing new. At one time, reconversion of the eight Finner *LSM(R)s 188* through *195* into Spinner rocketships with new Mark 51 launchers was anticipated.[3] By mid–April 1945, Vice Admiral Richmond Kelly Turner recommended "highest priority action" for LSM(R)s and other ship types fitted out as special fighter director ships for the radar picket stations, "mounting air and surface search radars with good CIC and powerful communications and maximum 40mm director controlled AA plus 20mm AA."[4] Those notions were supplanted by yet another proposal, where "the original twelve [LSM(R)s] … will probably be re-converted to their original LSM status and replaced by an additional twelve [Ultimate] LSM(R) [*sic*] of latest construction."[5]

Conjectures were finally dispelled in May 1945, however, when Fleet Admiral Nimitz promulgated conversions of the nine surviving "Interim" LSM(R)s, as Admiral Turner noted. "The LSM(R) turned in an altogether creditable performance and is considered here to stay. New LSM(R) [*sic*] will be equipped in a much better fashion to fulfill their mission and eventually the interim type [of LSM(R)] used at Okinawa will be utilized as ammunition carriers. Their capacious magazines, well insulated and ventilated, should make them ideal for this purpose."[6] That purpose would be to transport and supply rocket munitions for the "Ultimate" LSM(R)s during the two invasions of Imperial Japan under Operation Downfall.

Operation Downfall: Olympic and Coronet

From late 1944 into early 1945, the U.S. Joint Chiefs of Staff (JCS) pressed the strategic defeat of Japan through encirclement, blockade, and bombardment which was favored by Fleet Admiral Ernest King. Admiral Chester Nimitz also devised Operation Longtom to seize coastal areas of China, Korea and outlying Japanese islands to establish U.S. air and naval bases from which to intensify aerial raids and tighten sea lanes to isolate, strangle and destroy Japan's war-making capacity. But the JCS also acknowledged an invasion of the Japanese homeland was an option which was strongly favored by Generals George Marshall and Douglas MacArthur. So the question became: Which strategy would force Japanese unconditional surrender sooner?[7]

Between these contending prospects and their often-contentious proponents, the invasion of Japan prevailed and was codenamed Operation Downfall, which the JCS outlined in two phases: first, Operation Olympic would assault, capture and defend the southern island of Kyushu beginning X-Day, slated for 1 December 1945; three months later, Operation Coronet would invade the main island of Honshu, the heartland of Japan including Tokyo, on Y-Day, set for 1 March 1946.

On 3 April 1945 the JCS directed General MacArthur and Admiral Nimitz to coordinate detailed planning for Downfall; a week later, Admiral King appointed Admirals Raymond Spruance and Richmond K. Turner to command the initial amphibious and supporting forces for Olympic.

Through May 1945, MacArthur and Nimitz developed respective organizational guides and staff studies for army and navy forces in Operation Olympic. By the end of the month, logistical resources reserved for Operation Longtom were reassigned to Operation Olympic. The former plan was shelved indefinitely and all but cancelled on 25 May when the JCS issued the formal directive to implement plans for the invasion of Kyushu, but adjusted the assault date to 1 November due to operational weather concerns. The JCS also assigned General MacArthur primary responsibility over Operation Olympic while correlating naval and amphibious operations with Admiral Nimitz.[8] By 14 June Admiral Turner commenced planning for the Kyushu campaign, and just four days later on 18 June President Truman approved Operation Olympic. (Plans for Operation Coronet were only preliminary outlines when Japan surrendered.)

Operation Olympic would be the largest combined air-sea-land campaign of the war. Under Nimitz,[9] the Third and Fifth Fleets were the primary naval forces of more than 3,000 vessels. Admiral Halsey's Third Fleet would comprise carriers and battleships for air and surface fire support; Admiral Spruance's Fifth Fleet would comprise amphibious and gunfire supports to transport, land, and sustain troops fighting on southern Kyushu. Under the Fifth Fleet, Admiral Turner as Commander Amphibious Forces Pacific Fleet would command the Third, Fifth, and Seventh Amphibious Forces for the assault landings at Ariake Bay, Kushikino, and Miyazaki, respectively, by the Sixth Army under General Walter Krueger commanding more than 800,000 Army infantry and Marines.[10]

Under Operation Olympic, the nine surviving LSM(R)s (redesignated LSM(E) Ammo Carriers) were assigned to the Fifth Fleet, and since Nimitz preferred that ships continue to operate under their regular administrative flotilla and group commanders where possible, the former rocketships would remain under command of Lt. Comdr. John H. Fulweiler as Commander, LSM Group 27. At Pearl Harbor, these LSM(E)s were to load 5" SSR, 4.2" mortar, 40mm and 20mm ammunitions "to capacity," then report to ComPhibGrp13 under Rear Admiral Ralph O. Davis in Leyte, Philippines by 5 October 1945 for staging and rehearsals.[11] After mounting out under Task Force 42 with elements of Admiral Turner's Amphibious Advance Force (Task Force 41), they were to arrive off the southwestern Kyushu island of Koshiki Retto during U.S. Army landings on X-Day-minus-Four, then to other Kyushu invasion beaches as directed.[12]

LSM(R) Conversions in Pearl Harbor

Appropriately, as first of the class of rocketships, USS *LSM(R) 188* became the prototype (or "guinea pig"[13]) for conversion as the first ammunition ship, albeit circuitously.

After leaving Okinawa on 14 April 1945, the crew's morale slumped in part from the minimal ship maintenance and repairs since the deadly Japanese plane crash on 29 March, and because their fate lingered in limbo for weeks on end after arriving in the Ulithi advanced fleet base on 23 April. A sailor in *LSM(R) 188* commented in his diary on 26 April, "We might not go home but it will be a long time before this ship will be ready to see more action," then added on 7 May, "We are patched up enough to shove off now…. I sure hope we get off of this ship soon. Living conditions are terrible and nothing seems to be going just right." While en route to Pearl Harbor in convoy, he bitterly concluded by 19 May, "We are just a bunch of cripples."[14]

LSM(R) 188 reached Pearl Harbor on 7 June 1945, where ammunition was unloaded and diesel storage tanks de-fueled. By 12 June yard workers began clearing battle damage as reconversion plans were still being drafted. In dry dock, Navy Yard inspectors found the hull leaky, but otherwise in excellent condition. "Received word that we definitely would not go home," the sailor commented after arrival in Hawaii. "We'll get a while in a rest camp is all. Makes me very unhappy." By 19 June he wrote, "Still at Pearl Harbor and they have the ship all torn apart. We are sure of not getting home now. One of the men working on the ship found a finger this a.m. off of one of the boys that was killed but we did get most of that stuff

LSM(R) 191 after conversion into an Ammunition Carrier at Pearl Harbor circa September 1945. All rocket launchers were removed as well as the stern anchor and cradle. A movie screen is on the bow and a conventional LSM is tied alongside (U.S. Navy photograph by Lt. [jg] Laurie R. Russell).

off at Kerama Retto...." Finally, on 24 June, "We are tearing the main engines down for a complete overhaul and they are trying to work us to death on them...."[15]

The original conversion proposal by AdComPhibsPac suggested stowage for 30,000 5" SSR rockets in each ship. The maximum loaded mean draft for the converted LSM(R)s was limited to 8 feet. (This compares to the pre-conversion estimated loaded mean drafts of 6 feet, 6 inches at 968 tons for 188 Class LSM(R)s, and 6 feet, 10 inches at 1,008 tons for 196 Class LSM(R)s). However, it was found that the maximum number of rockets that could be carried without exceeding the maximum mean level draft was approximately 10,000 SSRs. Thus, the total projected cargo capacity of the nine LSM(R)s would provide only a 40 percent replacement of rockets due to displacement limitations.[16] Alterations further added two booms with kingposts, one port and one starboard, each with independent port and starboard cargo winches, to permit burtoning of loads to a point fifteen feet outboard of the ship's side for ammunition handling at sea and for a twenty-foot motorboat.[17] After mid–July, plans had been drafted and forwarded to the Bureau of Ships for reinforcing the tank deck and the general arrangements of the superstructure deck, main deck and hold.[18] Recommendation for crew manning levels for the nine ammo carriers was five officers and 59 enlisted.[19]

The nine LSM(R)s were never formally reclassified nor re-commissioned as ammunition ships or Ammo Carriers. Internal correspondence between Commander, Administrative Command, Amphibious Forces, U.S. Pacific Fleet (AdComPhibsPac) and Pearl Harbor Navy Yard continued referring to the rocketships during shipyard reconversion as LSM(R)s or simply as LSMs. Higher echelon reports, on the other hand, from CINCPAC and ComPhibsPac referred to them thereafter as either "Ammo Carriers" or "LSM(E)s," which replaced the parenthetical (R) for Rocket with (E) for Ammunition, per U.S. Navy parlance.[20]

Interestingly, LSM(A) with the parenthetical (A), also meaning Ammunition, was the most widely used classification at the unit level during the reconversions. An officer of the deck in *LSM(R) 198* reported on 28 July 1945, "being converted into an LSM(A)," while another OOD on *LSM(R) 199* noted 30 July 1945, "We are undergoing conversion from an LSM(R) to an LSM(A)." Similarly, USS *LSM(A) 196* was inserted throughout that ship's daily logs and monthly muster rolls from July to the end of October 1945. Even at the individual level, Gunnery Officer Ensign F. Donald Moore on *LSM(R) 189* noted in his diary on 10 July for example, "Moored portside to pier 55 Berth 15.5 Pearl Harbor undergoing conversion from LSM(R) to LSM(A)."[21] In the final months of 1945, however, references to LSM(E) and LSM(A) faded from correspondence and the original LSM(R) classification was resumed universally, even though these former rocketships no longer mounted rocket launchers.

In late June 1945, Commander Dennis L. Francis, while still Commander LSM Flotilla Nine, recommended refitting *LSM(R) 192* as an LSM(FF) flotilla flagship. His request was denied, however, on the basis that any ship modifications that increased personnel accommodations for staff officers and additional equipment would result in a corresponding decrease in ammunition lift. Moreover, since the numbers of rounds the ships were able to carry were far less than originally estimated, all nine LSM(R)s were urgently needed foremost as ammo carriers.[22]

Ammunition removal, de-fueling, and immediate repairs and conversions commenced as the LSM(R)s reported to AdComPhibsPac at Pearl Harbor: on 7 July, *LSM(R)s 189, 191, 192* and *193*; on 11 July, *LSM(R)s 196* and *197*; and on 25 July, *LSM(R)s 198* and *199*. All salt and fresh water, steam, air and electricity were supplied from the dockyard while under repairs. The first order of business was removing all Mark 36 launchers from the Finner ships and the remaining Mark 51 launchers from the Spinner ships. Meanwhile, LSM Flotilla Nine's former flagship *LC(FF) 535* would also undergo prolonged repairs and modifications at the Honolulu Harbor shipyard, after which she would serve as flagship for LSM(R) Flotilla 18 under Captain C. F. Macklin, Jr., with the new "Ultimate" LSM(R)s beginning 26 August 1945.

In dry dock, much work was shared by ships companies and yard workers alike. Fire watches were set during welding and whenever cutting torches were used. Ships' hulls were inspected for water tight integrity, skegs were repaired and sterns reinforced; old paint was chipped away from bottoms and then scraped and cleaned before non-corrosive plastic paint was applied. Stern anchors and their cradles and winches were removed. New internal lighting and circuits for magazine spaces were installed; fog oil heating systems and stowage were provided. Ordnance was either repaired or replaced, and yard arms were extended with revamped radio and radar electronics.

Ships official daily logs did not often record details of the conversion work being done, although OODs frequently noted that civilian yard workers were free to come and go around the clock. But personal diaries of those on board the LSM(R)s offer clues about the progression of the Navy Yard's work. Signalman Karl Matchett wrote on 16 July, "They have started to work on ship. We are at Berth 17, tied up to a pier close to the sub base…. They are taking our rocket launchers off, stern anchor and the Captain's cabin out, plus other things. They are making an ammunition ship out of us, to carry rockets for new rocket ships."[23] On 18 July Radioman Clyde Blue noted, "They sure are giving this ship an overhaul fixing the radio gear and getting some new stuff," and on 20 July, "The workers are working in the rocket compartments…."[24]

Signalman Matchett continued on 24 July, "Scraped paint and painted the worst parts around the conn. Workers on the ship all the time," and on 26 July, "Painters did most of the ship today—green, gray and brown camouflage colors. I talked 'big deal' with yard workers. Got a welding and burning outfit. Did my first burning job—fixing the flag bridge. I am a shipfitter now. Ha!" Resuming his diary on 3 August, "In dry dock now… We were all over the sides scraping the bottom and sides of the ship. Have it about all finished. Probably paint tomorrow," and the next day, "Had some scraping and brushing to do on ship," then finally on 5 August, "Workers finished painting the ship this morning."[25]

During the shipyard conversions, LSM(R) crews were granted ample liberty ashore where the USO sponsored numerous functions for officers and enlisted alike. In Oahu, officers could enjoy recreational activities of the Fleet Recreation Office at YMCA Camp Erdman, for example, while enlisted men often rested and relaxed at Camp Andrews, the U.S. Navy Recreation Camp at Nanakuli.[26] Signalman Karl Matchett from *LSM(R) 197* described one such liberty on 8 August 1945:

> Got to Camp Andrews about 0900. There are eight of us in this hut…. Can do anything we want to do here. Have a beach where we can swim, pool room, movies twice a day, canteen, good chow, recreation. Can wear anything we want to—which is usually a pair of trunks. Can go anywhere within a mile of camp. Have good showers. Can sleep whenever we want to. Sure is nice! Today, we played some basketball, wrestled, slept all afternoon, two showers. Will be here four days.[27]

Shipyard estimated timeframes for completion and RFS (Ready For Sailing) dates varied and were continually revised. On 6 August, finally, the Navy Yard's manager confidently reported all nine ships' dry dock repairs and reconversions would be completed by 27 August and RFS on 28 August.

War's End

On 14 August 1945, all shipyard work stopped and celebrations were everywhere. "Last night, at about 8:45, the Japanese news agency (Domehi) [Domei] declared that they had surrendered. Noise here lasted about twenty minutes ... sirens, horns, searchlights," described Karl Matchett. "However, as there was nothing official, things quieted down. Today, President Truman broadcast the message that the Japs had surrendered unconditionally. This was official and what everyone was waiting for. Noise really started and all the workers quit. [Clyde] Blue and I were at the main gate watching the excitement."[28]

LSM(R) 192's officer of the deck also noted at 1349 of 14 August 1945: "Official news received of Japan's acceptance of surrender terms. Yard workmen left ship for holiday." Ensign F. Donald Moore aboard *LSM(R) 189* wrote in his diary that day, "President Truman announced that surrender of Japan had been accepted. All work on ship cancelled unless it is necessary to make ship sea-worthy," and Clyde Blue in *LSM(R) 197* sounded hopeful in his diary:

> Well, about 1:30 p.m. we got the word and boy that was really good to my ears. They really raised Cain around here again today. We were notified today to prepare for sea at a word from the Commander. I don't know where but I believe it will be the states. It's hard to believe that there is no more war whatsoever.... Well, this is the Great V-J day that everyone has been looking for and now it's here. I sure wish I was back in the states to celebrate.[29]

The next couple days were eerily subdued at Pearl Harbor's Navy Yard as August 15 and 16 were declared impromptu holidays. "Surely is quiet around the yard after yesterday's excitement," observed Karl Matchett. On 16 August Clyde Blue also wrote, "It looks like we are going to move from here. They stopped all work on us," and Ensign Lawrence J. Low, Gunnery Officer on *LSM(R) 197* noted in his diary for 17 August: "... All work stopped on LSM(R)s.... Conversion on *LSM(R) 197* 95% complete."[30] Indeed, on 17 August Commander Service Force, U.S. Pacific Fleet (ComServPac) sent formal notice to Navy Yard, Pearl Harbor:

> STOP CONVERSION TO AMMO CARRIERS ... COMPLETE REPAIRS AND PARTIALLY COMPLETED ALT NECESSARY FOR SATISFACTORY OPERATION OF VESSELS X REQUEST EARLIEST POSSIBLE COMPLETION DATE...[31]

Ensigns Jack Shedd and David Mallery of *LSM(R) 196* summarized the thoughts and feelings of many on this day. "Plans at Pearl involved our reconversion to ammunition carriers for the new rocket ships and spelled an end to our career as a rocket ship. The reconversion was about three-quarters completed when the peace was announced. The final V-J announcement gave the crew not only the joy of seeing the end of the world struggle but also gave them the satisfaction of playing an active part in the last great phase of the war."[32]

CHAPTER 13

Homeward Bound

With peacetime, U.S. armed forces rapidly demobilized worldwide. LSM(R) officers and enlisted men were transferred to receiving stations for discharge from active duty; crews were mustered for change of command ceremonies and awards were bestowed for exemplary service. "It was an exciting time, the end of war," recalled Laurie R. Russell, Gunnery Officer on *LSM(R) 191*, and the public honored the returning veterans as *LSM(R) 197* Radioman Clyde Blue recalled while in a movie theatre: "Saw the newsreel on the Rocket ships going into the Okinawa battle. First time we had seen any of them."[1]

After celebrating the war's end, the Pearl Harbor Navy Shipyard resumed work finishing the incomplete conversions and repairs to the nine LSM(R)s and assuring their seaworthiness. "We made a ninety-mile trip to Maui one day and back the next just for an engine test as our engines were overhauled during our conversion period," explained Signalman Leonard Van-Oteghem in *LSM(R) 196*. As each was readied, a yard tugboat towed the rocket/ammo ship to Middle Loch to anchor amidst the new, and newly-arriving, "Ultimate" LSM(R) cousins. "*LSM(R) 401* moored Chinese fashion to port side," noted *LSM(R) 192*'s deck officer,[2] and Radioman Clyde Blue remarked, after visiting a buddy aboard nearby *LSM(R) 412*, "The new rocket ships are a real nice job…"[3]

The First…

The war ended before the nine reconverted LSM(R)s ever saw service as Ammo Carriers for the "Ultimate" LSM(R)s—with one unique exception.

LSM(R) 401 underwent extensive hull and ordnance repairs in Maalaea Bay anchorage at Maui, and to expedite work AdComPhibsPac ordered newly-converted ammo ship *LSM(R) 188* to sail under emergency orders on 30 August from Pearl Harbor to Maalaea Bay (the order to get underway was so sudden, in fact, that two men on authorized liberty missed ships movement). Once *LSM(R) 188* moored alongside *LSM(R) 401*, the next day work parties passed ammunition from the latter to the former for temporary stowage.[4]

Almost certainly unnoticed was this remarkably historic convergence: USS *LSM(R) 188* was first of her "Interim" class of rocket ships and progenitor of the entire LSM(R) series; first to be converted to an ammunition ship; the first *de facto* Ammo Carrier for the first of the "Ultimate" class of rocket ships USS *LSM(R) 401*, with both classes designed by Gibbs & Cox and built in Charleston Navy Yard, South Carolina.

LSM(R) 401 was the first of the new "Ultimate" LSM(R)s destined for the two planned U.S. invasions of homeland Japan under Operation Downfall: Operation Olympic in late 1945 and Operation Coronet in early 1946 (official U.S. Navy photograph).

... and Last

Conversion and repairs to *LSM(R) 199* were almost finished when inspected by Captain C. F. Macklin, Jr. Commander LSM(R) Flotilla Eighteen and Captain John A. Edwards, Commander LSM(R) Group Fifty-Two. The week before, Capt. Macklin and his flotilla staff had moved their gear aboard newly-renovated USS *LC(FF) 535*, former flagship of LSM Flotilla Nine under Commander Dennis L. Francis. Now, Edwards sought a temporary group flagship for his command as well. On 3 September 1945, Capt. Edwards requested authority from AdComPhibsPac to further modify *LSM(R) 199* so the group staff could continue functioning as an administrative unit for the 48 "Ultimate" rocket ships of LSM(R) Flotilla Eighteen. Requirements included accommodations for nine staff officers, office equipment, an additional flag bag, and refitting two ballast tanks for fresh water. Indeed, the following day the Captain and an inspection party embarked *LSM(R) 199* to inspect the progress on conversion of the forward handling room into a Staff Wardroom. But flagship conversion of this last "Interim" rocket ship fell to the wayside by mid–September when the Army entered discussions with the Navy over transporting troops from Hawaii to the continental United States.[5]

Scuttlebutt

LSM(R) sailors shared in the jubilations over Japan's surrender; hopes soared in the immediate afterglow, and dreams of finally going home would become reality. "V-J day here in Hawaii," wrote Clyde Blue on 1 September 1945, "Heard all the Tokio Bay Broadcasts [sic]…," adding a few days later, "Labor Day and lots of noise here. Big parade, lasted for two hours…," then on 7 September: "Well, today censorship is lifted for good and boy does that ever seem good…."[6] Weeks passed, however, without news about returning stateside, and with too much idle time and little to do, hopes grew jaded by spurious scuttlebutt that fed growing resentment.

In mid–September 1945 the army conferred with the navy about returning troops home. "The old man came back aboard today and said if we could carry 150 men we (LSM[R]) would all go back to the states this Friday the 21st," Clyde Blue recorded in his diary on 17 September. "Well, we figured out that we could carry 15 [sic] extra men besides the crew so we are supposed to load the men aboard Thursday. I guess this is it and I sure hope so. We will carry all the extra men in the rocket compartments and what few extra bunks we have in the [berthing] compartments."[7] The day after, Karl Matchett on LSM(R) 197 got wind of a related rumor he jotted in his diary: "Heard today that we are going back to Charleston from San Diego."[8]

Now no longer just idle rumors, excitement rose when preparations began in earnest on 18 September. "Well, today we went on a working party and started getting equipment for the trip," wrote Radioman Blue, while Karl Matchett commented after a long day: "…on a d… [sic] working party to get stores and provisions, and lots of them. Got back at 8:30 p.m." On LSM(R) 192 alone, working parties returned with 128 cots, 50 lifebelts and 420 pounds of bread. "Went on a working party and gone all day long," Blue added on 19 September: "We got 30 tons of food supplies for the trip. Sure hope nothing falls through on this deal…" But two days later rocket ship sailors were crestfallen upon hearing the trip was off: "I guess the deal has fallen under. Man is everyone ever fed up," wrote a sullen Clyde Blue.[9]

Despite disappointments, sailors still found diversions from their uncertain futures: "We played the [LSM(R)] 196 in softball and beat the hide off them," championed Clyde Blue on 25 September. "The losers bought all the beer and cokes and what a time we had," adding, "The CO has to report to Operations tomorrow." And this time the news they got was better than winning any sandlot softball game: "The old man was told today that he should be ready for sea by the 27th or 28th September and be ready to carry 100 men."[10]

Good news indeed arrived on 27 September from AdComPhibsPac:

WHEN RFS ABOUT 1500 28 SEPTEMBER FORM TASK UNIT 13.11.94 OTC IS LT. MACWILLIAMS ON LSM 196 [sic] X DEPART KEWALO BASIN PROCEED SAN DIEGO, CALIFORNIA X ON ARRIVAL SAN DIEGO REPORT BY DISPATCH TO COMWESSEAFRON X AWAIT FURTHER ORDERS FROM CINCPAC…[11]

The passage from Middle Loch, Pearl Harbor, to Kewalo Basin, Honolulu, was only a few hours, and by noon of 28 September the LSM(R)s were tied up. An hour later the former rocketships began embarking army enlisted contingents of 81 to 101 men, escorted by army officers. Lines were cast off around mid-afternoon and Task Unit 13.11.94 proceeded in column formation to international waters, guided by LSM(R) 196 as OTC per AdComPhibsPac order 272353 for San Diego, California.[12]

Hundreds of American GIs wait to embark LSM(R)s in Kewalo Basin, Honolulu, Hawaii, on 28 September 1945 for passage to the mainland United States. From Conns to sterns, traditional red and white "Homeward Bound" pennants flutter in the wind (U.S. Navy photograph by Lt. [jg] Laurie R. Russell).

Colorful signal flags fluttered and all ships' lights burned brightly under rippling traditional Homeward Bound Pennants. "The signalmen sewed this up and it was 1 foot per man, and officers had blue with a white star for each of them ... if memory serves me they had weather balloons tied on the end," recalled Peter C. Rendina from *LSM(R) 198*. Crews and passengers alike felt ebullient as some probably shared Clyde Blue's mixture of relief as well: "Sure glad to get the hell away from those Hawaiians."[13]

The task unit soon formed into Formation Able as three columns of three ships at 500-yard distances and intervals. After the first day at sea Clyde Blue noted on 29 September: "Steaming as usual. Few swells and lots of Doggies sick. Ha ... Ships are lit up like Christmas trees, movies topside. Getting into cooler weather now."[14] En route, ships frequently exchanged movies and shared projectors to entertain army passengers and navy crewmen.

But the task unit was plagued by daily breakdowns disrupting and slowing the voyage considerably. Despite the shipyard repairs at Pearl Harbor, or perhaps because work was hurriedly finished, mechanical and electrical problems befell each ship. On any given day, one or more LSM(R)s fell from formation as crews strained to effect repairs and resume convoy stations. On one occasion, a medical doctor was transferred between ships to treat an injured sailor.

The very survival of *LSM(R) 192* was threatened the second day at sea, on 30 September, as recalled by Storekeeper First Class Robert Landis:

While underway for the states, the starboard diesel engine caught on fire. The fire spread rapidly thru the passage ways and crew's quarters. All army personnel were brought up on main deck and were issued life jackets. They thought for sure they would have to abandon ship. However the damage control crew soon brought the fire under control. Within a few hours we were underway again on one engine and doing about seven knots.

Casualties were the chief boatswain's mate and a motor machinists mate, who suffered smoke inhalation while fire fighting and were treated by the ship's pharmacist's mate then returned to duty.[15]

Meanwhile, the convoy stopped while awaiting the status of *LSM(R) 192*, then proceeded onward at one-third speed after ordering *LSM(R)s 188* and *191* to stand by in case aid was needed. The latter two rocketships later rejoined formation while *LSM(R) 192* limped far behind, powered only by her port engine, but finally caught up with the task unit by mid-afternoon.

As the task unit struggled on its easterly course despite innumerable power failures and steering casualties, its final destination was changed the evening of 1 October when Commander Western Sea Frontier ordered the convoy to sail instead to San Pedro, California.

The fair seas and mild weather since departing Hawaii also changed, as Radioman Clyde Blue noted on 3 October: "Heard Detroit and Cubs game today, what a lousy game. Little over half way between Pearl and Pedro. It's awful cold out and the sea is very choppy and rough." Two days later he added: "It's really rough today. Cold also. Lost my doggie hat over the side. Doggies are sick and tossing their cookies in all directions."[16] His *LSM(R) 197* shipmate and lifelong friend Lawrence Willison also recalled, "Many of the army personnel became seasick during our return voyage to the U.S. These brought about many unsanitary and unpleasant conditions."[17] Not only were ships' galleys busy day and night feeding army passengers and navy crews, but enlisted men's heads grew full as well.

But *LSM(R) 192* never fully recovered after her engine room fire and suffered persistent breakdowns thereafter. Her crew struggled to repair the faulty starboard General Motors engine, but fire broke out once again after restarting it on 5 October so it was secured once more. Afterwards, the rocket ship slowly lost headway, so *LSM(R)s 188, 193* and *199* were ordered to fall astern the convoy as relay ships to maintain visual communications. The following day, finally, the task unit OTC ordered sister ships *LSM(R)s 192* and *193* to proceed independently at best possible speed while the remaining convoy closed and pressed onward. Calming weather and seas fortunately cooperated during the final leg home.

"Today's Sunday and we had inspection," Clyde Blue wrote on 7 October. "We have slowed down to 5 knots so as to pull into port at 0800 Monday morning. Detroit has won the last two games. Hope they win tomorrow. All I can dream of is fresh milk and fresh food."[18] That afternoon the task unit formed a single column assuming formation Baker with 300-yard intervals as California's remote San Nicolas Island was sighted some 20 miles off port bows.

Home at Last

The morning of 8 October 1945, *LSM(R)s 188, 189, 191, 196, 197, 198* and *199* passed from international to inland waters of the United States of America. Shortly after sunrise the

Top: "Welcome Home: A Job Well Done" greets arriving LSM(R)s in the Port of Los Angeles, San Pedro, California, on 8 October 1945. A military band played marches as newspaper reporters and cameramen covered the returning sailors and soldiers. *Bottom:* LSM(R)s *188, 189, 191, 192, 193, 196, 197, 198* and *199* tied dockside at Port of Los Angeles, San Pedro, California, on 8 October 1945 (U.S. Navy photograph by Lt. [jg] Laurie R. Russell).

ships entered the Port of Los Angeles, San Pedro, California, and moored portside to Berth 232-A-B at Terminal Island, then stood by until the arrival of *LSM(R)s 192* and *193* three hours later. After each ship was inspected and cleared by the Department of Agriculture and Customs, hundreds of army passengers were disembarked before noontime and greeted with a war heroes' welcome. A military band played marches as newspaper reporters with cameramen mingled among yard workers and bystanders. Robert Landis summed up the feelings of everyone when he wrote in his diary, "It feels so good to be back in the states," and Clyde Blue jotted impressions from that heady time: "Arrived here about 6:30 a.m. We docked and they had a band playing for us when the doggies got off the ship. Also took pictures of us and again we were in the papers. Had liberty and went to Long Beach. It sure is a nice town."[19]

After the din of excitement and celebration, the former rocketships cast off that afternoon and anchored at the Naval Operating Base's Inner Mole of Los Angeles Harbor.

In coming months, LSM(R) crews were pared severely as officers and enlisted were transferred singly or in groups to receiving stations and separation centers for discharge. Daily shipboard musters were held for remaining personnel as some took leaves home and others were granted liberty ashore. Change of command ceremonies were observed without fanfare. Work parties took on supplies and assured continued power and fresh water from adjacent ships or barges, and in one instance an LSM(R) went into dry dock for repairs. As compartments were cleaned and secured for decommissionings, the rocketships' skeleton crews were billeted in nearby barges and adjacent ships as temporary berthing and messing facilities. Soon, officers from the Sub Board of Inspection and Survey assessed material conditions of each ship; inventories were itemized then salvaged by the Naval Supply Depot. Both 40mm and 20mm gun mounts with spare barrels, as well as small arms and ammunition, were removed. The last remaining vestiges of the "Interim" LSM(R)s were their distinctive fire control towers and fantail 5"/38 gun mounts standing as silent sentinels. Decommissioning ceremonies were terse with officers and men at attention and rendering salutes as colors were struck and commissioning pennants hauled down. By early 1946, the nine surviving LSM(R)s were sold either to civilian maritime businesses or for scrap. In 1957, the three sunken LSM(R)s lost off Okinawa were donated by the Department of the Navy to the Government of the Ryukyus Islands.[20]

Appendices

*Containing **I.** "Interim" LSM(R) Characteristics and Performance; **II.** Crew Complements: LSM, "Interim" LSM(R), LSM(A)/LSM(E); **III.** Paint, Camouflage and Markings; **IV.** Ships Data*

I. "Interim" LSM(R) Characteristics and Performance

Length: (overall)	203 feet, 6 inches.
Beam: (maximum)	34 feet, 6 inches.
Draft: (mean, loaded)	*LSM(R)s 188–195*: 6 feet, 6 inches.
	LSM(R)s 196–199: 6 feet, 10 inches.
Engines:	Two General Motors 16-cylinder diesels, Model 16–278A, direct connected to clutch reverse gear.
	Emergency: 1800 BHP at 800 RPM.
	Continuous: 1440 BHP at 720 RPM.
	Directions of rotation:
	Starboard propeller clockwise,
	Port propeller counterclockwise.
Generators:	Two General Motors, 100 KW.
Displacement: (mean, loaded)	*LSM(R)s 188–195*: 968 tons.
	LSM(R)s 196–199: 1,008 tons.
Fresh Water Capacity:	53.45 tons (12,828 gallons).
Diesel Oil Capacity:	116.62 tons (32,618 gallons).
Cruising range:	4,900 nautical miles.
Cruising Speed:	12 knots.
Maximum Speed:	13.2 knots (maximum, loaded).
Armament:	*LSM(R)s 188–195*: 75 Mark 36 Rocket Launchers; 30 Mark 30 Rocket Launchers.
	LSM(R)s 196–199: 85 Mark 51 Rocket Launchers.
	Three single 20mm Oerlikon guns.
	Two single 40mm Bofor guns.
	One 5"/38 caliber Dual Purpose gun.
	Some LSM(R)s added .50 caliber machineguns.

Electronic Equipment:	SU-1 surface search radar.
	TCS-6 or -8 or -12 medium and high frequency radio telegraph and telephone operations transmitter-receivers.
	SCR-610 medium range FM radio transmitter-receiver.
	SCR-608T and SCR-608R medium range FM radio transmitter-receivers.
	TDE-2 or -3 medium to high frequency radio transmitters.
	RAO-2 or -3 or -4 radio-telegraph and AM radio-telephone signals receivers.
	RBL-3 or -6 radio longwave regenerative receivers.
	RBO recreational AM radio receiver.
	ABK-7 Identification Friend or Foe (IFF) transponder.
	BN Identification Friend or Foe (IFF) interrogator-responsor.
	Nancy gear: AM, C-3 infrared signaling telescope, X-12 infrared train light, "H" hood.
	Radio test equipment: LM-13 or -15 or -18, OBL-3, OE-8, OQ-2 or -3, QQ-3, OZ-1, Oscilloscope DuMont 245 or Hickok RFO-5.
	Remote radios: Wheelhouse, Radio Shack, Captain's Stateroom.
	Radio speakers: Officers' Wardroom and Crews' Quarters.
Auxiliary Equipment:	One Model "E" Smoke Generator, 100-gallon/hour Capacity, Todd Combustion Equipment.

II. Crew Complements: LSM, "Interim" LSM(R), LSM(A)/LSM(E)

LSM

Line Officers

Commanding Officer (Lieutenant)
Executive Officer and Navigator/First Lieutenant/Damage Control (Lieutenant [Junior Grade])
Gunnery Officer and Communications/Commissary and Stores (Ensign)
Engineer Officer and Assistant Damage Control (Ensign)

Enlisted

Seaman Branch: (22)	GM2c	SM2c
CBM	GM3c	SM3c
BM1c	FC3c	Sea1c [5]
BM2c	QM1c	Sea2c [6]
Cox	QM3c	
Artificer Branch: (10)	RdM2c	RM2c
EM1c	RdM3c [2]	RM3c
EM2c	RM1c	RT2c
EM3c		
Engine Room Force: (15)	MoMM2c [3]	F1c [3]
CMoMM	MoMM3c [3]	F2c [3]
MoMM1c [2]		
Special Branch: (3)	SK1c	PhM1c
Y2c		

Commissary Branch: (2)	SC1c	SC3c
Stewards Branch: (2)	StM1c	StM2c

Summary of Pay Grades:

Grade	Number
1	2
2	9
3	11
4	13
5	9
6	10

Total Officers: 4
Total Enlisted: 54
Total Complement: 58

"Interim" LSM(R)

Line Officers

Commanding Officer (Lieutenant)
Executive Officer and Navigator (Lieutenant [Junior Grade])
Gunnery Officer (Lieutenant [Junior Grade])
Engineer Officer (Ensign)
Communications and Assistant Gunnery Officer (Ensign)
First Lieutenant/Assistant First Lieutenant/ Watch Officer (Ensign)*
Assistant First Lieutenant (Ensign)*

Enlisted

Seaman Branch: (44)	GM1c	SM2c
CBM	GM2c [2]	SM3c
BM1c	GM3c [3]	FC2c
BM2c	QM1c	S1c [13]
Cox [2]	QM3c	S2c [14]
CGM		

Artificer Branch: (7)	RM3c	RdM2c
RM1c	RT2c	RdM3c [2]
RM2c		

Engine Room Force: (18)	MoMM3c [3]	EM3c
CMoMM	EM1c	F1c [3]
MoMM1c [2]	EM2c	F2c [3]
MoMM2c [3]		

Special Branch: (3)	SK1c	PhM1c
Y2c		

Commissary Branch: (2)	SC1c	SC3c

Stewards Branch: (2)	StM1c	StM2c

Summary of Pay Grades:

Grade	Number
1	3
2	10
3	13
4	15
5	17
6	18

Total Officers: 6 to 7*

Total Enlisted: 76
Total Complement: 82 to 83*

*The LSM(R)s' Line Officer complement was increased at commissionings with an additional Ensign variously designated First Lieutenant, Assistant First Lieutenant, or Watch Officer. USS *LSM(R) 189* was the exception with an additional two Ensigns both designated Assistant First Lieutenants. Source: U.S. Navy Deck Logs.

LSM(A)/LSM(E) Recommended Complement

Line Officers

Commanding Officer
Executive Officer
Communications Officer
Engineering Officer
Gunnery Officer

Enlisted

Seaman Branch: (31)	GM2c [2]	SM3c [2]
BM1c	GM3c	FC2c
BM2c	QM2c	S1c [13]
Cox	QM3c	S2c [5]
GM1c	SM2c	
Artificer Branch: (5)	RM3c	RdM3c
RM2c [2]	RdM2c	
Engine Room Force: (16)	MoMM2c [3]	EM3c
CMoMM	MoMM3c [4]	F1c [3]
MoMM1c	EM2c [2]	F2c
Special Branch: (3)	SK2c	PhM1c
Y2c		
Commissary Branch: (2)	SC1c	SC3c
Stewards Branch: (2)	StM1c	StM2c

Summary of Pay Grades:

Grade	Number
1	1
2	5
3	16
4	13
5	17
6	7

Total Officers: 5
Total Enlisted: 59
Total Complement: 64

Sources: *LSM Class Manual* (1944), Chapter 3, "Allocation of Personnel," 3–1 to 3–3; Chief of Naval Personnel Restricted Letter Pers-1042b-GB LSM/P16–1 dated 21 October 1944, with Enclosure Form NAVPERS 2128, Bureau of Naval Personnel, General Correspondence 1940–1945, Record Group 24, National Archives and Records A; The Commanding Officer, Minimum Compliment [*sic*] of Rates Required for Operation of *LSM (R) 197*, Serial 103, 21 August 1945.

III. Paint, Camouflage and Markings

At launchings in Charleston Navy Yard, South Carolina, the proto-LSM(R)s were still configured as conventional LSMs with a standard overall matte light gray base, and hull bottoms with boottops were painted matte black topped by a thin red line. 24-inch, block-type hull numbers in matte white paint without shading were on opposing sides of bows and sterns.

By shipyard commissioning, *LSM(R)s 188–199* were painted modified tropical camouflage Measure 31, Design 10L (L for Landing Craft) with "blended dots" transitioning colors. Navy paint directive called for 5-OG Ocean Green, 5-NG Navy Green, 20-G Deck Green, and BK Dull Black. En route to forward areas early in 1945, possibly at Pearl Harbor, the block hull numbers were enlarged to six feet in height in flat white paint per Pacific Fleet orders for increased visibility over greater distances.

Leading up to and throughout the Okinawa operation in 1945, LSM(R) deck forces routinely scraped and touched-up ships due to rust and weathering whenever time and opportunity permitted, causing camouflage patterns and colors to vary depending on paint supplies at hand and the dictates of the chief boatswain's mate. A subsequent Navy directive called for revised colors of Outside Green #1, #2, #3 and Brown #4, and most LSM(R)s generally followed the original shipyard patterns albeit with varying hues. In some cases the blended dots were painted over and thus sharpened the edges between colors; in one unusual instance, *LSM(R) 195* sported an inventive "scalloped" camouflage pattern seen between late March and early April 1945.

As the Okinawa campaign progressed, small credit markings were common among the LSM(R)s, usually painted in white symbols on the conning towers' Venturi shields. Markings included silhouettes of planes, boats, and palm tree islets under which hash marks indicated the numbers of island operations. Paintings of small Japanese flags in red and white were widespread, either as the rising sun symbol with outward rays, or as a single centered red disc, called a "meatball" in American parlance.

A few commanding officers permitted unique artworks painted on their ships. *LSM(R) 189* featured *MISS ROCKET* in large letters on the Conn atop a young lady with flowing locks in sailor's white hat wearing a bikini bathing suit and cradling a rocket in her arms, credited to Coxswain Adolfo "Tony" De La Torre. *LSM(R) 191* boasted *DRAGON LADY* in large letters on the Conn over the exotic femme fatale from the comic strip *Terry and the Pirates* by Milton Caniff, appropriated by Seaman First Class Raymond Barrett. On *LSM(R) 198* Radioman 2c (T) Louis Gobeille painted what came to be known informally by the crew as the "Lady in the Red Shoes," whose hair color and physical endowments were occasionally re-touched or embellished, shown reclining in a transparent veil on the left side of the 5"/38 gun mount. *BATTLIN' "BUGS"* was painted in large letters on the left side of another 5"/38 gun mount of an unidentified LSM(R) by an equally anonymous artist, and featured a Bugs Bunny-like cartoon character wearing boxing gloves in fighting stance. On the Conn of the flotilla's flagship *LC(FF) 535*, a round unit insignia representing LSM Flotilla Nine was painted by an unknown artist. A horned devil figure with a long, pointed tail wore a flowing cape while straddling a rocket, soaring over waters toward a Japanese pagoda, while he held forth a trident draping a pennant bearing the Roman numeral IX.

After returning to Pearl Harbor for re-conversion to Ammunition Carriers in preparation for the invasion of homeland Japan, the nine surviving LSM(R)s were repainted under a new Navy directive for temperate climate camouflage. Measure 31, Designs 5L and 8L used a "mottled green pattern" where Design 5L was applied to odd-numbered ships and Design 8L was applied to even-numbered ships. Paint callouts were 5-OG Ocean Green, 5-NG Navy Green, 20-G Deck Green, #4A Brown, and BK Dull Black, although one account suggested 5-H Haze Gray may have been included as well. This new camouflage scheme was in various stages of completion when the war ended in August 1945 but finished before the LSM(R)s returned stateside.

Upper left: LSM(R) 189, Miss Rocket, cover sketch from the ship's talent show program, "A Tragedy in Seven Acts" (undated). *Upper right: LSM(R) 191, Dragon Lady,* being painted by S1c Raymond Barrett (U.S. Navy photograph by Lt. [jg] Laurie R. Russell). *Lower left: LSM(R) 198, Lady in the Red Shoes,* with RM2c Louis Gobeille (U.S. Navy photograph, courtesy Louis Gobeille). *Lower right:* Credit Markings on conning towner's Venturi shield from unidentified LSM(R) (U.S. Navy photograph).

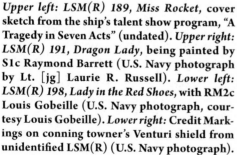

Sources: Naval History and Heritage Command website, Department of the Navy, Naval Historical Center, Photo #: 80-G-176521 Camouflage Measure 31, Design 10L (http://www.history.navy.mil/content/dam/nhhc/our-collections/photography/images/80-G-100000/80-G-176521), and Photo #: 80-G-176522 Camouflage Measure 31, Design 10L (http://www.history.navy.mil/content/dam/nhhc/our-collections/photography/images/80-G-100000/80-G-176522); Navy Department, Bureau of Ships, APA's AKA's, AP's, AK's, LSD's, LST's, LCI(L)'s, LCS(L)(3)'s, LCT(5)'s, LCT(6), LSM—Distinguished Numerals, Painting of, 20 May 1944, posted online at *U.S. Naval Camouflage* (blog) by Tracy White, Researcher@Large, http://www.researcheratlarge.com/Ships/S19-7/1944MayAuxiliaryHullNumbers.html; Office of the Commander, Amphibious Forces, Pacific Fleet, Transport Doctrine, Amphibious Forces, U.S. Pacific Fleet, Serial 0651, 18 September 1944, Chapter XXXVI Camouflage and Ship

Designating Letter and Number Painting Instructions, http://www.ibiblio.org/hyperwar/USN/ref/Transport/transport-36.html; Navy Department, Bureau of Ships, Amphibious Craft—Camouflage Measures, 20 February 1945, posted online at "US Naval Camouflage" (blog) by Tracy White, Researcher@Large, http://www.researcheratlarge.com/Ships/S19–7/1945_S19_631Amphib.html; Karl G. Matchett, untitled, unpublished diary, July 26, 1945, "Painters [in Pearl Harbor naval shipyard] did most of the ship [LSM(R) 197] today—green, gray and brown camouflage colors." For fuller discussions on U.S. Navy World War II camouflage, see Alan Raven, *The Development of Naval Camouflage 1914–1945* at ShipCamouflage.com website, http://www.shipcamouflage.com/development_of_naval_camouflage.htm; and C. Lee Johnson, *A Short History of U.S. Naval Camouflage in WWII* at "Ships of the U.S. Navy in WWII Dazzle Camouflage" website, http://usndazzle.com/1Web/Articles/Camo.html.

IV. Ships Data

LCT(7) 1688 redesignated LSM 188
Laid Down: 17 August 1944
Launched: 12 September 1944
Sponsor: Mrs. Olin D. Johnston
Commissioned: USS *LSM(R) 188* 15 November 1944
Commanding Officer: Lt. Harry C. Crist, USNR
Decommissioned: 23 January 1946
Stricken from U.S. Navy List: 7 February 1946
Fate: Sold 17 February 1948 [15 March 1948, $12,000] to National Metal and Steel Corporation, Terminal Island, CA, for scrap.

LCT(7) 1689 redesignated LSM 189
Laid Down: 17 August 1944
Launched: 12 September 1944
Sponsor: Mrs. John G. Fearing
Commissioned: USS *LSM(R) 189* 15 November 1944
Commanding Officer: Lt. James M. Stewart, USNR
Decommissioned: 31 January 1946
Stricken from U.S.Navy List: 25 February 1946
Fate: Sold 17 February 1948 [25 March 1948, $12,000] to National Metal and Steel Corporation, Terminal Island, CA, for scrap.

LCT(7) 1690 redesignated LSM 190
Laid Down: 27 August 1944
Launched: 21 September 1944
Sponsor: Mrs. John W. Fleming
Commissioned: USS *LSM(R) 190* 21 November 1944
Commanding Officer: Lt. Richard H. Saunders, USNR
War Loss: 4 May 1945
Fate: Donated to the Government of the Ryukyus Islands 10 July 1957.

LCT(7) 1691 redesignated LSM 191
Laid Down: 27 August 1944
Launched: 21 September 1944
Sponsor: Mrs. Henry R. Sweatman
Commissioned: USS *LSM(R) 191* 21 November 1944
Commanding Officer: Lt. (jg) John W. Loyer, USNR
Decommissioned: 12 February 1946
Stricken from U.S. Navy List: 26 February 1946
Fate: Sold 20 January 1948 for $15,000 to R. J. MacCallum, Compton, CA, converted to a barge. Registered by the West Coast Steamship Company, Los Angeles, CA, as freight barge *W-1*. Final disposition unknown after 1952.

LCT(7) 1692 redesignated LSM 192
Laid Down: 7 September 1944

Launched: 4 October 1944
Sponsor: Mrs. Mae D. Wilson
Commissioned: USS *LSM(R) 192* 22 November 1944
Commanding Officer: Lt. (jg) Neal B. Hadsell, USNR
Decommissioned: 26 February 1946
Stricken from U.S. Navy List: 12 March 1946
Fate: Sold 10 March 1948 [7 April 1948, $12,000] to Maritime Transport and Trading Company, Ltd.,
   New York, NY, scrapped 1963.

LCT(7) 1693 redesignated *LSM 193*
Laid Down: 7 September 1944
Launched: 4 October 1944
Sponsor: Mrs. Thelma Johnson Olsen
Commissioned: USS *LSM(R) 193* 22 November 1944
Commanding Officer: Lt. Donald E. Boynton, USNR
Decommissioned: 13 February 1946
Stricken from U.S. Navy List: 26 February 1946
Fate: Sold 20 January 1948 for $15,000 to R. J. MacCallum, Compton, CA, converted to a barge. Reg-
   istered in 1970 by Pioneering Towing Company, Seattle, WA, as freight barge *O & H 105*. Foundered
   off the Washington coast on February 10, 1976. Final disposition unknown.

LCT(7) 1694 redesignated *LSM 194*
Laid Down: 29 August 1944
Launched: 7 October 1944
Sponsor: Mrs. Andrew H. Pendarvis
Commissioned: USS *LSM(R) 194* 24 November 1944
Commanding Officer: Lt. (jg) Allan M. Hirshberg, USNR
War Loss: 4 May 1945
Fate: Donated to the Government of the Ryukyus Islands 10 July 1957.

LCT(7) 1695 redesignated *LSM 195*
Laid Down: 29 August 1944
Launched: 7 October 1944
Sponsor: Miss Winnie D. Knight
Commissioned: USS *LSM(R) 195* 24 November 1944
Commanding Officer: Lt. (jg) William E. Woodson, USNR
War Loss: 3 May 1945
Fate: Donated to the Government of the Ryukyus Islands 10 July 1957.

LCT(7) 1696 redesignated *LSM 196*
Laid Down: 13 September 1944
Launched: 12 October 1944
Sponsor: Mrs. Clarence T. Leinbach
Commissioned: USS *LSM(R) 196* 8 December 1944
Commanding Officer: Lt. Dennis D. O'Callaghan, USNR
Decommissioned: 26 March 1946
Stricken from U.S. Navy List: 17 April 1946
Fate: Sold 11 September 1947 [18 November 1947, $18,000] to A. G. Schoonmaker Company, New
   York, NY. Final disposition unknown.

LCT(7) 1697 redesignated *LSM 197*
Laid Down: 13 September 1944
Launched: 12 October 1944
Sponsor: Mrs. J. Melville Broughton
Commissioned: USS *LSM(R) 197* 8 December 1944
Commanding Officer: Lt. John "M" Cooper, USN

Decommissioned: 13 February 1946

Stricken from U.S. Navy List: 13 February 1946

Fate: Sold 3 February 1948 [$15,000] to Robert W. Erlbacher, Cape Girardeau, MO. Final disposition unknown.

LCT(7) 1698 redesignated LSM 198

Laid Down: 6 September 1944

Launched: 14 October 1944

Sponsor: Mrs. Myra Boynton Brown

Commissioned: USS *LSM(R) 198* 12 December 1944

Commanding Officer: Lt. George B. Timmerman, Jr., USNR

Decommissioned: 17 January 1946

Stricken from U.S. Navy List: 7 February 1946

Fate: Sold 17 February 1948 [1 March 1948, $12,000] to National Metal and Steel Corporation, Terminal Island, CA, for scrap.

LCT(7) 1699 redesignated LSM 199

Laid Down: 6 September 1944

Launched: 14 October 1944

Sponsor: Mrs. A. W. Walker, Jr.

Commissioned: USS *LSM(R) 199* 12 December 1944

Commanding Officer: Lt. Charles D. Cobb, USNR

Decommissioned: 1 February 1946

Stricken from U.S. Navy List: 26 February 1946

Fate: Sold 10 March 1948 [7 April 1948, $12,000] to Maritime Transport and Trading Company, Ltd., New York, NY. Final disposition unknown.

Sources: U.S. Navy Deck Logs; Norman Friedman, *U.S. Amphibious Ships and Craft*, Annapolis, MD: Naval Institute Press, 2005, 528; Rolf F. Illsley, *LSM-LSMR: WWII Amphibious Forces*, Paducah, KY: Turner Publishing Company, 1994, 57; Greg H. Williams, *World War II U.S. Navy Vessels in Private Hands*, Jefferson, NC: McFarland & Company, 2013) 59; bracketed sales dates and/or sales amounts cited from U.S. Department of Transportation, Maritime Administration, letter dated July 20, 1989 to Kelly K. Kirchner, provided courtesy Mr. Kirchner; Department of the Navy, Chief of Naval Operations, Donation of the sunken ... to the Government of the Ryukyus Islands, serial 1255P43B, 3 July 1957 with First Endorsement from Secretary of the Navy, serial 1256P43B, 10 July 1957.

Glossary

AA	Antiaircraft gun or gunfire, also called Flak and Ack-Ack	Ballistite	A double-base, single-grain rocket propellant
Abaft	Behind or to the rear of a ship	Battle Stations	General Quarters
		BB	Battleship
Action Report	Commanding officer's official record of specific action/s	Betty	Allied code name for the Japanese twin engine Mitsubishi G6M Navy bomber and transport
AdComPhibsPac	Administrative Command, Amphibious Forces, Pacific		
Aft/After	Toward, at, or near the stern of a ship	Black Gang	Enlisted men who work in the ship's engine room
After Steering	Steering Gear Flat with a "Trick Wheel" for emergency manual steering of a ship	BLT	Battalion Landing Team
		BM	Boatswains (or Bosun) Mate
		Bogey, Bogie	Unidentified radar target presumed an enemy aircraft, surface vessel, or submarine
AGC	Amphibious Force Flagship	Bow	Forward part of a ship
Adm	Admiral	Bridge	Raised platform from which ship is steered and navigated
AH	Hospital Ship		
AK; AKA; AKS	Cargo Ship; Attack Cargo Ship; General Stores-Issues Ship	BuOrd	U.S. Navy Bureau of Ordnance
		BuPers	U.S. Navy Bureau of Naval Personnel
AM	Minesweeper	BuShips	U.S. Navy Bureau of Ships
Amphib, Phib	Amphibian or amphibious	CA, CL	Cruiser
AO	Oiler	Caltech	California Institute of Technology in Pasadena, California, also called CIT
AP; APA	Transport; Attack Transport		
APD	High Speed Transport		
AR	Action Report; Aircraft Rocket	CAP	Combat Air Patrol; Civil Air Patrol
ARD	Auxiliary Repair Dock	Capt	Captain
ARG	Repair Ship, Internal Combustion Engines	CIC	Combat Information Center
		CINCPAC	Commander in Chief, Pacific Fleet
ARL	Repair Ship, Landing Craft		
ARS	Salvage Vessel	CINCPOA	Commander in Chief, Pacific Ocean Areas
ASCU	Air Support Control Unit		
ATB	Amphibious Training Base	Class	A group of ships of similar design which is named after the first or lead ship approved, built, or commissioned
ATF; ATR	Fleet Tugboat; Rescue Tugboat		
Athwartship	At right angles or transverse to the centerline or keel		

CNO	Chief of Naval Operations
CO	Commanding Officer
Com	Command (organization), Commander
Comdr	Commander
COMINCH	Commander in Chief
Commanding Officer	Captain of a ship regardless of rank, Skipper
ComServPac	Commander Service Force, U.S. Pacific Fleet
ComWesSeaFron	Commander Western Sea Frontier, U.S. Pacific Fleet
Conn, Conning Tower	Raised structure from which ship is steered and navigated
Cook-off/s	A secondary detonation from a nearby fire or explosion
Corpsman	Pharmacists Mate, Navy enlisted medic
Corsair	Chance-Vought F4U single-engine U.S. Navy and Marine carrier fighter
CTF	Commander Task Force
CTG	Commander Task Group
CTU	Commander Task Unit
Cumshaw	Something procured or bartered outside official U.S. Navy channels or regulations
CV; CVE	Aircraft Carrier; Escort Aircraft Carrier
DD	Destroyer
DE	Destroyer Escort
Deck Log	Log, logbook, or record of a ship's daily activities
Demonstration Landing	A feigned amphibious assault to deceive the enemy
DepNavOps	Deputy Chief of Naval Operations
Dinah	Allied code name for the Japanese twin engine Mitsubishi Ki-46 Army reconnaissance fighter-interceptor
Dispersion	A measure of the scatter of the impact points of a group of identical rockets fired under supposed identical conditions
DM; DMS	Light Minelayer; High Speed Minesweeper
DP, Dual Purpose	A naval gun designed for surface and air targets

DUKW	U.S. Army 4-wheel drive amphibious truck called a "Duck"
Ens	Ensign
EO	Engineering Officer
FD	Fighter Director
FIDO	Fighter Direction Officer
Finner	Informal term for a Fin-stabilized Rocket, rocket launcher, or LSM(R).
Five Flag, 5 Flag	Emergency signal flag indicating ship breakdown or man overboard
Flagbag	Container for stowage of signal flags and pennants
Flying Bridge	Uppermost Conning Tower station, also called the Bridge, Conn, Open Conn, or Open Bridge
Forecastle, Foc's'le	The forward upper portion of the hull
Frame	Ribs of a vessel numbered from forward to aft
Frances	Allied code name for the Japanese twin-engine Yokosuka P1Y Navy night fighter
GO	Gunnery Officer
GQ	General Quarters, Battle Stations
Guardmail	Intra-Navy correspondence, orders, and maps
Gun Tub	Circular steel gun shield to protect gunners
Gunwale	The junction of the deck and hull of a ship
Hamp/Hap	Allied code name for the Japanese single-engine Mitsubishi A6M Zero (or Zeke) Navy carrier fighter
Handy Billy	Portable gasoline-powered suction pump
Hanto	Japanese for peninsula
HCSR	High Capacity Spin-stabilized Rocket
HE	High Explosive
Head	A washroom, shower and toilet
HECP	Harbor Entrance Control Post
Hellcat	Grumman F6F single-engine U.S. Navy and Marine carrier fighter
HIJMS	His Imperial Japanese Majesty's Ship

Hook	Informal term for anchor	Liberty	Authorized absence of less than 48 hours
HQ	Headquarters		
HVAR	High Velocity Aircraft Rocket	Longitudinal	A forward-aft member parallel to the keel or centerline
IFF	Identify Friend or Foe radio signal		
		LSD	Landing Ship, Dock
IJA	Imperial Japanese Army	LSM	Landing Ship, Medium
IJAAF	Imperial Japanese Army Air Force	LSM(R)	Landing Ship, Medium (Rocket)
IJN	Imperial Japanese Navy	LST; LST(H)	Landing Ship, Tank; Landing Ship, Tank (Hospital)
I, ITEM	Greenwich Mean Time (GMT) plus 9 hours for Tokyo, Japan time zone		
		LSV	Landing Ship, Vehicle
		LT	Landing Team
JCS	U.S. Joint Chiefs of Staff	Lt	Lieutenant
Jill	Allied code name for the Japanese single-engine Nakajima B6N Navy carrier bomber	Lt Comdr	Lieutenant Commander
		Lt (jg)	Lieutenant (junior grade)
		LVT/LVT(A)	Landing Vehicle, Tracked (Armored)
Judy	Allied code name for the Japanese single-engine Yokosuka D4Y Navy carrier bomber	Main Deck	Well Deck, Tank Deck
		MarDiv	Marine Division
		Meatball	American slang for the Japanese Hinomaru national flag with the red disc on a white field
Kaiten	Japanese manned torpedoes		
Kate	Allied code name for the Japanese single-engine Nakajima B5N Navy carrier bomber		
		MIA	Missing In Action
		Midship	Center of ship
		Mil	¹⁄₆₄₀₀ of a complete circle or 0.056250 for calculating rocket dispersion
KIA	Killed In Action		
Knots	Speed in nautical miles per hour		
		Misaki, Mizaki	Japanese for cape (geographical)
Ko	Japanese for small bay or harbor		
		MM, mm	Millimeter
LC(FF)	Landing Craft (Force Flagship)	MoMM	Motor Machinists Mate, called a "Motor Mac"
		MPI	Mean Point of Impact
LCI	Landing Craft, Infantry	Muster Log	Roster of a ship's crew
LCI(G)	Landing Craft, Infantry (Gunboat)	Nate	Allied code name for the Japanese single-engine Nakajima Ki-27 Army fighter
LCI(L)	Landing Craft, Infantry (Large)		
LCI(M)	Landing Craft, Infantry (Mortar)		
		NavPers	Naval Personnel (document)
LCI(R)	Landing Craft, Infantry (Rocket)	NavWesPac	Naval Forces, Western Pacific
		NBC	Non-Battle Casualty
LCI(RCM)	Landing Craft, Infantry (Radar Counter Measures)	NGF; NGF(O)	Naval Gunfire; Naval Gunfire (Officer)
		Nick	Allied code name for the Japanese single-engine Kawasaki Ki-45 Army fighter
LCS	Landing Craft, Support (Large), Mark 3		
LCT	Landing Craft, Tank		
LCTR	British-built Landing Craft, Tank, Rocket	Oil King	Enlisted man in charge of fuel oil transfer and storage
LCVP	Landing Craft, Vehicle, Personnel	OOD, OD	Officer of the Deck
		Op Plan	Operations Plan
LD	Line of Departure	Oscar	Allied code name for the

	Japanese single-engine Nakajima Ki-43 Army fighter
OTC	Officer in Tactical Command
Pac	Pacific
PBM	Martin Mariner twin-engine U.S. Navy patrol bomber flying boat
PC; PCE; PCE(R)	Patrol Craft; Patrol Craft, Escort; Patrol Craft, Escort (Rescue)
Peggy	Allied code name for the Japanese twi- engine Mitsubishi Ki-67 Army bomber
PG; PGM	Patrol Gunboat; Patrol Motor Gunboat
Phib	Amphibious
PhM	Pharmacists Mate, Hospital Corpsman
Phone/Telephone Talker	Enlisted man on bridge who communicates with ship's gun batteries and repair parties using sound-powered microphone with helmet headset
PO	Petty Officer
POA	Pacific Ocean Areas
Point Bolo	Zampa Misaki (or Mizaki), the western Okinawa cape designated the central geographical coordinate for U.S. military operations
Port and Starboard	Half of a ship's crew alternate watch standing each day
POW	Prisoner of War
RCM	Radar Counter Measures
RCT	Regimental Combat Team
RdM	Radarman
Ready Service, RS	Locker or magazine for stowing readied ammunition and fully-assembled rockets less fuses
Retto	Japanese for a group of islands
RFS	Ready for Sailing
RM	Radioman
Rocketship	LSM(R)
SC	Submarine Chaser
SCR	Medium range FM radio transmitter-receiver
SFCP	Shore Fire Control Party
Shima, Jima	Japanese for island
SK	Storekeeper
Skeg	A fin-like projection from the bottom stern for stability and protection of the rudders, propellers and shafts
Skipper	Commanding Officer
SM	Signalman
SOPA	Senior Officer Present Afloat
Spinner	Informal term for a Spin-stabilized Rocket, rocket launcher, or LSM(R)
SSR	Spin-stabilized Rocket
Steerageway	Minimum speed
Stern	The rear or fantail of a ship
StM	Stewards Mate
SU-1	Surface search radar
Superstructure	All ship's structure, equipment and fittings except rmament extending above the hull
TBF/TBM	Grumman/General Motors Avenger single-engine U.S. Navy carrier torpedo bomber
TBS	Talk Between Ships voice radio network
TF	Task Force
TG	Task Group
TH	Territory of Hawaii
Tony	Allied code name for the Japanese single-engine Kawasaki Ki-61 Army fighter
Transverse	At right angles to the keel or centerline, athwartship
TU	Task Unit
USS	United States Ship
Val	Allied code name for the Japanese single-engine Aichi D3A Navy carrier bomber
VF	Navy or Marine Corps fighter plane
VMF	Marine Corps fighter squadron
VOF	Navy or Marine Corps observation fighter plane
VT	Variable Timed antiaircraft ammunition, also called Proximity Shells
Wan	Japanese for large bay or harbor
War Diary	Monthly summary of activities

Weigh	To lift an anchor off the bottom	XO	Executive Officer
Well Deck	Tank Deck or Main Deck for vehicles	YMS	Yard Minesweeper
Wherry	A light twelve-foot boat with a transom stern and a 7-man capacity pulled by 2 or 3 men, each using 2 oars	Zampa Misaki (or Mizaki)	Cape Zampa, codenamed Point Bolo by U.S. forces
WIA	Wounded In Action	Zeke, Zero	Allied code name for the Japanese single-engine Mitsubishi A6M Navy carrier fighter

Chapter Notes

Introduction

1. "Picture of the Week," *LIFE* 18, no. 16 (1945): 32–33, erroneously identified as an LCT(R).

2. Robert W. Landis, *Ship's Log USS LSM(R) 192*, unpublished diary; Paul S. Vaitses Jr., *In the Rockets' Red Glare* (unpublished manuscript), 1.

3. Richard Hillyer, "Meanest Ships Afloat," *Sea Classics* 2, no. 2 (1979), Cover, 22.

4. John C. Merrill, Jr., "Rocket-Firing Guinea Pigs," *Our Navy*, First of March, 1952, 12.

5. Commander, LSM Flotilla Nine, Action Report–Ie Shima and Southeastern Okinawa, 2 April through 20 April 1945, Serial 0010, 21 April 1945, 1st Endorsement, Serial 0018, 17 May 1945.

6. The National Archives, United Kingdom, DEFE 2/1327, Appendix "C" to C. R. 2626/45; Warship, vol. IV (1980), John Roberts, ed., *Amphibious Fire Support* by Norman Friedman, 199–205, Conway Maritime Press/Naval Institute Press, Annapolis, MD. See Chapter 8 "Fire Support," 242–246, Norman Friedman, *U.S. Amphibious Ships and Craft* (Annapolis, MD: Naval Institute Press, 2002).

7. George C. Dyer, Vice Admiral, USN (Ret.), *The Amphibians Came to Conquer: The Story of Admiral Richmond Kelly Turner*, vol. 1 (Washington, D.C.: U.S. Government Printing Office, 1969), 268–269.

8. Donald E. Graves, *Sir William Congreve and the Rocket's Red Glare*, Historical Arms Series No. 23 (Alexandria Bay, NY: Museum Restoration Service, 1989).

9. Norman Friedman, *U.S. Amphibious Ships and Craft: An Illustrated Design History* (Annapolis, MD: Naval Institute Press, 2002), 228–230.

10. Sam J. Tangredi, Captain, U.S. Navy (Ret.), "Breaking the Anti-Access Wall," *Proceedings* 141 (2015), 40–45.

11. Friedman, *U.S. Amphibious Ships and Craft*, 228–230.

12. Joel R. Davidson, *The Unsinkable Fleet: The Politics of U.S. Navy Expansion in World War II* (Annapolis, MD: Naval Institute Press, 1996), 185.

13. Buell, *Master of Sea Power*, 419, 423.

14. Robert Ross Smith. Chapter 1, "The Debate Over Luzon," in *Triumph In the Philippines, The War in the Pacific, United States Army in World War II*. Washington, D.C.: U.S. Government Printing Office, 1963.

15. Buell, *Master of Sea Power*, 447–448.

16. Samuel Eliot Morison. *Victory in the Pacific 1945*. vol. 14, 4–5, of *History of United States Naval Operations in World War II*. Boston: Little, Brown, 1960; Smith, *Triumph In the Philippines*, Chapter 1, "The Debate Over Luzon."

17. Frederick J. Hovde, "The Spinner Family," in *Rockets, Guns and Targets*, ed. John E. Burchard (Boston: Little, Brown, 1948), 200–201; Paul S. Vaitses Jr., *In the Rockets' Red Glare* (unpublished manuscript), 9, 23; Neal B. Hadsell conversation with author.

18. Commander, Amphibious Forces, U.S. Pacific Fleet, Amphibious Gunnery Bulletin No. 2–Assault of Okinawa, Serial 0391, 24 May 1945, 5.

Chapter 1

1. Rear Admiral Charles M. ("Savvy") Cooke was Admiral (later Fleet Admiral) King's "top planning officer": Samuel Eliot Morison, *Breaking The Bismarcks Barrier*, vol. 6, 9–11, of *History of United States Naval Operations in World War II* (Boston: Little, Brown, 1950); Samuel Eliot Morison, *The Invasion of France and Germany*, vol. 11, of *History of United States Naval Operations in World War II* (Boston: Little, Brown, 1957), 54.

2. Vice Admiral Frederick J. Horne, USN, Vice Chief of Naval Operations, "was CNO in every way save title alone": Thomas B. Buell, *Master of Sea Power: A Biography of Fleet Admiral Ernest J. King* (Boston: Little, Brown, 1980), 221.

3. Commander In Chief Confidential Memo FFI/S82–3 Serial 03092, 6 September 1944.

4. Buford Rowland and William B. Boyd, *U.S. Navy Bureau of Ordnance in World War II* (Washington, D.C.: U.S. Government Printing Office, 1953), 319.

5. "the ultimate wartime fire support craft": Friedman, *U.S. Amphibious Ships and Craft*, 246.

6. Gibbs & Cox, Inc., "(b) Conversion of LSM Landing Craft to Rocket Ships—Three Types," (i) LSM(R), paragraph 129, 1–53 to 1–54, n.d.; Frank O. Braynard, *By Their Works Ye Shall Know Them: The Life and Ships of William Francis Gibbs 1886–1967* (N.p.: Gibbs & Cox, Inc., private limited printing, 1968), 116–119.

7. Gibbs & Cox, Inc., "(b) Conversion of LSM Landing Craft to Rocket Ships—Three Types," (i) LSM(R), paragraph 129, 1–54 to 1–55; Braynard, *By Their Works Ye Shall Know Them*, 116–119.

8. Bureau of Ships Confidential Letter C-LSM/L9–3(440), "LSM Rocket Ship," 7 October 1944.

9. DEFE 2/1327, Appendix C to C.R. 2626/45, The National Archives, United Kingdom; Norman Friedman, "Amphibious Fire Support," in *Warship*, vol. 4, ed. John Roberts (Annapolis, MD: Conway Maritime Press/Naval Institute Press, 1980), 199–205; Friedman, *U.S. Amphibious Ships and Craft*, 242–246.

10. Gibbs & Cox, Inc., "(b) Conversion of LSM Landing Craft to Rocket Ships—Three Types," (i) LSM(R), paragraph 129, 1–54 to 1–55; Braynard, *By Their Works Ye Shall Know Them*, 116–119.

11. Joel R. Davidson, *Unsinkable Fleet: The Politics of U.S. Navy Expansion in World War II* (Annapolis, MD: Naval Institute Press, 1996), 135.

12. A. D. Baker III, ed., *Allied Landing Craft of World War Two* (Annapolis, MD: Naval Institute Press, 1985).

13. Jim McNeil, *Charleston's Navy Yard: A Picture History* (Charleston: Coker Craft Press, Inc., 1985), 102, 127; Fritz P. Hamer, *Charleston Reborn: A Southern City, Its Navy Yard and World War II* (Charleston: The History Press, 2005), 41–42, 50; Navy Department, Memorandum, Office of Procurement and Material, Price Revision Division, PM320/CAB/hc, August 14, 1944, to Lt. Comdr. E. F. McGuire, Subject: Dravo Corporation, Papers of Mark E. Andrews, Harry S. Truman Library, Independence, Missouri. In contrast, Andrews reported on productivity in a Midwest LSM shipyard:

> Labor: From the inspection trip which took in practically all operations at both [Dravo Corporation, Delaware] yards, my general impression is that the Neville Island operation is probably as efficient as the average shipyard although there are evidences of considerable loafing which at the time I went through the yards probably ran to about 25% total of those supposedly on a job. At Wilmington it was apparent that there was less efficiency than at Neville Island. Insofar as yard and outfitting labor is concerned, there seemed to be about one-third of the personnel who were working energetically. Another third seemed to be giving attention to their work and the remaining one-third did not seem to be particularly interested in the work at hand. In the various shops at both plants, efficiency seemed to be normal and would compare favorably with similar enterprises in a regular manufacturing establishment.

14. "Except for *LSM 231, 232,* and *306–309, LSM 1–336* were ordered as *LCT(7) 1501–1830,* within the LCT series. Ships were all completed as LSMs, and 1944 orders certainly described them as LSMs rather than LCT(7)s. The precise date of the changeover is not clear": Friedman, *U.S. Amphibious Ships and Craft,* 634; Cf. Stephen S. Roberts, *United States Navy in World War II: Shipbuilding Programs and Contracts, 1938–1945,* FISCAL YEAR 1944:1945 Combatant Building Program (Use all authorized combatant tonnage), http://www.shipscribe.com/shiprefs/usnprog/fy4445.html: *LCT(7)s 1501–1625: LSMs 1–125* Brown Ship Building Company, Houston, Texas; *LCT(7)s 1626–1700: LSMs 126–200* U.S. Navy Yard, Charleston, South Carolina; *LCT(7)s 1701–1720: LSMs 233–252* Western Pipe and Steel Company, San Pedro, California; *LCT(7)s 1721–1750: LSMs 201–230* Dravo Corporation, Wilmington, Delaware; *LCT(7)s 1751–1803:* (ex-*LSMs 251–303) LSMs 253–305* initially contracted to Bethlehem Hingham then withdrawn and re-contracted between Federal Ship Building and Dry Dock Company, Newark, New Jersey and Charleston Navy Yard, Charleston, South Carolina; *LCT(7)s 1804–1830: LSMs 310–336* Pullman Standard Car and Manufacturing Company, Chicago, Illinois.

15. Dravo Corporation, Wilmington, DE: *LSMs 201–232; LSMs 414–446;* Navy Yard Charleston, Charleston, SC: *LSMs 126–200; LSMs 295–309; LSMs 389–413; LSMs 553–558;* Federal Ship Building and Dry Dock Company, Newark, NJ: *LSMs 253–294;* Pullman Standard Car and Manufacturing Company, Chicago, IL: *LSMs 310–353;* Brown Ship Building Company, Houston, TX: *LSMs 1–125; LSMs 354–388; LSMs 459–552;* Western Pipe and Steel Company, San Pedro, CA: *LSMs 233–252; LSMs 447–458.*

16. Braynard, *By Their Works Ye Shall Know Them,* 116–119.

17. The LCT(7) redesignation to LSM was probably promulgated no later than 22 November 1943 according to three sources:

   1) Department of the Navy, *Ship's Data, U.S. Naval Vessels,* vol. 2 (Washington, D.C.: U.S. Government Printing Office, 1949);

   2) Navy Department, Bureau of Ships, 22 November 1943, *Detail Specifications for Building Landing Ship Medium LSM 1 to 353, formerly designated Landing Craft, Tank, MK VII LCT(7) 1501 Class, NavShips (451)* (Washington, D.C.: U.S. Government Printing Office, 1943);

   3) "Ship designation changed from LCT(7) to LSM in accordance with Sup Ship NY Letter to G&C Dated Nov. 29,

1943. *LCT(7) 1501–1830/S28* (126678-D3)": LSM Class, Brown Shipbuilding Company, Houston, Texas, Design and Engineering By Gibbs & Cox, Inc., New York City, 1944: Dr. No. LSM-01010–1, General Arrangement of Outboard Profile, Bureau of Ships Plan Number LSM(1)S0103–112380, Alt. 8; Dr. No. LSM-01010–2, General Arrangement of Hold & Main Deck, Bureau of Ships Plan Number LSM(1)S0103–112366 Alt. 10; Dr. No. LSM-01010–3, General Arrangement Superstructure Deck, Bridges & Focsle Deck, Bureau of Ships Plan Number LSM(1)-S0103–112367 Alt. 9.

18. LSM Class Manual, March 1, 1944, O2–1 to O2–2.

19. "The evocative DUKW designation was derived from the army's alphabetical symbols for 4-wheel drive and the year the vehicle entered service, 1942. D indicated 1942, U indicated amphibious, K indicated front-wheel drive, and W indicated rear-wheel drive": LSM Class Manual, March 1, 1944, 1–1; Friedman, *U.S. Amphibious Ships and Craft,* 623, n. 10.

20. William L. McGee, *The Amphibians are Coming!,* vol. 1 (Santa Barbara: BMC Publications, 2000), 34–35; Rolf F. Illsley, *LSM-LSMR WWII Amphibious Forces,* vol. 1 (Paducah, KY: Turner Publishing Company, 1994), 18; "Welcome Aboard," *United States Atlantic Fleet, Amphibious Training Base, Little Creek, Virginia* (ca. 1944–1945).

21. Bureau of Naval Personnel Information Bulletin, "Insignia Authorized for Amphibious Forces" (July 1944, no. 328), 68.

22. Neal B. Hadsell letter to author January 5, 1995.

23. Daniel E. Barbey, Vice Admiral, USN, *MacArthur's Amphibious Navy: Seventh Amphibious Force Operations 1943–1945* (Annapolis, MD: Naval Institute Press, 1969), 47.

24. George C. Dyer, Vice Admiral, USN (Ret.), *The Amphibians Came to Conquer: The Story of Admiral Richmond Kelly Turner,* vol. 1 (Washington, D.C.: U.S. Government Printing Office, 1969), 268–269.

25. Vaitses, *In the Rockets' Red Glare,* 1, 4.

26. McNeil, *Charleston's Navy Yard: A Picture History,* 99–100.

27. Admiral Jules James Papers, East Carolina Manuscript Collection, J. Y. Joyner Library, East Carolina University, Greenville, North Carolina, excerpted article dated 25 August 1944.

28. Allison Gray letter to author February 6, 1996.

29. Bruce A. McDaniel letter to author July 9, 2001.

30. Vaitses, *In the Rockets' Red Glare,* 4.

31. 1st Endorsement on Lt. H.G. Carrison ltr of 18 Dec 1944 serial 07 LSMFlot9/S73–1/44, 4 January 1945.

32. Allan M. Hirshberg undated letter to author ca. October 1995.

33. James M. Stewart letter to author November 2, 1994.

34. James M. Stewart, *90 Day Naval Wonder* (Bellevue, WA: Trees, Inc., 2003).

35. Lieutenant (Junior Grade) Neal B. Hadsell, D-V(G), USNR 238756, Restricted Orders, File No. FE25–4/P16–4/MM/OO, Change of Duty.

36. Vaitses, *In the Rockets' Red Glare,* 5–6.

37. Bruce A. McDaniel undated letter to author ca. January 1996.

38. Lyle Tennis letter to author dated November 7, 1996.

39. Muster Rolls (BuPers Files), USS *LSM(R) 188* thru USS *LSM(R) 199.*

40. Vaitses, *In the Rockets' Red Glare,* 4.

41. Allan M. Hirshberg undated letter to author ca. October 1995.

42. C.W. Snyder, "Rocket Weapons as Developed and Used in World War II," in *Rocket and Underwater Ordnance,* Summary Technical Report of the National Defense Research Committee, Division 3, vol. 1, ed. Eliot B. Bradford (Washington, D.C.: Columbia University Press, 1946), 115.

43. Albert B. Christman, *Sailors, Scientists and Rockets,* vol. 1 (Washington, D.C.: U.S. Government Printing Office, 1971), 97.

44. Christman, *Sailors, Scientists and Rockets*, 50–51.

45. Christman, *Sailors, Scientists and Rockets*, 97.

46. Caltech scientists and engineers often referred to rockets and launchers as either "Finners," meaning Fin-stabilized, or "Spinners," meaning Spin-stabilized. Thus, LSM(R)s also came to be called either "Finner" or "Spinner" rocketships, just as Huse similarly refers to LSM(R)s as either "F-ships" or "S-ships": C.W. Snyder, "General Theory of Rocket Performance," in *Rocket and Underwater Ordnance*, Summary Technical Report of the National Defense Research Committee, Division 3, vol. 1, ed. Eliot B. Bradford (Washington, D.C.: Columbia University Press, 1946), 215; Hovde, *Rockets, Guns and Targets*, 202.

47. Rowland and Boyd, *U.S. Navy Bureau of Ordnance in World War II*, 26.

48. "Contract Numbers," in *Rocket and Underwater Ordnance*, Summary Technical Report of the National Defense Research Committee, Division 3, vol. 1, ed. Eliot B. Bradford, 368–369.

49. Frederick J. Hovde, "Initial Work and Tests 1940–1941," in *Rockets, Guns and Targets*, ed. John E. Burchard (Boston: Little, Brown, 1948), 19.

50. Christman, *Sailors, Scientists and Rockets*, 114.

51. J. D. Gerrard-Gough and Albert B. Christman, *The Grand Experiment at Inyokern*, vol. 2 (Washington, D.C.: U.S. Government Printing Office, 1978), 3.

52. Conway W. Snyder, "Caltech's Other Rocket Project: Personal Recollections," *Engineering & Science*, Spring 1991, 2–13; Judith Goodstein, *Millikan's School: A History of the California Institute of Technology* (New York: W.W. Norton, 1991), 425.

53. Although the 5.0-inch AR (Aircraft Rocket) was made obsolete by Caltech's 5.0-inch HVAR (High Velocity Aircraft Rocket), the former continued to be used extensively due to insufficient quantities of the latter until spring 1945: C.W. Snyder, "Service Designs of Fin-Stabilized Rockets for Aircraft Armament," in *Rocket and Underwater Ordnance*, Summary Technical Report of the National Defense Research Committee, Division 3, vol. 1, ed. Eliot B. Bradford (Washington, D.C.: Columbia University Press, 1946), 170–171, 175.

54. C.W. Snyder, "Service Designs of Fin-Stabilized Rockets for Surface Warfare," in *Rocket and Underwater Ordnance*, Summary Technical Report of the National Defense Research Committee, Division 3, vol. 1, ed. Eliot B. Bradford (Washington, D.C.: Columbia University Press, 1946), 151.

55. "Dispersion is a measure of the scatter of the impact points of a group of identical rockets fired under supposedly identical conditions." Rocket scatter may be calculated in mils for lateral dispersion and/or range dispersion. Generally speaking, a mil is a unit of measurement equaling $\frac{1}{6400}$ of a complete circle; for practical purposes, this may be understood as 1 mil equaling 1-yard deflection (or variation) for every thousand yards of range: C.W. Snyder, "Exterior Ballistics of Fin-Stabilized Rockets," in *Rocket and Underwater Ordnance*, Summary Technical Report of the National Defense Research Committee, Division 3, vol. 1, ed. Eliot B. Bradford (Washington, D.C.: Columbia University Press, 1946), 276.

56. C.W. Snyder, "Service Designs of Fin-Stabilized Rockets for Surface Warfare," in *Rocket and Underwater Ordnance*, Summary Technical Report of the National Defense Research Committee, Division 3, vol. 1, ed. Eliot B. Bradford (Washington, D.C.: Columbia University Press, 1946), 151–152.

57. L. E. H. Maund, Rear Admiral (Ret.), *Assault from the Sea* (London: Methuen, 1949), 90; J. D. Ladd, *Assault from the Sea 1939–1945* (New York: Hippocrene, 1976), 175, 182.

58. "Landing Craft and Auxiliary Vessels," in *The Design and Construction of British Warships 1939–1945: The Official Record*, vol. 3, ed. D. K. Brown (London: Conway Maritime Press, 1996), 56.

59. U.S. LCT(R) Group, September 1943-October 1944, War Diary, u.d; After this unit was dissolved, some former American LCTR sailors were later transferred to the Pacific where they reported aboard the new "Ultimate" LSM(R)s.

60. Taylor Peck, *Round-Shot to Rockets* (Annapolis, MD: Naval Institute Press, 1949), 244–245.

61. C.W. Snyder, "Military Needs Which Rockets Can Meet," in *Rocket and Underwater Ordnance*, Summary Technical Report of the National Defense Research Committee, Division 3, vol. 1, ed. Eliot B. Bradford (Washington, D.C.: Columbia University Press, 1946), 118.

62. C.W. Snyder, "Service Designs of Spin-Stabilized Rockets," in *Rocket and Underwater Ordnance*, Summary Technical Report of the National Defense Research Committee, Division 3, vol. 1, ed. Eliot B. Bradford (Washington, D.C.: Columbia University Press, 1946), 196.

63. C.W. Snyder, "General Theory of Rocket Performance," in *Rocket and Underwater Ordnance*, Summary Technical Report of the National Defense Research Committee, Division 3, vol. 1, ed. Eliot B. Bradford (Washington, D.C.: Columbia University Press, 1946), 218.

64. C.W. Snyder, "Military Needs Which Rockets Can Meet," in *Rocket and Underwater Ordnance*, Summary Technical Report of the National Defense Research Committee, Division 3, vol. 1, ed. Eliot B. Bradford (Washington, D.C.: Columbia University Press, 1946), 117–125.

65. C.W. Snyder, "General Theory of Rocket Performance," in *Rocket and Underwater Ordnance*, Summary Technical Report of the National Defense Research Committee, Division 3, vol. 1, ed. Eliot B. Bradford (Washington, D.C.: Columbia University Press, 1946), 216.

66. C.W. Snyder, "Service Designs of Spin-Stabilized Rockets," in *Rocket and Underwater Ordnance*, Summary Technical Report of the National Defense Research Committee, Division 3, vol. 1, ed. Eliot B. Bradford (Washington, D.C.: Columbia University Press, 1946), 199–200; Charles C. Lauritsen, William A. Fowler and B. M. Norton, "Spin-Stabilized Rockets," in *Ballistic Data: Fin-Stabilized and Spin-Stabilized Rockets*, Office of Scientific Research and Development, National Defense Research Committee, Division 3, Section L, ed. Joseph Foladare (Pasadena: California Institute of Technology, 1946), 333–390.

67. Rowland and Boyd, *U.S. Navy Bureau of Ordnance in World War II*, 317.

68. LSMs as LCT(7)s: *LSM 188 = LCT(7) 1688; LSM 189 = LCT(7) 1689; LSM 190 = LCT(7) 1690; LSM 191 = LCT(7) 1691; LSM 192 = LCT(7) 1692; LSM 193 = LCT(7) 1693; LSM 194 = LCT(7) 1694; LSM 195 = LCT(7) 1695; LSM 196 = LCT(7) 1696; LSM 197 = LCT(7) 1697; LSM 198 = LCT(7) 1698; LSM 199 = LCT(7) 1699*

69. CNO Confidential Letter Op-23-E-AMC 10–12 Serial 0599523 (SC) S82–3 Doc. 138166, 13 October 1944, "Subject: LSM Rocket Ship."

70. CNO Restricted Letter Op-23-S-jk Serial 335123, 18 October 1944, Recommendation for new classification LSM(R) and reclassification of LSMs, with attached Secretary of the Navy First Endorsement Approval Op-23-S-jk Serial 335223, 20 October 1944: Note standard U.S. Navy hyphenated hull designations, e.g., *LSM-188* reclassified *LSM(R)-188*.

71. Chief of Naval Personnel, Pers-1042b-GB, LSM/16–1, Restricted, 21 October 1944, LSM—Officer and Enlisted Complement, with Restricted NavPers 2128, Complement of *LSM(R) 188–199*, Approved 21 October 1944, Enclosure to Pers-1042b-GB of 21 October 1944.

72. Lawrence J. Low letter to author September 20, 1998.

73. Ships Launching Files, *LSMs 188 thru 199*. Records of Naval Districts and Shore Establishments 1942–1945, Record Group 181, National Archives and Records Administration (NARA), Atlanta.

74. Undocking Report of *LSM 190* and *LSM 191*, U.S. Navy Yard Charleston, S.C., 21 September 1944; Launching Report of *LSM 196* and *LSM 197*, U.S. Navy Yard Charleston, S.C., 12 October 1944.

75. "Interim" LSM(R) beachings and retractings occurred only once: 16 June 1945 by *LSM(R)s 189, 191* and *192* at Samar, Philippine Islands.

76. Vaitses, *In the Rockets' Red Glare,* 2.

77. Neal B. Hadsell letter to author January 5, 1995.

78. Weekly Progress Report from Commandant, Navy Yard, USS *LSM 188,* USS *LSM 189,* USS *LSM 190,* 16 October 1944, Bureau of Ships General Correspondence 1940–1945.

79. Friedman's remark about the LST program applies equally to the LSMs and LSM(R)s: "... As in several other amphibious programs, work was accelerated by beginning construction while building drawings were being completed ...": Friedman, *US Amphibious Ships and Craft,* 120.

80. Progress Report from Prospective Commanding Officer, USS *LSM 194,* 13 October 1944.

81. Cf. *LSM 188* thru *LSM 195,* Weekly Progress Report by Prospective Commanding Officer.

82. U.S. Navy Deck Log, USS *LSM(R) 189.*

83. Cf. Bureau of Ships (BuShips) Files, *LSMs/LSM(R)s 188* thru *199.*

84. Charles C. Lauritsen, William A. Fowler and B. M. Norton, "Firing Systems," in *Rocket Launchers for Surface Use,* ed. Paul E. Lloyd (Pasadena: California Institute of Technology, 1946), 20–21.

85. Charles C. Lauritsen, William A. Fowler and B. M. Norton, "Aircraft Launchers for Fin-Stabilized Rockets," in *Firing of Rockets from Aircraft: Launchers, Sights, Flight Tests,* ed. Catherine C. Campbell (Pasadena: California Institute of Technology, 1946), 1–2.

86. Friedman, *U.S. Amphibious Ships and Craft,* 246.

87. Charles C. Lauritsen, William A. Fowler and B. M. Norton, "CIT Launcher Catalog," in *Rocket Launchers for Surface Use,* ed. Paul E. Lloyd (Pasadena: California Institute of Technology, 1946), 110–113; Department of the Navy, Bureau of Ordnance, *Missile Launchers and Related Equipment Catalog OP 1855,* 1 June 1953, 319–320.

88. Hovde, *Rockets, Guns and Targets,* 202; C.W. Snyder, "Military Needs Which Rockets Can Meet," in *Rocket and Underwater Ordnance,* Summary Technical Report of the National Defense Research Committee, Division 3, vol. 1, ed. Eliot B. Bradford (Washington, D.C.: Columbia University Press, 1946), 118; C.W. Snyder, "Rocket Heads," in *Rocket and Underwater Ordnance,* Summary Technical Report of the National Defense Research Committee, Division 3, vol. 1, ed. Eliot B. Bradford (Washington, D.C.: Columbia University Press, 1946), 128; C.W. Snyder, "General Theory of Rocket Performance," in *Rocket and Underwater Ordnance,* Summary Technical Report of the National Defense Research Committee, Division 3, vol. 1, ed. Eliot B. Bradford (Washington, D.C.: Columbia University Press, 1946), 216.

89. 5.0-inch Fin-stabilized Aircraft (AR) rockets with an approximate range of 4000-yards fired at a 45° quadrant elevation (QE) had mean dispersions ranging from under 20 mils to over 30 mils. By comparison, 5.0-inch Spin-stabilized (SSR) Rockets with an approximate range of 5000-yards fired at a 45° QE had mean dispersions of less than 10 mils to almost 20 mils: C.W. Snyder, "Military Needs Which Rockets Can Meet," in *Rocket and Underwater Ordnance,* Summary Technical Report of the National Defense Research Committee, Division 3, vol. 1, ed. Eliot B. Bradford (Washington, D.C.: Columbia University Press, 1946), 121; C.W. Snyder, "Service Designs of Fin-Stabilized Rockets for Aircraft Armament," in *Rocket and Underwater Ordnance,* Summary Technical Report of the National Defense Research Committee, Division 3, vol. 1, ed. Eliot B. Bradford (Washington, D.C.: Columbia University Press, 1946), 173; Charles C. Lauritsen, William A. Fowler and B. M. Norton, "Fin-Stabilized Rockets," in *Ballistic Data: Fin-Stabilized and Spin-Stabilized Rockets,* Office of Scientific Research and Development, National Defense Research Committee, Division 3, Section L, ed. Joseph Foladare (Pasadena: California Institute of Technology, 1946), 138.

90. Aircraft Rocket (AR) specifications, characteristics and other data varied with Mark and Mod designations: C.W. Snyder, "Service Designs of Fin-Stabilized Rockets for Aircraft Armament," in *Rocket and Underwater Ordnance,* Summary Technical Report of the National Defense Research Committee, Division 3, vol. 1, ed. Eliot B. Bradford (Washington, D.C.: Columbia University Press, 1946), 172–173; Charles C. Lauritsen, William A. Fowler and B. M. Norton, "Fin-Stabilized Rockets," in *Ballistic Data: Fin-Stabilized and Spin-Stabilized Rockets,* Office of Scientific Research and Development, National Defense Research Committee, Division 3, Section L, ed. Joseph Foladare (Pasadena: California Institute of Technology, 1946), 119–143.

91. C.W. Snyder, "Service Designs of Fin-Stabilized Rockets for Aircraft Armament," in *Rocket and Underwater Ordnance,* Summary Technical Report of the National Defense Research Committee, Division 3, vol. 1, ed. Eliot B. Bradford (Washington, D.C.: Columbia University Press, 1946), 165–195: "... [T]he base of the AA common shell was boat-tailed and bored out to take a motor adapter and became the 5.0-in. Rocket Head Mk. 1 ...," 171; "Probably more ARs were fired with the 5.0-in. Mk. 1 head than with all others ...," 175.

92. C.W. Snyder, "Rocket Fuzes," in *Rocket and Underwater Ordnance,* Summary Technical Report of the National Defense Research Committee, Division 3, vol. 1, ed. Eliot B. Bradford (Washington, D.C.: Columbia University Press, 1946), 130–131. C.W. Snyder, "Service Designs of Fin-Stabilized Rockets for Aircraft Armament," in *Rocket and Underwater Ordnance,* Summary Technical Report of the National Defense Research Committee, Division 3, vol. 1, ed. Eliot B. Bradford (Washington, D.C.: Columbia University Press, 1946), 175.

93. Lawrence J. Low letter to author May 30, 1996.

94. C.W. Snyder, "Motor Design," in *Rocket and Underwater Ordnance,* Summary Technical Report of the National Defense Research Committee, Division 3, vol. 1, ed. Eliot B. Bradford (Washington, D.C.: Columbia University Press, 1946), 262–266.

95. Charles C. Lauritsen, William A. Fowler and B. M. Norton, "Fin-Stabilized Rockets," in *Ballistic Data: Fin-Stabilized and Spin-Stabilized Rockets,* Office of Scientific Research and Development, National Defense Research Committee, Division 3, Section L, ed. Joseph Foladare (Pasadena: California Institute of Technology, 1946), 119–143.

96. CIT Secret Memorandum, "Status of Rocket Ships leaving Pearl Harbor, T.H., from 21 Jan 45 to 15 Feb 45," 21 February 1945.

97. Henry E. Guerlac, *Radar in World War II: The History of Modern Physics 1800–1950,* vol. 1 (Los Angeles: Tomash Publishers/American Institute of Physics, 1987), 415–419.

98. Seventeen men manned the 5" 38 gun in *LSM(R) 191*: Laurie R. Russell letter to author November 27, 1995.

99. Office of the Commandant Confirmation of Telephone Conversation LSM(R)/S8(R)(M-2), 8 November 1944.

100. U.S. Navy Deck Log, USS *LSM(R) 188.*

101. *LSM(R) 188,* The Commanding Officer, Memo, Structural Firing Report, 11280368, 21 November 1944.

102. Burton E. Weed, "LSM 'R' 188," unpublished typescript.

103. U.S. Navy Deck Log, USS *LSM(R) 188.*

104. U.S. Navy Deck Logs: USS *LSM(R) 192,* USS *LSM(R) 193,* USS *LSM(R) 194,* USS *LSM(R) 195.*

105. Vaitses, *In the Rockets' Red Glare,* 9–10.

106. Gibbs & Cox, Inc., "(b): Conversion of LSM Landing Craft [*sic*] to Rocket Ships—Three Types (ii) LSM(R)—Scheme 'E,' paragraph 130," 1–54 to 1–55; Braynard, *By Their Works Ye Shall Know Them,* 116–119.

107. CNO Confidential Letter Op-23-E-AMC 10–12, Serial 0599523 (SC) S82–3, Doc. 138166, 13 October 1944, "Subject: LSM Rocket Ship."

108. Bureau of Ships Confidential Letter C-LSM(R)188–199/S74(519L), File "S82–3," 4 November 1944, Secretary of

the Navy/Chief of Naval Operations; See Chief of Bureau of Ordnance, LSM(R)(Rela), Confidential, "*LSM(R) 196–199–* (Scheme E)–Installation of Rocket Launchers Mark 51," 21 December 1944.

109. Lawrence J. Low letter to author May 30, 1996; Department of the Navy, Bureau of Ordnance, *Missile Launchers and Related Equipment Catalog OP 1855*, 1 June 1953, 323–324.

110. Lawrence J. Low letter to author May 30, 1996.

111. Charles C. Lauritsen, William A. Fowler and B.M. Norton, "Automatic Launchers," in *Rocket Launchers for Surface Use*, ed. Paul E. Lloyd (Pasadena: California Institute of Technology, 1946), 15–18; See "CIT Launcher Catalog," in *Rocket Launchers for Surface Use*, 160–165.

112. Friedman, *U.S. Amphibious Ships and Craft*, 246.

113. Spin-stabilized Rocket (SSR) specifications, characteristics and related data varied with Mark and Mod designations: C.W. Snyder, "Service Designs of Spin-Stabilized Rockets," in *Rocket and Underwater Ordnance*, Summary Technical Report of the National Defense Research Committee, Division 3, vol. 1, ed. Eliot B. Bradford (Washington, D.C.: Columbia University Press, 1946), 196–207; Charles C. Lauritsen, William A. Fowler and B.M. Norton, "Spin-Stabilized Rockets," in *Ballistic Data: Fin-Stabilized and Spin-Stabilized Rockets*, Office of Scientific Research and Development, National Defense Research Committee, Division 3, Section L, ed. Joseph Foladare (Pasadena: California Institute of Technology, 1946), 333–390.

114. Charles C. Lauritsen, William A. Fowler and B.M. Norton, "Spin-Stabilized Rockets," in *Ballistic Data: Fin-Stabilized and Spin-Stabilized Rockets*, Office of Scientific Research and Development, National Defense Research Committee, Division 3, Section L, ed. Joseph Foladare (Pasadena: California Institute of Technology, 1946), 348, and Cf. Range Table, 355.

115. C.W. Snyder, "Rocket Fuzes," in *Rocket and Underwater Ordnance*, Summary Technical Report of the National Defense Research Committee, Division 3, vol. 1, ed. Eliot B. Bradford (Washington, D.C.: Columbia University Press, 1946), 137; C.W. Snyder, "Service Designs of Spin-Stabilized Rockets," in *Rocket and Underwater Ordnance*, Summary Technical Report of the National Defense Research Committee, Division 3, vol. 1, ed. Eliot B. Bradford (Washington, D.C.: Columbia University Press, 1946), 199, 203.

116. Lawrence J. Low letter to author May 30, 1996.

117. CIT Secret Memorandum, "Status of Rocket Ships leaving Pearl Harbor, T.H., from 21 Jan 45 to 15 Feb 45," 21 February 1945.

118. Hovde, *Rockets, Guns and Targets*, 200–201.

119. E.W. Price, C.L. Horine and C.W. Snyder, "Eaton Canyon: A History of Rocket Motor Research and Development in the Caltech-NDRC-Navy Rocket Program, 1941–1946," 34th AIAA/ASME/SAE/ASEE Joint Propulsion Conference & Exhibit, July 13–15, 1998, Cleveland, OH; Commandant, Navy Yard LSM(R)/S79(R)(M-5) to Chief of Bureau of Ordnance, "Confirmation of Telephone Conversation," 3 December 1944.

120. Commandant, Navy Yard LSM(R)/S79(R)(M-5) to Chief of Bureau of Ordnance, "Confirmation of Telephone Conversation," 3 December 1944.

121. Chief of Bureau of Ordnance, LSM(R)(Rela), Confidential, "LSM(R) 196–199–(Scheme E)–Installation of Rocket Launchers Mark 51," 21 December 1944; Commandant, Navy Yard Confidential Letter A7–3/LSM(R)/S78(R) (N-1-4-42) to Chief, Bureau of Ordnance, "Rocket Launchers Mk. 51—Correction of Defects," 17 December 1944.

122. Acceptance Trials reports of USS *LSM(R) 196*, USS *LSM(R) 197*, USS *LSM(R) 198*, USS *LSM(R) 199*, n.d.

123. Weekly Progress Report from Prospective Commanding Officer, USS *LSM(R) 196*, 8 December 1944; Weekly Progress Report from Prospective Commanding Officer, USS *LSM(R) 197*, 8 December 1944.

124. U.S. Navy Deck Logs: USS *LSM(R) 196*, USS *LSM(R) 197*, USS *LSM(R) 198*, USS *LSM(R) 199*.

125. Operations and Gunnery Officer, LSM Flotilla Nine, Lieut. H. G. Carrison, Proof and Structural Firing of *LSM(R)s 198* and *199*, LSM Flot 9/S73–1/44, Ser: 07, 18 December 1944; Gunnery Officer, USS *LSM(R) 198*, Lt.(jg) Raymond H. Dick, O-V(S), USNR, Gunnery Officer, Report of Structural Rocket Firing of *LSM(R) 198* on 16 December 1944, Serial 10, 18 December 1944; Gunnery Officer, USS *LSM(R) 199*, Ens. Benton F. Murphy, O-V(S), USNR, Gunnery Officer, Report of Structural Firing of *LSM(R) 199* on 16 December 1944, n.d.

126. Operations and Gunnery Officer, LSM Flotilla Nine, Lieut. H. G. Carrison, Proof and Structural Firing of *LSM(R)s 198* and *199*, LSM Flot 9/S73–1/44, Ser: 07, 18 December 1944: "…[C]onsiderable difficulty was experienced due largely to the inconsistency of dimensions found on the launchers. Proper functioning of the launchers was attained only after considerable time was spent performing miscellaneous modifications. It is recommended that on future launchers Mk. 51, the experience gained from this installation be applied at the point of manufacture"; Office of the Commandant, United States Navy Yard, Charleston, S.C., Confidential Letter, A7–3/LSM(R)/S78(R)(N-1-4-42), Rocket Launchers Mk. 51—Correction of Defects, 17 December 1944.

127. Operations and Gunnery Officer, LSM Flotilla Nine, Lieut. H. G. Carrison, Proof and Structural Firing of *LSM(R)s 198* and *199*, LSM Flot 9/S73–1/44, Ser: 07, 18 December 1944.

128. *LSM(R) 198*, Bureau of Ordnance Routing Slip, handwritten entry of 6 January 1945.

129. James M. Stewart letter to author November 2, 1994.

Chapter 2

1. Neal B. Hadsell conversation with author August 10, 1998; Paul S. Vaitses, Jr., *In the Rockets' Red Glare* (unpublished manuscript), 9, 23.

2. Wesley Murbach letter to author April 24, 1996; Bureau of Ships (BuShips) Files, USS *LSM(R) 196*.

3. 29 November 1944 Lieutenant Commander John H. Fulweiler, USNR, assumed tactical command as Commander LSM(R) Group 27 (ComLSM (R) Grp27) hoisting command pennant on temporary flagship USS *LSM(R) 188* as OTC (Officer-in-Tactical-Command) and SOPA (Senior Officer Present Afloat).

4. 1 December 1944 Commander Dennis L. Francis, USN, Commanding Officer, LSM Flotilla Nine hoisted command pennant on temporary flagship USS *LSM(R) 193* as OTC and SOPA.

5. Lt. Dennis D. O'Callaghan, USNR, Commanding Officer, USS *LSM(R) 196* as OTC.

6. Lt. H. G. Carrison, USN, Operations and Gunnery Officer, LSM Flotilla Nine in USS *LSM(R) 199* as OTC.

7. Robert W. Landis email to author June 5, 2002.

8. George E. Passey letter to author December 8, 1995.

9. "Seaman Edward Bleakley Has Been Declared Dead" (newspaper clipping).

10. *The Bluejackets' Manual 1943* (Annapolis, MD: United States Naval Institute, 1943), 797–798; Edward Briand letter to author April 25, 1996; James M. Stewart undated letter to author ca. May 1996.

11. Laurie R. Russell letter to author May 22, 1996.

12. Allan M. Hirshberg undated letter to author ca. October 1995.

13. Vaitses, *In the Rockets' Red Glare*, 13.

14. Reports of Arrival Inspections and Reports of Departure Inspections. Bureau of Ships General Correspondence 1940–1945, Record Group 19, National Archives and Records Administration (NARA).

15. J. D. Gerrard-Gough and Albert B. Christman, *The*

Grand Experiment at Inyokern, vol. 2 (Washington, D.C.: U.S. Government Printing Office, 1978), 78.

16. Neal B. Hadsell conversation with author August 10, 1998.

17. Vaitses, *In the Rockets' Red Glare*, 16–17.

18. Neal B. Hadsell letter to author January 5, 1995.

19. U.S. Navy Deck Log, USS *LSM(R) 192*.

20. Robert W. Landis, *Ship's Log USS LSM(R) 192*, unpublished diary.

21. Reports of Arrival Inspections and Reports of Departure Inspections. Bureau of Ships General Correspondence 1940–1945, Record Group 19, National Archives and Records Administration (NARA).

22. Edward Briand letter to author April 25, 1996: Some if not all of these rockets were assembled en route after leaving Panama and before arriving in San Diego, California.

23. USS *LSM 186* Commanding Officer Lt. Henry O. Bergkamp, USNR, later assumed command of *LSM(R) 197* on 1 May 1945.

24. U.S. Navy Deck Log, USS *LSM(R) 192*, 5 January 1945, per "LSM Flot. 9 Operation Order 1–45."

25. U.S. Navy Deck Log, USS *LSM(R) 196*, 5 January 1945.

26. David Mallery and Jack Shedd, Ensigns, USNR, *The History of USS LSM(R) 196*, unpublished typescript ca. October 1945.

27. Leonard A. VanOteghem, *Events About and in the Area of Our Ship, the USS LSM(R) 196 and our Unit of 12 LSM(R)s*, unpublished diary.

28. U.S. Navy Deck Log, USS *LSM(R) 197*, 7 January 1945, per "order ND11/A4–3 serial number 0–94."

29. 1st Endorsement on Lt. H.G. Carrison ltr of 18 Dec 1944, serial 07, LSMFlot9/S73–1/44, 4 January 1945.

30. George E. Passey letter to author November 26, 1995.

31. Lieut. H.G. Carrison, Proof and Structural Firing of *LSM(R)s 198* and *199*, LSM Flot 9/S73–1/44, Ser: 07, 18 December 1944; 1st Endorsement on Lt. H. G. Carrison ltr of 18 Dec 1944, serial 07, LSMFlot9/S73–1/44, 4 January 1945.

32. *Rockets, Guns and Targets*, ed. John E. Burchard (Boston: Little, Brown, 1948), 39, 41, 185, 201.

33. Office of the Commandant, United States Navy Yard, Charleston, S.C., Confidential Letter, A7–3/LSM(R)/S78(R) (N-1–4-42), Rocket Launchers Mk. 51—Correction of Defects, 17 December 1944.

34. 1345 hours: U.S. Navy Deck Log, USS *LSM(R) 199*.

35. Gerrard-Gough and Christman, *The Grand Experiment at Inyokern*, 171–172.

36. USS *LSM(R) 199*, Report of Departure Inspection on 18 January 1945, S3–1(7), Serial IB-367, 11 February 1945.

37. CIT Memorandum, OEC 1.2, "Tests of the Mk 35, Mk 50, 2 Mk 51 Launchers aboard an LCI(L)," 25 January 1945; HCSR 5.0-inch rockets were acquired due to "emergency need" from nearby launcher tests on USS *LCI(L) 1086*.

38. 1st Endorsement on Lt. H. G. Carrison ltr of 18 Dec 1944, serial 07, LSMFlot9/S73–1/44, 4 January 1945.

39. U.S. Navy Deck Log, USS *LSM(R) 198*, 26 January 1945: "Seven (7) .50 cal. machine guns delivered aboard complete," and .50 caliber AP with .50 caliber tracer ammunition taken aboard 3 February 1945; See also U.S. Navy Deck Log, USS *LSM(R) 189*, 31 January and 1 February 1945; U.S. Navy Deck Log, USS *LSM(R) 190*, 3 February 1945; U.S. Navy Deck Log, USS *LSM(R) 194*, 1 February 1945.

40. Bruce A. McDaniel undated letter to author ca. March 1997.

41. *LSM(R)s 189* (21–22 Jan 1945), *197* (22–23 Jan 1945), *192* (24–26 Jan 1945), *190* (30 Jan-3 Feb 1945), *188* (30 Jan-3 Feb 1945), *199* (7–8 Feb 1945) repaired in *ARDC 3* (Auxiliary Floating Dry Dock).

42. U.S. Navy Deck Logs, USS *LSM(R)s 191, 192, 196*; VanOteghem, *Events About and in the Area of Our Ship*.

43. Frederick J. Hovde, "Organization and Administrative History," in *Rockets, Guns and Targets*, ed. John E. Burchard

(Boston: Little, Brown, 1948), 41; Hovde, "The Spinner Family," in *Rockets, Guns and Targets*, 201; CIT Telegram, F. L. Hovde, Div. 3, OEM:OSRD:NDRC:Div. 3, 1153800.001, 18 January 1945.

44. CIT Confidential Memorandum, OEC 1.1, A. S. Gould, "Inspection and Repair of Mk 51 Automatic Launchers on *LSM(R) 199*," 23 January 1945.

45. CIT Secret Memorandum, CIT OMC 11.1, "Report on Trip to Pearl Harbor, T. H., from 19 January 1945 to 17 February 1945," 22 February 1945.

46. Lawrence J. Low letter to author May 30, 1996.

47. Commander Administrative Command, Amphibious Forces, U.S. Pacific Fleet (AdComPhibsPac), War Diary, January 1945, Training Order No. A14–45, LSM Training Group 13.10.3; U.S. Navy Deck Log, USS *LSM(R) 190*.

48. R. D. Heinl Jr., Lt. Col., USMC, "The Most Shot-At Island in the Pacific," *Proceedings* 73, no. 4 (1947): 397–399.

49. Mallery and Shedd, *The History of USS LSM(R) 196*.

50. CIT Secret Memorandum, CIT OMC 11.1, "Report on Trip to Pearl Harbor, from 19 January 1945 to 17 February 1945," 22 February 1945; Sears' memorandum cites *LSM(R) 196* with 252 successful rocket firings of 268 attempts, and *LSM(R) 197* with 115 successful rocket firings of 121 attempts, but these numbers appear transposed since they do not correspond with the reported quantities of rockets stowed in each ship by their respective U.S. Navy Deck Logs.

51. Paul S. Vaitses Jr., letter to author August 26, 1996.

52. "Elsie Tease" was a clever onomatopoeic on LCTs.

53. *Allied Landing Craft of World War Two*, ed. A. D. Baker III (Annapolis, MD: Naval Institute Press, 1985).

54. John A. McNeill, *The Voyage of the 159* (Wilmington, NC: self-published, 1995), 74.

55. Commander Administrative Command, Amphibious Forces, U.S. Pacific Fleet (AdComPhibsPac), War Diary, January 1945, Secret Movement Order #5–45, Serial 0092, 29 January 1945; U.S. Navy Deck Logs of LSM(R)s and LCS(L)s.

56. Jack E. Johnson, Lieutenant, USNR, *Thirty-seven Days in a Bathtub, or How to Cross the Pacific in an L.C.T.*, unpublished typescript ca. 1945.

57. Ron Swanson, "LCT Convoys: Across the Pacific Under Their Own Power," in *Flotilla* 5, no. 1 (2004): LCT Flotilla 23 departed Pearl Harbor 3 February 1945; LCT Flotilla 31 departed Pearl Harbor 15 February 1945; Flotilla 33 departed Pearl Harbor 1 March 1945; See Robin L. Rielly, *Kamikaze Patrol: The LCS(L)(3) 61 at War* (self-published, 1996), 36, 41–46; Robin L. Rielly, *Mighty Midgets at War: The Saga of the LCS(L) Ships from Iwo Jima to Vietnam* (Central Point, OR: Hellgate Press, 2000), 39–43.

58. U.S. Navy Deck Log, USS *LCS(L)(3) #40*, 3 February 1945, LCT Flotilla 23:

LCT Group 67: LCT(6)s 699, 794, 806, 807, 832, 902, 903, 1051, 1133, 1178, 1309, 1313;

LCT Group 68: LCT(6)s 700, 701, 757, 758, 759, 762, 797, 761, 798, 1369, 1192, 760;

LCT Group 69: LCT(6)s 837, 838, 880, 881, 882, 906, 907, 1083, 1084, 1102, 1103, 1104.

59. Commander, LSM(R) Group Twenty-Seven, Flotilla Nine, War Diary, 3 February 1945, AdComPhibsPac Secret Order No. 5–45 Serial 0092 of 29 January 1945: "Task Group is to proceed to Eniwetok via Johnston Island and Majuro, Marshall Islands."

60. USS *LCS(L)(3) #40*, Collision, Report of, LCS40/FE25/L11–1, Serial No. 86, 6 February 1945; U.S. Navy Deck Log, USS *LCS(L)(3) 40*, 6 February 1945; U.S. Navy Deck Log, USS *LCS(L)(3) 44*, 6 February 1945; Johnson, *Thirty-seven Days in a Bathtub*.

61. Landis, *Ship's Log USS LSM(R) 192*.

62. Samuel Eliot Morison. *Coral Sea, Midway and Submarine Actions*, vol. 4, 251–252, 263, of *History of United States Naval Operations in World War II*. Boston: Little, Brown, 1949.

63. Allen B. Koltun letter to author November 20, 1996.

64. Commander, LSM(R) Group Twenty-Seven, Flotilla Nine, War Diary, 19 February 1945: Inexplicably, Lt. Comdr. John H. Fulweiler remarked, "This completes the longest over water cruise made by LCTs, no major engine trouble experienced."

65. Landis, *Ship's Log USS LSM(R) 192.*

66. Landis, *Ship's Log USS LSM(R) 192.*

67. *The Bluejackets' Manual 1943* (Annapolis, MD: United States Naval Institute, 1943), 284, 848.

68. McNeill, *The Voyage of the 159*, 75–76.

69. Harold Catchpole letter to author December 27, 1996.

70. Jack E. Johnson letter to author June 6, 1996.

71. Actual date 21 February 1945.

72. Dispatch provided courtesy James M. Stewart.

73. Commander Administrative Command, Amphibious Forces, U.S. Pacific Fleet (AdComPhibsPac), War Diary, February 1945, Secret Movement Order, AdComPhibsPac No. 9–45, Serial 00119, 7 February 1945 for Task Organization 13.11.14; in accordance with ComPhibsPac letter serial 00044 of 19 January 1945 and AdComPhibsPac 270806, CinCPac 281927, January, AdComPhibsPac Movement Order No. 5–45.

74. Commander Administrative Command, Amphibious Forces, U.S. Pacific Fleet (AdComPhibsPac), War Diary, February 1945.

75. Commander Administrative Command, Amphibious Forces, U.S. Pacific Fleet (AdComPhibsPac), War Diary, February 1945, Secret Movement Order, AdComPhibsPac No. 9–45, Serial 00119, 7 February 1945. LSM(R) commanders were instructed to tow LCTs at lengths of 300 feet, walk out one foot of cable each hour for 48 hours, then reverse the process.

76. Mallery and Shedd, *The History of USS LSM(R) 196.*

77. Frank Buxton and Bill Owen, *Radio's Golden Age: The Programs and the Personalities* (New York: Easton Valley Press, 1966), 393–394.

78. Clyde Blue, *Publication Sight Book*, unpublished diary.

79. Blue, *Publication Sight Book.*

80. Commander, LSM(R) Group Twenty-Seven, Flotilla Nine, War Diary, Enclosure (B), Amphibious Forces, United States Pacific Fleet, Task Group Thirteen Point Eleven, Movement Order, AdComPhibsPac No. 9–45, Serial 00119, 7 February 1945, 1–3; Enclosure (C), From Port Director, Majuro to Commander LSM(R) Flotilla 9, Routing Instructions, Reference AdComPhibsPac Movement Order No. 9–45, 21 February 1945.

81. Samuel Eliot Morison. *Aleutians, Gilberts and Marshalls.* vol. 7, 282–283, 306–307, of *History of United States Naval Operations in World War II*. Boston: Little, Brown, 1951.

82. Anonymous, "L.S.M. 'R' 188," unpublished diary.

83. Blue, *Publication Sight Book.*

84. U.S. Navy Deck Log, USS *LSM(R) 188*, 28 Feb 1945, Port Director's Sailing Orders Navy 3237-AL-3/THB/wdc of 28 February 1945 for Ulithi in Eniwetok-Ulithi Convoy #45 in company with Task Unit 96.3.22; U.S. Navy Deck Log, USS *LSM(R) 195.*

85. USS *LSM(R) 197*, Inventory of Ammunition, LSM(R) 197/A13/A5–1/JMC;wr, Serial 25, 4 March 1945.

86. USS *LSM(R) 197*, Casualty Control Drills—report of, LSM(R)197/A5–9/JMC;wr, Serial 26, 4 March 1945.

87. U.S. Navy Deck Log, USS *LSM(R) 192.*

88. U.S. Navy Deck Log, USS *LSM(R) 198.*

89. Blue, *Publication Sight Book.*

90. Anonymous, "L.S.M. 'R' 188," unpublished diary.

91. Samuel Eliot Morison. *Leyte.* vol. 12, 47–50, of *History of United States Naval Operations in World War II*. Boston: Little, Brown, 1958.

92. VanOteghem, *Events About and in the Area of Our Ship.*

93. Blue, *Publication Sight Book.*

94. Blue, *Publication Sight Book.*

95. Anonymous, "L.S.M. 'R' 188," unpublished diary.

96. Commander, LSM(R) Group Twenty-Seven, Flotilla

Nine, War Diary, Enclosure (D), Port Director's Office, Ulithi, Routing Instructions: Ulithi-Kossol, A4–3/9, 7 March 1945, 1–3.

97. Commander, LSM(R) Group Twenty-Seven, Flotilla Nine, War Diary, Enclosure (D), Port Director's Office, Ulithi, Routing Instructions: Ulithi-Kossol, A4–3/9, 7 March 1945, 1–3.

98. Mallery and Shedd, *The History of USS LSM(R) 196.*

99. Blue, *Publication Sight Book.*

100. Anonymous, "L.S.M. 'R' 188," unpublished diary.

101. Landis, *Ship's Log USS LSM(R) 192.*

102. Mallery and Shedd, *The History of USS LSM(R) 196.*

103. USS *LC(FF) 367* was originally designated the LSM Flotilla Nine flagship: Commander Amphibious Forces, U.S. Pacific Fleet (ComPhibsPac), Operation Plan No. A1–45 (OpPlan No. A1–45), Serial 000120, 9 February 1945, Change No. ONE, 11 March 1945, 5, 14, 18.

104. Harold J. Ball, *My Autobiography* (unpublished typescript, 1992), 27.

105. Harold J. Ball letter to author July 5, 1996.

106. Ball, *My Autobiography*, 23.

107. Ball, *My Autobiography*, 26–27.

108. Commander, LSM(R) Group Twenty-Seven, Flotilla Nine, War Diary, Enclosure (E),

Port Director's Office, Kossol Roads, Sailing Orders, Convoy Destination: G1–15 (Kossol Section), 1–4, n.d.

109. Landis, *Ship's Log USS LSM(R) 192.*

110. Blue, *Publication Sight Book.*

111. Mallery and Shedd, *The History of USS LSM(R) 196.*

112. U.S. Navy Deck Log, USS *LSM(R) 199*, 0225 hours.

113. U.S. Navy Deck Log, USS *LSM(R) 198*, 0340 hours.

114. Blue, *Publication Sight Book.*

115. Commander, Amphibious Group Seven (CTG 51.1), Action Report, Capture of Okinawa Gunto, Phases 1 and 2, Serial 0172, 26 May 1945 (II)-2 (III)-1.

Chapter 3

1. Commander, Amphibious Group One (CTF 52), Action Report, Operations Against Okinawa Gunto including the Capture of Kerama Retto and the Eastern Islands of Okinawa, March 21 to and including April 20, 1945, Serial 053, 1 May 1945, V-(H)-9.

2. Commander, Amphibious Group Seven (CTG 51.1), Action Report, Capture of Okinawa Gunto, Phases 1 and 2, Serial 0172, 26 May 1945 (I)-19.

3. CTG 51.1, Action Report (III)-5 to (III)-8 (III)-12.

4. Clyde Blue, *Publication Sight Book*, unpublished diary.

5. Blue, *Publication Sight Book.*

6. John P. Wickser, "With the 'Little Boys'" (address, The Thursday Club, New York, December 9, 1971).

7. Undated dispatch ca. 19–20 March 1945, "Edited by LSM(R) Group Twenty-Seven Staff."

8. Blue, *Publication Sight Book.*

9. Blue, *Publication Sight Book.*

10. Robert W. Landis, *Ship's Log USS LSM(R) 192*, unpublished diary.

11. Blue, *Publication Sight Book.*

12. Bruce A. McDaniel undated letter to author ca. January 1996.

13. CTF 52, Action Report, V-(E)-1.

14. CTF 52, Action Report, V-(E)-2.

15. Commander Amphibious Group Seven, Task Group 51.1, Attack Order A701–45, Serial 0005, 13 March 1945, Annex A (A)-1: Note original sequences of assault landings.

16. CTG 51.1, Action Report (V)(D)-2.

17. Task Group 51.1, Attack Order (E)(I)-4.

18. CTG 51.1, Action Report (V)-(F)-2.

19. Commander Amphibious Forces, U.S. Pacific Fleet (ComPhibsPac), Operation Plan No. A1–45 (OpPlan No. A1–45), Serial 000120, 9 February 1945 (H)(XIII)-12 to -14: Ad-

miral Kiland was codenamed "Viceroy" in "Boxthorn" *Mount McKinley*; Admiral Turner was "Anzac" in "Delegate" *Eldorado*; Admiral Blandy was "Trojan" in "Crisscross" *Estes*.

20. Task Group 51.1, Attack Order (E)-2: *LSM(R)s 194* and *195* were originally scheduled for the Aka Shima attack with LSM(R) Unit Two (TU 52.21.2), but were subsequently cross-assigned to LSM(R) Unit One (TU 52.21.1) for the Zamami Shima attack under Lt. Comdr. Fulweiler.

21. Commander, LSM Flotilla Nine, Action Report, Battle of Kerama Retto and Okinawa Shima, 26 March through 1 April 1945, Serial 004, 2 April 45, Enclosure (C), "Rocket Firing LSM(R) Unit 2."

22. Task Group 51.1, Attack Order (B) (II)-2.

23. CTG 51.1, Action Report (V)-(C)-2.

24. Task Group 51.1, Attack Order (E)(I)-2.

25. USS *LCI(M)-807*, Action Report at Okinawa Shima in Okinawa Gunto 26 March 1945, Serial 139, 7 April 1945.

26. U.S. Navy Deck Log, USS *LSM(R) 198*.

27. Blue, *Publication Sight Book.*

28. CTG 51.1, Action Report (II)-11 (III)-19.

29. David Mallery and Jack Shedd, Ensigns, USNR, *The History of USS LSM(R) 196*, unpublished typescript ca. October 1945.

30. Bruce A. McDaniel undated letter to author ca. February 1997.

31. Mallery and Shedd, *The History of USS LSM(R) 196*.

32. Harold J. Ball, *My Autobiography* (unpublished typescript, 1992), 29; Harold J. Ball letter to author June 1, 1999.

33. Commander, LSM Flotilla Nine, War Diary, 26 March 1945.

34. LSM Flotilla Nine, Battle of Kerama Retto and Okinawa, 4, 6.

35. LSM Flotilla Nine, Battle of Kerama Retto and Okinawa, Second Endorsement, Serial 0260, 14 June 1945, 1–2.

36. LSM Flotilla Nine, Battle of Kerama Retto and Okinawa, Enclosure (B), "Rocket Firing Plan (Corrected 24 March)."

37. Roy E. Appleman, James M. Burns, Russell A. Gugeler, and John Stevens, *Okinawa: The Last Battle* (Washington, D.C.: U.S. Government Printing Office, 1948), 54.

38. Task Group 51.1, Attack Order (B)(II)-2 to -3.

39. Commander, Amphibious Group Seven, Task Group 51.1, Attack Order A701–45, Serial 0005, 13 March 1945, Annex (E), Ship's Gunfire Support Plan (E)(I)-1.

40. Landis, *Ship's Log USS LSM(R) 192.*

41. Commander, Amphibious Group Seven, Task Group 51.1, Attack Order A701–45, Serial 0005, 13 March 1945, Annex (E), Ship's Gunfire Support Plan (E)(I)-1.

42. LSM Flotilla Nine, Battle of Kerama Retto and Okinawa, Enclosure (B), "Rocket Firing Plan (Corrected 24 March)."

43. Commander, Amphibious Group Seven, Task Group 51.1, Attack Order A701–45, Serial 0005, 13 March 1945, Annex (E), Ship's Gunfire Support Plan (E)(I)-1.

44. LSM Flotilla Nine, Battle of Kerama Retto and Okinawa, Enclosure (B), "Rocket Firing Plan (Corrected 24 March)."

45. LSM Flotilla Nine, Battle of Kerama Retto and Okinawa, 4: Commander Francis reported approximately 1400 Fin-stabilized Rockets expended by *LSM(R)s 191, 192, 193* and *194* against Zamami Shima on 26 March 1945.

46. LSM Flotilla Nine, Battle of Kerama Retto and Okinawa, 1, 4; CTG 51.1, Action Report (II)-11 (III)-20.

47. Landis, *Ship's Log USS LSM(R) 192*; Paul S. Vaitses Jr., *In the Rockets' Red Glare* (unpublished manuscript), 57: "Meanwhile the other ships which had been following us [*LSM(R) 193*] in column were making their rocket runs. One by one they rejoined us."

48. Wickser, "With the 'Little Boys.'"

49. CTG 51.1, Action Report (V)-(C)-5.

50. Commander, Task Force Fifty-One, Commander Am-

phibious Forces, U.S. Pacific Fleet, Report on Okinawa Gunto Operation from 17 February to 17 May 1945, Serial 01400, 25 July 1945, (V)(C)-16.

51. Landis, *Ship's Log USS LSM(R) 192*

52. U.S. Navy Deck Log, USS *LSM(R) 192*, 26 March 1945.

53. LSM(R) Flotilla Nine, Destruction on Night Patrol—Commendation for, Serial 123, 7 April 1945: LSM(R) Flotilla Nine should read LSM Flotilla Nine, and Commander Francis' rank mistakenly reads "LT. COMDR"; See Commander, LSM Flotilla Nine, War Diary, 26 March 1945, 7.

54. Mallery and Shedd, *The History of USS LSM(R) 196.*

55. LSM Flotilla Nine, Battle of Kerama Retto and Okinawa, 5.

56. Blue, *Publication Sight Book.*

57. U.S. Navy Deck Log, USS *LSM(R) 192*, 0000–0400, 27 March 1945.

58. U.S. Navy Deck Log, USS *LSM(R) 194*, 26–27 March 1945; Wickser, "With the 'Little Boys.'"

59. Wickser misidentifies USS *Halligan* as USS *Harrington*, which never existed in the U.S. Navy.

60. Possibly Ensign Richard L. Gardner, USS *Halligan*'s senior non-casualty surviving officer, since the only other surviving but injured officer, Ensign Bert Jameyson, Assistant Engineering Officer, was probably below decks: Commander Amphibious Group Seven, Report of Loss or Damage to USS *Halligan* (DD584), Serial 0028, April 1, 1945.

61. Harold Catchpole letter to Mrs. William Woodson, February 25, 1996.

62. U.S. Navy Deck Log, USS *LSM(R) 194*: "The surviving Radar Gear was apparently jettisoned."

63. CTF 52, Action Report (III)-5.

64. U.S. Navy Deck Log, USS *LSM(R) 194*; Commander Amphibious Group Seven, Report of Loss or Damage to USS *Halligan* (DD584), Serial 0028, April 1, 1945: The investigation concluded the commanding officer of USS *Halligan* strayed into unswept waters where the destroyer most likely exploded upon striking a mine; Cf. Second Endorsement 2 May 1945 from Commander Amphibious Group One [Admiral Blandy, CTF 52], 2.

65. U.S. Navy Deck Log, USS *LSM(R) 195.*

66. LSM Flotilla Nine, Battle of Kerama Retto and Okinawa, 7; Commander, LSM Flotilla Nine, War Diary, 26 March 1945, 6.

67. Allan M. Hirshberg undated letter to author ca. November 1995.

68. LSM Flotilla Nine, Battle of Kerama Retto and Okinawa, Enclosure (D).

69. Sometimes simply noted "Orange Z"; north of Aware on Tokashiki Shima, a simultaneous assault was made on Tokashiki village, "Purple Z-1" beach; at midday, Americans landed on Kuba Shima's "Red Z" and Amuro Shima's "Amber Z" beaches before and after noontime, respectively.

70. LSM Flotilla Nine, Battle of Kerama Retto and Okinawa, Enclosure (D), "Firing Order L-5 for LSM(R) Unit 1."

71. Appleman et al., *Okinawa: The Last Battle*, 55–56.

72. Task Group 51.1, Attack Order (B)(II)-3 to -4.

73. Commander, LSM Flotilla Nine, War Diary, 27 March 1945.

74. CTG 51.1, Action Report (III)-30.

75. LSM Flotilla Nine, Battle of Kerama Retto and Okinawa, 5.

76. LSM Flotilla Nine, Battle of Kerama Retto and Okinawa, Second Endorsement, Serial 0260, 14 June 1945 to ComLSMFlot 9 Secret ltr. A12/(ml) Serial 004, 2 April 1945, 1–2.

77. Mallery and Shedd, *The History of USS LSM(R) 196.*

78. Leonard A. VanOteghem, *Events About and in the Area of Our Ship, the USS LSM(R) 196 and our Unit of 12 LSM(R)s*, unpublished diary.

79. Landis, *Ship's Log USS LSM(R) 192*

80. Ronald R. MacKay, Sr., interview with author August 28, 1999.

81. CTG 51.1, Action Report (III)-32, 0820 hours.

82. VanOteghem, *Events About and in the Area of Our Ship*; U.S. Navy Deck Log, USS *LSM(R) 198*. At 1310 of 28 March 1945, *Tolman DM 28* was attacked by eight motor torpedo boats while patrolling station P10, or "Peter 10": CTF 52, Action Report, IV-(A)-1; CTG 51.1, Action Report (III)-37 to (III)-38.

83. Anonymous, "L.S.M. 'R' 188," unpublished diary.

84. Blue, *Publication Sight Book*.

85. U.S. Navy Deck Log, USS *LSM(R) 196*; Peter Maslowski, *Armed with Cameras: The American Military Photographers of World War Two* (New York: The Free Press, 1993), 219.

86. CTF 52, Action Report, III-10.

87. F. Donald Moore, *Quartermaster's Log*, unpublished diary.

88. Moore, *Quartermaster's Log*.

89. Moore, *Quartermaster's Log*.

90. Burton E. Weed, "LSM 'R' 188," unpublished typescript.

91. U.S. Navy Deck Log, USS *LSM(R) 188*. "0400 Ceased firing. DM 29 crossed line of fire."

92. Bill Zinzow, ed., untitled, USS *Henry A. Wiley DM-29* 101 (2001), 6; Bill Zinzow email to author January 8, 2003; USS *Henry A. Wiley (DM 29)*, Report of the Capture of Okinawa Gunto, Phase One and Two, Serial 058, 2 July 1945.

93. USS *LSM(R) 189*, Attack by enemy small boats on 29 March 1945 off Okinawa Island, Serial 0101, 3 April 1945, 1.

94. LSM Flotilla Nine, Destruction of Japanese Suicide Boats on Night Patrol–Commendation for, Serial 125, 7 April 1945.

95. CTG 51.1, Action Report (V)-(C)-4); CTF 52 Action Report, V-(G)-2 to -3.

96. Commanding Officer, USS *LSM(R) 188*, Battle Report, Serial 33, 30 March 1945, 1; See LSM Flotilla Nine, Battle of Kerama Retto and Okinawa, Enclosure (G). *LSM(R) 188* reported her patrol station was "Peter Nine" (P9), "About eight miles east [*sic*] of the town of Naha." However, station P9 was many miles due north of Naha, hence *LSM(R) 188* was more likely patrolling parallel with the western Hagushi coastline opposite the Kadena, Yonton, and Machinato airfields.

97. Harold Franssen telephone interview with author January 1, 2013.

98. Commanding Officer, USS *LSM(R) 188*, Battle Report, Serial 33, 30 March 1945, 1: "Time: 0557 (time verified by damaged radar timing clock) although Radar Man says clock was five minutes slow."

99. Commander, LSM Flotilla Nine, Battle Damage Report of USS *LSM(R) 188*, Serial 015, 5 April 1945.

100. USS *LSM(R) 188*, Battle Report, Serial 33, 30 March 1945.

101. Commander, LSM Flotilla Nine, Battle Damage Report of USS *LSM(R) 188*, Serial 015, 5 April 1945, 1, paragraph (f).

102. Harold Franssen telephone interview with author January 1, 2013.

103. Burton E. Weed, "LSM 'R' 188," unpublished typescript.

104. Burton E. Weed, "LSM 'R' 188," unpublished typescript.

105. Burton E. Weed, "LSM 'R' 188," unpublished typescript.

106. Anonymous, "L.S.M. 'R' 188," unpublished diary.

107. USS *LSM(R) 188* killed in action and died from wounds in action 29 March 1945: S1c Gilmer E. Adams; S1c Alvin M. Anderson; S1c George E. Brooks; S1c William A. Cooper; RM3c James R. Flasher; StM1c Weldon Lemon; FC3c Carroll B. Ligon; GM2c Carl T. Loos; S1c William P. Mader; S1c Robert A. McPheron; GM1c Albert F. Miller; Cox

Joseph P. Olewnik; S1c Edwin M. Prada; S1c Jack H. Slease; S2c "A" "J" Smith; S1c William D. Wright; PhM1c Harold C. Zahn. Compiled from the following sources: U.S. Navy Deck Log, USS *LSM(R) 188*, 31 March 1945; Muster Rolls, USS *LSM(R) 188*; Commander, LSM Flotilla Nine, Battle Damage Report of USS *LSM(R) 188*, Serial 015, 5 April 1945; USS *LSM(R) 188*, Battle Report, Serial 33, 30 March 1945; Rolf F. Illsley, LSM-LSMR WWII Amphibious Forces, vol. II (Paducah, KY: Turner Publishing Company, 1997), 72.

108. Commanding Officer, USS *LSM(R) 188*, Battle Report, Serial 33, 30 March 1945, 3.

109. Mallery and Shedd, *The History of USS LSM(R) 196*.

110. Commander, LSM Flotilla Nine, Battle Damage Report of USS *LSM(R) 188*, Serial 015, 5 April 1945.

111. Lawrence Willison, "LSM(R) 188," unpublished typescript.

112. Vaitses, *In the Rockets' Red Glare*, 67–68.

113. Robert W. Landis letter to author December 12, 1999.

114. Samuel Eliot Morison. *Victory in the Pacific 1945*. vol. 14, 135, of *History of United States Naval Operations in World War II*. Boston: Little, Brown, 1960; CTF 52, Action Report, IV-(A)-1.

115. LSM Flotilla Nine, Battle of Kerama Retto and Okinawa.

116. Task Group 51.1, Attack Order (E)(I)-4.

117. Amphibious Reconnaissance Battalion, FMF, Pacific, In the Field, 17 March 1945, Annex Able –OPNS Orders–ICEBERG, 1–8.

118. CTG 51.1, Action Report (V)-(I)-2 (III)-66; CTF 51, "Report on Okinawa Gunto Operation"(V)-(D)-6; Robert Sherrod, *History of Marine Corps Aviation in World War II* (Washington: Combat Forces Press, 1952), 377, 454.

119. Vaitses, *In the Rockets' Red Glare*, 69–70, 77.

120. Commander, LCI(L) Flotilla Fourteen (CTU 51.1.16), Action Report for Kerama Retto and Keise Shima Operations, Serial 0534, 27 April 1945,7; LSM Flotilla Nine, Battle of Kerama Retto and Okinawa, First Endorsement, Serial 0594, 18 May 1945 to ComLSMFlot 9 A12/(ml) Serial 004, 2 April 1945, 1–2.

121. Blue, *Publication Sight Book*.

122. Bruce A. McDaniel undated letter to author ca. February 1997.

123. Van Oteghem, *Events About and in the Area of Our Ship*.

124. Bruce A. McDaniel undated letter to author ca. February 1997.

125. Commanding Officer, USS *LSM(R) 196*, Damage to this vessel by shelling from beach of Okinawa near Naha on 1 April 1945 at 0040, Report of, Serial 20, 8 April 1945, Enclosure (A).

126. Bruce A. McDaniel letter to author September 8, 1998.

Chapter 4

1. In 480 BC Xerxes I of Persia commanded a combined army and navy reputedly numbering a million men with over 1200 ships for the amphibious invasion of Ancient Greece: Victor Davis Hanson, "Remembering Okinawa: Dealing with Suicide Bombers—60 Years Ago," Victor Davis Hanson's Private Papers, Tribune Media Services, April 6, 2005, http://victorhanson.com/wordpress/?p=4436.

2. Commander, Task Force Fifty-One, Commander Amphibious Forces, U.S. Pacific Fleet, Report on Okinawa Gunto Operation from 17 February to 17 May 1945, Serial 01400, 25 July 1945 (I)-5 (I)-7.

3. Commander, Amphibious Forces, U.S. Pacific Fleet (ComPhibsPac), Operation Plan No. A1–45 (OpPlan No. A1–45), Serial 000120, 9 February 1945 (G)-13 thru (G)-15; See CTF 51, *Report on Okinawa Gunto Operation* (V)(C)-25.

4. ComPhibsPac, *OpPlan A1–45*, Schedule of Fires, Appendix III to Annex (G), Target Area 7777.

5. Commander, LSM Flotilla Nine, Action Report, Battle of Kerama Retto and Okinawa Shima, 26 March through 1 April 1945, Serial 004, 2 April 45, Enclosure (E).

6. Roy E. Appleman et al., *Okinawa: The Last Battle*, 208–213.

7. LSM Flotilla Nine, Battle of Kerama Retto and Okinawa, Enclosure (E).

8. Paul S. Vaitses Jr., *In the Rockets' Red Glare* (unpublished manuscript), 72–73.

9. Robert W. Landis, *Ship's Log USS LSM(R) 192*, unpublished diary.

10. F. Donald Moore, *Quartermaster's Log*, unpublished diary.

11. LSM Flotilla Nine, Battle of Kerama Retto and Okinawa, 6.

12. ComPhibsPac, *OpPlan A1–45* (G)-13 thru (G)-15; See CTF 51, *Report on Okinawa Gunto Operation* (V)(C)-25.

13. LSM Flotilla Nine, Battle of Kerama Retto and Okinawa; LSM Flotilla Nine, Combat Rocket Fire Performed 1 April 1945—Observed results of, Serial 0003, 10 April 1945, 6, Enclosure (F).

14. LSM Flotilla Nine, Battle of Kerama Retto and Okinawa, Enclosure (F).

15. Lawrence J. Low, untitled, unpublished diary, notebook and sketches: *LSM(R) 197* loaded 504 rockets.

16. John P. Wickser, "With the 'Little Boys'" (address, The Thursday Club, New York, December 9, 1971).

17. David Mallery and Jack Shedd, Ensigns, USNR, *The History of USS LSM(R) 196*, unpublished typescript ca. October 1945.

18. LSM Flotilla Nine, Battle of Kerama Retto and Okinawa, 6.

19. Commander, LSM Flotilla Nine, Combat Rocket Fire Performed 1 April 1945—Observed results of, Serial 0003, 10 April 1945.

20. Robert W. Cox undated letter to author ca. 1995.

21. Mallery and Shedd, *The History of USS LSM(R) 196*.

22. Clyde Blue, *Publication Sight Book*, unpublished diary; Wickser, "With the 'Little Boys.'"

23. Commander, Task Force Fifty-One, Commander Amphibious Forces, U.S. Pacific Fleet, Report on Okinawa Gunto Operation from 17 February to 17 May 1945, Serial 01400, 25 July 1945 (V)(C)-20. See Commander, Amphibious Group Twelve (Commander Southern Attack Force–CTF 55), Report on the Capture of Okinawa Gunto Phase I and II, 14 March–9 June 1945, Serial 0287, 31 July 1945 (V)(C)-20.

24. CTF 51, *Report on Okinawa Gunto Operation* (V)(C)-7; Commander LCI(R) Flotilla Sixteen, Action Report–Invasion of the Okinawa Group Liu Chius, 26 March to 21 June 1945, Serial No. 35, 15 July 1945, 34. Commander Coffin disputed this contention: "Lack of information, and misinformation, as to the capabilities of the LCI(R)s resulted in their non-employment and consequent loss of their fire power in support missions for about six weeks after L-Day. Conversation [*sic*] with Army and Marine personnel indicated that much earlier use would have been made of the LCI(R)s had more information been available as to their capabilities and had they been made available for fire support missions."

25. LSM Flotilla Nine, War Diary, 3–4 April 1945.

26. LSM Flotilla Nine, War Diary, 2 April 1945.

27. Blue, *Publication Sight Book*.

28. CTF 51, *Report on Okinawa Gunto Operation* (III)-15.

29. U.S. Navy Deck Log, USS *LSM(R) 198*.

30. Commander, LSM Flotilla Nine, Action Report–Ie Shima and Southeastern Okinawa, 2 April through 20 April 1945, Serial 0010, 21 April 1945, 4.

31. Commander, LSM(R) Group Twenty-Seven, Flotilla Nine, War Diary, 3 April 1945: "While on patrol off POINT BOLO, *LSM(R) 196* destroyed one enemy plane (probably a Val) with automatic weapons fire."

32. Mallery and Shedd, *The History of USS LSM(R) 196*.

33. Compiled from Bruce A. McDaniel undated letters to author ca. January 1996 and March 1997.

34. Landis, *Ship's Log USS LSM(R) 192*.

35. U.S. Navy Deck Log, USS *LSM(R) 188*.

36. Landis, *Ship's Log USS LSM(R) 192*.

37. Compiled from Neal B. Hadsell letters to author January 5, 1995 and January 17, 1995.

38. Dick Boak, Ensign Thomas Boak letter to his wife, June 13, 1945, unpublished typescript.

39. Commander, LSM(R) Group Twenty-Seven, Flotilla Nine, War Diary, 5 April 1945; CTF 51, *Report on Okinawa Gunto Operation* (V)(C)-74.

40. F. Donald Moore telephone conversation with author November 1, 1995. U.S. Navy Deck Logs for April 1945 from *LSM(R)s 190, 194* and *195* were lost when these ships were sunk in May 1945, so it remains uncertain whether any or all of the Mark 30 outboard launchers were removed from *LSM(R)s 190* and *194*, but *LSM(R) 195* noted her Mark 30 launchers were removed in her final action report. Interestingly, USS *LSM(R) 189* former Gunnery Officer Ensign F. Donald Moore asserted his rocketship, alone among the LSM(R)s, fired rockets from the Mark 30 launchers in combat, although the author has found no corroborating documentation.

41. CTF 51, *Report on Okinawa Gunto Operation* (III)-16 to -17.

42. CTF 51, *Report on Okinawa Gunto Operation* (III)-17.

43. CTF 51, *Report on Okinawa Gunto Operation* Part (IV), Summary of Naval Actions Against Enemy Aircraft, 14–34.

44. Commander, Task Flotilla 5 (Commander Task Group 51.5), Action Report, Capture of Okinawa Gunto, 26 March to 21 June 1945, Serial 0894, 20 July 1945, A9; CTF 51, *Report on Okinawa Gunto Operation* (III)-22.

45. Leonard A. VanOteghem, *Events About and in the Area of Our Ship, the USS LSM(R) 196 and our Unit of 12 LSM(R)s*, unpublished diary.

46. Blue, *Publication Sight Book*.

47. Lawrence J. Low, untitled, unpublished diary, notebook and sketches; See LSM Flotilla Nine, *Ie Shima and Southeastern Okinawa*, 2; Commander, LSM(R) Group Twenty-Seven, Flotilla Nine, War Diary.

48. Commander, LSM Flotilla Nine, Destruction of enemy plane–credit and commendation for, Serial 137, 17 April 1945.

49. Wickser, "With the 'Little Boys'"; See Commander, LSM Flotilla Nine, *Ie Shima and Southeastern Okinawa*, 2; Commander, LSM(R) Group Twenty-Seven, Flotilla Nine, War Diary.

50. CTF 51, *Report on Okinawa Gunto Operation* (III)-27.

51. Commander, Amphibious Forces, U.S. Pacific Fleet, Amphibious Gunnery Bulletin No. 2–Assault of Okinawa, Serial 0391, 24 May 1945, 9.

52. Landis, *Ship's Log USS LSM(R) 192*.

53. Commander, LSM(R) Group Twenty-Seven, Flotilla Nine, War Diary, 11 April 1945.

54. Landis, *Ship's Log USS LSM(R) 192*.

55. U.S. Navy Deck Log, USS *LSM(R) 192*.

Chapter 5

1. Commander, LSM Flotilla Nine, Action Report–Ie Shima and Southeastern Okinawa, 2 April through 20 April 1945, Serial 0010, 21 April 1945, 1.

2. Commander, LCI(L) Flotilla Fourteen, War Diary, April 1945, Serial 0804, 23 May 1945.

3. Commander, LCI Flotilla Twenty-One, Action Report, Invasion of Okinawa Jima, Nansei Shoto Group, 25 March 1945 through 10 April 1945, Serial 0001, 10 April 1945.

4. Commander, Task Flotilla 5 (Commander Task Group 51.5), Action Report, Capture of Okinawa Gunto, 26 March to 21 June 1945, Serial 0894, 20 July 1945, Enclosure (A), 1. Captain Moosbrugger was temporarily promoted to Commodore on 6 April 1945.

5. Commander, LSM(R) Group Twenty-Seven, Flotilla Nine, War Diary, 5 April 45; Commander, Task Force Fifty-One, Commander Amphibious Forces, U.S. Pacific Fleet, Report on Okinawa Gunto Operation from 17 February to 17 May 1945, Serial 01400, 25 July 1945 (V)(C)-74.

6. Robin L. Rielly, *Kamikazes, Corsairs, and Picket Ships: Okinawa 1945* (Drexel Hill, PA: Casemate Publishers, 2008), 109.

7. Commander, LSM Flotilla Nine, War Diary, 6 April 1945; Commander, LSM(R) Group Twenty-Seven, Flotilla Nine, 6 April 1945.

8. CTG 51.5, Action Report, Enclosure A, 8–11; CTF 51, *Report on Okinawa Gunto Operation*, (II)-17; Commander, Amphibious Forces, U.S. Pacific Fleet, Suicide Plane Attacks, Serial 00470, 7 July 1945, 6; Commander in Chief, U.S. Pacific Fleet and Pacific Ocean Areas, Operations in the Pacific Ocean Areas during the Month of April 1945, Annex A, 51–52.

9. CTF 51, *Report on Okinawa Gunto Operation* (II)-17; Commander, Task Flotilla 5 (Commander Task Group 51.5), Action Report, Capture of Okinawa Gunto, 26 March to 21 June 1945, Serial 0894, 20 July 1945, 9, 11; Commander, Amphibious Group One (Task Force 52), Operation Order A6–45, Serial 000166, 16 March 1945.

10. CTG 51.5, Action Report, 9, 17; Rielly, *Kamikazes, Corsairs, and Picket Ships: Okinawa 1945*, 151, 296.

11. Commander, LSM Flotilla Nine, War Diary, April 1945; Commander Fifth Amphibious Force (CTF 51 and 31), Report of Capture of Okinawa Gunto Phases 1 and 2 for period 17 May 1945 to 21 June 1945, Serial 0268, 4 July 45 (I)-5.

12. USS *Little* (DD-803), Report of Action Between USS *Little* (DD803) and Enemy aircraft on May 3, 1945 (E.I.D.), 7 May 1945, 2: "…commonly referred to by DD pickets as 'The Pall Bearers') …"; USS *Luce* (DD 522), Action report on Ryukyus Operation 24 March–4 May 1945, 4 May 1945, 8: "Small craft assigned the *Luce* quickly became known as pallbearer"; Theodore Roscoe, *Destroyer Operations in World War II* (Annapolis, MD: United States Naval Institute, 1953), 478–479; Ron Surels, *DD 522: Diary of a Destroyer* (Plymouth, NH: Valley Graphics, Inc., 1994), 111: "We called them 'meat-wagons'"; Earl Blanton, *Boston—to Jacksonville (41,000 Miles by Sea)* (Seaford, VA: Goose Creek Publications, 1991), 92: "I never knew until after the war that the LCS(L)s were known by destroyermen as the 'Pall Bearers.'"

13. ComPhibsPac, *OpPlan A1–45* (K)-(II)-2 (K)-(II)-7; Commander, Amphibious Group One (Task Force 52), Operation Order A6–45, Serial 000166, 16 March 1945, 3; CTG 51.5, Action Report, 8.

14. Admiral Richmond Kelly Turner, USN, "Problems of Unified Command in the Marianas, Okinawa, and (Projected) Kyushu Operations" (address, Air War College, Maxwell Field, Alabama, 11 February 1947), 6–7.

15. Commander, Amphibious Group One (Task Force 52), Operation Order A6–45, Serial 000166, 16 March 1945; E. B. Potter, *Admiral Arleigh Burke* (New York: Random House, 1990), 228: Prior to the Okinawa operation, Captain Arleigh Burke expressed his concerns to Admiral Turner that the Radar Picket Station destroyer coverage was inadequate.

16. Denis Warner and Peggy Warner, *The Sacred Warriors: Japan's Suicide Legions* (New York: Van Norstrand Reinhold Company, 1982), 198.

17. Edwin P. Hoyt, *The Kamikazes: Suicide Squadrons of World War II* (Short Hills, NJ: Burford Books, 1983), 266.

18. CTG 51.5, Action Report, A9.

19. Rielly, *Kamikazes, Corsairs, and Picket Ships: Okinawa 1945*, 109.

20. James Belote and William Belote, *Typhoon of Steel: The Battle for Okinawa* (New York: Harper & Row, 1970), 104.

21. Samuel Eliot Morison. *Victory in the Pacific 1945*. vol. 14, 197, 233, of *History of United States Naval Operations in World War II*. Boston: Little, Brown, 1960; Robin L. Rielly,

Kamikaze Attacks of World War II, 190. Another account reported 406 Japanese aircraft sortied in *Kikusui* No. 1: Japanese Monograph No. 86, 5th Air Fleet Operations, Feb-Aug 1945, Document No. 41010, Annexed Table No. 1, "Strength used in the *Kikusui* Operations."

22. Fleet Admiral Chester W. Nimitz, USN, "Command Summary of Fleet Admiral Chester W. Nimitz, USN, Nimitz 'Graybook,'" 7 December 1941–31 August 1945, vol. 6, Running Estimate and Summary maintained by CINCPAC staff covering the period 1 January 1945 to 1 July 1945, U.S. Naval War College Naval Historical Collection, 342, https://www.usnwc.edu/archives; CTF 51, *Report on Okinawa Gunto Operation* (V)(E)-36.

23. Robin L. Rielly, *Kamikaze Attacks of World War II*, Appendix 1; Samuel Eliot Morison. *Victory in the Pacific 1945*, Appendix II, 390; CTF 51, Action Report, Part (III), 22, Part (V) Section (H), 5 to 10.

24. Commander, LSM(R) Group Twenty-Seven, Flotilla Nine, War Diary, 11 April 1945.

25. Norman Friedman, *U.S. Amphibious Ships and Craft: An Illustrated Design History* (Annapolis, MD: Naval Institute Press, 2002), 246.

26. Lawrence Willison e-mail to author December 7, 2000.

27. Lawrence J. Low telephone conversation with author January 29, 1996; Lawrence J. Low letter to author November 11, 2000.

28. Paul S. Vaitses Jr., *In the Rockets' Red Glare* (unpublished manuscript), 92–93.

29. Leonard A. VanOteghem, *Events About and in the Area of Our Ship, the USS LSM(R) 196 and our Unit of 12 LSM(R)s*, unpublished diary.

30. John P. Wickser, "With the 'Little Boys'" (address, The Thursday Club, New York, December 9, 1971), 14.

31. Robin L. Rielly, *Kamikaze Attacks of World War II*, Appendix 1; Samuel Eliot Morison, *Victory in the Pacific 1945*, Appendix II, 390; CTF 51, Action Report, Part (III), 22, Part (V) Section (H), 5 to 10.

32. Fleet Admiral Chester W. Nimitz, USN, "Command Summary of Fleet Admiral Chester W. Nimitz, USN, Nimitz 'Graybook,'" 7 December 1941–31 August 1945, vol. 6, Running Estimate and Summary maintained by CINCPAC staff covering the period 1 January 1945 to 1 July 1945, U.S. Naval War College Naval Historical Collection, 358, https://www.usnwc.edu/archives.

33. Clyde Blue, *Publication Sight Book*, unpublished diary.

34. Blue, *Publication Sight Book*.

35. Karl G. Matchett, untitled, unpublished diary.

36. U.S. Navy Deck Log, USS *LSM(R) 198*.

37. Lawrence J. Low telephone conversation with author January 29, 1996; Lawrence J. Low, untitled, unpublished diary, notebook and sketches.

38. Blue, *Publication Sight Book*.

39. Andrew Adams, ed., *Born to Die: The Cherry Blossom Squadrons* (Los Angeles: Ohara Publications, Inc., 1973), 45, 47.

40. Francis Lihosit Collection courtesy Rex A. Knight; Rex A. Knight, *Riding on Luck: The Saga of the USS Lang (DD-399)* (Central Point, OR: Hellgate Press, 2001), 230.

41. USS *LSM(R) 197*, Confidential Memorandum, Japanese Buzz Bomb Seen While Under Attack on Patrol on 12 April 1945—description of, Serial 04, 23 April 1945. See USS *Stanly* (DD 478), Occupation of Okinawa Gunto, 25 March–13 April 1945, Serial 087, 17 April 1945, Enclosure (E), Drawing of Japanese "Buzz Bomb."

42. Japanese Monograph No. 86, 5th Air Fleet Operations Feb-Aug 1945, 51.

43. Adams, ed., *Born to Die: The Cherry Blossom Squadrons*, 44–45, 91–93.

44. USS *Stanly* (DD 478), War Diary, April 1945.

45. Lawrence J. Low, untitled, unpublished diary, notebook and sketches; Knight, *Riding on Luck*, 199, 230; Francis Lihosit Collection.

46. USS *Mannert L. Abele*, Action Report from 20 March through 12 April 1945, including damage to and loss of ship, 14 April 1945.

47. Commanding Officer, USS *LSM(R) 189*, General Action Report, Battle of Okinawa–12 April 1945, Serial 0102, 15 April 1945, 2. Three weeks later, Lt. Stewart commented, "It seems apparent that our ships cannot stop the planes from suicidal attacks or jet propelled and piloted bombs. One jet propelled bomb hit a destroyer [*Mannert L. Abele DD 733*] amidships and she sank in two minutes, on 12 April, 1945. On 3 May, 1945 [*sic*, should read 4 May 1945] another destroyer [*Shea DM 30*], along-side us, took a hit in the same place. The last I saw of her she was heading toward shore in a cloud of smoke. Neither of these vessels fired more than a few bursts of 20MM at the missiles that struck them. Both jet propelled bombs were released from Bettys. Another fact that I wish to point out, is that in the attack of 12 April, 1945, we had no air coverage and the Jap pilots could plan their approach and make their preparation as they chose. In the latest attack of 3 May, 1945 [*sic*], we had a CAP over head which shot the Betty down, however, the jet propelled bomb was still successfully launched and accomplished its mission ... If the Japanese continue these suicidal attacks, the price we are paying in ships, men and equipment is reaping them a huge reward." Commanding Officer, USS *LSM(R) 189*, Report of anti-aircraft action by surface vessels–Forwarding of, Serial 0110, 1 May 1945, Enclosure (A), 1.

48. James M. Stewart letter to Mrs. Alton Parker, May 31, 1997, in the author's possession.

49. Commanding Officer, USS *LSM(R) 189*, General Action Report, Battle of Okinawa–12 April 1945, Serial 0102, 15 April 1945, 5.

50. Laurie R. Russell letter to author 20 October 1995.

51. Newspaper article, "Lt. Harmon Tells Of Jap Plane Attack"; "Sturdy Rocket Ship Proves Its Mettle," *Navy News*, August 1945.

52. F. Donald Moore, *Quartermaster's Log*, unpublished diary.

53. Commanding Officer, USS *LSM(R) 189*, General Action Report, Battle of Okinawa–12 April 1945, Serial 0102, 15 April 1945, First Endorsement, 20 April 1945; See Second Endorsement, 24 April 1945.

54. Commander Parker letter 18 April 1945 to Commanding Officer, USS *LSM(R) 190*.

55. And misquoted, most notably by Norman Friedman, *U.S. Destroyers: An Illustrated Design History* (Annapolis, MD: Naval Institute Press, 1985), 177; and by Owen Gault, "Worth Their Weight in Gold! The Saga of the LSMs," *Sea Classics*, October 1979, vol. 2, no. 5; See Headquarters of the Commander in Chief, United States Fleet, Radar Pickets and Methods of Combating Suicide Attacks Off Okinawa March-May 1945, Secret Information Bulletin No. 24, 65.

56. USS *Mannert L. Abele*, Action Report from 20 March through 12 April 1945, including damage to and loss of ship, no serial, 14 April 1945, Enclosure (A), 13: "It is also the opinion of this officer that the small LSM(R)s are literally worth their weight in gold as support vessels but larger forty millimeter batteries should be installed and the number [*sic*] assigned each picket be increased to a minimum of four. Maneuvering to remain close to supports is difficult but not impossible."

57. USS *Mannert L. Abele*, Action Report from 20 March through 12 April 1945, including damage to and loss of ship, no serial, 14 April 1945, Enclosure (B), 2.

58. Commanding Officer, USS *LSM(R) 189*, General Action Report, Battle of Okinawa–12 April 1945, Serial 0102, 15 April 1945.

59. Commander, LSM Flotilla Nine, Destruction of enemy planes—credit and commendation for, Serial 152, 25 April 1945.

60. Commanding Officer, USS *LSM(R) 189*, General Action Report, Battle of Okinawa–12 April 1945, Serial 0102, 15 April 1945, Third Endorsement, 17 May 45.

61. James M. Stewart, *90 Day Naval Wonder* (Bellevue, WA: Trees, Inc., 2003), 68.

62. Rolf F. Illsley, *LSM-LSMR WWII Amphibious Forces*, vol. 1 (Paducah: Turner Publishing Company, 1994), 50; Department of the Navy, Bureau of Naval Personnel, Navy Unit Commendation Awarded the USS *LSM(R) 189*, 22 June 1949.

63. Belote and Belote, *Typhoon of Steel*, 162; Japanese Monograph No. 86, 5th Air Fleet Operations, Feb-Aug 1945, 56, 64, Document No. 41010; Warner and Warner, *The Sacred Warriors*, 227, Footnote 1; Rielly, *Kamikaze Attacks of World War II*, 210, 236.

64. Rielly, *Kamikaze Attacks of World War II*, Appendix 1; Samuel Eliot Morison, *Victory in the Pacific 1945*, Appendix II, 390; CTF 51, Action Report, Part (III), 22, Part (V) Section (H), 5 to 10.

65. Joe B. Smith letter to author January 9, 1997.

66. Roy Moceri telephone conversations with author October 26–27, 2001; Laurie R. Russell email to author October 23, 2001.

67. Commanding Officer, USS *LSM 191* [*sic*], Action Report–1 April Thru 19 April 1945, 19 April 1945.

68. U.S. Navy Deck Log, USS *LSM(R) 191*: "1655–USS *Hobson* confirmed the fact that this vessel shot down an enemy plane"; USS *Hobson*, Report of Action Report, Invasion of Okinawa, 19 March 1945 to 28 April 1945, Serial 014–45, 1 May 1945, 3, 28: "*LSM(R) 191* reported shooting down one Val at this time," and "*LSM(R) 191* shot down one plane during these attacks."

69. Roy Moceri undated letter to author ca. October 2001.

70. Commanding Officer, USS *LSM 191* [*sic*], Action Report–1 April Thru 19 April 1945, 19 April 1945.

71. Joe B. Smith letter to author January 9, 1997.

72. USS *LSM(R) 191*, Secret Dispatch from *Hobson* DMS 26 to Commander Task Force 51, 18 April 1945.

73. Commander, Mine Division Fifty-Eight (Commander Task Unit Fifty Two Point Three Point Two), Serial 020, 7 May 1945, First Endorsement to Report of Action, Invasion of Okinawa, 19 March 1945 to 28 April 1945, Serial 014–45, 1 May 1945, 1.

74. Fleet Admiral Chester W. Nimitz, USN, "Command Summary of Fleet Admiral Chester W. Nimitz, USN, Nimitz 'Graybook,'" 7 December 1941–31 August 1945, vol. 6, Running Estimate and Summary maintained by CINCPAC staff covering the period 1 January 1945 to 1 July 1945, U.S. Naval War College Naval Historical Collection, 379, https://www.usnwc.edu/archives.

75. Commander, LSM Flotilla Nine, Action Report–Ie Shima and Southeastern Okinawa, 2 April through 20 April 1945, Serial 0010, 21 April 1945, 3, 6; Lt. Comdr. Fulweiler briefly noted this 18 April 1945 incident in Commander, LSM(R) Group Twenty-Seven, Flotilla Nine, War Diary: "... while on station [*LSM(R)*] *194* shot down at 1914—one plane (Betty)."

76. USS *LSM(R) 194*, Action Report–Battle of Okinawa–4 May 1945, Serial: F9–06, 6 May 1945, 3.

77. Captain Moosbrugger was temporarily promoted to Commodore on 6 April 1945.

78. Commanding Officer, USS *LSM 279*, Action Report RE: Ruyuko [*sic*] Campaign 30 April–26 May 1945–Submission of, Serial: 27–45, 26 May 1945, Appendix One, CTG 52.21 OP Plan #2103–45, Serial: 0014, 30 April 1945.

79. *LSM(R) 191* embarked a medical officer stationed ⅔ distance to RPS 2 from 30 April until 2 May 1945, although CTG 52.21 OP Plan #2103–45 directed LSM(R)s with medical officers stationed ⅔ distances to RPSs 3, 7, 9, 10, and 12.

80. U.S. Navy Deck Log, USS *LSM(R) 199*.

81. Commander, LSM(R) Group Twenty-Seven, Flotilla Nine, War Diary; See Commander, LSM Flotilla Nine, War Diary.

82. CTG 51.5, Action Report, A16.

83. Commander, LSM Flotilla Nine, Action Report—Ie Shima and Southeastern Okinawa, 2 April through 20 April 1945, Serial 0010, 21 April 1945, 7, 9–10.

84. Commanding Officer, USS *LCS(L)(3) 15*, Survivors, Appreciation from, 25 April 1945.

85. U.S. Navy Deck Log, USS *LSM(R) 193*; USS *Wadsworth* (*DD 516*), War Diary, April 1945; Paul S. Vaitses Jr., *In the Rockets' Red Glare* (unpublished manuscript), 97: Vaitses recalls a twin-engine Betty bomber.

86. Vaitses, *In the Rockets' Red Glare*, 97; U.S. Navy Deck Log, USS *LSM(R) 193*.

87. USS *Wadsworth* (*DD 516*), War Diary, April 1945.

88. "The Galloping Ghost of Nansei Shoto," *Combat Information Center* 2, no. 3 (1945): 46–47.

89. Sources dispute numbers and types of Japanese aircraft in *Kikusui* No. 4: Japanese Monograph No. 86, 5th Air Fleet Operations, Feb-Aug 1945, 65–67, Document No. 41010; Warner and Warner, *The Sacred Warriors*, 231; Rielly, *Kamikaze Attacks of World War II*, 210, 248.

90. Rielly, *Kamikaze Attacks of World War II*, Appendix 1; Samuel Eliot Morison, *Victory in the Pacific 1945*, Appendix II, 390; CTF 51, Action Report, Part (III), 22, Part (V) Section (H), 5 to 10.

91. Vaitses, *In the Rockets' Red Glare*, 97–99; U.S. Navy Deck Log, USS *LSM(R) 193*.

92. Commander, LSM(R) Group Twenty-Seven, Flotilla Nine, War Diary, 28 April 1945.

93. VanOteghem, *Events About and in the Area of Our Ship*.

94. Commanding Officer, USS *LSM(R) 197*, Special Patrol–report of, Serial 42, 28 April 1945.

95. Blue, *Publication Sight Book*.

96. Commander, LSM(R) Group Twenty-Seven, Flotilla Nine, War Diary, April 1945.

97. "Lt. Harmon Tells Of Jap Plane Attack"; CTF 51, *Report on Okinawa Gunto Operation* (III)-68 (IV)-49.

98. USS *Wadsworth* (*DD 516*), War Diary, April 1945.

99. USS *Wadsworth* (*DD 516*), Action Report for Invasion of Okinawa Jima, Serial 028, 24 June 1945, 34–35.

100. Robert W. Landis, *Ship's Log USS LSM(R) 192*, unpublished diary.

101. Mallery and Shedd, *The History of USS LSM(R) 196*.

102. Leonard A. VanOteghem, *Events About and in the Area of Our Ship, the USS LSM(R) 196 and our Unit of 12 LSM(R)s*, unpublished diary.

103. Donald L. Ball, *Fighting Amphibs: The LCS(L)s in World War II* (Williamsburg, VA: Mill Neck Publications, 1997), 189; Robin L. Rielly, *Mighty Midgets at War: The Saga of the LCS(L) Ships from Iwo Jima to Vietnam* (Central Point, OR: Hellgate Press, 2000), 143.

104. USS *LCS(L)(3) 67*, Ship's History and Records, compiled by Lieutenant John Palmer Murphy USNR, 15.

105. Rielly, *Kamikazes, Corsairs, and Picket Ships: Okinawa, 1945*, Appendix I, 351–353.

106. Warner and Warner, *The Sacred Warriors*, 234; Samuel Eliot Morison, *Victory in the Pacific 1945*, 250.

Chapter 6

1. Commander, Amphibious Group Four (Commander Task Force 53)(Commander Task Group 51.21), Report of Participation in the Capture of Okinawa Gunto–Phases I and II, Serial 0252, 20 July 1945 (III)-39 (III)-41.

2. CTF 53, *Report* (V)(C)-25 to –26.

3. CTF 53, *Report* (I)(B)-10 to –14.

4. CTF 53, *Report* (V)(A)-4.

5. Commander, Task Force Fifty-One, Commander Amphibious Forces, U.S. Pacific Fleet, Report on Okinawa Gunto Operation from 17 February to 17 May 1945, Serial 01400, 25 July 1945, (I)-1; Commander, Amphibious Forces, U.S. Pacific Fleet (ComPhibsPac), Operation Plan No. A1–45 (OpPlan No. A1–45), Serial 000120, 9 February 1945 (A)-1.

6. Roy E. Appleman, James M. Burns, Russell A. Gugeler, and John Stevens, *Okinawa: The Last Battle* (Washington, D.C.: U.S. Government Printing Office, 1948), 149–150.

7. Commander, LSM Flotilla Nine, Action Report–Ie Shima and Southeastern Okinawa, 2 April through 20 April 1945, Serial 0010, 21 April 1945.

8. Commander, LSM Flotilla Nine, Rockets for harassing fire–use on Ie Shima and recommendations regarding future employment, Serial 008, 19 April 1945 (a), CTG 52.21 OpPlan 2101–45, Serial 006, 13 April 1945, "Patrol Sectors" sketch.

9. LSM Flotilla Nine, *Ie Shima and Southeastern Okinawa*, Annex Able, Appendix I, "Schedule of Patrol and Target Assignments."

10. Commander, Amphibious Group Twelve (Commander Southern Attack Force–CTF 55), Report on the Capture of Okinawa Gunto Phase I and II, 14 March–9 June 1945, Serial 0287, 31 July 1945 (V)(C)-2.

11. Commander, LSM Flotilla Nine, Rockets for harassing fire–use on Ie Shima and recommendations regarding future employment, Serial 008, 19 April 1945, 1, 2; LSM Flotilla Nine, *Ie Shima and Southeastern Okinawa*.

12. LSM Flotilla Nine, *Ie Shima and Southeastern Okinawa*, Enclosure (B), 2.

13. Clyde Blue, *Publication Sight Book*, unpublished diary.

14. Robert W. Landis, *Ship's Log USS LSM(R) 192*, unpublished diary.

15. LSM Flotilla Nine, *Ie Shima and Southeastern Okinawa*, Counter Battery Plan (Annex George).

16. Leonard A. VanOteghem, *Events About and in the Area of Our Ship, the USS LSM(R) 196 and our Unit of 12 LSM(R)s*, unpublished diary.

17. Lawrence J. Low letter to author December 7, 1998.

18. Robert W. Cox undated letter to author ca. 1996.

19. Blue, *Publication Sight Book*.

20. Blue, *Publication Sight Book*.

21. CTF 53, *Report* (III)-41.

22. CTF 53, *Report* (V)(C)-19. "Destructive bombardment of Ie Shima was canceled to prepare for other required dispositions of the Fire Support Ships."

23. U.S. Navy Deck Log, USS *LSM(R) 199*.

24. LSM Flotilla Nine, *Ie Shima and Southeastern Okinawa*, Enclosure (B), 1.

25. Lawrence J. Low, untitled, unpublished diary, notebook and sketches.

26. Blue, *Publication Sight Book*.

27. LSM Flotilla Nine, *Ie Shima and Southeastern Okinawa*, Enclosure (B), 2.

28. LSM Flotilla Nine, *Ie Shima and Southeastern Okinawa*, Enclosure (B), 2.

29. LSM Flotilla Nine, *Ie Shima and Southeastern Okinawa*, Enclosure (B). 3.

30. CTF 53, *Report* (V)(C)-8.

31. Commander, LSM Flotilla Nine, Action Report–Ie Shima and Southeastern Okinawa, 2 April through 20 April 1945, Serial 0010, 21 April 1945, Enclosure (F), New Attack Formations.

32. LSM Flotilla Nine, *Ie Shima and Southeastern Okinawa*, 3.

33. Blue, *Publication Sight Book*.

34. CTF 53, *Report* (V)(C)-26.

35. Landis, *Ship's Log USS LSM(R) 192*; See USS *Bowers* (*DE 637*), Action Report of the USS *Bowers* (*DE 637*), 1–24 April 1945, Serial No. 003, 15 May 1945.

36. CTF 53, *Report* (IV)(B)-4 to -5.

37. CTF 53, *Report* (III)-44.

38. Blue, *Publication Sight Book*.

39. LSM Flotilla Nine, *Ie Shima and Southeastern Okinawa*, 3: "The night patrols of the surrounding waters prevented any personnel movement or mine laying activities."

40. CTF 53, *Report* (V)(C)-19 to 20.

41. Blue, *Publication Sight Book.*

42. Commander, LSM Flotilla Nine, War Diary, 17 April 1945.

43. Commanding Officer, USS *LSM(R) 197*, Action Report, Battle of Okinawa Shima and Ie Shima, 1 April 1945 through 20 April 1945, Serial 03, 22 April 1945, 2.

44. Bruce A. McDaniel undated letter to author ca. January 1996.

45. David Mallery and Jack Shedd, Ensigns, USNR, *The History of USS LSM(R) 196*, unpublished typescript ca. October 1945.

46. Commander, Amphibious Group One (CTF 52), Action Report, Operations Against Okinawa Gunto including the Capture of Kerama Retto and the Eastern Islands of Okinawa, March 21 to and including April 20, 1945, Serial 053, 1 May 1945 (III)-34 to -36; CTF 53, *Report* (III)-45.

47. Blue, *Publication Sight Book.*

48. Jeter A. Isley and Philip A. Crowl, *The U.S. Marines and Amphibious War* (Princeton: Princeton University Press, 1951), 563, 568; Benis M. Frank and Henry I Shaw, Jr., *Victory and Occupation: History of U.S. Marine Corps Operations in World War II*, vol. 5 (Washington, D.C.: U.S. Government Printing Office, 1968), 193.

49. CTF 52, Action Report V-(C)-14.

50. CTF 52, Action Report V-(C)-14.

51. LSM Flotilla Nine, *Ie Shima and Southeastern Okinawa*, Part VI (D), 9; CTF 52, Action Report, V-(D)-7, paragraph 16, V-(D)-2 to -3, paragraph 6.

52. LSM Flotilla Nine, *Ie Shima and Southeastern Okinawa*, 3.

53. LSM Flotilla Nine, *Ie Shima and Southeastern Okinawa*, Part V (B), 7.

54. Mallery and Shedd, *The History of USS LSM(R) 196.*

55. CTF 52, Action Report, V-(C)-14.

56. CTF 51, *Report on Okinawa Gunto Operation* (V)(C)-9, paragraph (C).

57. Roy E. Appleman et al., *Okinawa: The Last Battle*, 207; Chas. S. Nichols, Jr., Major, USMC, and Henry I. Shaw, *Okinawa: Victory in the Pacific* (Washington, D.C.: U.S. Government Printing Office, 1955), 126.

Chapter 7

1. Robin L. Rielly, *Kamikaze Attacks of World War II* (Jefferson, NC: McFarland, 2010), Appendix 1; Samuel Eliot Morison. *Victory in the Pacific 1945.* vol. 14, Appendix II, 390, of *History of United States Naval Operations in World War II.* Boston: Little, Brown, 1960; Commander, Task Force Fifty-One, Commander Amphibious Forces, U.S. Pacific Fleet, Report on Okinawa Gunto Operation from 17 February to 17 May 1945, Serial 01400, 25 July 1945, Part (III), 22, Part (V), Section (H), 5 to 10.

2. "(commonly referred to by DD pickets as 'The Pall Bearers')...": USS *Little* (DD-803), Report of Action Between USS *Little* (DD803) and Enemy aircraft on May 3, 1945 (E.I.D.), 7 May 1945, 2.

3. Commanding Officer, USS *LSM(R) 195*, Action Report–Battle of Okinawa, 3 May 1945, Serial F9–05, 5 May 1945; Commanding Officer, USS *LSM(R) 195*, USS *LSM(R) 195*: Amplifying Report on Loss of, 7 June 1945; USS *LSM(R) 195* former Signalman Terence W. Listen related to the author that Lt. Woodson made repeated requests through the chain of command to either remove the rockets from topside launchers to stow them below decks or toss the projectiles over the side, but permission was never forthcoming.

4. USS *Little*, Report of Action Between USS *Little* (DD803), and Enemy aircraft on May 3, 1945 (E.L.D.), 7 May 1945: "This scheme was followed very closely in the ensuing action."

5. One group was flying toward RPS 9, the other was moving toward RPS 10, and "Both raids were apparently coordinated": USS *Bache*, Action Report, Okinawa Jima Operation, 16 March 1945 to 2 June 1945, Serial 0126, 2 June 1945.

6. USS *Little*, Report of Action Between USS *Little* (DD 803), and Enemy aircraft on May 3, 1945 (E.L.D.), 7 May 1945.

7. Commanding Officer, USS *LSM(R) 195*, Action Report–Battle of Okinawa, 3 May 1945, Serial F9–05, 5 May 1945; Commanding Officer, USS *LSM(R) 195*, USS *LSM(R) 195*: Amplifying Report on Loss of, 7 June 1945.

8. Harold Catchpole letter to Mrs. William Woodson February 25, 1996.

9. Frank Pizur, Letters to the Editor, *Alligator Alley*, No. 25, April 1996, 13.

10. LSM(R) 195, Action Report; LSM(R) 195, *Amplifying Report*; Laurie R. Russell letter to author October 20, 1995: "Yes, I believe that the large number of rocket motors on board did complicate fighting fires on the [*LSM(R)s*] 190, 194 & 195. The heads (5"-38 projectiles), however, contributed less damage. They were inherently more stable, especially in the unfused state, as they were in storage."

11. Harold Catchpole letter to author December 27, 1996.

12. Harold Catchpole letter to author December 27, 1996.

13. *LSM(R) 195*, Action Report, 1.

14. *LSM(R) 195*, Action Report, 3: Lt. Woodson noted Y2c Catchpole "aided greatly in bringing wounded to the raft, even though it kept him dangerously close to the blazing ship."

15. Frank Pizur, Letters to the Editor, *Alligator Alley*, No. 25, April 1996, 13.

16. Harold Catchpole letter to author December 27, 1996.

17. Harold Catchpole letter to author December 27, 1996; Frank Pizur, Letters to the Editor, *Alligator Alley*, No. 25, April 1996, 13.

18. "Rocket—A Dog Story," by John H. Fulweiler, is an essay of unknown publication about a cocker spaniel mascot on USS *LSM(R) 194* named "Rocket." However, the story is problematic because it relates an evening enemy air attack that sank the rocketship at dusk of 4 May 1945, but *LSM(R 194* was attacked and sunk during the morning of 4 May 1945. Interestingly, while USS *Bache* searched for survivors and dead from *LSM(R) 195*, the destroyer recovered an unnamed dog at 2313 of 3 May 1945. In conversation with former S1c (Coxswain) John B. Francis on 13 May 2015, he affirmed "Rocket the Dog" was in fact the mascot of USS *LSM(R) 195*. See Rolf F. Illsley, *LSM-LSMR WWII Amphibious Forces*, vol. 2 (Paducah: Turner Publishing Company, 1997), 82; U.S. Navy Deck Log, USS *Bache* DD 470, 3–4 May 1945.

19. Muster Rolls (BuPers Files), USS *LSM(R) 195*; See Commander, Task Force Fifty-One, Commander Amphibious Forces, U.S. Pacific Fleet, Report on Okinawa Gunto Operation from 17 February to 17 May 1945, Serial 01400, 25 July 1945, Part (V), Special Reports, Section (H), Medical Report (V)(H)-2.

20. "County Man Wins Silver Star Medal," July 20 [1945].

21. *LSM(R) 195*, Action Report, First and Second Endorsements, 12 May 1945.

22. USS *LSM(R) 195* killed in action and died from wounds in action 3 May 1945: Ensign James R. McKelvey; S2c (RM) William J. Burke; S2c Karl L. Dickens; GM3c Joseph A. Hale; EM3c (T) Hyman Kernes; Ensign Thomas H. Milliken; F1c George J. Ruhlman; PhM2c Daniel W. Styles; F1c James Tallery, Jr. Compiled from the following sources: Muster Rolls (BuPers Files), USS *LSM(R) 195*; USS *LSM(R) 195*, Action Report–Battle of Okinawa, 3 May 1945, Serial F9–05, 5 May 1945; Commanding Officer, USS *LSM(R) 195*, USS *LSM(R) 195*: Amplifying Report on Loss of, 7 June 1945; Rolf F. Illsley, *LSM-LSMR WWII Amphibious Forces*, vol. 2 (Paducah: Turner Publishing Company, 1997), 72; Navy Department, State Summary of War Casualties, Casualty Section, Office of Public Information (1946).

23. USS *Ingraham*, Action Report–Okinawa Gunto Oper-

ation for period from 29 April through 4 May 1945, Serial 004, 8 May 1945, 8.

24. USS *Morrison*, Action Report of the USS *Morrison* (*DD560*) For Period 21 March 1945 to 4 May 1945, Serial None, 11 May 1945.

25. John P. Wickser, "With the 'Little Boys'" (address, The Thursday Club, New York, December 9, 1971).

26. Wickser; Commanding Officer, USS *LSM(R) 194*, Action Report–Battle of Okinawa–4 May 1945, Serial: F9–06, 6 May 1945.

27. *LCS 21* identified the plane as a Val dive bomber, but *LCS 31* reported a Japanese float type plane hit the *LSM(R) 194*: USS *LCS(L)(3) 21*, Action, Report of, 6 May 1945, 2; USS *LCS(L)(3) 31*, Action Report (4 May 1945), 9 May 1945, 2; Navy Department, Bureau of Naval Personnel [Commanding Officer, USS *LSM(R) 194*], Pers 8249 mvb, 15 June 1945.

28. Wickser.

29. Ibid.

30. Ibid.

31. USS *Ingraham*, Action Report, 9.

32. Wickser.

33. Allan M. Hirshberg letter to Steven Gatto May 6, 1994.

34. Ibid.

35. Wickser.

36. U.S. Navy Deck Log, USS *LCS(L)(3) 21*; USS *LCS(L)(3) 21*, Action, Report of, 6 May 1945; USS *LCS(L)(3) 21*, Action, Report of, 6 May 1945.

37. Wickser; John H. Fulweiler "Rocket—A Dog Story."

38. USS *Ingraham*, Action Report, 9.

39. Commanding Officer, USS *LSM(R) 194*, Action Report–Battle of Okinawa–4 May 1945, Serial: F9–06, 6 May 1945, First Endorsement, Commander, LSM(R) Group Twenty-Seven, Flotilla Nine, 12 May 1945.

40. USS *LSM(R) 194* killed in action and died from wounds in action 4 May 1945: S1c (RM) Albert J. Arnhold; S1c Edward T. Bleakley; S1c Joseph T. Callen; S2c Boyd L. Carr; S2c Leonard P. Collins; MoMM2c (T) John R. Despard; S1c Clarence L. Ellis; MoMM3c (T) Asa E. Fitts; F1c Edward J. Kuligowski; F1c (MOMM) Herbert Meyerowitz; F1c (MoMM) Keith A. Place; PhM1c (T) Earl "D" Ridgeway; Cox (T) John W. Smith; SK3c (T) Hayden E. Thomas (LSM(R) Group 27 Staff). Compiled from the following sources: Muster Rolls (BuPers Files), USS *LSM(R) 194*; USS *LSM(R) 194*, Action Report–Battle of Okinawa–4 May 1945, Serial: F9–06, 6 May 1945; Rolf F. Illsley, *LSM-LSMR WWII Amphibious Forces*, vol. 2 (Paducah: Turner Publishing Company, 1997), 72; Navy Department, State Summary of War Casualties, Casualty Section, Office of Public Information (1946).

41. USS *Luce* (*DD 522*), Action report on Ryukyus Operation 24 March–4 May 1945, 4 May 1945, 8: "Small craft assigned the *Luce* quickly became known as pallbearer"; Ron Surels, *DD 522: Diary of a Destroyer* (Plymouth, NH: Valley Graphics, Inc., 1994), 104, 111: "We called them 'meatwagons.'"

42. "Sturdy Rocket Ship Proves Its Mettle, Took Three Jap Suicide Planes to Equal Score," *Navy News*, August 1945; "Lt. Harmon Tells Of Jap Plane Attack": "One morning in May the vessels in our group were raided by 18 Japanese planes. Two of them peeled off and dived into a destroyer [USS *Luce*]. Others came after us."

43. The Executive Officer, USS *LSM(R) 190*, Action Report–Battle of Okinawa, 4 May 1945, Serial F9–04, 5 May 1945.

44. *LSM(R) 190*, Action Report, 1; Earl Blanton, *Boston—to Jacksonville (41,000 Miles by Sea)* (Seaford, VA: Goose Creek Publications, 1991), 91; USS *LCS(L)(3) 118*, Action Report, Serial 02, 8 May 1945; U.S. Navy Deck Log, USS *LCS(L)(3) 84*; USS *LCS(L)(3) 84*, Action Report, Invasion of Okinawa Shima, 7 April 1945–12 May 1945, May 29, 1945; U.S. Navy Deck Log, USS *LCS(L)(3)81*. Accounts vary widely: *LCS 118* noted the first attack as a diving near miss at

0814; *LCS 84* recorded the plane crashed at 0823; *LCS 81* identified a Val striking the rocket ship's fantail at 0826.

45. "Lt. Harmon Tells of Jap Plane Attack"; "Sturdy Rocket Ship Proves Its Mettle, Took Three Jap Suicide Planes to Equal Score," *Navy News*, August 1945.

46. *LSM(R) 190*, Action Report.

47. *Ibid.*

48. *Ibid.*

49. *Ibid.*

50. *Ibid.*

51. *Ibid.*

52. Commanding Officer, USS *LCS(L)(3) 84*, Action Report, Invasion Okinawa Shima, 7 April 1945–12 May 1945, May 29, 1945, 13. See USS *LCS(L)(3) 118*, Action Report, Serial 02, 8 May 1945, "Comments and Recommendations," 3–4.

53. "USS *LSM(R) 190* Log," Revision, File: LogLSMR190, 20 May 1991, unpublished typescript.

54. Rolf F. Illsley, *LSM-LSMR WWII Amphibious Forces*, vol. 1 (Paducah: Turner Publishing Company, 1994), 50; Department of the Navy, Bureau of Naval Personnel, Navy Unit Commendation Awarded the USS *LSM(R) 190*, 23 June 1949.

55. USS *LSM(R) 190* killed in action and died from wounds in action 4 May 1945: Ensign Stuart C. Bjorklund; EM2c Arthur A. Armstrong; S1c Joseph H. Carpenter; S1c Henry A. Cherney; MoMM3c (T) Herbert L. Colclough; FCO3c Cecil C. Cox; GM1c Thomas J. Dutton, Jr.; GM1c John D. Hasbrouck; GM3c (T) James Karanutsos, Jr.; S1c James A. Massi; S2c Ralph Sheneman, Jr.; Cox (T) Ivan L. Sturgeon; S1c William R. Toy; GM2c Francis L. Whaley. Compiled from the following sources: Muster Rolls (BuPers Files), USS *LSM(R) 190*; USS *LSM(R) 190*, Action Report–Battle of Okinawa, 4 May 1945, Serial F9–04, 18 August 1945; Rolf F. Illsley, *LSM-LSMR WWII Amphibious Forces*, vol. 2 (Paducah: Turner Publishing Company, 1997), 72; Navy Department, State Summary of War Casualties, Casualty Section, Office of Public Information (1946).

56. Commanding Officer, USS *LSM(R) 192*, Action Report of, Serial 001, 6 May 1945.

57. Russell Wydeen letter to author October 9, 1995.

58. USS *Cowell* (*DD 547*), War Diary, May 1945; USS *Gwin* (*DM 33*), Report of Capture of Phases I and II, Okinawa Gunto, Serial 025, 4 July 1945; USS *Gwin* (*DM 33*), War Diary, 1945.

59. *LSM(R) 192*, Action Report.

60. Russell Wydeen letter to author October 9, 1995; Commanding Officer, USS *LSM(R) 192*, Action Report of, Serial 001, 6 May 1945: "The only casualty was Histed, William F., F1c, 959 31 04, second loader on the 20 mm gun that was damaged. He sustained two badly lacerated fingers and a broken bone in one finger."

61. Ronald R. MacKay, Sr., tape recorded interview with author July 14, 2001.

62. *LSM(R) 192*, Action Report.

63. Neal B. Hadsell letter to author January 5, 1995.

64. Commanding Officer, USS *LSM(R) 192*, Action Report of, Serial 001, 6 May 1945, First Endorsement, Serial: 0026, 7 June 1945.

65. Rielly, *Kamikaze Attacks of World War II*, Appendix 1; Samuel Eliot Morison, *Victory in the Pacific 1945*, Appendix II, 390; CTF 51, *Report on Okinawa Gunto Operation*, Part (III), 22, and Part (V) Section (H), 5 to 10.

66. U.S. Navy Deck Log, USS *LSM(R) 191*; USS *Lowry* (*DD 770*), Action Report–Report of Capture of Okinawa Gunto, Serial No. 021, 30 June 1945; USS *Henry A. Wiley* (*DM 29*), Report of the Capture of Okinawa Gunto, Phase One and Two, Serial: (058), 2 July 1945; USS *LCS(L)(3) 54*, Report of the Capture of Okinawa Gunto, Phases One and Two, Serial 116–45, 25 June 1945; USS *LCS(L)(3) 55*, Action Report, Surprise attack by Jap Torpedo Plane off Tori Shima, 10 May 1945, Serial No. 93, 11 May 1945.

67. Paul S. Vaitses Jr., *In the Rockets' Red Glare* (unpublished manuscript), 111.

68. Commanding Officer, USS *LSM(R) 193*, Action Report, Battle of Okinawa 11 May 1945, Serial 007, 13 May 1945.

69. USS *Evans* (*DD 552*), Action Report, Anti-aircraft action off Okinawa, 11 May 1945, Serial 004, 22 May 1945, 4.

70. Commanding Officer, USS *LSM(R) 193*, Action Report, Battle of Okinawa 11 May 1945, Serial 007, 13 May 1945; Revised Form for Reporting A.A. Action by Surface Ships, USS *LSM(R) 193*, 11 May 1945.

71. Commanding Officer, USS *LSM(R) 193*, Action Report, Battle of Okinawa 11 May 1945, Serial 007, 13 May 1945.

72. Ibid.

73. USS *Hugh W. Hadley* (*DD 774*), Action Report: Action against enemy aircraft attacking this ship, while on Radar Picket Station Number Fifteen, off Okinawa, Nansei Shoto, 11 May 1945, Serial 066, 15 May 1945, 3.

74. Vaitses, *In the Rockets' Red Glare*, 117.

75. Commanding Officer, USS *LSM(R) 193*, Action Report, Battle of Okinawa 11 May 1945, Serial 007, 13 May 1945.

76. Ibid.

77. Vaitses, *In the Rockets' Red Glare*, 119–120.

78. Commanding Officer, USS *LSM(R) 193*, Action Report, Battle of Okinawa 11 May 1945, Serial 007, 13 May 1945.

79. USS *Hugh W. Hadley* (*DD 774*), Action Report: Action against enemy aircraft attacking this ship, while on Radar Picket Station Number Fifteen, off Okinawa, Nansei Shoto, 11 May 1945, Serial 066, 15 May 1945, Battle Damage and Damage Control–report of (Enclosure C of Reference [a]), Serial No. 069, 22 May 1945, 2.

80. USS *Hugh W. Hadley* (*DD 774*), Action Report: Action against enemy aircraft attacking this ship, while on Radar Picket Station Number Fifteen, off Okinawa, Nansei Shoto, 11 May 1945, Serial 066, 15 May 1945, Enclosure (A), Action Report, 15 May 1945, 3.

81. Commanding Officer, USS *LSM(R) 193*, Action Report, Battle of Okinawa 11 May 1945, Serial 007, 13 May 1945.

82. Commanding Officer, USS *LSM(R) 193*, Action Report, Battle of Okinawa 11 May 1945, Serial 007, 13 May 1945, First Endorsement, 17 May 1945.

83. Commanding Officer, USS *LSM(R) 193*, Action Report, Battle of Okinawa 11 May 1945, Serial 007, 13 May 1945, Second Endorsement, 21 May 1945.

84. Commanding Officer, USS *LSM(R) 193*, Action Report, Battle of Okinawa 11 May 1945, Serial 007, 13 May 1945, Fourth Endorsement, 3 June 1945.

85. Rolf F. Illsley, *LSM-LSMR WWII Amphibious Forces*, vol. 1 (Paducah: Turner Publishing Company, 1994), 51.

86. Commanding Officer, USS *LSM(R) 197*, Action Report–Radar Picket Station Nine (9), Okinawa, 12 May 1945 thru 15 May 1945, Serial 05, 17 May 1945.

87. Ibid.

88. Lawrence J. Low letter to author January 10, 2003.

89. Accounts varied widely. For examples, *LSM(R) 197* reported two Vals; *Cowell* reported three Vals; *Bache's* initial battle damage report cited two Vals, but her latter action report cited three Vals: Commanding Officer, USS *LSM(R) 197*, Action Report–Radar Picket Station Nine (9), Okinawa, 12 May 1945 thru 15 May 1945, Serial 05, 17 May 1945, 2; USS *Cowell* (*DD 547*), War Diary, May 1945, 4; USS *Bache* (*DD 470*) Battle Damage Report, Serial 002, 21 May 1945,1; USS *Bache* (*DD 470*), Action Report–Okinawa Jima Operation, 16 March 1945 to 2 June 1945, Serial (0126), 2 June 1945, 7.

90. Commanding Officer, USS *LSM(R) 197*, Action Report–Radar Picket Station Nine (9), Okinawa, 12 May 1945 thru 15 May 1945, Serial 05, 17 May 1945.

91. Clyde Blue, *Publication Sight Book*, unpublished diary.

92. The Commanding Officer, USS *LCS 87*, Destruction of Enemy Aircraft by USS *LSM (R) 197*–confirmation of, Serial 48, 19 May 1945; Commander, LSM(R) Group 27, Flotilla Nine, War Diary, 13 May 1945: "During an evening air attack on Radar Picket Station 5 [*sic*], [*LSM(R)*] *197* destroyed one enemy plane."

93. *LSM(R) 197* reported this Val crashed into *Bache's* starboard side.

94. Blue, *Publication Sight Book*.

95. Commanding Officer, USS *LSM(R) 197*, Action Report–Radar Picket Station Nine (9), Okinawa, 12 May 1945 thru 15 May 1945, Serial 05, 17 May 1945.

96. Lawrence J. Low letter to author January 10, 2003.

97. Commanding Officer, USS *LSM(R) 197*, Action Report–Radar Picket Station Nine (9), Okinawa, 12 May 1945 thru 15 May 1945, Serial 05, 17 May 1945.

98. USS *Cowell*, War Diary, May 1945.

99. Commanding Officer, USS *LSM(R) 197*, Action Report–Radar Picket Station Nine (9), Okinawa, 12 May 1945 thru 15 May 1945, Serial 05, 17 May 1945, First Endorsement, Commander, LSM Flotilla Nine, Serial 0037, 26 May 1945.

100. Commanding Officer, USS *LSM(R) 197*, Action Report–Radar Picket Station Nine (9), Okinawa, 12 May 1945 thru 15 May 1945, Serial 05, 17 May 1945.

101. Blue, *Publication Sight Book*.

102. USS *Cowell*, War Diary, May 1945.

103. Dick Boak, Ensign Thomas Boak letter to his wife, June 13, 1945, unpublished typescript; Earl Blanton, *Boston—to Jacksonville (41,000 Miles by Sea)* (Seaford, VA: Goose Creek Publications, 1991), 97; Ronald R. MacKay, Sr., interview by author July 14, 2001; U.S. Navy Deck Log, USS *LCS(L)(3) 12*, 16 May 1945: "2045 Secured from General Quarters. While changing No. 2 40 MM gun from director to local control, 8 rounds were accidentally fired. No casualties."

104. Commander, LSM(R) Group 27, Flotilla Nine, War Diary, May 1945.

105. Vaitses, *In the Rockets' Red Glare*, 124.

106. Commander, Amphibious Forces, U.S. Pacific Fleet, Amphibious Gunnery Bulletin No. 2–Assault of Okinawa, Serial 0391, 24 May 1945, 5.

107. Commander, LSM Flotilla Nine, Action Report–Ie Shima and Southeastern Okinawa, 2 April through 20 April 1945, Serial 0010, 21 April 1945, 1st Endorsement, Commander Task Group 51.5, Serial 0018, 17 May 1945.

108. Commander, Task Force Fifty-One, Commander Amphibious Forces, U.S. Pacific Fleet, Report on Okinawa Gunto Operation from 17 February to 17 May 1945, Serial 01400, 25 July 1945 (V)(H)-2, subparagraph 11; Commander, Task Flotilla 1 (Commander Task Group 51.5), Action Report, Capture of Okinawa Gunto, 26 March to 21 June 1945, Serial 0894, 20 July 1945, 12; Commander, LSM Flotilla Nine (CTU 32.9.12), Action Report–Submission of, Serial 0045, 15 June 1945, First Endorsement, Enclosures (A) through (F): "On 30 April a pool of ten doctors from APAs was made available to the Screen Commander. These were placed aboard the picket supports to make their assistance more effective..." See also Ron MacKay, Jr., "The Towing and Medical LSMs at Okinawa: Part I," *Alligator Alley*, No. 69, June 2008, 29; Ron MacKay, Jr., "The Towing and Medical LSMs at Okinawa: Part II," *Alligator Alley*, No. 70, October 2008, 29.

109. Commanding Officer, USS *LSM(R) 189*, General Action Report, Battle of Okinawa–12 April 1945, Serial 0102, 15 April 1945, Second Endorsement, 24 April 1945.

110. Commander, LSM Flotilla Nine, War Diary, April 1945. Commodore Moosbrugger, USS *Biscayne*, 22, 25, 28, 30 April 1945; Vice Admiral Turner, USS *Eldorado*, 26 April 1945.

111. Commander, LSM Flotilla Nine, War Diary, 28 April 1945: "CTG 51.5 advised in dispatch number 281420 Z that ten junior Medicos will be available for assignment to ships of this command on 29 April." Lt. William J. Devlin, 231010, MC, USNR; Lt. George E. Roch, 280140, MC, USNR; Lt. E. C. Weiford, 167755, MC, USNR; Lt. (jg) Leland G. Brown, 182742, MC, USNR; Lt. (jg) Dayton R. Clark, 324769, MC, USNR; Lt. (jg) Joseph L. Goldner, 166460, MC, USNR; Lt. (jg) Philip C. Lynch, 143065, MC, USNR; Lt. (jg) J. T. McBurney, 425064, MC, USNR; Lt. (jg) Joseph M. Ryan, 183039, MC, USNR; Lt. (jg) Mitch Yanow, 362685, MC,

USNR, LSM Group 7, Staff Medical Officer, in USS *LSM 14* since 24 June 1944.

112. Commander, LSM Flotilla Nine, War Diary, April 1945: "Plan for new station assignments is as follows: 5 LSM(R)s on RADAR PICKET stations to act as support ships, 4 LSMs to take stations ⅔ distance to RADAR PICKET stations to act as Support and Medical ships, 6 LSMs to take station ⅓ distance to RADAR PICKET stations to act as Tow-Medical ships. This in accordance with CTG 52.21 OP PLAN number 2103–45 dated 30 April 1945."

113. Commanding Officer, USS *LSM(R) 189*, General Action Report, Battle of Okinawa–12 April 1945, Serial 0102, 15 April 1945, Second Endorsement, 24 April 1945; See First Endorsement, 20 April 1945.

114. USS *LSM 279*, Action Report RE: Ruyuko [*sic*] Campaign 30 April–26 May 1945–Submission of, Serial: 27–45, 26 May 1945, Appendix One, CTG 52.21 OP Plan #2103–45, Serial: 0014, 30 April 1945.

115. CTF 51, *Report on Okinawa Gunto Operation* (V)(H)-2, subparagraph 11; *PGMs 9, 10* and *20* backfilled the losses of *LSM(R)s 190, 194* and *195* after 5 May 1945.

116. USS *LSM 279*, Action Report RE: Ruyuko Campaign 30 April–26 May 1945–Submission of, Serial 27–45, 26 May 1945.

117. USS *LSM 167*, Action Report, Occupation of Okinawa Shima, 30 April 1945 to 23 May 1945, 24 May 1945.

118. USS *LSM 82*, Action Report, period 30 April–26 May 1945, Serial 0245, 26 May 1945.

119. Commander, LSM Flotilla Nine (CTU 32.9.12), Action Report–Submission of, Serial 0045, 15 June 1945, First Endorsement, Enclosures (A) through (F).

Chapter 8

1. Commander, LSM(R) Group 27, Flotilla Nine, War Diary, May 1945, 4.

2. Roy E. Appleman, James M. Burns, Russell A. Gugeler, and John Stevens, *Okinawa: The Last Battle* (Washington, D.C.: U.S. Government Printing Office, 1948); Chas. S. Nichols, Jr., Major, USMC, and Henry I. Shaw, *Okinawa: Victory in the Pacific* (Washington, D.C.: U.S. Government Printing Office, 1955); Benis M. Frank and Henry I Shaw, Jr., *Victory and Occupation: History of U.S. Marine Corps Operations in World War II*, vol. 5 (Washington, D.C.: U.S. Government Printing Office, 1968).

3. Tenth Army Action Report, Ryukyus, 26 March to 30 June 1945, 3 September 1945, 11-V-10.

4. Commander Fifth Amphibious Force (CTF 51 and 31), Report of Capture of Okinawa Gunto Phases 1 and 2 for period 17 May 1945 to 21 June 1945, Serial 0268, 4 July 45 (V)-12 to (V)-13 and (III)-70. After mid–May 1945, NGF commanders and commands changed frequently.

5. Commander, Amphibious Group Twelve (Commander Southern Attack Force–CTF 55), Report on the Capture of Okinawa Gunto Phase I and II, 14 March–9 June 1945, Serial 0287, 31 July 1945 (V) (C) -5 and -6; Tenth Army, Action Report, 11-V-9.

6. Commander, LSM(R) Group 27, Flotilla Nine, War Diary, 21 May 1945, 3: "*LSM(R) 192* and *193* were ordered by CTF 51 to report to CTG 51.19 for Fire Support Missions on the southeastern side of Okinawa."

7. CTG 51.19, *Report of Participation in Operations Against Okinawa Shima*, I/II-Page 1.

8. CTF 51 and 31, Report of Capture of Okinawa Gunto (V)-14.

9. Commander, Cruiser Division Six (CTG 51.19), Report of Participation in Operations Against Okinawa Shima, Nansei Shoto from 13 May to 27 May 1945 (period during which ConCruDiv6 was CTG 51.19 and SOPA Eastern Okinawa), Serial 0016, 6 June 1945,VI/VIII- 6 to -7.

10. CTG 51.19, *Report of Participation in Operations Against Okinawa Shima*, I/II-Page 1.

11. Commander, Small Craft Eastern Okinawa, CTU 32.9.7 (Commander LCI Flotilla Twenty-One), Action Report, Operations at Okinawa Jima, Nansei Shoto, 1 May through 31 May 1945, Serial 005, 1 June 1945; CTG 51.19, *Report of Participation in Operations Against Okinawa Shima*, VI/VIII-Page 8.

12. Commander, LSM(R) Group 27, Flotilla Nine, War Diary, May 1945.

13. Commander, Task Force Fifty-One, Commander Amphibious Forces, U.S. Pacific Fleet, Report on Okinawa Gunto Operation from 17 February to 17 May 1945, Serial 01400, 25 July 1945 (I)-3 (I)-6 (III)-111.

14. Donald L. Ball, *Fighting Amphibs: The LCS(L)s in World War II* (Williamsburg, VA: Mill Neck Publications, 1997), 152–153.

15. Commander, LSM Flotilla Nine, War Diary, April 1945, Serial 021, 1 May 1945, and note references on 24 April, 26 April, and 29 April 1945; Commander, LSM(R) Group 27, Flotilla Nine, War Diary, May 1945: "13 May 1945 … Under CTF 51's [*sic*] a new Task Organization this Unit was designated 51.9.12 [*sic*], under 51.9.1 [*sic*] (Captain Aylward)…," should read 52.9.12 [Commander Francis, LSM(R) Picket Supports] and 52.9.1 [LSM(R) Picket Support Gunboats] respectively. Captain Aylward was CTG 52.9 as Commander, LCS(L) Flotilla Three and Gunboats and Mortar Support Flotillas.

16. Roy E. Appleman et al., *Okinawa: The Last Battle*, 377, 392; Frank and Shaw, *Victory and Occupation*, 270; Nichols and Shaw, *Okinawa: Victory in the Pacific*, 196–198; Edmund G. Love, *The Hourglass: A History of the 7th Infantry Division in World War II* (Washington, D.C.: Infantry Journal Press, 1950), 411.

17. U.S. Navy Deck Log, USS *LSM(R) 192*: 22 May 1945 entry mistakenly cites Hagushi.

18. Commander, LSM(R) Group 27, Flotilla Nine, War Diary, 22 May 1945, 4: "[*LSM(R)*s] *193* and *191* assigned by CTG 31.19 to give Fire Support to 184th Infantry…," but *191* should read *192*.

19. CTG 51.19, *Report of Participation in Operations Against Okinawa Shima*, III-Page 15; CTF 51 and 31, Report of Capture of Okinawa Gunto (V)-19: 22 May 1945, Eastern Okinawa day direct support were USS *St. Louis*, USS *Portland*, USS *H. L. Edwards*, USS *Rooks*, USS *Twiggs*, and USS *Vicksburg*; Eastern Okinawa night direct support ships were the same less USS *Rooks*.

20. Love, *The Hourglass*, 411–414.

21. U.S. Navy Deck Log, USS *LSM(R) 193*: TA [Tactical Area] 8468–8368.

22. Headquarters, 7th Infantry Division teletype message addressed to USS *LSM(R) 192*, 22 May 1945.

23. TA 8968 covers vicinity of China village on Chinen Hanto peninsula, however, rocket attacks in TA 8968 are not affirmed by U.S. Navy Deck Logs of USS *LSM(R) 192* or USS *LSM(R) 193*. See CTG 51.19, *Report of Participation in Operations Against Okinawa Shima*, III-Page 15. TA 8468–8268 is north-northwest of Tsuwanuku village.

24. CTG 51.19, *Report of Participation in Operations Against Okinawa Shima*, III-Page 15.

25. Commander, LSM(R) Group 27, Flotilla Nine, War Diary, 22 May 1945.

26. Robert W. Landis, *Ship's Log USS LSM(R) 192*, unpublished diary: May 22, 1945 entry mistakenly cites Naha, Okinawa's capital, which is on the west coast.

27. CTG 51.19, *Report of Participation in Operations Against Okinawa Shima*, III-Page 16.

28. CTG 51.19, *Report of Participation in Operations Against Okinawa Shima*, III-Page 16; CTF 51 and 31, Report of Capture of Okinawa Gunto (V)-19 to -20: 23 May 1945, Eastern Okinawa day direct support included USS *St. Louis*, USS *Portland*, USS *Rooks*, USS *Vicksburg*, USS *Beale*, USS *San Francisco*, and USS *H.L. Edwards*; Eastern Okinawa night direct support were the same except USS *St. Louis* and USS *Rooks*.

29. Love, *The Hourglass*, 418.

30. U.S. Navy Deck Log, USS *LSM(R) 193*: TA 8468–8368.

31. U.S. Navy Deck Log, USS *LSM(R) 193*: TA 9272.

32. CTG 51.19, *Report of Participation in Operations Against Okinawa Shima*, III-Page 16.

33. U.S. Navy Deck Log, USS *LSM(R) 192*: Target areas for 23 May 1945 are unclear and reports of the numbers of rockets expended are inconsistent.

34. Commander, LSM(R) Group 27, Flotilla Nine, War Diary, 4.

35. Landis, *Ship's Log USS LSM(R) 192*: Naha is mistakenly cited.

36. Landis, *Ship's Log USS LSM(R) 192*.

37. HQ 7th Infantry Division/10th Army, 23 May 1945.

38. Love, *The Hourglass*, 418–419, 421.

39. CTG 51.19, *Report of Participation in Operations Against Okinawa Shima*, III-Page 17; CTF 51 and 31, Report of Capture of Okinawa Gunto (V)-20 to -21: 24 May 1945, Eastern Okinawa day direct support were USS *San Francisco*, USS *Vicksburg*, USS *Callaghan*, USS *Portland*, USS *H. L. Edwards*, USS *Irwin*, USS *Beale*, and USS *Tuscaloosa*; Eastern Okinawa night direct support were USS *Callaghan*, USS *Preston*, USS *Irwin*, and USS *Vicksburg*; special assignments as "Flycatchers" were USS *San Francisco* and USS *Portland*.

40. Love, *The Hourglass*, 422–423.

41. U.S. Navy Deck Log, USS *LSM(R) 193*: TA 8467A.

42. U.S. Navy Deck Log, USS *LSM(R) 193*.

43. Love, *The Hourglass*, 423–424.

44. U.S. Navy Deck Log, USS *LSM(R) 192*.

45. U.S. Navy Deck Log, USS *LSM(R) 193*.

46. U.S. Navy Deck Log, USS *LSM(R) 193*: TA 8366M.

47. U.S. Navy Deck Log, USS *LSM(R) 192*: The numbers of rockets expended are not recorded.

48. U.S. Navy Deck Log, USS *LSM(R) 193*: TA 9274.

49. Landis, *Ship's Log USS LSM(R) 192*.

50. Commander, LSM(R) Group 27, Flotilla Nine, War Diary, 24 May 1945.

51. CTU 32.9.7, *Operations at Okinawa Jima*, 5.

52. CTG 51.19, *Report of Participation in Operations Against Okinawa Shima*, III-Page 17.

53. CTG 51.19, *Report of Participation in Operations Against Okinawa Shima*, III-Page 18.

54. Samuel Eliot Morison. *Victory in the Pacific 1945.* vol. 14, 199–200, of *History of United States Naval Operations in World War II.* Boston: Little, Brown, 1960.

55. CTU 32.9.7, *Operations at Okinawa Jima*, 5.

56. CTG 51.19, *Report of Participation in Operations Against Okinawa Shima*, III-Page 20.

57. CTG 51.19, *Report of Participation in Operations Against Okinawa Shima*, III-Page 20.

58. CTF 51 and 31, Report of Capture of Okinawa Gunto (V)-21: 25 May 1945, Eastern Okinawa day direct support were USS *West Virginia*, USS *Vicksburg*, USS *Irwin*, USS *Callaghan*, USS *Rooks*, USS *San Francisco*, USS *Tuscaloosa*, and USS *Preston*; Eastern Okinawa night direct support were USS *Preston*, USS *West Virginia*, USS *Tuscaloosa*, USS *Irwin*, and USS *Rooks*; USS *San Francisco* was on special assignment as a "Flycatcher."

59. CTG 51.19, *Report of Participation in Operations Against Okinawa Shima*, III-Page 21.

60. CTG 51.19, *Report of Participation in Operations Against Okinawa Shima*, III-Page 22 and V-Page 3: "A few minutes after 0900, *LSM 192* [*sic*] reported shooting down one *Oscar* which it was claimed was not fired on by any other ship."

61. CTG 51.19, *Report of Participation in Operations Against Okinawa Shima*, III-Page 22.

62. U.S. Navy Deck Log, USS *LSM(R) 193*; Commander, LSM(R) Group 27, Flotilla Nine, War Diary, 4: "[*LSM(R)*s] *192* and *193* rendered Fire Support and Spotting for Army. By dispatch CTG 51.5 released all LSM(R)s from Radar Picket Duty."

63. Love, *The Hourglass*, 425–426.

64. Ammunition acquisition not recorded in U.S. Navy Deck Logs for USS *LSM(R) 192* or USS *LSM(R) 193*.

65. U.S. Navy Deck Log, USS *LSM(R) 193*: TA 8566 Uncle.

66. CTG 51.19, *Report of Participation in Operations Against Okinawa Shima*, III-Page 19: note typographical error: TA 7367M is on the Oroku Peninsula in western Okinawa, so TA 8367M is the more likely target for the reported LSM(R) fire immediately west of Tsuwanuku village.

67. CTG 51.19, *Report of Participation in Operations Against Okinawa Shima*, III-Page 19: LSM(R) records do not indicate rocket runs or rocket fires during 25 May 1945.

68. U.S. Navy Deck Logs for USS *LSM(R) 192* and USS *LSM(R) 193* note 57 and 58 rounds expended respectively.

69. CTG 51.19, *Report of Participation in Operations Against Okinawa Shima*, III-Page 23.

70. U.S. Navy Deck Log, USS *LSM(R) 193*: TA 8570 Q.

71. CTG 51.19, *Report of Participation in Operations Against Okinawa Shima*, III-Page 23.

72. U.S. Navy Deck Log, USS *LSM(R) 193*: TA 8668 R.

73. U.S. Navy Deck Log, USS *LSM(R) 193*: TA 8667 J; TA 8767 G, F, K.

74. CTG 51.19, *Report of Participation in Operations Against Okinawa Shima*, III-Page 23; U.S. Navy Deck Log, USS *LSM(R) 193*.

75. U.S. Navy Deck Log, USS *LSM(R) 193*: TA 8570 T.

76. U.S. Navy Deck Log, USS *LSM(R) 193*: TA 8367 N.

77. CTF 51 and 31, Report of Capture of Okinawa Gunto (V)-22: 26 May 1945, Eastern Okinawa day direct support were USS *Vicksburg*, USS *West Virginia*, USS *Preston*, USS *Tuscaloosa*, USS *Paul Hamilton*, USS *Rooks*, and USS *Irwin*; Eastern Okinawa night direct support were USS *Vicksburg*, USS *West Virginia*, USS *Paul Hamilton*, USS *San Francisco*, and USS *Twiggs*; no "Flycatcher" special assignments cited this date for the East side.

78. CTF 51 and 31, Report of Capture of Okinawa Gunto (III)-27.

79. U.S. Navy Deck Log, USS *LSM(R) 192*: location is unclear for 1600–1800.

80. CTG 51.19, *Report of Participation in Operations Against Okinawa Shima*, III-Page 23 to 24; William J. Veigele, *PC Patrol Craft of World War II* (Santa Barbara, CA: Astral Publishing Co., 1998), 222.

81. U.S. Navy Deck Log, USS *LSM(R) 193*: TA 8625 L is beyond the coastline of Okinawa proper and likely a typographical error.

82. U.S. Navy Deck Log, USS *LSM(R) 192*: location is unclear for 1600–1800.

83. Roy E. Appleman et al., *Okinawa: The Last Battle*, 381.

84. U.S. Navy Deck Log, USS *LSM(R) 193*: TA 9374 Love.

85. Commander, LSM(R) Group 27, Flotilla Nine, War Diary, 26 May 1945.

86. CTG 51.19, *Report of Participation in Operations Against Okinawa Shima*, III-Page 25.

87. CTF 51 and 31, Report of Capture of Okinawa Gunto (V)-22 to (V)-23: 27 May 1945, Eastern Okinawa day direct support were USS *San Francisco*, USS *Vicksburg*, USS *West Virginia*, USS *Paul Hamilton*, USS *Rooks*, and USS *Preston*; Eastern Okinawa night direct support were USS *West Virginia*, USS *Portland*, USS *San Francisco*, USS *Paul Hamilton*, and USS *Rooks*; USS *Callaghan* was on special assignment as a "Flycatcher."

88. U.S. Navy Deck Log, USS *LSM(R) 193*: TA 8766 Jig.

89. U.S. Navy Deck Log, USS *LSM(R) 192*.

90. Love, *The Hourglass*, 412–413.

91. U.S. Navy Deck Log, USS *LSM(R) 193*: TA 8567.

92. Headquarters 7th Infantry Division teletype message addressed to USS *LSM(R) 192*, 27 May 1945.

93. U.S. Navy Deck Log, USS *LSM(R) 193*: TA 8966 D.

94. U.S. Navy Deck Log, USS *LSM(R) 193*: TA 9067 KQ.

95. U.S. Navy Deck Log, USS *LSM(R) 193*: TA 8766 NI; TA 8566 BC.

96. CTG 51.19, *Report of Participation in Operations Against Okinawa Shima*, III-Page 25. TA 8565DE is immediately inland and southwest of Sashiki village in Baten Ko.

97. CTF 51 and 31, Report of Capture of Okinawa Gunto (III)-29.

98. Target Areas 8766 and 9067 are adjacent to Sashiki and China villages, respectively: Commander, Battleship Division Four, Action Report, Capture of Okinawa Gunto, Continuation of Phase One, 18 May through 10 June 1945, Serial 0314, 22 June 1945, Part III, Page 4, Enclosure (A).

99. CTG 51.19, *Report of Participation in Operations Against Okinawa Shima*, VI/VIII-Page 6 to 7.

100. U.S. Navy Deck Log, USS *LSM(R) 193*: TA 9174 J.

101. Roy E. Appleman et al., *Okinawa: The Last Battle*, 362.

102. CTU 32.9.7, *Operations at Okinawa Jima*, 5: "*LSM(R) 192* and *193* continued working with the Army"; CTF 51 and 31, Report of Capture of Okinawa Gunto (V)-23 to (V)-24: 28 May 1945, Eastern Okinawa day direct support were USS *Portland*, USS *New Orleans*, USS *West Virginia*, USS *Callaghan*, USS *Paul Hamilton*, and USS *Rooks*; Eastern Okinawa night direct support were USS *West Virginia*, USS *Portland*, USS *Rooks*, USS *New Orleans*, and USS *Putnam*; USS *Callaghan* was on special assignment as a "Flycatcher."

103. Battleship Division Four, *Capture of Okinawa Gunto*, Part III, Page 5, Enclosure (A).

104. CTF 51 and 31, Report of Capture of Okinawa Gunto (III)-33; Roy E. Appleman et al., *Okinawa: The Last Battle*, 391: "Before 30 May, "...there was no real conviction in the American command that the Japanese were actually engaged in a withdrawal from Shuri."

105. U.S. Navy Deck Log, USS *LSM(R) 193*: TA 8967D; TA 8967 V; TA 8967 Q.

106. U.S. Navy Deck Log, USS *LSM(R) 193*.

107. Commander, LSM(R) Group 27, Flotilla Nine, War Diary, 28 May 1945.

108. U.S. Navy Deck Log, USS *LSM(R) 193*: TA 8361 A, B, F, G, K, L.

109. CTU 32.9.7, *Operations at Okinawa Jima*, 5: "*LSM(R) 192* continued as fire support for the Army in Baten Ko."

110. Battleship Division Four, *Capture of Okinawa Gunto* (Part III), Page 5, Enclosure (A); CTF 51 and 31, Report of Capture of Okinawa Gunto,(V)-24: 29 May 1945, Eastern Okinawa day direct support were USS *Rooks*, USS *New Orleans*, USS *West Virginia*, USS *Putnam*, USS *Callaghan*, and USS *Portland*; Eastern Okinawa night direct support were USS *West Virginia*, USS *New Orleans*, USS *Portland*, and USS *Callaghan*; USS *Laws* was on special assignment as a "Flycatcher."

111. Roy E. Appleman et al., *Okinawa: The Last Battle*, 392–394, 422.

112. U.S. Navy Deck Log, USS *LSM(R) 192*: 1st Lt. Carr, USA, Sgt. Hayworth, USA, Sgt. Meyer, USA, disembarked; 1st Lt. O'Brien, USA, Sgt. Yagerson, USA, embarked. Sergeant Meyer is recorded embarking twice on 29 May 1945 at 0855 and 0910.

113. Robert W. Landis email to author January 30, 2005.

114. Ronald R. MacKay, Sr., letter to author July 14, 1977.

115. CTU 32.9.7, *Operations at Okinawa Jima*, 6: "*LSM(R) 192* continued as fire support for the Army in Baten Ko."

116. CTF 51 and 31, Report of Capture of Okinawa Gunto (III)-39.

117. Battleship Division Four, *Capture of Okinawa Gunto*, Part III, Page 5, Enclosure (A); CTF 51 and 31, Report of Capture of Okinawa Gunto (V)-25: 30 May 1945, Eastern Okinawa day direct support were USS *Portland*, USS *New Orleans*, USS *Laws*, USS *Preston*, USS *Putnam*, and USS *West Virginia*; Eastern Okinawa night direct support were USS *West Virginia*, USS *New Orleans*, USS *Laws*, USS *Callaghan*, and USS *Portland*; USS *Preston* was on special assignment as a "Flycatcher."

118. U.S. Navy Deck Log, USS *LSM(R) 192*: The numbers of AR rockets expended on 30 May 1945 are not recorded.

119. U.S. Navy Deck Log, USS *LSM(R) 193*.

120. CTU 32.9.7, *Operations at Okinawa Jima*, 6: "*LSM(R) 192* and *LSM(R) 193* worked with the 7th Infantry Division again as fire support ships."

121. Battleship Division Four, *Capture of Okinawa Gunto*, Part III, Page 6 Pages, Enclosure (A); CTF 51 and 31, Report of Capture of Okinawa Gunto (V)-25 to (V)-26: 31 May 1945, Eastern Okinawa day direct support were USS *New Orleans*, USS *Laws*, USS *Preston*, USS *Portland*, USS *West Virginia*, and USS *Callaghan*; Eastern Okinawa night direct support were USS *Portland*, USS *West Virginia*, USS *H.L. Edwards*, USS *Preston*, and USS *Laws*; USS *New Orleans* was on special assignment as a "Flycatcher."

122. CTF 51 and 31, Report of Capture of Okinawa Gunto (III)-42.

123. Commander, LSM(R) Group 27, Flotilla Nine, War Diary, 31 May 1945.

124. U.S. Navy Deck Log, USS *LSM(R) 193*: TA 9274 Y.

125. U.S. Navy Deck Log, USS *LSM(R) 192*: "Captain of *LSM(R) 193* aboard to check radio message which they could not decode." The message was neither cited nor characterized.

126. Landis, *Ship's Log USS LSM(R) 192*. U.S. forces officially declared the end of organized resistance on Okinawa on 21 June 1945.

127. Battleship Division Four, *Capture of Okinawa Gunto*, Part IV, Page 3, Enclosure (A).

128. Documentation citing command organizations are often error-laden and contradictory. See U.S. Navy Deck Log, USS *LSM(R) 191*, 21 May 1945, 1200: "Detached from Task Force 51.21 [Admiral Cobb, SOPA Ie Shima and Northern Okinawa] and reassigned to Task Force 51.22 [Admiral Hill, SOPA Hagushi]" (Task Force should read Task Group); Commander, LSM(R) Group 27, Flotilla Nine, War Diary, 21 May 1945: "*LSM(R)s 189* and *191* were ordered by CTF 51 to report to CTG 51.21 [Admiral Cobb, SOPA Ie Shima and Northern Okinawa] for similar [Fire Support] Missions on southwestern side of Okinawa"; Commander, LSM(R) Group 27, Flotilla Nine, War Diary, 22 May 1945: "*LSM(R)s 189* and *191* assigned by CTG 31.21 [Admiral Cobb, SOPA Ie Shima and Northern Okinawa] to CTU 32.9.4 [Commander Coffin, Southern Support Gunboats] remained at Hagushi" (CTG 31.21 should read CTG 51.21, and CTU 32.9.4 should read CTU 52.9.4, because Admiral Spruance as Commander Fifth Fleet was not relieved by Admiral Halsey as Commander Third Fleet until 28 May 1945); Commanding Officer, USS *LSM 189* [*sic*], Fire support rendered by *LSM(R)s 189* and *191* on south-western part of Okinawa from 22 May 1945 to 2 June 1945, "Subject named ships were detached 22 May 1945 at 1200 by Commander, LSM Flotilla Nine, for temporary duty CTF 55, who in turn assigned us to Cmdr. Bailliere, CTU 52.9.4 aboard *LCI (FF) 370*." Reference to Commander Bailliere is in error: Commander Coffin was CTU 52.9.4 in flagship USS *LC(FF) 370*, Commander Bailliere was CTU 52.9.7, Eastern Gunboats in flagship USS *LC(FF) 679*: CTF 51, *Report on Okinawa Gunto Operation* (I)-3 (I)-7) (III)-48 (III)-111. Effective 18 April 1945, CTF 55 was dissolved and re-designated CTG 51.22 and CTF 53 was dissolved and re-designated CTG 51.21, but CTG 51.19 was not affected.

129. CTF 51 and 31, Report of Capture of Okinawa Gunto (V)-13.

130. CTF 55, Report on the Capture of Okinawa Gunto (V)(C)-20; See Vice Admiral Turner's reference in CTF 51, Report on Okinawa Gunto Operation, Part (V), Special Reports, Section (C), Naval Ordnance and Gunnery–Support Craft (V)(C)-20).

131. Commander, LCI(R) Flotilla Sixteen, Action Report–Invasion of the Okinawa Group Liu Chius, 26 March to 21 June 1945, Serial No. 35, 15 July 1945. Curiously, Commander Coffin does not cite *LSM(R)s 189* or *191* in his report; F.

Donald Moore, *Quartermaster's Log*, unpublished diary, 21 May 1945: "1345 Reported to *LCI* [*sic*] *370* [Cmdr. Coffin's flagship] for fire support duty."

132. CTF 51, "Report on Okinawa Gunto Operation"(I)-3 (I)-6 (III)-111.

133. Ball, *Fighting Amphibs*, 152–153.

134. Commander, LSM Flotilla Nine, War Diary, 1 May 1945: Note 24 April, 26 April, and 29 April 1945; See Commander, LSM(R) Group 27, Flotilla Nine, War Diary, May 1945: "13 May 1945… Under CTF 51's [*sic*] a new Task Organization this Unit was designated 51.9.12 [*sic*], under 51.9.1 [*sic*] (Captain Aylward)…," should read 52.9.12 for Commander Francis as LSM(R) Picket Supports and 52.9.1 for LSM(R) Picket Support Gunboats respectively. Captain Aylward was CTG 52.9 for Commander LCS(L) Flotilla Three and Gunboats and Mortar Support Flotillas.

135. CTF 51, Report on Okinawa Gunto Operation (V) (C)-7.

136. LCI(R) Flotilla Sixteen, Action Report, 34, 37.

137. Commander, LSM(R) Group 27, Flotilla Nine, War Diary, 25 May 1945.

138. Roy E. Appleman et al., *Okinawa: The Last Battle*, 317.

139. Phillips D. Carlton, Major, USMCR, *The Conquest of Okinawa: An Account of the Sixth Marine Division*, Historical Division, Headquarters, U.S. Marine Corps, 1947; Frank and Shaw, *Victory and Occupation*, 244–256.

140. Naval Gunfire Support, Sixth Marine Division, 19 May 1945 to 19 June 1945, incomplete supplement to Headquarters, III Corps Artillery, Third Amphibious Corps, Naval Gunfire Report, Okinawa Operation, 23 April 1945. Note LSM(R) misidentified as LSM(M) on 26 May 1945.

141. CTF 51 and 31, Report of Capture of Okinawa Gunto (V)-14.

142. CTF 51 and 31, Report of Capture of Okinawa Gunto (V)-22: 26 May 1945, Western Okinawa daytime direct support were USS *Laws*, USS *Wichita*, USS *Idaho*, USS *Hall*, USS *Mississippi*, USS *New York*, USS *Vincennes*, USS *New Orleans*, USS *Picking*, USS *Twiggs*; Western Okinawa nighttime direct support included USS *Mississippi*, USS *Vincennes*, USS *Beale*, USS *Wichita*, and USS *Louisville*.

143. Moore, *Quartermaster's Log*.

144. USS *LSM 189*, Fire support rendered by *LSM(R)s 189 and 191*: TA 7073.

145. USS *LSM 189*, Fire support rendered by *LSM(R)s 189 and 191*: TAs 7370, 7271, 7270, 7369.

146. Frank and Shaw, *Victory and Occupation*, 251.

147. Nichols and Shaw, *Okinawa: Victory in the Pacific*, 209.

148. Roy E. Appleman et al., *Okinawa: The Last Battle*, 427–428.

149. Moore, *Quartermaster's Log*.

150. U.S. Navy Deck Log, USS *LSM(R) 191*, time of attack 1520; Moore, *Quartermaster's Log*, time of attack 1528.

151. USS *LSM 189*, Fire support rendered by *LSM(R)s 189 and 191*.

152. Moore, *Quartermaster's Log*.

153. Sixth Marine Division, Naval Gunfire Support, 26 May 1945.

154. Moore, *Quartermaster's Log*.

155. U.S. Navy Deck Log, USS *LSM(R) 189*, 26 May 1945; *LSM(R) 189* in TAs 7167 and 7267; *LSM(R) 191* in TAs 7166 and 7266.

156. Frank and Shaw, *Victory and Occupation*, 311, 323; Nichols and Shaw, *Victory in the Pacific*, 221, 228.

157. Moore, *Quartermaster's Log*; USS LSM 189, Fire support rendered by *LSM(R)s 189 and 191*.

158. USS *LSM 189*, Fire support rendered by *LSM(R)s 189 and 191*; Cf. U.S. Navy Deck Log, USS *LSM(R) 191*, 26 May 1945: "1907 Secured from GQ. Total ammunition expended: 83 rounds, 40mm; 70 rounds, 20mm; 400 rounds, .50 caliber; 14 rounds, 5"/38." See also Commander, LSM(R) Group 27, Flotilla Nine, War Diary, 26 May 1945: "On detached duty

189 and *191* in support of Sixth Marine Division delivered 212 Rockets, 5 inch and automatic weapon fire on assigned target areas on Southwestern Okinawa"; Naval Gunfire Support Sixth Marine Division, 26 May 1945: Unidentified vessel "#1" fired 400 4.2" mortar rounds, unidentified vessel "#2" fired 200 4.2" mortar rounds, however, none of the original twelve "Interim" LSM(R)s were fitted with 4.2" mortars.

159. Moore, *Quartermaster's Log*.

160. Commander, LSM(R) Group 27, Flotilla Nine, War Diary, 26 May 1945.

161. USS *LSM 189*, Fire support rendered by *LSM(R)s 189 and 191*; Naval Gunfire Support Sixth Marine Division, 26 May 1945: "1 hour concentrated neutralization fire—Unobserved…"

162. U.S. Navy Deck Log, USS *LSM(R) 189*: CTF 55.94 should read CTG 52.9.4.

163. U.S. Navy Deck Log, USS *LSM(R) 189*.

164. Moore, *Quartermaster's Log*.

165. Moore, *Quartermaster's Log*.

166. Sixth Marine Division, Naval Gunfire Support, 27 May 1945; CTF 51 and 31, Report of Capture of Okinawa Gunto (V)-22 to (V)-23: 27 May 1945, Western Okinawa daytime direct support included USS *Mississippi*, USS *Barton*, USS *New York*, USS *Beale*, USS *Vincennes*, USS *Tuscaloosa*, USS *Laws*, USS *Louisville*, and USS *Twiggs*; Western Okinawa nighttime direct support included USS *Barton*, USS *New York*, USS *Vincennes*, USS *Louisville*, and USS *Wilson*.

167. CTF 51 and 31, Report of Capture of Okinawa Gunto (III)-29.

168. U.S. Navy Deck Log, USS *LSM(R) 189*: TA 7073.

169. Moore, *Quartermaster's Log*.

170. Sixth Marine Division, Naval Gunfire Support, 27 May 1945.

171. U.S. Navy Deck Log, USS *LSM(R) 191*.

172. Edward Bowden conversation with author October 30, 1995.

173. USS *LSM 189*, Fire support rendered by *LSM(R)s 189 and 191*.

174. Sixth Marine Division, Naval Gunfire Support, 27 May 1945.

175. U.S. Navy Deck Log, USS *LC(FF) 535*: TA 7884.

176. U.S. Navy Deck Log, USS *LSM(R) 189*, 27 May 1945; Commander, LSM(R) Group 27, Flotilla Nine, War Diary, 27 May 1945. "Commander, LSM(R) Group Twenty-Seven temporarily embarked on [*LSM(R)*] *189*."

177. U.S. Navy Deck Log, USS *LSM 189*: TAs 7167, 7166, 7266, 7267; See USS *LSM 189*, Fire support rendered by *LSM(R)s 189 and 191*.

178. Moore, *Quartermaster's Log*.

179. Ibid.

180. Sixth Marine Division, Naval Gunfire Support, 27 May 1945.

181. U.S. Navy Deck Log, USS *LSM(R) 189*: TA 7267.

182. Moore, *Quartermaster's Log*.

183. Moore, *Quartermaster's Log*; U.S. Navy Deck Log, USS *LSM(R) 189*: TA 7361.

184. Moore, *Quartermaster's Log*.

185. U.S. Navy Deck Log, USS *LSM(R) 191*: Ammunition expended 300 rockets, 16—5" shells, 575—40mm shells; See Naval Gunfire Support Sixth Marine Division, 27 May 1945; Commander, LSM(R) Group 27, Flotilla Nine, War Diary, 27 May 1945: "On detached duty [*LSM(R)*] *189* delivered 147 Rockets, 5 inch and automatic weapon fire in assigned area. [*LSM(R)*] *191* on a particularly exposed mission delivered 7 hours of call fire, 575 rounds of 40mm. At 1800 both Ships [*sic*] fired total of 600 Rockets in assigned area [*sic*]."

186. Moore, *Quartermaster's Log*.

187. Ibid.

188. U.S. Navy Deck Log, USS *LSM(R) 189*.

189. Commander, LSM(R) Group 27, Flotilla Nine, War Diary, 27 May 1945.

190. Moore, *Quartermaster's Log.*
191. Ibid.
192. Moore, *Quartermaster's Log*; U.S. Navy Deck Log, USS *LSM(R) 189*: TA 7073.
193. CTF 51 and 31, Report of Capture of Okinawa Gunto (V)-23 to (V)-24: 28 May 1945, Western Okinawa daytime direct support included USS *Mississippi*, USS *Wilson*, USS *Idaho*, USS *Vicksburg*, USS *Beale*, USS *Tuscaloosa*, USS *Louisville*, and USS *Twiggs*; Western Okinawa nighttime direct support included USS *Wilson*, USS *New York*, USS *Idaho*, USS *Louisville*, and USS *Mississippi.*
194. Sixth Marine Division, Naval Gunfire Support, 28 May 1945.
195. Roy E. Appleman et al., *Okinawa: The Last Battle*, 428.
196. CTF 51 and 31, Report of Capture of Okinawa Gunto (III)-33.
197. U.S. Navy Deck Log, USS *LSM(R) 189*: TAs 7162 and 7267 are the identified target areas, however, TA 7162 is a typographical error because this grid area lies about 1500 yards offshore from Itoman, hence the likely target area designations were TA 7167 and TA 7267 for Gushi village.
198. *LSM(R) 189* records her rocket run from 1240–1245, but *LSM(R) 191* records *LSM(R) 189*'s rocket run earlier at 1230: U.S. Navy Deck Log, USS *LSM(R) 189* and U.S. Navy Deck Log, USS *LSM(R) 191.*
199. U.S. Navy Deck Log, USS *LSM(R) 191*: Rocket run recorded at 1331 but a typographical error that should read 1231; ship's log also records rockets fired from 1235 to 1248, although F. Donald Moore's *Quartermaster's Log* notes *LSM(R) 191* commenced rocket fire at 1255.
200. U.S. Navy Deck Log, USS *LSM(R) 189*: TA 7267.
201. Moore, *Quartermaster's Log.*
202. Ibid.
203. U.S. Navy Deck Log, USS *LSM(R) 189*: TA 7168.
204. Moore, *Quartermaster's Log*: "1538 *LSM(R) 191* commenced firing" ... "1541 Run completed."
205. Commander, LSM(R) Group 27, Flotilla Nine, War Diary.
206. Moore, *Quartermaster's Log*; See Muster Rolls (BuPers Files), USS *LSM(R) 189*, 30 April 1945 and 31 May 1945.
207. Sixth Marine Division, Naval Gunfire Support, 29 May 1945.
208. CTF 51 and 31, Report of Capture of Okinawa Gunto (V)-24 to (V)-25): 29 May 1945, Western Okinawa daytime direct support included USS *New York*, USS *Idaho*, USS *Wilson*, USS *Picking*, USS *Tuscaloosa*, USS *Louisville*, and USS *Barton*; Western Okinawa nighttime direct support included USS *Idaho*, USS *Barton*, USS *San Francisco*, USS *Vincennes*, and USS *Picking.*
209. Commander, LSM(R) Group 27, Flotilla Nine, War Diary.
210. U.S. Navy Deck Log, USS *LSM(R) 189*: TAs 7364 and 7365.
211. Moore, *Quartermaster's Log*; U.S. Navy Deck Log, USS *LSM(R) 191* records her rocket fire commenced 1120.
212. Moore, *Quartermaster's Log.*
213. Sixth Marine Division, Naval Gunfire Support, 29 May 1945: "2 LSM(R)'s, Coverage And Targets, #1—7365 W X R Y–7364 D E..."
214. U.S. Navy Deck Log, USS *LSM(R) 189.*
215. Sixth Marine Division, Naval Gunfire Support, 29 May 1945: TAs 7167 and 7267.
216. Moore, *Quartermaster's Log.*
217. Sixth Marine Division, Naval Gunfire Support, 29 May 1945: "2 LSM(R)'s–Coverage And Targets: #2—7167 M N O S T–7267 K L P Q U V."
218. Commander, LSM(R) Group 27, Flotilla Nine, War Diary, 29 May 1945: "[*LSM(R)*s] 189 and 191 fired 900 Rockets at fortified Ridge."
219. U.S. Navy Deck Log, USS *LSM(R) 191.*
220. Moore, *Quartermaster's Log.*
221. Ibid.
222. Moore, *Quartermaster's Log*; Commander, LSM(R) Group 27, Flotilla Nine, War Diary: "On detached duty, *LSM(R)*s 189 and 191 at Hagushi."
223. Commander, LSM(R) Group 27, Flotilla Nine, War Diary.
224. Commander, LSM(R) Group 27, Flotilla Nine, War Diary, 1 June 1945.
225. Commander, LSM(R) Group 27, Flotilla Nine, War Diary, 2 June 1945: "*LSM(R)*s 189 and 191 under orders of CTG 31.21 [SOPA, Ie Shima and Northern Okinawa] gave fire support to Marines on southwestern coast of Okinawa..."
226. U.S. Navy Deck Log, USS *LSM(R) 189*: TA 6974.
227. Commander, LSM(R) Group 27, Flotilla Nine, War Diary, 2 June 1945.

Chapter 9

1. Clyde Blue, *Publication Sight Book*, unpublished diary.
2. Ibid.
3. Commander, Task Force Fifty-One, Commander Amphibious Forces, U.S. Pacific Fleet, Report on Okinawa Gunto Operation from 17 February to 17 May 1945, Serial 01400, 25 July 1945 (V)(C)-7, -20; See Commander, Amphibious Group Twelve (Commander Southern Attack Force–CTF 55), Report on the Capture of Okinawa Gunto Phase I and II, 14 March–9 June 1945, Serial 0287, 31 July 1945 (V)(C)-20.
4. CTF 51, Report on Okinawa Gunto Operation (V)(C)-20: "No support tasks were performed after Love Day until 14 May due to navigational limitations in the southern sector and the lack of concentrated defenses in the northern portions of the island."
5. CTF 51 and 31, Report of Capture of Okinawa Gunto (II)-2; Pursuant to Commander, Fifth Amphibious Force, Operation Order A210–45 (Com5thPhibFor OpOrd A210–45).
6. Commander Amphibious Group Four, Commander Task Group 31.25, Report of Participation in the Capture of Okinawa Gunto—Capture of Iheya Shima and Aguni Shima, Serial 0327, 3 August 1945 (III)-9.
7. Blue, *Publication Sight Book*; CTF 51 and 31, Report of Capture of Okinawa Gunto (III)-21: "Evening Red Alerts began at 1420 and continued through the night with an estimated total of 60 enemy planes participating up to 2400."
8. Leonard A. VanOteghem, *Events About and in the Area of Our Ship, the USS LSM(R) 196 and our Unit of 12 LSM(R)s*, unpublished diary.
9. CTF 55, Report on the Capture of Okinawa Gunto (III)-47.
10. David Mallery and Jack Shedd, Ensigns, USNR, *The History of USS LSM(R) 196*, unpublished typescript ca. October 1945.
11. CTU 31.25.4 (Commander Gunboat Support), Commander, LSM Flotilla Nine, Action Report–Iheya Shima and Aguni Shima, Capture of–Support Gunboat Phase, Serial 0041, 13 June 1945, 2, Reference (b) LSM Flotilla Nine Support Gunboat Plan #2540–45, Enclosure (B), Serial 0038, 26 May 1945, 1–3, Annex (D), Annex (S), Annex (C).
12. A cogent outline of Operation Iceberg, Phase III, is History of Planning Division, Army Service Forces (ASF), Volume 10, Planning Division, Office of Director of Plans and Operations, Army Service Forces, War Department.
13. Many secondary sources are inconsistent, ambiguous, or inaccurate regarding Phase III, Operation Iceberg operational planning, timeframes, and decisions regarding the outlying islands of Okinawa, e.g., Chas. S. Nichols, Jr., Major, USMC, and Henry I. Shaw, *Okinawa: Victory in the Pacific* (Washington, D.C.: U.S. Government Printing Office, 1955), 23, 259, 266; Benis M. Frank and Henry I Shaw, Jr., *Victory and Occupation: History of U.S. Marine Corps Operations in World War II*, vol. 5 (Washington, D.C.: U.S. Government Printing Office, 1968), 58, 196–197, 240–241, 347–348, 378,

381; Roy E. Appleman, James M. Burns, Russell A. Gugeler, and John Stevens, *Okinawa: The Last Battle* (Washington, D.C.: U.S. Government Printing Office, 1948), 259–260, 419; Simon Bolivar Buckner, Jr., Papers, 1944–45, Dwight D. Eisenhower Library, 22 April 1945, 25 April 1945, 27 April 1945, 4–7 May 1945, 11 May 1945, 14–16 May 1945, also published under *Seven Stars: The Okinawa Battle Diaries of Simon Bolivar Buckner, Jr., and Joseph Stillwell*, ed. Nicholas Evan Sarantakes (College Station: Texas A&M University Press, 2004).

14. History of Planning Division, *Army Service Forces*, 42–43: January 1945 Okino Daito Shima (IIIa) and Kume Shima (IIIb) were postponed indefinitely; April 1945 Miyako Shima (IIIc) was postponed indefinitely; May 1945 Tokuno Shima (IIIe) was postponed indefinitely; June 1945 Kikai Shima (IIId) was postponed indefinitely. Mid-May 1945 Miyako, Tokuno, and Kikai islands remained contingent upon whether Operation Longtom or Operation Olympic was executed. Of these islands, Kume Island alone would be assaulted and captured by U.S. forces by late June 1945.

15. Simon Bolivar Buckner, Jr., Papers, 1944–45, Dwight D. Eisenhower Library, 4 May 1945.

16. CTF 51, "Report on Okinawa Gunto Operation" (V)(D)-7, paragraph 10; Frank and Shaw, *Victory and Occupation*, 348; Nichols and Shaw, *Okinawa: Victory in the Pacific*, 243.

17. CTF 51, Report on Okinawa Gunto Operation (V)(D)-7, paragraph 11; Robert Sherrod, *History of Marine Corps Aviation in World War II* (Washington, D.C.: Combat Forces Press, 1952), 403, 453: Marine Air Warning Squadron 6 on Katchin Hanto, Taka Banare, and Ike Banare.

18. CTF 51, Report on Okinawa Gunto Operation (III)-91 (V)(D)-7; Frank and Shaw, *Victory and Occupation*, 348; Nichols and Shaw, *Okinawa: Victory in the Pacific*, 243; Sherrod, *History of Marine Corps Aviation in World War II*, 449: Marine Air Warning Squadron 1.

19. Commander, Amphibious Forces, U.S. Pacific Fleet (ComPhibsPac), Operation Plan No. A1–45 (OpPlan No. A1–45), Serial 000120, 9 February 1945, 32.

20. Frank and Shaw, *Victory and Occupation*, 347–348; Headquarters Tenth Army, Okinawa, Tactical Study of Phase III, Section II, Tentative Operations Order No. 11–45, Iceberg IIId—FRICTION, 16–17 May 1945.

21. Combat Team Eight, Second Marine Division, Action Report, Iheya and Aguni Operations, n.d., III-1 and IV-1.

22. Commanding General, Iheya-Aguni Landing Force, In the Field, Action Report, Capture of Iheya Shima and Aguni Shima, Forwarding of, Serial 00479, 25 June 45, 2–3.

23. CTG 31.25, Capture of Iheya Shima and Aguni Shima, (III)-9.

24. Sherrod, *History of Marine Corps Aviation in World War II*, 401. See Headquarters Tenth Army, Okinawa, Tactical Study of Phase III, Section II, Tentative Operations Order No. 11–45, Iceberg IIId—FRICTION.

25. CTU 31.25.4, Iheya Shima and Aguni Shima, 1–2, 14, 16.

26. CTU 31.25.4, Iheya Shima and Aguni Shima,14.

27. CTU 31.25.4, Iheya Shima and Aguni Shima, 2.

28. VanOteghem, *Events About and in the Area of Our Ship.*

29. Blue, *Publication Sight Book.*

30. Lawrence J. Low, untitled, unpublished diary, notebook and sketches.

31. Commander, Amphibious Group Four (Commander Task Force 53) (Commander Task Group 51.21), Report of Participation in the Capture of Okinawa Gunto—Phases I and II, Serial 0252, 20 July 45 (III)-58.

32. CTF 51 and 31, Report of Capture of Okinawa Gunto (II)-2.

33. CTG 31.25, Capture of Iheya Shima and Aguni Shima (III)-10.

34. CTU 31.25.4, Iheya Shima and Aguni Shima, 15.

35. CTG 31.25, Capture of Iheya Shima and Aguni Shima (III)-11.

36. CTF 51 and 31, Report of Capture of Okinawa Gunto (II)-3.

37. CTF 51 and 31, Report of Capture of Okinawa Gunto (III)-46.

38. Commanding General, Iheya-Aguni Landing Force, 3.

39. USS *Paul Hamilton* (DD590), War Diary–June 1945, Serial 031, 10 July 1945, 1: "It is believed that the Japanese at Iheya Retto must have seen the minesweeping unit and the gunfire support ships as they approached the objective."

40. CTG 31.25, Capture of Iheya Shima and Aguni Shima (III)-11.

41. Lawrence J. Low, untitled, unpublished diary, notebook and sketches.

42. VanOteghem, *Events About and in the Area of Our Ship.*

43. Blue, *Publication Sight Book.*

44. CTG 31.25, Capture of Iheya Shima and Aguni Shima (III)-2; CTF 55, Report on the Capture of Okinawa Gunto, (III)—54 and (V)(B)—10; CTF 51 and 31, Report of Capture of Okinawa Gunto (III)-46; Buckner, *Papers*, 2 June 1945.

45. CTF 55, Report on the Capture of Okinawa Gunto (III)—54.

46. Blue, *Publication Sight Book.*

47. CTU 31.25.4, Iheya Shima and Aguni Shima, 5.

48. Commanding Officer, USS LSM(R) 197, Action Report—Battle of Iheya Shima and Aguni Shima, 30 May 1945 through 10 June 1945, Serial 07, 12 June 1945.

49. CTG 31.25, Capture of Iheya Shima and Aguni Shima (II)-8.

50. CTG 31.25, Capture of Iheya Shima and Aguni Shima (III)—14.

51. CTG 31.25, Capture of Iheya Shima and Aguni Shima (VI)—4.

52. Combat Team Eight, Iheya and Aguni Operations, VII—7.

53. Combat Team Eight, Iheya and Aguni Operations, Annex A, First Battalion, Eighth Marines, Second Marine Division, Action Report, Iheya and Aguni Operations, VII—13.

54. Combat Team Eight, Iheya and Aguni Operations, VII—1.

55. Commanding General, Iheya-Aguni Landing Force, 3; CTG 31.25, Capture of Iheya Shima and Aguni Shima (III)-13. Paraphrase of secret despatch from CTG 31.25 to TG 31.25 on 2 June 1945 at 1323: WITH THE FOLLOWING CHANGES IN TIMES OF EVENTS MY MAILGRAM 290705 SORTIE AND MOVEMENT ORDER EFFECTIVE X FROM HAGUSHI ANCHORAGE GET UNDERWAY 0150 JUNE 3 X TIME OF ARRIVAL AT POINT JACK IS 0930 X AT 0745 TU 31.25.2 IS DETACHED.

56. CTG 31.25, Capture of Iheya Shima and Aguni Shima (III)—15.

57. Combat Team Eight, Iheya and Aguni Operations, VII—2.

58. Combat Team Eight, Iheya and Aguni Operations, VII—2 to VII—3.

59. CTG 31.25, Capture of Iheya Shima and Aguni Shima (VI)—2.

60. Commanding Officer, Marine Fighting Squadron Three Hundred Eleven, War Diary, June 1945; Commanding Officer, Marine Fighting Squadron Four Forty One, War Diary, June 1945: "Two aircraft failed to attack the target due to pilot error and one because of electrical failure." See Commanding Officer, Headquarters, Marine Aircraft Group 31, War Diary, June 1945: seven strike aircraft from VMF 311 and eight strike aircraft from VMF 441.

61. Combat Team Eight, Iheya and Aguni Operations, VII—2 to VII—3.

62. CTG 31.25, Capture of Iheya Shima and Aguni Shima (III)—3.

63. CTF 55, Report on the Capture of Okinawa Gunto (III)—55.

64. Combat Team Eight, Iheya and Aguni Operations, VII—4.

65. CTG 31.25, Capture of Iheya Shima and Aguni Shima (III)–15 to (III)–16; Combat Team Eight, Iheya and Aguni Operations, Annex I, Amphibian Tractor Group, Action Report, Iheya Shima Operation, VII—1. Scheduled landing times: 1st Wave—H Hour; 2nd Wave—H plus 5; 3rd Wave—H plus 8; 4th Wave—H plus 18; 5th Wave—H plus 28.

66. CTU 31.25.4, Iheya Shima and Aguni Shima, 5.

67. Commanding Officer, USS *LSM(R) 198*, Action Report, Iheya—Aguni Operation, 30 May–10 June, 1945, Serial 004, 12 June 1945.

68. U.S. Navy Deck Log, USS *LSM(R) 199*.

69. CTU 31.25.4, Iheya Shima and Aguni Shima, 10–11: "The *LSM(R) 196* fired its first salvo (108 rockets) to adequately cover the near edge of assigned target area and in doing so allowed about 10% to fall on the reef..." See Commanding Officer, USS *LSM(R) 196*, Action Report, Capture of Iheya Shima and Aguni Shima–30 May 1945 to 12 June 1945, Serial 003, 12 June 1945; Commanding Officer, USS *LSM(R) 197*, Action Report—Battle of Iheya Shima and Aguni Shima, 30 May 1945 through 10 June 1945, Serial 07, 12 June 1945; Commanding Officer, USS *LSM(R) 198*, Action Report, Iheya—Aguni Operation, 30 May— 10 June, 1945, Serial 004, 12 June 1945; Commanding Officer, USS *LSM(R) 199*, Action Report—Invasion of Iheya Shima and Aguni Shima, 3 June through 9 June 1945, Serial (002–45), 12 June 1945.

70. Commanding Officer, USS *LSM(R) 198*, Action Report, Iheya—Aguni Operation, 30 May— 10 June, 1945, Serial 004, 12 June 1945.

71. Commander Francis' citation of 1034 indicating the end of the Support Gunboats' fire was almost certainly a transposition that should likely read 1043; Cf. CTU 31.25.4, Iheya Shima and Aguni Shima, 2 and 5; CTG 31.25, Capture of Iheya Shima and Aguni Shima, (III)—3: Admiral Reifsnider closely substantiated the approximate time of 1043: "1044–CTU 31. 25.41 [LCS Division 8] reported all scheduled fires completed."

72. CTU 31.25.4, Iheya Shima and Aguni Shima, 12.

73. CTU 31.25.4, Iheya Shima and Aguni Shima, 5.

74. CTG 31.25, Capture of Iheya Shima and Aguni Shima, (III)—3.

75. CTG 31.25, Capture of Iheya Shima and Aguni Shima, (III)-3: 3 June 1945, "1052–LVT on shore hit by undetermined friendly fire 1 KIA 1 WIA."

76. CTG 31.25, Capture of Iheya Shima and Aguni Shima (III)-23.

77. CTG 31.25, Capture of Iheya Shima and Aguni Shima (III)-23 to (III)-24 (III)-30 to (III)-31; See USS *Paul Hamilton* (DD590), War Diary–June 1945, Serial 031, 10 July 1945, TCS Log, page 191 at 1023 time: "We have been decided [*sic*] to inform you about rockets being fired on boats."

78. USS *Daly* (DD519), War Diary, June 1945.

79. CTG 31.25, Capture of Iheya Shima and Aguni Shima, (III)-31.

80. CTG 31.25, Capture of Iheya Shima and Aguni Shima, (VI)-10.

81. Nichols and Shaw, *Okinawa: Victory in the Pacific*, 244, footnote 147: "CT 8, 2nd MarDiv AR-Iheya and Aguni Operations. n.d. The only casualties in the Iheya operation were two Marines killed and 16 wounded by short NGF [naval gunfire] rounds and aerial rockets"; Frank and Shaw, *Victory and Occupation*, 348: "The only Marine casualties of the two amphibious assaults were sustained at Iheya: 2 Marines were killed and 16 wounded by aerial rockets and short rounds of naval gunfire."

82. CTG 31.25, Capture of Iheya Shima and Aguni Shima, (III)-15 to -16: Battalion Landing Team 3/8 landings on RED Beach One: 1042–First wave landed; 1045–Second wave landed; 1050–Third wave landed; 1056–Fourth wave landed; 1105–Fifth wave landed.

83. Combat Team Eight, Iheya and Aguni Operations, VII-1; See CTG 31.25, Capture of Iheya Shima and Aguni Shima (III) –3 and (III)–15 to -16.

84. Combat Team Eight, Iheya and Aguni Operations, Annex C, Third Battalion, Combat Team 8, Second Marine Division, Action Report, Iheya Jima Operation, 11 June 1945, Chapter VII, 6; Combat Team Eight, Iheya and Aguni Operations, VII -2 to -3: per Colonel Clarence R. Wallace, Commander Combat Team Eight, "Although eight VFs were on station for airstrikes during the daylight hours, no strikes were called during the operation."

85. Combat Team Eight, Iheya and Aguni Operations, Annex C, Third Battalion, Combat Team 8, Second Marine Division, Action Report, Iheya Jima Operation, 11 June 1945, Chapter VII, 7–8.

86. Combat Team Eight, Iheya and Aguni Operations, Annex C, Third Battalion, Combat Team 8, Second Marine Division, Action Report, Iheya Jima Operation, 11 June 1945, Chapter IX, 10.

87. CTG 31.25, Capture of Iheya Shima and Aguni Shima, (III)-15 to -16. Battalion Landing Team 2/8 landings on RED Beach Two: 1047–First wave landed; 1050–Second wave landed; (no Third wave); 1101–Fourth wave landed; 1105–Fifth wave landed.

88. Combat Team Eight, Iheya and Aguni Operations, VII—1; CTG 31.25, Capture of Iheya Shima and Aguni Shima (III) –3 and (III)-15 to -16.

89. Combat Team Eight, Iheya and Aguni Operations, Annex B, Battalion Landing Team 2/8, Regimental Combat Team 8, Second Marine Division, Fleet Marine Force, In The Field, Action Report, Iheya Jima, Chapter VII, 11.

90. Combat Team Eight, Iheya and Aguni Operations, Annex I, Amphibian Tractor Group, Action Report, Iheya Operation, VII—1. See Commanding Officer, Second Amphibian Tractor Battalion, Fleet Marine Force, Pacific, In The Field, Action Report, Nansei Shoto, Phase Two, Serial 00502, 16 July 1945, 8.

91. Combat Team Eight, Iheya and Aguni Operations, Annex I, Amphibian Tractor Group, Action Report, Iheya Shima Operation, I-1, II-1.

92. Combat Team Eight, Iheya and Aguni Operations, Annex B, Battalion Landing Team 2/8, Regimental Combat Team 8, Second Marine Division, Fleet Marine Force, In The Field, Action Report, Iheya Shima, Chapter VII, 11–12, 15.

93. Commanding General, Iheya-Aguni Landing Force, 5. KIA (Killed in Action), WIA (Wounded in Action), and MIA (Missing in Action) are typically U.S. battle casualties from enemy hostile actions and not friendly fire, i.e., NBC (Non-Battle Casualties).

94. Commanding General, Iheya-Aguni Landing Force, 5–6.

95. Combat Team Eight, Iheya and Aguni Operations, IX—1.

96. Combat Team Eight, Iheya and Aguni Operations, X—1.

97. CTU 31.25.4, Iheya Shima and Aguni Shima, Addendum to Support Gunboat Plan #2540-45 for Phase II [*sic*], Aguni Shima, 1–2.

98. CTU 31.25.4, Iheya Shima and Aguni Shima, 5, 16–17.

99. CTG 31.25, Capture of Iheya Shima and Aguni Shima (III)—16.

100. CTG 31.25, Capture of Iheya Shima and Aguni Shima (VI)—4.

101. Blue, *Publication Sight Book*.

102. Lawrence J. Low, untitled, unpublished diary, notebook and sketches.

103. Compiled from Bruce A. McDaniel's undated letter to author ca. January 1996 and letter to author July 31, 1999; Lawrence J. Low, untitled, unpublished diary, notebook and sketches: "Gakiya and Maetomari declared open towns for civilians to escape pre-invasion bombardment and shelling."

104. Commanding Officer, USS *LSM(R) 198*, Action Report, Iheya—Aguni Operation, 30 May–10 June, 1945, Serial 004, 12 June 1945.

105. CTU 31.25.4, Iheya Shima and Aguni Shima, 17.

106. CTG 31.25, Capture of Iheya Shima and Aguni Shima (III)—16.

107. Commanding Officer, USS *LSM(R) 198*, Action Report, Iheya—Aguni Operation, 30 May–10 June, 1945, Serial 004, 12 June 1945.

108. LCS(L)(3) Flotilla Four, Group Ten, Composite Action Report–Capture of Iheya Shima and Aguni Shima, Ryukyu Retto, 3 June and 9 June 1945, Serial 041, 11 June 1945, T.U. 31.25.41 and Commander LCS(L) (3) Group Ten, Annex Baker to Com LCS(L) (3) Group Ten Operation Order No. A2–45, Instructions for Flycatcher Operations, Serial 0010, 30 May 1945; CTU 31.25.4, Iheya Shima and Aguni Shima, 2, 17.

109. CTG 31.25, Capture of Iheya Shima and Aguni Shima, (III)—19–20.

110. CTG 31.25, Capture of Iheya Shima and Aguni Shima, (III)—21.

111. CTG 31.25, Capture of Iheya Shima and Aguni Shima (III)—4.

112. CTG 31.25, Capture of Iheya Shima and Aguni Shima (III)—20.

113. CTU 31.25.4, Iheya Shima and Aguni Shima, 6–7; CTF 55, *Report on the Capture of Okinawa Gunto* (III)—55.

114. Blue, *Publication Sight Book*.

115. CTG 31.25, Capture of Iheya Shima and Aguni Shima (III)—5.

116. CTF 55, Report on the Capture of Okinawa Gunto (V) (B)—13.

117. CTG 31.25, Capture of Iheya Shima and Aguni Shima (III)—24.

118. CTG 31.25, Capture of Iheya Shima and Aguni Shima (III)—5.

119. CTU 31.25.4, Iheya Shima and Aguni Shima, 7.

120. Blue, *Publication Sight Book*.

121. CTU 31.25.4, Iheya Shima and Aguni Shima, 14–17.

122. CTU 31.25.4, Iheya Shima and Aguni Shima, 7, 14–17; CTG 31.25, Capture of Iheya Shima and Aguni Shima (III)—6.

123. CTG 31.25, Capture of Iheya Shima and Aguni Shima (III)—6.

124. VanOteghem, *Events About and in the Area of Our Ship*.

125. Blue, *Publication Sight Book*.

126. U.S. Navy Deck Log, USS *LSM(R) 199*.

127. CTU 31.25.4, Iheya Shima and Aguni Shima, 3.

128. CTG 31.25, Capture of Iheya Shima and Aguni Shima (VI)—2: per Commander C.E. Perkins, Commander Air Support Control Unit, Amphibious Group Four, "After the Iheya Operation, estimates of expected opposition at Aguni were revised, and plans for the air strike changed in some respects; in the interest of conservatism, all runs were made parallel to the beach, and the point of aim was moved inland 1000 yards when the first boat wave was 400 yards from shore."

129. CTF 51 and 31, Report of Capture of Okinawa Gunto (II)-5 to -7.

130. CTG 31.25, Capture of Iheya Shima and Aguni Shima (II)-1 to –7.

131. CTU 31.25.4, Iheya Shima and Aguni Shima, 8.

132. CTU 31.25.4, Iheya Shima and Aguni Shima, 14.

133. Commanding Officer, USS *LSM(R) 198*, Action Report, Iheya—Aguni Operation, 30 May–10 June, 1945, Serial 004, 12 June 1945; CTF 51 and 31, Report of Capture of Okinawa Gunto (III)-61.

134. CTF 51 and 31, Report of Capture of Okinawa Gunto (III)-60 and see (III)-6.

135. Lawrence J. Low, untitled, unpublished diary, notebook and sketches.

136. Commanding Officer, USS *LSM(R) 198*, Action Report, Iheya—Aguni Operation, 30 May–10 June, 1945, Serial 004, 12 June 1945.

137. CTF 51 and 31, Report of Capture of Okinawa Gunto (V)-63.

138. CTF 51 and 31, Report of Capture of Okinawa Gunto (V)-63 and (V)-81.

139. Commanding Officer, USS *LSM(R) 198*, Action Report, Iheya—Aguni Operation, 30 May–10 June, 1945, Serial 004, 12 June 1945.

140. Blue, *Publication Sight Book*.

141. CTU 31.25.4, Iheya Shima and Aguni Shima, 14–15.

142. CTF 51 and 31, Report of Capture of Okinawa Gunto (V)-82, and see 8 June 1945.

143. CTF 51 and 31, Report of Capture of Okinawa Gunto (V)-63.

144. Commanding Officer, USS *LSM(R) 198*, Action Report, Iheya—Aguni Operation, 30 May–10 June, 1945, Serial 004, 12 June 1945.

145. U.S. Navy Deck Log, USS *LSM(R) 197*.

146. Commanding Officer, USS *LSM(R) 198*, Action Report, Iheya—Aguni Operation, 30 May–10 June, 1945, Serial 004, 12 June 1945.

147. CTU 31.25.4, Iheya Shima and Aguni Shima, 8.

148. CTG 31.25, Capture of Iheya Shima and Aguni Shima (III)-6.

149. CTG 31.25, Capture of Iheya Shima and Aguni Shima (III)-32.

150. CTU 31.25.4, Iheya Shima and Aguni Shima, 16.

151. CTG 31.25, Capture of Iheya Shima and Aguni Shima (III)-32.

152. CTG 31.25, Capture of Iheya Shima and Aguni Shima (II)-8.

153. CTF 51 and 31, Report of Capture of Okinawa Gunto (V)-81.

154. CTG 31.25, Capture of Iheya Shima and Aguni Shima (VI)-4 to -5.

155. VanOteghem, *Events About and in the Area of Our Ship*.

156. Combat Team Eight, Iheya and Aguni Operations, VII—7.

157. Combat Team Eight, Iheya and Aguni Operations, Annex A, First Battalion, Eighth Marines, Second Marine Division, Action Report, Iheya and Aguni Operations, n.d., VII-13 to -14.

158. CTG 31.25, Capture of Iheya Shima and Aguni Shima (III)-7 and (III)-32: Admiral Reifsnider inexplicably cites his execution of landing signal at 0350 and 0452.

159. Combat Team Eight, Iheya and Aguni Operations, I—1.

160. Combat Team Eight, Iheya and Aguni Operations, Annex J, Second Amphibian Tractor Battalion, Action Report, Aguni Operation, n.d., 3.

161. CTG 31.25, Capture of Iheya Shima and Aguni Shima (VI)-1.

162. CTG 31.25, Capture of Iheya Shima and Aguni Shima (VI)-2; CTF 51 and 31, Report of Capture of Okinawa Gunto (V)-64 and (V)-82, 9 June 1945.

163. Commanding Officer, Marine Fighting Squadron Three Hundred Eleven, War Diary, June 1945, notes 8 aircraft; Commanding Officer, Marine Fighting Squadron Four Forty One, War Diary, June 1945, notes 14 aircraft.

164. LCS(L)(3) Flotilla Four, Group Ten, Composite Action Report–Capture of Iheya Shima and Aguni Shima, Ryukyu Retto, 3 June and 9 June 1945, Serial 041, 11 June 1945, Enclosure (A), 4 to 5.

165. CTU 31.25.4, Iheya Shima and Aguni Shima, Addendum to Support Gunboat Plan #2540–45 for Phase II [*sic*], Aguni Shima, 1, 7 June 1945. Records are unclear who the observers were.

166. Ibid.

167. CTU 31.25.4, Iheya Shima and Aguni Shima, Addendum to Support Gunboat Plan #2540–45 for Phase II [*sic*], Aguni Shima, 1, 7 June 1945.

168. CTU 31.25.4, Iheya Shima and Aguni Shima, Adden-

dum to Support Gunboat Plan #2540–45 for Phase II [*sic*], Aguni Shima, 1–2, 7 June 1945; Norman Friedman, *U.S. Amphibious Ships and Craft: An Illustrated Design History* (Annapolis, MD: Naval Institute Press, 2002), 238. LCI(M) 4.2-inch mortars were fixed in elevation and train while mortar charges were adjusted for range/s.

169. CTU 31.25.4, Iheya Shima and Aguni Shima, Addendum to Support Gunboat Plan #2540–45 for Phase II [*sic*], Aguni Shima, 2, 7 June 1945.

170. CTU 31.25.4, Iheya Shima and Aguni Shima, 3.

171. CTU 31.25.4, Iheya Shima and Aguni Shima, 11: Numeral 7 overtypes numeral 6 in the original document and other mistyping, erasures and smudges are also evident.

172. CTU 31.25.4, Iheya Shima and Aguni Shima, 11: USS *LSM(R) 199* is cited twice but no citation of USS *LSM(R) 198*.

173. CTU 31.25.4, Iheya Shima and Aguni Shima, 11: Most likely USS *LSM(R) 198*, not USS *LSM(R) 199*.

174. CTU 31.25.4, Iheya Shima and Aguni Shima, 11.

175. Commanding Officer, USS *LSM(R) 198*, Action Report, Iheya—Aguni Operation, 30 May–10 June, 1945, Serial 004, 12 June 1945.

176. CTU 31.25.4, Iheya Shima and Aguni Shima, 8.

177. CTU 31.25.4, Iheya Shima and Aguni Shima, 12.

178. CTF 55, Report on the Capture of Okinawa Gunto (III)—59.

179. Commanding Officer, USS *LSM(R) 198*, Action Report, Iheya—Aguni Operation, 30 May–10 June, 1945, Serial 004, 12 June 1945.

180. Combat Team Eight, Iheya and Aguni Operations, Annex J, Second Amphibian Tractor Battalion, Action Report, Aguni Operation, n.d., 1–2: First Wave—12 LVT(2)s, 12 LVT(A)4s; Second Wave—12 LVT(4)s, 2 LVT(2)s; Third Wave—12 LVT(4)s; Fourth Wave—11 LVT(4)s.

181. Combat Team Eight, Iheya and Aguni Operations, Annex J, Second Amphibian Tractor Battalion, Action Report, Aguni Operation, n.d., 1–2.

182. CTG 31.25, Capture of Iheya Shima and Aguni Shima (VI)-8.

183. Combat Team Eight, Iheya and Aguni Operations, Annex A, First Battalion, Eighth Marines, Second Marine Division, Action Report, Iheya and Aguni Operations, n.d., VII—2; CTG 31.25, Capture of Iheya Shima and Aguni Shima (III)-7: "0612—First wave hit the beach—no opposition. Remaining waves hit beach on schedule." See Combat Team Eight, Iheya and Aguni Operations, Annex J, Second Amphibian Tractor Battalion, Action Report, Aguni Operation, n.d., 4: 1st Wave crossed line of departure 0542 and hit beach 0613; 2nd Wave crossed line of departure 0549 and hit beach 0617; 3rd Wave crossed line of departure 0557 and hit beach 0623; 4th Wave crossed line of departure 0607 and hit beach 0633.

184. Combat Team Eight, Iheya and Aguni Operations, Annex J, Second Amphibian Tractor Battalion, Action Report, Aguni Operation, n.d., 4; Commanding Officer, Second Amphibian Tractor Battalion, Fleet Marine Force, Pacific, In The Field, Action Report, Nansei Shoto, Phase Two, Serial 00502, 16 July 1945, 13.

185. Combat Team Eight, Iheya and Aguni Operations, Annex A, First Battalion, Eighth Marines, Second Marine Division, Action Report, Iheya and Aguni Operations, n.d., VII–3.

186. Combat Team Eight, Iheya and Aguni Operations, Annex A, First Battalion, Eighth Marines, Second Marine Division, Action Report, Iheya and Aguni Operations, n.d., VII–4.

187. Combat Team Eight, Iheya and Aguni Operations, Annex J, Second Amphibian Tractor Battalion, Action Report, Aguni Operation, n.d., 5; See Commanding Officer, Headquarters, Second Amphibian Tractor Battalion, Fleet Marine Force, Pacific, In The Field, Action Report, Nansei Shoto, Phase Two, Serial 00502, 16 July 1945, 14.

188. Blue, *Publication Sight Book*.

189. CTG 31.25, Capture of Iheya Shima and Aguni Shima (VI)-1.

190. Commanding General, Iheya-Aguni Landing Force, Chapter X, 6.

191. CTF 51 and 31, Report of Capture of Okinawa Gunto (V)-81.

192. Commanding Officer, USS *LSM(R) 198*, Action Report, Iheya—Aguni Operation, 30 May–10 June, 1945, Serial 004, 12 June 1945.

193. CTF 51 and 31, Report of Capture of Okinawa Gunto (V)-81.

194. Compiled from Bruce A. McDaniel undated letter to author ca. January 1996 and letter to author July 31, 1999.

195. Blue, *Publication Sight Book*; Lawrence J. Low, untitled, unpublished diary, notebook and sketches: "Took position in anchorage as smoke screen and AA screen ship. Air raid in evening. Ships in anchorage bring down friendly plane (Hellcat) with AA fire. Pilot rescued."

196. CTF 51 and 31, Report of Capture of Okinawa Gunto (III)-66; CTG 31.25, Capture of Iheya Shima and Aguni Shima (III)-35; U.S. Navy Deck Log, USS *LSM(R) 196*; Commanding Officer, USS *LSM(R) 196*, Action Report, Capture of Iheya Shima and Aguni Shima—30 May 1945 to 12 June 1945, Serial 003, 12 June 1945; Commanding Officer, USS *LSM(R) 197*, Action Report—Battle of Iheya Shima and Aguni Shima, 30 May 1945 through 10 June 1945, Serial 07, 12 June 1945; Commanding Officer, USS *LSM(R) 198*, Action Report, Iheya—Aguni Operation, 30 May—10 June, 1945, Serial 004, 12 June 1945; U.S. Navy Deck Log, USS *LSM(R) 198*; Commanding Officer, USS *LSM(R) 199*, Action Report—Invasion of Iheya and Aguni Shima, 3 June through 9 June 1945, Serial (002–45), 12 June 1945; U.S. Navy Deck Log, USS *LSM(R) 199*.

197. CTF 51 and 31, Report of Capture of Okinawa Gunto (V)-81.

198. CTU 31.25.4, Iheya Shima and Aguni Shima, 15.

199. Blue, *Publication Sight Book*.

200. CTF 51 and 31, Report of Capture of Okinawa Gunto (V)-81.

201. CTG 31.25, Capture of Iheya Shima and Aguni Shima (VI)-5.

202. Combat Team Eight, Iheya and Aguni Operations, Annex A, First Battalion, Eighth Marines, Second Marine Division, Action Report, Iheya and Aguni Operations, n.d., VII-6.

203. Combat Team Eight, Iheya and Aguni Operations, Annex A, First Battalion, Eighth Marines, Second Marine Division, Action Report, Iheya and Aguni Operations, n.d., IX-1.

204. CTG 31.25, Capture of Iheya Shima and Aguni Shima (III)-7.

205. CTF 55, Report on the Capture of Okinawa Gunto (V)(B)-11.

206. CTU 31.25.4, Iheya Shima and Aguni Shima, 16.

207. Commanding Officer, USS *LSM(R) 197*, Action Report—Battle of Iheya Shima and Aguni Shima, 30 May 1945 through 10 June 1945, Serial 07, 12 June 1945; Commanding Officer, USS *LSM(R) 198*, Action Report, Iheya—Aguni Operation, 30 May—10 June, 1945, Serial 004, 12 June 1945.

208. Blue, *Publication Sight Book*.

209. CTU 31.25.4, Iheya Shima and Aguni Shima, 9, 17.

210. CTG 31.25, Capture of Iheya Shima and Aguni Shima (III)-8.

211. CTU 31.25.4, Iheya Shima and Aguni Shima, Commander, Amphibious Group Four, File No. A16–3(1), Serial 0314, 23 July 1945, 1st Endorsement on ComLSMFlotNINE (CTU 31.25.4) ltr. LSM-Flot9/A12/wsc, Ser. 0041, of 13 June 45.

212. Lawrence J. Low, untitled, unpublished diary, notebook and sketches.

213. CTU 31.25.4, Iheya Shima and Aguni Shima, 17–18.

214. CTU 31.25.4, Iheya Shima and Aguni Shima, 12–13.

215. CTU 31.25.4, Iheya Shima and Aguni Shima, 12.

216. CTU 31.25.4, Iheya Shima and Aguni Shima, 12.
217. CTU 31.25.4, Iheya Shima and Aguni Shima, 13.
218. CTU 31.25.4, Iheya Shima and Aguni Shima, 18.

Chapter 10

1. Clyde Blue, *Publication Sight Book*, unpublished diary.
2. Ibid.
3. USS *Auburn* arrived at Okinawa 31 May 1945 to which Vice Admiral Hill (Com5thPhibFor and CTF 31) shifted his flag and administration from USS *Ancon* at 1300 of 3 June 1945, after which the latter amphibious headquarters ship departed Okinawa.
4. Commander Fifth Amphibious Force (CTF 51 and 31), Report of Capture of Okinawa Gunto Phases 1 and 2 for period 17 May 1945 to 21 June 1945, Serial 0268, 4 July 45 (V)-12: "Fire support ships of TF 32 were at all times assigned to one of the following Task Groups: Western Fire Support Group, Covering and Standby Fire Support Group, Logistics Group, and Eastern Fire Support Group."
5. Commander, Amphibious Group Twelve (Commander Southern Attack Force–CTF 55), Report on the Capture of Okinawa Gunto Phase I and II, 14 March–9 June 1945, Serial 0287, 31 July 1945 (V)(C)-5 to -6: "At 1000 [of 11 June 1945] the following change in Naval gunfire control became effective: CTF 32 assumed control of all naval gunfire support exercising direct control for both sides of the island; all requests for fire support formerly made to CTG 32.14 to be made to CTF 32." See CTF 51 and 31, Report of Capture of Okinawa Gunto (III)-70 and (V)-12 to -13.
6. CTF 51 and 31, Report of Capture of Okinawa Gunto (V)-34 to -35: 13 June 1945, "Day Direct Support Assignments, Special Assignments: 2 LSM(R)s with 7th Div., 2 LSM(R)s with 1st MarDiv. Night Direct Support Assignments, Special Assignments: *Beale* with IIIPhibCorps, 2 LSM(R)s with 7th Div., *Barton* 'Flycatcher' on east side, *H. L. Edwards* 'Flycatcher' on west side."
7. Commanding Officer, USS *LSM(R) 197*, Rocket Bombardment of Southern Okinawa—13 June to 15 June 1945, Serial 08, 16 June 1945.
8. Commanding Officer, USS *LSM(R) 198*, Action Report, Southern Okinawa Fire Support and Rocket Bombardment, 13–15 June 1945, Serial 005, 17 June 1945.
9. LSM(R) 197, *Rocket Bombardment of Southern Okinawa*: TA 8055.
10. LSM(R) 197, *Rocket Bombardment of Southern Okinawa*: TA 7851.
11. Commander, LCI(R) Flotilla Sixteen, Action Report–Invasion of the Okinawa Group Liu Chius, 26 March to 21 June 1945, Serial No. 35, 15 July 1945, 21: *LCI(R)s 643, 647, 648 (F)* [Flagship], *649, 708, 709*.
12. Commander, LCI(R) Group 47, General Action Report for the Capture of Okinawa Gunto, Phases One and Two, from 1 April to 22 June 1945, 0126, 27 June 1945; Commander, LCI(R) Group 47, War Diary, June 1945.
13. Lawrence J. Low, untitled, unpublished diary, notebook and sketches.
14. LSM(R) 197, *Rocket Bombardment of Southern Okinawa*: TAs 7856, 7957.
15. *LSM(R) 197's* records are inconsistent for attack times vis-à-vis numbers of rockets fired: Cf. U.S. Navy Deck Log, USS *LSM(R) 197*, 0941–72 rockets; 1026–10 rockets; 1045–204 rockets; 1135 maneuvered to fire rockets on area 7957; *LSM(R) 197, Rocket Bombardment of Southern Okinawa*, 0942—84 rockets; 1047—210 rockets; 1115—202 rockets; 1155—202 rockets; U.S. Navy Deck Log, USS *LSM(R) 198*, 0942–86 rockets; 0958–82 rockets; 1029–64 rockets; 1056–98 rockets; 1116–74 rockets; 1136–98 rockets; 1156–85 rockets.
16. *LSM(R) 198, Southern Okinawa Fire Support*.
17. *LSM(R) 197, Rocket Bombardment of Southern Okinawa*; *LSM(R) 198, Southern Okinawa Fire Support*: TA 7953.
18. *LSM(R) 197, Rocket Bombardment of Southern Okinawa*: TA 7957.
19. *LSM(R) 197's* records are inconsistent for attack times vis-à-vis numbers of rockets fired:
  Cf. U.S. Navy Deck Log, USS *LSM(R) 197*, 1357—108 rockets; 1445—95 rockets; 1609—unreported number of rockets; 1611—"rocket run completed firing of one deck load"; *LSM(R) 197, Rocket Bombardment of Southern Okinawa*, 1402—110 rockets; 1453—102 rockets; 1607—110 rockets;
  U.S. Navy Deck Log, USS *LSM(R) 198*, 1345—58 rockets; 1409—80 rockets; 1425—62 rockets; 1608—77 rockets.
20. *LSM(R) 198, Southern Okinawa Fire Support*.
21. Louis Gobeille email to author October 11, 2004.
22. U.S. Navy Deck Log, USS *LSM(R) 197*: TA 7756M "to Grid line 57"; *LSM(R) 197, Rocket Bombardment of Southern Okinawa*: TAs 7756 M to 7956 D.
23. *LSM(R) 197, Rocket Bombardment of Southern Okinawa*: TAs 7856, 7956.
24. *LSM(R) 198, Southern Okinawa Fire Support*.
25. U.S. Navy Deck Log, USS *LSM(R) 197*: TA 8360.
26. Cf. LCI(R) Flotilla Sixteen, Action Report, 21.
27. Commander, LCI(R) Group 47, General Action Report for the Capture of Okinawa Gunto, Phases One and Two, from 1 April to 22 June 1945, 0126, 27 June 1945, 11; Commander, LCI(R) Group 47, War Diary, June 1945.
28. Blue, *Publication Sight Book*.
29. CTF 51 and 31, Report of Capture of Okinawa Gunto (V)-35: 14 June 1945, "Day Direct Support Assignments, Special Assignments: 5 LCI(R) (RCM) with 7th Div.2 LSM(R) with 1st MarDiv. Night Direct Support Assignments, Special Assignments: 2 LSM(R) with 7th Div. 2 LSM(R) with 1st MarDiv. *Preston* 'Flycatcher' on east side. *Barton* 'Flycatcher' on west side."
30. U.S. Navy Deck Log, USS *LSM(R) 197*: "Operating under CTU 32.20.4 in *LCI 646* and with Hdqtrs [*sic*] 7th Marine Infantry Division." Both *LSM(R)s 197* and *198* supported the Seventh Infantry Division, U.S. Army. USS *LCI(R) 646* (TG 32.20.6) is not corroborated this date by Commander Coffin as CTU 32.20: LCI(R) Flotilla Sixteen, Action Report, 21.
31. LCI(R) Flotilla Sixteen, Action Report, 21.
32. *LSM(R) 197, Rocket Bombardment of Southern Okinawa*.
33. *LSM(R) 198, Southern Okinawa Fire Support*.
34. U.S. Navy Deck Log, USS *LSM(R) 197*: TA 7856DEN; *LSM(R) 197, Rocket Bombardment of Southern Okinawa*: TA 7856.
35. *LSM(R) 197's* records are inconsistent for attack times. Cf. U.S. Navy Deck Log, USS *LSM(R) 197*, times 0946, 1028, 1040, 1114; *LSM(R) 197, Rocket Bombardment of Southern Okinawa*, times 0950, 1025, 1052, 1114; U.S. Navy Deck Log, USS *LSM(R) 198*, times 0936, 1030, 1054, 1115.
36. *LSM(R) 197, Rocket Bombardment of Southern Okinawa*; U.S. Navy Deck Log, USS *LSM(R) 198*.
37. U.S. Navy Deck Log, USS *LSM(R) 198*. Specific target areas are not identified.
38. *LSM(R) 197, Rocket Bombardment of Southern Okinawa*: TA 7856.
39. *LSM(R) 197's* records are inconsistent for attack times. Cf. U.S. Navy Deck Log, USS *LSM(R) 197*, times 1312, 1329, 1355, 1446, 1508; *LSM(R) 197, Rocket Bombardment of Southern Okinawa*, times 1312, 1332, 1358, 1448, 1510; U.S. Navy Deck Log, USS *LSM(R) 198*, times 1325, 1352, 1428, 1446.
40. *LSM(R) 197, Rocket Bombardment of Southern Okinawa*.
41. U.S. Navy Deck Log, USS *LSM(R) 198*.
42. Ibid.
43. U.S. Navy Deck Log, USS *LSM(R) 197*: TA 7556 VWX; *LSM(R) 197, Rocket Bombardment of Southern Okinawa*: TA 7556.
44. *LSM(R) 197's* records are inconsistent for rocket-firing

time. U.S. Navy Deck Log, USS *LSM(R) 197*, time 1841; *LSM(R) 197, Rocket Bombardment of Southern Okinawa*, time 1845.

45. U.S. Navy Deck Log, USS *LSM(R) 197*: TAs 7555 to 7856.

46. *LSM(R) 197, Rocket Bombardment of Southern Okinawa*: TA 7756.

47. *LSM(R) 197, Rocket Bombardment of Southern Okinawa*: TAs 7455, 7555, 7756, 7657, 7557.

48. *LSM(R) 197, Rocket Bombardment of Southern Okinawa*: TA 7856.

49. *LSM(R) 198, Southern Okinawa Fire Support*.

50. Blue, *Publication Sight Book*.

51. TA 8460.

52. Commander, LCI(R) Group 47, General Action Report for the Capture of Okinawa Gunto, Phases One and Two, from 1 April to 22 June 1945, 0126, 27 June 1945, 11; Commander, LCI(R) Group 47, War Diary, June 1945.

53. CTF 51 and 31, Report of Capture of Okinawa Gunto (V)-36: 15 June 1945, "Day Direct Support Assignments, Special Assignments: 2 LSM(R) & 5 LCI(R) (RCM) with 7th Div., 2 LSM(R) with 1st MarDiv. Night Direct Support Assignments, Special Assignments: *Laws* with IIIPhibCorps. *Rooks* 'Flycatcher' on east side. *H. L. Edwards* 'Flycatcher' on west side."

54. U.S. Navy Deck Log, USS *LSM(R) 197*.

55. U.S. Navy Deck Log, USS *LSM(R) 197*: TAs 7856 to 7455.

56. *LSM(R) 197, Rocket Bombardment of Southern Okinawa*.

57. *LSM(R) 198, Southern Okinawa Fire Support*.

58. Louis Gobeille emails to author October 6, 2004 and October 11, 2004: "The event with the American pilot I told you about was perhaps the most rewarding one. We hit the target and he let us know about it."

59. U.S. Navy Deck Log, USS *LSM(R) 197*: TA 7255.

60. *LSM(R) 198, Southern Okinawa Fire Support*.

61. U.S. Navy Deck Log, USS *LSM(R) 197*; *LSM(R) 197, Rocket Bombardment of Southern Okinawa*: TA 7856 at 0925.

62. U.S. Navy Deck Log, USS *LSM(R) 197*; *LSM(R) 197, Rocket Bombardment of Southern Okinawa*, time 0950.

63. U.S. Navy Deck Log, USS *LSM(R) 197*; *LSM(R) 197, Rocket Bombardment of Southern Okinawa*, time 1014.

64. U.S. Navy Deck Log, USS *LSM(R) 197*, time 1217; *LSM(R) 197, Rocket Bombardment of Southern Okinawa*, time 1218.

65. *LSM(R) 197*'s records are inconsistent regarding the afternoon rocket run times of 15 June 1945: Cf. U.S. Navy Deck Log, USS *LSM(R) 197*; *LSM(R) 197, Rocket Bombardment of Southern Okinawa*.

66. Lawrence J. Low, untitled, unpublished diary, notebook and sketches.

67. Ibid.

68. Lawrence J. Low, untitled, unpublished diary, notebook and sketches. See Commander, LCI(R) Group 47, General Action Report for the Capture of Okinawa Gunto, Phases One and Two, from 1 April to 22 June 1945, 0126, 27 June 1945: "Army advised that their [LSM(R)s'] work had been highly satisfactory."

69. *LSM(R) 197, Rocket Bombardment of Southern Okinawa*.

70. *LSM(R) 198, Southern Okinawa Fire Support*.

71. *LSM(R) 197, Rocket Bombardment of Southern Okinawa*.

72. CTF 51 and 31, Report of Capture of Okinawa Gunto (V)-34 to -35: 13 June 1945, "Day Direct Support Assignments, Special Assignments: 2 LSM(R)s with 7th Div., 2 LSM(R)s with 1st MarDiv. Night Direct Support Assignments, Special Assignments: *Beale* with IIIPhibCorps, 2 LSM(R)s with 7th Div., *Barton* 'Flycatcher' on east side, *H. L. Edwards* 'Flycatcher' on west side."

73. Commanding Officer, USS *LSM(R) 196*, Rocket Bom-

bardment of Southern Okinawa–13 June to 15 June 1945, Serial 004, 16 June 1945.

74. Commanding Officer, USS *LSM(R) 199*, Action Report—rocket firing on Southern Okinawa 13, 14, and 15 June 1945, Serial (003–45), 15 June 1945: Lieutenant Cobb slightly misspoke when he added, "Operated with *LSM(R)s 196, 197*, and *198* under control of Headquarters First Marine Division," because the LSM(R)s variously supported both the Army and Marines during this period.

75. U.S. Navy Deck Log, USS *LSM(R) 199*: "Ship is assigned to task group 51.5," however, *LSM(R)s 196, 197, 198, 199* were not designated as screening ships *per se* during this period. See Commander, Task Flotilla 5 (Commander Task Group 51.5), Action Report, Capture of Okinawa Gunto, 26 March to 21 June 1945, Serial 0894, 20 July 1945.

76. U.S. Navy Deck Log, USS *LSM(R) 199*: "0814 All stopped, all hands manned 2-R [*sic*] station to load rockets."

77. U.S. Navy Deck Log, USS *LSM(R) 196*; *LSM(R) 196, Rocket Bombardment of Southern Okinawa*; *LSM(R) 199, Rocket firing on Southern Okinawa*.

78. David Mallery and Jack Shedd, Ensigns, USNR, *The History of USS LSM(R) 196*, unpublished typescript ca. October 1945.

79. U.S. Navy Deck Log, USS *LSM(R) 199*: TAs 7258EIJ and 7358 GHI; *LSM(R) 196, Rocket Bombardment of Southern Okinawa*: TA 7358.

80. *LSM(R) 199*'s records are only slightly mismatched regarding rocket firing times on Nagusuku: *LSM(R) 199, Rocket firing on Southern Okinawa*, of 1100, 1120, 1159, 1235; U.S. Navy Deck Log, USS *LSM(R) 199*, of 1100, 1120, 1159, 1255.

81. *LSM(R) 196, Rocket Bombardment of Southern Okinawa*, 1153–1330. However, U.S. Navy Deck Log, USS *LSM(R) 196* records rocket run firing times of 1052–1121 expending 202 rockets, and expending an unspecified number of rockets at 1153.

82. *LSM(R) 199, Rocket firing on Southern Okinawa*.

83. *LSM(R) 196, Rocket Bombardment of Southern Okinawa*: TA 7558.

84. U.S. Navy Deck Log, USS *LSM(R) 199*: "1300–put 200 rockets into grid location 7558... Prominent bluff in grid location 7856 Peter [south of Mabuni] was used as point of aim."

85. U.S. Navy Deck Log, USS *LSM(R) 199*: Grid area 7852 is the noted target area but likely a typographical error because TA 7657 is more plausible.

86. *LSM(R) 196, Rocket Bombardment of Southern Okinawa*: TA 7657.

87. *LSM(R) 199, Rocket firing on Southern Okinawa*. Numbers of rockets fired on Komesu are not recorded, but 796 SSRs were expended during 13 June 1945.

88. Commanding General, First Marine Division, Action Report, Nansei Shoto Operation, 1 April–30 June, 1945, submission of, 10 July, 1945, 14; Benis M. Frank and Henry I Shaw, Jr., *Victory and Occupation: History of U.S. Marine Corps Operations in World War II*, vol. 5, 340 (Washington, D.C.: U.S. Government Printing Office, 1968): "Two rocket launching craft took positions off the southern tip of Okinawa to rake reverse slope defenses of the Thirty-Second Army. More than 800 5-inch rockets ripped into the towns of Makabe and Komesu in an hour's time alone."

89. U.S. Navy Deck Log, USS *LSM(R) 199*: "1537–1538 GQ, secured from GQ and manned R-2 [*sic*] stations."

90. U.S. Navy Deck Log, USS *LSM(R) 199*.

91. CTF 51 and 31, Report of Capture of Okinawa Gunto (V)-35: 14 June 1945, "Day Direct Support Assignments, Special Assignments: 5 LCI(R) (RCM) with 7th Div. 2 LSM(R) with 1st MarDiv. Night Direct Support Assignments, Special Assignments: 2 LSM(R) with 7th Div. 2 LSM(R) with 1st MarDiv. *Preston* 'Flycatcher' on east side. *Barton* 'Flycatcher' on west side."

92. U.S. Navy Deck Log, USS *LSM(R) 199*: Rendezvous grid area TA 7580 is an error.

93. *LSM(R) 199, Rocket firing on Southern Okinawa.*

94. *LSM(R) 196*'s records are problematic regarding target areas, firing times, and rocket expenditures, viz., *LSM(R) 196, Rocket Bombardment of Southern Okinawa:* "14 June—0702–0750: 317 rockets fired into grid area 1459," but grid area 1459 is a typographical error and most likely TA 7459, i.e., between Kunishi, Nagusuku, and Makabe; U.S. Navy Deck Log, USS *LSM(R) 196*, "0708 Commenced firing. 0727 Ceased firing. 100 rockets expended." No further rocket firing times or rocket expenditures are recorded between 0702 and 0750. See also U.S. Navy Deck Log, USS *LSM(R) 199.*

95. U.S. Navy Deck Log, USS *LSM(R) 199:* TA 7459.

96. *LSM(R) 196, Rocket Bombardment of Southern Okinawa:* TA 7457.

97. U.S. Navy Deck Log, USS *LSM(R) 199:* "Grid target King Love Peter Queen."

98. U.S. Navy Deck Log, USS *LSM(R) 196.*

99. *LSM(R) 196, Rocket Bombardment of Southern Okinawa:* TA 7557.

100. U.S. Navy Deck Log, USS *LSM(R) 196.*

101. U.S. Navy Deck Log, USS *LC(FF) 535.*

102. U.S. Navy Deck Log, USS *LSM(R) 199:* "Grid area 7456 Roger William Xray [*sic*]."

103. *LSM(R) 199, Rocket firing on Southern Okinawa.*

104. U.S. Navy Deck Log, USS *LSM(R) 199:* Pvt. Burrows, Cpl. Acherman, Tech Sgt Carson and Lt. Burman.

105. Robert W. Cox undated letter to author ca. November 1995.

106. Robert W. Cox undated letter to author ca. November 1995.

107. U.S. Navy Deck Log, USS *LSM(R) 199:* TA 7256 DEIJO.

108. U.S. Navy Deck Log, USS *LSM(R) 199:* TA 7657 GHILMNQRSUWX.

109. U.S. Navy Deck Log, USS *LSM(R) 199:* TA 7257; *LSM(R) 199, Rocket firing on Southern Okinawa:* 1,282 SSRs were expended 14 June 1945.

110. *LSM(R) 196, Rocket Bombardment of Southern Okinawa:* "2145—107 rockets into grid area 2145." Note time and grid area coincide, hence the latter 2145 is clearly a typographical error. Note also U.S. Navy Deck Log, USS *LSM(R) 196* records 100 rockets fired at 2145.

111. U.S. Navy Deck Log, USS *LSM(R) 199:* "2131 Underway on various courses and speeds keeping station in grid area 7580 awaiting instructions," but TA 7580 is a typographical error.

112. CTF 51 and 31, Report of Capture of Okinawa Gunto (V)-36: 15 June 1945, "Day Direct Support Assignments, Special Assignments: 2 LSM(R) & 5 LCI(R) (RCM) with 7th Div., 2 LSM(R) with 1st MarDiv. Night Direct Support Assignments, Special Assignments: *Laws* with IIIPhibCorps. *Rooks* 'Flycatcher'on east side. *H. L. Edwards* 'Flycatcher'on west side."

113. U.S. Navy Deck Log, USS *LSM(R) 199.*

114. U.S. Navy Deck Log, USS *LSM(R) 199:* "1st Lt. E.J. Burman; Acheman–Corp., T/S T.P. Cunson and Pvt. Burrow."

115. *LSM(R) 196, Rocket Bombardment of Southern Okinawa:* TAs 7457, 7557.

116. *LSM(R) 196, Rocket Bombardment of Southern Okinawa.*

117. Leonard A. Van Oteghem, *Events About and in the Area of Our Ship, the USS LSM(R) 196 and our Unit of 12 LSM(R)s,* unpublished diary.

118. U.S. Navy Deck Log, USS *LSM(R) 199:* TA 7456 PQR.

119. U.S. Navy Deck Log, USS *LSM(R) 199:* TA 7658.

120. Target unidentified.

121. U.S. Navy Deck Log, USS *LSM(R) 199:* TA 7557 N and TA 7657 Oboe.

122. U.S. Navy Deck Log, USS *LSM(R) 199:* "1553 Fired rockets into area 7559," but the original notation shows extra spacing between "Fired" and "rockets," suggesting that the numbers of rockets were unknown at the time but intended for insertion later.

123. U.S. Navy Deck Log, USS *LSM(R) 199:* TA 7556; *LSM(R) 199, Rocket firing on Southern Okinawa:* 1284 SSRs were expended 15 June 1945, however, the precise time of the final rocket attack remains uncertain due to the anomalous notation, "1627 Fired."

124. U.S. Navy Deck Log, USS *LSM(R) 199.*

125. *LSM(R) 199, Rocket firing on Southern Okinawa.*

126. Commanding General, Headquarters, III Amphibious Corps, Action Report, Ryukyus Operation Phases I and II (Okinawa), 1 June to 30 June, 1945, serial 0270, 1 July 1945, Chapter VII, Naval Gunfire Support, 80; See Commanding General, First Marine Division, Action Report, Nansei Shoto Operation, 1 April–30 June, 1945, submission of, 10 July, 1945, Phase III, Naval Gunfire Support Annex, Special Action Report, Nansei Shoto, 2.

127. Blue, *Publication Sight Book.*

128. CTF 51 and 31, Report of Capture of Okinawa Gunto (V)-36 to -37: 16 June 1945, "Day Direct Support Assignments, Special Assignments: 5 LCI(R) (RCM) with 7th Div., *Laws* with IIIPhibCorps; Night Direct Support Assignments, Special Assignments: *Laws* with IIIPhibCorps. *Irwin* 'Flycatcher'on west side."

129. Blue, *Publication Sight Book.*

130. CTF 51 and 31, Report of Capture of Okinawa Gunto (V)-37: 17 June 1945, "Day Direct Support Assignments, Special Assignments: 5 LCI(R) (RCM) & 2 LSM(R) with 7th Div., 2 LSM(R) with 1st MarDiv.; Night Direct Support Assignments, Special Assignments: *H. L. Edwards* 'Flycatcher'on east side. *Irwin* 'Flycatcher'on west side." CTF 31 mistakenly records the four Spinners continuing gunfire support this date.

131. Lawrence J. Low, untitled, unpublished diary, notebook and sketches.

132. Blue, *Publication Sight Book.*

133. Lawrence J. Low, untitled, unpublished diary, notebook and sketches.

134. VanOteghem, *Events About and in the Area of Our Ship.*

Chapter 11

1. Commander, LSM(R) Group 27, Flotilla Nine, War Diary.

2. Commander Fifth Amphibious Force (CTF 51 and 31), Report of Capture of Okinawa Gunto Phases 1 and 2 for period 17 May 1945 to 21 June 1945, Serial 0268, 4 July 45 (III)-51.

3. F. Donald Moore, *Quartermaster's Log,* unpublished diary; U.S. Navy Deck Log, USS *LSM(R) 192,* Dispatches 31007, 312317, 010301.

4. Moore, *Quartermaster's Log.*

5. Robert W. Landis, *Ship's Log USS LSM(R) 192,* unpublished diary.

6. CTF 51 and 31, Report of Capture of Okinawa *Gunto* III)-51; Moore, *Quartermaster's Log:* "0908 All ships in formation, on course 180° (T) enroute to Leyte. Convoy consists of *LSD 8* and *13,* 8 *LSM(R)s* [*sic*] and *DE 664*," however, the task unit actually comprised 2 LSDs, 1 DE, 1 PCS, 2 SCs, 6 LSMs, and 4 LSM(R)s.

7. Commander, LSM(R) Group 27, Flotilla Nine, War Diary.

8. Commander, LSM(R) Group 27, Flotilla Nine, War Diary.

9. Moore, *Quartermaster's Log.*

10. Commander, LSM(R) Group 27, Flotilla Nine, War Diary.

11. Commander, LSM(R) Group 27, Flotilla Nine, War Diary.

12. Commander, LSM(R) Group 27, Flotilla Nine, War Diary.

13. CTF 51 and 31, Report of Capture of Okinawa Gunto (III)-86.

14. Mike Grogan, "This Dogged Veteran's 'Tail' Told Through Memories of a Shipmate," *Alligator Alley* no. 30, July 1997, 11–12.

15. Commander, LSM(R) Group 27, Flotilla Nine, War Diary.

16. USS *Antares AKS 3.*

17. CTF 51 and 31, Report of Capture of Okinawa Gunto (III)-88.

18. Clyde Blue, *Publication Sight Book*, unpublished diary.

19. Leonard A. VanOteghem, *Events About and in the Area of Our Ship, the USS LSM(R) 196 and our Unit of 12 LSM(R)s,* unpublished diary.

20. Lawrence J. Low, untitled, unpublished diary, notebook and sketches; David Mallery and Jack Shedd, Ensigns, USNR, *The History of USS LSM(R) 196,* unpublished typescript ca. October 1945.

21. USS *Sproston*, Anti-submarine Action by USS *Sproston* (*DD577*), 28–29 June, 1945–Report of, Serial 022, 8 July 1945; USS *Sproston* (*DD577*), War Diary, June 1945: *Sproston* variously misidentified the amphibious landing ships as *LCI 535, LCS 55, LCS 555, LCI 555, LSM 196, LSM 197*. See also Ron MacKay, Jr., "LSM(R) Sub Hunters: Part 1," *Alligator Alley*, no. 77, February 2011, 7; Ron MacKay, Jr., "LSM(R) Sub Hunters: Part 2," *Alligator Alley*, no. 78, June 2011, 11.

22. U.S. Navy Deck Log, USS *LSM(R) 196.*

23. USS *Endymion* (*ARL-9*), Action Report, Torpedoing of USS *Endymion* (*ARL-9*) 21 June 1945, Serial 0009, 23 June 1945; Imperial Japanese Navy Page, "HIJMS Submarine *I-36* Tabular Record of Movement," *Sensuikan! Operational Histories of Japanese Submarines in WW II,* http://www.combinedfleet.com/I-36.htm.

24. Lawrence J. Low, untitled, unpublished diary, notebook and sketches.

25. USS *Sproston*, *Anti-submarine Action*, IV-3: "*LSM 196* [sic] had only one engine operational limiting speed to 9 knots," however, USS *LSM(R) 196* indicated no engine problems at this time, but USS *LC(FF) 535* did suffer recurring engine breakdowns.

26. USS *Sproston*, *Anti-submarine Action*, IV-3.

27. USS *Sproston*, *Anti-submarine Action*, IV-3.

28. U.S. Navy Deck Log, USS *Sproston* (*DD577*): departure at "2115" should read "2215."

29. Bruce A. McDaniel recollections compiled from letter to author October 30, 2001 and undated letters to author ca. January 1996, March 1997, November 2000, and June 2003.

30. Blue, *Publication Sight Book*: ship misidentified as *YMS 482*. See Paul H. Silverstone, *US Warships of World War II* (New York: Doubleday & Company, Inc., 1965), 231.

31. U.S. Navy Deck Log, USS *LC(FF) 535*, "2230 … Target identified as *YMS 382*"; U.S. Navy Deck Log, USS *LSM(R) 197*, "2312 … Target identified as *YMS 2*."

32. U.S. Navy Deck Logs, USS *YMS 268*, USS *YMS 441*, USS *YMS 468.*

33. USS *Sproston*, *Anti-submarine Action*, IV-3.

34. Imperial Japanese Navy Page, "HIJMS Submarine *I-36* Tabular Record of Movement," *Sensuikan! Operational Histories of Japanese Submarines in WW II,* http://www.combinedfleet.com/I-36.htm.

35. Lawrence J. Low, untitled, unpublished diary, notebook and sketches; VanOteghem, *Events About and in the Area of Our Ship.*

36. Karl G. Matchett, untitled, unpublished diary.

37. Commander, LSM(R) Group 27, Flotilla Nine, War Diary.

Chapter 12

1. Clyde Blue, *Publication Sight Book*, unpublished diary.

2. Karl G. Matchett, untitled, unpublished diary.

3. Commanding Officer, USS *LSM(R) 188*, Battle Report, Serial 33, 30 March 1945, 5.

4. Fleet Admiral Chester W. Nimitz, USN, "Command Summary of Fleet Admiral Chester W. Nimitz, USN, Nimitz 'Graybook,'" 7 December 1941–31 August 1945, vol. 6, Running Estimate and Summary maintained by CINCPAC staff covering the period 1 January 1945 to 1 July 1945, U.S. Naval War College Naval Historical Collection, 381, https://www.usnwc.edu/archives.

5. "Landing Ships Medium (Rocket)," *Rocket* 1, no. 1, April 1945, Office of the Chief of Naval Operations, 8.

6. Commander Amphibious Forces, U.S. Pacific Fleet, Amphibious Gunnery Bulletin No. 2–Assault of Okinawa, Serial 0391, 24 May 1945, 5.

7. John Ray Skates, *The Invasion of Japan: Alternative to the Bomb* (Columbia: University of South Carolina Press, 1995), 55.

8. Benis M. Frank and Henry I Shaw, Jr., *Victory and Occupation: History of U.S. Marine Corps Operations in World War II*, vol. 5 (Washington, D.C.: U.S. Government Printing Office, 1968), 399.

9. CINCPAC-CINCPOA Tentative Operation Plan 10–45, 8 August 1945.

10. Frank and Shaw, *Victory and Occupation*, 404.

11. Commander, Amphibious Forces, U.S. Pacific Fleet, LST, LSM, LST and LSM Flotilla and Group Commanders, Assembly of for OLYMPIC, Revision No. 2, Serial 000338, 7 August 1945.

12. Commander, Amphibious Forces, U.S. Pacific Fleet, Commander Task Force Forty, Operation Plan No. A11–45 (Advance Draft), Serial 000344, 10 August 1945, Annex (G)–Naval Gunfire Support Plan, p. (G) (IV) -1.

13. John C. Merrill, Jr., "Rocket-Firing Guinea Pig," *Our Navy*, First of March 1952: "The guinea pig LSM(R)s were at Pearl Harbor when the atomic bombs rocked the Enemy into final defeat. They were being converted into rocket carrying ships for the new LSM(R)s which were arriving from the states …"

14. Anonymous, "L.S.M. 'R' 188," unpublished diary.

15. Anonymous, "L.S.M. 'R' 188," unpublished diary.

16. Commander, Administrative Command, Amphibious Forces, U.S. Pacific Fleet, Serial 02933, July 10, 1945, First Endorsement to ComLSMFlot 9 ltr. (Conf.) S28, 29 June 1945, Conversion of *LSM(R) 192* to LSM(FF)–Recommendation on, 1–2.

17. U.S. Navy Yard, Pearl Harbor, T. H., Memorandum to: Planning Superintendent, LSM188–Winches for Transfer of Ammunition At Sea and Boat Handling, 14 June 1945; Navy Yard, Navy Number 128 (One Two Eight), *LSM 188*–Conversion to Ammunition Carrier–Winches–Procurement of, Serial Y-02102–90, 26 June 1945.

18. Commander, Administrative Command, Amphibious Forces, U.S. Pacific Fleet, *LSM(R) 188–199*, Conversion to Ammo Carriers, Serial 03383, July 21, 1945.

19. The Commanding Officer [*LSM(R) 197*], Minimum Compliment [sic] of Rates Required for Operation of *LSM (R) 197*, Serial 103, 21 August 1945.

20. U.S. Navy ship designations were first codified and evolved during the twentieth century yet remain inconsistently applied to this day. See full discussion at "Ship Nomenclature and Ship Types," Dictionary of American Naval Fighting Ships, Naval History and Heritage Command website, http://www.history.navy.mil/danfs/ship_nomenclature.htm.

21. F. Donald Moore, *Quartermaster's Log*, unpublished diary.

22. Commander, Administrative Command, Amphibious Forces, U.S. Pacific Fleet, Serial 02933, July 10, 1945, First Endorsement to ComLSMFlot 9 ltr. (Conf.) S28, 29 June 1945, Conversion of *LSM(R) 192* to LSM(FF)–Recommendation on, 1–2.

23. Matchett, *diary*.

24. Blue, *Publication Sight Book.*
25. Matchett, *diary.*
26. Gwenfread Allen, *Hawaii's War Years 1941–1945* (Kailua, HI: Pacific War Classics, Pacific Monogram, 1999), 285; See also John C. Merrill and Ralph L. Lowenstein, *Viva Journalism! The Triumph of Print in the Media Revolution* (Bloomington: Author House, 2010), 88–89.
27. Matchett, *diary.*
28. Matchett, *diary.*
29. Blue, *Publication Sight Book.*
30. Matchett, *diary;* Blue, *Publication Sight Book;* Lawrence J. Low, untitled, unpublished diary, notebook and sketches.
31. Commander, Service Force, U.S. Pacific Fleet (ComServPac) 17 August 1945, teletype message.
32. David Mallery and Jack Shedd, Ensigns, USNR, *The History of USS LSM(R) 196,* unpublished typescript ca. October 1945.

Chapter 13

1. Laurie R. Russell, email to author October 23, 2001; Clyde Blue, *Publication Sight Book,* unpublished diary.
2. U.S. Navy Deck Log, USS *LSM(R) 192.*
3. Leonard A. VanOteghem, *Events About and in the Area of Our Ship, the USS LSM(R) 196 and our Unit of 12 LSM(R)s,* unpublished diary; Blue, *Publication Sight Book.*
4. LSM(R) Flotilla Eighteen, War Diary; U.S. Navy Deck Log, USS *LSM(R) 188.*

5. Commander, LSM(R) Group Fifty-Two, Temporary Flagship, Serial No. 63, 5 September 1945; U.S. Navy Deck Log, USS *LC(FF) 535;* U.S. Navy Deck Log, USS *LSM(R) 199.*
6. Blue, *Publication Sight Book.*
7. Ibid.
8. Karl G. Matchett, untitled, unpublished diary; Blue, *Publication Sight Book.*
9. U.S. Navy Deck Log, USS *LSM(R) 192;* Matchett, *diary;* Blue, *Publication Sight Book.*
10. Blue, *Publication Sight Book.*
11. Administrative Command, Amphibious Forces, Pacific (AdComPhibsPac), 27 September 1945 teletype message: RFS is Ready for Sailing.
12. U.S. Navy Deck Log, USS *LSM(A) 196.*
13. Peter C. Rendina letter to author April 23, 1996; Blue, *Publication Sight Book.*
14. Blue, *Publication Sight Book.*
15. Robert W. Landis, *Ship's Log USS LSM(R) 192,* unpublished diary; U.S. Navy Deck Log, USS *LSM(R) 192.*
16. Blue, *Publication Sight Book.*
17. Lawrence Willison email to author June 26, 2013.
18. Blue, *Publication Sight Book.*
19. Ibid.
20. Department of the Navy, Chief of Naval Operations, Donation of the sunken … to the Government of the Ryukyus Islands, serial 1255P43B, 3 July 1957 with First Endorsement from Secretary of the Navy, serial 1256P43B, 10 July 1957.

Bibliography

I. *Primary Sources*

NARA Record Group 19: Bureau of Ships General Correspondence 1940–1945

Acceptance Trials reports of USS *LSM(R) 196*, USS *LSM(R) 197*, USS *LSM(R) 198*, USS *LSM(R) 199*, u.d.

Bureau of Ships Confidential Letter C-LSM/L9-3(440), "LSM Rocket Ship," 7 October 1944.

Bureau of Ships (BuShips) Files, *LSMs/LSM(R)s 188* through*199*.

Commander, Administrative Command, Amphibious Forces, U.S. Pacific Fleet, Conversion of *LSM(R) 192* to LSM(FF)—Recommendation on, Serial 02933, July 10, 1945, First Endorsement to ComLSMFlot 9 ltr. (Conf.) S28, 29 June 1945, Conversion of *LSM(R) 192* to LSM(FF).

Commander, Administrative Command, Amphibious Forces, U.S. Pacific Fleet, *LSM(R) 188–199*, Conversion to Ammo Carriers, Serial 03383, 21 July 1945.

CNO Restricted Letter Op-23-S-jk Serial 335123, 18 October 1944, Recommendation for new classification LSM(R) and reclassification of LSMs with attached Secretary of the Navy First Endorsement Approval Op-23-S-jk Serial 335223, 20 October 1944.

Commander In Chief Confidential Memo FFI/S82-3 Serial 03092, 6 September 1944.

Launching Report of *LSM 196* and *LSM 197*, U.S. Navy Yard Charleston, S.C., 12 October 1944.

LSM(R) 188, The Commanding Officer, Memo, Structural Firing Report, 11280368, 21 November 1944.

Navy Yard, Navy Number 128 (One Two Eight), *LSM 188*—Conversion to Ammunition Carrier—Winches—Procurement of, Serial Y-02102–90, 26 June 1945.

Office of the Commandant Confirmation of Telephone Conversation LSM(R)/S8(R)(M-2), 8 November 1944.

Undocking Report of *LSM 190* and *LSM 191*, U.S. Navy Yard Charleston, S.C., 21 September 1944.

U.S. Navy Yard, Pearl Harbor, T.H., Memorandum to: Planning Superintendent, *LSM 188*—Winches for Transfer of Ammunition At Sea and Boat Handling, 14 June 1945.

Weekly Progress Report from Prospective Commanding Officer, USS *LSM(R) 196*, 8 December 1944.

USS *LSM(R) 199*, Report of Departure Inspection on 18 January 1945, S3–1(7), Serial IB-367, 11 February 1945.

Weekly Progress Report from Commandant, Navy Yard, USS *LSM 188*, USS *LSM 189*, USS *LSM 190*, 16 October 1944.

Weekly Progress Report from Prospective Commanding Officer, USS *LSM(R) 197*, 8 December 1944.

NARA Record Group 24: Records of the Bureau of Naval Personnel

Chief of Naval Personnel, Pers-1042b-GB, LSM/16-1, Restricted, 21 October 1944, LSM—Officer and Enlisted Complement, with Restricted NavPers 2128, Complement of *LSM(R) 188–199*, Approved 21 October 1944, Enclosure to Pers-1042b-GB of 21 October 1944.

Muster Rolls (BuPers Files): USS *LSM(R) 188* through USS *LSM(R) 199* (1944–1946).

Muster Rolls (BuPers Files): USS *LC(FF) 535* (1944–1945).

U.S. Navy Deck Logs (BuPers Files): USS *LSM(R) 188* through USS *LSM(R) 199* (1944–1946);

U.S. Navy Deck Logs (BuPers Files): USS *LC(FF) 535* (1944–1945).

Additional Ships' U.S. Navy Deck Logs

Amphibious force flagships (AGC): *Eldorado, Estes, Biscayne, Mt. McKinley.*

Battleships (BB): *Arkansas.*

Cargo ships (AK): *Antares.*

Destroyer escorts (DE): *Levy, Parks.*

Destroyers (DD): *Ammen, Bache, Barton, Bryant, Cowell, Dyson, Farenholt, Hall, Hudson, Kimberly, Lang, Nicholson, Putnam, Russell, Van Valkenburgh, Wadsworth.*

High speed minesweepers (DMS): *Ellyson, Forrest.*

High speed transports (APD): *Gilmer, Pavlic, Ringness, Sims.*

Landing craft, infantry (LCI): *560.*

Landing craft, support (LCS): *11, 12, 13, 14, 15, 17, 19, 20, 21, 22, 23, 24, 25, 32, 34, 35, 37, 38, 39, 40, 44, 51, 53, 54, 55, 57, 61, 62, 63, 81, 83, 84, 85, 86, 87, 88, 110.*

Landing ships, dock (LSD): *Gunston Hall.*

Landing ships, medium (LSM): *14, 82, 167, 222, 228, 279.*

Light minelayers (DM): *Adams, Gwin, J. William Ditter, Tolman, H. A. Wiley.* Minesweepers (AM): *Spear.*

Motor minesweepers (YMS): *268, 441, 468*.
Ocean tugs, fleet (ATF): *Molala, Tekesta, Yuma*.
Patrol craft, escort (rescue) (PCE(R): *852, 853, 854, 855*.
Patrol motor gunboats (PGM): *9, 10, 17, 20*.
Repair ships (AR): *Egeria, Clamp*.
Submarine chasers (SC): *1028, 1311*.
Transports (AP): *Crescent City*.

NARA Record Group 38: Records of the Office of Chief of Naval Operations

Commander, LSM Flotilla Nine, Action Report, Battle of Kerama Retto and Okinawa Shima, 26 March through 1 April 1945, Serial 004, 2 April 45.

Commander, LSM Flotilla Nine, Action Report—Ie Shima and Southeastern Okinawa, 2 April through 20 April 1945, Serial 0010, 21 April 1945.

Commander, LSM Flotilla Nine, Battle Damage Report of USS *LSM(R) 188*, Serial 015, 5 April 1945.

Commander, LSM Flotilla Nine, Combat Rocket Fire Performed 1 April 1945—Observed results of, Serial 0003, 10 April 1945.

Commander, LSM Flotilla Nine, CTU 31.25.4 (Commander Gunboat Support), Action Report—Iheya Shima and Aguni Shima, Capture of—Support Gunboat Phase, Serial 0041, 13 June 1945.

Commander, LSM Flotilla Nine (CTU 32.9.12), Action Report—Submission of, Serial 0045, 15 June 1945, First Endorsement, Enclosures (A) through (F).

Commander, LSM Flotilla Nine, Destruction of Japanese Suicide Boats on Night Patrol—Commendation for, Serial 125, 7 April 1945.

Commander, LSM Flotilla Nine, Rockets for harassing fire—use on Ie Shima and recommendations regarding future employment, Serial 008, 19 April 1945, (a), CTG 52.21 OpPlan 2101–45, Serial 006, 13 April 1945.

Commander, LSM Flotilla Nine, Support Gunboat Plan #2540–45, Enclosure (B), Serial 0038, 26 May 1945, Annex (D), D-1 to D-2, Annex (S), S-1 to S-2, Annex (C), C-1; Addendum to Support Gunboat Plan #2540–45 for Phase II, Aguni Shima, 1–2, 7 June 1945.

Commander, LSM Flotilla Nine, War Diary, March-April 1945.

Commander, LSM(R) Group Twenty-Seven, Flotilla Nine, War Diary, February-July 1945.

Commanding Officer, USS *LSM(R) 188*, Battle Report, Serial 33, 30 March 1945.

Commanding Officer, USS *LSM(R) 189*, Attack by enemy small boats on 29 March 1945 off Okinawa Island, Serial 0101, 3 April 1945.

Commanding Officer, USS *LSM(R) 189*, General Action Report, Battle of Okinawa—12 April 1945, Serial 0102, 15 April 1945.

Commanding Officer, USS *LSM(R) 192*, Action Report of, Serial 001, 6 May 1945.

Commanding Officer, USS *LSM(R) 193*, Action Report, Battle of Okinawa 11 May 1945, Serial 007, 13 May 1945.

Commanding Officer, USS *LSM(R) 194*, Action Report–Battle of Okinawa–4 May 1945, Serial F9–06, 6 May 1945.

Commanding Officer, USS *LSM(R) 195*, Action Report—Battle of Okinawa, 3 May 1945, Serial F9–05, 5 May 1945.

Commanding Officer, USS *LSM(R) 195*, USS *LSM(R) 195*: Amplifying Report on Loss of, 7 June 1945.

Commanding Officer, USS *LSM(R) 196*, Damage to this vessel by shelling from beach of Okinawa near Naha on 1 April 1945 at 0040, Report of, Serial 20, 8 April 1945.

Commanding Officer, USS *LSM(R) 196*, Action Report, Capture of Iheya Shima and Aguni Shima—30 May 1945 to 12 June 1945, Serial 003, 12 June 1945.

Commanding Officer, USS *LSM(R) 196*, Rocket Bombardment of Southern Okinawa—13 June to 15 June 1945, Serial 004, 16 June 1945.

Commanding Officer, USS *LSM(R) 197*, Action Report, Battle of Okinawa Shima and Ie Shima, 1 April 1945 through 20 April 1945, Serial 03, 22 April 1945.

Commanding Officer, USS *LSM(R) 197*, Special Patrol—report of, Serial 42, 28 April 1945.

Commanding Officer, USS *LSM(R) 197*, Action Report—Radar Picket Station Nine (9), Okinawa, 12 May 1945 through 15 May 1945, Serial 05, 17 May 1945.

Commanding Officer, USS *LSM(R) 197*, Action Report—Battle of Iheya Shima and Aguni Shima, 30 May 1945 through 10 June 1945, Serial 07, 12 June 1945.

Commanding Officer, USS *LSM(R) 197*, Rocket Bombardment of Southern Okinawa—13 June to 15 June 1945, Serial 08, 16 June 1945.

Commanding Officer, USS *LSM(R) 198*, Action Report, Iheya—Aguni Operation, 30 May—10 June, 1945, Serial 004, 12 June 1945.

Commanding Officer, USS *LSM(R) 198*, Action Report, Southern Okinawa Fire Support and Rocket Bombardment, 13–15 June 1945, Serial 005, 17 June 1945.

Commanding Officer, USS *LSM(R) 199*, Action Report—Invasion of Iheya Shima and Aguni Shima, 3 June through 9 June 1945, Serial (002–45), 12 June 1945.

Commanding Officer, USS *LSM(R) 199*, Action Report—rocket firing on Southern Okinawa 13, 14, and 15 June 1945, Serial (003–45), 15 June 1945.

Executive Officer, USS *LSM(R) 190*, Action Report—Battle of Okinawa, 4 May 1945, Serial F9–04, 5 May 1945.

Gunnery Officer, USS *LSM(R) 198*, Lt.(jg) Raymond H. Dick, O-V(S), USNR, Gunnery Officer, Report of Structural Rocket Firing of *LSM(R) 198* on 16 December 1944, Serial 10, 18 December 1944.

Gunnery Officer, USS *LSM(R) 199*, Ens. Benton F. Murphy, O-V(S), USNR, Gunnery Officer, Report of Structural Firing of *LSM(R) 199* on 16 December 1944, u.d.

Operations and Gunnery Officer, LSM Flotilla Nine, Lieut. H. G. Carrison, Proof and Structural Firing of *LSM(R)s 198* and *199*, LSM Flot 9/S73–1/44, Ser: 07, 18 December 1944, with 1st Endorsement, LSM-Flot9/S73–1/44, 4 January 1945 from D. L. Francis.

Related Documents in the Author's Possession

Commander, LSM Flotilla Nine, Destruction on Night Patrol—Commendation for, Serial 123, 7 April 1945.

Commander, LSM Flotilla Nine, Destruction of enemy

plane—credit and commendation for, Serial 137, 17 April 1945.

Commander, LSM Flotilla Nine, Destruction of enemy planes—credit and commendation for, Serial 152, 25 April 1945.

Commander, LSM(R) Group Twenty-Seven, Flotilla Nine dispatch ca. 19–20 March 1945.

Commander, LSM(R) Group Fifty-Two, Temporary Flagship, Serial No. 63, 5 September 1945.

The Commanding Officer, Minimum Compliment [sic] of Rates Required for Operation of LSM (R) 197, Serial 103, 21 August 1945.

Commanding Officer, USS LCS(L)(3)-15, Survivors, Appreciation from, 25 April 1945.

Commanding Officer, USS LCS 87, Destruction of Enemy Aircraft by USS LSM (R) 197—confirmation of, Serial 48, 19 May 1945.

Commanding Officer, USS LSM(R) 189, Report of anti-aircraft action by surface vessels—Forwarding of, Serial 0110, 1 May 1945.

Commanding Officer, USS LSM 191, Action Report—1 April through 19 April 1945, 19 April 1945.

Commanding Officer, USS Mannert L. Abele, letter to Commanding Officer, USS LSM(R) 190, 18 April 1945.

Department of the Navy, Bureau of Naval Personnel, Navy Unit Commendation Awarded the USS LSM(R) 189, 22 June 1949.

Department of the Navy, Bureau of Naval Personnel, Navy Unit Commendation Awarded the USS LSM(R) 190, 23 June 1949.

Lieutenant (Junior Grade) Neal B. Hadsell, D-V(G), USNR 238756, Restricted Orders, File No. FE25-4/P16-4/MM/OO, Change of Duty.

LSMR [sic] Group Twenty-Seven, Flotilla Nine, 17 May 1945.

Navy Department, Bureau of Naval Personnel [Commanding Officer, USS LSM(R) 194], Pers 8249 mvb, 15 June 1945.

Revised Form for Reporting A.A. Action by Surface Ships, USS LSM(R) 193,11 May 1945.

USS LSM(R) 191, Secret Dispatch from Hobson DMS 26 to Commander Task Force 51, 18 April 1945.

USS LSM(R) 197, Casualty Control Drills—report of, LSM(R)197/A5-9/JMC;wr, Serial 26, 4 March 1945.

USS LSM(R) 197, Inventory of Ammunition, LSM(R) 197/A13/A5-1/JMC;wr, Serial 25, 4 March 1945.

USS LSM(R) 197, Confidential Memorandum, Japanese Buzz Bomb Seen While Under Attack on Patrol on 12 April 1945—description of, Serial 04, 23 April 1945.

Additional Official Reports

CINCPAC-CINCPOA Tentative Operation Plan 10–45, 8 August 1945.

Commander in Chief, U.S. Pacific Fleet and Pacific Ocean Areas, Operations in the Pacific Ocean Areas during the Month of April 1945.

Commander, Amphibious Forces, U.S. Pacific Fleet (ComPhibsPac), Operation Plan No. A1–45 (OpPlan No. A1–45), Serial 000120, 9 February 1945.

Commander, Amphibious Forces, U.S. Pacific Fleet, Amphibious Gunnery Bulletin No. 2—Assault of Okinawa, Serial 0391, 24 May 1945.

Commander, Amphibious Forces, U.S. Pacific Fleet, Suicide Plane Attacks, Serial 00470, 7 July 1945.

Commander, Amphibious Forces, U.S. Pacific Fleet, LST, LSM, LST and LSM Flotilla and Group Commanders, Assembly of for OLYMPIC, Revision No. 2, Serial 000338, 7 August 1945.

Commander, Amphibious Forces, U.S. Pacific Fleet, Commander Task Force Forty,

Operation Plan No. A11–45 (Advance Draft), Serial 000344, 10 August 1945.

Commander, Administrative Command, Amphibious Forces, U.S. Pacific Fleet (AdComPhibsPac), War Diary.

Commander, Amphibious Group One (Task Force 52), Operation Plan No. A106–45, Serial 00032, 5 March 1945.

Commander, Amphibious Group One (Task Force 52), Operation Order A6–45, Serial 000166, 16 March 1945.

Commander, Amphibious Group One (CTF 52), Action Report, Operations Against Okinawa Gunto including the Capture of Kerama Retto and the Eastern Islands of Okinawa, March 21 to and including April 20, 1945, Serial 053, 1 May 1945.

Commander, Amphibious Group Four (CTG 51.21), SOPA Ie Shima and Northern Okinawa, Operation Plan ComPhibGrp4 No. A407–45, Serial 00223, 28 April 1945.

Commander, Amphibious Group Four (Commander Task Force 53) (Commander Task Group 51.21), Report of Participation in the Capture of Okinawa Gunto—Phases I and II, Serial 0252, 20 July 45.

Commander, Amphibious Group Four, Commander Task Group 31.25, Report of Participation in the Capture of Okinawa Gunto—Capture of Iheya Shima and Aguni Shima, Serial 0327, 3 August 1945.

Commander, Amphibious Group Seven, Task Group 51.1, Attack Order A701–45, Serial 0005, 13 March 1945.

Commander, Amphibious Group Seven, Report of Loss or Damage to USS Halligan (DD584), Serial 0028, April 1, 1945.

Commander, Amphibious Group Seven (CTG 51.1), Action Report, Capture of Okinawa Gunto, Phases 1 and 2, Serial 0172, 26 May 1945.

Commander, Amphibious Group Twelve (Commander Southern Attack Force—CTF 55), Report on the Capture of Okinawa Gunto Phase I and II, 14 March–9 June 1945, Serial 0287, 31 July 1945.

Commander, Task Force Fifty-One, Commander Amphibious Forces, U.S. Pacific Fleet, Report on Okinawa Gunto Operation from 17 February to 17 May 1945, Serial 01400, 25 July 1945.

Commander, Fifth Amphibious Force (CTF 51 and 31), Report of Capture of Okinawa Gunto Phases 1 and 2 for period 17 May 1945 to 21 June 1945, Serial 0268, 4 July 45.

Commander, Fifth Fleet, Action Report, Ryukyus Operation through 27 May 1945, Serial 0333, 21 June 1945.

Commander, Battleship Division Four, Action Report, Capture of Okinawa Gunto, Continuation of Phase One, 18 May through 10 June 1945, Serial 0314, 22 June 1945.

Commander, Cruiser Division Six (CTG 51.19), Report of Participation in Operations Against Okinawa Shima, Nansei Shoto from 13 May to 27 May 1945 (period during which ConCruDiv6 was CTG 51.19 and SOPA Eastern Okinawa), Serial 0016, 6 June 1945.

Commander, Destroyer Squadron Twenty-Three, Commander Task Unit 31.25.3, Action Report for Iheya Shima and Aguni Shima Operation—Forwarding of, Serial 074, 17 June 1945.

Commander, Task Flotilla 5 (Commander, Task Group 51.5), Action Report, Capture of Okinawa Gunto, 26 March to 21 June 1945, Serial 0894, 20 July 1945.

Commander, Southern Support Craft—CTG 55.11 (Commander LCS(L) Flotilla Three), Action Report, Invasion of Okinawa Jima (Initial Assault), 1 April 1945, Serial 00055, 12 May 1945.

Commander, LST Flotilla Six, Action Report, Assault and Occupation of Iheya Shima and Aguni Shima, Ryukyu Islands, Nansei Shoto, 1–10 June 1945, Serial 0145, 24 June 1945.

Commander, LST Flotilla Six, War Diary, June 1945, Serial 0156, 1 July 1945.

Commander, LCI(G) Flotilla Six, Report of capture of Okinawa Gunto, Phases 1 and 2, Serial 0401, 19 July 1945.

Commander, LCI(L) Flotilla Fourteen (CTU 51.1.16), Action Report for Kerama Retto and Keise Shima Operations, Serial 0534, 27 April 1945.

Commander, LCI(L) Flotilla Fourteen, War Diary, April 1945, Serial 0804, 23 May 1945.

Commander, LCI(R) Flotilla Sixteen, Action Report—Invasion of the Okinawa Group Liu Chius, 26 March to 21 June 1945, Serial No. 35, 15 July 1945.

Commander, LCI(R) Group 47, General Action Report for the Capture of Okinawa Gunto, Phases One and Two, from 1 April to 22 June 1945, 0126, 27 June 1945.

Commander, LCI Flotilla Twenty-One, Action Report, Invasion of Okinawa Jima, Nansei Shoto Group, 25 March 1945 through 10 April 1945, Serial 0001, 10 April 1945.

Commander, Small Craft Eastern Okinawa, CTU 32.9.7 (Commander LCI Flotilla Twenty-One), Action Report, Operations at Okinawa Jima, Nansei Shoto, 1 May through 31 May 1945, Serial 005, 1 June 1945.

Commander, LCI(L) Group 67, Flotilla Twenty-Three, Action Report, Invasion of Okinawa Jima, Period 11 April 1945 through 30 April 1945, Serial 31–45, 1 May 1945.

Commander, LCI(M) Group 41 (CTU 31.25.43), Action Report—Iheya Shima, 30 May–8 June 1945, Serial 02, 9 June 1945.

Commander, LCI Group 42, Flotilla 14 and Commander Task Unit 31.25.42, Action Report, Invasions of Iheya Shima and Aguni Shima, Period 30 May 1945 through 10 June 1945, Serial 21–45, 10 June 1945.

Commander, LCS(L) Flotilla Three, War Diary, 22 January to 1 April 1945, Serial 0138, 1 June 1945.

Commander, LCS(L)(3) Flotilla Four, Group Ten, Composite Action Report—Capture of Iheya Shima and Aguni Shima, Ryukyu Retto, 3 June and 9 June 1945, Serial 041, 11 June 1945, T.U. 31.25.41 and Commander LCS(L) (3) Group Ten, Annex Baker to Com

LCS(L) (3) Group Ten Operation Order No. A2–45, Instructions for Flycatcher Operations, Serial 0010, 30 May 1945.

Headquarters of the Commander in Chief, United States Fleet, Radar Pickets and Methods of Combating Suicide Attacks Off Okinawa March-May 1945, Secret Information Bulletin No. 24.

LCS(L)(3) Group 12, War Diary, June 1945, Serial 042, 9 July 1945.

United States Fleet, Fifth Fleet, TF 51 Joint Expeditionary Force, TG 51.21 SOPA Ie Shima and Northern Okinawa, and ComPhibGrp 4, Operation Plan ComPhibGrp 4 No. A407–45, Serial 00223, 28 April 1945.

United States Pacific Fleet and Pacific Ocean Areas, Information Bulletin, Okinawa Gunto, CINCPAC-CINCPOA Bulletin No. 161–44, 15 November 1944, Supplement No. 1, Serial DIS-171105, 15 December 1944.

U.S. LCT(R) Group, September 1943-October 1944, War Diary, u.d.

Additional Ships' Action Reports

Battleships (BB): *Arkansas.*

Cargo ships (AK): *Antares.*

Cruisers (CA): *Portland, Tuscaloosa.*

Destroyer escorts (DE): *Bowers, Edmonds, England, Fieberling, Oberrender, Stern.*

Destroyers (DD): *Bache, Beale, Brown, Callaghan, Colhoun, Converse, Cowell, Daly, Drexler, Evans, Foote, Fullam, Gainard, Hugh W. Hadley, Halligan, Paul Hamilton, Harry E. Hubbard, Hudson, Ingraham, Isherwood, Laffey, Lang, Little, Lowry, Luce, Mannert L. Abele, Morrison, Mustin, Nicholson, Pringle, Sproston, Stanly, Thatcher, Twiggs.*

Fleet tugs (AT): *Tawakoni.*

High speed transports (APD): *Loy, Ringness.*

Landing craft, infantry (LCI): 34, 73, 351, 352, 353, 354, 355, 356, 452, 657, 801, 806, 807, 810, 1058.

Landing craft, support (LCS): 14, 15, 21, 25, 31, 32, 34, 37, 51, 52, 54, 55, 56, 57, 61, 62, 66, 67, 82, 83, 84, 87, 88, 110, 116, 118.

Landing ships, dock (LSD): *Oak Hill.*

Landing ships, medium (LSM): 14, 82, 167, 222, 228, 279.

Minelayers (DM): *Gwin, J. William Ditter, Tolman, Shea, H. A. Wiley.*

Minesweepers (DMS): *Hobson, Macomb.*

Patrol motor gunboats (PGM): 9, 20.

Repair ship, landing craft (ARL): *Endymion.*

Transports (AP): *Henrico, Montrose, Telfair.*

Additional Ships' War Diaries

Cargo ships (AK): *Suffolk.*

Destroyer escorts (DE): *Snyder.*

Destroyers (DD): *Ammen, Aulick, Bennett, Bennion, Boyd, Bradford, Brown, Brush, Bryant, Charles Ausburne, Converse, Cowell, Daly, Dyson, H. L. Edwards, Farenholt, Foote, Douglas H. Fox, Fullam, Gainard, Gregory, Guest, Hugh W. Hadley, Harry E. Hubbard, Hudson, Irwin, Lang, Lowry, Massey, Mustin, James C. Owens, Paul Hamilton, William D. Porter, Prichett, Purdy, Putnam, Shubrick, Sproston, Stanly, Sterett, Wadsworth, Walke.*

Fleet tugs (AT): *Arikara, Cree, Lipan, Tawakoni.*

High speed transports (APD): *Barber, Ringness.*
Landing craft, support (LCS): *34, 54, 55, 62, 64, 65, 66, 67, 110, 117.*
Landing ships, dock (LSD): *Oak Hill, Epping Forest.*
Minelayers (DM): *H. F. Bauer, T. E. Fraser, Gwin, Shea, R. H. Smith.*
Minesweepers (DMS): *Ellyson, Jeffers, Macomb.*
Patrol motor gunboats (PGM): *10.*
Repairs ships (AR): *Deliver, Egeria.*
Transports (AP): *Montrose, Karnes, Lauderdale.*

NARA Record Group 74: Bureau of Ordnance General Correspondence 1940–1945

Bureau of Ordnance (BuOrd) Files, *LSMs/LSM(R)s 188* through *199.*
CNO Confidential Letter Op-23-E-AMC 10–12, Serial 0599523 (SC) S82–3, Doc. 138166, 13 October 1944, "Subject: LSM Rocket Ship."
Commandant, Navy Yard LSM(R)/S79(R)(M-5) to Chief of Bureau of Ordnance, "Confirmation of Telephone Conversation," 3 December 1944.
Commandant, Navy Yard Confidential Letter A7–3/LSM(R)/S78(R)(N-1-4-42) to Chief, Bureau of Ordnance, "Rocket Launchers Mk. 51—Correction of Defects," 17 December 1944.
Chief of Bureau of Ordnance, LSM(R)(Rela), Confidential, "*LSM(R) 196–199*—(Scheme E)—Installation of Rocket Launchers Mark 51," 21 December 1944.

NARA Record Group 80: General Records of the Department of the Navy

Bureau of Ships Confidential Letter C-*LSM(R)188–199*/S74(519L), File "S82–3," 4 November 1944, Secretary of the Navy/Chief of Naval Operations.

NARA Record Group 127: Records of the United States Marine Corps

Combat Team Eight, Second Marine Division, Action Report, Iheya and Aguni Operations, n.d.
Commander, Amphibious Forces, U.S. Pacific Fleet, Amphibious Gunnery Bulletin No. 2—Assault of Okinawa, Serial 0391, 24 May 1945.
Commanding General, First Marine Division, Action Report, Nansei Shoto Operation, 1 April–30 June, 1945, submission of, 10 July, 1945.
Commanding General, Headquarters, III Amphibious Corps, Action Report, Ryukyus Operation Phases I and II (Okinawa), 1 June to 30 June, 1945, serial 0270, 1 July 1945.
Commanding General, Tactical Air Force, Tenth Army, Action Report, Phase I, Nansei Shoto, Period 8 December 1944 to 30 June 1945 Incl., 12 July 1945.
Commanding General, Tactical Air Force, Tenth Army, War Diary, June 1945, 10 July 1945.
Commanding General, Headquarters, Second Marine Aircraft Wing, War Diary, June 1945, 10 July 1945.
Commanding General, Iheya-Aguni Landing Force, In the Field, Action Report, Capture of Iheya Shima and Aguni Shima, Forwarding of, Serial 00479, 25 June 45.
Commanding Officer, Headquarters, Marine Aircraft Group-31, War Diary, June 1945.

Commanding Officer, Marine Fighting Squadron Three Hundred Eleven, War Diary, June 1945.
Commanding Officer, Marine Fighting Squadron Four Forty One, War Diary, June 1945.
Commanding Officer, Second Amphibian Tractor Battalion, Fleet Marine Force, Pacific, In the Field, Action Report, Nansei Shoto, Phase Two, Serial 00502, 16 July 1945.
Commanding Officer, USS *LSM 189* [*sic*], Fire support rendered by *LSM(R)s 189* and *191* on south-western part of Okinawa from 22 May 1945 to 2 June 1945—summary of.
Headquarters, III Corps Artillery, Third Amphibious Corps, Naval Gunfire Report, Okinawa Operation, 23 April 1945, with incomplete supplemental Naval Gunfire.
Serial 0124, 3 June 1945, Stack Area 370, Row D, Compartment 05, Shelf 03, Box 248.
Support, Sixth Marine Division, 19 May 1945 to 19 June 1945, Stack Area 370, Row D, Compartment 05, Shelf 04, Box 257.

NARA Record Group 181: Records of Naval Districts and Shore Establishments 1942–1945

Material and Inspection Reports of Radio Apparatus, June-August 1945, *LSMs 188, 189, 191, 192, 193, 196, 197, 198, 199.*
Ships Launching Files, *LSMs 188* through *199.*

NARA Record Group 227: Records of the Office of Scientific Research and Development

CIT Confidential Memorandum, OEC 1.1, A.S. Gould, "Inspection and Repair of Mk 51 Automatic Launchers on *LSM(R) 199*," 23 January 1945.
CIT Memorandum, OEC 1.2, "Tests of the Mk 35, Mk 50, 2 Mk 51 Launchers aboard an LCI(L)," 25 January 1945.
CIT Secret Memorandum, "Status of Rocket Ships leaving Pearl Harbor, T.H., from 21 Jan 45 to 15 Feb 45," 21 February 1945.
CIT Secret Memorandum, CIT OMC 11.1, "Report on Trip to Pearl Harbor, T.H., from 19 January 1945 to 17 February 1945," 22 February 1945.
CIT Telegram, F. L. Hovde, Div. 3, OEM:OSRD: NDRC:Div. 3, 1153800.001, 18 January 1945.
Office of the Commandant, United States Navy Yard, Charleston, S.C., Confidential Letter, A7–3/LSM(R)/S78(R)(N-1-4-42), Rocket Launchers Mk. 51—Correction of Defects, 17 December 1944.

NARA Record Group 407: Records of the Adjutant General's Office

Commanding General, XXIV Corps Action Report, Ryukyus, 1 April 1945–30 June 1945, n.d.
Commanding General, 77th Infantry Division, U.S. Army, Action Report—Ie Shima, n.d.
General Headquarters, United States Army Forces, Pacific, APO 500, Antiaircraft Artillery Activities in the Pacific War, 1946.
Headquarters 77th Infantry Division in the Field, APO

77, G-2 Estimate of the Situation—Iceberg Kerama Retto, 20 March 1945.

Headquarters 77th Infantry Division in the Field, APO 77, G-2 Summary, No. 8, 1 April to 1 June 1945.

Tenth Army Action Report, Ryukyus, 26 March to 30 June 1945, 3 vols., 3 September 1945.

Headquarters, United States Marine Corps

Amphibious Reconnaissance Battalion, FMF, Pacific, In the Field, 17 March 1945, Annex Able—OPNS Orders—ICEBERG: Official Papers Unit, History and Museums Division, Headquarters, U.S. Marine Corps, Washington, D.C. 20374–0580.

Navy Library, Washington Navy Yard

Department of the Navy, Bureau of Ordnance. *Missile Launchers and Related Equipment Catalog OP 1855.* 1 June 1953.

Department of the Navy. *Ships' Data, U.S. Naval Vessels.* vol. 2. Washington, D.C.: U.S. Government Printing Office, 1949.

Navy Department, Bureau of Ships. *Detail Specifications for Building Landing Ship Medium LSM 1 to 353, formerly designated Landing Craft, Tank, MK VII LCT(7) 1501 Class, NavShips (451).* 22 November 1943.

Navy Department, State Summary of War Casualties, Casualty Section, Office of Public Information, 1946.

Library of Congress

Japanese Monograph No. 83, Naval Operations in the Okinawa Area, 1945.

Japanese Monograph No. 86, 5th Air Fleet Operations, Feb.-Aug. 1945.

Combined Arms Research Library (CARL)

Headquarters Tenth Army, Okinawa, Tactical Study of Phase III, Section II, Tentative Operations Order No. 11–45, Iceberg IIId—FRICTION, accessed at Combined Arms Research Library (CARL) Digital Library, WWII Operational Documents. http://cgsc.cdm. oclc.org.

History of Planning Division, Army Service Forces (ASF), Volume 10, Planning Division, Office of Director of Plans and Operations, Army Service Forces, War Department, accessed at Combined Arms Research Library (CARL) Digital Library, WWII Operational Documents. http://cgsc.contentdm.oclc.org/cdm/.

British Official Files

DEFE 2/1327, Appendix C to C.R. 2626/45, The National Archives, United Kingdom.

Other Official Documents

Ayres, Warren J., Lieutenant, USNR. "Fighting Amphibians (The Alligator Song)." Official Song U.S. Naval Amphibious Training Base, Little Creek, VA.

The Bluejackets' Manual 1943. Annapolis: United States Naval Institute, 1943.

Booklet of General Plans, *LSM(R) 188–195*, Design and Engineering by Gibbs & Cox, Inc., New York City, 1944.

Gibbs & Cox, Inc. "(b) Conversion of LSM Landing Craft to Rocket Ships—Three Types," section (i) LSM(R), paragraph 129, pages 1–53 to 1–56. Enclosures courtesy of Donald G. Cavanaugh, Administrator, Gibbs & Cox, Inc., with cover letter April 19, 2000.

LSM Class Manual, March 1, 1944.

LSM Class, Brown Shipbuilding Company, Houston, Texas, design and engineering by Gibbs & Cox, Inc., New York City. 1944. Dr. No. LSM-01010–1, General Arrangement of Outboard Profile, Bureau of Ships Plan Number LSM(1)S0103–112380, Alt. 8.

_____. 1944. Dr. No. LSM-01010–2, General Arrangement of Hold & Main Deck, Bureau of Ships Plan Number LSM(1)S0103–112366 Alt. 10.

_____. 1944. Dr. No. LSM-01010–3, General Arrangement Superstructure Deck, Bridges & Focsle Deck, Bureau of Ships Plan Number LSM(1)-S0103–112367 Alt. 9.

Navy Department, Office of the Chief of Naval Operations. *Allied Landing Craft and Ships.* ONI 226, Supplement No. 1. Washington, D.C.: U.S. Government Printing Office, 1945.

"Welcome Aboard." *United States Atlantic Fleet, Amphibious Training Base, Little Creek, Virginia* (ca. 1944–1945).

Unpublished Works

Ball, Harold J. "My Autobiography," 1992. Unpublished typescript.

Blue, Clyde. "Publication Sight Book." Unpublished diary.

Boak, Dick. Ensign Thomas Boak letter to his wife, June 13, 1945. Unpublished typescript.

Johnson, Jack E., Lieutenant, USNR. "Thirty-seven Days in a Bathtub, or How to Cross the Pacific in an L.C.T." Unpublished typescript.

Landis, Robert W. "Ship's Log USS *LSM(R) 192*." Unpublished diary.

Low, Lawrence J. Untitled. Unpublished diary, notebook and sketches.

"*L.S.M. 'R' 188*." Unpublished diary (anonymous).

Mallery, David, and Jack Shedd, Ensigns, USNR. "The History of USS *LSM(R) 196*," circa October 1945. Unpublished typescript.

Matchett, Karl G. Untitled. Unpublished diary.

Moore, F. Donald. "Quartermaster's Log." Unpublished diary.

Nuber, William, Roy Bailes, and Gordon Etter. "USS *LSM(R) 190* Log," Revision, File: LogLSMR190, 20 May 1991. Unpublished typescript.

"USS *Wadsworth DDS16*." Unpublished typescript (anonymous).

Vaitses, Paul S., Jr. "In the Rockets' Red Glare." Unpublished manuscript.

VanOteghem, Leonard A. "Events About and in the Area of Our Ship, the USS *LSM(R) 196* and our Unit of 12 LSM(R)s." Unpublished diary.

Weed, Burton E. "*LSM 'R' 188*." Unpublished typescript.

Wickser, John P. "With the Little Boys." Address presented to the Thursday Club, New York, December 9, 1971.

Willison, Lawrence. "*LSM(R) 188*." Unpublished typescript.

Winslow, Abner T. "Account of Air Attack Off Ie Shima—16 April 1945." Unpublished typescript.

Public Collections

Mark E. Andrews Papers, Harry S. Truman Library, Independence, Missouri.

Admiral Jules James Papers, East Carolina Manuscript Collection, J. Y. Joyner Library, East Carolina University, South Carolina.

Simon Bolivar Buckner, Jr., Papers, 1944–45, Dwight D. Eisenhower Library.

Private Collections

Francis Lihosit Collection (USS *Lang*).

II. Secondary Sources

Books

Adams, Andrew, ed. *Born to Die: The Cherry Blossom Squadrons*. By the Hagoromo Society of Kamikaze Divine Thunderbolt Corps Survivors. Introduction by Andrew Adams. Edited and supplemented by Andrew Adams. Translation by Nobuo Asahi and the Japan Technical Company. Los Angeles: Ohara Publications, Inc., 1973.

Andersen, Roy S. *Three Minutes Off Okinawa: The Sinking of the Radar Picket Destroyer The USS Mannert L. Abele by Japanese Kamikaze Aircraft*. Worchester, MA: The Jana Press, 2007.

Appleman, Roy E., James M. Burns, Russell A. Gugeler, and John Stevens. *Okinawa: The Last Battle*. The War in the Pacific, United States Army in World War II. Washington, D.C.: U.S. Government Printing Office, 1948.

Astor, Gerald. *Operation Iceberg: The Invasion and Conquest of Okinawa in World War II*. New York: Donald I. Fine, 1995.

Baker, A.D., III, ed. *Allied Landing Craft of World War Two*. Annapolis: Naval Institute Press, 1985.

Baker, Elijah, III. *Introduction to Steel Shipbuilding*, 2nd ed. New York: McGraw-Hill, 1953.

Ball, Donald L. *Fighting Amphibs: The LCS(L)s in World War II*. Williamsburg, VA: Mill Neck Publications, 1997.

Barbey, Daniel E., Vice Admiral, USN. *MacArthur's Amphibious Navy: Seventh Amphibious Force Operations 1943–1945*. Annapolis: Naval Institute Press, 1969.

Barker, Arthur J. *Suicide Weapon*. Ballantine's Illustrated History of the Violent Century, Weapons Book No. 22. New York: Ballantine Books, 1971.

Baudot, Marcel, Henri Bernard, Hendrik Brugmans, Michael R. D. Foot, and Hans-Adolf Jacobsen, eds. *The Historical Encyclopedia of World War II*. New York: Facts On File, 1980.

Baumler, Raymond A. *Ten Thousand Men and One Hundred Thirty "Mighty Midget" Ships (The USS LCS(L)s in World War II)*. Rockville, MD: PIP Printing, 1991.

Baxter, James Phinney. *Scientists Against Time*. Boston: Little, Brown, 1948.

Belote, James, and William Belote. *Typhoon of Steel: The Battle for Okinawa*. New York: Harper & Row, 1970.

Birindelli, James Benson, Captain, USNR (Ret.). *Land-ing Ship Medium (LSM), Landing Ship Medium Rocket (LSMR) Ships' Histories*. Washington, D.C.: Naval Historical Center, Washington Navy Yard, n.d.

Bix, Herbert P. *Hirohito and the Making of Modern Japan*. New York: HarperCollins, 2000.

Blanton, Earl. *Boston—to Jacksonville (41,000 Miles by Sea)*. Seaford, VA: Goose Creek Publications, 1991.

Boyd, Carl, and Akihiko Yoshida. *The Japanese Submarine Force and World War II*. Annapolis: Naval Institute Press, 2002.

Bradford, Eliot B., ed. *Rocket and Underwater Ordnance*. Summary Technical Report of the National Defense Research Committee, Division 3, vol. 1. Washington, D.C.: Columbia University Press, 1946.

Braynard, Frank O. *By Their Works Ye Shall Know Them: The Life and Ships of William Francis Gibbs 1886–1967*. N.p.: Gibbs & Cox, Inc., private limited printing, 1968.

Brown, D. K., RCNC, ed. *Landing Craft and Auxiliary Vessels: The Design and Construction of British Warships 1939–1945: The Official Record*, vol. 3. London: Conway Maritime Press, 1996.

Buell, Thomas B. *Master of Sea Power: A Biography of Fleet Admiral Ernest J. King*. Boston: Little, Brown, 1980.

Bunker, John. *Heroes in Dungarees: The Story of the Merchant Marine in World War II*. Annapolis: Naval Institute Press, 1995.

Burchard, John E., ed. *Rockets, Guns and Targets: Rockets, Target Information, Erosion Information, and Hypervelocity Guns Developed During World War II by the Office of Scientific Research and Development*. Boston: Little, Brown, 1948.

Bureau of Yards and Docks. *Building the Navy's Bases in World War II: History of the Bureau of Yards and Docks and the Civil Engineer Corps 1940–1946*. Washington, D.C.: U.S. Government Printing Office, 1947.

Buxton, Frank, and Bill Owen. *Radio's Golden Age: The Programs and the Personalities*. New York: Easton Valley Press, 1966.

Campbell, Catherine C., ed. *Firing of Rockets from Aircraft: Launchers, Sights, Flight Tests*. Pasadena: California Institute of Technology, 1946.

Cannon, M. Hamlin. *Leyte: The Return to the Philippines*. The War in the Pacific, United States Army in World War II. Washington, D.C.: U.S. Government Printing Office, 1954.

Carlton, Phillips D., Major, USMCR. *The Conquest of Okinawa: An Account of the Sixth Marine Division*. Historical Division, Headquarters, U.S. Marine Corps, 1947.

Carpenter, Dorr, and Norman Polmar. *Submarines of the Imperial Japanese Navy*. Annapolis: Naval Institute Press, 1986.

Cass, Bevan G., ed. *History of the Sixth Marine Division*. Washington, D.C.: Infantry Journal Press, 1948.

Charney, John G. *USS Ingraham DD694 1944–1945*. Oakmont, PA: American Eagle Printing, n.d.

Christman, Albert B. *Sailors, Scientists and Rockets: Origins of the Navy Rocket Program and of the Naval Ordnance Test Station, Inyokern*. History of the Naval Weapons Center, China Lake, California, vol. 1. Washington, D.C.: U.S. Government Printing Office, 1971.

Clark, Curt. *Acceleration Zero to Ninety: An Autobiography by Curt Clark*. San Diego, CA: self-published, n.d.

Davidson, Joel R. *The Unsinkable Fleet: The Politics of U.S. Navy Expansion in World War II.* Annapolis: Naval Institute Press, 1996.

Dyer, George C., Vice Admiral, USN (Ret.). *The Amphibians Came to Conquer: The Story of Admiral Richmond Kelly Turner.* 2 vols. Washington, D.C.: U.S. Government Printing Office, 1969.

Feifer, George. *Tennozan: The Battle of Okinawa and the Atomic Bomb.* New York: Ticknor & Fields, 1992.

Foladare, Joseph, ed. *Ballistic Data: Fin-Stabilized and Spin-Stabilized Rockets.* Office of Scientific Research and Development, National Defense Research Committee, Division 3, Section L. Pasadena: California Institute of Technology, 1946.

Foster, Simon. *Okinawa 1945: Final Assault on the Empire.* London: Arms and Armour Press, 1994.

Francillon, Rene J. *Japanese Aircraft of the Pacific War.* Annapolis: Naval Institute Press, 1979.

_____. *Japanese Navy Bombers of World War Two.* Garden City, NY: Doubleday, 1968.

Frank, Benis M. *Okinawa: Touchstone to Victory.* Ballantine's Illustrated History of the Violent Century, Battle Book No. 12. New York: Ballantine Books, 1969.

_____, and Henry I. Shaw, Jr. *Victory and Occupation.* History of U.S. Marine Corps Operations in World War II. vol. 5. Historical Branch, G-3 Division, Headquarters, U.S. Marine Corps. Washington, D.C.: U.S. Government Printing Office, 1968.

Friedman, Norman. *Naval Radar.* London: Conway Maritime Press, 1981.

_____. *U.S. Amphibious Ships and Craft: An Illustrated Design History.* Annapolis: Naval Institute Press, 2002.

_____. *U.S. Destroyers: An Illustrated Design History.* Annapolis: Naval Institute Press, 1985.

_____. *U.S. Naval Weapons.* London: Conway Maritime Press, 1983.

Gerrard-Gough, J.D., and Albert B. Christman. *The Grand Experiment at Inyokern: Narrative of the Naval Ordnance Test Station During the Second World War and the Immediate Postwar Years.* History of the Naval Weapons Center, China Lake, California, vol. 2. Washington, D.C.: U.S. Government Printing Office, 1978.

Giberson, Art. *Eyes of the Fleet: A History of Naval Photography.* Niceville, FL: Wind Canyon Books, 2000.

Goodstein, Judith. *Millikan's School: A History of the California Institute of Technology.* New York: W.W. Norton, 1991.

Gow, Ian. *Okinawa 1945: Gateway to Japan.* Garden City, NY: Doubleday, 1985.

Graves, Donald E. *Sir William Congreve and the Rocket's Red Glare.* Historical Arms Series No. 23. Alexandria Bay, NY: Museum Restoration Service, 1989.

Guerlac, Henry E. *Radar in World War II: The History of Modern Physics 1800–1950.* 2 vols. Los Angeles: Tomash Publishers/American Institute of Physics, 1987.

Hagerman, George, and Roy Fisher, eds. *The Story of the USS* Wadsworth *DD 516: A Fighting Ship.* N.p.: The Wadsworth Association, 1989.

Hamer, Fritz P. *Charleston Reborn: A Southern City, Its Navy Yard and World War II.* Charleston, S.C.: The History Press, 2005.

Hata, Ikuhiko, and Yasuho Izawa. *Japanese Naval Aces and Fighter Units in World War II.* Annapolis: Naval Institute Press, 1989.

Hata, Ikuhiko, Yasuho Izawa, and Christopher Shores. *Japanese Army Air Force Fighter Units and their Aces 1931–1945.* London: Grub Street, 2002.

Hayes, Grace Person. *The History of the Joint Chiefs of Staff in World War II: The War Against Japan.* Annapolis: Naval Institute Press, 1982.

Hoyt, Edwin P. *The Kamikazes: Suicide Squadrons of World War II.* Short Hills, N.J.: Burford Books, 1983.

Huber, Thomas M. *Okinawa 1945.* Havertown, PA: Casemate, 2001.

Illsley, Rolf F. *LSM-LSMR WWII Amphibious Forces.* Vol. 1. Paducah, KY: Turner Publishing Company, 1994.

_____. *LSM-LSMR WWII Amphibious Forces.* Vol. 2. Paducah, KY: Turner Publishing Company, 1997.

Inoguchi, Rikihei, Captain, and Commander Tadashi Nakajima, with Roger Pineau. *The Divine Wind: Japan's Kamikaze Force in World War II.* Annapolis: Naval Institute Press, 1958.

Isley, Jeter A., and Philip A. Crowl. *The U.S. Marines and Amphibious War.* Princeton: Princeton University Press, 1951.

Jentschura, Hansgeorg, Dieter Jung, and Peter Mickel. *Warships of the Imperial Japanese Navy, 1869–1945.* Annapolis: Naval Institute Press, 1982.

Joint Board on Scientific Information Policy. *U.S. Rocket Ordnance: Development and Use in World War II.* Washington, D.C.: U.S. Government Printing Office, 1946.

Karig, Walter, Russell L. Harris, and Frank A. Manson. *Battle Report: Victory in the Pacific.* New York: Rinehart and Company, 1949.

Knight, Rex A. *Riding on Luck: The Saga of the USS Lang (DD-399).* Central Point, OR: Hellgate Press, 2001.

Ladd, J. D. *Assault from the Sea 1939–1945.* New York: Hippocrene Books, 1976.

Lindberg, Michael, and Daniel Todd. *Anglo-American Shipbuilding in World War II.* Westport, CT: Praeger, 2004.

Lloyd, Paul E., ed. *Rocket Launchers for Surface Use.* Pasadena: California Institute of Technology, 1946.

Lorelli, John A. *To Foreign Shores: U.S. Amphibious Operations in World War II.* Annapolis: Naval Institute Press, 1995.

Lott, Arnold S. *Brave Ship, Brave Men.* Annapolis: Naval Institute Press, 1964.

Love, Edmund G. *The Hourglass: A History of the 7th Infantry Division in World War II.* Washington, D.C.: Infantry Journal Press, 1950.

Maund, L. E. H., Rear Admiral (Ret.). *Assault from the Sea.* London: Methuen & Co., 1949.

McGee, William L. *The Amphibians are Coming!* Vol. 1. Santa Barbara: BMC Publications, 2000.

McNeil, Jim. *Charleston's Navy Yard: A Picture History.* Charleston, S.C.: Coker Craft Press, Inc., 1985.

McNeill, John A. *The Voyage of the 159.* Wilmington, N.C.: self-published, 1995.

Merrill, John C., and Ralph L. Lowenstein. *Viva Journalism! The Triumph of Print in the Media Revolution.* Bloomington, IN: Author House, 2010.

Mikesh, Robert C. *Broken Wings of the Samurai: The Destruction of the Japanese Airforce.* Annapolis: Naval Institute Press, 1993.

Miller, John A. *Men and Volts at War: The Story of General Electric in World War II*. New York: McGraw-Hill, 1947.

Morison, Samuel Eliot. *History of United States Naval Operations in World War II*. 15 vols. Boston: Little, Brown, 1947–62.

_____. *The Two-Ocean War*. Boston: Little, Brown, 1963.

Nichols, Chas. S., Jr., Major, USMC, and Henry I. Shaw. *Okinawa: Victory in the Pacific*. Historical Branch, G-3 Division, Headquarters, U.S. Marine Corps. Washington, D.C.: U.S. Government Printing Office, 1955.

Ota, Masahide. *This was the Battle of Okinawa*. Naha, Okinawa: Naha Shuppan Sha [Naha Publishing Company], 1981.

Parton, James, ed. *Impact: The Army Air Forces' Confidential Picture History of World War II*. 8 vols. New York: James Parton and Company, 1980.

Peck, Taylor. *Round-Shot to Rockets: A History of the Washington Navy Yard and U.S. Naval Gun Factory*. Annapolis: Naval Institute Press, 1949.

Potter, E.B. *Admiral Arleigh Burke*. New York: Random House, 1990.

_____. *Nimitz*. Annapolis: Naval Institute Press, 1976.

Rielly, Robin L. *American Amphibious Gunboats in World War II*. Jefferson, NC: McFarland, 2013.

_____. *Kamikaze Attacks of World War II*. Jefferson, NC: McFarland, 2010.

_____. *Kamikazes, Corsairs, and Picket Ships: Okinawa, 1945*. Drexel Hill, PA: Casemate Publishers, 2008.

_____. *Kamikaze Patrol: The LCS(L)(3) 61 at War*. N.p.: self-published, 1996.

_____. *Mighty Midgets at War: The Saga of the LCS(L) Ships from Iwo Jima to Vietnam*. Central Point, OR: Hellgate Press, 2000.

Roberts, John, ed. *Warship*. Vol. 4. Annapolis: Conway Maritime Press/Naval Institute Press, 1980.

Rohwer, Jürgen. *Axis Submarine Successes of World War Two*. Annapolis: Naval Institute Press, 1999.

Roscoe, Theodore. *United States Destroyer Operations in World War II*. Annapolis: Naval Institute Press, 1953.

Rowland, Buford, and William B. Boyd. *U.S. Navy Bureau of Ordnance in World War II*. Washington, D.C.: U.S. Government Printing Office, 1953.

Sarantakes, Nicholas Evan, ed. *Seven Stars: The Okinawa Battle Diaries of Simon Bolivar Buckner, Jr., and Joseph Stillwell*. College Station: Texas A&M University Press, 2004.

Sherrod, Robert. *History of Marine Corps Aviation in World War II*. Washington, D.C.: Combat Forces Press, 1952.

_____. *On To Westward: The Battles of Saipan and Iwo Jima*. Baltimore: The Nautical & Aviation Publishing Company of America, 1990.

Silverstone, Paul H. *U.S. Warships of World War II*. New York: Doubleday, 1965.

Skates, John Ray. *The Invasion of Japan: Alternative to the Bomb*. Columbia: University of South Carolina Press, 1995.

Smith, Robert Ross. *Triumph In the Philippines*. The War in the Pacific, United States Army in World War II. Washington, D.C.: U.S. Government Printing Office, 1963.

Staton, Michael. *The Fighting Bob: A Wartime History of the USS Robley D. Evans (DD-552)*. Bennington, VT: Merriam Press, 2001.

Stewart, James M. *90 Day Naval Wonder*. Bellevue, WA: Trees, Inc., 2003.

Surels, Ron. *DD 522: Diary of a Destroyer*. Plymouth, NH: Valley Graphics, 1994.

Sweeney, Charles W., with James A. Antonucci and Marion K. Antonucci. *War's End: An Eyewitness Account of America's Last Atomic Mission*. New York: Avon Books, 1997.

Timenes, Nicolai Jr. *Defense Against Kamikaze Attacks in World War II and Its Relevance to Anti-Ship Missile Defense*. Arlington, VA: Center for Naval Analysis, Operations Evaluation Group, 1970.

Thorpe, Donald W. *Japanese Army Air Force Camouflage and Markings: World War II*. Fallbrook, CA: Aero Publishers, Inc., 1968.

Treadwell, Theodore R. *Splinter Fleet: The Wooden Subchasers of World War II*. Annapolis: Naval Institute Press, 2000.

The United States Strategic Bombing Survey [Pacific], Naval Analysis Division, OPNAV-P-03–100. *Interrogations of Japanese Officials Volume 1*. Washington, D.C.: U.S. Government Printing Office, 1945.

_____. Naval Analysis Division, OPNAV-P-03-100. *Interrogations of Japanese Officials Volume 2*. Washington, D.C.: U.S. Government Printing Office, 1945.

Veesenmeyer, Jeffrey R. *Kamikaze Destroyer: USS Hugh W. Hadley (DD774)*. Bennington, VT: Merriam Press, 2014.

Veigele, William J. *PC Patrol Craft of World War II*. Santa Barbara: Astral Publishing Company, 1998.

Warner, Denis, and Peggy Warner. *The Sacred Warriors: Japan's Suicide Legions*. New York: Van Nostrand Reinhold Company, 1982.

Welch, W. P. *Mechanical Shock on Naval Vessels*. Bureau of Ships, Navy Department, NAVSHIPS 250–660-26. Washington, D.C.: U.S. Government Printing Office, 1946.

White, Laurie Woodson. *LSM(R) 195*. Liberty, SC: self-published, 2002.

Williams, Greg H. *World War II U.S. Navy Vessels in Private Hands*. Jefferson, NC: McFarland, 2013.

Yahara, Hiromichi. *The Battle for Okinawa*. New York: John Wiley and Sons, 1995.

Y'Blood, William T. *The Little Giants: U.S. Escort Carriers Against Japan*. Annapolis: Naval Institute Press, 1987.

Articles

"Amphibs to Fore in '44." *Bureau of Naval Personnel Information Bulletin*, no. 323 (1944): 10–12.

"Building Door-to-Door Invasions." *Bureau of Naval Personnel Information Bulletin*, no. 320 (1943): 36–39.

"County Man Wins Silver Star Medal," July 20 [1945] (n.p.).

Donovan, Robert J. "On Dec. 7, 1941, the U.S. Had Not One Missile; By End of War Millions Had Been Fired; The Armed Forces Tell of the Conquest." *New York Herald Tribune*, March 31, 1946.

Friedman, Norman. "Amphibious Fire Support." *Warship*, vol. 4, John Roberts, ed. (1980), 199–205.

"The Galloping Ghost of Nansei Shoto." *C.I.C.* 2, no. 3 (1945): 46–47.

Gault, Owen. "Worth Their Weight in Gold! The Saga of the LSMs." *Sea Classics* 2, no. 5 (1979): 4–20.

"Governor Surprised At Navy Yard Speed In Turning Out LSMs." *Charleston News & Courier.* September 13, 1944.

"Honors Will Be Given Governor At Yard Today." *Charleston Evening Post.* September 12, 1944.

Grogan, Mike. "This Dogged Veteran's 'Tail' Told Through Memories of a Shipmate." *Alligator Alley* no. 30 (1997): 11–12.

Heinl, R. D. Jr., Lieutenant Colonel, USMC. "The Most Shot-At Island in the Pacific." *Proceedings* 73, no. 4 (1947): 397–399.

Hillyer, Richard. "Meanest Ships Afloat." *Sea Classics* 2, no. 2 (1979): 22–31, 79.

Inoguchi, Rikihei, Captain, former IJN, and Commander Tadashi Nakajima, former IJN. "The Kamikaze Corps." *Proceedings* (1953): 932–945.

"Insignia Authorized for Amphibious Forces." *Bureau of Naval Personnel Information Bulletin*, no. 328 (1944): 68.

"'Interim' LSM(R)s Tested in Combat." *Rocket* 1, no. 2 (1945): 5–6.

"Landing Ships Medium (Rocket)." *Rocket* 1, no. 1 (1945): 8.

"LSMs Christened, Quickly Placed In Commission." *Charleston News & Courier.* November 22, 1944.

"LSM(R)s at Okinawa." *Rocket* 1, no. 3 (1945): 2–4.

MacKay, Ron Jr. "LSM(R) Sub Hunters: Part 1." *Alligator Alley* no. 77 (2011): 7.

———. "LSM(R) Sub Hunters: Part 2." *Alligator Alley* no. 78 (2011): 11.

———. "The Towing and Medical LSMs at Okinawa: Part I." *Alligator Alley* no. 69 (2008): 29.

———. "The Towing and Medical LSMs at Okinawa: Part II." *Alligator Alley* no. 70 (2008): 29.

McMillian, I. E., Commander, USN. "Gunfire Support Lessons Learned in World War II." *Proceedings* (1948): 978–989.

Merrill, John C. Jr. "Rocket-Firing Guinea Pig." *Our Navy* (1952).

"Navy Yard Christens Second Pair of LSMs Within 24 Hours." *Charleston News & Courier.* November 23, 1944.

Paro, E. E., Captain, USN. "Okinawa Operation." *Proceedings* (1946): 60–67.

"Picture Of The Week." *LIFE* 18, no. 16 (1945): 32–33.

Pizur, Frank. Letters to the Editor. *Alligator Alley* no. 25 (1996): 13.

"Rockets." *Bureau of Naval Personnel Information Bulletin*, no. 335 (1945): 20–23.

Scott, J. Davis, Commander, USNR. "No Hiding Place— Off Okinawa." *Proceedings* (1957): 1208–1213.

Shaw, Richard. "A Veterans Story: Surviving a Kamikaze Attack." *Sun Advocate*, March 11, 2004. http://www.sunad.com/index.php?tier=1&article_id=4542.

"6 LSMs in 6 Days To Be Launched, Beginning Today." *Charleston News & Courier.* October 7, 1944.

"Sturdy Rocket Ship Proves Its Mettle, Took Three Jap Suicide Planes to Equal Score." *Navy News* (1945).

Swanson, Ron, ed. "LCT Convoys: Across the Pacific Under Their Own Power." *Flotilla: Newsletter of the LCT Flotillas of World War II* 5, no. 1 (2004): 1, 6.

Tangredi, Sam J., Captain, U.S. Navy (Ret.). "Breaking the Anti-Access Wall." *Proceedings* (2015): 40–45.

"2 Landing Ships Commissioned." *Charleston News & Courier.* November 25, 1944.

Yokoi, Toshiyuki, Rear Admiral, former IJN. "Kamikazes and the Okinawa Campaign." *Proceedings* (1954): 504–513.

Zinzow, Bill, ed. *USS Henry A. Wiley DM-29*, no. 101, untitled (2001): 4–6.

Addresses and Recollections

Price, E. W., C. L. Horine, and C. W. Snyder. "Eaton Canyon: A History of Rocket Motor Research and Development in the Caltech-NDRC-Navy Rocket Program, 1941–1946." 34th AIAA/ASME/SAE/ASEE Joint Propulsion Conference & Exhibit (1998).

Snyder, Conway W. "Caltech's Other Rocket Project: Personal Recollections." *Engineering & Science*, Spring (1991): 3–13.

Turner, Richmond Kelly, Admiral, USN. "Problems of Unified Command in the Marianas, Okinawa, and (Projected) Kyushu Operations." Air War College, Maxwell Field, Alabama (1947).

Internet Sources

Imperial Japanese Navy Page. "HIJMS Submarine I-36 Tabular Record of Movement." *Sensuikan! Operational Histories of Japanese Submarines in WW II*, http://www.combinedfleet.com/I-36.htm.

Johnson, C. Lee, "Ships of the U.S. Navy in WWII 'Dazzle' Camouflage," http://usndazzle.com/1Web/Index.

National Association of USS LCS(L) 1–130, http://www.mightymidgets.org/.

Naval History and Heritage Command. "Ship Nomenclature and Ship Types." *Dictionary of American Naval Fighting Ships*, http://www.history.navy.mil/danfs/ship_nomenclature.htm.

Naval History and Heritage Command. "Our Collections." http://www.history.navy.mil/search.html?q=LSM+Camouflage.

Nimitz, Chester W. *Command Summary of Fleet Admiral Chester W. Nimitz, USN.* 8 vols. U.S. Naval War College Naval Historical Collection. https://www.usnwc.edu/archives.

Office of the Commander, Amphibious Forces, Pacific Fleet, Transport Doctrine, Amphibious Forces, U.S. Pacific Fleet, Serial 0651, 18 September 1944. Hyper-War: A HyperText History of the Second World War, http://www.ibiblio.org/hyperwar/USN/ref/Transport/index.html#contents.

Palatas, Michael D., Commander, USN, ed. "A Summary of Admiral Arleigh Burke's After Battle Reports." *Conference Proceedings on Military Education for the 21st Century Warrior* (1998): 8–89 to 8–94, http://calhoun.nps.edu/handle/10945/36410.

ShipCamouflage.com, http://www.shipcamouflage.com/.

Tracy White, Researcher @ Large (blog), http://researcheratlarge.blogspot.com/2008/05/day-1.html.

Tracy White, Researcher @ Large (website), http://www.researcheratlarge.com/, "U.S. Naval Camouflage," http://www.researcheratlarge.com/Ships/S 19–7/index.html.

United States Navy in World War II. "U.S. Navy Shipbuilding Programs and Contracts, 1938–1945." *FISCAL YEAR 1944: 1945 Combatant Building Program*, http://www.shipscribe.com/shiprefs/usnprog/fy4445.html.

U.S. Naval Technical Mission to Japan. "Series S: Ships and Related Targets." *Target Report—Japanese Suicide Craft*, January 1946, Index No. S-02, http://www.fischer-tropsch.org/primary_documents/gvt_reports/USNAVY/USNTMJ%20Reports/USNTMJ-200H-0555–0601%20Report%20S-02.pdf.

USS Landing Craft Infantry National Association, http://www.usslci.com/html.

USS LSM-LSMR Association, http://lsmlsmr.org/.

Vance, Corbett, G., Lieutenant Colonel, USMC. "Operation Iceberg: Campaigning in the Ryukyus: An Operational Analysis." Final Report, Naval War College, 1998. http://www.dtic.mil/cgi-bin/GetTRDoc?AD=ADA348863.

Zee, Richard, Lieutenant Colonel, USMC. "Operational Perspectives of the Okinawa Campaign (Operation Iceberg)." Final Report, Naval War College, 1994. http://oai.dtic.mil/oai/oai?verb=getRecord&metadataPrefix=html&identifier=ADA283557.

Correspondences and Interviews

Harold J. Ball, *LC(FF)-535*, letters to author July 5, 1996 and June 1, 1999.

Edward E. Bowden, *LSM(R) 191*, conversation with author October 30, 1995.

J. Edward Briand, *LSM(R) 189*, letter to author April 25, 1996.

Harold Catchpole, *LSM(R) 195*, letter to author December 27, 1996; copy of Harold Catchpole letter to Mrs. William Woodson February 25, 1996 provided courtesy Mr. Catchpole.

John B. Francis, *LSM(R) 195*, conversation with author May 13, 2015.

Louis Gobeille, *LSM(R) 198*, email letters to author October 6, 2004 and October 11, 2004.

Allison Gray, *LSM(R) 188*, letter to author February 6, 1996.

Neal B. Hadsell, *LSM(R) 192*, letters to author January 5, 1995, January 17, 1995, and conversation with author August 10, 1998.

Allan M. Hirshberg, *LSM(R) 194*, undated letters to author circa October 1995 and November 1995.

Jack E. Johnson, LCT Flotilla Commander, letter to author June 6, 1996.

Allen B. Koltun, *SC 1028*, letter to author November 20, 1996.

Robert W. Landis, *LSM(R) 192*, letters to author December 12, 1999 and January 30, 2005; email to author June 5, 2002.

Lawrence J. Low, *LSM(R) 197*, letters to author May 30, 1996, 30 June 1996, September 20, 1998, December 7, 1998, November 11, 2000, January 10, 2003, and telephone conversation with author January 29, 1996.

Ronald R. MacKay, Sr., *LSM(R) 192*, letter to author July 14, 1977 and tape recorded interview with author July 14, 2001.

Bruce A. McDaniel, *LSM(R) 196*, letters to author undated circa January 1996, undated circa February 1997, undated circa March 1997, September 8, 1998, July 31, 1999, undated circa November 2000, July 9, 2001, October 30, 2001, July 15, 2002, undated circa June 2003, and conversations with author circa 2010.

Roy Moceri, *LSM(R) 191*, telephone conversations with author October 26–27, 2001 and undated letter to author circa October 2001.

F. Donald Moore, *LSM(R) 189*, telephone conversation with author November 1, 1995.

Wesley Murbach, *LSM(R) 193*, letter to author April 24, 1996.

George E. Passey, *LSM(R) 199*, letters to author November 26, 1995 and December 8, 1995.

Laurie R. Russell, *LSM(R) 191*, letters to author 20 October 1995, 27 November 1995, May 22, 1996, and email to author October 23, 2001.

Joe B. Smith, *LSM(R) 191*, letter to author January 9, 1997.

James M. Stewart, *LSM(R) 189*, letter to author 2 November 1994 and undated letter circa May 1996.

Lyle Tennis, *LSM(R) 190*, letter to author November 7, 1996.

Paul S. Vaitses, Jr., *LSM(R) 193*, letter to author August 26, 1996.

Russell Wydeen, *LSM(R) 192*, letter to author October 9, 1995.

Index

Numbers in **bold italics** indicate pages with illustrations